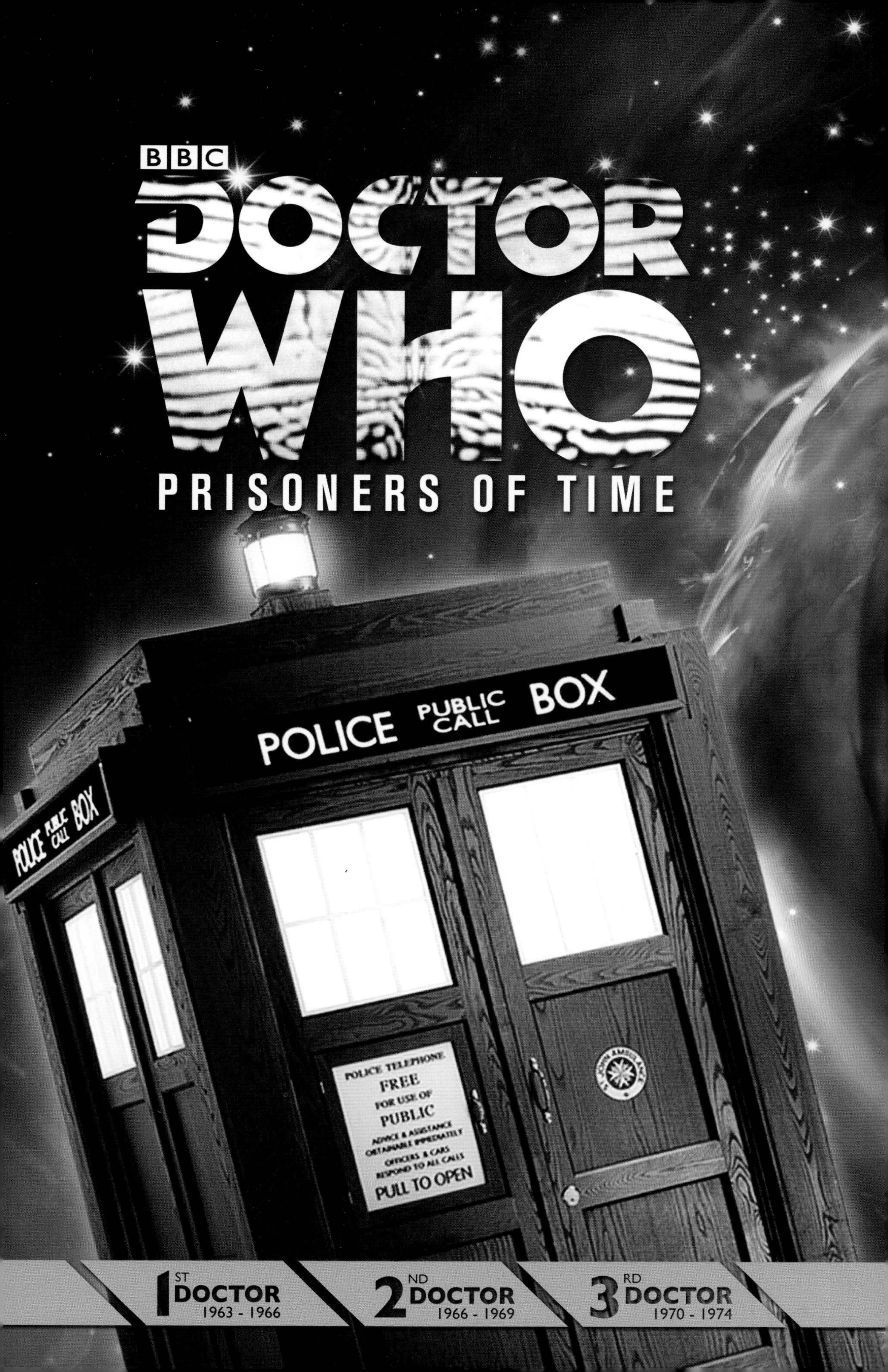
BBC
DOCTOR WHO
PRISONERS OF TIME
POLICE PUBLIC CALL BOX
POLICE PUBLIC CALL BOX
POLICE TELEPHONE
FREE
FOR USE OF
PUBLIC
ADVICE & ASSISTANCE
OBTAINABLE IMMEDIATELY
OFFICERS & CARS
RESPOND TO ALL CALLS
PULL TO OPEN
1ST DOCTOR 1963 - 1966
2ND DOCTOR 1966 - 1969
3RD DOCTOR 1970 - 1974

BBC

DOCTOR WHO

PRISONERS OF TIME

Cover by
DAVE SIM
Cover Colors by
CHARLIE KIRCHOFF
Collection Edits by
JUSTIN EISINGER and
ALONZO SIMON
Collection Design by
TOM B. LONG

ISBN: 978-1-61377-824-1 16 15 14 13 1 2 3 4

IDW founded by Ted Adams, Alex Garner, Kris Oprisko, and Robbie Robbins

IDW®

Ted Adams, CEO & Publisher
Greg Goldstein, President & COO
Robbie Robbins, EVP/Sr. Graphic Artist
Chris Ryall, Chief Creative Officer/Editor-in-Chief
Matthew Ruzicka, CPA, Chief Financial Officer
Alan Payne, VP of Sales
Dirk Wood, VP of Marketing
Lorelei Bunjes, VP of Digital Services

Special thanks to Kate Bush, Georgie Britton, Brian Minchin, Richard Cookson, Matt Nichols, and Ed Casey at BBC Worldwide for their invaluable assistance.

Originally published as DOCTOR WHO: PRISONERS OF TIME issues #1–12.

4TH DOCTOR 1974 - 1981 | 5TH DOCTOR 1981 - 1984 | 6TH DOCTOR 1984 - 1986 | 7TH DOCTO 1987 - 19

Written by
**SCOTT
&
DAVID
TIPTON**

Art by
**SIMON FRASER,
LEE SULLIVAN,
MIKE COLLINS, GARY ERSKINE,
PHILIP BOND, JOHN RIDGWAY,
KEV HOPGOOD, ROGER LANGRIDGE,
DAVID MESSINA** with **GIORGIA SPOSITO,
ELENA CASAGRANDE,
MATTHEW DOW SMITH,**
and **KELLY YATES**

Colors by
**CHARLIE KIRCHOFF, GARY CALDWELL,
PHIL ELLIOTT, SCARLETGOTHICA,**
and **ARIANNA FLOREAN** with
AZZURRA M. FLOREAN

Letters by
TOM B. LONG
Series Edits by
DENTON J. TIPTON

8TH DOCTOR 1996   **9**TH DOCTOR 2005   **10**TH DOCTOR 2005 - 2010   **11**TH DOCTOR 2010 - 2013

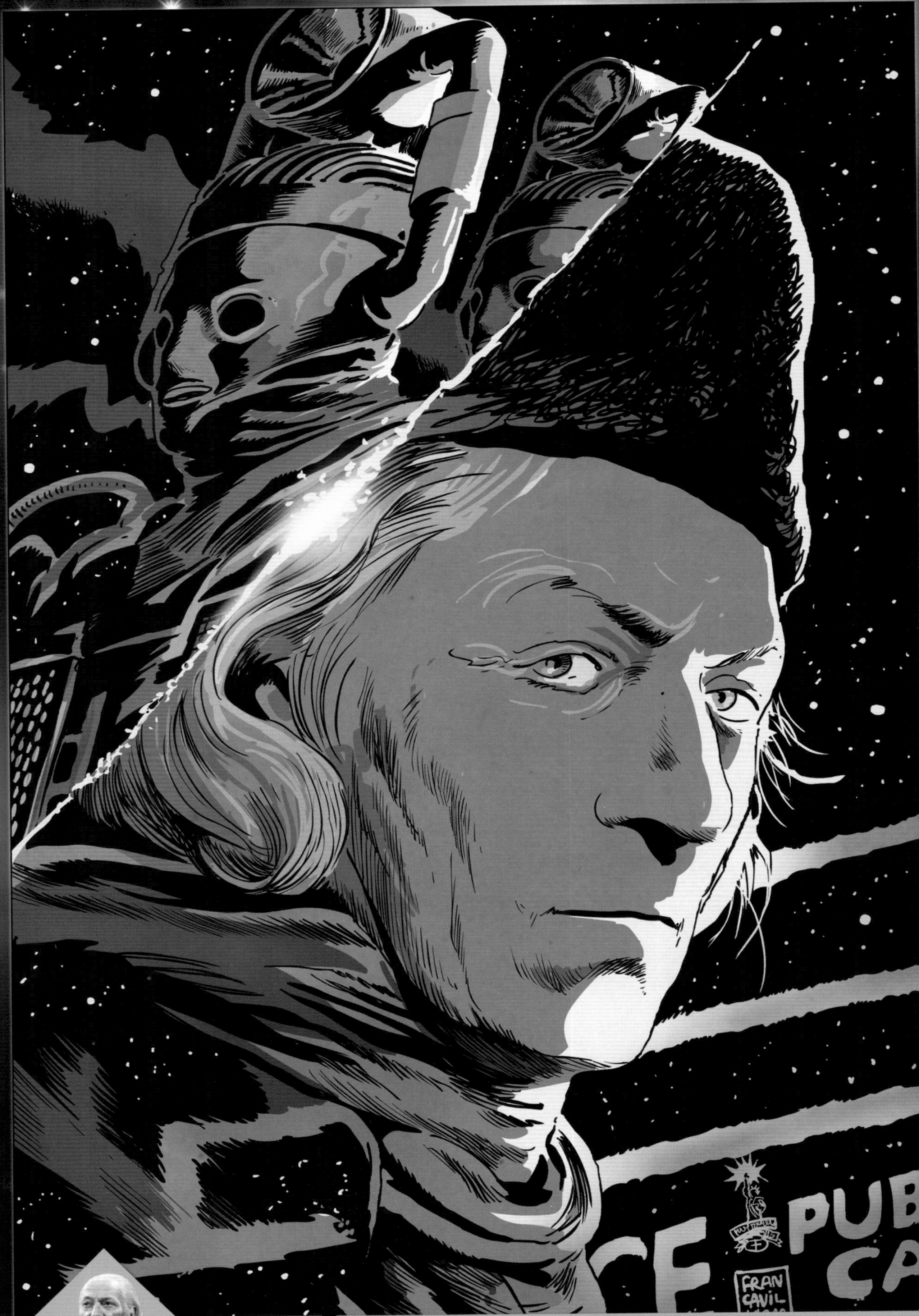

1ST DOCTOR
1963 - 1966

CHAPTER I "Unnatural Selection"

Cover Art by Francesco Francavilla

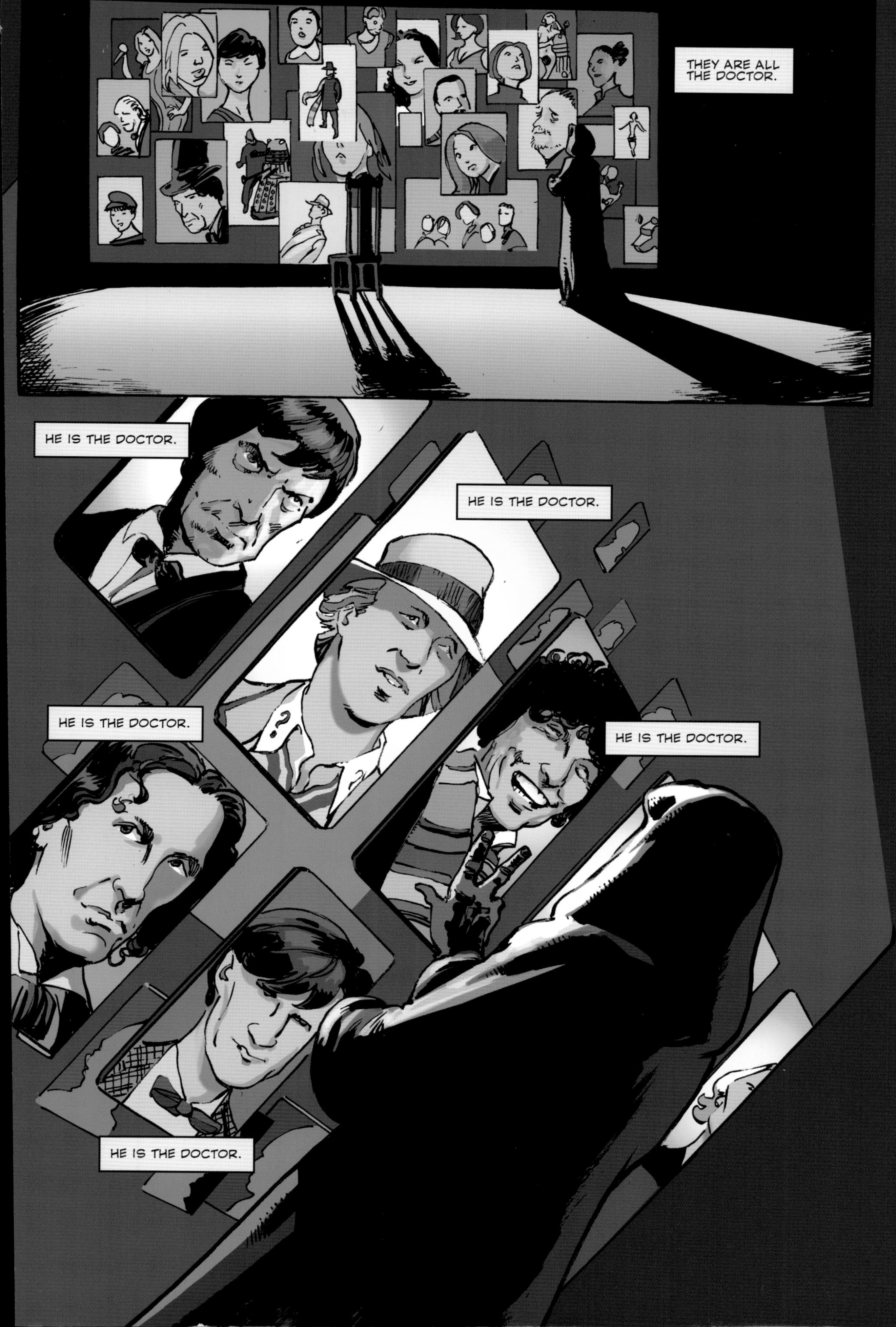
THEY ARE ALL THE DOCTOR.
HE IS THE DOCTOR.
HE IS THE DOCTOR.
HE IS THE DOCTOR.
HE IS THE DOCTOR.
HE IS THE DOCTOR.

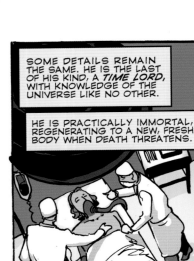

SOME DETAILS REMAIN THE SAME. HE IS THE LAST OF HIS KIND, A *TIME LORD*, WITH KNOWLEDGE OF THE UNIVERSE LIKE NO OTHER.

HE IS PRACTICALLY IMMORTAL, REGENERATING TO A NEW, FRESH BODY WHEN DEATH THREATENS.

HE TRAVELS THROUGH TIME AND SPACE IN THE *TARDIS*, ENABLING HIM TO BE LITERALLY ANYWHERE, ANYTIME, WITHOUT RHYME OR REASON.

SOMETIMES HE IS AN EDUCATOR.

SOMETIMES HE IS A SOLDIER.

SOMETIMES HE IS A MADMAN.

SOMETIMES HE IS THE ONCOMING STORM.

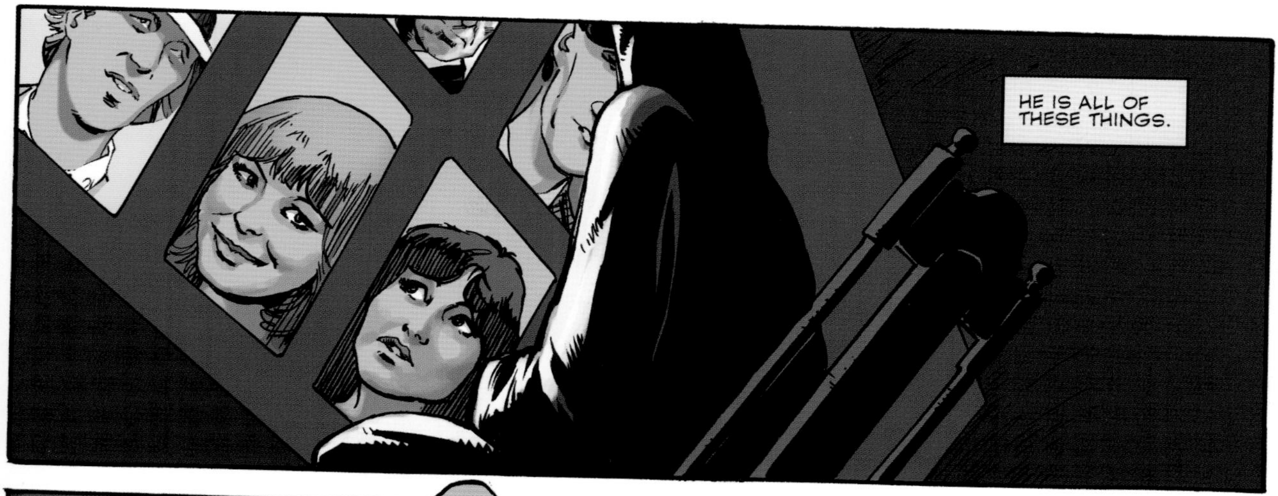
HE IS ALL OF THESE THINGS.

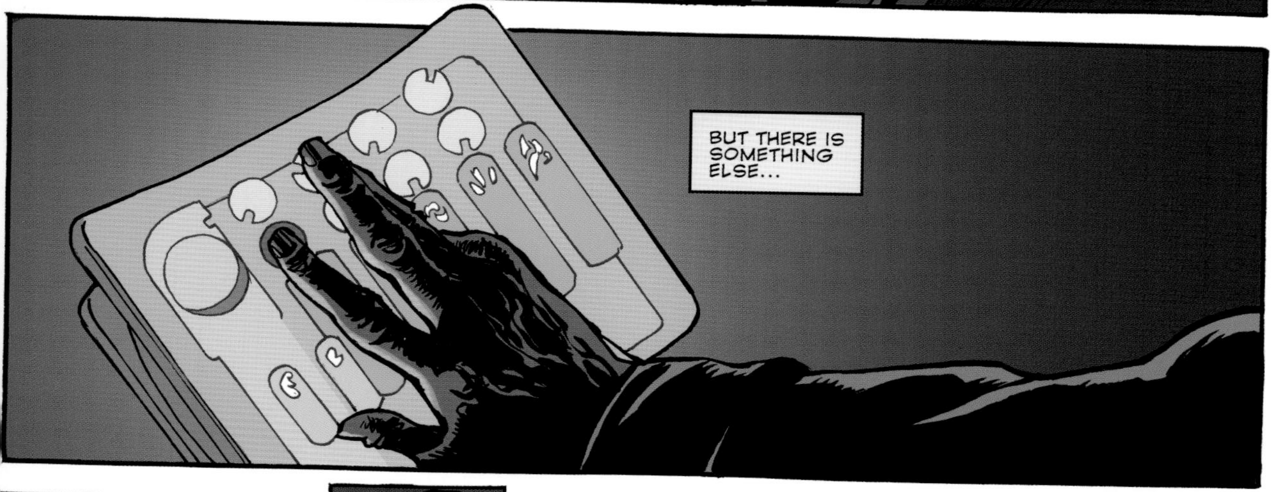
BUT THERE IS SOMETHING ELSE...

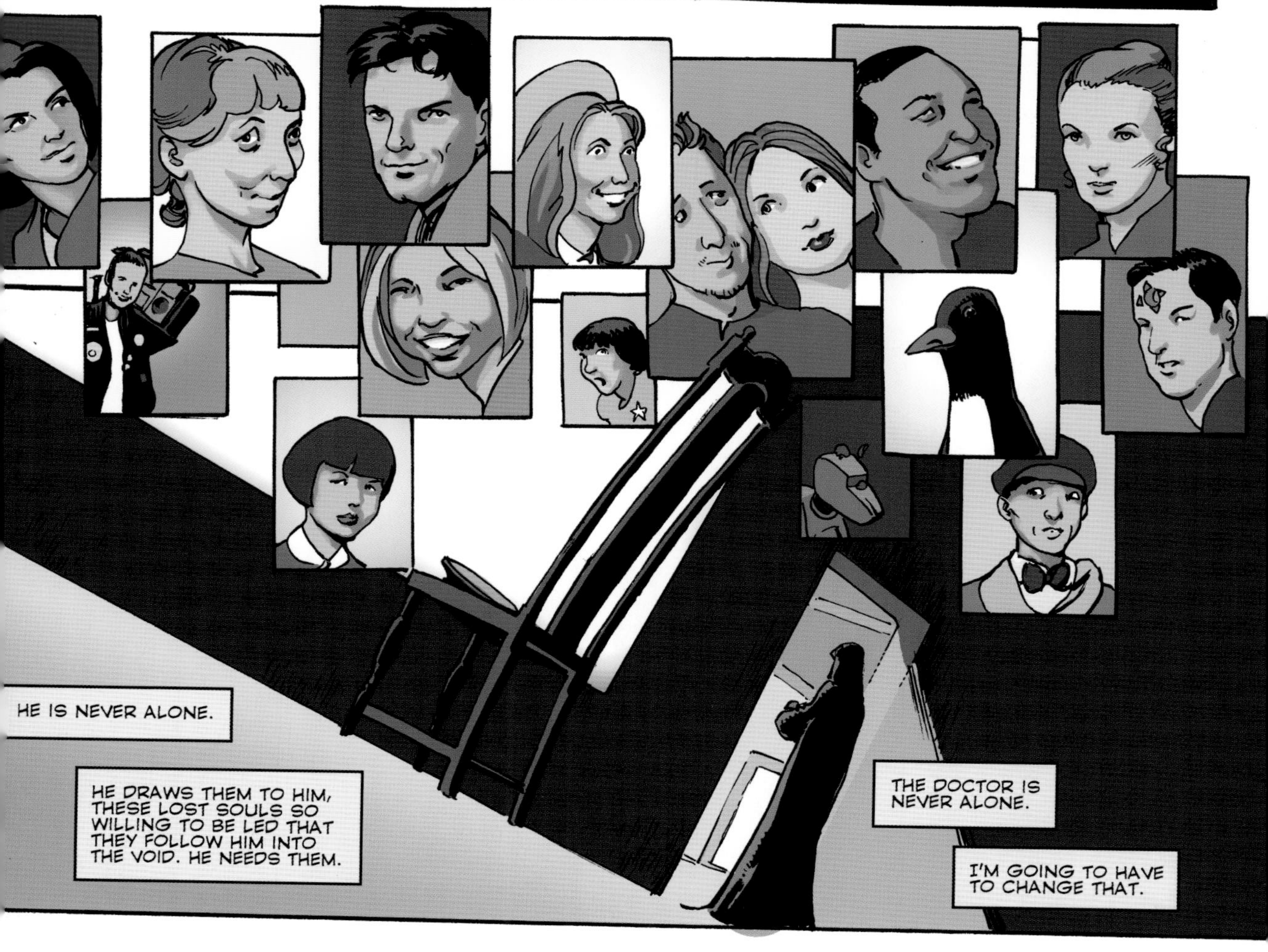
HE IS NEVER ALONE.
HE DRAWS THEM TO HIM, THESE LOST SOULS SO WILLING TO BE LED THAT THEY FOLLOW HIM INTO THE VOID. HE NEEDS THEM.
THE DOCTOR IS NEVER ALONE.
I'M GOING TO HAVE TO CHANGE THAT.

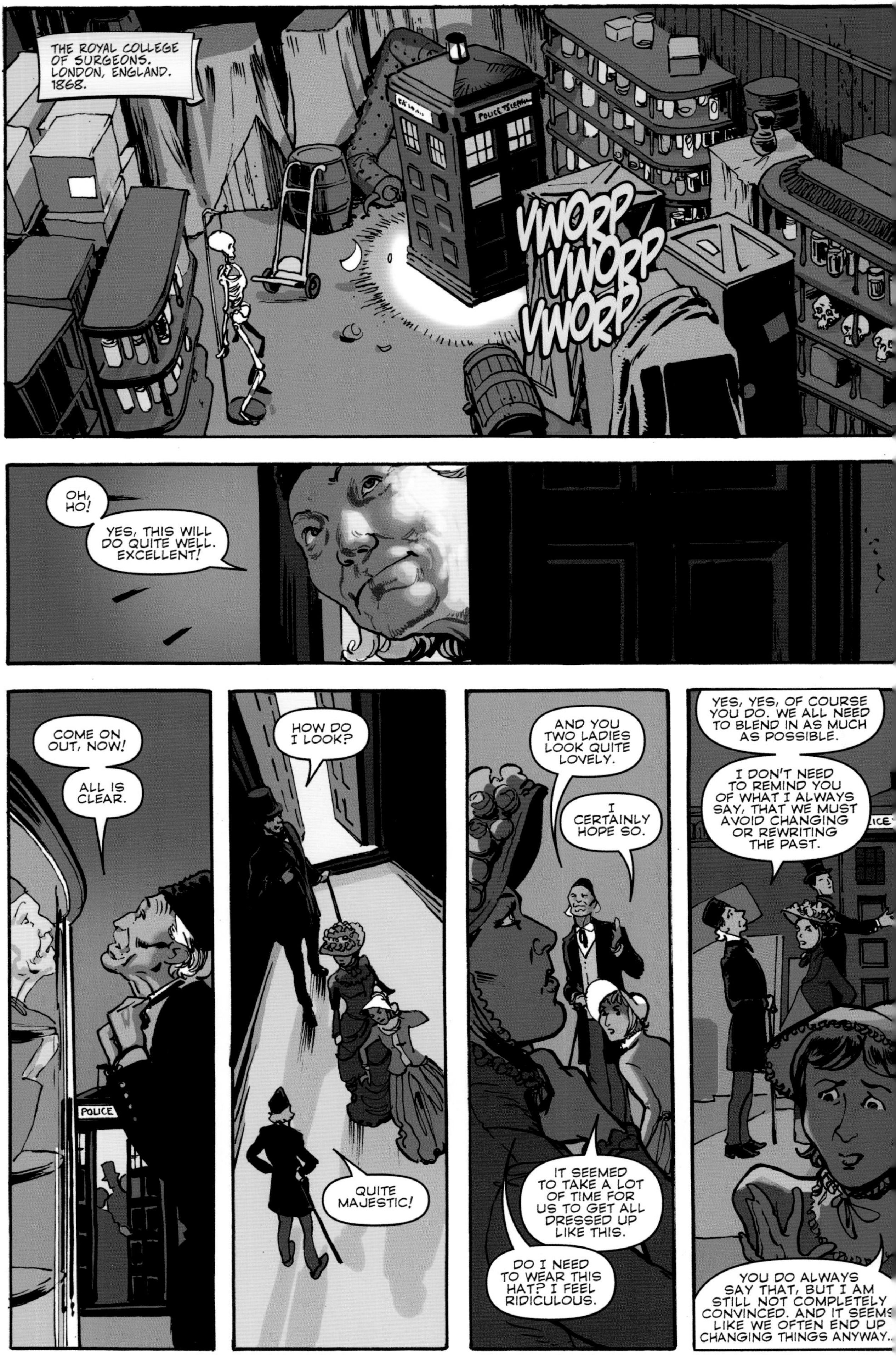
THE ROYAL COLLEGE OF SURGEONS. LONDON, ENGLAND. 1868.
VWORP VWORP VWORP
OH, HO!
YES, THIS WILL DO QUITE WELL. EXCELLENT!
COME ON OUT, NOW!
ALL IS CLEAR.
POLICE
HOW DO I LOOK?
QUITE MAJESTIC!
AND YOU TWO LADIES LOOK QUITE LOVELY.
I CERTAINLY HOPE SO.
IT SEEMED TO TAKE A LOT OF TIME FOR US TO GET ALL DRESSED UP LIKE THIS.
DO I NEED TO WEAR THIS HAT? I FEEL RIDICULOUS.
YES, YES, OF COURSE YOU DO. WE ALL NEED TO BLEND IN AS MUCH AS POSSIBLE.
I DON'T NEED TO REMIND YOU OF WHAT I ALWAYS SAY, THAT WE MUST AVOID CHANGING OR REWRITING THE PAST.
YOU DO ALWAYS SAY THAT, BUT I AM STILL NOT COMPLETELY CONVINCED. AND IT SEEMS LIKE WE OFTEN END UP CHANGING THINGS ANYWAY...

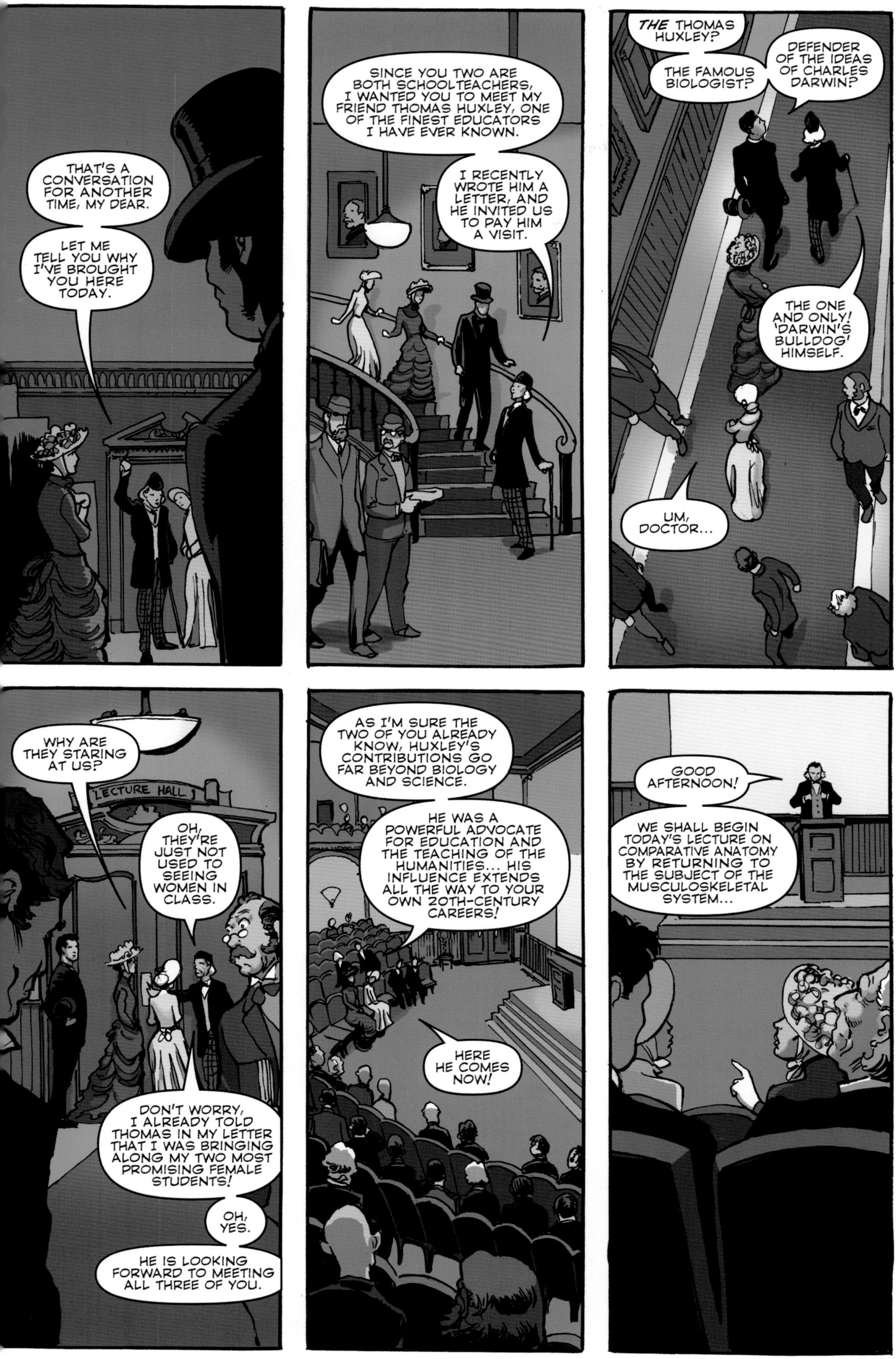
THAT'S A CONVERSATION FOR ANOTHER TIME, MY DEAR.
LET ME TELL YOU WHY I'VE BROUGHT YOU HERE TODAY.
SINCE YOU TWO ARE BOTH SCHOOLTEACHERS, I WANTED YOU TO MEET MY FRIEND THOMAS HUXLEY, ONE OF THE FINEST EDUCATORS I HAVE EVER KNOWN.
I RECENTLY WROTE HIM A LETTER, AND HE INVITED US TO PAY HIM A VISIT.
THE THOMAS HUXLEY?
THE FAMOUS BIOLOGIST?
DEFENDER OF THE IDEAS OF CHARLES DARWIN?
THE ONE AND ONLY! 'DARWIN'S BULLDOG' HIMSELF.
UM, DOCTOR...
WHY ARE THEY STARING AT US?
LECTURE HALL
OH, THEY'RE JUST NOT USED TO SEEING WOMEN IN CLASS.
DON'T WORRY, I ALREADY TOLD THOMAS IN MY LETTER THAT I WAS BRINGING ALONG MY TWO MOST PROMISING FEMALE STUDENTS!
OH, YES.
HE IS LOOKING FORWARD TO MEETING ALL THREE OF YOU.
AS I'M SURE THE TWO OF YOU ALREADY KNOW, HUXLEY'S CONTRIBUTIONS GO FAR BEYOND BIOLOGY AND SCIENCE.
HE WAS A POWERFUL ADVOCATE FOR EDUCATION AND THE TEACHING OF THE HUMANITIES... HIS INFLUENCE EXTENDS ALL THE WAY TO YOUR OWN 20TH-CENTURY CAREERS!
HERE HE COMES NOW!
GOOD AFTERNOON!
WE SHALL BEGIN TODAY'S LECTURE ON COMPARATIVE ANATOMY BY RETURNING TO THE SUBJECT OF THE MUSCULOSKELETAL SYSTEM...

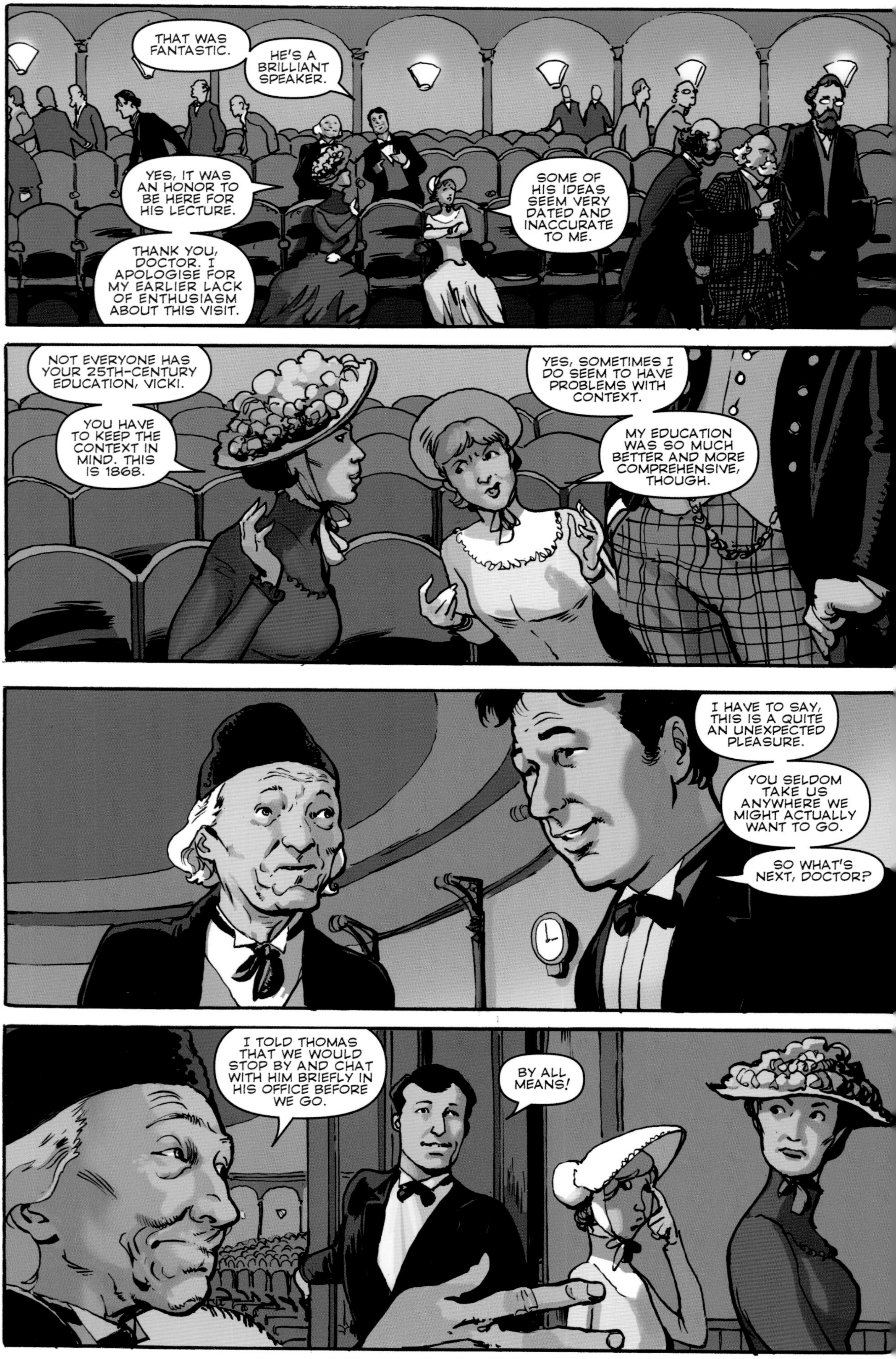

THAT WAS FANTASTIC.
HE'S A BRILLIANT SPEAKER.
YES, IT WAS AN HONOR TO BE HERE FOR HIS LECTURE.
THANK YOU, DOCTOR. I APOLOGISE FOR MY EARLIER LACK OF ENTHUSIASM ABOUT THIS VISIT.
SOME OF HIS IDEAS SEEM VERY DATED AND INACCURATE TO ME.
NOT EVERYONE HAS YOUR 25TH-CENTURY EDUCATION, VICKI.
YOU HAVE TO KEEP THE CONTEXT IN MIND. THIS IS 1868.
YES, SOMETIMES I DO SEEM TO HAVE PROBLEMS WITH CONTEXT.
MY EDUCATION WAS SO MUCH BETTER AND MORE COMPREHENSIVE, THOUGH.
I HAVE TO SAY, THIS IS A QUITE AN UNEXPECTED PLEASURE.
YOU SELDOM TAKE US ANYWHERE WE MIGHT ACTUALLY WANT TO GO.
SO WHAT'S NEXT, DOCTOR?
I TOLD THOMAS THAT WE WOULD STOP BY AND CHAT WITH HIM BRIEFLY IN HIS OFFICE BEFORE WE GO.
BY ALL MEANS!

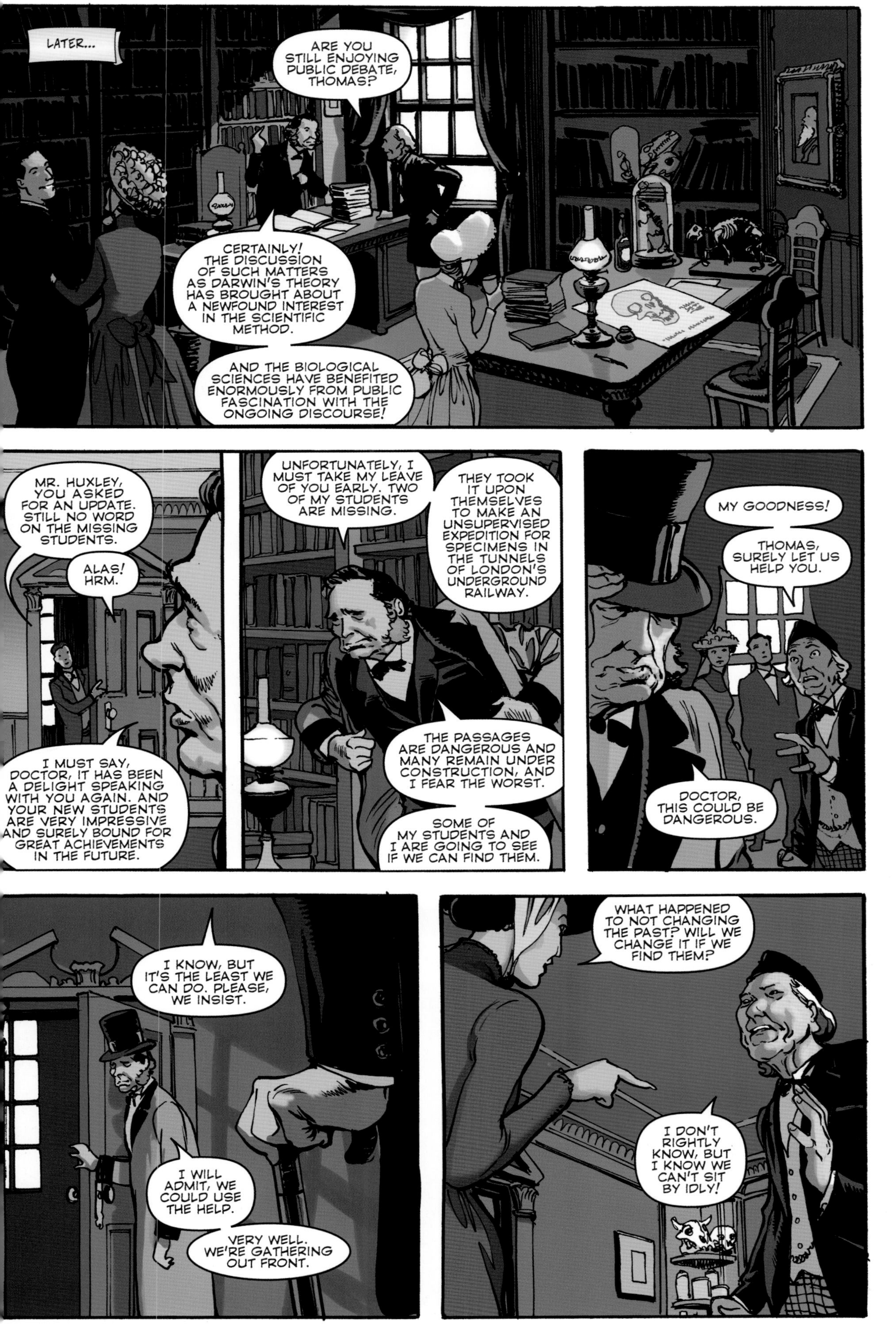
LATER...
ARE YOU STILL ENJOYING PUBLIC DEBATE, THOMAS?
CERTAINLY! THE DISCUSSION OF SUCH MATTERS AS DARWIN'S THEORY HAS BROUGHT ABOUT A NEWFOUND INTEREST IN THE SCIENTIFIC METHOD.
AND THE BIOLOGICAL SCIENCES HAVE BENEFITED ENORMOUSLY FROM PUBLIC FASCINATION WITH THE ONGOING DISCOURSE!
MR. HUXLEY, YOU ASKED FOR AN UPDATE. STILL NO WORD ON THE MISSING STUDENTS.
ALAS! HRM.
I MUST SAY, DOCTOR, IT HAS BEEN A DELIGHT SPEAKING WITH YOU AGAIN. AND YOUR NEW STUDENTS ARE VERY IMPRESSIVE AND SURELY BOUND FOR GREAT ACHIEVEMENTS IN THE FUTURE.
UNFORTUNATELY, I MUST TAKE MY LEAVE OF YOU EARLY. TWO OF MY STUDENTS ARE MISSING.
THEY TOOK IT UPON THEMSELVES TO MAKE AN UNSUPERVISED EXPEDITION FOR SPECIMENS IN THE TUNNELS OF LONDON'S UNDERGROUND RAILWAY.
THE PASSAGES ARE DANGEROUS AND MANY REMAIN UNDER CONSTRUCTION, AND I FEAR THE WORST.
SOME OF MY STUDENTS AND I ARE GOING TO SEE IF WE CAN FIND THEM.
MY GOODNESS!
THOMAS, SURELY LET US HELP YOU.
DOCTOR, THIS COULD BE DANGEROUS.
I KNOW, BUT IT'S THE LEAST WE CAN DO. PLEASE, WE INSIST.
I WILL ADMIT, WE COULD USE THE HELP.
VERY WELL. WE'RE GATHERING OUT FRONT.
WHAT HAPPENED TO NOT CHANGING THE PAST? WILL WE CHANGE IT IF WE FIND THEM?
I DON'T RIGHTLY KNOW, BUT I KNOW WE CAN'T SIT BY IDLY!

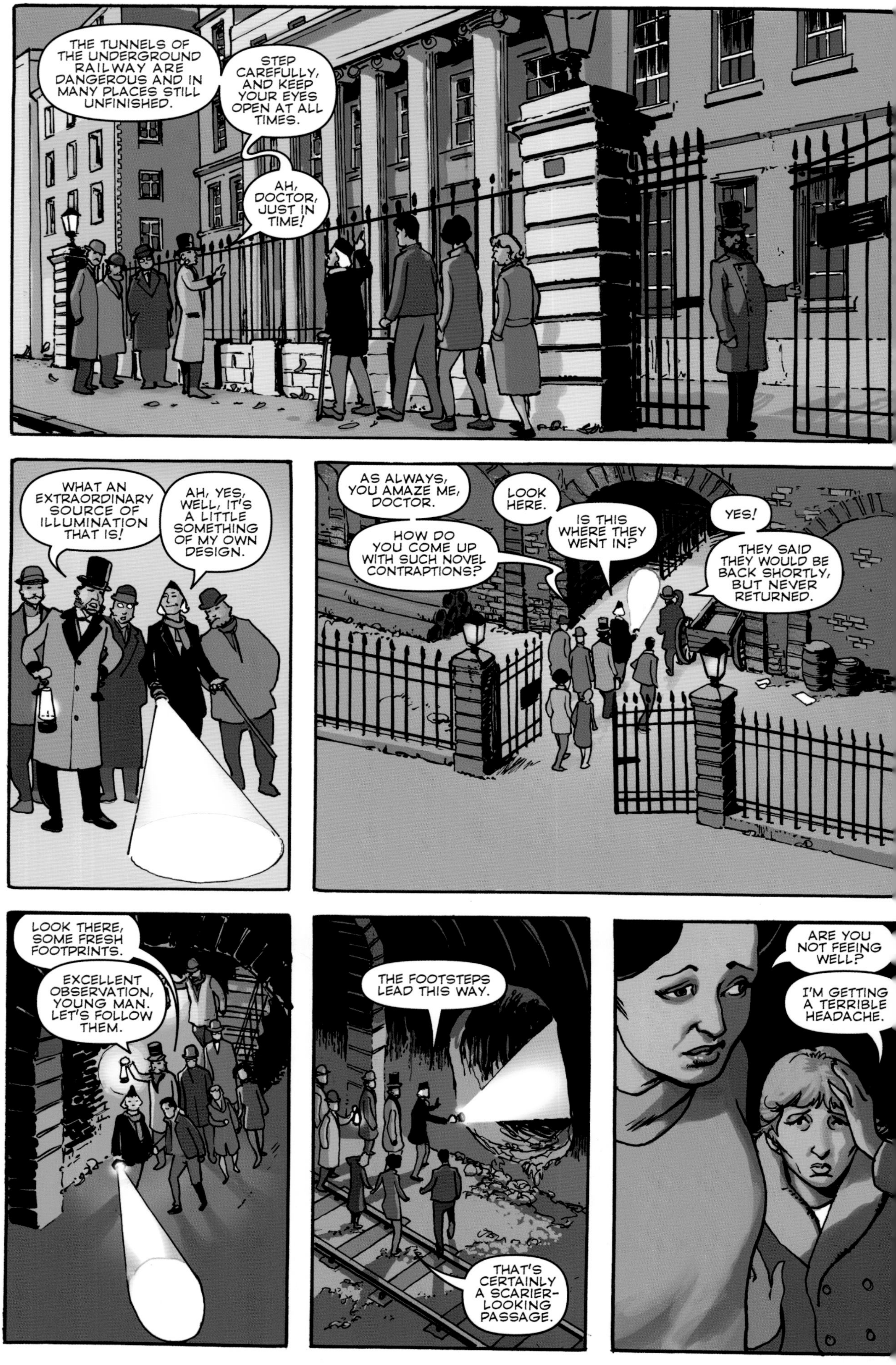
THE TUNNELS OF THE UNDERGROUND RAILWAY ARE DANGEROUS AND IN MANY PLACES STILL UNFINISHED.
STEP CAREFULLY, AND KEEP YOUR EYES OPEN AT ALL TIMES.
AH, DOCTOR, JUST IN TIME!
WHAT AN EXTRAORDINARY SOURCE OF ILLUMINATION THAT IS!
AH, YES, WELL, IT'S A LITTLE SOMETHING OF MY OWN DESIGN.
AS ALWAYS, YOU AMAZE ME, DOCTOR.
HOW DO YOU COME UP WITH SUCH NOVEL CONTRAPTIONS?
LOOK HERE.
IS THIS WHERE THEY WENT IN?
YES!
THEY SAID THEY WOULD BE BACK SHORTLY, BUT NEVER RETURNED.
LOOK THERE, SOME FRESH FOOTPRINTS.
EXCELLENT OBSERVATION, YOUNG MAN. LET'S FOLLOW THEM.
THE FOOTSTEPS LEAD THIS WAY.
THAT'S CERTAINLY A SCARIER-LOOKING PASSAGE.
ARE YOU NOT FEEING WELL?
I'M GETTING A TERRIBLE HEADACHE.

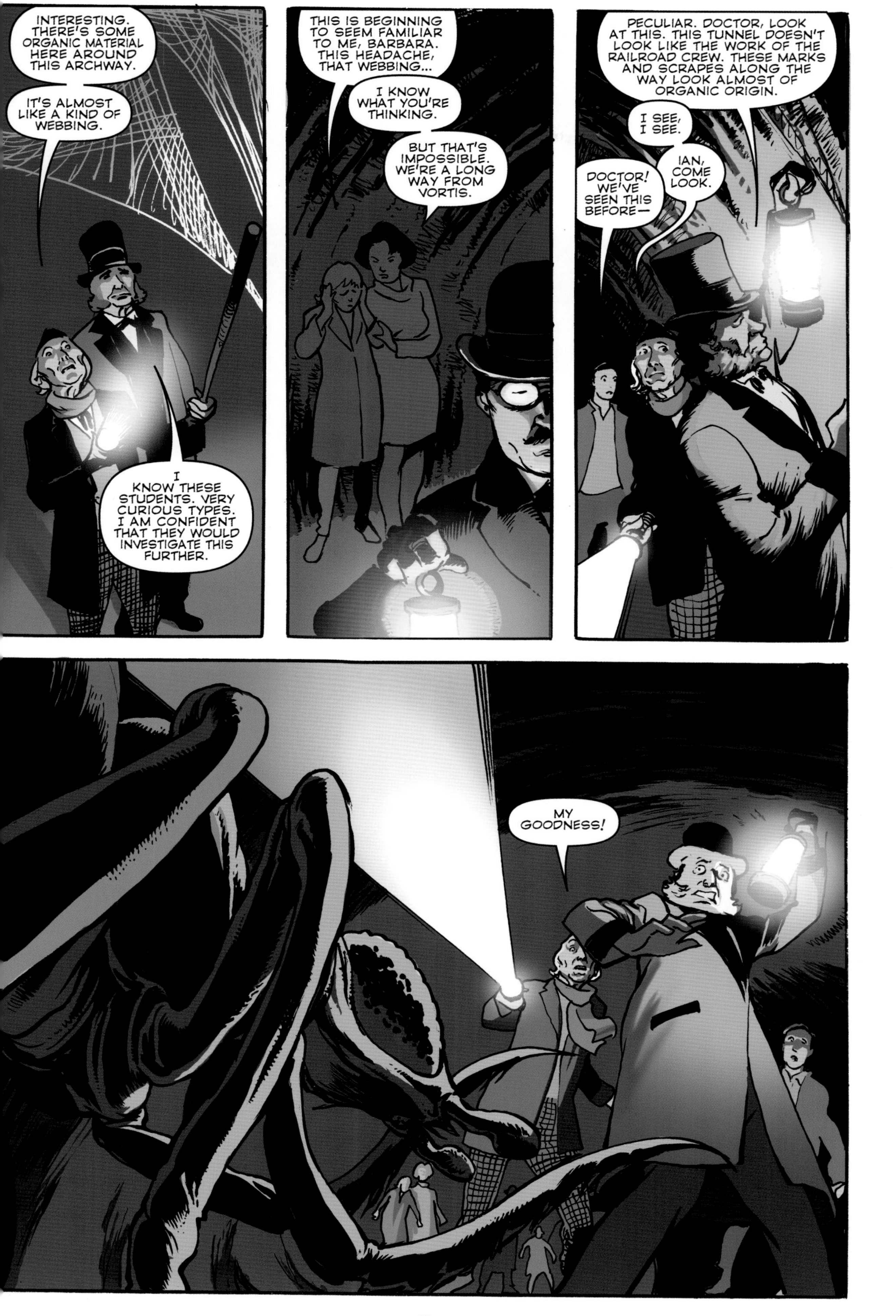
INTERESTING. THERE'S SOME ORGANIC MATERIAL HERE AROUND THIS ARCHWAY.
IT'S ALMOST LIKE A KIND OF WEBBING.
I KNOW THESE STUDENTS. VERY CURIOUS TYPES. I AM CONFIDENT THAT THEY WOULD INVESTIGATE THIS FURTHER.
THIS IS BEGINNING TO SEEM FAMILIAR TO ME, BARBARA. THIS HEADACHE, THAT WEBBING...
I KNOW WHAT YOU'RE THINKING.
BUT THAT'S IMPOSSIBLE. WE'RE A LONG WAY FROM VORTIS.
PECULIAR. DOCTOR, LOOK AT THIS. THIS TUNNEL DOESN'T LOOK LIKE THE WORK OF THE RAILROAD CREW. THESE MARKS AND SCRAPES ALONG THE WAY LOOK ALMOST OF ORGANIC ORIGIN.
I SEE, I SEE.
IAN, COME LOOK.
DOCTOR! WE'VE SEEN THIS BEFORE—
MY GOODNESS!

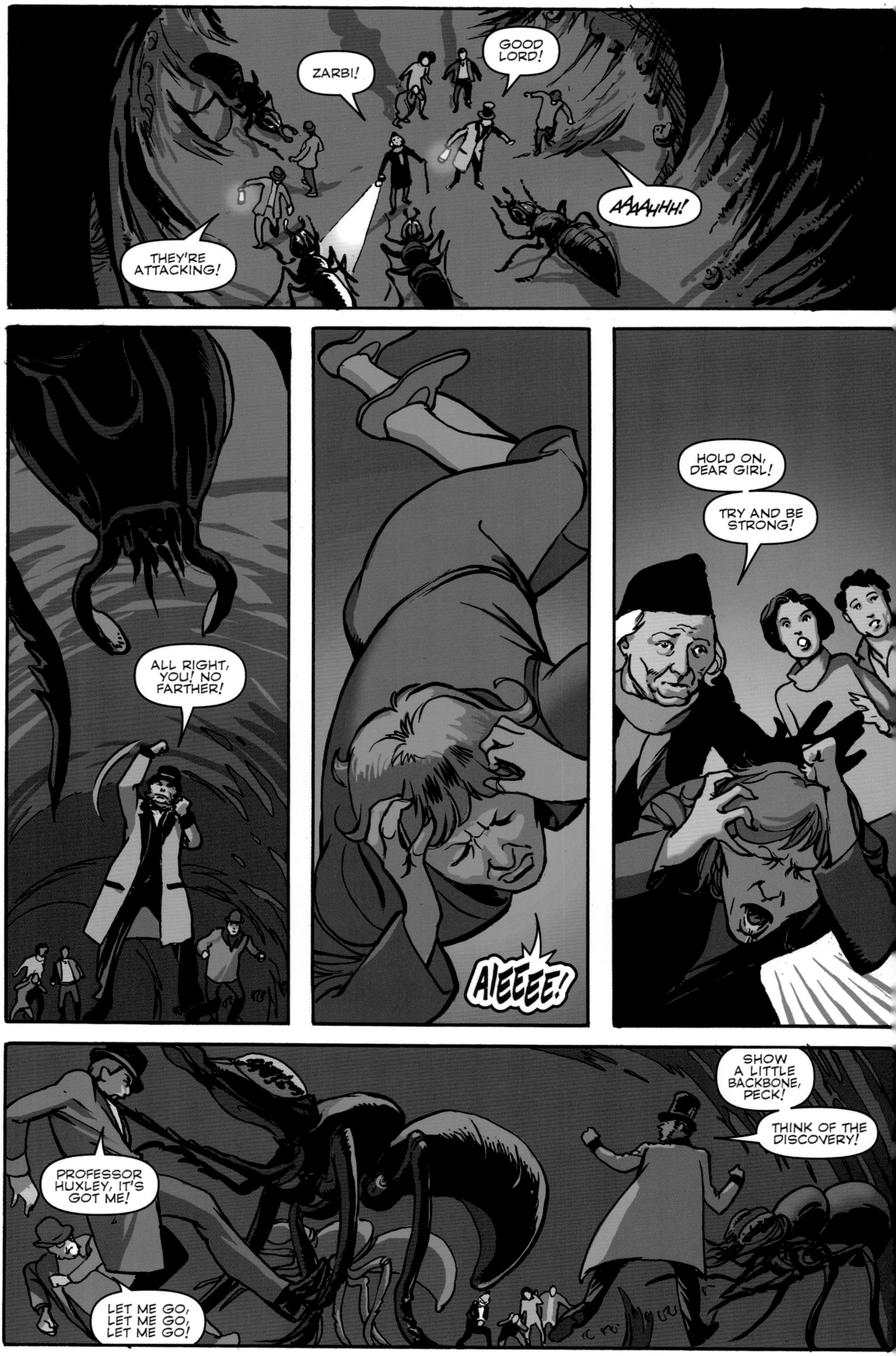

ZARBI!
GOOD LORD!
THEY'RE ATTACKING!
AAAAHHH!
ALL RIGHT, YOU! NO FARTHER!
AIEEEE!
HOLD ON, DEAR GIRL!
TRY AND BE STRONG!
PROFESSOR HUXLEY, IT'S GOT ME!
LET ME GO, LET ME GO, LET ME GO!
SHOW A LITTLE BACKBONE, PECK!
THINK OF THE DISCOVERY!

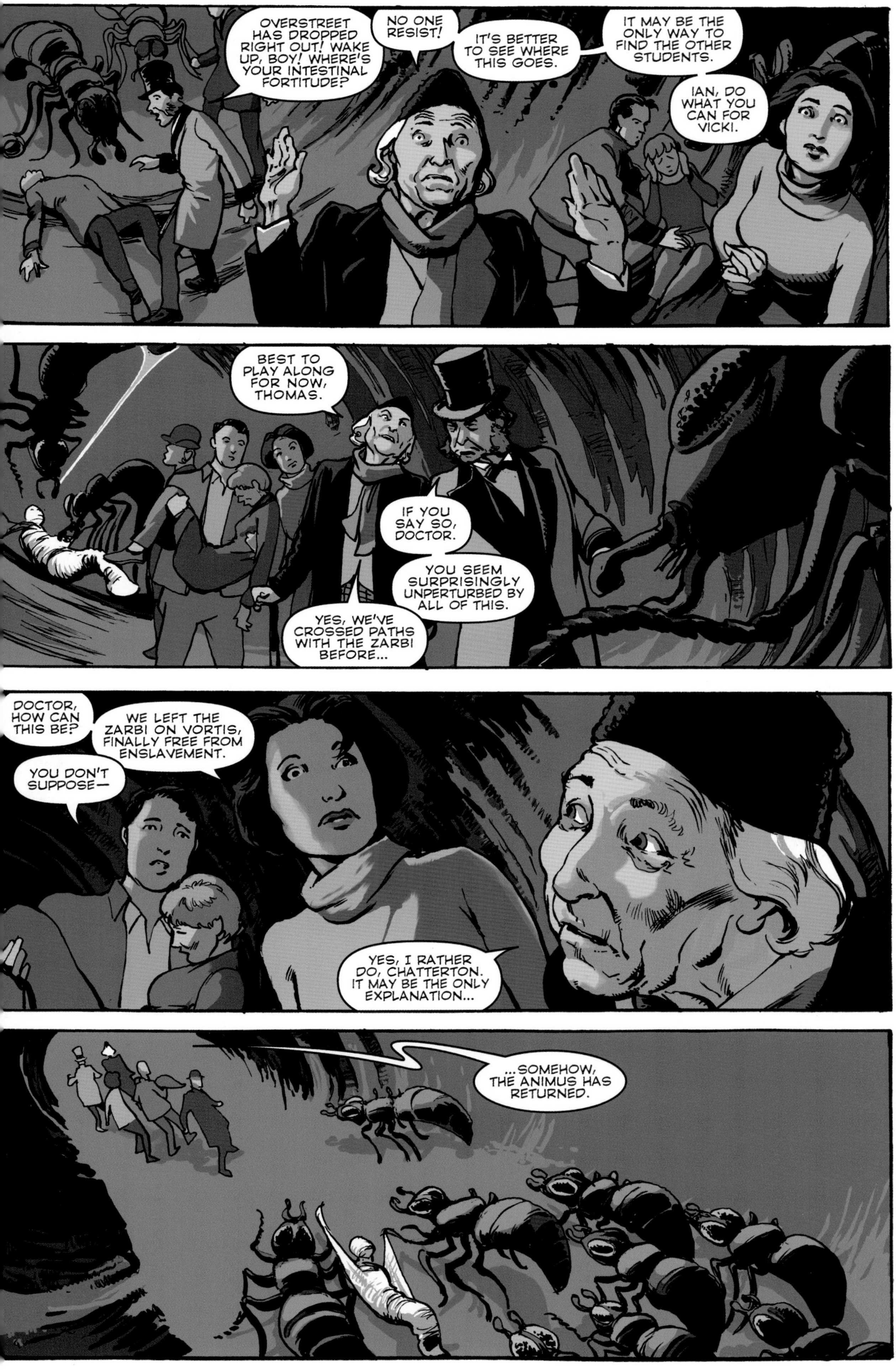
OVERSTREET HAS DROPPED RIGHT OUT! WAKE UP, BOY! WHERE'S YOUR INTESTINAL FORTITUDE?
NO ONE RESIST!
IT'S BETTER TO SEE WHERE THIS GOES.
IT MAY BE THE ONLY WAY TO FIND THE OTHER STUDENTS.
IAN, DO WHAT YOU CAN FOR VICKI.
BEST TO PLAY ALONG FOR NOW, THOMAS.
IF YOU SAY SO, DOCTOR.
YOU SEEM SURPRISINGLY UNPERTURBED BY ALL OF THIS.
YES, WE'VE CROSSED PATHS WITH THE ZARBI BEFORE...
DOCTOR, HOW CAN THIS BE?
WE LEFT THE ZARBI ON VORTIS, FINALLY FREE FROM ENSLAVEMENT.
YOU DON'T SUPPOSE—
YES, I RATHER DO, CHATTERTON. IT MAY BE THE ONLY EXPLANATION...
...SOMEHOW, THE ANIMUS HAS RETURNED.

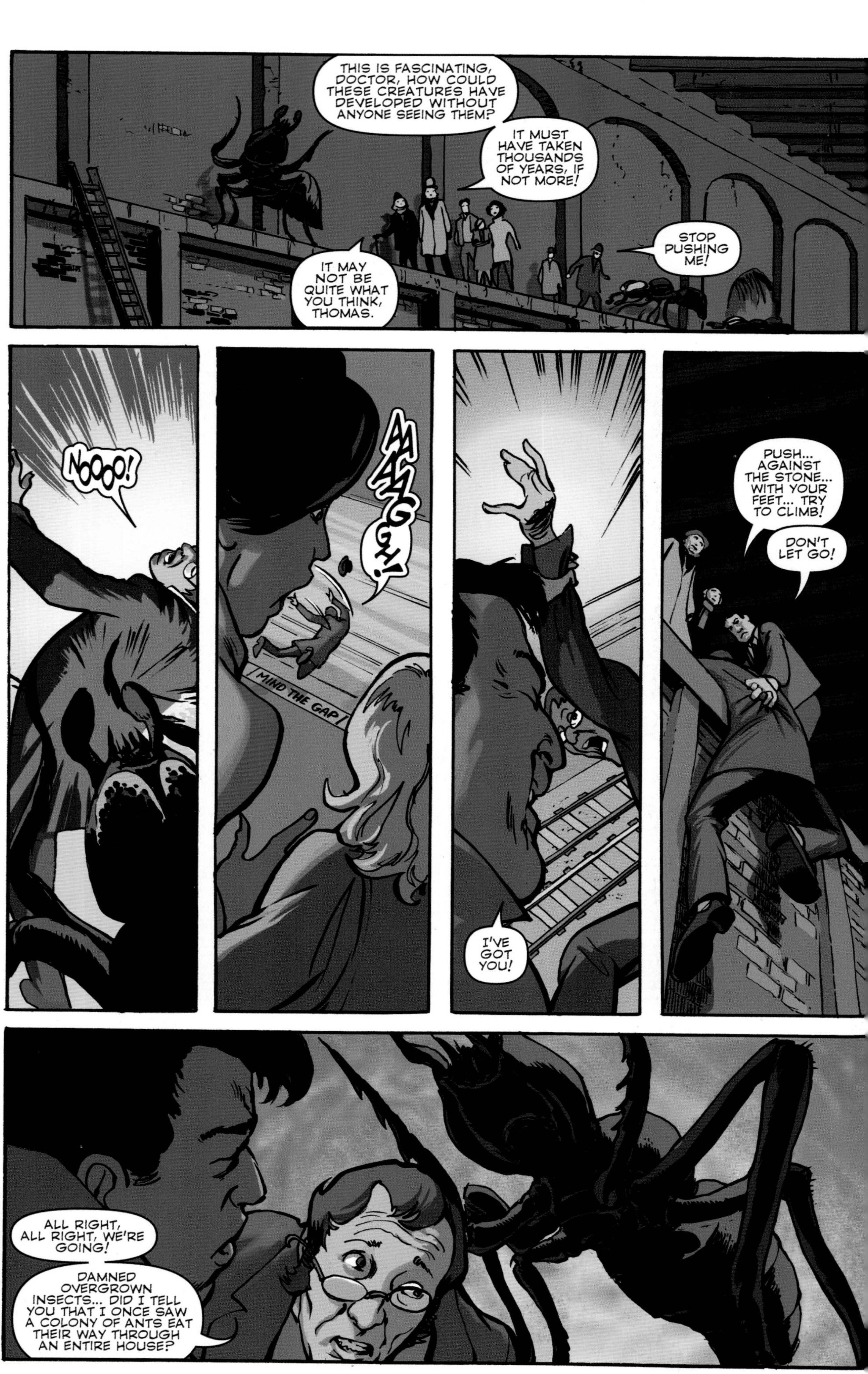

THIS IS FASCINATING, DOCTOR, HOW COULD THESE CREATURES HAVE DEVELOPED WITHOUT ANYONE SEEING THEM?
IT MUST HAVE TAKEN THOUSANDS OF YEARS, IF NOT MORE!
IT MAY NOT BE QUITE WHAT YOU THINK, THOMAS.
STOP PUSHING ME!
NOOOO!
AAAGGH!
MIND THE GAP
I'VE GOT YOU!
PUSH... AGAINST THE STONE... WITH YOUR FEET... TRY TO CLIMB!
DON'T LET GO!
ALL RIGHT, ALL RIGHT, WE'RE GOING!
DAMNED OVERGROWN INSECTS... DID I TELL YOU THAT I ONCE SAW A COLONY OF ANTS EAT THEIR WAY THROUGH AN ENTIRE HOUSE?

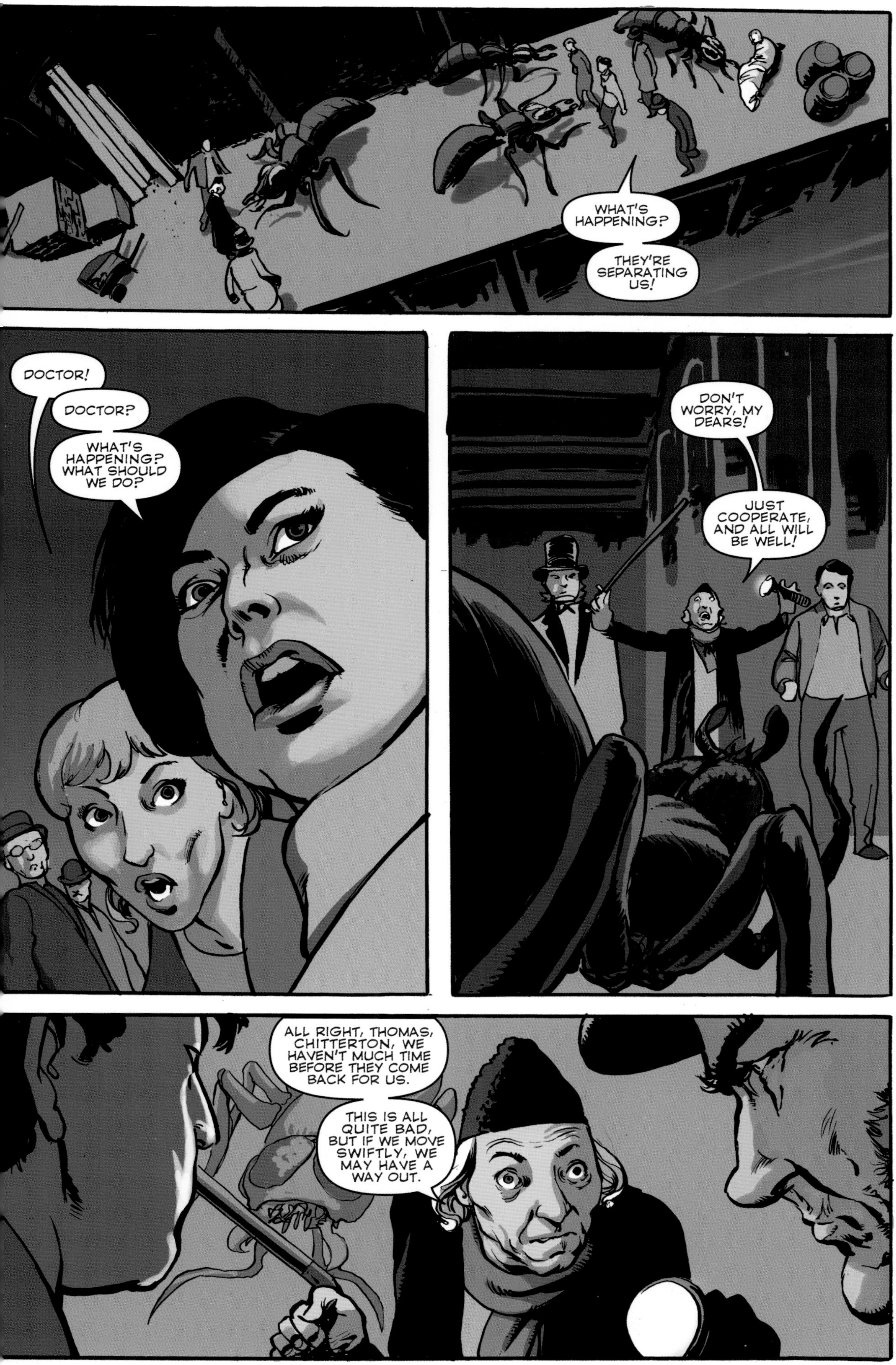
WHAT'S HAPPENING?
THEY'RE SEPARATING US!
DOCTOR!
DOCTOR?
WHAT'S HAPPENING? WHAT SHOULD WE DO?
DON'T WORRY, MY DEARS!
JUST COOPERATE, AND ALL WILL BE WELL!
ALL RIGHT, THOMAS, CHITTERTON, WE HAVEN'T MUCH TIME BEFORE THEY COME BACK FOR US.
THIS IS ALL QUITE BAD, BUT IF WE MOVE SWIFTLY, WE MAY HAVE A WAY OUT.

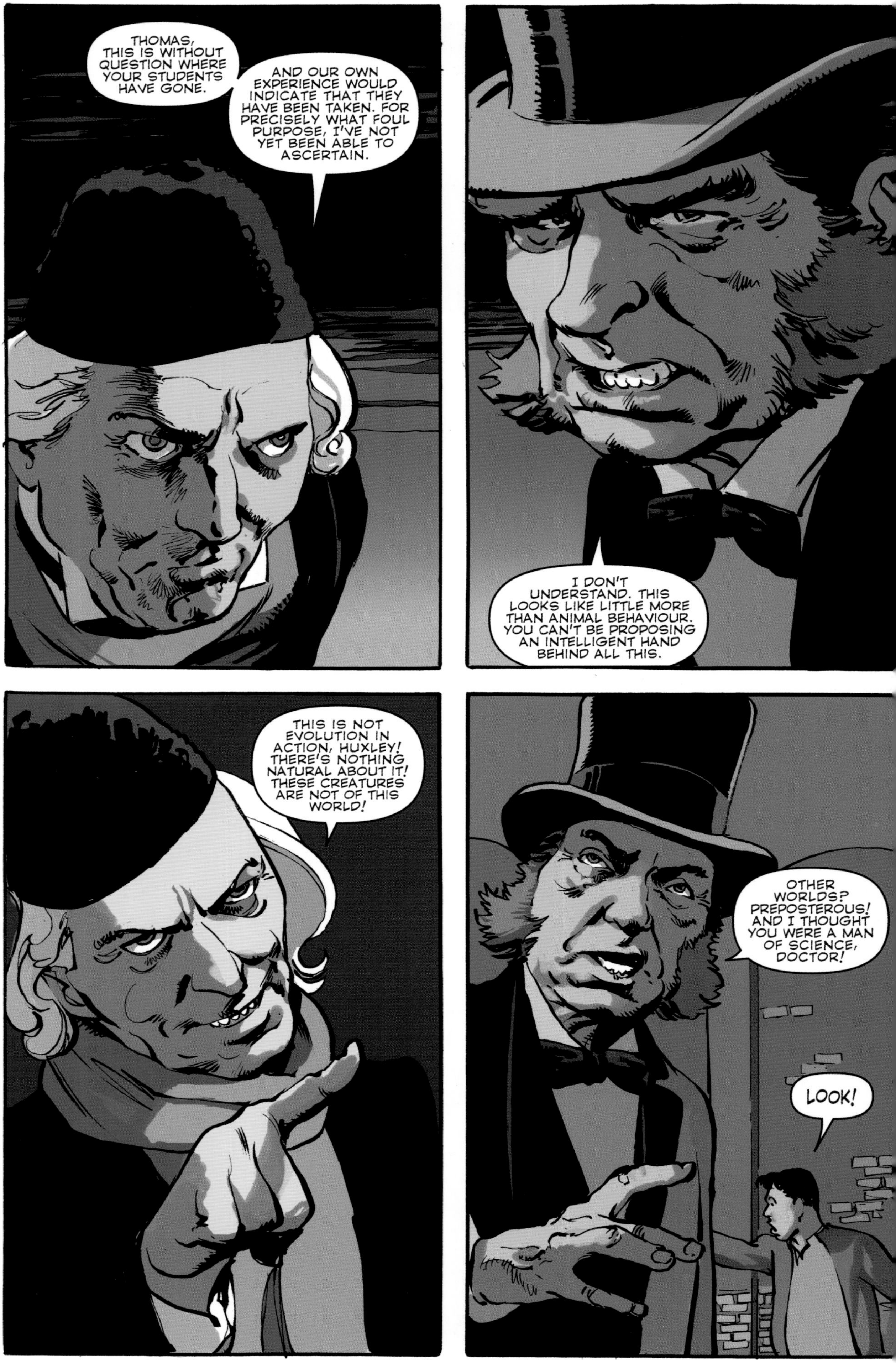
THOMAS, THIS IS WITHOUT QUESTION WHERE YOUR STUDENTS HAVE GONE.
AND OUR OWN EXPERIENCE WOULD INDICATE THAT THEY HAVE BEEN TAKEN. FOR PRECISELY WHAT FOUL PURPOSE, I'VE NOT YET BEEN ABLE TO ASCERTAIN.
I DON'T UNDERSTAND. THIS LOOKS LIKE LITTLE MORE THAN ANIMAL BEHAVIOUR. YOU CAN'T BE PROPOSING AN INTELLIGENT HAND BEHIND ALL THIS.
THIS IS NOT EVOLUTION IN ACTION, HUXLEY! THERE'S NOTHING NATURAL ABOUT IT! THESE CREATURES ARE NOT OF THIS WORLD!
OTHER WORLDS? PREPOSTEROUS! AND I THOUGHT YOU WERE A MAN OF SCIENCE, DOCTOR!
LOOK!

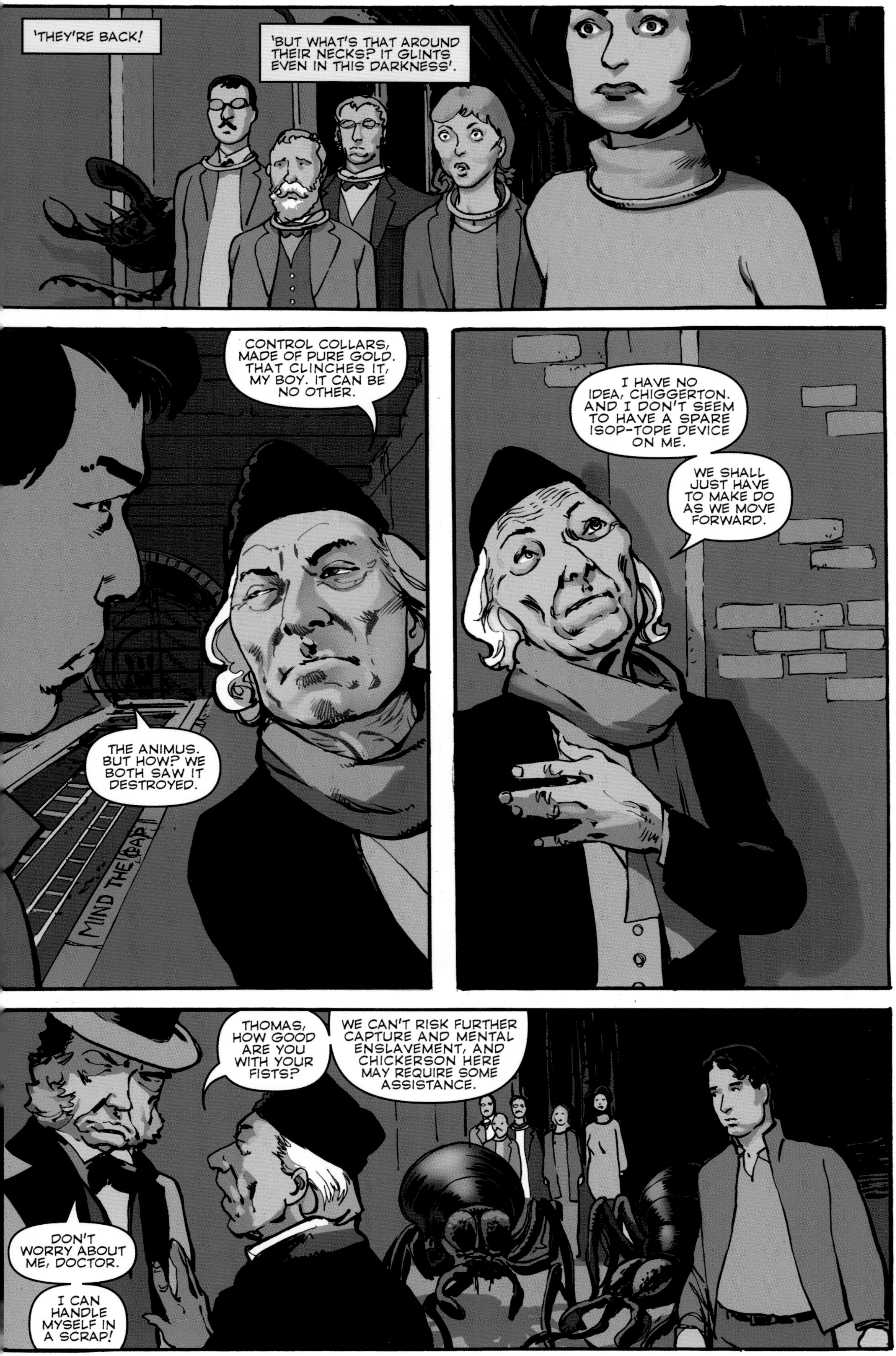
'THEY'RE BACK!
'BUT WHAT'S THAT AROUND THEIR NECKS? IT GLINTS EVEN IN THIS DARKNESS'.
CONTROL COLLARS, MADE OF PURE GOLD. THAT CLINCHES IT, MY BOY. IT CAN BE NO OTHER.
THE ANIMUS. BUT HOW? WE BOTH SAW IT DESTROYED.
MIND THE GAP
I HAVE NO IDEA, CHIGGERTON. AND I DON'T SEEM TO HAVE A SPARE ISOP-TOPE DEVICE ON ME.
WE SHALL JUST HAVE TO MAKE DO AS WE MOVE FORWARD.
THOMAS, HOW GOOD ARE YOU WITH YOUR FISTS?
WE CAN'T RISK FURTHER CAPTURE AND MENTAL ENSLAVEMENT, AND CHICKERSON HERE MAY REQUIRE SOME ASSISTANCE.
DON'T WORRY ABOUT ME, DOCTOR.
I CAN HANDLE MYSELF IN A SCRAP!

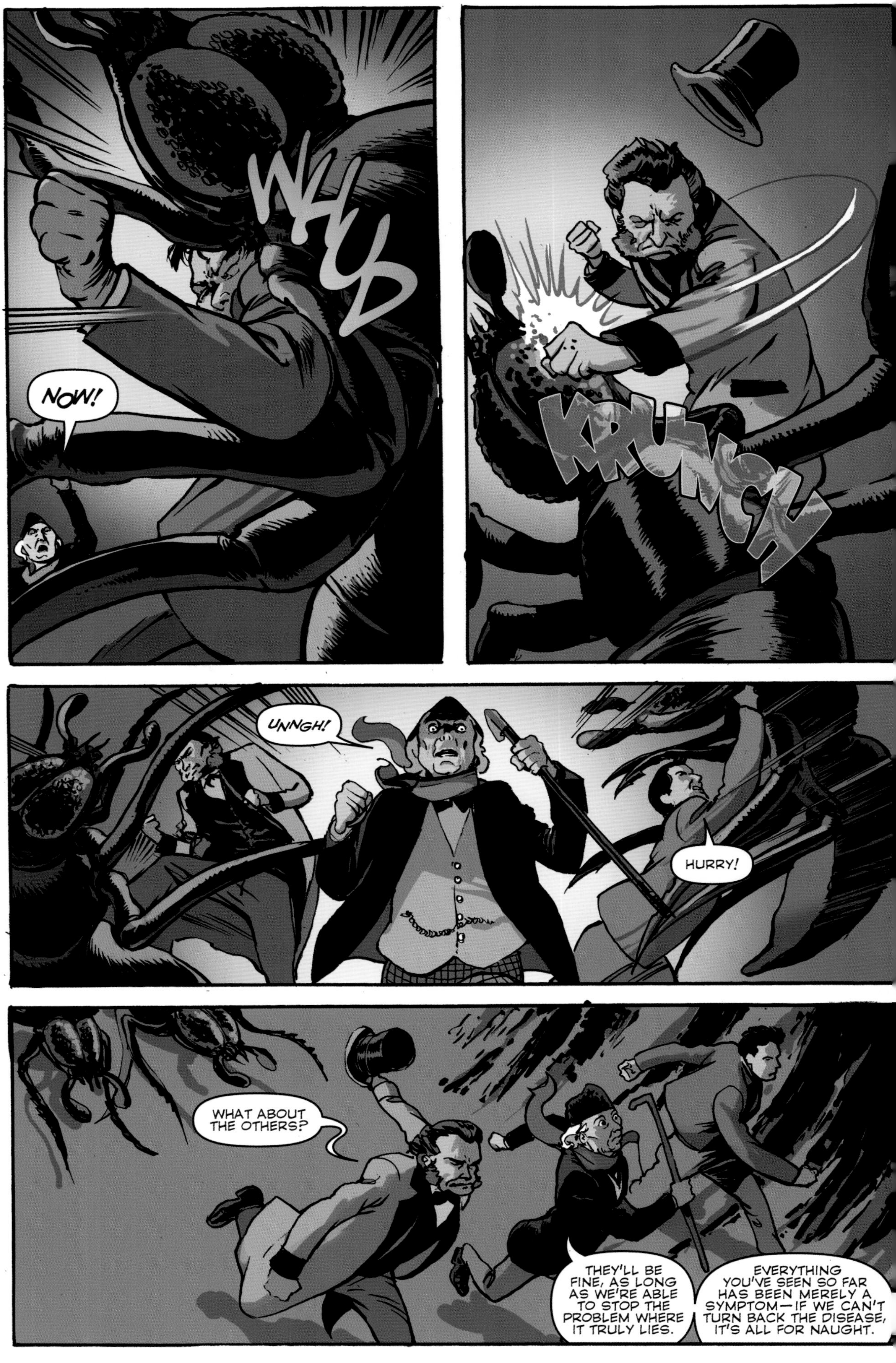
WHUD
NOW!
KRUNCH
UNNGH!
HURRY!
WHAT ABOUT THE OTHERS?
THEY'LL BE FINE, AS LONG AS WE'RE ABLE TO STOP THE PROBLEM WHERE IT TRULY LIES.
EVERYTHING YOU'VE SEEN SO FAR HAS BEEN MERELY A SYMPTOM—IF WE CAN'T TURN BACK THE DISEASE, IT'S ALL FOR NAUGHT.

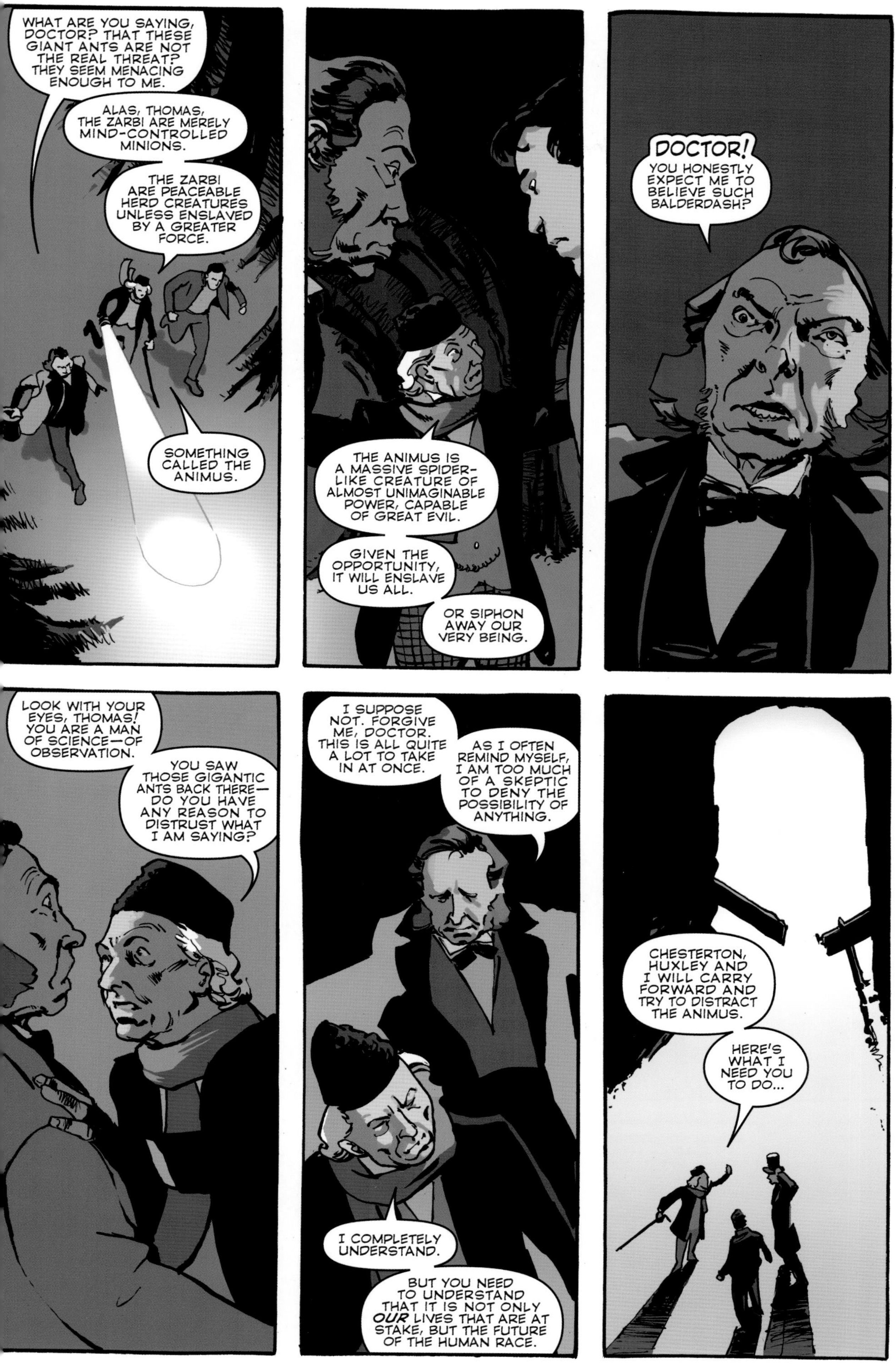

WHAT ARE YOU SAYING, DOCTOR? THAT THESE GIANT ANTS ARE NOT THE REAL THREAT? THEY SEEM MENACING ENOUGH TO ME.
ALAS, THOMAS, THE ZARBI ARE MERELY MIND-CONTROLLED MINIONS.
THE ZARBI ARE PEACEABLE HERD CREATURES UNLESS ENSLAVED BY A GREATER FORCE.
SOMETHING CALLED THE ANIMUS.
THE ANIMUS IS A MASSIVE SPIDER-LIKE CREATURE OF ALMOST UNIMAGINABLE POWER, CAPABLE OF GREAT EVIL.
GIVEN THE OPPORTUNITY, IT WILL ENSLAVE US ALL.
OR SIPHON AWAY OUR VERY BEING.
DOCTOR! YOU HONESTLY EXPECT ME TO BELIEVE SUCH BALDERDASH?
LOOK WITH YOUR EYES, THOMAS! YOU ARE A MAN OF SCIENCE—OF OBSERVATION.
YOU SAW THOSE GIGANTIC ANTS BACK THERE—DO YOU HAVE ANY REASON TO DISTRUST WHAT I AM SAYING?
I SUPPOSE NOT. FORGIVE ME, DOCTOR. THIS IS ALL QUITE A LOT TO TAKE IN AT ONCE.
AS I OFTEN REMIND MYSELF, I AM TOO MUCH OF A SKEPTIC TO DENY THE POSSIBILITY OF ANYTHING.
I COMPLETELY UNDERSTAND.
BUT YOU NEED TO UNDERSTAND THAT IT IS NOT ONLY OUR LIVES THAT ARE AT STAKE, BUT THE FUTURE OF THE HUMAN RACE.
CHESTERTON, HUXLEY AND I WILL CARRY FORWARD AND TRY TO DISTRACT THE ANIMUS.
HERE'S WHAT I NEED YOU TO DO...

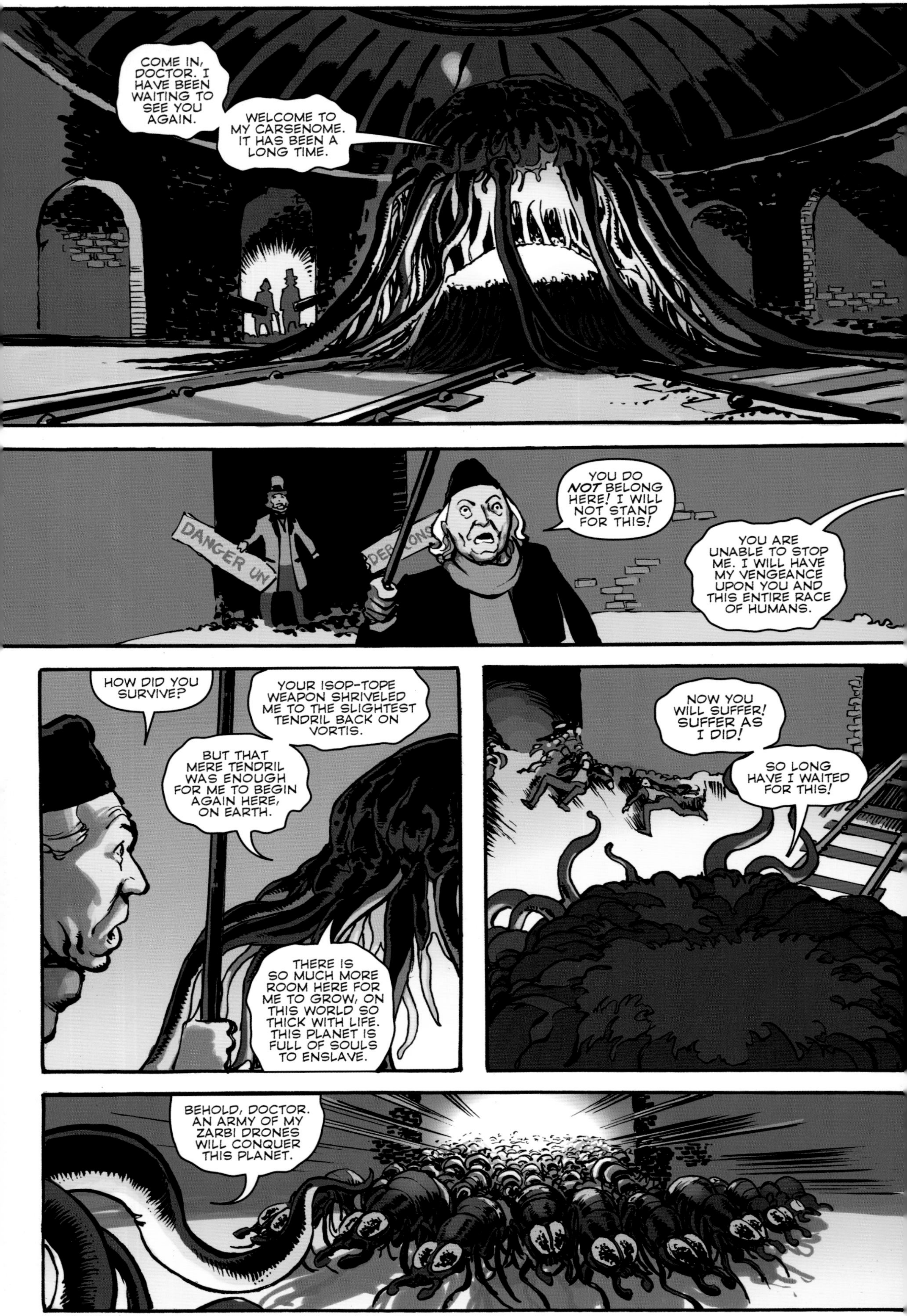
COME IN, DOCTOR. I HAVE BEEN WAITING TO SEE YOU AGAIN.
WELCOME TO MY CARSENOME. IT HAS BEEN A LONG TIME.
DANGER UN
DER CONS
YOU DO *NOT* BELONG HERE! I WILL NOT STAND FOR THIS!
YOU ARE UNABLE TO STOP ME. I WILL HAVE MY VENGEANCE UPON YOU AND THIS ENTIRE RACE OF HUMANS.
HOW DID YOU SURVIVE?
YOUR ISOP-TOPE WEAPON SHRIVELED ME TO THE SLIGHTEST TENDRIL BACK ON VORTIS.
BUT THAT MERE TENDRIL WAS ENOUGH FOR ME TO BEGIN AGAIN HERE, ON EARTH.
THERE IS SO MUCH MORE ROOM HERE FOR ME TO GROW, ON THIS WORLD SO THICK WITH LIFE. THIS PLANET IS FULL OF SOULS TO ENSLAVE.
NOW YOU WILL SUFFER! SUFFER AS I DID!
SO LONG HAVE I WAITED FOR THIS!
BEHOLD, DOCTOR. AN ARMY OF MY ZARBI DRONES WILL CONQUER THIS PLANET.

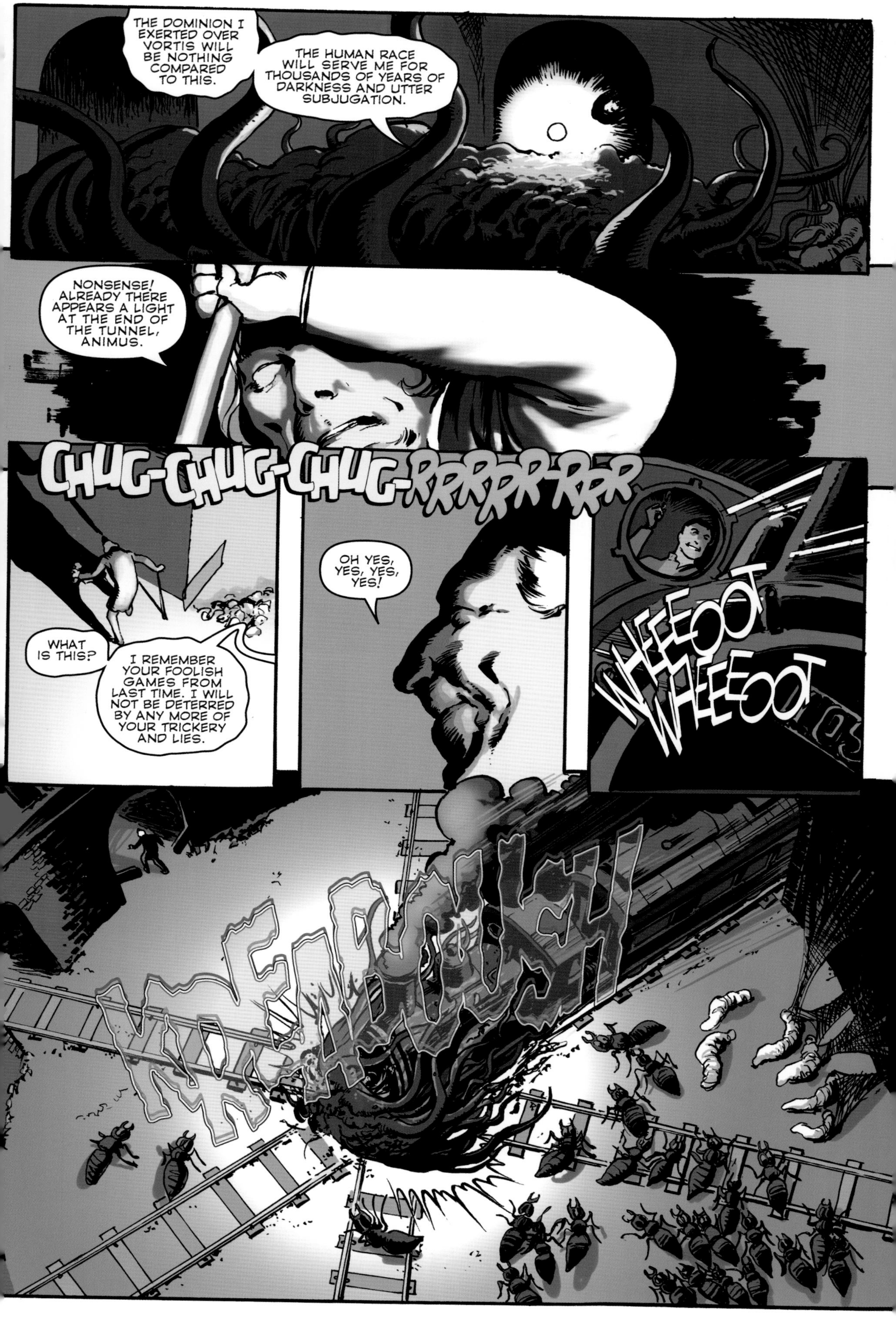

THE DOMINION I EXERTED OVER VORTIS WILL BE NOTHING COMPARED TO THIS.
THE HUMAN RACE WILL SERVE ME FOR THOUSANDS OF YEARS OF DARKNESS AND UTTER SUBJUGATION.
NONSENSE! ALREADY THERE APPEARS A LIGHT AT THE END OF THE TUNNEL, ANIMUS.
CHUG-CHUG-CHUG-RRRRR-RRR
WHAT IS THIS?
I REMEMBER YOUR FOOLISH GAMES FROM LAST TIME. I WILL NOT BE DETERRED BY ANY MORE OF YOUR TRICKERY AND LIES.
OH YES, YES, YES, YES!
WHEEEOOT WHEEEOOT

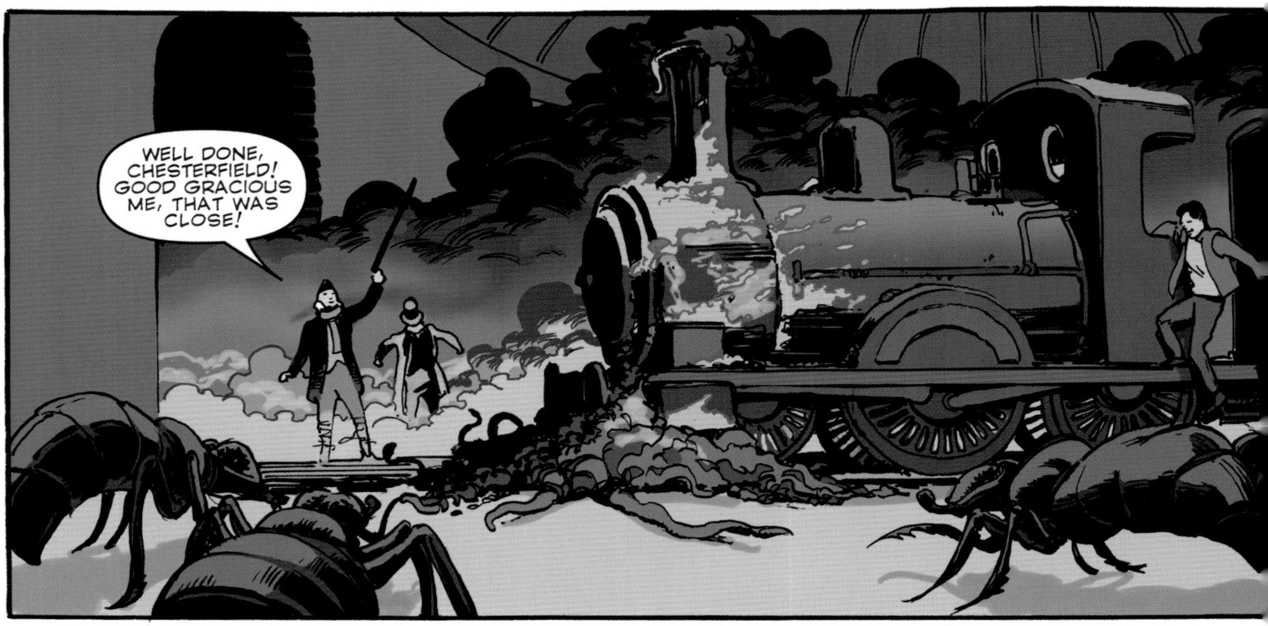
WELL DONE, CHESTERFIELD! GOOD GRACIOUS ME, THAT WAS CLOSE!

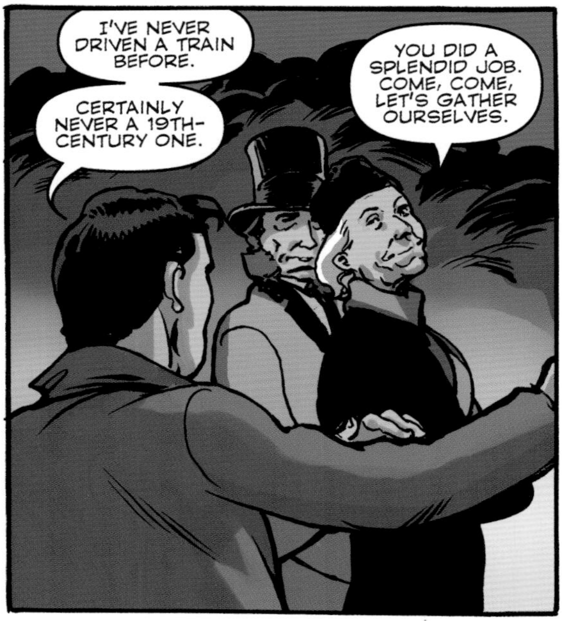
I'VE NEVER DRIVEN A TRAIN BEFORE.
CERTAINLY NEVER A 19TH-CENTURY ONE.
YOU DID A SPLENDID JOB. COME, COME, LET'S GATHER OURSELVES.

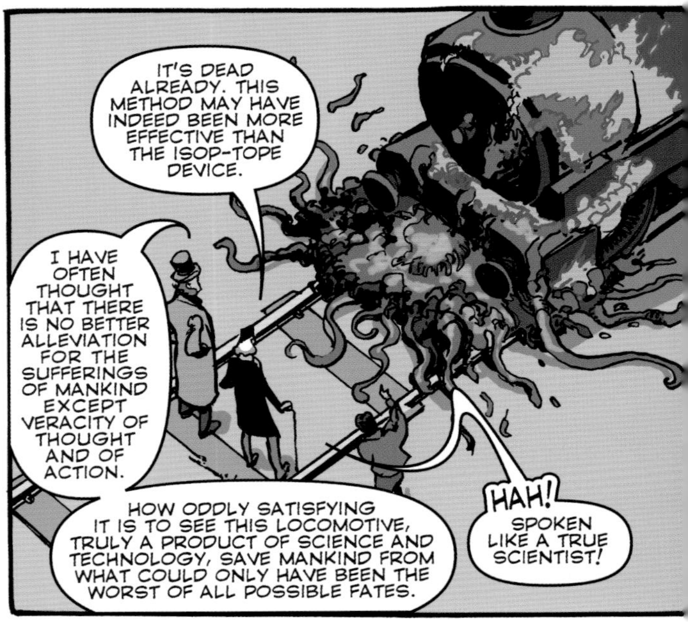
IT'S DEAD ALREADY. THIS METHOD MAY HAVE INDEED BEEN MORE EFFECTIVE THAN THE ISOP-TOPE DEVICE.
I HAVE OFTEN THOUGHT THAT THERE IS NO BETTER ALLEVIATION FOR THE SUFFERINGS OF MANKIND EXCEPT VERACITY OF THOUGHT AND OF ACTION.
HOW ODDLY SATISFYING IT IS TO SEE THIS LOCOMOTIVE, TRULY A PRODUCT OF SCIENCE AND TECHNOLOGY, SAVE MANKIND FROM WHAT COULD ONLY HAVE BEEN THE WORST OF ALL POSSIBLE FATES.
HAH! SPOKEN LIKE A TRUE SCIENTIST!

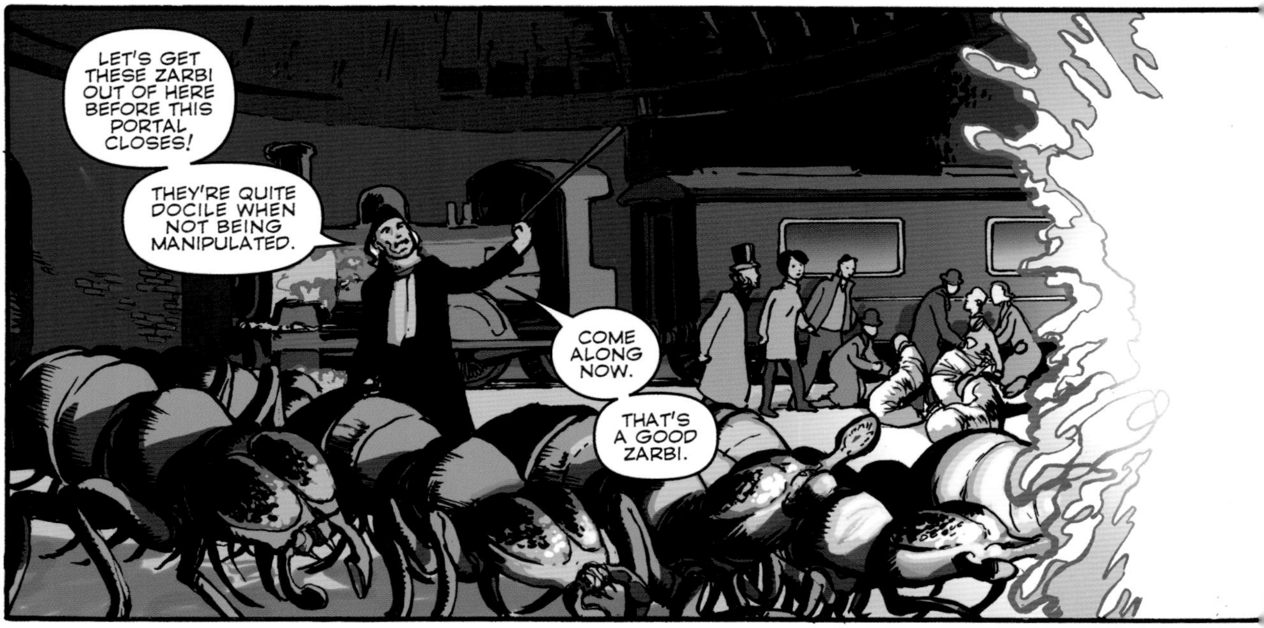
LET'S GET THESE ZARBI OUT OF HERE BEFORE THIS PORTAL CLOSES!
THEY'RE QUITE DOCILE WHEN NOT BEING MANIPULATED.
COME ALONG NOW.
THAT'S A GOOD ZARBI.

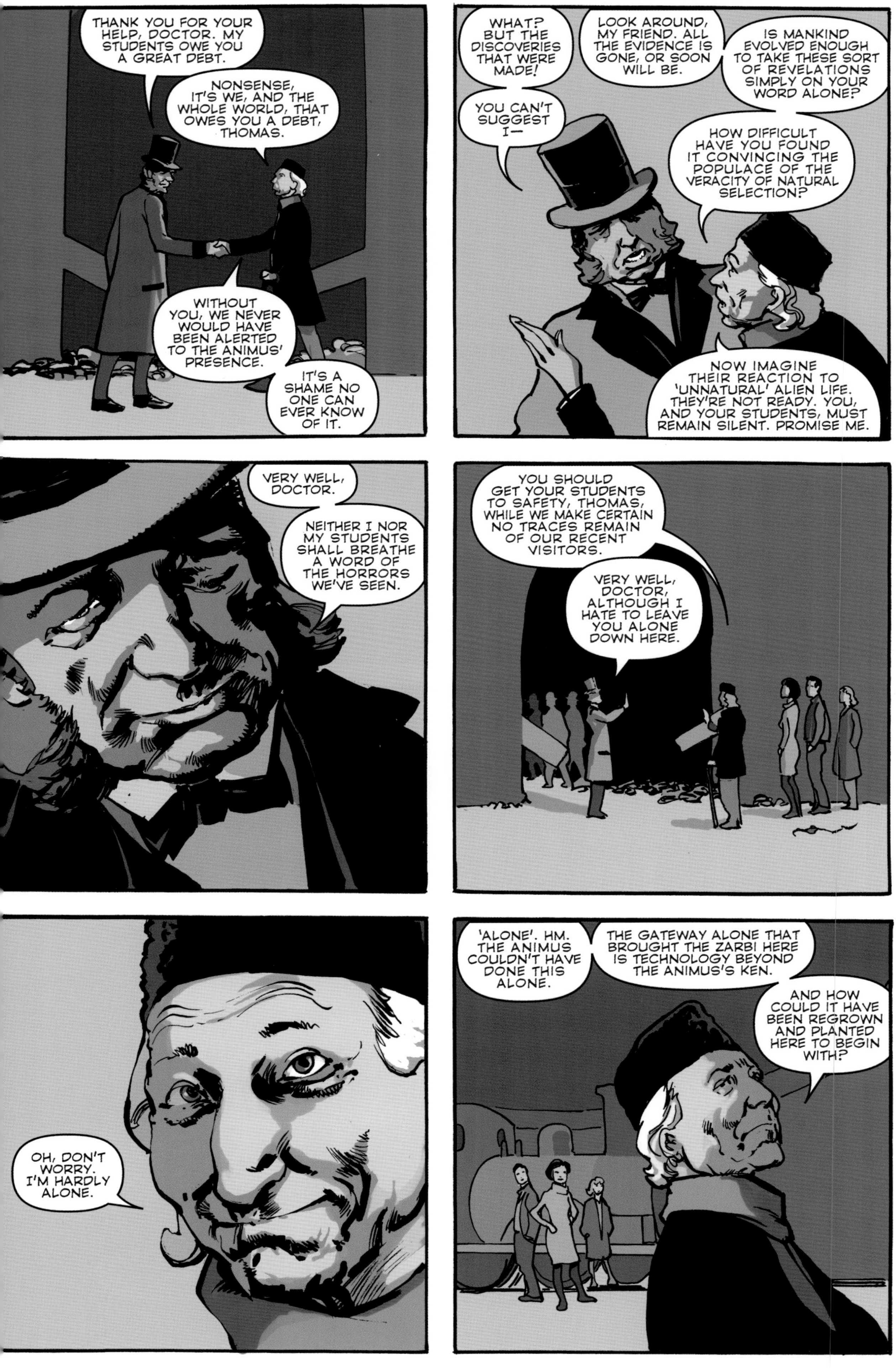
THANK YOU FOR YOUR HELP, DOCTOR. MY STUDENTS OWE YOU A GREAT DEBT.
NONSENSE, IT'S WE, AND THE WHOLE WORLD, THAT OWES YOU A DEBT, THOMAS.
WITHOUT YOU, WE NEVER WOULD HAVE BEEN ALERTED TO THE ANIMUS' PRESENCE.
IT'S A SHAME NO ONE CAN EVER KNOW OF IT.
WHAT? BUT THE DISCOVERIES THAT WERE MADE!
YOU CAN'T SUGGEST I—
LOOK AROUND, MY FRIEND. ALL THE EVIDENCE IS GONE, OR SOON WILL BE.
IS MANKIND EVOLVED ENOUGH TO TAKE THESE SORT OF REVELATIONS SIMPLY ON YOUR WORD ALONE?
HOW DIFFICULT HAVE YOU FOUND IT CONVINCING THE POPULACE OF THE VERACITY OF NATURAL SELECTION?
NOW IMAGINE THEIR REACTION TO 'UNNATURAL' ALIEN LIFE. THEY'RE NOT READY. YOU, AND YOUR STUDENTS, MUST REMAIN SILENT. PROMISE ME.
VERY WELL, DOCTOR.
NEITHER I NOR MY STUDENTS SHALL BREATHE A WORD OF THE HORRORS WE'VE SEEN.
YOU SHOULD GET YOUR STUDENTS TO SAFETY, THOMAS, WHILE WE MAKE CERTAIN NO TRACES REMAIN OF OUR RECENT VISITORS.
VERY WELL, DOCTOR, ALTHOUGH I HATE TO LEAVE YOU ALONE DOWN HERE.
OH, DON'T WORRY. I'M HARDLY ALONE.
'ALONE'. HM. THE ANIMUS COULDN'T HAVE DONE THIS ALONE.
THE GATEWAY ALONE THAT BROUGHT THE ZARBI HERE IS TECHNOLOGY BEYOND THE ANIMUS'S KEN.
AND HOW COULD IT HAVE BEEN REGROWN AND PLANTED HERE TO BEGIN WITH?

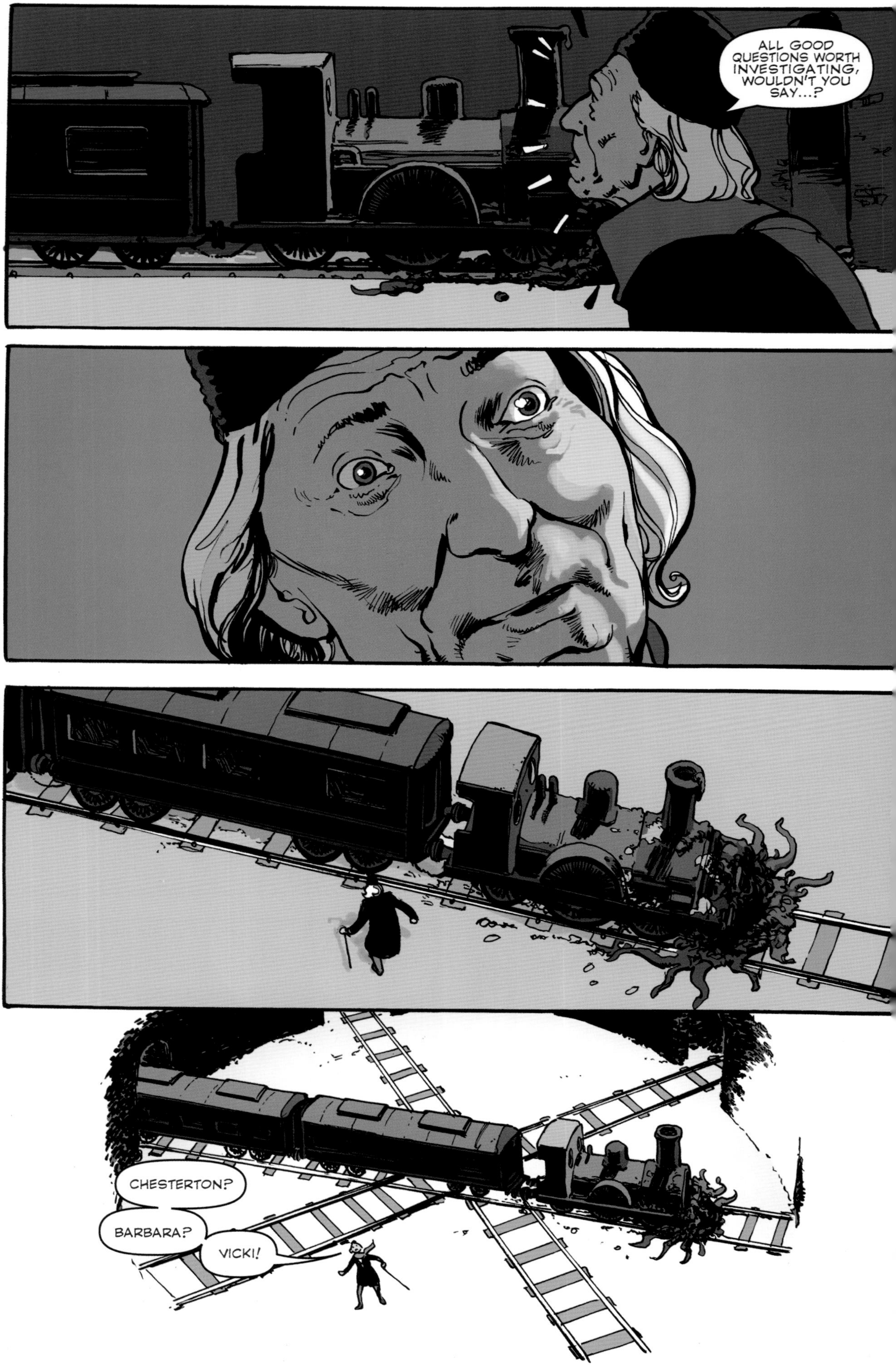
ALL GOOD QUESTIONS WORTH INVESTIGATING, WOULDN'T YOU SAY...?
CHESTERTON?
BARBARA?
VICKI!

REFLECTIONS OF TIME

Wherein prominent Whovians past and present muse upon the Doctor's history in comic form.

It's all too easy to poke fun at the early *Doctor Who* comic strips published in *TV Comic*, or even to dismiss them entirely. If we were to use the solar system to represent the entire body of *Doctor Who* adventures, with the TV series itself being the Sun around which everything else rotates, the comic strip stories from the 1960s would be somewhere out beyond Pluto, insignificant, overlooked and forgotten. And that's rather a shame, really.

I first encountered the First Doctor's strip adventures when I was invited to write the supporting features for Marvel UK's *Doctor Who Classic Comics* in the early 1990s. I wasn't quite old enough to have read them on their original publication, so it was with some excitement that I visited the British Library's newspaper archive in London to unearth this forgotten, alternative version of *Doctor Who*. "I'm reading them so that you don't have to," I used to joke to people at the time. The stories had little in common with the style of the TV series that they were supposedly emulating and the plots were often extremely simplistic and full of contradictions. Yet, despite my derogatory jibe, as I slowly worked my way through one dusty bound volume of *TV Comic* after another, I did develop quite an affection for these forgotten adventures.

These days, the writers, producers and editors of all *Doctor Who* spin-off stories, be they comic strips, novels or audio dramas, strive to make their adventures as authentic as possible, so much so that they could

feasibly fit seamlessly in between episodes of the TV series. Indeed, they *have* to be authentic as the BBC insist upon it and check each story for any inaccuracies or inconsistencies. It was a different world back in the 1960s...

When the Doctor made his comic strip debut in the first part of *The Klepton Parasites*, published in *TV Comic* on November 14, 1964, he did indeed resemble William Hartnell. And just like the first episode of the TV series, his police box TARDIS was located in a junk yard. But that's just about where any similarity with the TV series ended. Instead of his familiar TV companions, the Doctor was joined in his travels by young brother and sister, John and Gillian, who were apparently his grandchildren. Worse still, they addressed their grandfather not as 'Doctor' but 'Dr. Who'!

Despite the outer space settings, the First Doctor's adventures with John and Gillian were more of the fairytale variety rather than the science-fiction and historical adventure of the TV serials. The Pied Piper of Hamelin, the Ancient Mariner and even Father Christmas all make appearances—with the latter manufacturing toy TARDIS police boxes to deliver to

the Earth's children as Christmas presents. Even the Daleks, such an essential element of *Doctor Who*'s success, were absent due to copyright restrictions, their place taken by the robotic Trods who whizzed around on caterpillar tracks.

This all seems a far cry from the TV series. And yet, there is an undeniable charm to these whimsical, unsophisticated stories that have their origins in simpler times. I think that the *Doctor Who* universe would be a little less interesting without the likes of the Trods, John and Gillian, and their grandfather Dr. Who.

—John Ainsworth
producer, director, and script
editor for Big Finish Productions

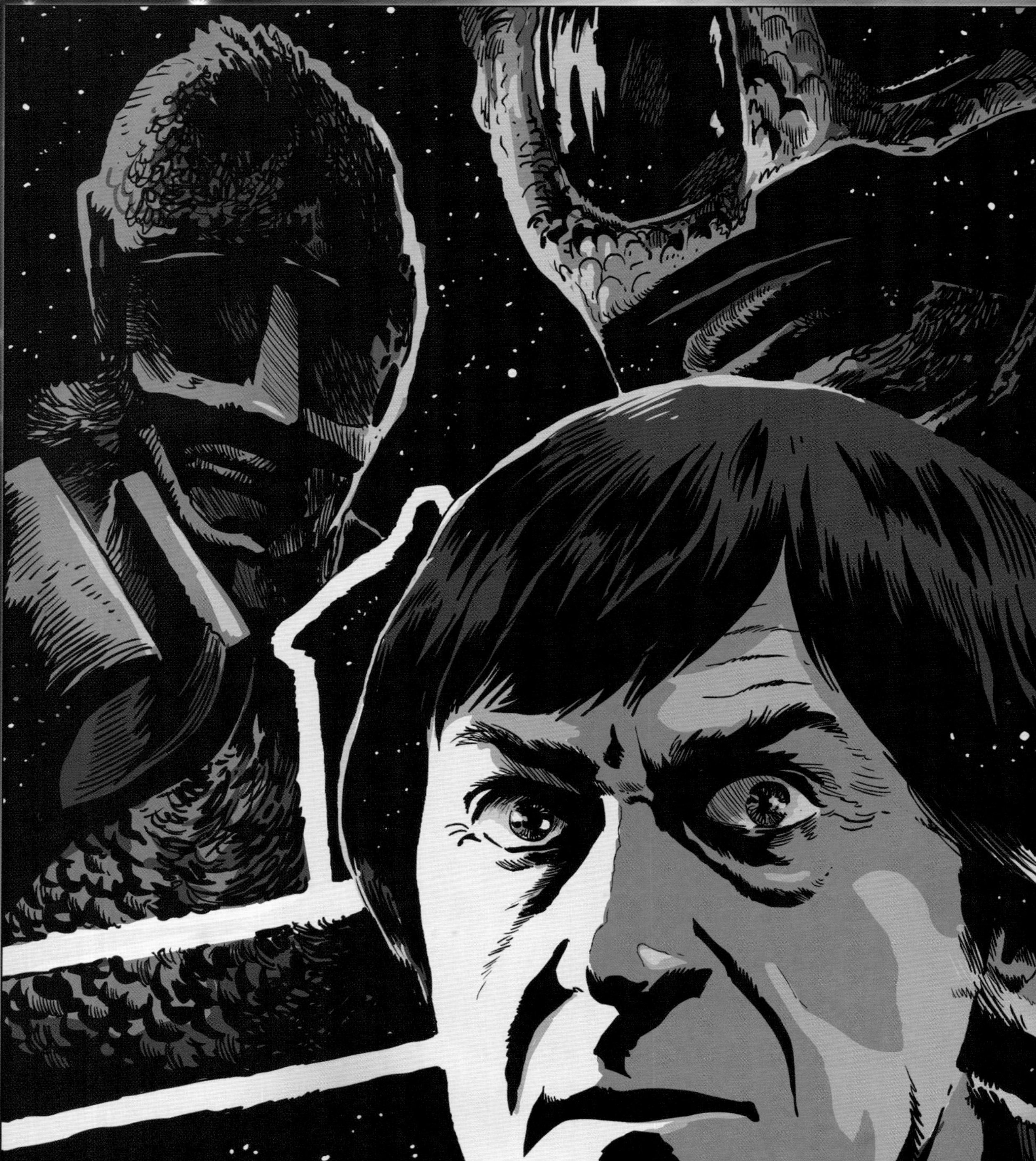

LIC
BOX
FRAN CAVIL

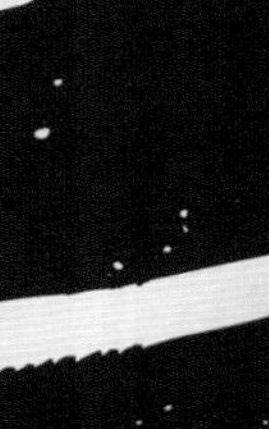

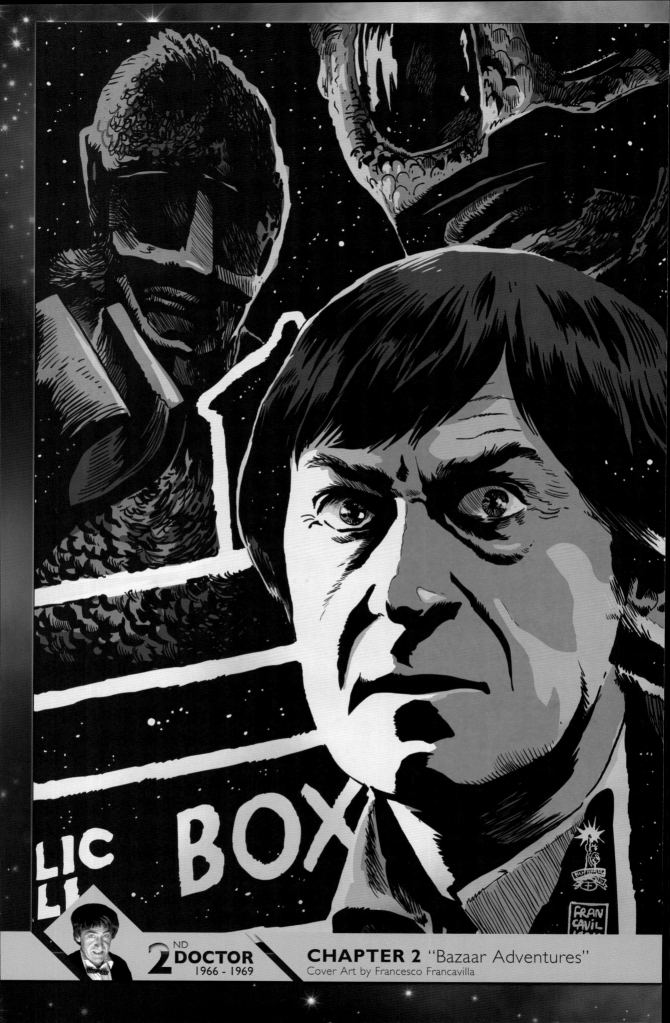

2ND DOCTOR
1966 - 1969

CHAPTER 2 "Bazaar Adventures"

Cover Art by Francesco Francavilla

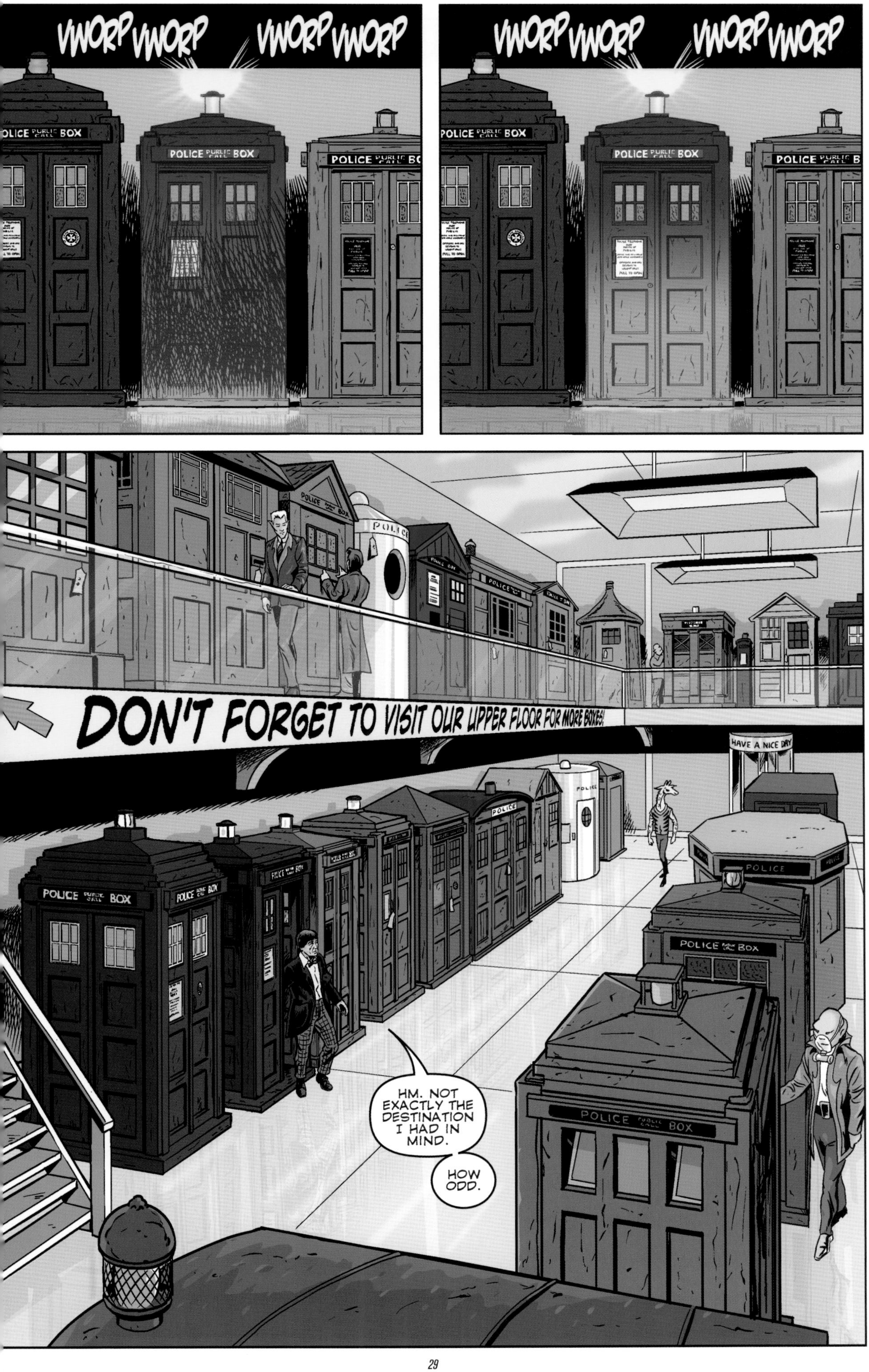
VWORP VWORP
VWORP VWORP
VWORP VWORP
VWORP VWORP
DON'T FORGET TO VISIT OUR UPPER FLOOR FOR MORE BOXES!
HAVE A NICE DAY
HM. NOT EXACTLY THE DESTINATION I HAD IN MIND.
HOW ODD.

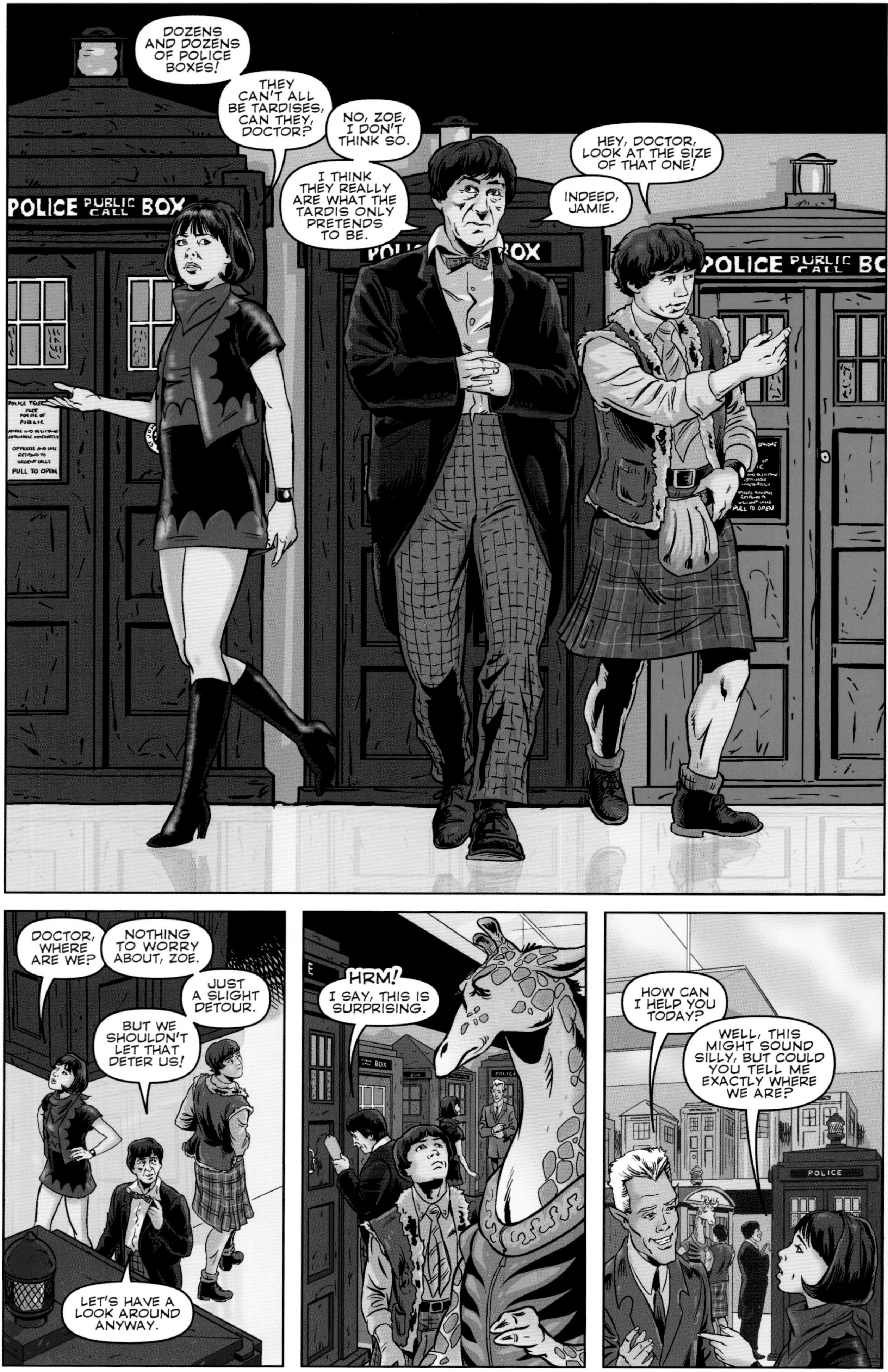
DOZENS AND DOZENS OF POLICE BOXES!
THEY CAN'T ALL BE TARDISES, CAN THEY, DOCTOR?
NO, ZOE, I DON'T THINK SO.
I THINK THEY REALLY ARE WHAT THE TARDIS ONLY PRETENDS TO BE.
HEY, DOCTOR, LOOK AT THE SIZE OF THAT ONE!
INDEED, JAMIE.
POLICE PUBLIC CALL BOX
PULL TO OPEN
DOCTOR, WHERE ARE WE?
NOTHING TO WORRY ABOUT, ZOE.
JUST A SLIGHT DETOUR.
BUT WE SHOULDN'T LET THAT DETER US!
LET'S HAVE A LOOK AROUND ANYWAY.
HRM!
I SAY, THIS IS SURPRISING.
HOW CAN I HELP YOU TODAY?
WELL, THIS MIGHT SOUND SILLY, BUT COULD YOU TELL ME EXACTLY WHERE WE ARE?
POLICE

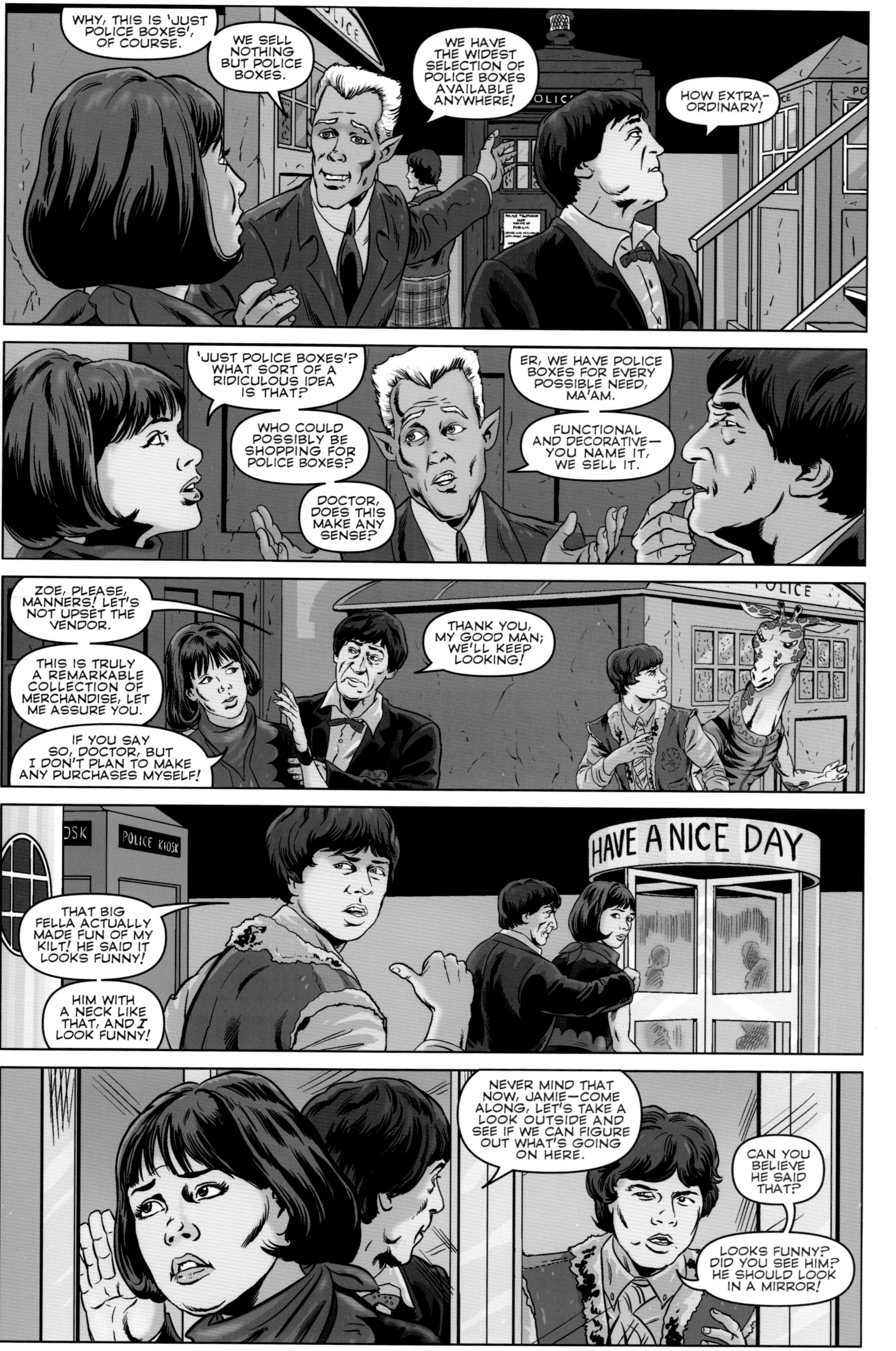
WHY, THIS IS 'JUST POLICE BOXES', OF COURSE.
WE SELL NOTHING BUT POLICE BOXES.
WE HAVE THE WIDEST SELECTION OF POLICE BOXES AVAILABLE ANYWHERE!
HOW EXTRA-ORDINARY!
'JUST POLICE BOXES'? WHAT SORT OF A RIDICULOUS IDEA IS THAT?
WHO COULD POSSIBLY BE SHOPPING FOR POLICE BOXES?
DOCTOR, DOES THIS MAKE ANY SENSE?
ER, WE HAVE POLICE BOXES FOR EVERY POSSIBLE NEED, MA'AM.
FUNCTIONAL AND DECORATIVE— YOU NAME IT, WE SELL IT.
ZOE, PLEASE, MANNERS! LET'S NOT UPSET THE VENDOR.
THIS IS TRULY A REMARKABLE COLLECTION OF MERCHANDISE, LET ME ASSURE YOU.
THANK YOU, MY GOOD MAN; WE'LL KEEP LOOKING!
IF YOU SAY SO, DOCTOR, BUT I DON'T PLAN TO MAKE ANY PURCHASES MYSELF!
POLICE KIOSK
HAVE A NICE DAY
THAT BIG FELLA ACTUALLY MADE FUN OF MY KILT! HE SAID IT LOOKS FUNNY!
HIM WITH A NECK LIKE THAT, AND *I* LOOK FUNNY!
NEVER MIND THAT NOW, JAMIE—COME ALONG, LET'S TAKE A LOOK OUTSIDE AND SEE IF WE CAN FIGURE OUT WHAT'S GOING ON HERE.
CAN YOU BELIEVE HE SAID THAT?
LOOKS FUNNY? DID YOU SEE HIM? HE SHOULD LOOK IN A MIRROR!

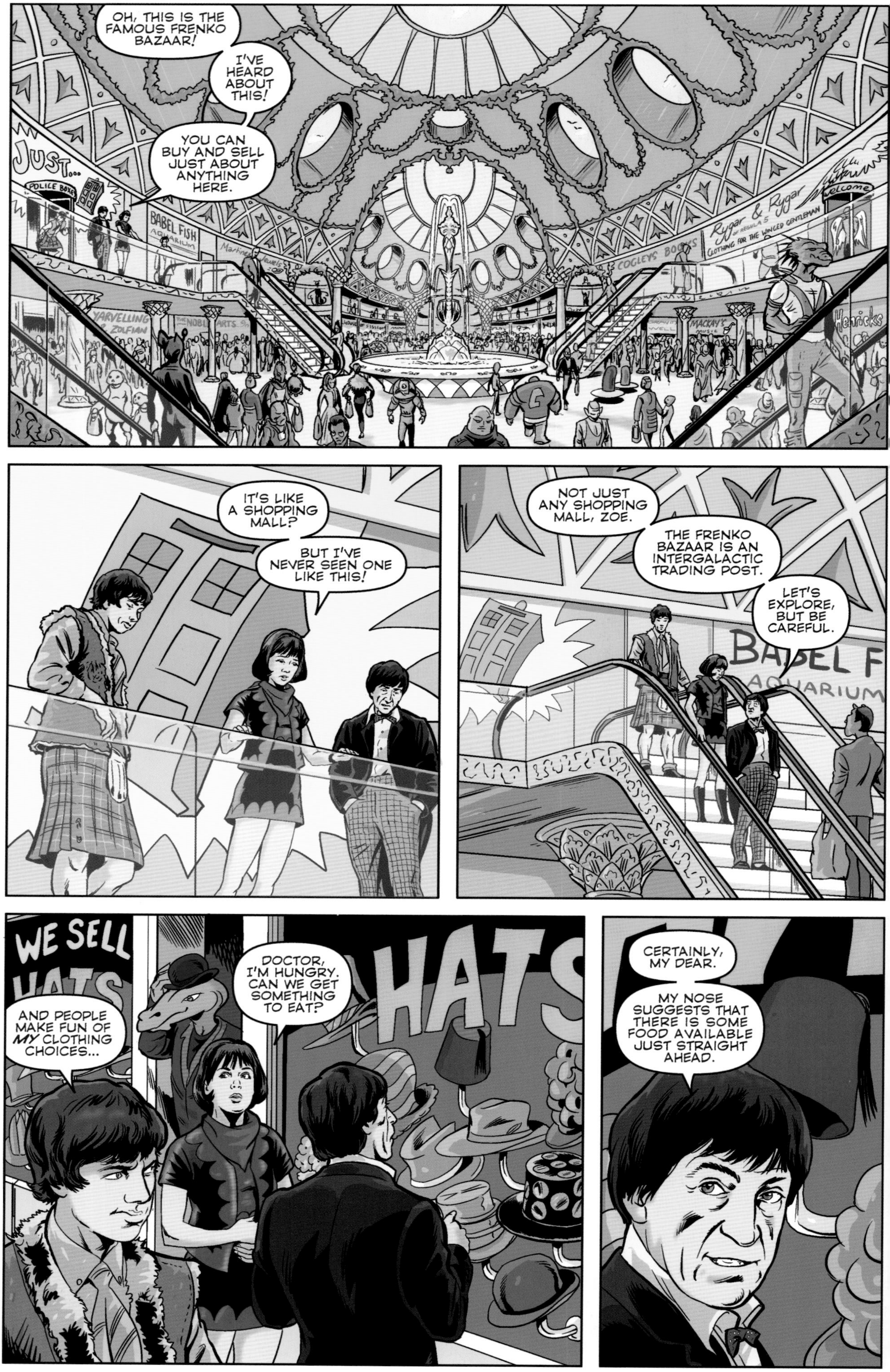

OH, THIS IS THE FAMOUS FRENKO BAZAAR!
I'VE HEARD ABOUT THIS!
YOU CAN BUY AND SELL JUST ABOUT ANYTHING HERE.
JUST...
POLICE BOXES
BABEL FISH AQUARIUM
COGLEYS BOOKS
Rygar & Rygar of Regula 5
CLOTHING FOR THE WINGED GENTLEMAN
Welcome
YARVELLING & ZOLFIAN
Henricks
IT'S LIKE A SHOPPING MALL?
BUT I'VE NEVER SEEN ONE LIKE THIS!
NOT JUST ANY SHOPPING MALL, ZOE.
THE FRENKO BAZAAR IS AN INTERGALACTIC TRADING POST.
LET'S EXPLORE, BUT BE CAREFUL.
BABEL F
AQUARIUM
WE SELL HATS
HATS
AND PEOPLE MAKE FUN OF *MY* CLOTHING CHOICES...
DOCTOR, I'M HUNGRY. CAN WE GET SOMETHING TO EAT?
CERTAINLY, MY DEAR.
MY NOSE SUGGESTS THAT THERE IS SOME FOOD AVAILABLE JUST STRAIGHT AHEAD.

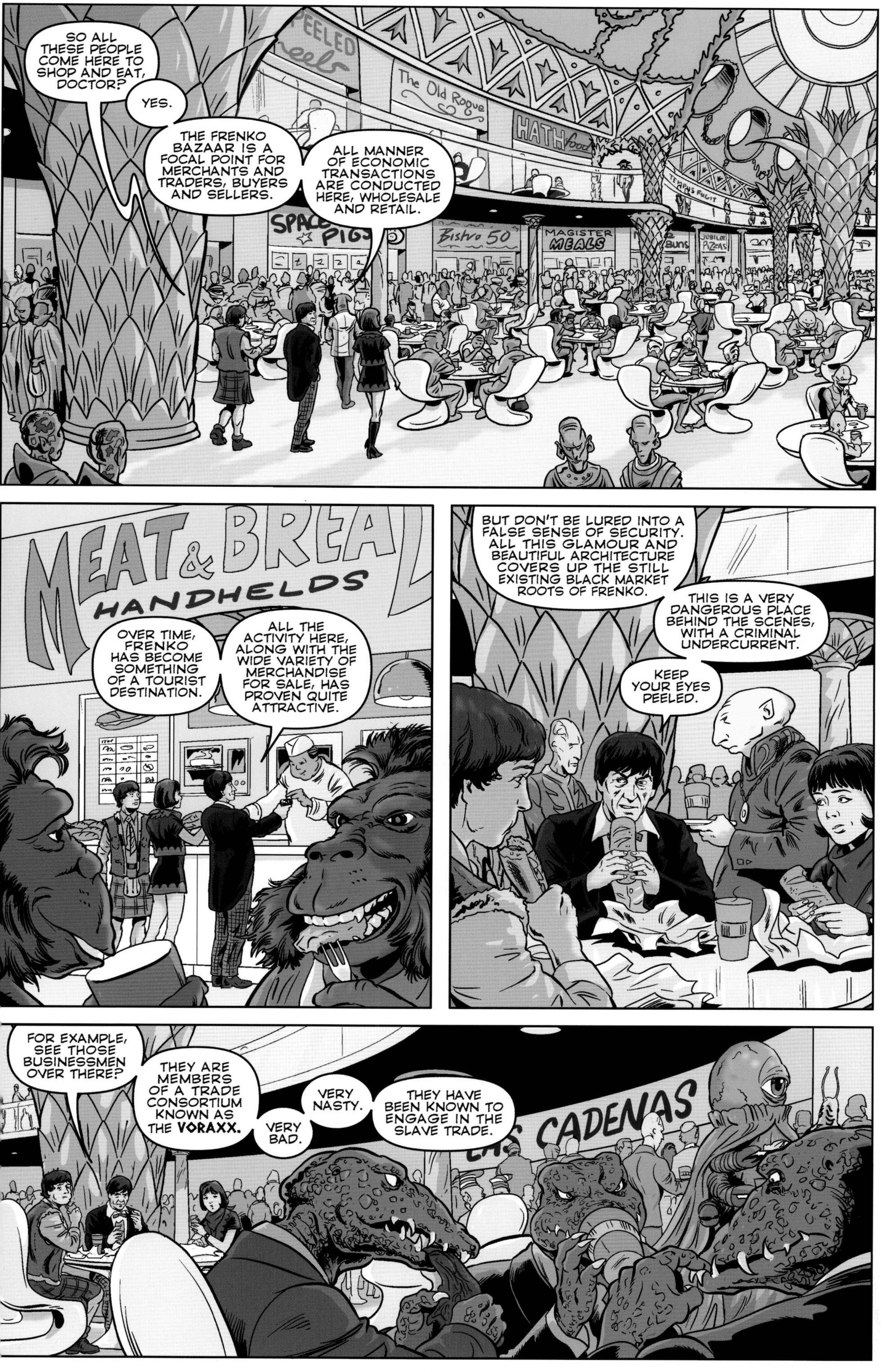

SO ALL THESE PEOPLE COME HERE TO SHOP AND EAT, DOCTOR?
YES.
THE FRENKO BAZAAR IS A FOCAL POINT FOR MERCHANTS AND TRADERS, BUYERS AND SELLERS.
ALL MANNER OF ECONOMIC TRANSACTIONS ARE CONDUCTED HERE, WHOLESALE AND RETAIL.
The Old Rogue
Bistro 50
MAGISTER MEALS
HANDHELDS
OVER TIME, FRENKO HAS BECOME SOMETHING OF A TOURIST DESTINATION.
ALL THE ACTIVITY HERE, ALONG WITH THE WIDE VARIETY OF MERCHANDISE FOR SALE, HAS PROVEN QUITE ATTRACTIVE.
BUT DON'T BE LURED INTO A FALSE SENSE OF SECURITY. ALL THIS GLAMOUR AND BEAUTIFUL ARCHITECTURE COVERS UP THE STILL EXISTING BLACK MARKET ROOTS OF FRENKO.
THIS IS A VERY DANGEROUS PLACE BEHIND THE SCENES, WITH A CRIMINAL UNDERCURRENT.
KEEP YOUR EYES PEELED.
FOR EXAMPLE, SEE THOSE BUSINESSMEN OVER THERE?
THEY ARE MEMBERS OF A TRADE CONSORTIUM KNOWN AS THE **VORAXX.**
VERY BAD.
VERY NASTY.
THEY HAVE BEEN KNOWN TO ENGAGE IN THE SLAVE TRADE.

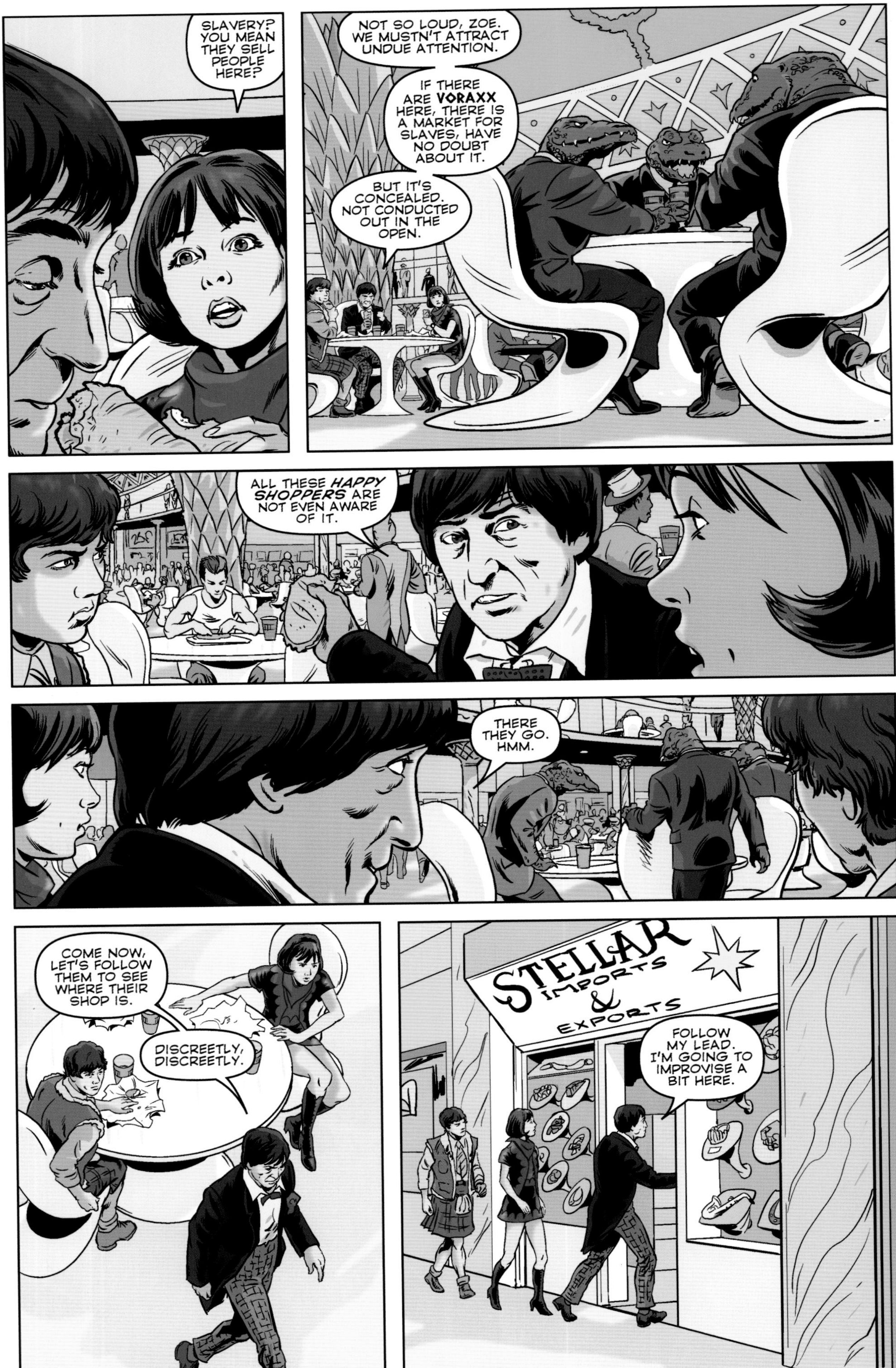

SLAVERY? YOU MEAN THEY SELL PEOPLE HERE?
NOT SO LOUD, ZOE. WE MUSTN'T ATTRACT UNDUE ATTENTION.
IF THERE ARE VORAXX HERE, THERE IS A MARKET FOR SLAVES, HAVE NO DOUBT ABOUT IT.
BUT IT'S CONCEALED. NOT CONDUCTED OUT IN THE OPEN.
ALL THESE HAPPY SHOPPERS ARE NOT EVEN AWARE OF IT.
THERE THEY GO. HMM.
COME NOW, LET'S FOLLOW THEM TO SEE WHERE THEIR SHOP IS.
DISCREETLY, DISCREETLY.
STELLAR IMPORTS & EXPORTS
FOLLOW MY LEAD. I'M GOING TO IMPROVISE A BIT HERE.

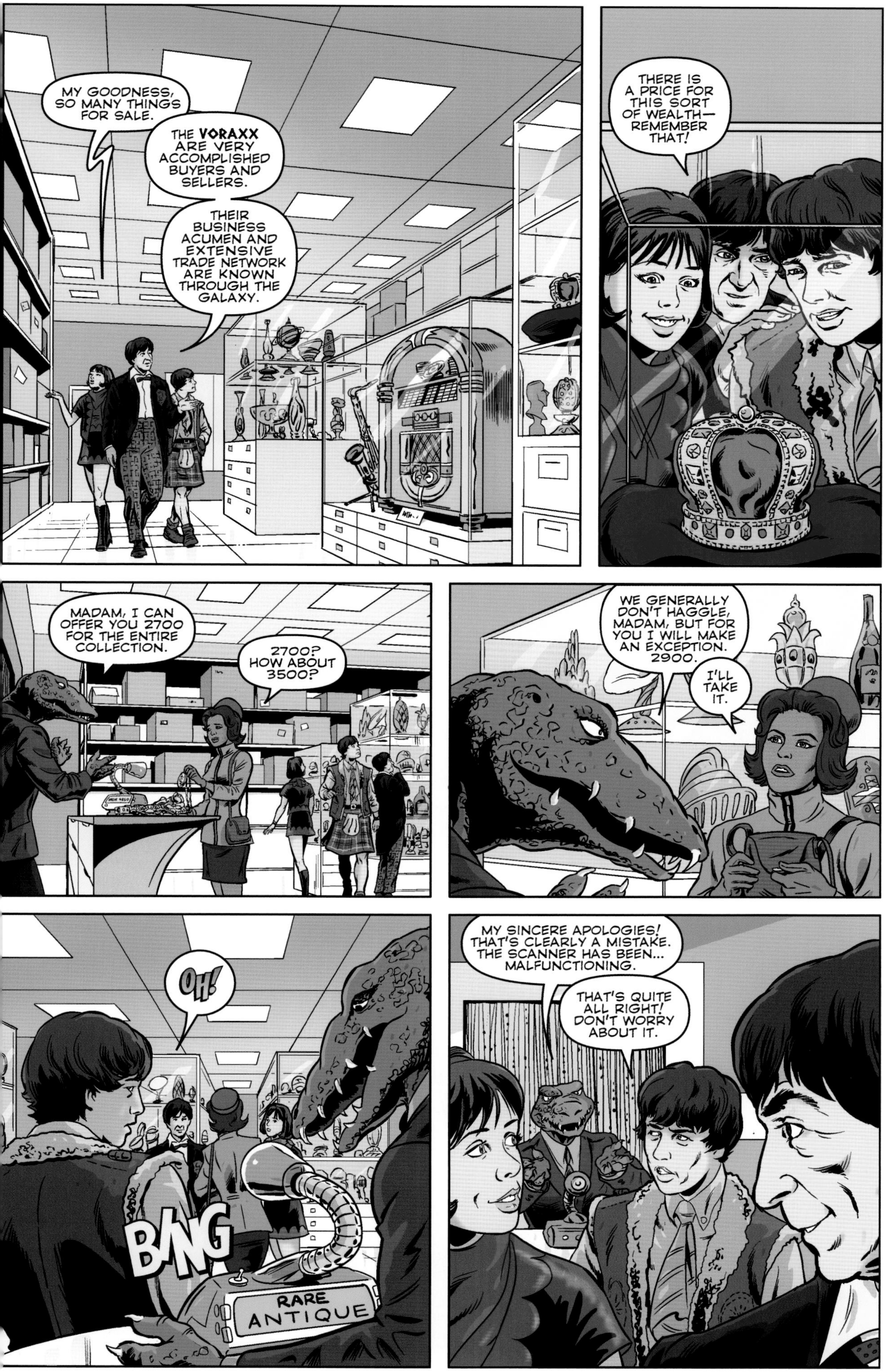
MY GOODNESS, SO MANY THINGS FOR SALE.
THE VORAXX ARE VERY ACCOMPLISHED BUYERS AND SELLERS.
THEIR BUSINESS ACUMEN AND EXTENSIVE TRADE NETWORK ARE KNOWN THROUGH THE GALAXY.
THERE IS A PRICE FOR THIS SORT OF WEALTH— REMEMBER THAT!
MADAM, I CAN OFFER YOU 2700 FOR THE ENTIRE COLLECTION.
2700? HOW ABOUT 3500?
WE GENERALLY DON'T HAGGLE, MADAM, BUT FOR YOU I WILL MAKE AN EXCEPTION. 2900.
I'LL TAKE IT.
OH!
BING
RARE ANTIQUE
MY SINCERE APOLOGIES! THAT'S CLEARLY A MISTAKE. THE SCANNER HAS BEEN... MALFUNCTIONING.
THAT'S QUITE ALL RIGHT! DON'T WORRY ABOUT IT.

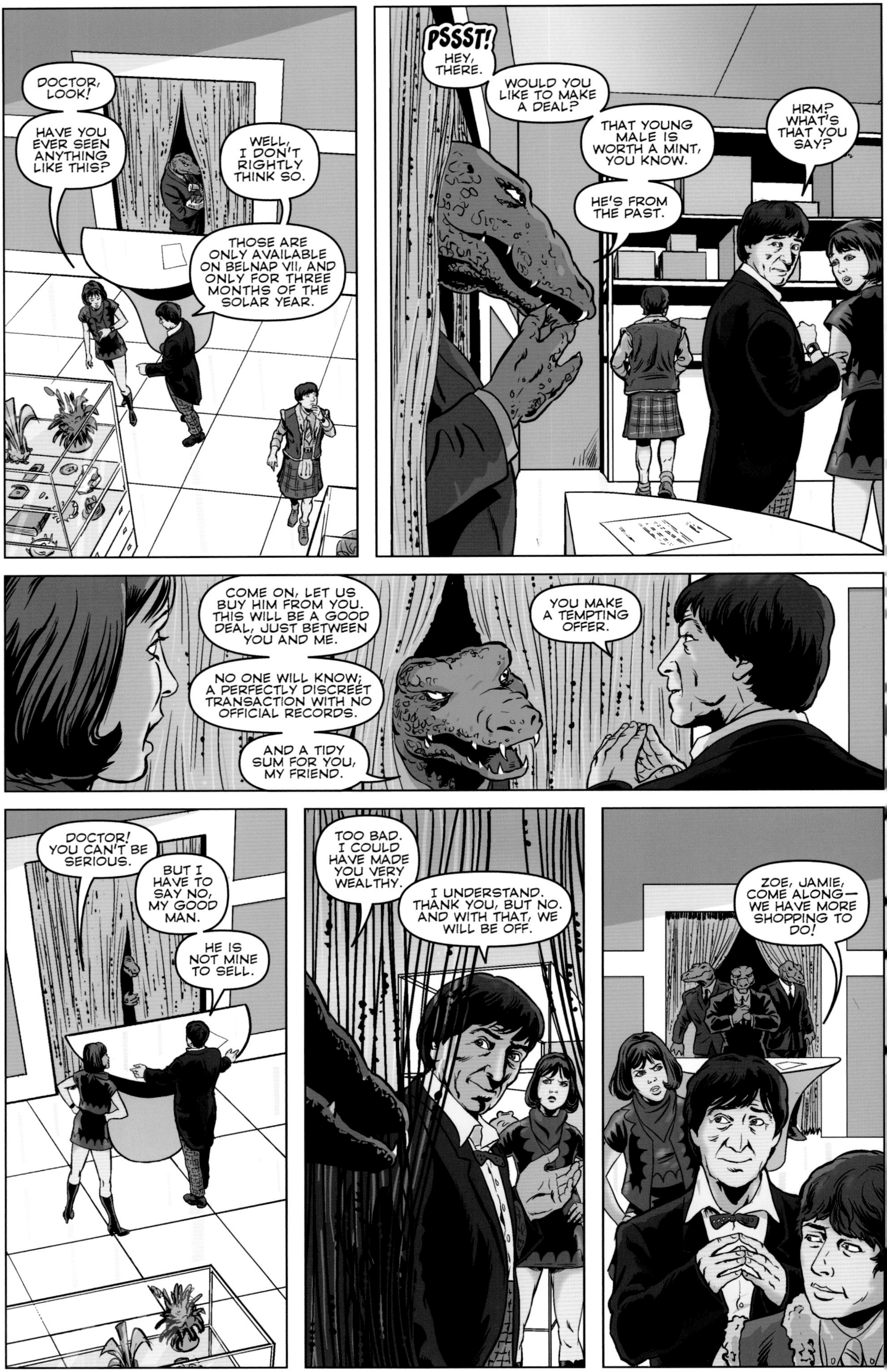
DOCTOR, LOOK!
HAVE YOU EVER SEEN ANYTHING LIKE THIS?
WELL, I DON'T RIGHTLY THINK SO.
THOSE ARE ONLY AVAILABLE ON BELNAP VII, AND ONLY FOR THREE MONTHS OF THE SOLAR YEAR.
PSSST!
HEY, THERE.
WOULD YOU LIKE TO MAKE A DEAL?
THAT YOUNG MALE IS WORTH A MINT, YOU KNOW.
HE'S FROM THE PAST.
HRM? WHAT'S THAT YOU SAY?
COME ON, LET US BUY HIM FROM YOU. THIS WILL BE A GOOD DEAL, JUST BETWEEN YOU AND ME.
NO ONE WILL KNOW; A PERFECTLY DISCREET TRANSACTION WITH NO OFFICIAL RECORDS.
AND A TIDY SUM FOR YOU, MY FRIEND.
YOU MAKE A TEMPTING OFFER.
DOCTOR! YOU CAN'T BE SERIOUS.
BUT I HAVE TO SAY NO, MY GOOD MAN.
HE IS NOT MINE TO SELL.
TOO BAD. I COULD HAVE MADE YOU VERY WEALTHY.
I UNDERSTAND. THANK YOU, BUT NO. AND WITH THAT, WE WILL BE OFF.
ZOE, JAMIE, COME ALONG— WE HAVE MORE SHOPPING TO DO!

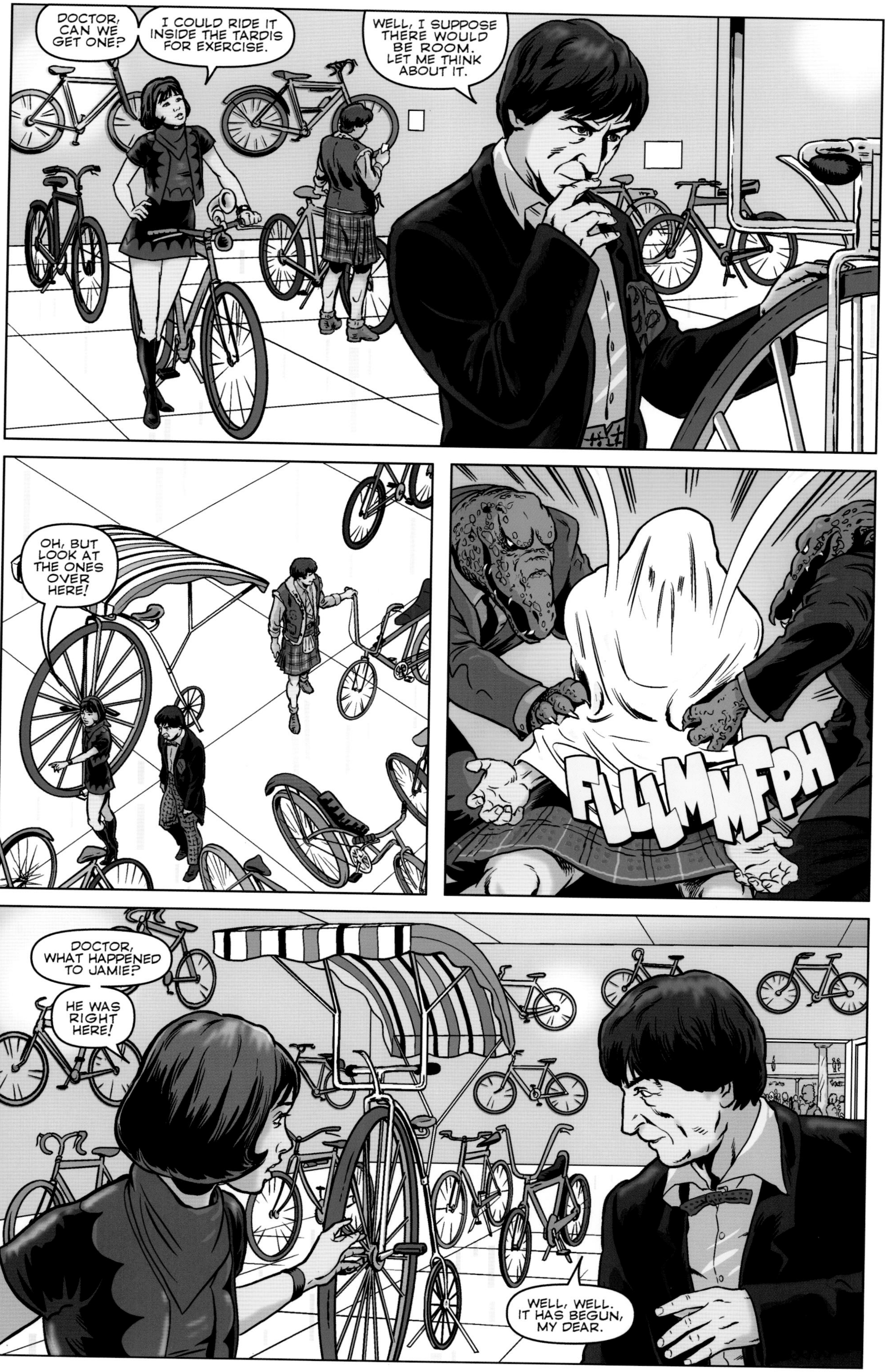
DOCTOR, CAN WE GET ONE?
I COULD RIDE IT INSIDE THE TARDIS FOR EXERCISE.
WELL, I SUPPOSE THERE WOULD BE ROOM. LET ME THINK ABOUT IT.
OH, BUT LOOK AT THE ONES OVER HERE!
FLLLMMFPH
DOCTOR, WHAT HAPPENED TO JAMIE?
HE WAS RIGHT HERE!
WELL, WELL. IT HAS BEGUN, MY DEAR.

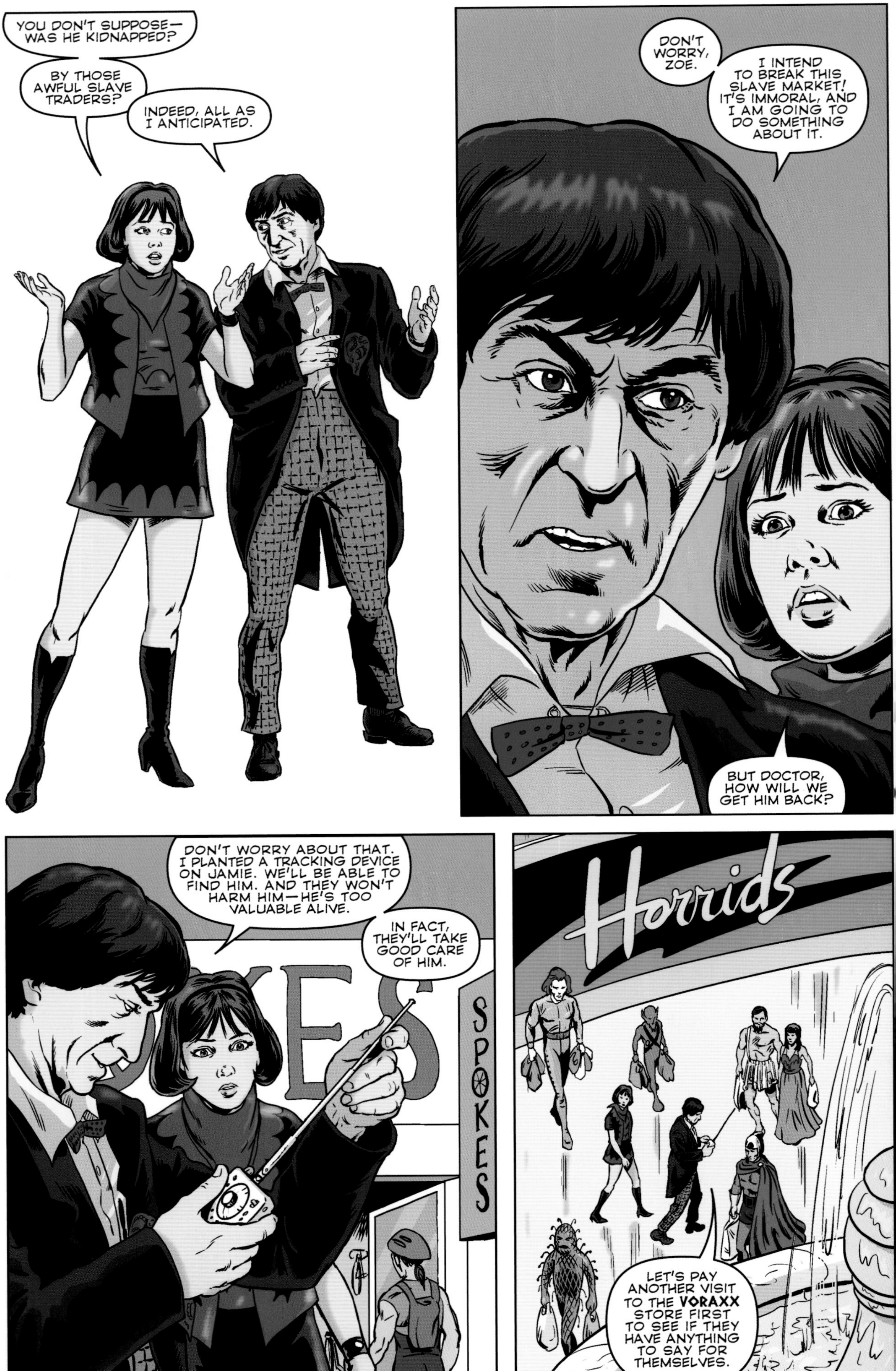
YOU DON'T SUPPOSE— WAS HE KIDNAPPED?
BY THOSE AWFUL SLAVE TRADERS?
INDEED, ALL AS I ANTICIPATED.
DON'T WORRY, ZOE.
I INTEND TO BREAK THIS SLAVE MARKET! IT'S IMMORAL, AND I AM GOING TO DO SOMETHING ABOUT IT.
BUT DOCTOR, HOW WILL WE GET HIM BACK?
DON'T WORRY ABOUT THAT. I PLANTED A TRACKING DEVICE ON JAMIE. WE'LL BE ABLE TO FIND HIM. AND THEY WON'T HARM HIM—HE'S TOO VALUABLE ALIVE.
IN FACT, THEY'LL TAKE GOOD CARE OF HIM.
SPOKES
Horrids
LET'S PAY ANOTHER VISIT TO THE **VORAXX** STORE FIRST TO SEE IF THEY HAVE ANYTHING TO SAY FOR THEMSELVES.

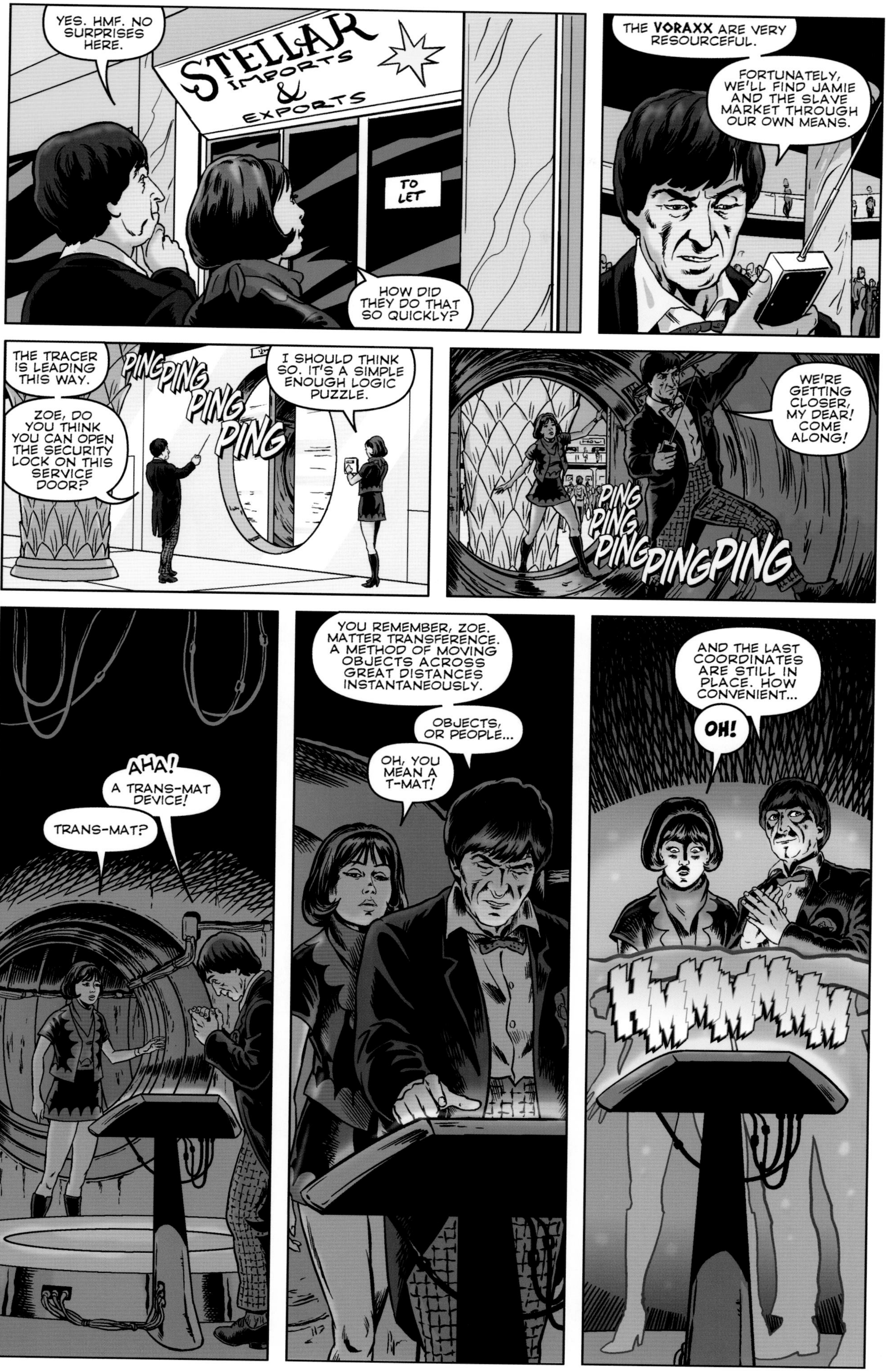

YES. HMF. NO SURPRISES HERE.
STELLAR IMPORTS & EXPORTS
TO LET
HOW DID THEY DO THAT SO QUICKLY?
THE VORAXX ARE VERY RESOURCEFUL.
FORTUNATELY, WE'LL FIND JAMIE AND THE SLAVE MARKET THROUGH OUR OWN MEANS.
THE TRACER IS LEADING THIS WAY.
PING PING PING PING
ZOE, DO YOU THINK YOU CAN OPEN THE SECURITY LOCK ON THIS SERVICE DOOR?
I SHOULD THINK SO. IT'S A SIMPLE ENOUGH LOGIC PUZZLE.
WE'RE GETTING CLOSER, MY DEAR! COME ALONG!
PING PING PING PING PING
AHA!
A TRANS-MAT DEVICE!
TRANS-MAT?
YOU REMEMBER, ZOE. MATTER TRANSFERENCE. A METHOD OF MOVING OBJECTS ACROSS GREAT DISTANCES INSTANTANEOUSLY.
OBJECTS, OR PEOPLE...
OH, YOU MEAN A T-MAT!
AND THE LAST COORDINATES ARE STILL IN PLACE. HOW CONVENIENT...
OH!
HMMMMMM

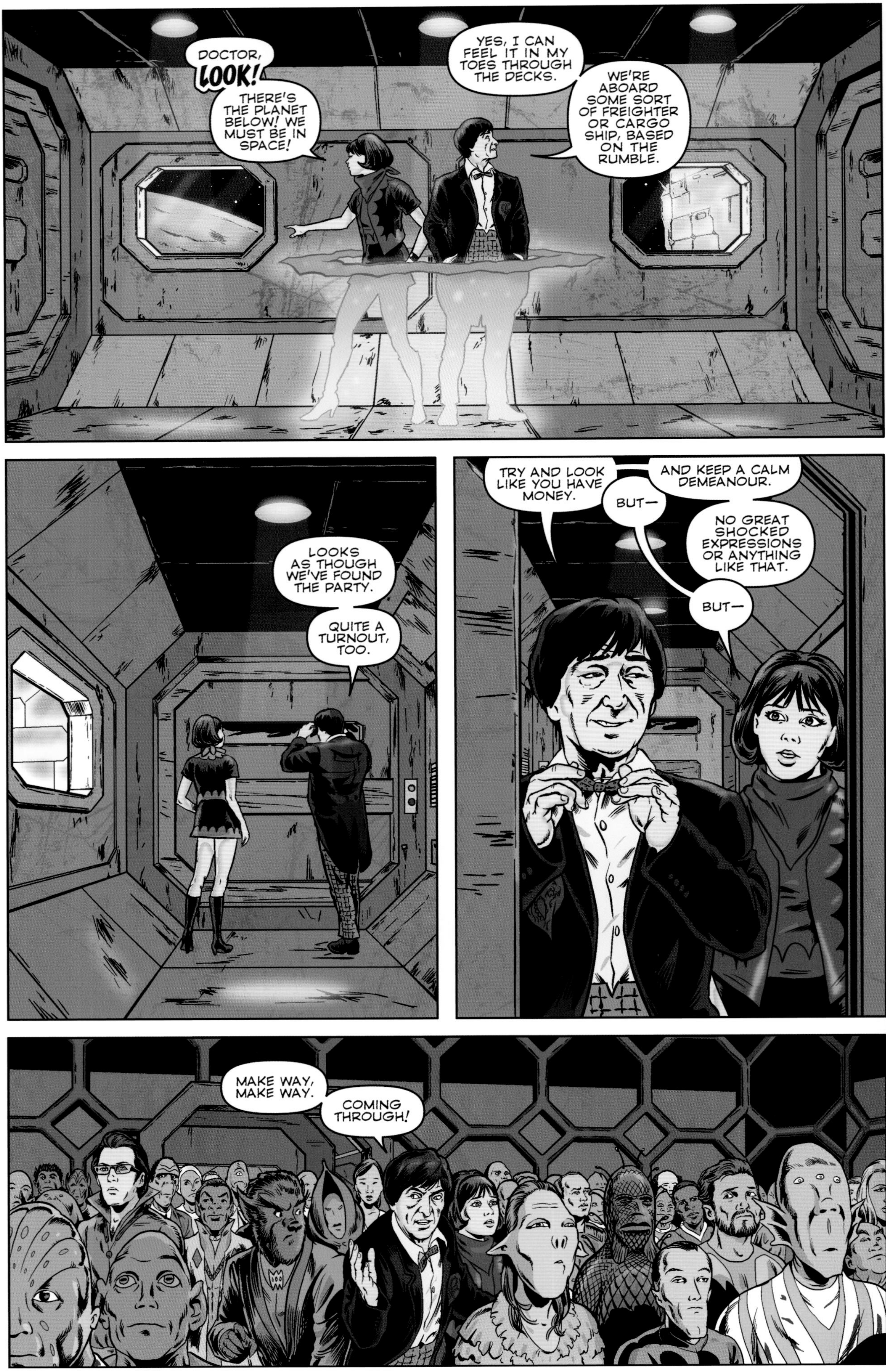
DOCTOR, LOOK!
THERE'S THE PLANET BELOW! WE MUST BE IN SPACE!
YES, I CAN FEEL IT IN MY TOES THROUGH THE DECKS.
WE'RE ABOARD SOME SORT OF FREIGHTER OR CARGO SHIP, BASED ON THE RUMBLE.
LOOKS AS THOUGH WE'VE FOUND THE PARTY.
QUITE A TURNOUT, TOO.
TRY AND LOOK LIKE YOU HAVE MONEY.
BUT—
AND KEEP A CALM DEMEANOUR.
NO GREAT SHOCKED EXPRESSIONS OR ANYTHING LIKE THAT.
BUT—
MAKE WAY, MAKE WAY.
COMING THROUGH!

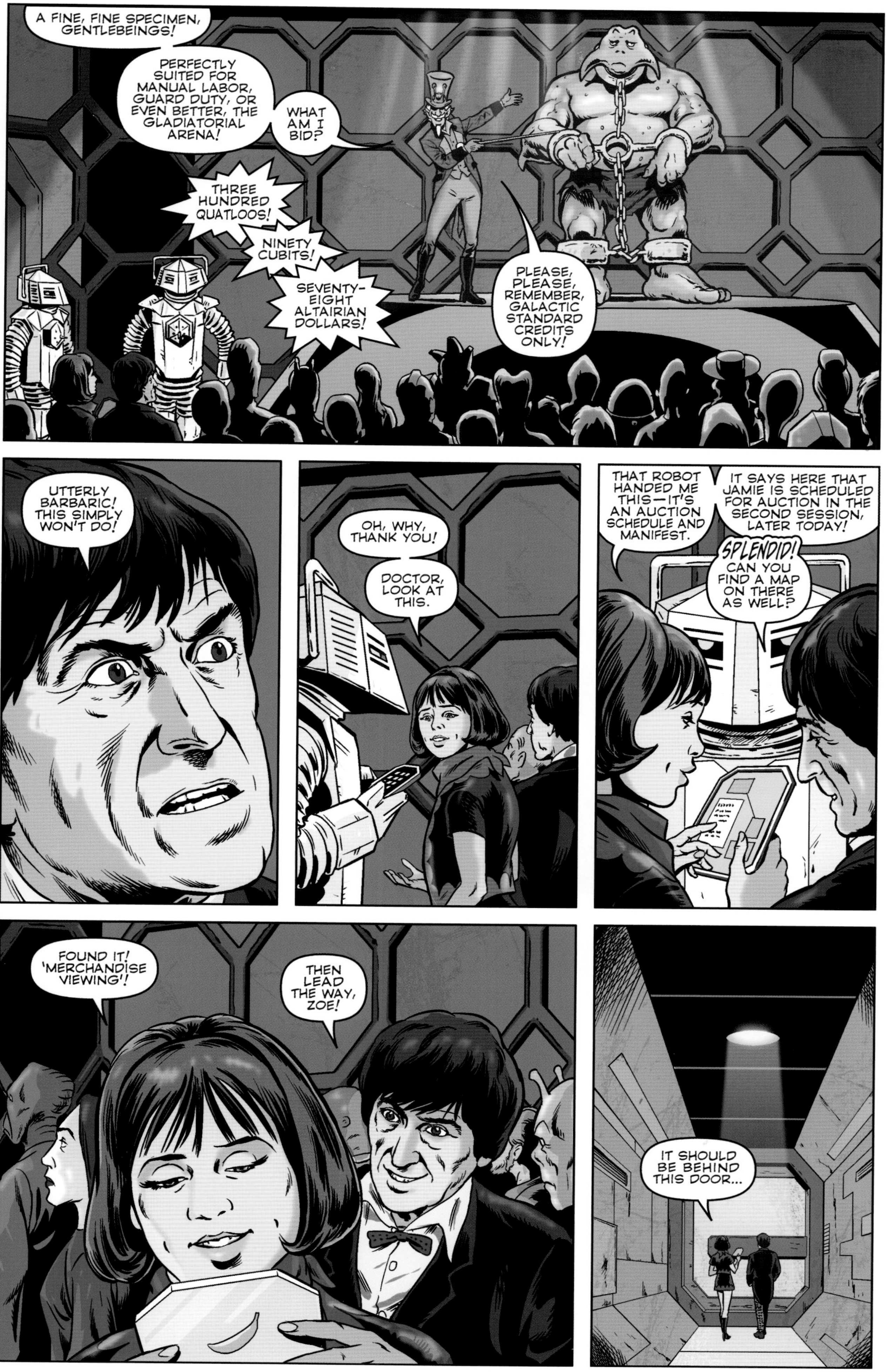
A FINE, FINE SPECIMEN, GENTLEBEINGS!
PERFECTLY SUITED FOR MANUAL LABOR, GUARD DUTY, OR EVEN BETTER, THE GLADIATORIAL ARENA!
WHAT AM I BID?
THREE HUNDRED QUATLOOS!
NINETY CUBITS!
SEVENTY-EIGHT ALTAIRIAN DOLLARS!
PLEASE, PLEASE, REMEMBER, GALACTIC STANDARD CREDITS ONLY!
UTTERLY BARBARIC! THIS SIMPLY WON'T DO!
OH, WHY, THANK YOU!
DOCTOR, LOOK AT THIS.
THAT ROBOT HANDED ME THIS—IT'S AN AUCTION SCHEDULE AND MANIFEST.
IT SAYS HERE THAT JAMIE IS SCHEDULED FOR AUCTION IN THE SECOND SESSION, LATER TODAY!
SPLENDID! CAN YOU FIND A MAP ON THERE AS WELL?
FOUND IT! 'MERCHANDISE VIEWING'!
THEN LEAD THE WAY, ZOE!
IT SHOULD BE BEHIND THIS DOOR...

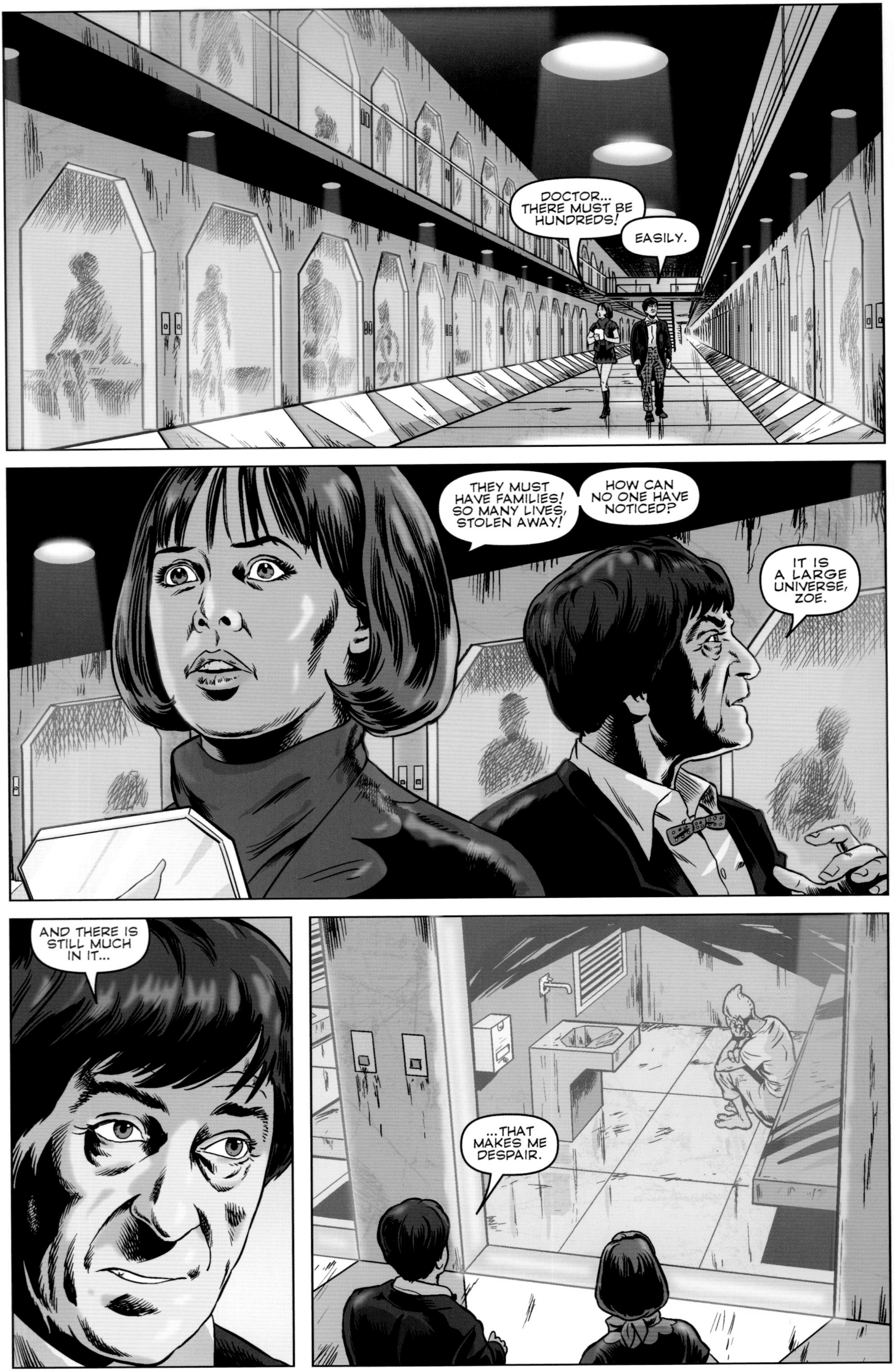
DOCTOR... THERE MUST BE HUNDREDS!
EASILY.
THEY MUST HAVE FAMILIES! SO MANY LIVES, STOLEN AWAY!
HOW CAN NO ONE HAVE NOTICED?
IT IS A LARGE UNIVERSE, ZOE.
AND THERE IS STILL MUCH IN IT...
...THAT MAKES ME DESPAIR.

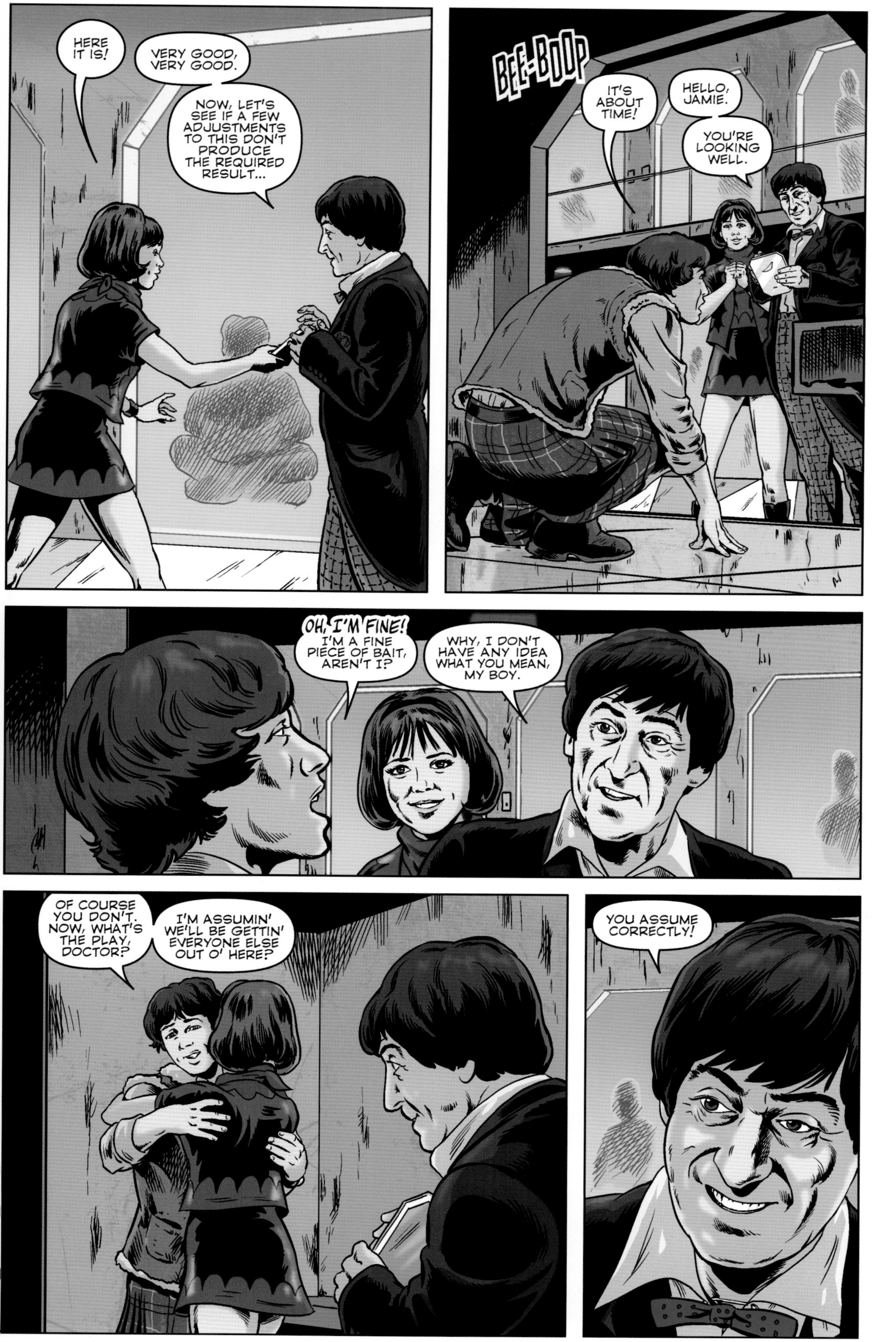
HERE IT IS!
VERY GOOD, VERY GOOD.
NOW, LET'S SEE IF A FEW ADJUSTMENTS TO THIS DON'T PRODUCE THE REQUIRED RESULT...
BEE-BOOP
IT'S ABOUT TIME!
HELLO, JAMIE.
YOU'RE LOOKING WELL.
OH, I'M FINE! I'M A FINE PIECE OF BAIT, AREN'T I?
WHY, I DON'T HAVE ANY IDEA WHAT YOU MEAN, MY BOY.
OF COURSE YOU DON'T. NOW, WHAT'S THE PLAY, DOCTOR?
I'M ASSUMIN' WE'LL BE GETTIN' EVERYONE ELSE OUT O' HERE?
YOU ASSUME CORRECTLY!

LET'S SEE IF I CAN'T WIDEN THE RANGE ON THIS...

BEE-BOOP

BEE-BOOP

BEE-BOOP

COME ON! WE'RE GETTIN' YOU OUT OF HERE! LET'S GET A MOVE ON!

HURRY!

THERE'S NO POINT. WE CAN'T STOP THEM. THEY'LL JUST SLAUGHTER US.

AND EVEN IF WE DID SURVIVE, WE CAN'T GET OUT, AND WE CAN'T GET HOME.

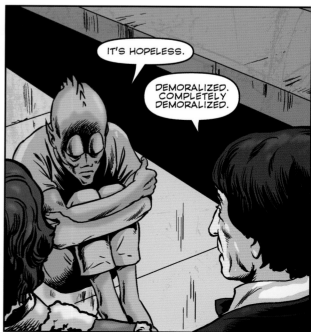

IT'S HOPELESS.

DEMORALIZED. COMPLETELY DEMORALIZED.

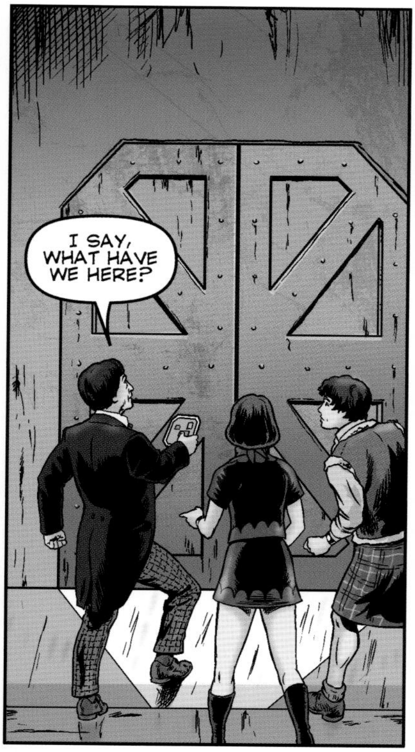
I SAY, WHAT HAVE WE HERE?

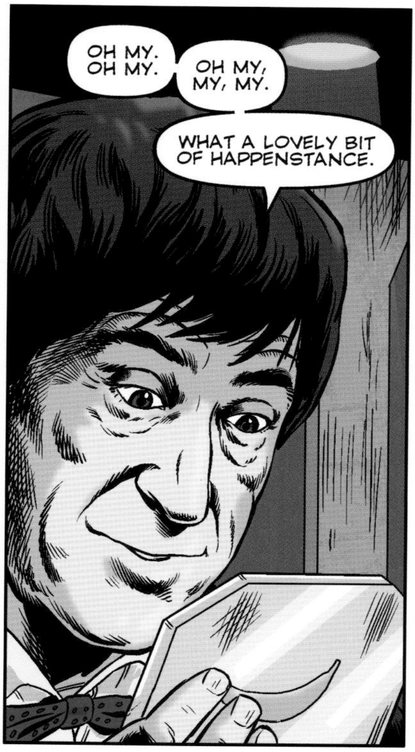
OH MY. OH MY.
OH MY, MY, MY.
WHAT A LOVELY BIT OF HAPPENSTANCE.

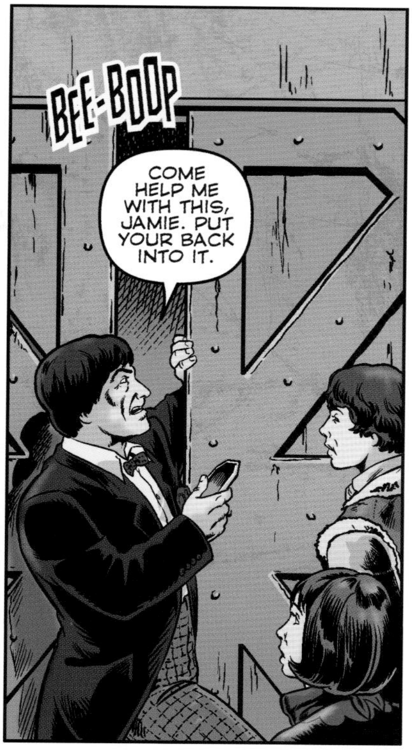
BEE-BOOP
COME HELP ME WITH THIS, JAMIE. PUT YOUR BACK INTO IT.

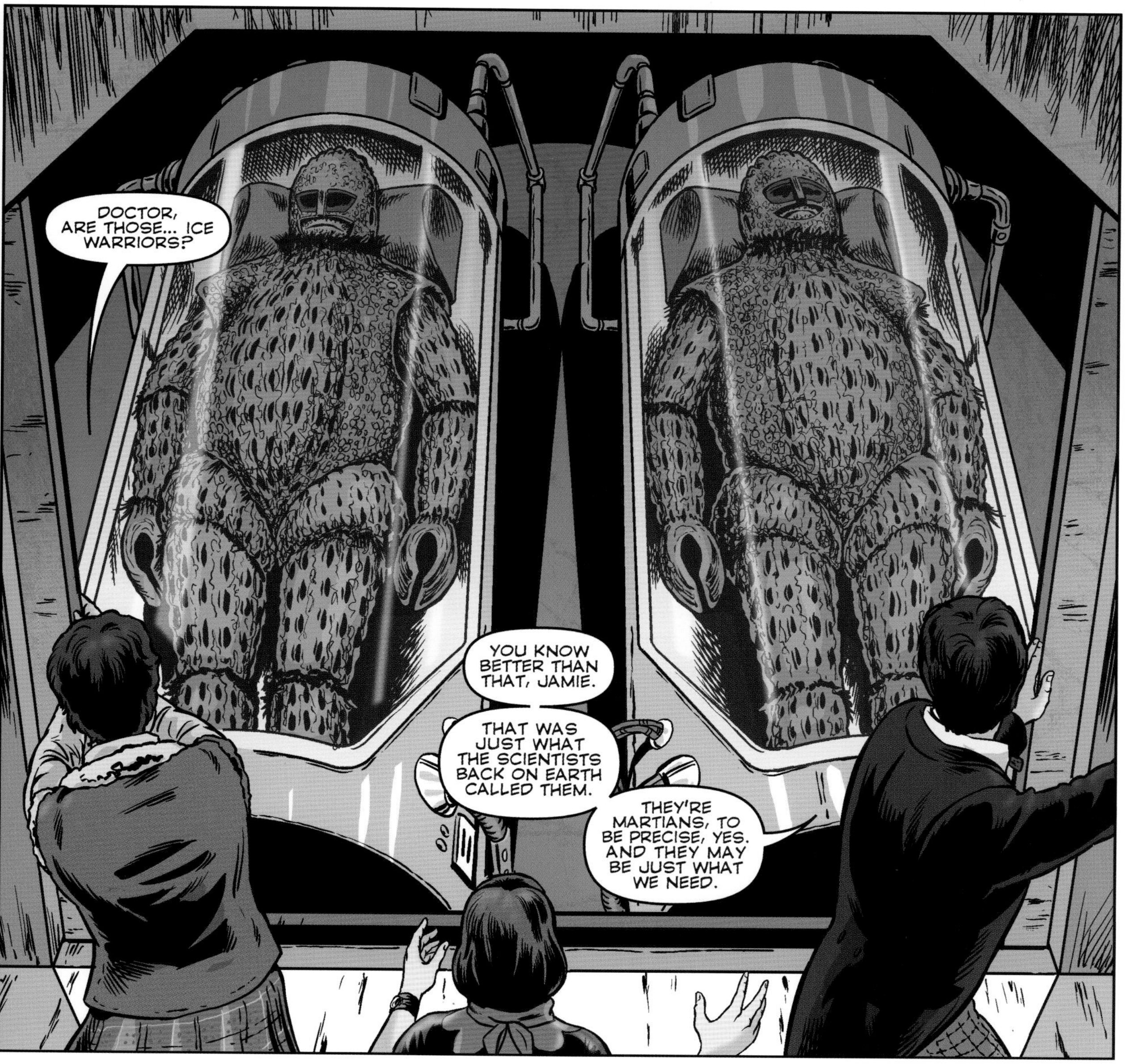
DOCTOR, ARE THOSE... ICE WARRIORS?
YOU KNOW BETTER THAN THAT, JAMIE.
THAT WAS JUST WHAT THE SCIENTISTS BACK ON EARTH CALLED THEM.
THEY'RE MARTIANS, TO BE PRECISE, YES. AND THEY MAY BE JUST WHAT WE NEED.

...WHERE... ARE WE?

YOU ARE CAPTIVES ABOARD A SLAVER SHIP.

ARE YOU... OUR ENSSSS- SLAVER?

NOT AT ALL. I CAN FREE YOU.

THERE ARE MANY HERE HELD ENSLAVED, BUT THEY LACK THE WILL TO RISE UP. THEY NEED INSPIRATION.

I AM CALLED... ARAXUS... HELP ME UP... AND I WILL TURN YOUR RABBLE INTO AN ARMY.

BUZZZ BUZZZ BUZZZ BUZZZ

ALERT! ALERT! MERCHANDISE HAS ESCAPED THEIR CELLS!

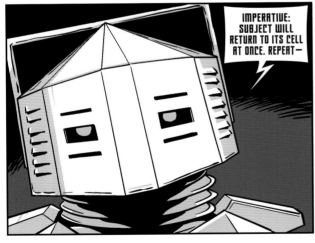

IMPERATIVE: SUBJECT WILL RETURN TO ITS CELL AT ONCE. REPEAT—

KLAANG

BZZT BZZT

LET USSSSSSS FIGHT!

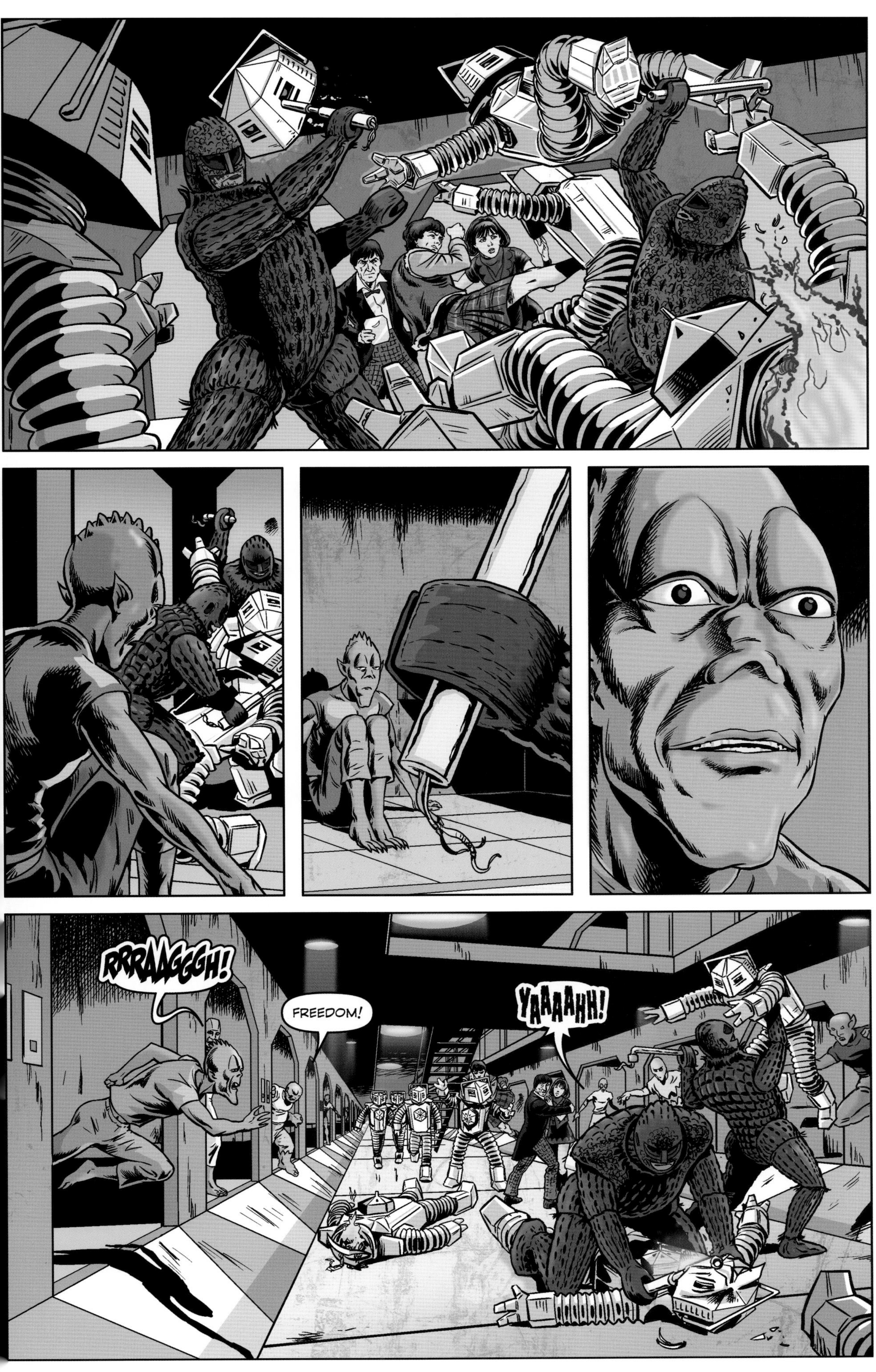
RRRAAGGGH!
FREEDOM!
YAAAAHH!

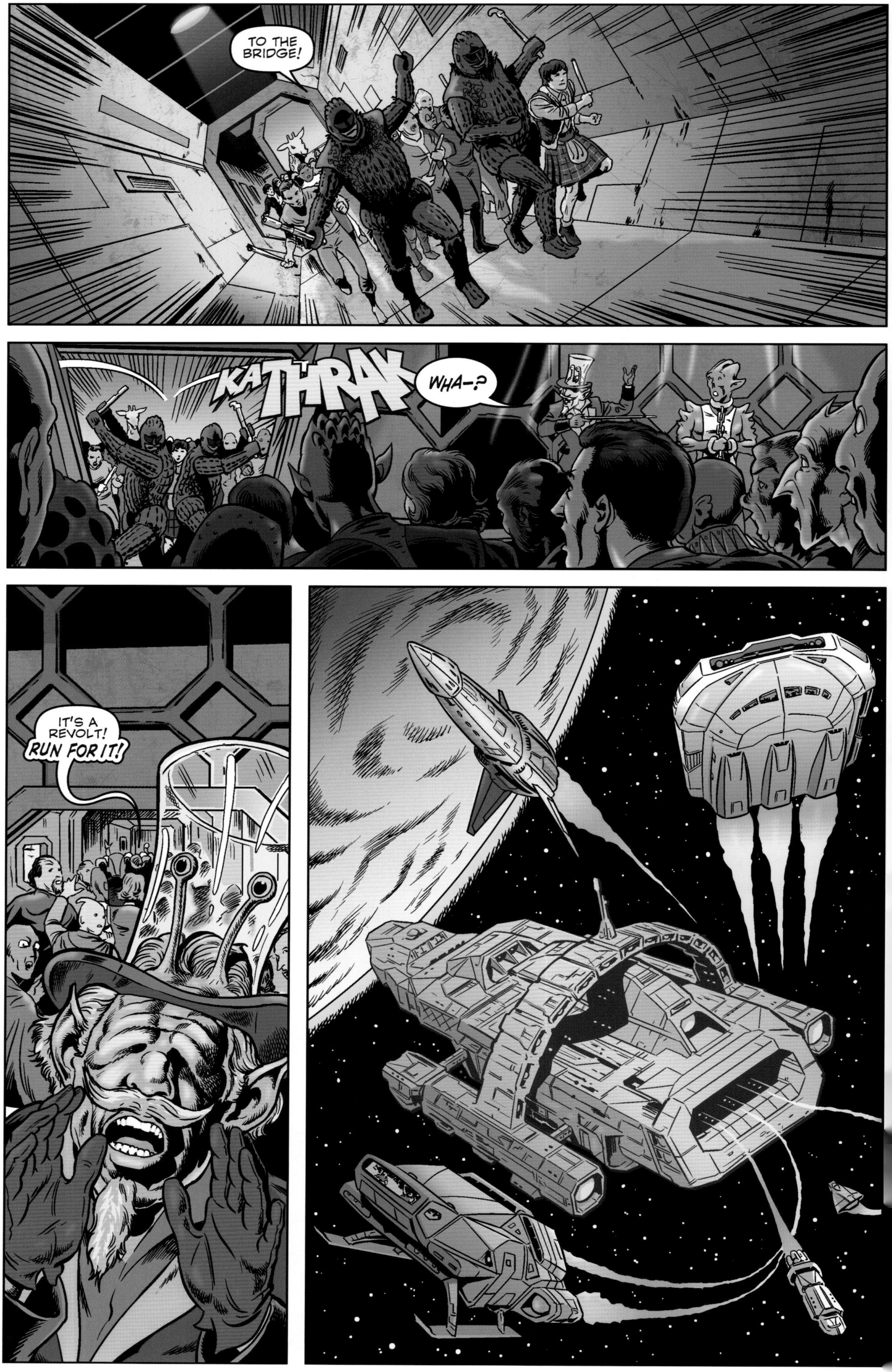
TO THE BRIDGE!
KATHRAK
WHA-?
IT'S A REVOLT! RUN FOR IT!

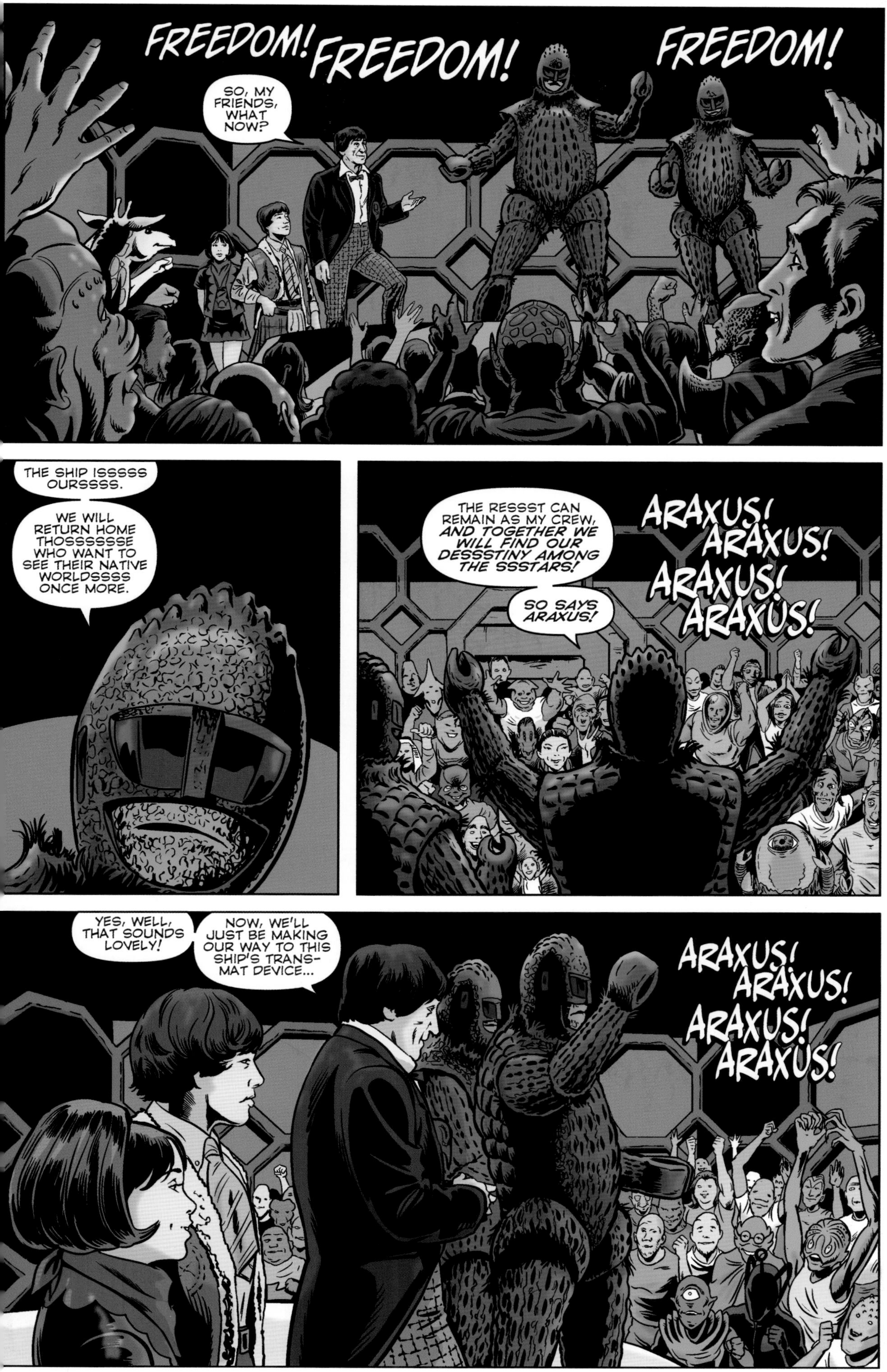
FREEDOM! FREEDOM! FREEDOM!
SO, MY FRIENDS, WHAT NOW?
THE SHIP ISSSSS OURSSSS.
WE WILL RETURN HOME THOSSSSSSE WHO WANT TO SEE THEIR NATIVE WORLDSSSS ONCE MORE.
THE RESSST CAN REMAIN AS MY CREW, AND TOGETHER WE WILL FIND OUR DESSSTINY AMONG THE SSSTARS!
SO SAYS ARAXUS!
ARAXUS! ARAXUS! ARAXUS! ARAXUS!
YES, WELL, THAT SOUNDS LOVELY!
NOW, WE'LL JUST BE MAKING OUR WAY TO THIS SHIP'S TRANS-MAT DEVICE...
ARAXUS! ARAXUS! ARAXUS! ARAXUS!

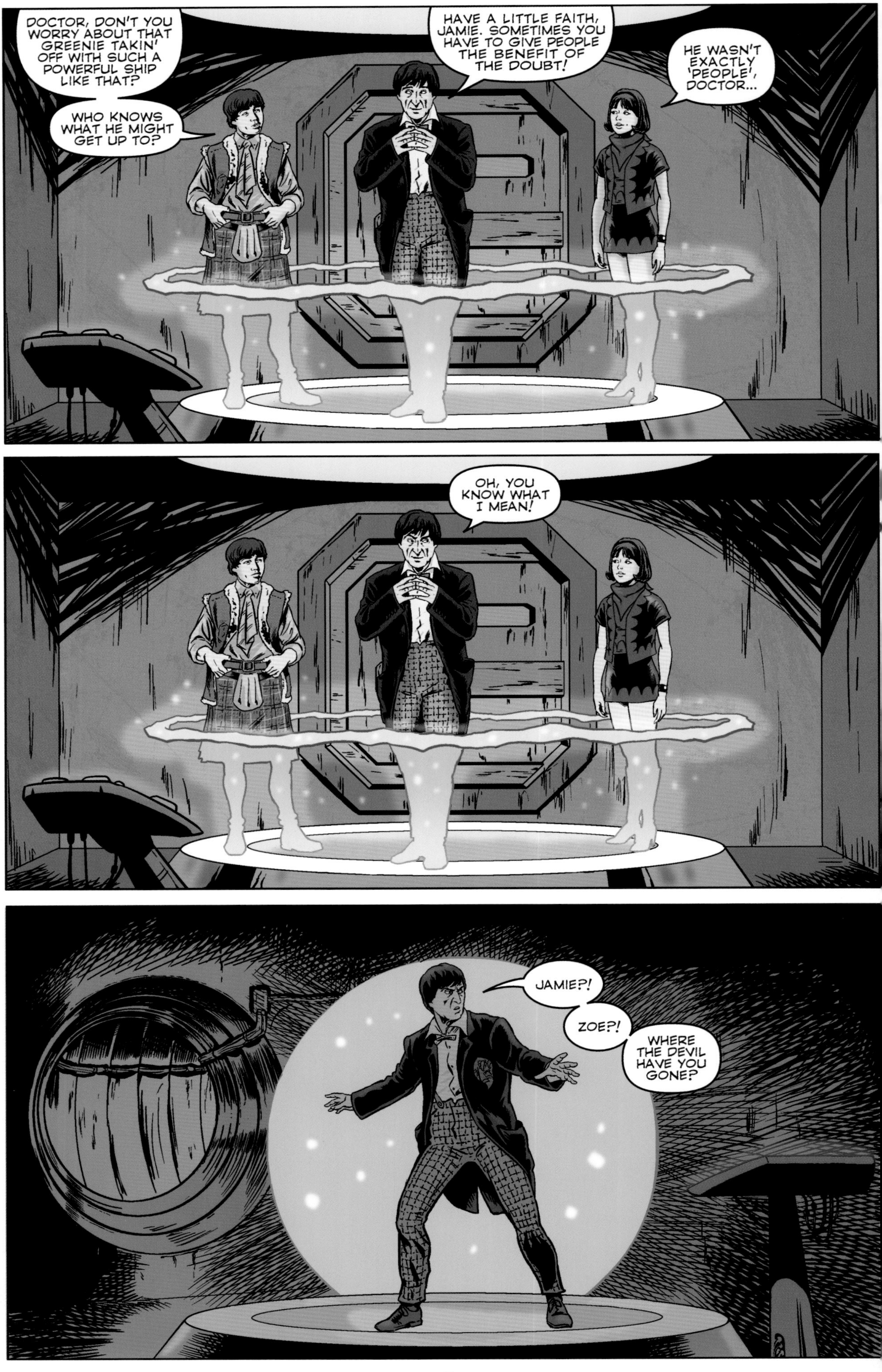
DOCTOR, DON'T YOU WORRY ABOUT THAT GREENIE TAKIN' OFF WITH SUCH A POWERFUL SHIP LIKE THAT?
WHO KNOWS WHAT HE MIGHT GET UP TO?
HAVE A LITTLE FAITH, JAMIE. SOMETIMES YOU HAVE TO GIVE PEOPLE THE BENEFIT OF THE DOUBT!
HE WASN'T EXACTLY 'PEOPLE', DOCTOR...
OH, YOU KNOW WHAT I MEAN!
JAMIE?!
ZOE?!
WHERE THE DEVIL HAVE YOU GONE?

REFLECTIONS OF TIME

Wherein prominent Whovians past and present muse upon the Doctor's history in comic form.

With the arrival of the Second Doctor in *TV Comic's Doctor Who* strip—a transformation that was given no explanation—the tone of the series moved away from the fairy tale whimsy of the First Doctor's stories, and began to adopt the action-adventure tropes common to 1960s TV shows such as *The Avengers* and *Danger Man*. With the addition of the Daleks, the Cybermen, the Quarks, and companion Jamie McCrimmon, the strip also had more in common with *Doctor Who* on television—superficially at least.

In truth, there was one significant difference that set the Doctor's strip exploits apart from his TV adventures. In their bid to appeal to a younger audience, the strip writers attempted to boil the ethos of *Doctor Who* down to a very black-and-white formula of good versus evil. In so doing, they unfortunately managed to almost completely miss the underlying message of the series and the nature of the Doctor's character. Of course, the Doctor was seen to oppose evil, in its many forms, on a weekly basis in the TV series. However, violence was the Doctor's last resort, always favoring a peaceful resolution to any conflict wherever possible. In the pages of *TV Comic*, though, the Doctor was rarely so coy and was regularly seen to dispense harsh justice to his opponents. Worse still, he seemed to relish it. This somewhat worrying attitude is concisely demonstrated by the now infamous "Die, hideous creature. Die!" sequence in the 1967 strip adventure *Master of Spiders*. The Doctor builds himself a ray gun—something that would be unconscionable in the TV series—and decides to test it out by obliterating a robotic spider and its human operator within whilst uttering the notorious line. Not only does this demonstrate the Doctor's cavalier disregard for the sanctity of life, but also implies 'ugly' equals 'evil'—a disturbing subliminal message prevalent in the *Doctor Who* strip adventures of the time.

As part of my research for Marvel's *Doctor Who: Classic Comics* in the early 1990s, I was allowed access to some of the original correspondence that had taken place between the publishers of *TV Comic* and the BBC. Then, as now, story outlines for the *Doctor Who* strips had to be submitted to the BBC for approval. It was interesting to note that the authors of the stories would often propose two alternative endings to an adventure. One would tend to lean towards a more reasonable conclusion with the Doctor making at least some attempt to negotiate a peaceful settlement between opposing factions, while the other, usually favored by the authors, would see the Doctor enthusiastically dispatching the enemy by bludgeoning them to death with hammers, or some such. The job of approving these storylines in the late 1960s fell to the then junior script editor, Terrance Dicks. Not surprisingly, in his replies to *TV Comic*, Dicks would always strongly recommend adopting the more conciliatory conclusion to the story, the tone of his letters, however, betraying his astonishment that the authors might even think it appropriate to portray the Doctor as some kind of vigilante. Thank goodness Terrance Dicks understood *Doctor Who* even if the strip writers didn't, otherwise we might be enjoying a very different kind of *Doctor Who* today.

—John Ainsworth
producer, director,
and script editor
for Big Finish
Productions

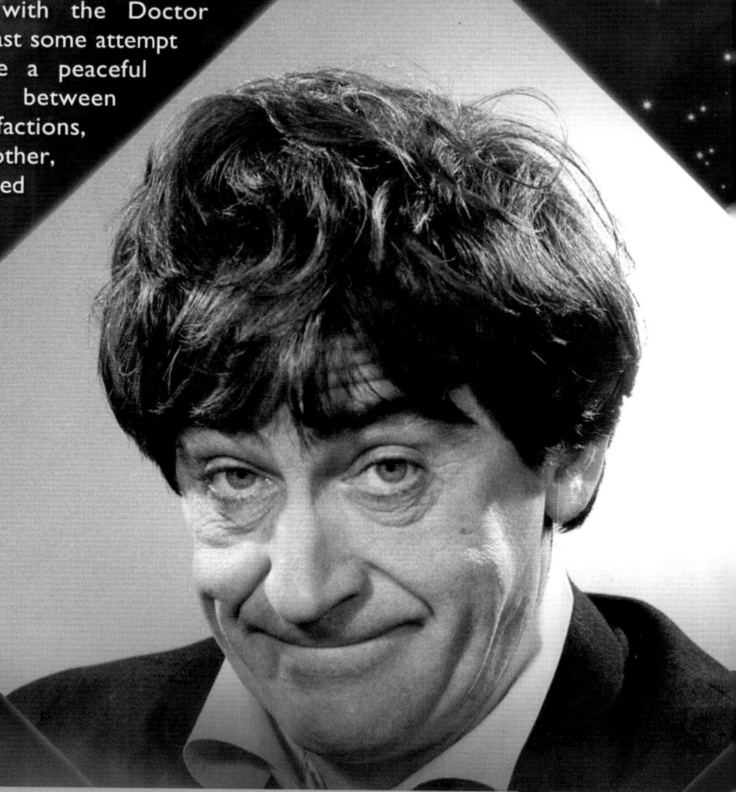

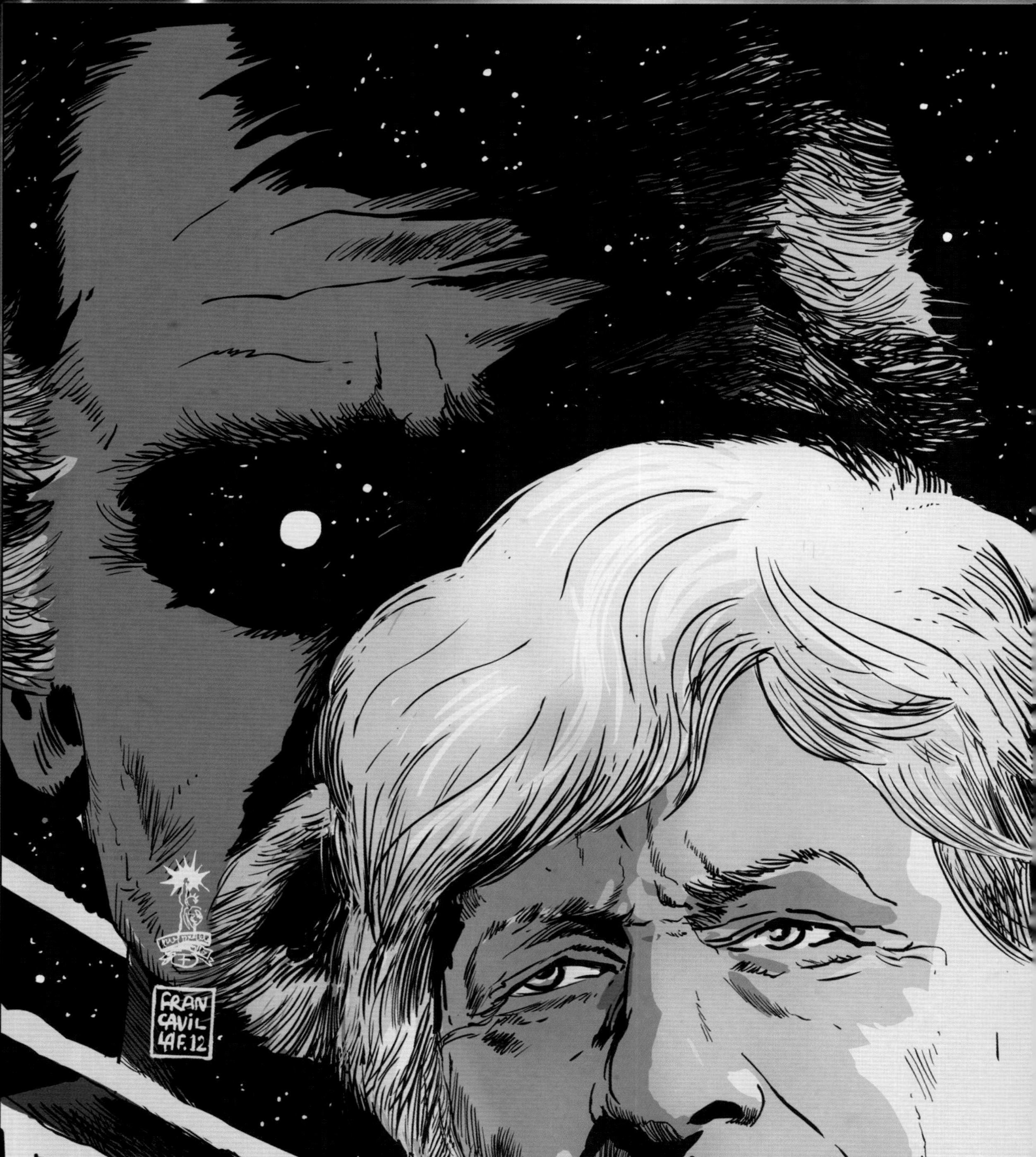

FRAN CAVIL LAF. 12
POLICE
PUBLIC
CALL

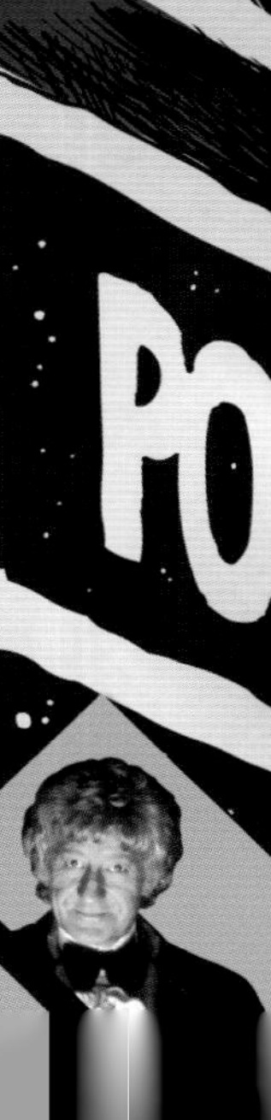

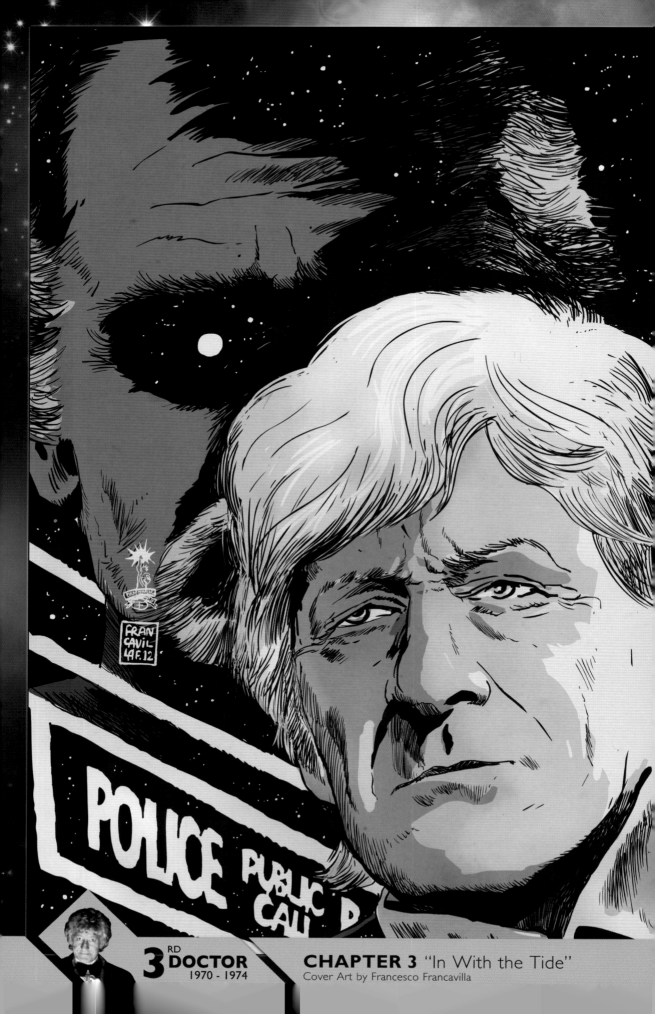

3RD DOCTOR
1970 - 1974

CHAPTER 3 "In With the Tide"
Cover Art by Francesco Francavilla

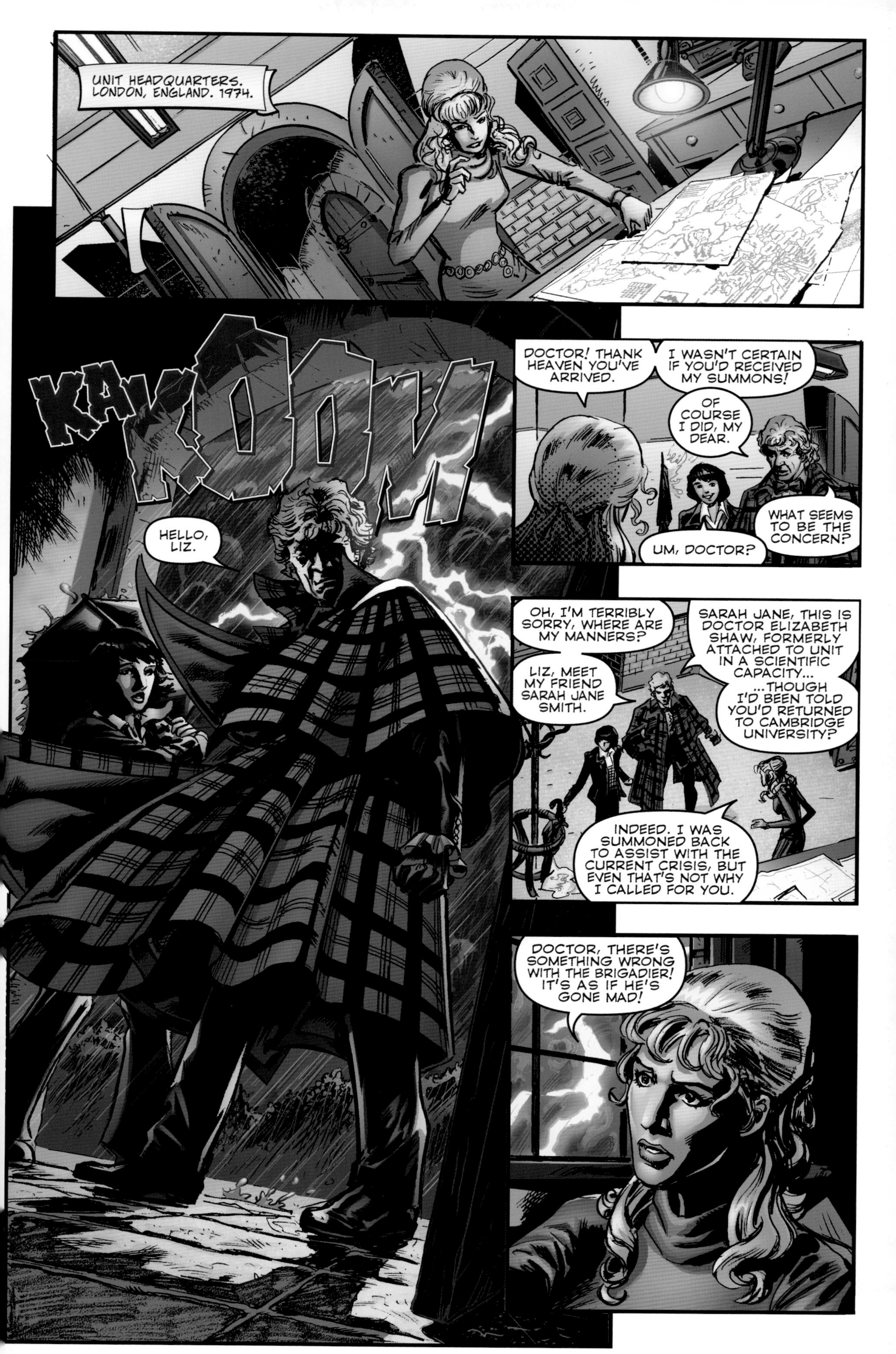
UNIT HEADQUARTERS. LONDON, ENGLAND. 1974.
KAKKOOM
HELLO, LIZ.
DOCTOR! THANK HEAVEN YOU'VE ARRIVED.
I WASN'T CERTAIN IF YOU'D RECEIVED MY SUMMONS!
OF COURSE I DID, MY DEAR.
WHAT SEEMS TO BE THE CONCERN?
UM, DOCTOR?
OH, I'M TERRIBLY SORRY, WHERE ARE MY MANNERS?
LIZ, MEET MY FRIEND SARAH JANE SMITH.
SARAH JANE, THIS IS DOCTOR ELIZABETH SHAW, FORMERLY ATTACHED TO UNIT IN A SCIENTIFIC CAPACITY...
...THOUGH I'D BEEN TOLD YOU'D RETURNED TO CAMBRIDGE UNIVERSITY?
INDEED. I WAS SUMMONED BACK TO ASSIST WITH THE CURRENT CRISIS, BUT EVEN THAT'S NOT WHY I CALLED FOR YOU.
DOCTOR, THERE'S SOMETHING WRONG WITH THE BRIGADIER! IT'S AS IF HE'S GONE MAD!

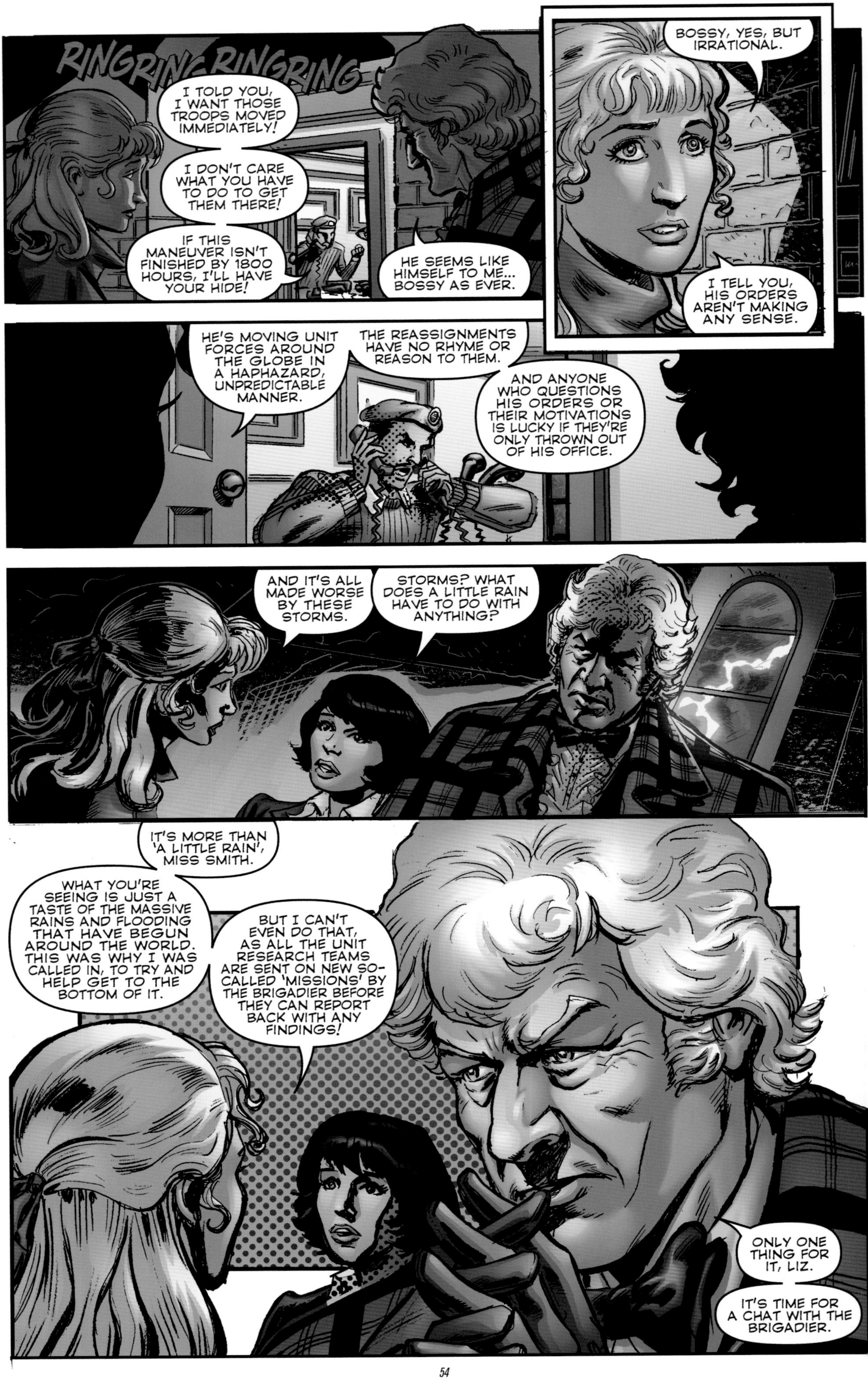

RINGRING RINGRING
I TOLD YOU, I WANT THOSE TROOPS MOVED IMMEDIATELY!
I DON'T CARE WHAT YOU HAVE TO DO TO GET THEM THERE!
IF THIS MANEUVER ISN'T FINISHED BY 1800 HOURS, I'LL HAVE YOUR HIDE!
HE SEEMS LIKE HIMSELF TO ME... BOSSY AS EVER.
BOSSY, YES, BUT IRRATIONAL.
I TELL YOU, HIS ORDERS AREN'T MAKING ANY SENSE.
HE'S MOVING UNIT FORCES AROUND THE GLOBE IN A HAPHAZARD, UNPREDICTABLE MANNER.
THE REASSIGNMENTS HAVE NO RHYME OR REASON TO THEM.
AND ANYONE WHO QUESTIONS HIS ORDERS OR THEIR MOTIVATIONS IS LUCKY IF THEY'RE ONLY THROWN OUT OF HIS OFFICE.
AND IT'S ALL MADE WORSE BY THESE STORMS.
STORMS? WHAT DOES A LITTLE RAIN HAVE TO DO WITH ANYTHING?
IT'S MORE THAN 'A LITTLE RAIN', MISS SMITH.
WHAT YOU'RE SEEING IS JUST A TASTE OF THE MASSIVE RAINS AND FLOODING THAT HAVE BEGUN AROUND THE WORLD. THIS WAS WHY I WAS CALLED IN, TO TRY AND HELP GET TO THE BOTTOM OF IT.
BUT I CAN'T EVEN DO THAT, AS ALL THE UNIT RESEARCH TEAMS ARE SENT ON NEW SO-CALLED 'MISSIONS' BY THE BRIGADIER BEFORE THEY CAN REPORT BACK WITH ANY FINDINGS!
ONLY ONE THING FOR IT, LIZ.
IT'S TIME FOR A CHAT WITH THE BRIGADIER.

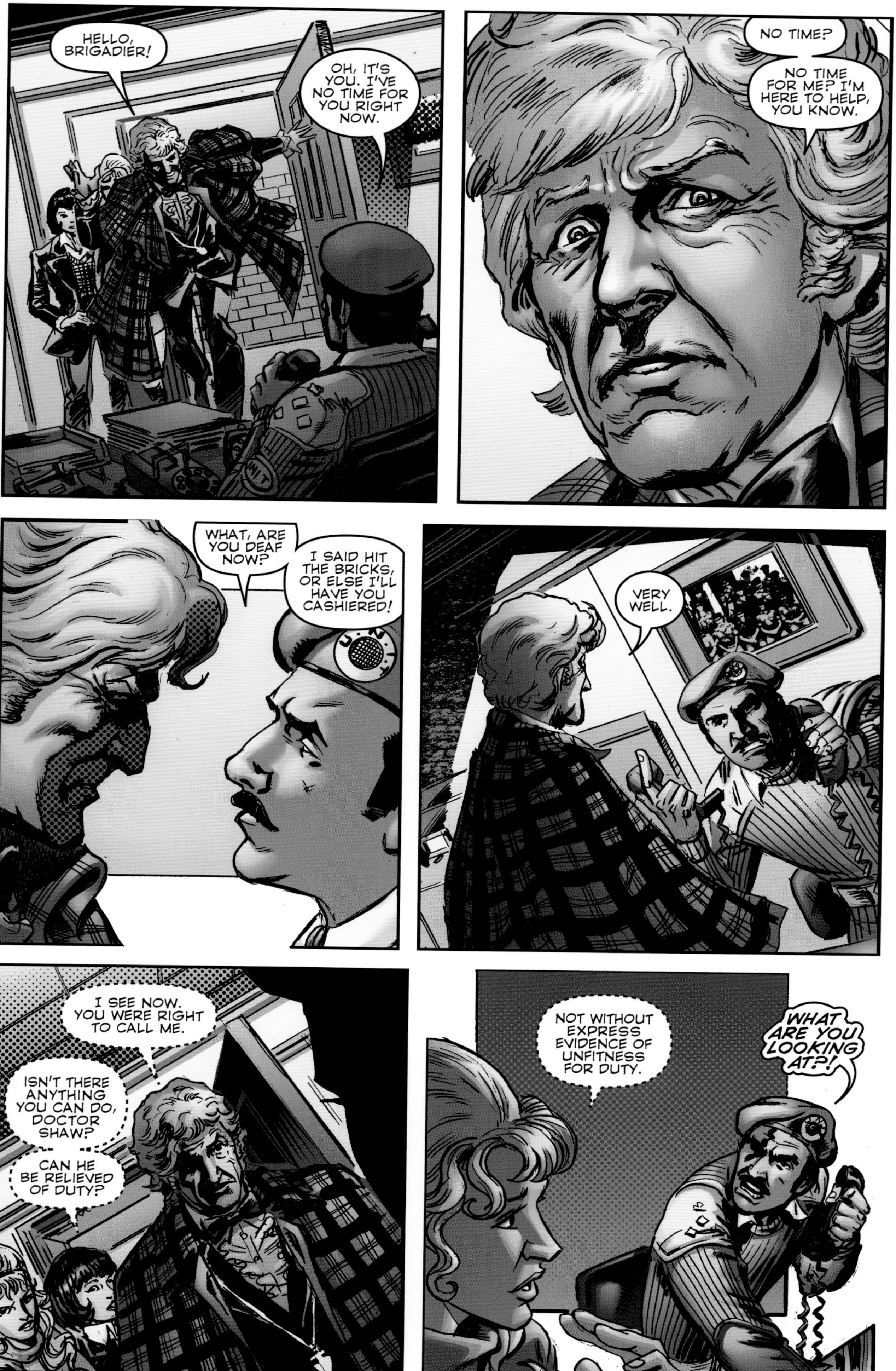

HELLO, BRIGADIER!
OH, IT'S YOU. I'VE NO TIME FOR YOU RIGHT NOW.
NO TIME?
NO TIME FOR ME? I'M HERE TO HELP, YOU KNOW.
WHAT, ARE YOU DEAF NOW?
I SAID HIT THE BRICKS, OR ELSE I'LL HAVE YOU CASHIERED!
VERY WELL.
I SEE NOW. YOU WERE RIGHT TO CALL ME.
ISN'T THERE ANYTHING YOU CAN DO, DOCTOR SHAW?
CAN HE BE RELIEVED OF DUTY?
NOT WITHOUT EXPRESS EVIDENCE OF UNFITNESS FOR DUTY.
WHAT ARE YOU LOOKING AT?!

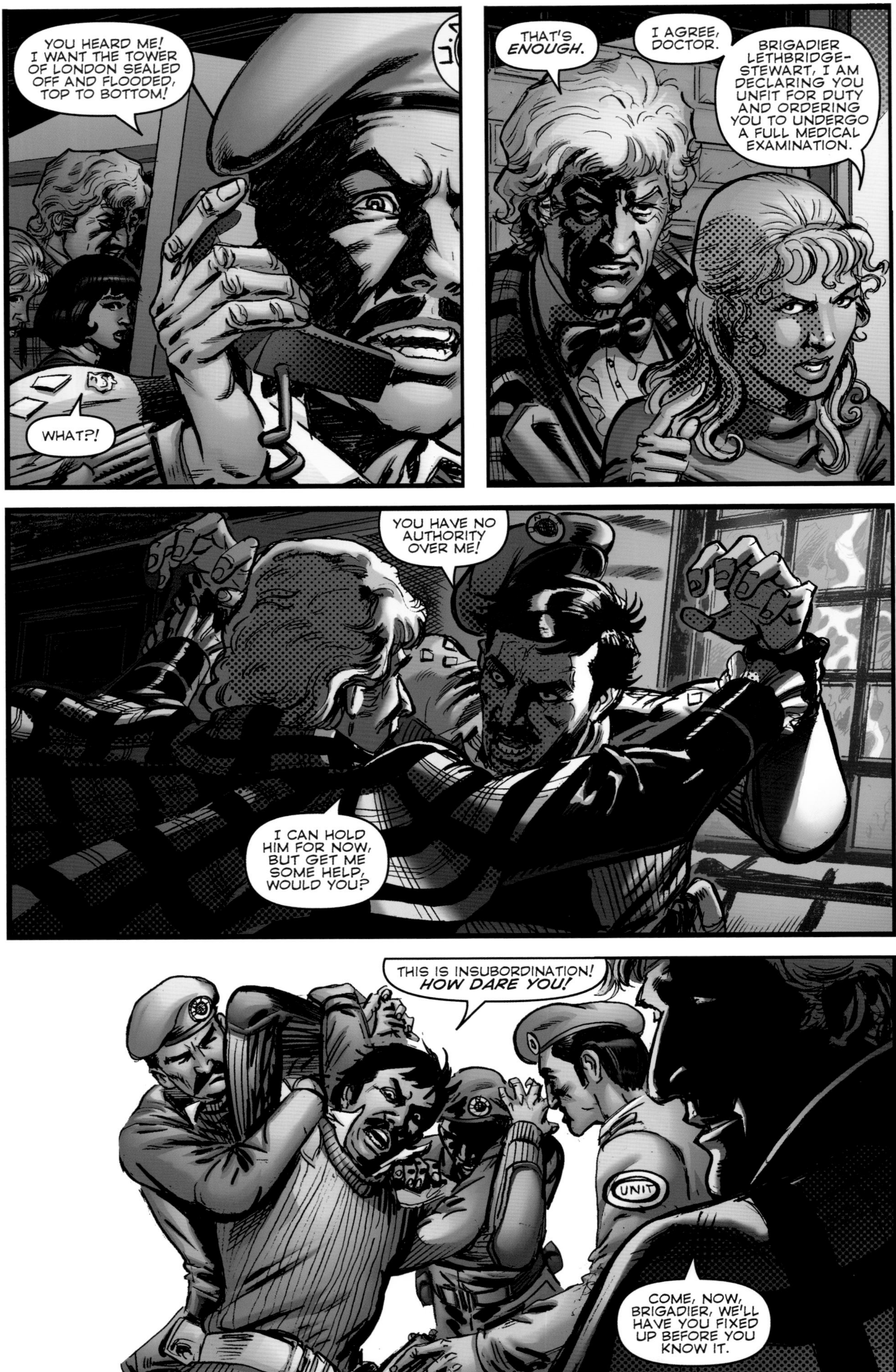
YOU HEARD ME! I WANT THE TOWER OF LONDON SEALED OFF AND FLOODED, TOP TO BOTTOM!
WHAT?!
THAT'S ENOUGH.
I AGREE, DOCTOR.
BRIGADIER LETHBRIDGE-STEWART, I AM DECLARING YOU UNFIT FOR DUTY AND ORDERING YOU TO UNDERGO A FULL MEDICAL EXAMINATION.
YOU HAVE NO AUTHORITY OVER ME!
I CAN HOLD HIM FOR NOW, BUT GET ME SOME HELP, WOULD YOU?
THIS IS INSUBORDINATION! HOW DARE YOU!
UNIT
COME, NOW, BRIGADIER, WE'LL HAVE YOU FIXED UP BEFORE YOU KNOW IT.

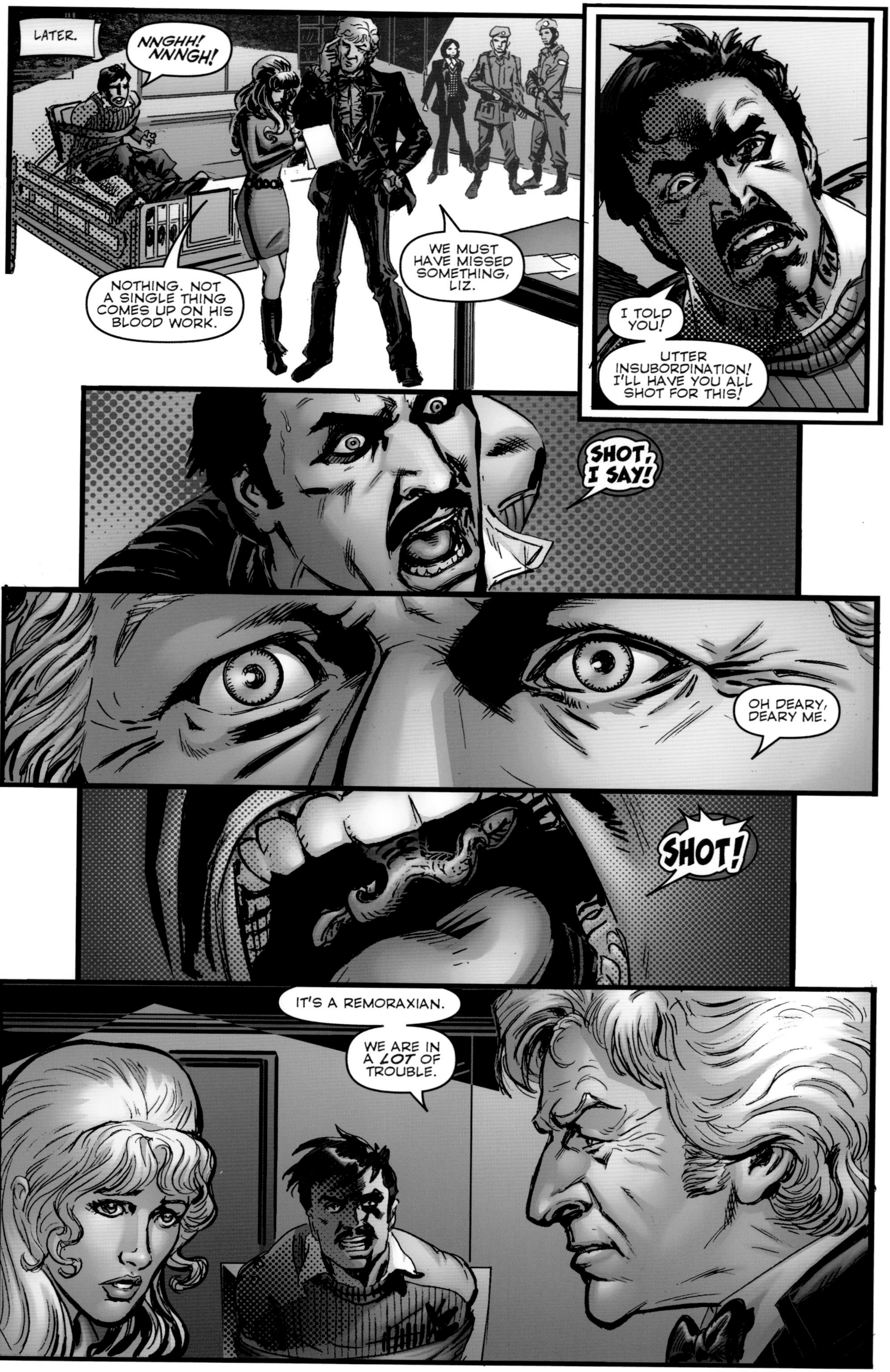
LATER.
NNGHH! NNNGH!
NOTHING. NOT A SINGLE THING COMES UP ON HIS BLOOD WORK.
WE MUST HAVE MISSED SOMETHING, LIZ.
I TOLD YOU!
UTTER INSUBORDINATION! I'LL HAVE YOU ALL SHOT FOR THIS!
SHOT, I SAY!
OH DEARY, DEARY ME.
SHOT!
IT'S A REMORAXIAN.
WE ARE IN A *LOT* OF TROUBLE.

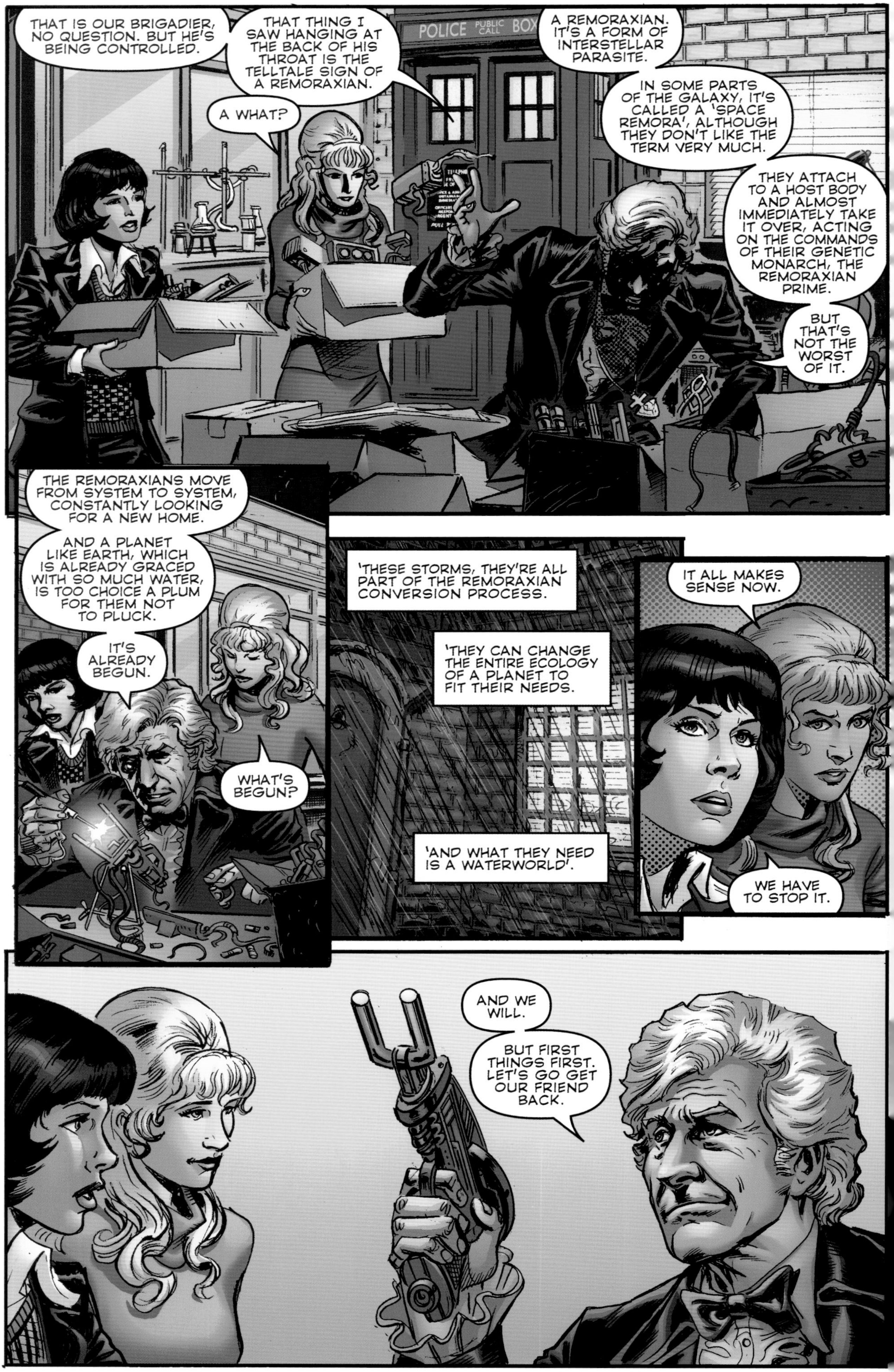

THAT IS OUR BRIGADIER, NO QUESTION. BUT HE'S BEING CONTROLLED.
THAT THING I SAW HANGING AT THE BACK OF HIS THROAT IS THE TELLTALE SIGN OF A REMORAXIAN.
A WHAT?
A REMORAXIAN. IT'S A FORM OF INTERSTELLAR PARASITE.
IN SOME PARTS OF THE GALAXY, IT'S CALLED A 'SPACE REMORA', ALTHOUGH THEY DON'T LIKE THE TERM VERY MUCH.
THEY ATTACH TO A HOST BODY AND ALMOST IMMEDIATELY TAKE IT OVER, ACTING ON THE COMMANDS OF THEIR GENETIC MONARCH, THE REMORAXIAN PRIME.
BUT THAT'S NOT THE WORST OF IT.
POLICE PUBLIC CALL BOX
THE REMORAXIANS MOVE FROM SYSTEM TO SYSTEM, CONSTANTLY LOOKING FOR A NEW HOME.
AND A PLANET LIKE EARTH, WHICH IS ALREADY GRACED WITH SO MUCH WATER, IS TOO CHOICE A PLUM FOR THEM NOT TO PLUCK.
IT'S ALREADY BEGUN.
WHAT'S BEGUN?
'THESE STORMS, THEY'RE ALL PART OF THE REMORAXIAN CONVERSION PROCESS.
'THEY CAN CHANGE THE ENTIRE ECOLOGY OF A PLANET TO FIT THEIR NEEDS.
'AND WHAT THEY NEED IS A WATERWORLD'.
IT ALL MAKES SENSE NOW.
WE HAVE TO STOP IT.
AND WE WILL.
BUT FIRST THINGS FIRST. LET'S GO GET OUR FRIEND BACK.

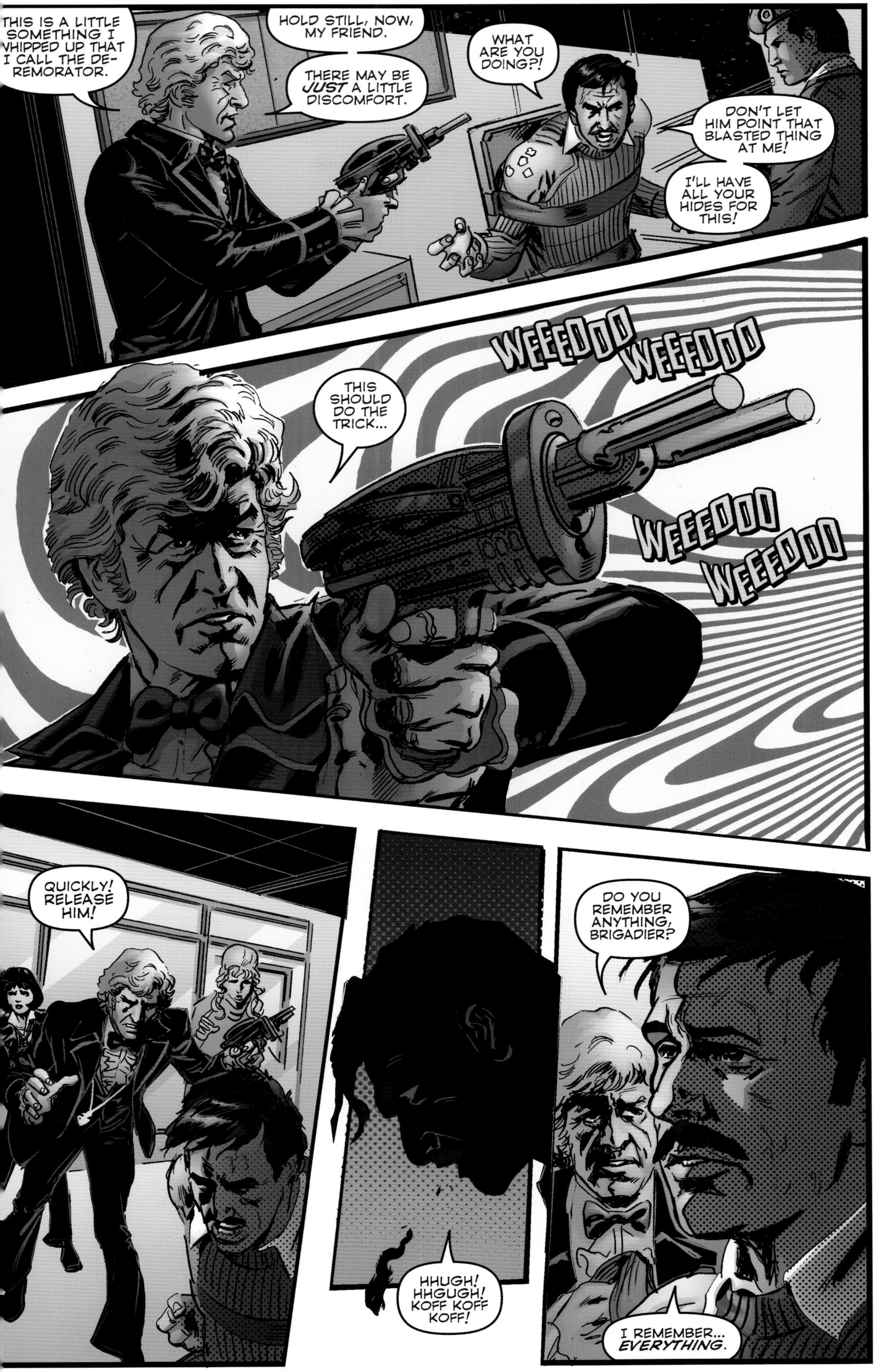
THIS IS A LITTLE SOMETHING I WHIPPED UP THAT I CALL THE DE-REMORATOR.
HOLD STILL, NOW, MY FRIEND.
THERE MAY BE JUST A LITTLE DISCOMFORT.
WHAT ARE YOU DOING?!
DON'T LET HIM POINT THAT BLASTED THING AT ME!
I'LL HAVE ALL YOUR HIDES FOR THIS!
THIS SHOULD DO THE TRICK...
WEEEDOO WEEEDOO
WEEEDOO WEEEDOO
QUICKLY! RELEASE HIM!
HHUGH! HHGUGH! KOFF KOFF KOFF!
DO YOU REMEMBER ANYTHING, BRIGADIER?
I REMEMBER... EVERYTHING.

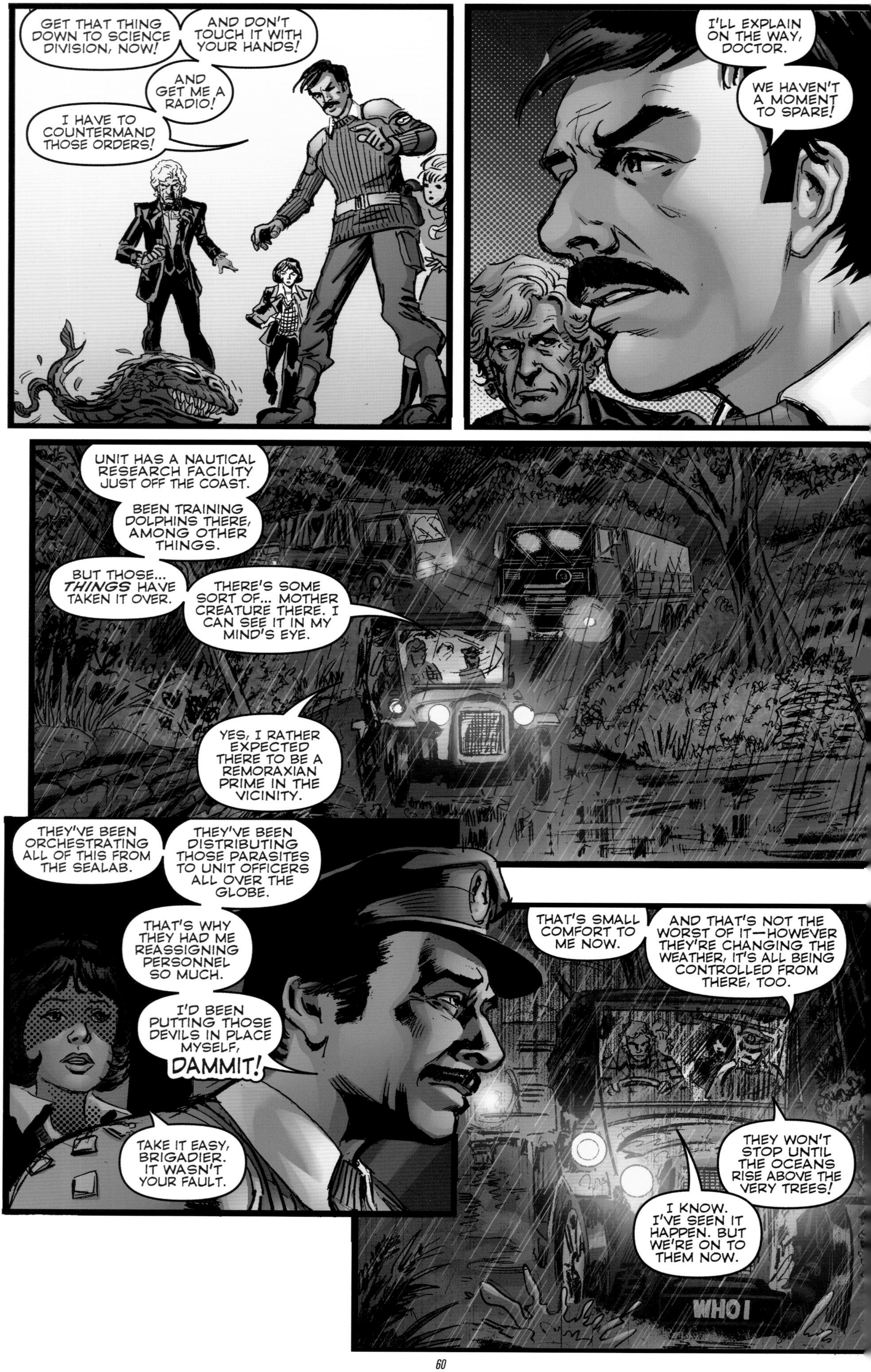
GET THAT THING DOWN TO SCIENCE DIVISION, NOW!
AND DON'T TOUCH IT WITH YOUR HANDS!
AND GET ME A RADIO!
I HAVE TO COUNTERMAND THOSE ORDERS!
I'LL EXPLAIN ON THE WAY, DOCTOR.
WE HAVEN'T A MOMENT TO SPARE!
UNIT HAS A NAUTICAL RESEARCH FACILITY JUST OFF THE COAST.
BEEN TRAINING DOLPHINS THERE, AMONG OTHER THINGS.
BUT THOSE... THINGS HAVE TAKEN IT OVER.
THERE'S SOME SORT OF... MOTHER CREATURE THERE. I CAN SEE IT IN MY MIND'S EYE.
YES, I RATHER EXPECTED THERE TO BE A REMORAXIAN PRIME IN THE VICINITY.
THEY'VE BEEN ORCHESTRATING ALL OF THIS FROM THE SEALAB.
THEY'VE BEEN DISTRIBUTING THOSE PARASITES TO UNIT OFFICERS ALL OVER THE GLOBE.
THAT'S WHY THEY HAD ME REASSIGNING PERSONNEL SO MUCH.
I'D BEEN PUTTING THOSE DEVILS IN PLACE MYSELF, DAMMIT!
TAKE IT EASY, BRIGADIER. IT WASN'T YOUR FAULT.
THAT'S SMALL COMFORT TO ME NOW.
AND THAT'S NOT THE WORST OF IT—HOWEVER THEY'RE CHANGING THE WEATHER, IT'S ALL BEING CONTROLLED FROM THERE, TOO.
THEY WON'T STOP UNTIL THE OCEANS RISE ABOVE THE VERY TREES!
I KNOW. I'VE SEEN IT HAPPEN. BUT WE'RE ON TO THEM NOW.
WHO I

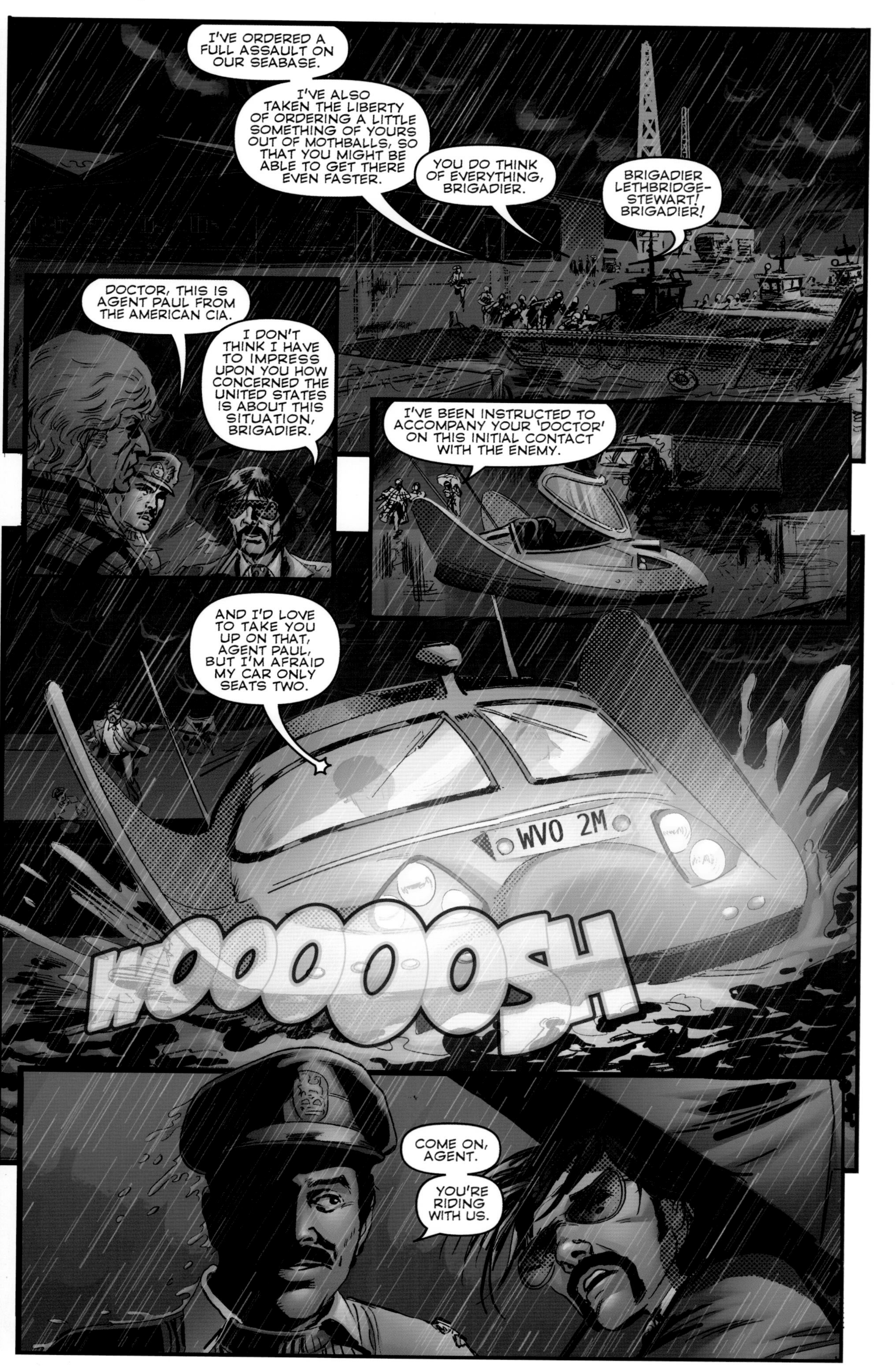
I'VE ORDERED A FULL ASSAULT ON OUR SEABASE.
I'VE ALSO TAKEN THE LIBERTY OF ORDERING A LITTLE SOMETHING OF YOURS OUT OF MOTHBALLS, SO THAT YOU MIGHT BE ABLE TO GET THERE EVEN FASTER.
YOU DO THINK OF EVERYTHING, BRIGADIER.
BRIGADIER LETHBRIDGE-STEWART! BRIGADIER!
DOCTOR, THIS IS AGENT PAUL FROM THE AMERICAN CIA.
I DON'T THINK I HAVE TO IMPRESS UPON YOU HOW CONCERNED THE UNITED STATES IS ABOUT THIS SITUATION, BRIGADIER.
I'VE BEEN INSTRUCTED TO ACCOMPANY YOUR 'DOCTOR' ON THIS INITIAL CONTACT WITH THE ENEMY.
AND I'D LOVE TO TAKE YOU UP ON THAT, AGENT PAUL, BUT I'M AFRAID MY CAR ONLY SEATS TWO.
WVO 2M
WOOOOOOSH
COME ON, AGENT.
YOU'RE RIDING WITH US.

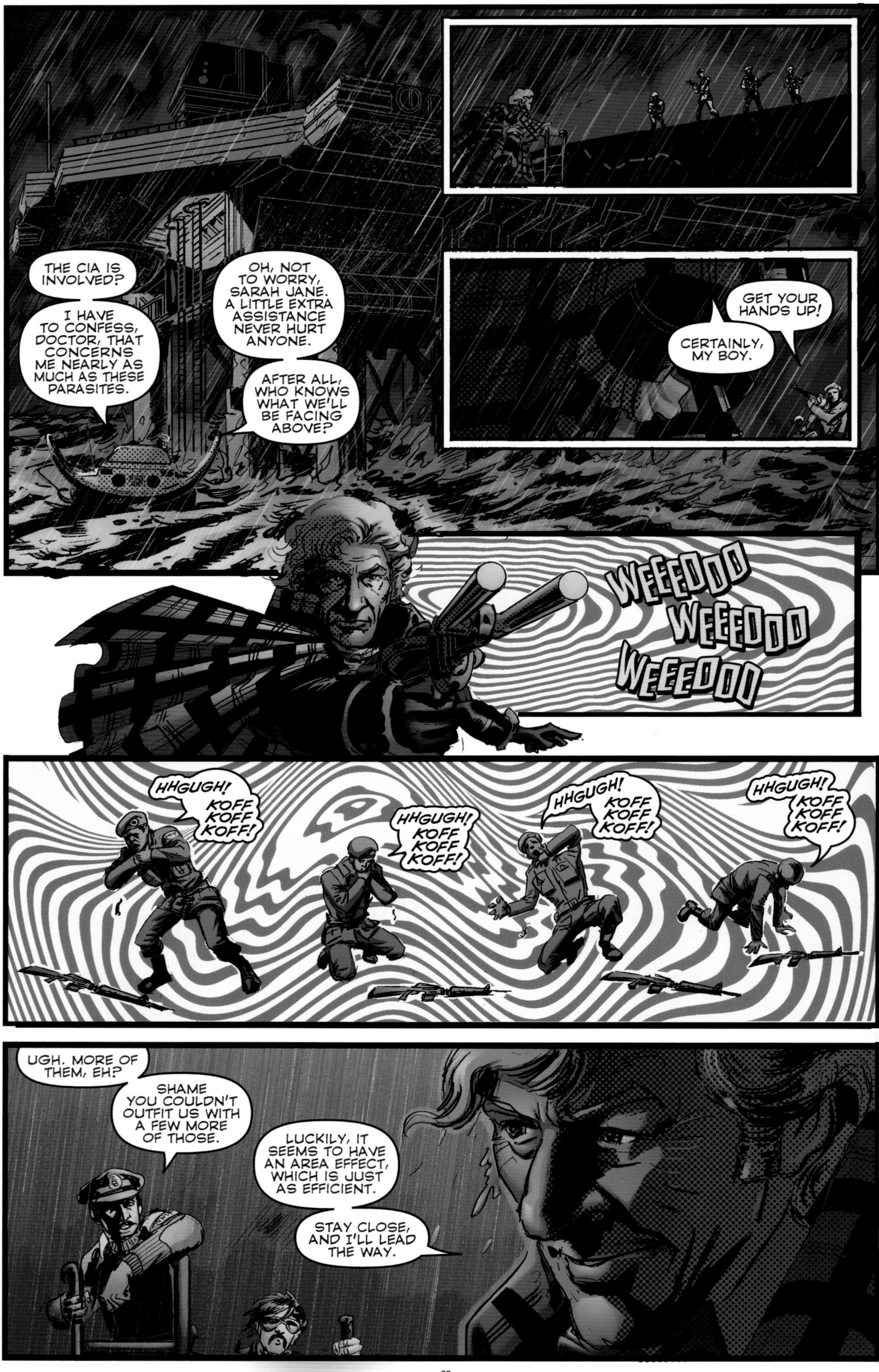
THE CIA IS INVOLVED?
I HAVE TO CONFESS, DOCTOR, THAT CONCERNS ME NEARLY AS MUCH AS THESE PARASITES.
OH, NOT TO WORRY, SARAH JANE. A LITTLE EXTRA ASSISTANCE NEVER HURT ANYONE.
AFTER ALL, WHO KNOWS WHAT WE'LL BE FACING ABOVE?
GET YOUR HANDS UP!
CERTAINLY, MY BOY.
WEEEDOO WEEEDOO WEEEDOO
HHGUGH! KOFF KOFF KOFF!
HHGUGH! KOFF KOFF KOFF!
HHGUGH! KOFF KOFF KOFF!
HHGUGH! KOFF KOFF KOFF!
UGH. MORE OF THEM, EH?
SHAME YOU COULDN'T OUTFIT US WITH A FEW MORE OF THOSE.
LUCKILY, IT SEEMS TO HAVE AN AREA EFFECT, WHICH IS JUST AS EFFICIENT.
STAY CLOSE, AND I'LL LEAD THE WAY.

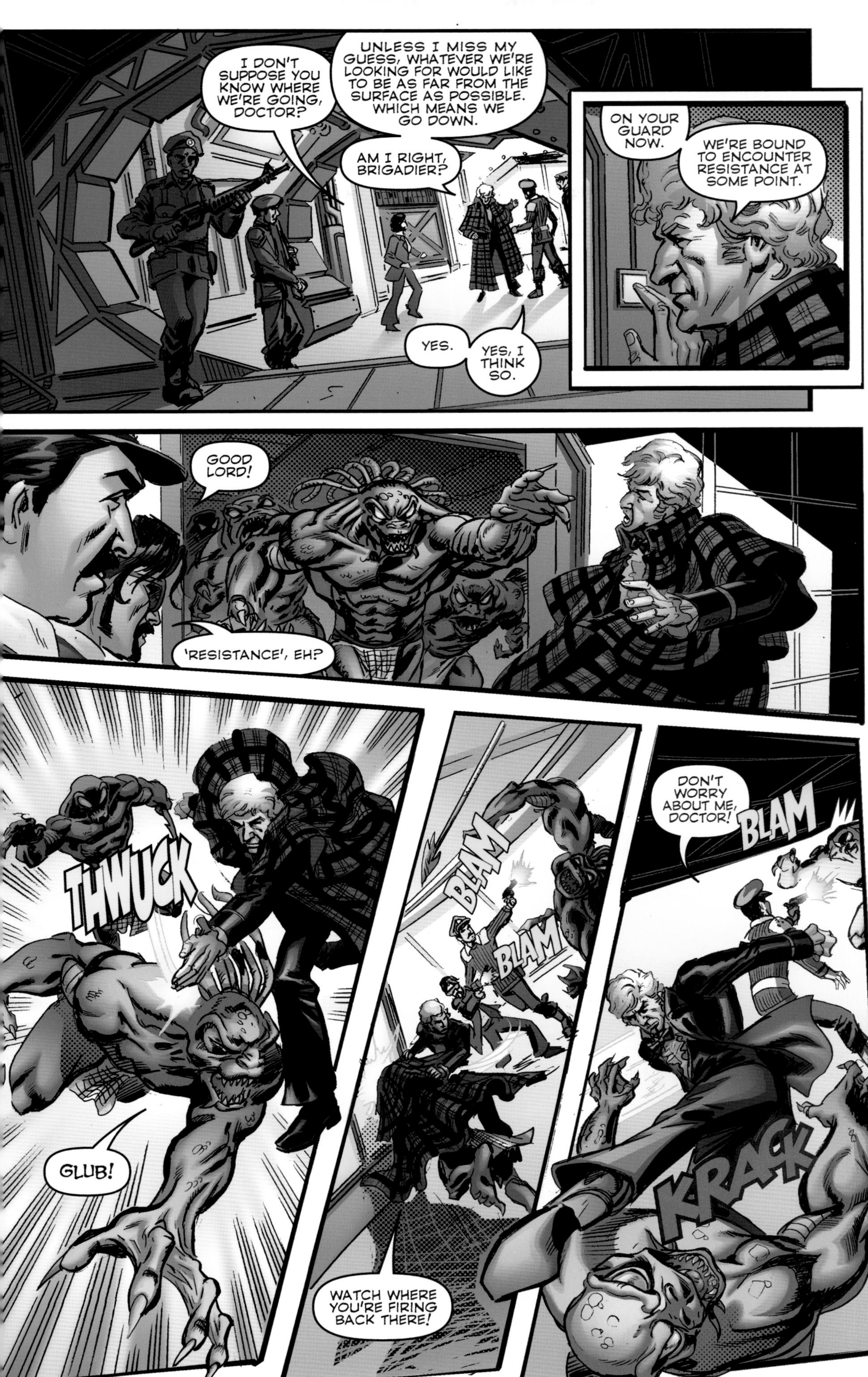
I DON'T SUPPOSE YOU KNOW WHERE WE'RE GOING, DOCTOR?
UNLESS I MISS MY GUESS, WHATEVER WE'RE LOOKING FOR WOULD LIKE TO BE AS FAR FROM THE SURFACE AS POSSIBLE. WHICH MEANS WE GO DOWN.
AM I RIGHT, BRIGADIER?
YES.
YES, I THINK SO.
ON YOUR GUARD NOW.
WE'RE BOUND TO ENCOUNTER RESISTANCE AT SOME POINT.
GOOD LORD!
'RESISTANCE', EH?
THWUCK
GLUB!
BLAM
BLAM
WATCH WHERE YOU'RE FIRING BACK THERE!
DON'T WORRY ABOUT ME, DOCTOR!
BLAM
KRACK

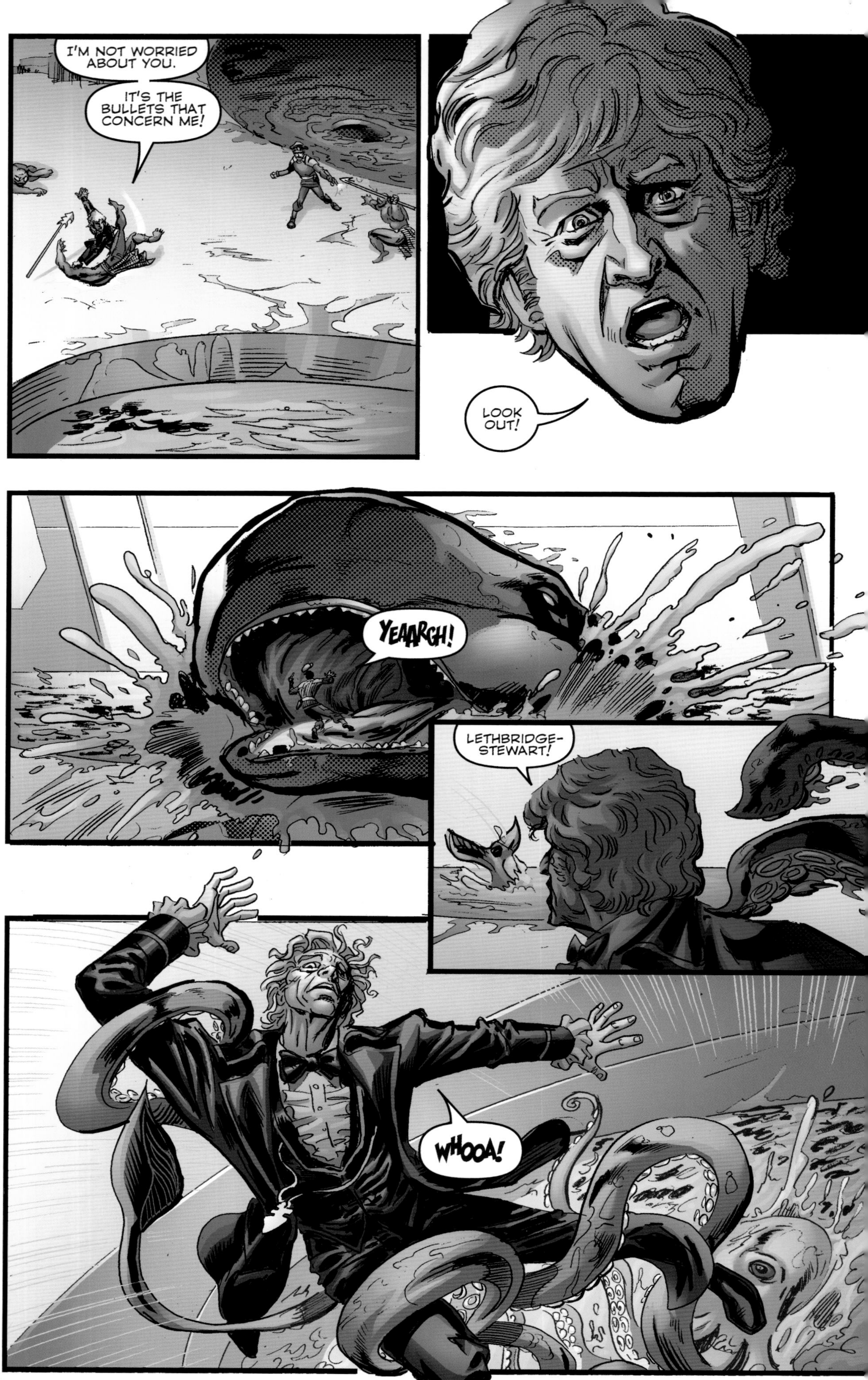
I'M NOT WORRIED ABOUT YOU.
IT'S THE BULLETS THAT CONCERN ME!
LOOK OUT!
YEAARGH!
LETHBRIDGE-STEWART!
WHOOA!

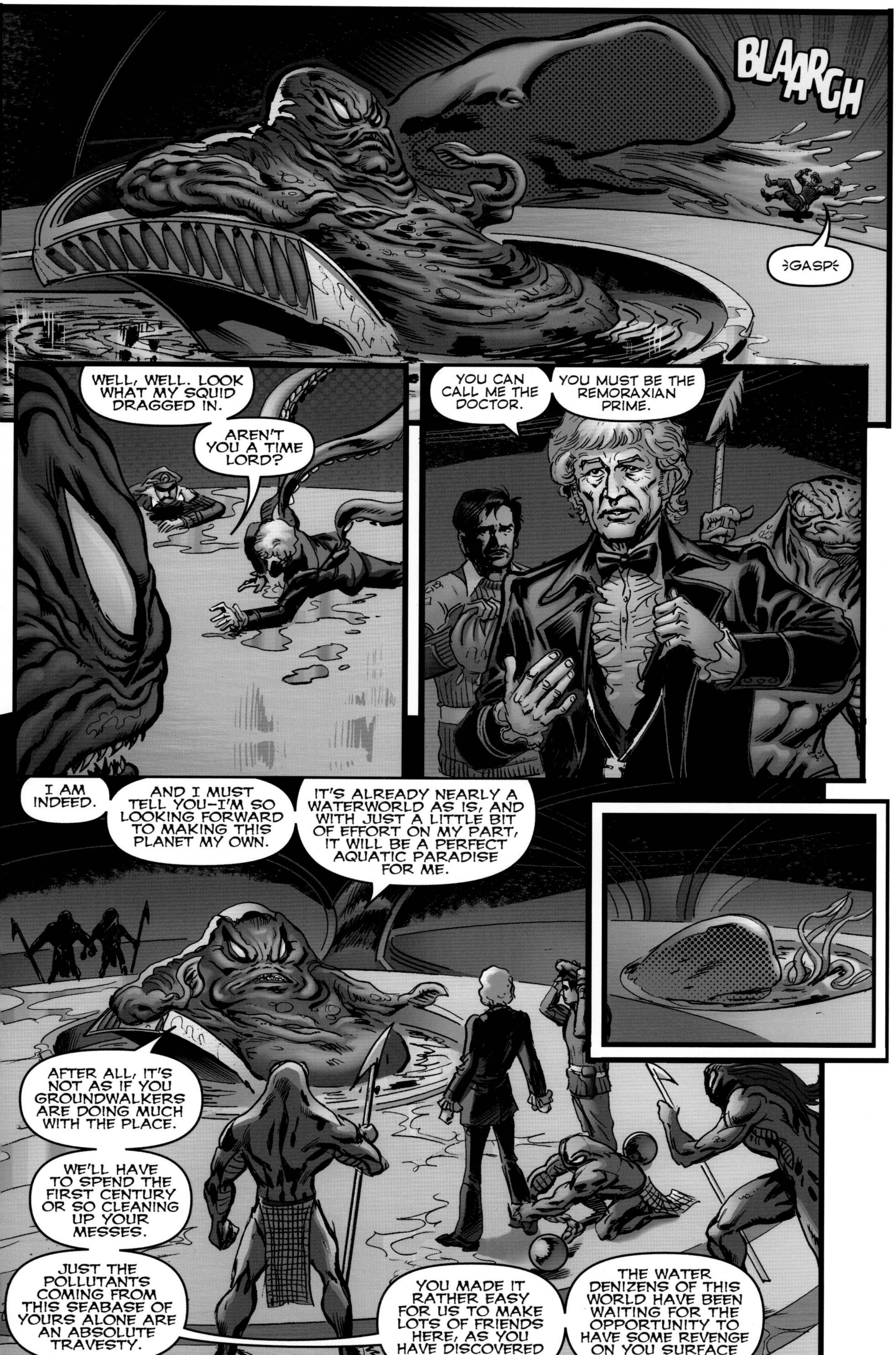
BLAARGH
GASP
WELL, WELL. LOOK WHAT MY SQUID DRAGGED IN.
AREN'T YOU A TIME LORD?
YOU CAN CALL ME THE DOCTOR.
YOU MUST BE THE REMORAXIAN PRIME.
I AM INDEED.
AND I MUST TELL YOU–I'M SO LOOKING FORWARD TO MAKING THIS PLANET MY OWN.
IT'S ALREADY NEARLY A WATERWORLD AS IS, AND WITH JUST A LITTLE BIT OF EFFORT ON MY PART, IT WILL BE A PERFECT AQUATIC PARADISE FOR ME.
AFTER ALL, IT'S NOT AS IF YOU GROUNDWALKERS ARE DOING MUCH WITH THE PLACE.
WE'LL HAVE TO SPEND THE FIRST CENTURY OR SO CLEANING UP YOUR MESSES.
JUST THE POLLUTANTS COMING FROM THIS SEABASE OF YOURS ALONE ARE AN ABSOLUTE TRAVESTY.
YOU MADE IT RATHER EASY FOR US TO MAKE LOTS OF FRIENDS HERE, AS YOU HAVE DISCOVERED FIRSTHAND.
THE WATER DENIZENS OF THIS WORLD HAVE BEEN WAITING FOR THE OPPORTUNITY TO HAVE SOME REVENGE ON YOU SURFACE DWELLERS.

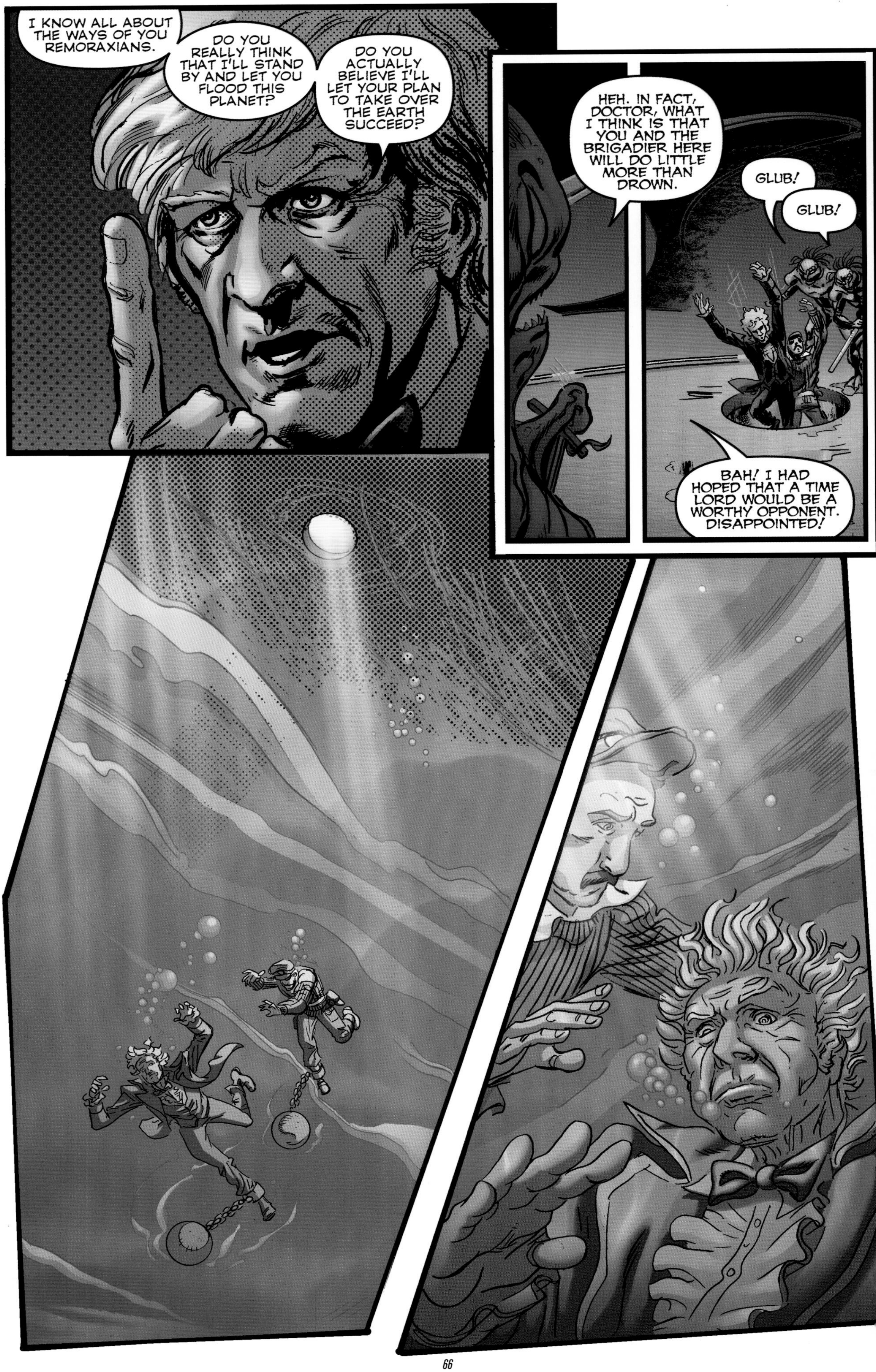
I KNOW ALL ABOUT THE WAYS OF YOU REMORAXIANS.
DO YOU REALLY THINK THAT I'LL STAND BY AND LET YOU FLOOD THIS PLANET?
DO YOU ACTUALLY BELIEVE I'LL LET YOUR PLAN TO TAKE OVER THE EARTH SUCCEED?
HEH. IN FACT, DOCTOR, WHAT I THINK IS THAT YOU AND THE BRIGADIER HERE WILL DO LITTLE MORE THAN DROWN.
GLUB!
GLUB!
BAH! I HAD HOPED THAT A TIME LORD WOULD BE A WORTHY OPPONENT. DISAPPOINTED!

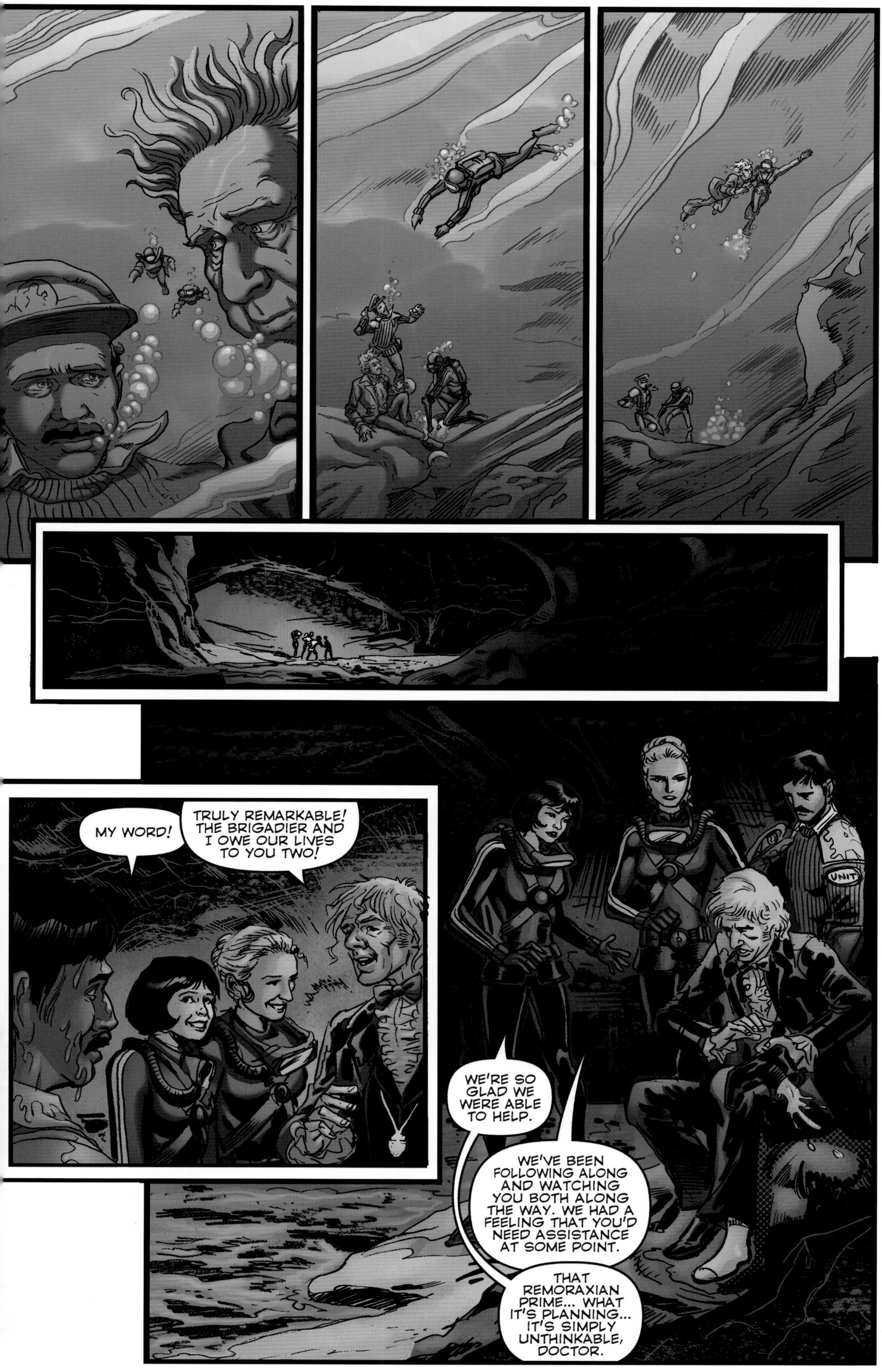

MY WORD!
TRULY REMARKABLE! THE BRIGADIER AND I OWE OUR LIVES TO YOU TWO!
WE'RE SO GLAD WE WERE ABLE TO HELP.
WE'VE BEEN FOLLOWING ALONG AND WATCHING YOU BOTH ALONG THE WAY. WE HAD A FEELING THAT YOU'D NEED ASSISTANCE AT SOME POINT.
THAT REMORAXIAN PRIME... WHAT IT'S PLANNING... IT'S SIMPLY UNTHINKABLE, DOCTOR.

THAT IT IS, SARAH JANE. WE MUST STOP HIM AS QUICKLY AS POSSIBLE.

WHERE IS THE REST OF OUR TASK FORCE?

MANY HAVE BEEN CAPTURED OR KILLED.

HERE UP AHEAD, AGENT PAUL FROM THE CIA HAS ESTABLISHED A TEMPORARY COMMAND CENTER FOR OUR REMAINING FORCES.

GENTLEMEN! I SEE DR. SHAW AND MISS SMITH WERE ABLE TO RESCUE YOU FROM YOUR PREDICAMENT.

THEY WERE MOST INSISTENT ON FOLLOWING YOU.

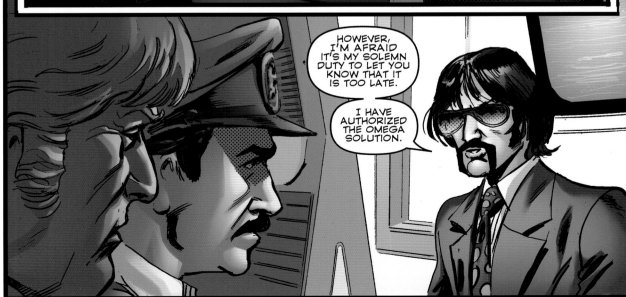

HOWEVER, I'M AFRAID IT'S MY SOLEMN DUTY TO LET YOU KNOW THAT IT IS TOO LATE.

I HAVE AUTHORIZED THE OMEGA SOLUTION.

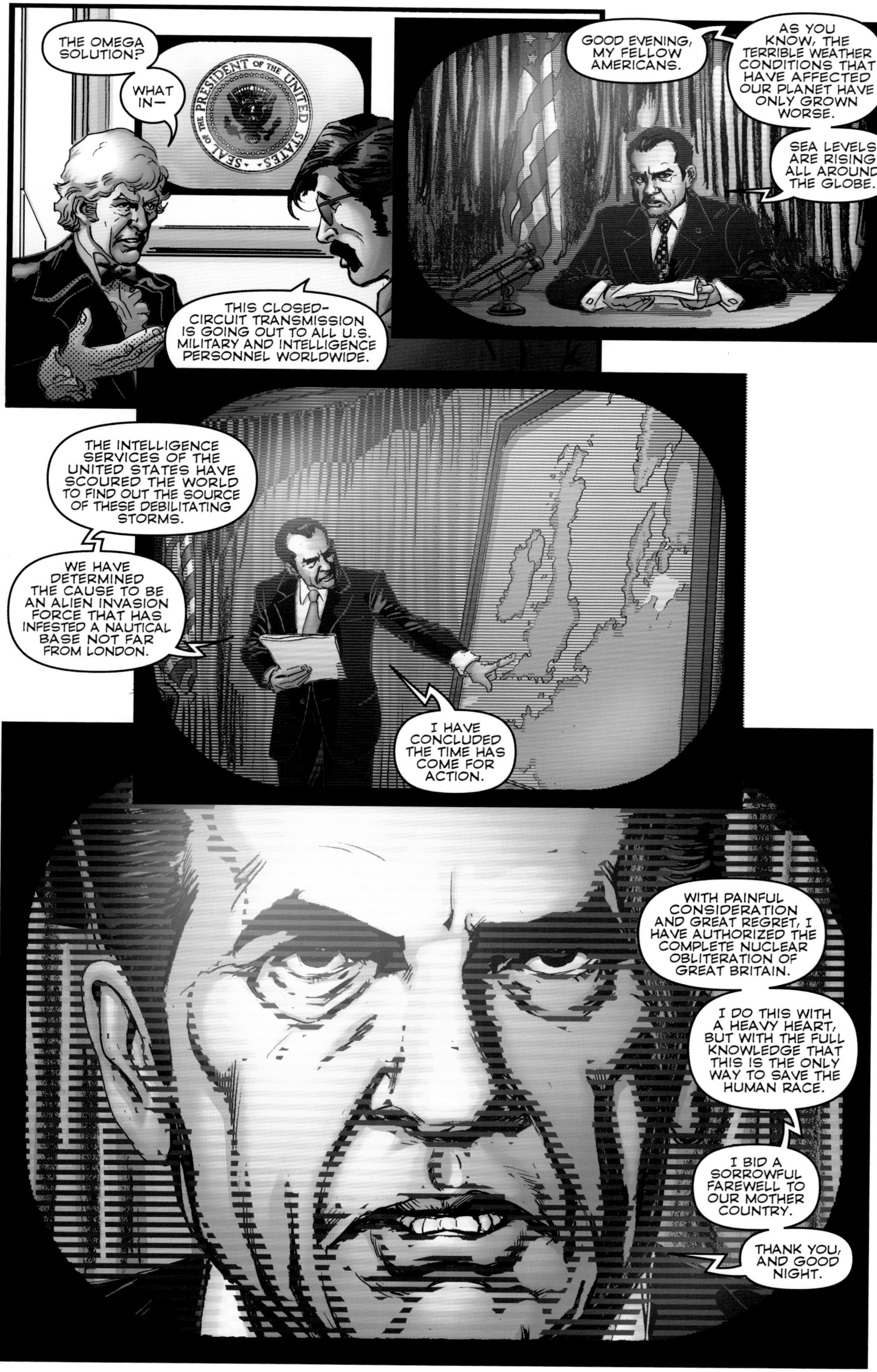
THE OMEGA SOLUTION?
WHAT IN—
SEAL OF THE PRESIDENT OF THE UNITED STATES
THIS CLOSED-CIRCUIT TRANSMISSION IS GOING OUT TO ALL U.S. MILITARY AND INTELLIGENCE PERSONNEL WORLDWIDE.
GOOD EVENING, MY FELLOW AMERICANS.
AS YOU KNOW, THE TERRIBLE WEATHER CONDITIONS THAT HAVE AFFECTED OUR PLANET HAVE ONLY GROWN WORSE.
SEA LEVELS ARE RISING ALL AROUND THE GLOBE.
THE INTELLIGENCE SERVICES OF THE UNITED STATES HAVE SCOURED THE WORLD TO FIND OUT THE SOURCE OF THESE DEBILITATING STORMS.
WE HAVE DETERMINED THE CAUSE TO BE AN ALIEN INVASION FORCE THAT HAS INFESTED A NAUTICAL BASE NOT FAR FROM LONDON.
I HAVE CONCLUDED THE TIME HAS COME FOR ACTION.
WITH PAINFUL CONSIDERATION AND GREAT REGRET, I HAVE AUTHORIZED THE COMPLETE NUCLEAR OBLITERATION OF GREAT BRITAIN.
I DO THIS WITH A HEAVY HEART, BUT WITH THE FULL KNOWLEDGE THAT THIS IS THE ONLY WAY TO SAVE THE HUMAN RACE.
I BID A SORROWFUL FAREWELL TO OUR MOTHER COUNTRY.
THANK YOU, AND GOOD NIGHT.

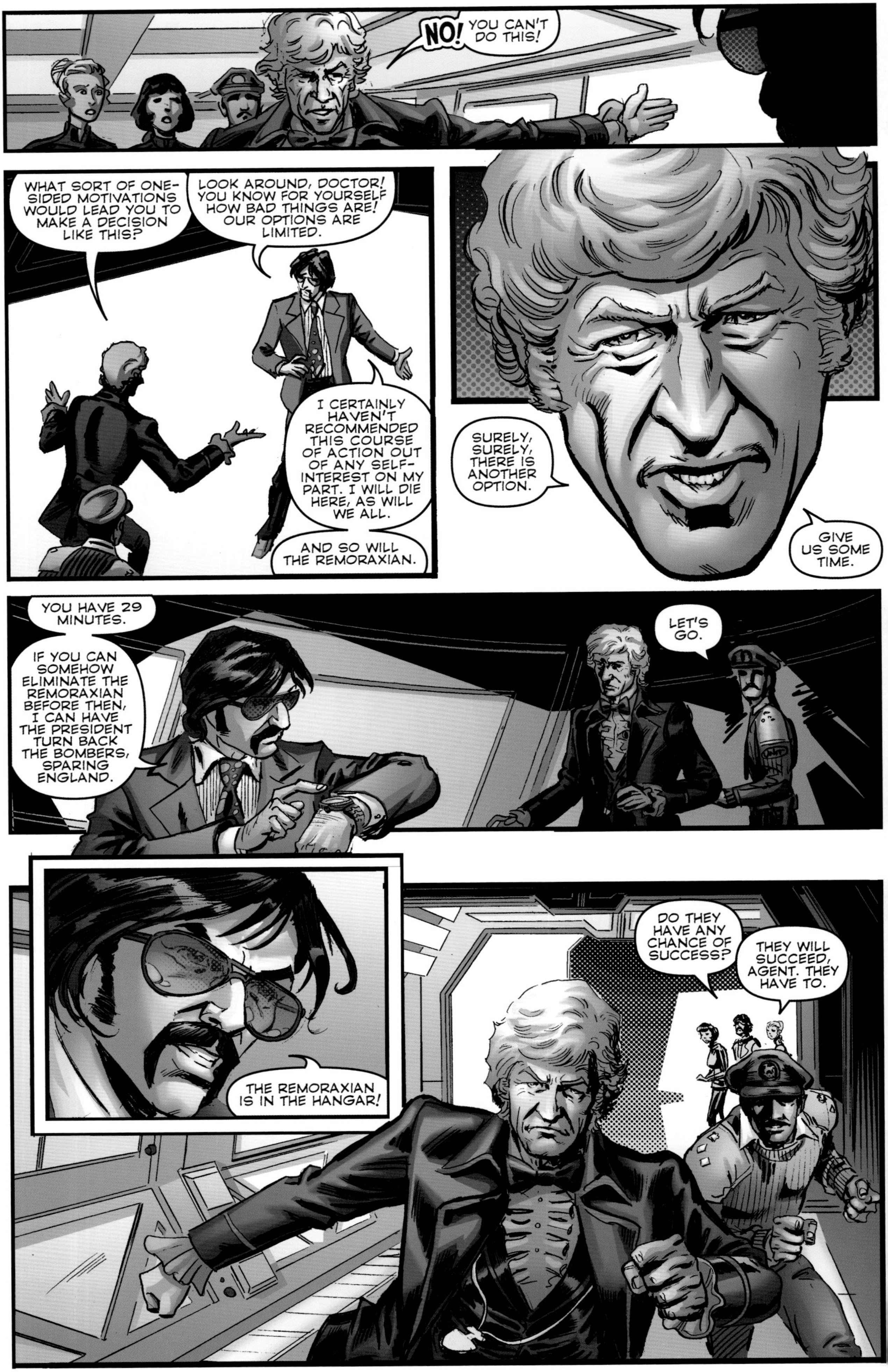
NO! YOU CAN'T DO THIS!
WHAT SORT OF ONE-SIDED MOTIVATIONS WOULD LEAD YOU TO MAKE A DECISION LIKE THIS?
LOOK AROUND, DOCTOR! YOU KNOW FOR YOURSELF HOW BAD THINGS ARE! OUR OPTIONS ARE LIMITED.
I CERTAINLY HAVEN'T RECOMMENDED THIS COURSE OF ACTION OUT OF ANY SELF-INTEREST ON MY PART. I WILL DIE HERE, AS WILL WE ALL.
AND SO WILL THE REMORAXIAN.
SURELY, SURELY, THERE IS ANOTHER OPTION.
GIVE US SOME TIME.
YOU HAVE 29 MINUTES.
IF YOU CAN SOMEHOW ELIMINATE THE REMORAXIAN BEFORE THEN, I CAN HAVE THE PRESIDENT TURN BACK THE BOMBERS, SPARING ENGLAND.
LET'S GO.
THE REMORAXIAN IS IN THE HANGAR!
DO THEY HAVE ANY CHANCE OF SUCCESS?
THEY WILL SUCCEED, AGENT. THEY HAVE TO.

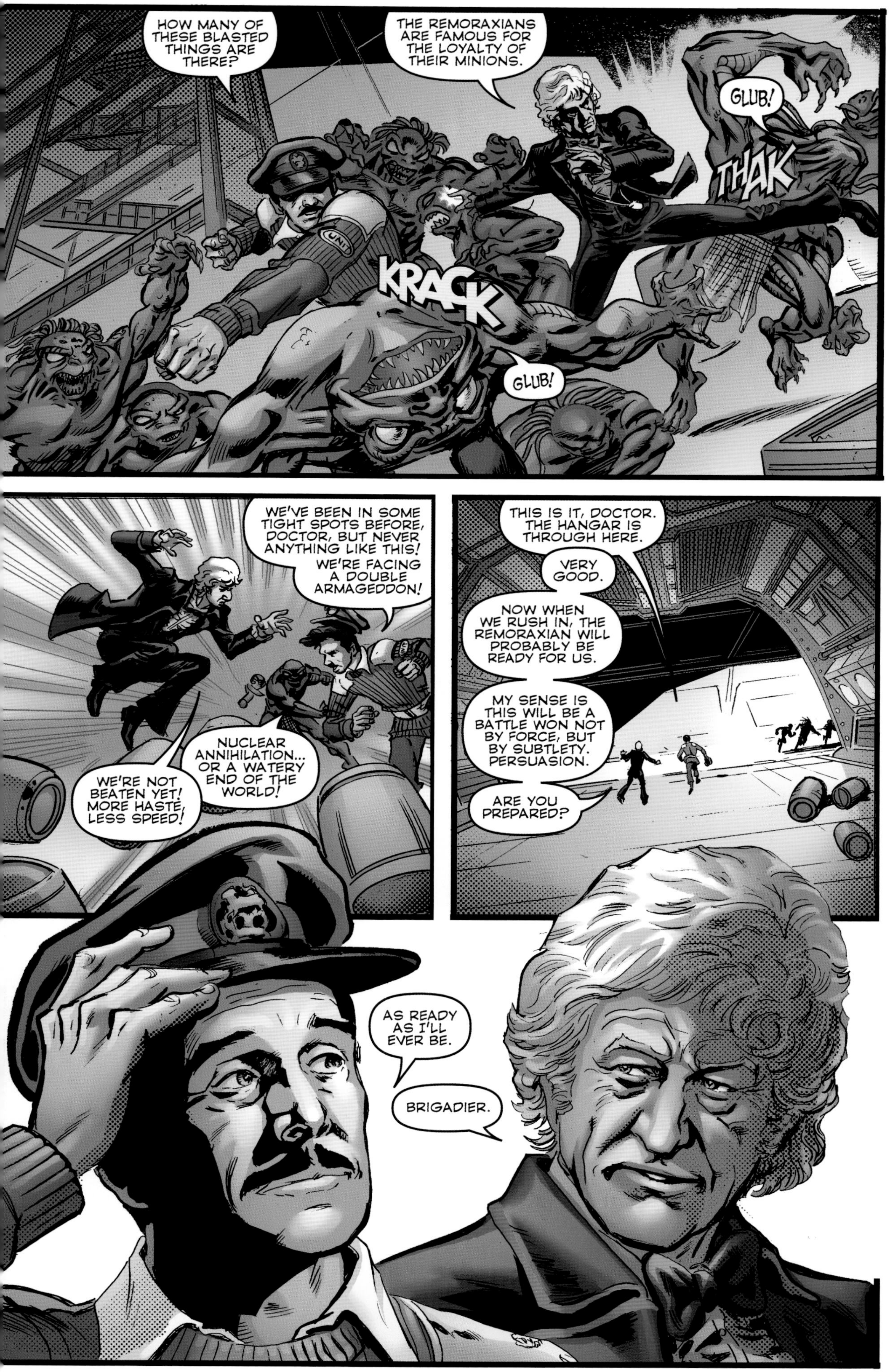
HOW MANY OF THESE BLASTED THINGS ARE THERE?
THE REMORAXIANS ARE FAMOUS FOR THE LOYALTY OF THEIR MINIONS.
GLUB!
THAK
KRACK
GLUB!
WE'VE BEEN IN SOME TIGHT SPOTS BEFORE, DOCTOR, BUT NEVER ANYTHING LIKE THIS!
WE'RE FACING A DOUBLE ARMAGEDDON!
NUCLEAR ANNIHILATION... OR A WATERY END OF THE WORLD!
WE'RE NOT BEATEN YET! MORE HASTE, LESS SPEED!
THIS IS IT, DOCTOR. THE HANGAR IS THROUGH HERE.
VERY GOOD.
NOW WHEN WE RUSH IN, THE REMORAXIAN WILL PROBABLY BE READY FOR US.
MY SENSE IS THIS WILL BE A BATTLE WON NOT BY FORCE, BUT BY SUBTLETY. PERSUASION.
ARE YOU PREPARED?
AS READY AS I'LL EVER BE.
BRIGADIER.

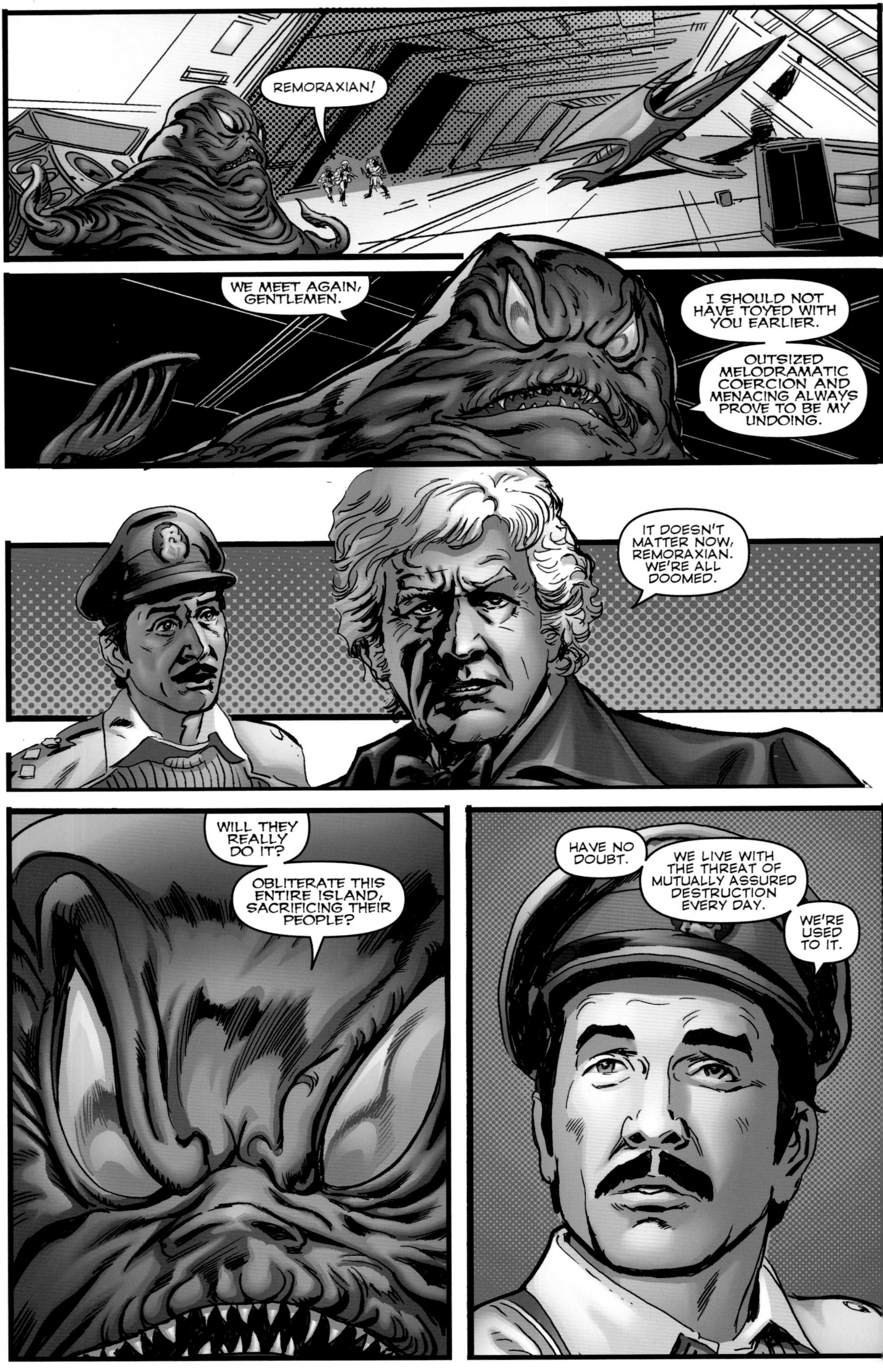
REMORAXIAN!
WE MEET AGAIN, GENTLEMEN.
I SHOULD NOT HAVE TOYED WITH YOU EARLIER.
OUTSIZED MELODRAMATIC COERCION AND MENACING ALWAYS PROVE TO BE MY UNDOING.
IT DOESN'T MATTER NOW, REMORAXIAN. WE'RE ALL DOOMED.
WILL THEY REALLY DO IT?
OBLITERATE THIS ENTIRE ISLAND, SACRIFICING THEIR PEOPLE?
HAVE NO DOUBT.
WE LIVE WITH THE THREAT OF MUTUALLY ASSURED DESTRUCTION EVERY DAY.
WE'RE USED TO IT.

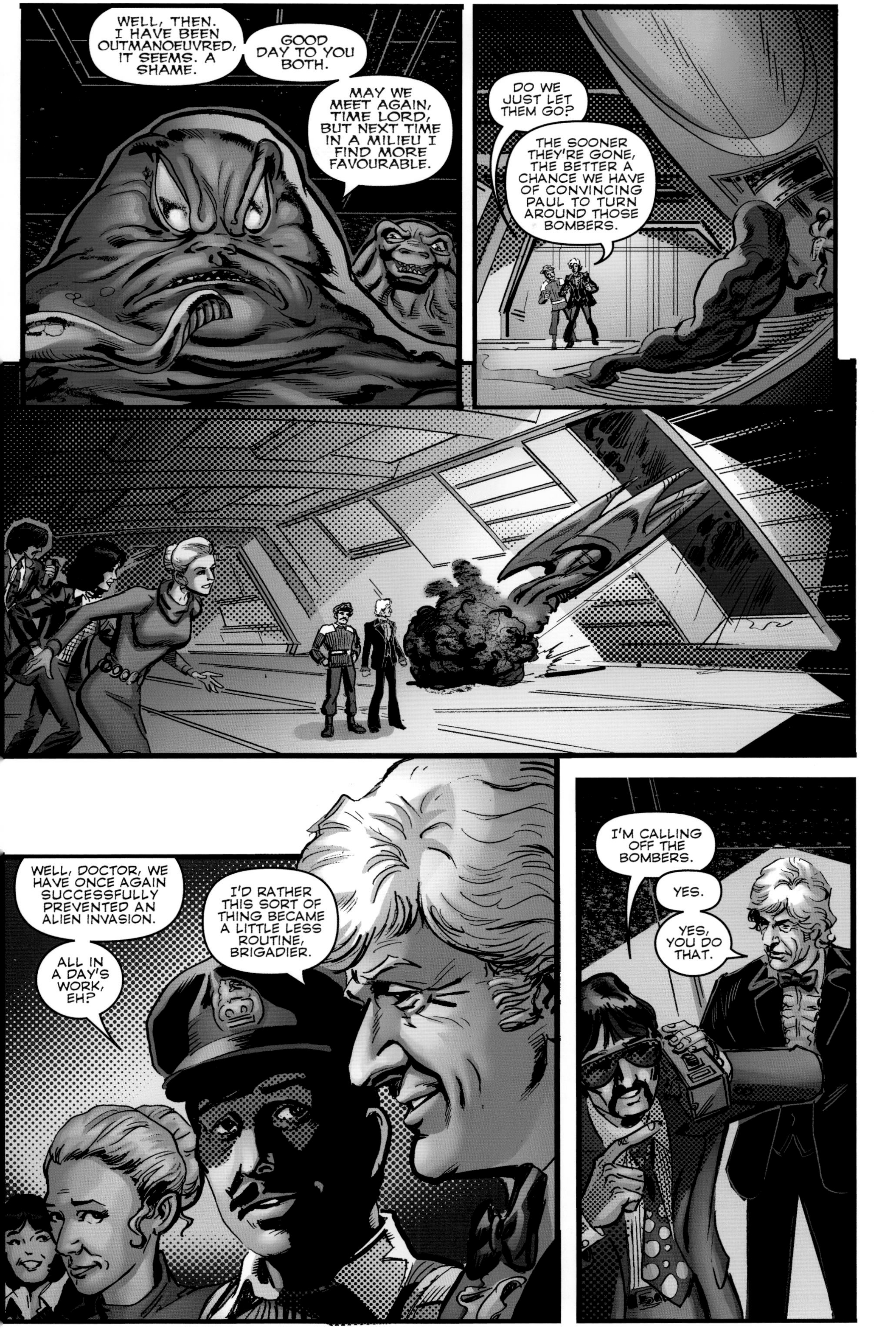

WELL, THEN. I HAVE BEEN OUTMANOEUVRED, IT SEEMS. A SHAME.
GOOD DAY TO YOU BOTH.
MAY WE MEET AGAIN, TIME LORD, BUT NEXT TIME IN A MILIEU I FIND MORE FAVOURABLE.
DO WE JUST LET THEM GO?
THE SOONER THEY'RE GONE, THE BETTER A CHANCE WE HAVE OF CONVINCING PAUL TO TURN AROUND THOSE BOMBERS.
WELL, DOCTOR, WE HAVE ONCE AGAIN SUCCESSFULLY PREVENTED AN ALIEN INVASION.
ALL IN A DAY'S WORK, EH?
I'D RATHER THIS SORT OF THING BECAME A LITTLE LESS ROUTINE, BRIGADIER.
I'M CALLING OFF THE BOMBERS.
YES.
YES, YOU DO THAT.

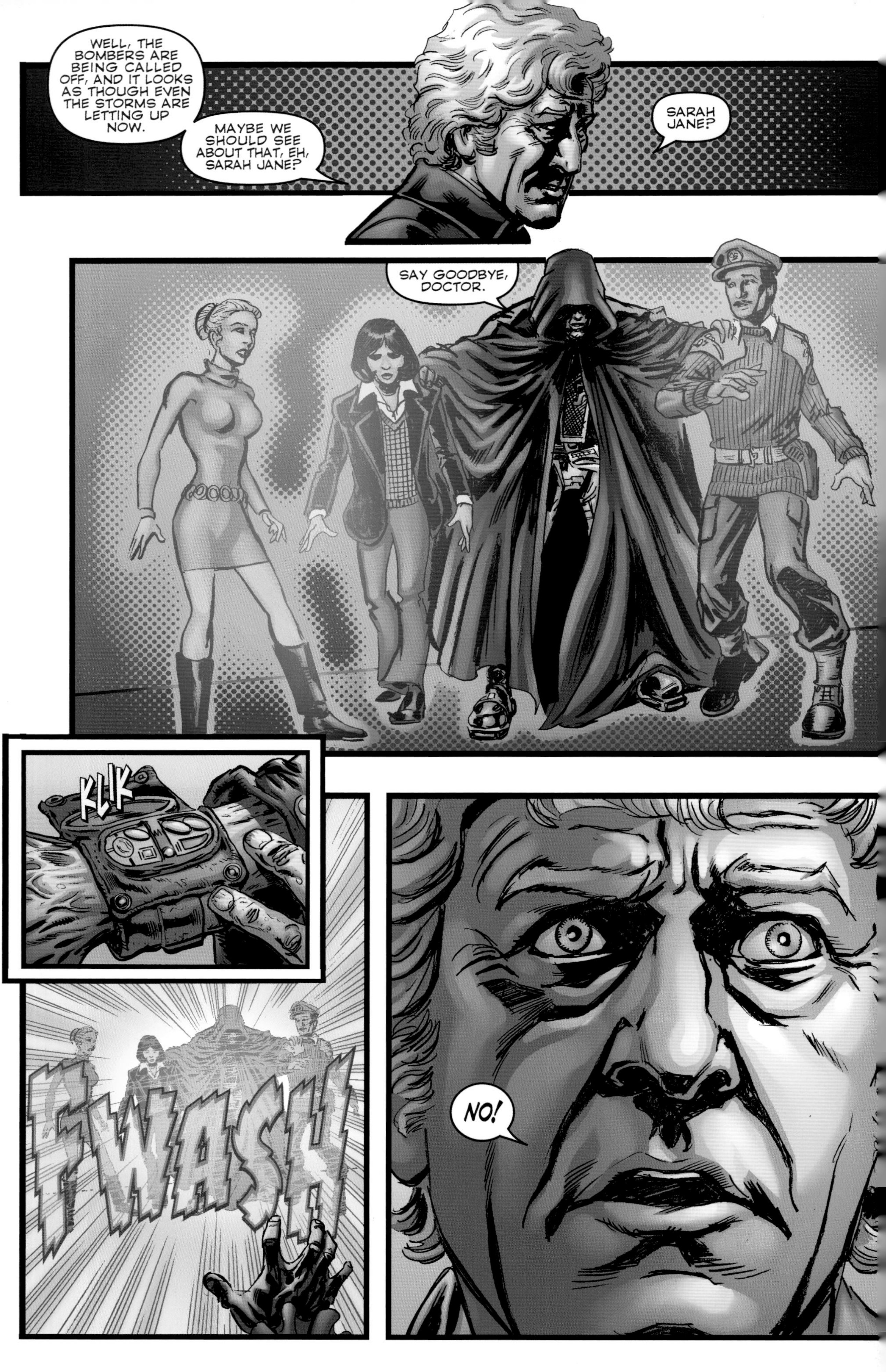

WELL, THE BOMBERS ARE BEING CALLED OFF, AND IT LOOKS AS THOUGH EVEN THE STORMS ARE LETTING UP NOW.
MAYBE WE SHOULD SEE ABOUT THAT, EH, SARAH JANE?
SARAH JANE?
SAY GOODBYE, DOCTOR.
KLIK
FWASH
NO!

REFLECTIONS OF TIME

Wherein prominent Whovians past and present muse upon the Doctor's history in comic form.

As the television show *Doctor Who* celebrates its 50th anniversary, it's worth remembering that November 2013 will also celebrate another anniversary—the 49th of the adventures of the Doctor in comic-strip form. Oh yes, indeed, 14th November 1964 saw the publication of the first instalment of 'The Klepton Parasites' in the British weekly *TV Comic*, starting an unbroken run of stories and resulting in the series being the longest-running comic strip based on a TV show in the world.

The stories featured the First Doctor and the unique-to-the-strip companions John and Gillian, his pre-teen grandchildren. *TV Comic*, you see, was very much aimed at that market, younger girls and boys for whom television was still a luxurious novelty which they could watch cartoons and adventure shows on. So the *Doctor Who* strip reflected that youthfulness—and although the stories were often fun, colourful, and witty, they were also rather simplistic and, frankly, daft. This theme continued through the Second Doctor and early Third Doctor strips until, in 1971, in issue 999 of *TV Comic*, the strip ended. Not because *Doctor Who* wasn't popular, but because it was too popular.

Therefore the publishers created a new weekly science-fiction-themed comic called *Countdown*, and *Doctor Who* was the heart and soul of that new publication. *Countdown* was aimed more at 10- to 14-year-olds, and the strip changed to accommodate that, thus beginning the maturity and incredible storytelling that all of today's 2013 comic strips owe their heritage to. Written by the likes of Dick O'Neill and Dennis Hooper and drawn by Gerry Haylock, Frank Langford, and Harry Lindfield, the Third Doctor strips, whilst not being tied too closely into what was being seen on screen at the time, still consisted of adventures that would not patronise or belittle their audience. Science fiction really had not been this much fun before.

The whimsy and outrageous nonsense that never truly 'felt' like *Doctor Who* in *TV Comic* was gone—and in its place, adventure and thrills were commonplace. However, the sci-fi basis of *Countdown* soon had to reflect the action-thriller shows of the mid-1970s and the magazine changed its name to accommodate this, becoming *TV Action*. Nevertheless, the *Doctor Who* strip maintained a steadfast high quality despite this, and when *TV Action* went the way of the dodo around Christmas 1973 and *Doctor Who* returned to its original home in *TV Comic*, that grown-up feel remained. Indeed, other than a slight blip towards the end of the '70s, it resisted the rest of *TV Comic's* lure of childishness, and those Third and Fourth Doctor strips in *TV Comic* are absolutely the jewels in its crown.

Ultimately, Marvel Comics' UK division made a successful bid to take *Doctor Who* away from *TV Comic*, and in 1979 *Doctor Who Weekly* was launched, the comic strip a central focus of the magazine—where it remains today in the renamed *Doctor Who Magazine*.

So as you read today's *Doctor Who* strips which clearly echo and celebrate the show that spawned them, be eternally grateful to those trail-blazing Third Doctor strips from *Countdown* and *TV Action*—because without them, the viability of a good, intelligent, and sophisticated *Doctor Who* IDW comic book might never have been proven.

—Gary Russell,
author, former BBC Drama script editor, former *Doctor Who Magazine* editor,
and producer for Big Finish Productions

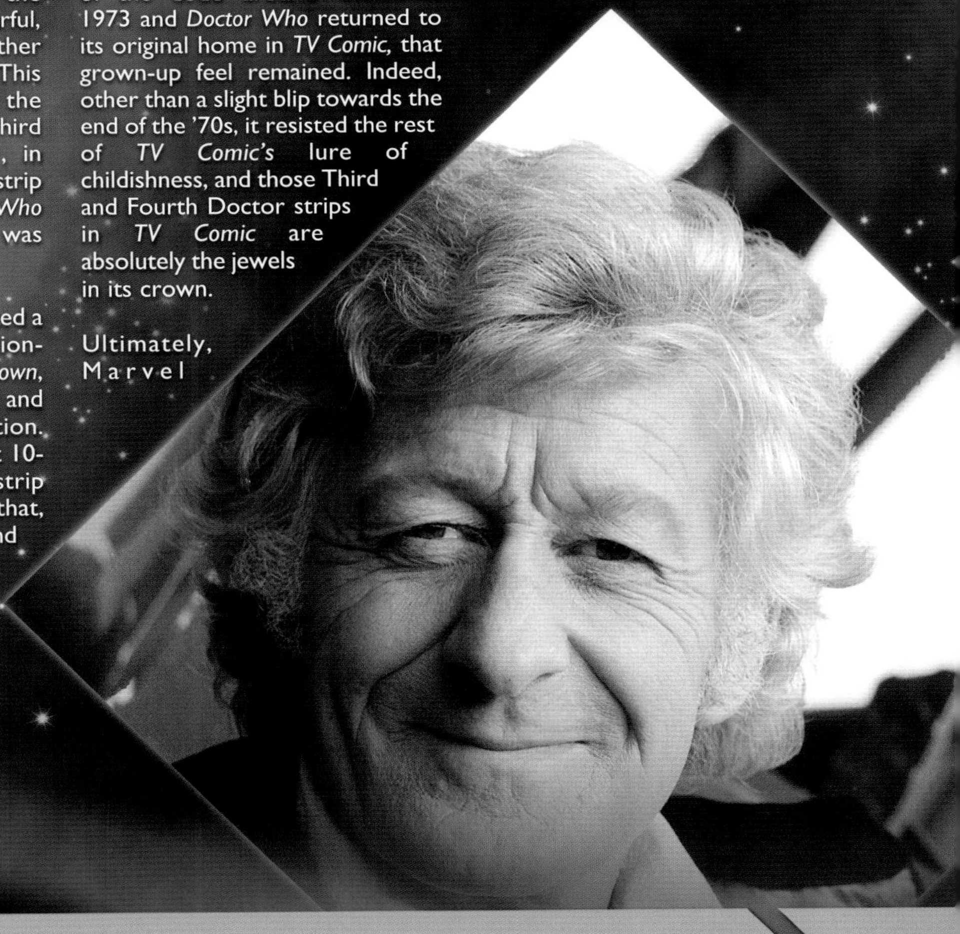

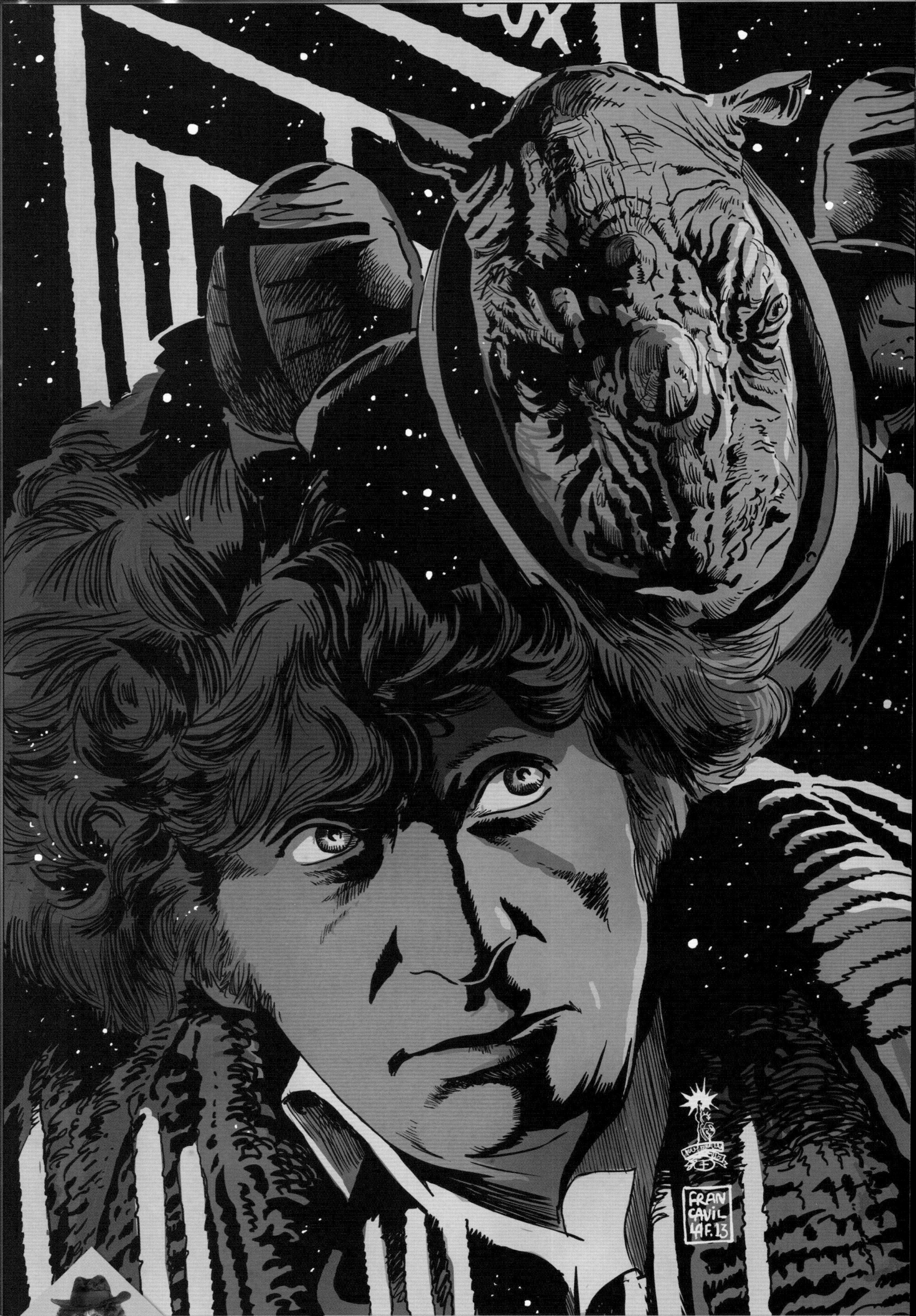
FRAN
CAVIL
14 F.13

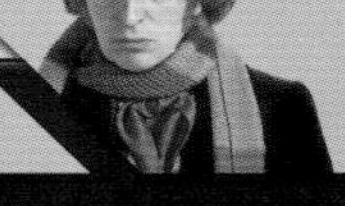

4TH DOCTOR
1974 - 1981

CHAPTER 4 "A Rare Gem"

Cover Art by Francesco Francavilla

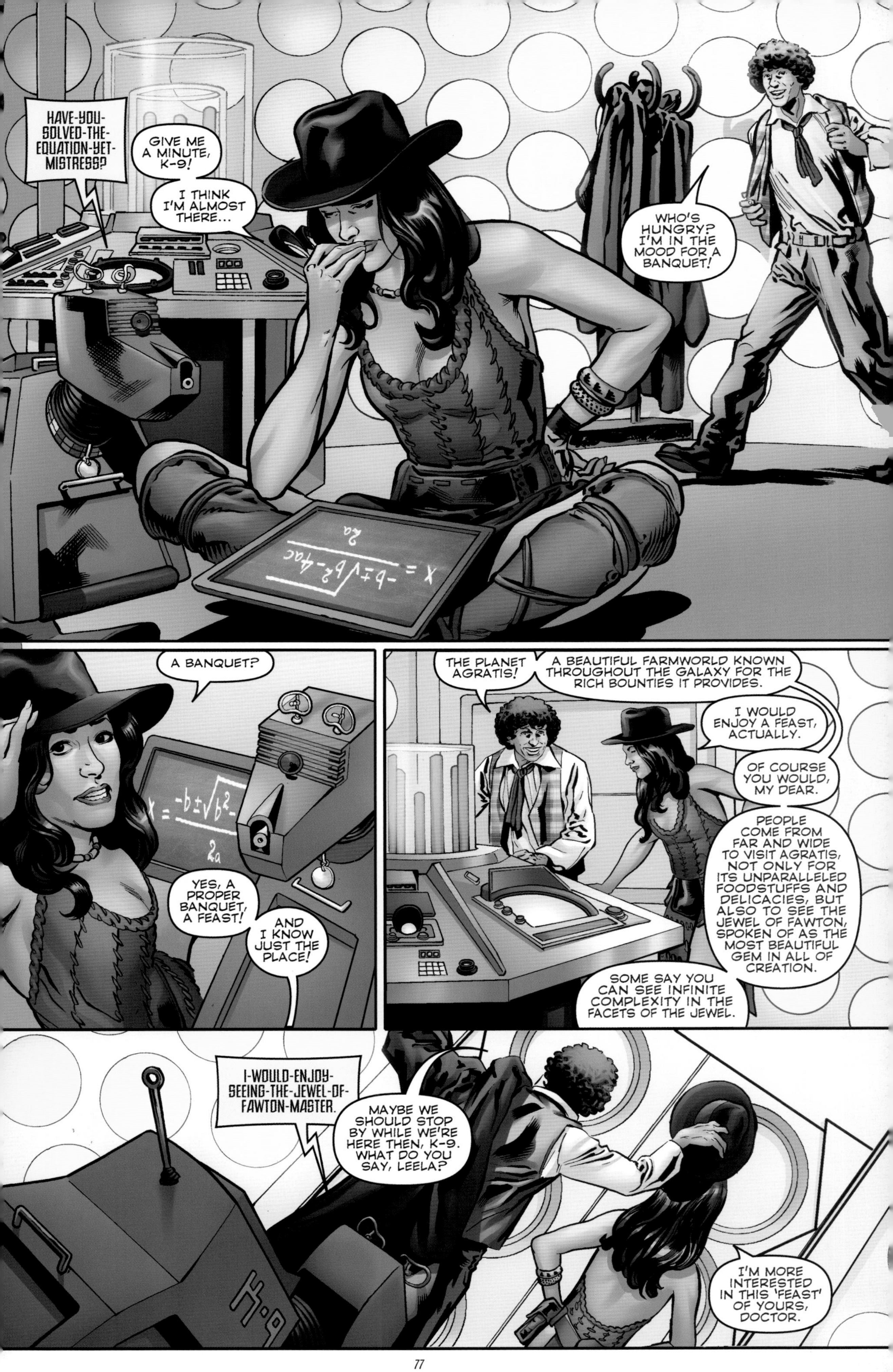
HAVE-YOU-SOLVED-THE-EQUATION-YET-MISTRESS?
GIVE ME A MINUTE, K-9!
I THINK I'M ALMOST THERE...
WHO'S HUNGRY? I'M IN THE MOOD FOR A BANQUET!
A BANQUET?
YES, A PROPER BANQUET, A FEAST!
AND I KNOW JUST THE PLACE!
THE PLANET AGRATIS!
A BEAUTIFUL FARMWORLD KNOWN THROUGHOUT THE GALAXY FOR THE RICH BOUNTIES IT PROVIDES.
I WOULD ENJOY A FEAST, ACTUALLY.
OF COURSE YOU WOULD, MY DEAR.
PEOPLE COME FROM FAR AND WIDE TO VISIT AGRATIS, NOT ONLY FOR ITS UNPARALLELED FOODSTUFFS AND DELICACIES, BUT ALSO TO SEE THE JEWEL OF FAWTON, SPOKEN OF AS THE MOST BEAUTIFUL GEM IN ALL OF CREATION.
SOME SAY YOU CAN SEE INFINITE COMPLEXITY IN THE FACETS OF THE JEWEL.
I-WOULD-ENJOY-SEEING-THE-JEWEL-OF-FAWTON-MASTER.
MAYBE WE SHOULD STOP BY WHILE WE'RE HERE THEN, K-9. WHAT DO YOU SAY, LEELA?
I'M MORE INTERESTED IN THIS 'FEAST' OF YOURS, DOCTOR.
K-9

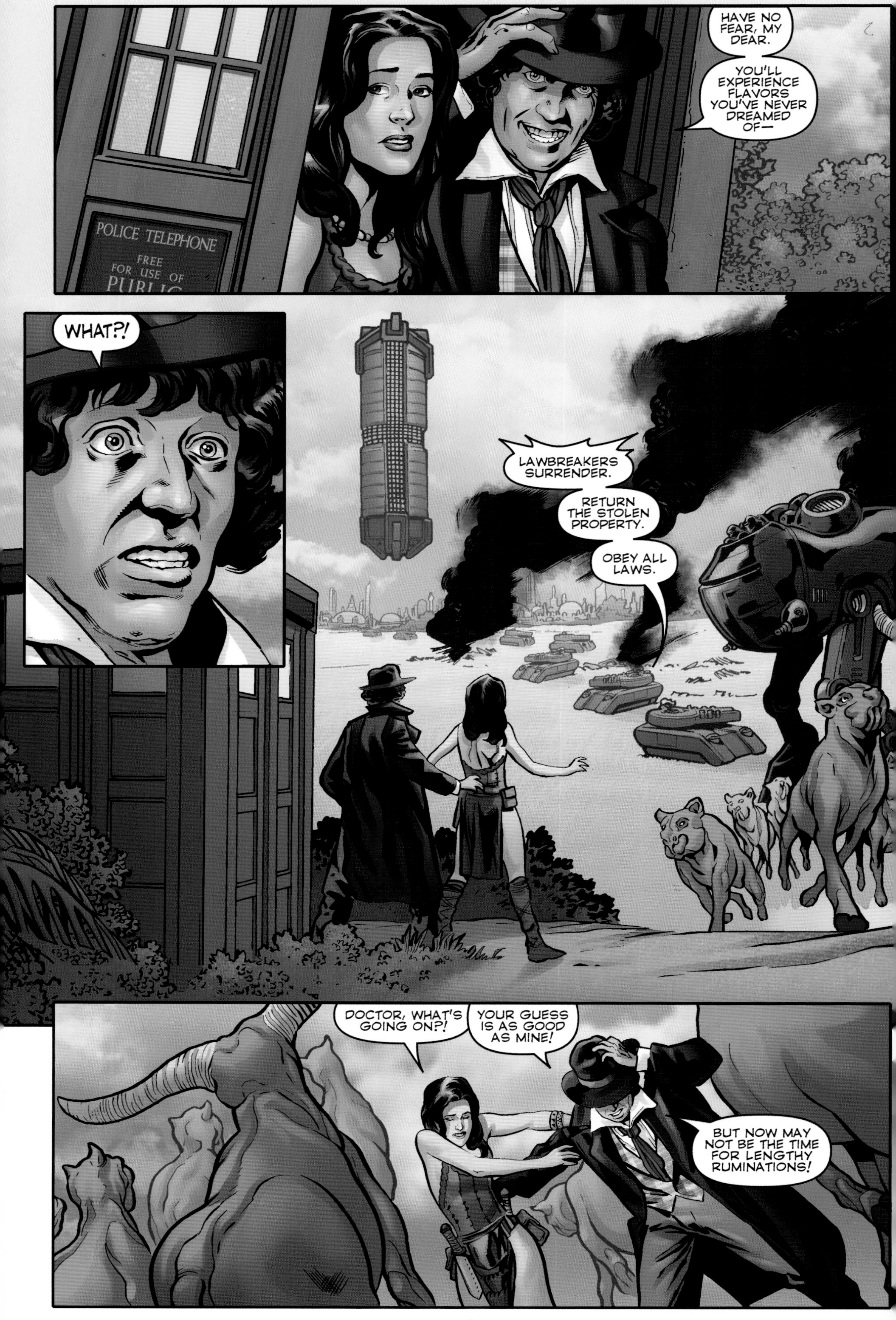
HAVE NO FEAR, MY DEAR.
YOU'LL EXPERIENCE FLAVORS YOU'VE NEVER DREAMED OF—
POLICE TELEPHONE FREE FOR USE OF PUBLIC
WHAT?!
LAWBREAKERS SURRENDER.
RETURN THE STOLEN PROPERTY.
OBEY ALL LAWS.
DOCTOR, WHAT'S GOING ON?!
YOUR GUESS IS AS GOOD AS MINE!
BUT NOW MAY NOT BE THE TIME FOR LENGTHY RUMINATIONS!

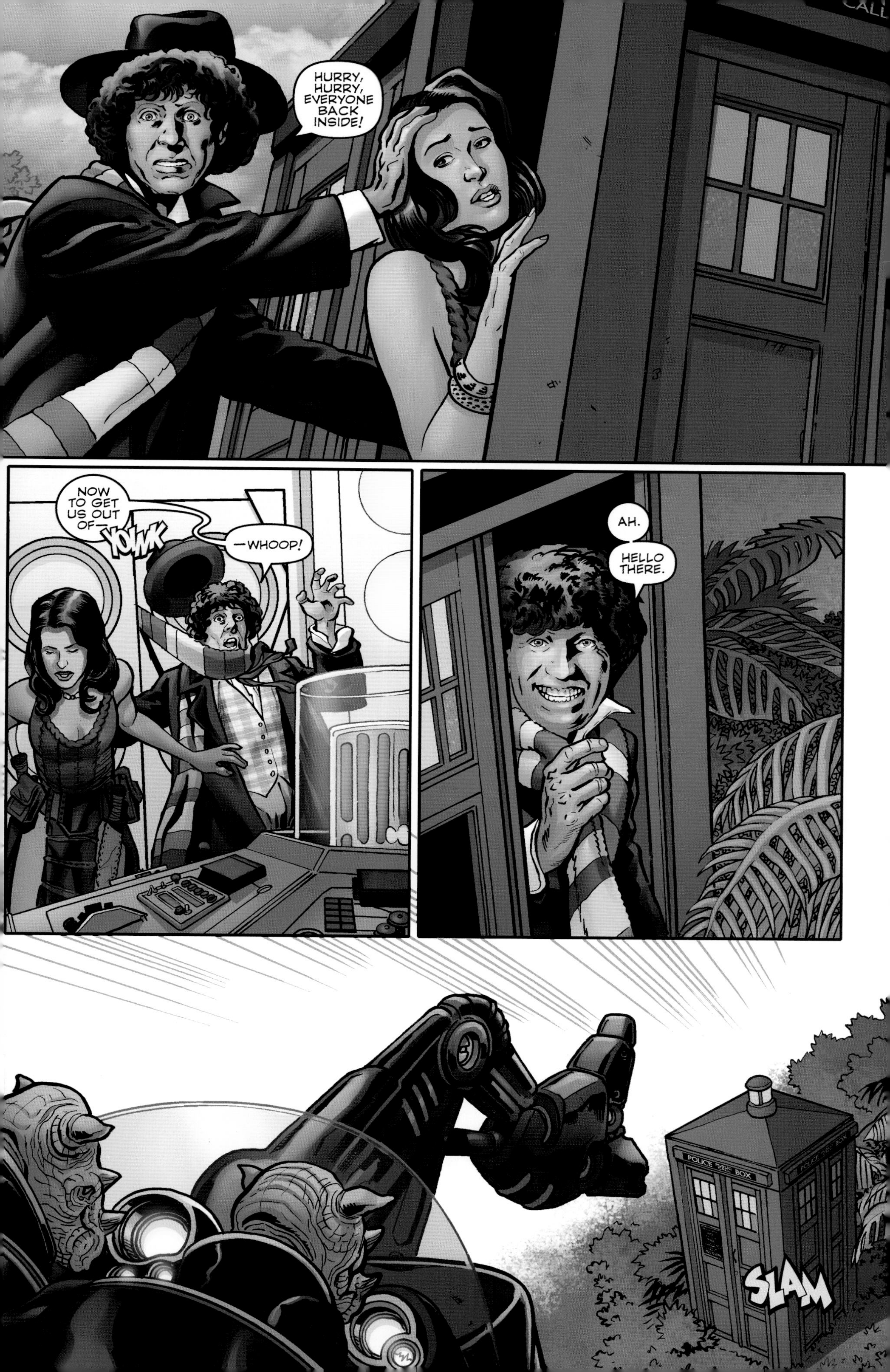

HURRY, HURRY, EVERYONE BACK INSIDE!
NOW TO GET US OUT OF—
YOWK
—WHOOP!
AH.
HELLO THERE.
POLICE BOX
SLAM

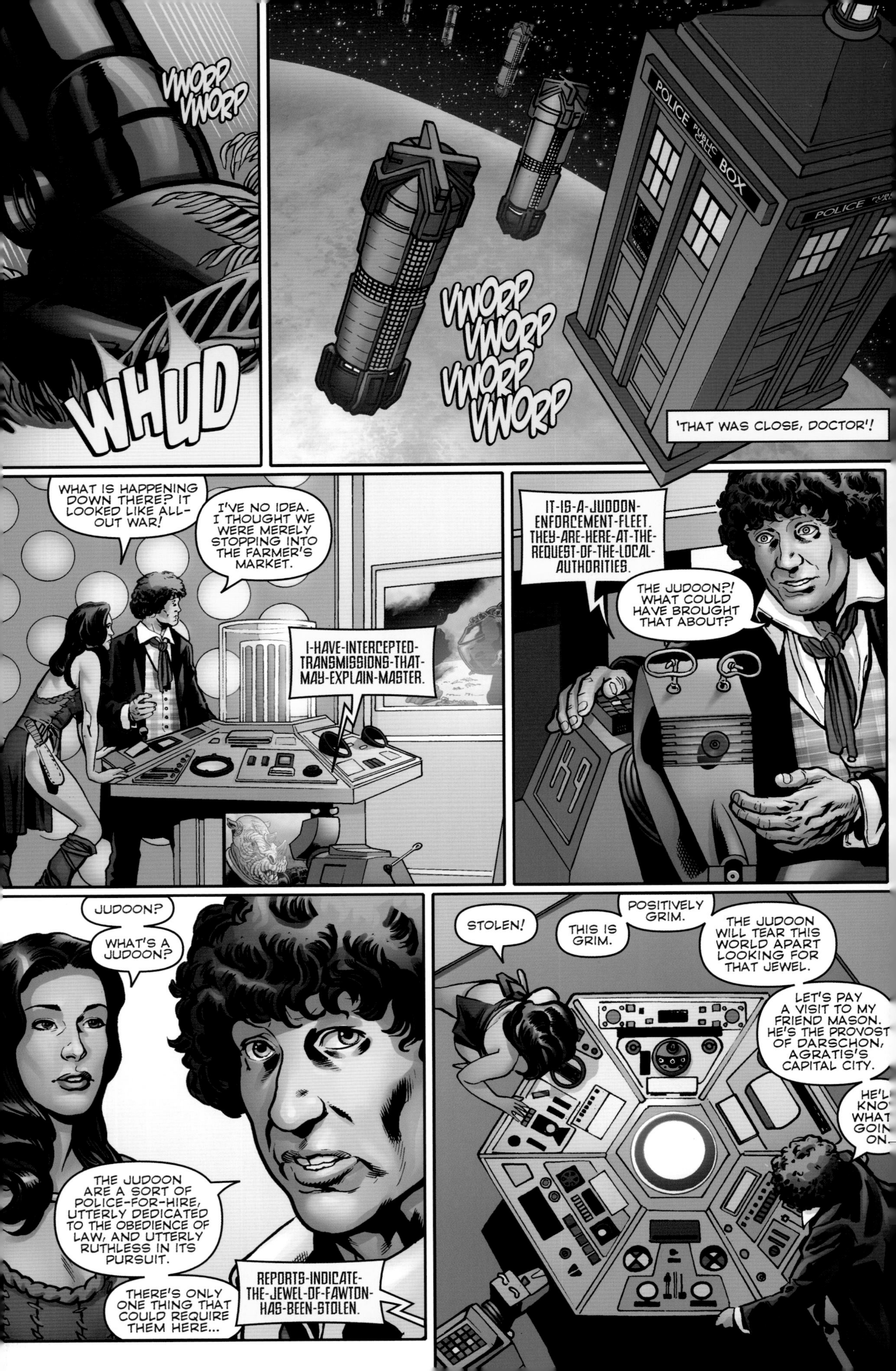
VWORP VWORP
WHUD
VWORP VWORP VWORP VWORP
POLICE PUBLIC CALL BOX
'THAT WAS CLOSE, DOCTOR'!
WHAT IS HAPPENING DOWN THERE? IT LOOKED LIKE ALL-OUT WAR!
I'VE NO IDEA. I THOUGHT WE WERE MERELY STOPPING INTO THE FARMER'S MARKET.
I-HAVE-INTERCEPTED-TRANSMISSIONS-THAT-MAY-EXPLAIN-MASTER.
IT-IS-A-JUDOON-ENFORCEMENT-FLEET. THEY-ARE-HERE-AT-THE-REQUEST-OF-THE-LOCAL-AUTHORITIES.
THE JUDOON?! WHAT COULD HAVE BROUGHT THAT ABOUT?
JUDOON?
WHAT'S A JUDOON?
THE JUDOON ARE A SORT OF POLICE-FOR-HIRE, UTTERLY DEDICATED TO THE OBEDIENCE OF LAW, AND UTTERLY RUTHLESS IN ITS PURSUIT.
THERE'S ONLY ONE THING THAT COULD REQUIRE THEM HERE...
REPORTS-INDICATE-THE-JEWEL-OF-FAWTON-HAS-BEEN-STOLEN.
STOLEN!
THIS IS GRIM.
POSITIVELY GRIM.
THE JUDOON WILL TEAR THIS WORLD APART LOOKING FOR THAT JEWEL.
LET'S PAY A VISIT TO MY FRIEND MASON. HE'S THE PROVOST OF DARSCHON, AGRATIS'S CAPITAL CITY.

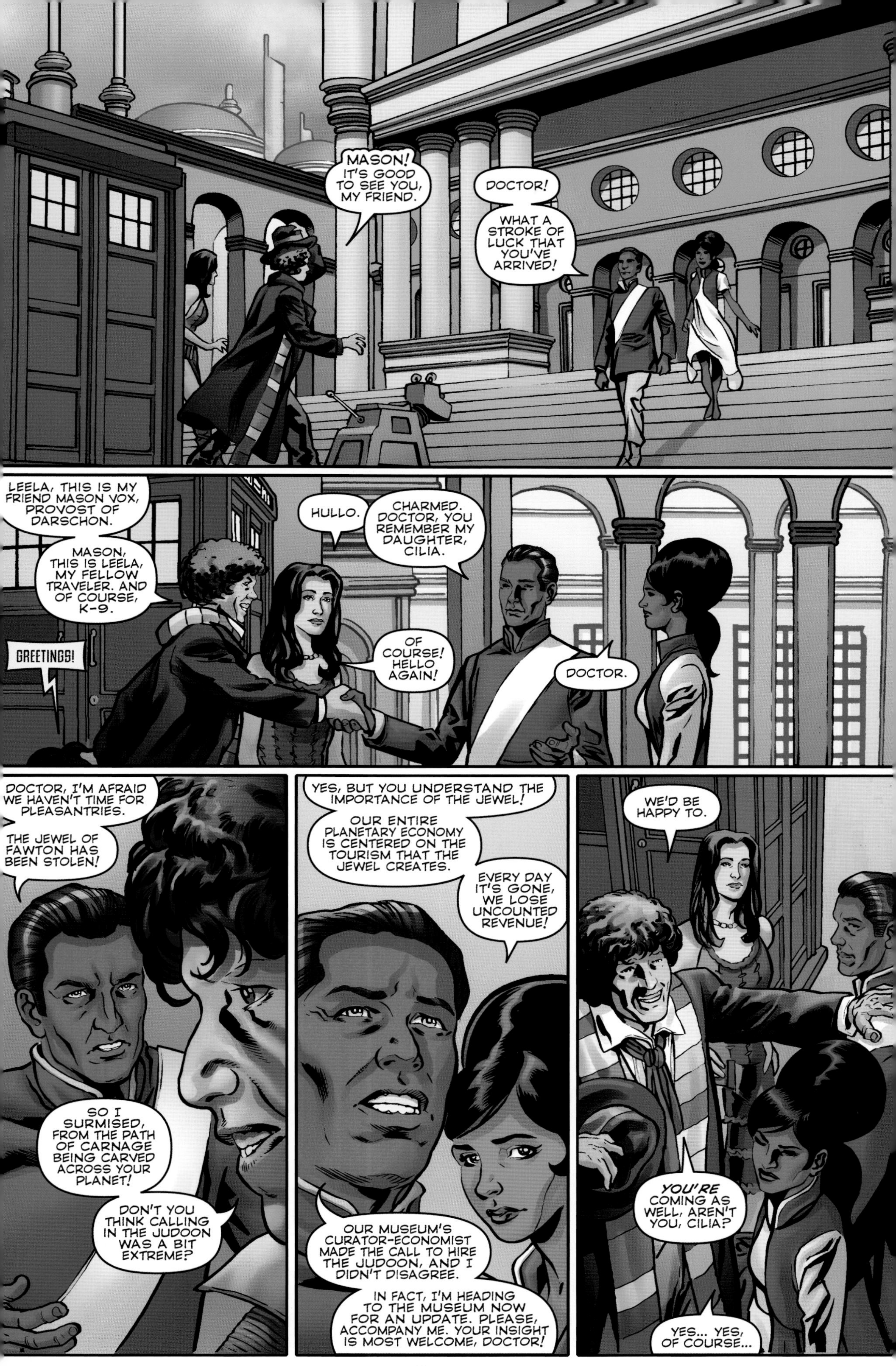
MASON! IT'S GOOD TO SEE YOU, MY FRIEND.
DOCTOR!
WHAT A STROKE OF LUCK THAT YOU'VE ARRIVED!
LEELA, THIS IS MY FRIEND MASON VOX, PROVOST OF DARSCHON.
MASON, THIS IS LEELA, MY FELLOW TRAVELER. AND OF COURSE, K-9.
GREETINGS!
HULLO.
CHARMED. DOCTOR, YOU REMEMBER MY DAUGHTER, CILIA.
OF COURSE! HELLO AGAIN!
DOCTOR.
DOCTOR, I'M AFRAID WE HAVEN'T TIME FOR PLEASANTRIES.
THE JEWEL OF FAWTON HAS BEEN STOLEN!
SO I SURMISED, FROM THE PATH OF CARNAGE BEING CARVED ACROSS YOUR PLANET!
DON'T YOU THINK CALLING IN THE JUDOON WAS A BIT EXTREME?
YES, BUT YOU UNDERSTAND THE IMPORTANCE OF THE JEWEL!
OUR ENTIRE PLANETARY ECONOMY IS CENTERED ON THE TOURISM THAT THE JEWEL CREATES.
EVERY DAY IT'S GONE, WE LOSE UNCOUNTED REVENUE!
OUR MUSEUM'S CURATOR-ECONOMIST MADE THE CALL TO HIRE THE JUDOON, AND I DIDN'T DISAGREE.
IN FACT, I'M HEADING TO THE MUSEUM NOW FOR AN UPDATE. PLEASE, ACCOMPANY ME. YOUR INSIGHT IS MOST WELCOME, DOCTOR!
WE'D BE HAPPY TO.
YOU'RE COMING AS WELL, AREN'T YOU, CILIA?
YES... YES, OF COURSE...

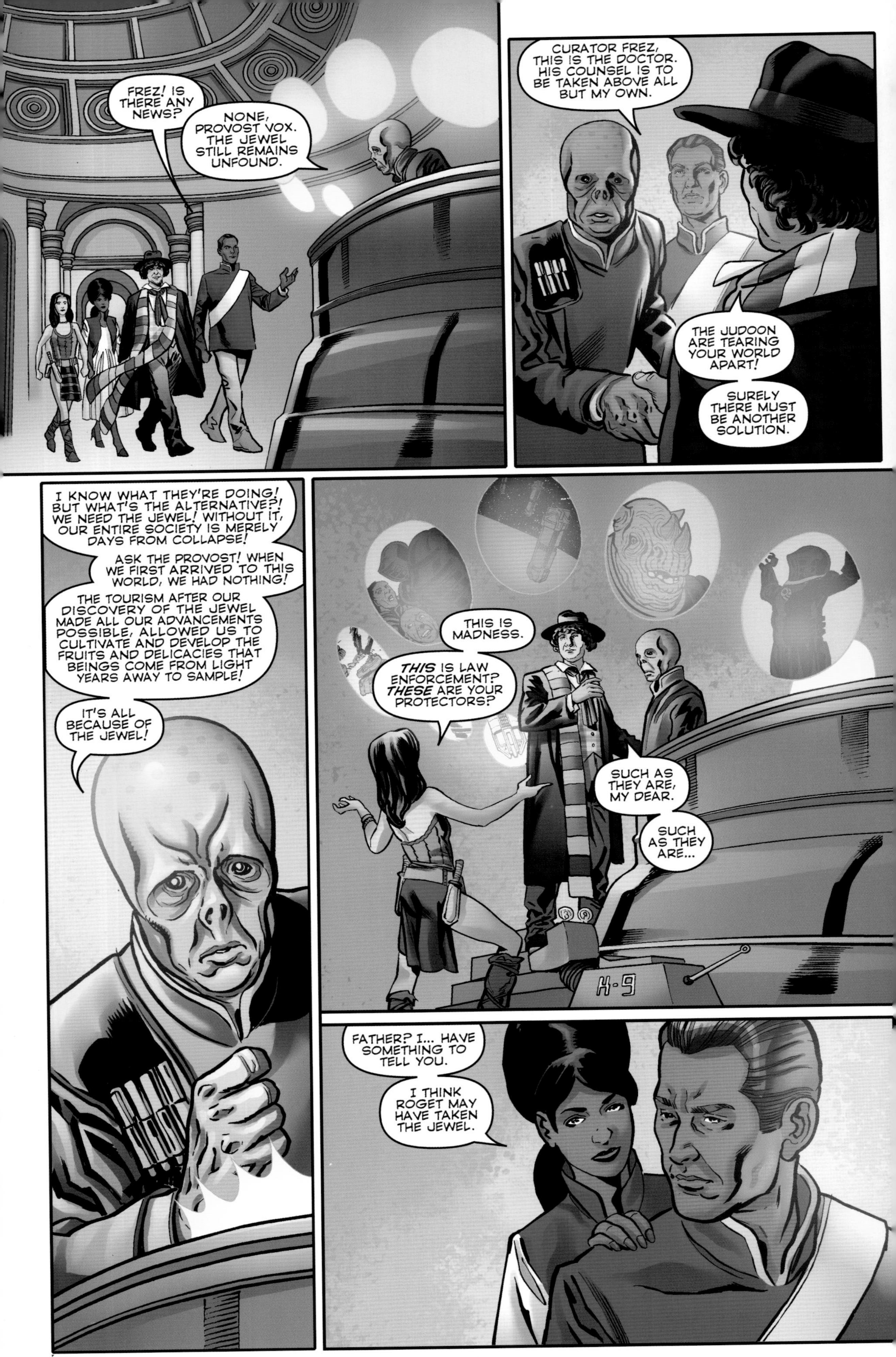

FREZ! IS THERE ANY NEWS?
NONE, PROVOST VOX. THE JEWEL STILL REMAINS UNFOUND.
CURATOR FREZ, THIS IS THE DOCTOR. HIS COUNSEL IS TO BE TAKEN ABOVE ALL BUT MY OWN.
THE JUDOON ARE TEARING YOUR WORLD APART!
SURELY THERE MUST BE ANOTHER SOLUTION.
I KNOW WHAT THEY'RE DOING! BUT WHAT'S THE ALTERNATIVE?! WE NEED THE JEWEL! WITHOUT IT, OUR ENTIRE SOCIETY IS MERELY DAYS FROM COLLAPSE!
ASK THE PROVOST! WHEN WE FIRST ARRIVED TO THIS WORLD, WE HAD NOTHING!
THE TOURISM AFTER OUR DISCOVERY OF THE JEWEL MADE ALL OUR ADVANCEMENTS POSSIBLE, ALLOWED US TO CULTIVATE AND DEVELOP THE FRUITS AND DELICACIES THAT BEINGS COME FROM LIGHT YEARS AWAY TO SAMPLE!
IT'S ALL BECAUSE OF THE JEWEL!
THIS IS MADNESS.
THIS IS LAW ENFORCEMENT? *THESE* ARE YOUR PROTECTORS?
SUCH AS THEY ARE, MY DEAR.
SUCH AS THEY ARE...
K-9
FATHER? I... HAVE SOMETHING TO TELL YOU.
I THINK ROGET MAY HAVE TAKEN THE JEWEL.

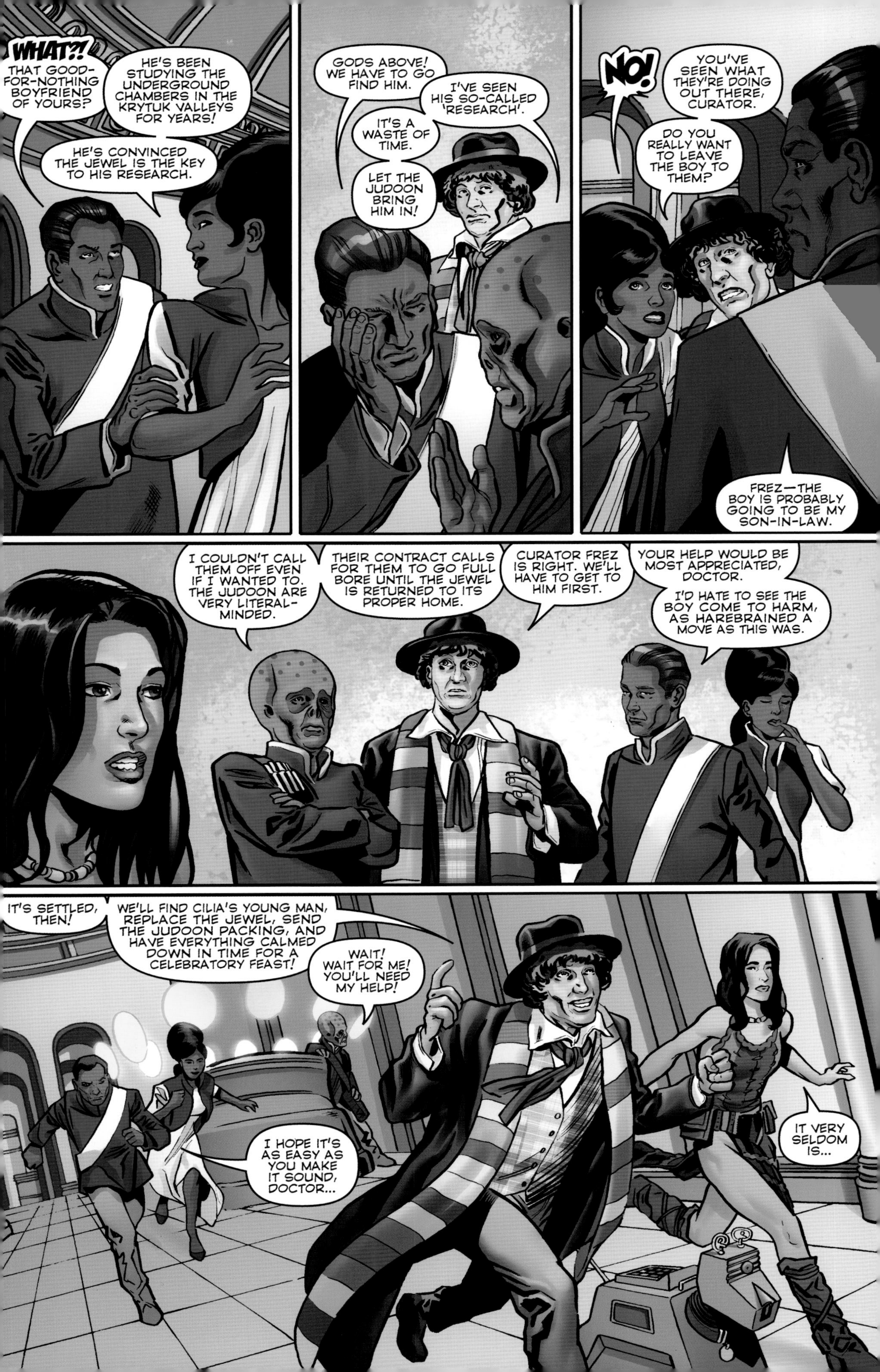
WHAT?! THAT GOOD-FOR-NOTHING BOYFRIEND OF YOURS?
HE'S BEEN STUDYING THE UNDERGROUND CHAMBERS IN THE KRYTUK VALLEYS FOR YEARS!
HE'S CONVINCED THE JEWEL IS THE KEY TO HIS RESEARCH.
GODS ABOVE! WE HAVE TO GO FIND HIM.
I'VE SEEN HIS SO-CALLED 'RESEARCH'.
IT'S A WASTE OF TIME.
LET THE JUDOON BRING HIM IN!
NO!
YOU'VE SEEN WHAT THEY'RE DOING OUT THERE, CURATOR.
DO YOU REALLY WANT TO LEAVE THE BOY TO THEM?
FREZ—THE BOY IS PROBABLY GOING TO BE MY SON-IN-LAW.
I COULDN'T CALL THEM OFF EVEN IF I WANTED TO. THE JUDOON ARE VERY LITERAL-MINDED.
THEIR CONTRACT CALLS FOR THEM TO GO FULL BORE UNTIL THE JEWEL IS RETURNED TO ITS PROPER HOME.
CURATOR FREZ IS RIGHT. WE'LL HAVE TO GET TO HIM FIRST.
YOUR HELP WOULD BE MOST APPRECIATED, DOCTOR.
I'D HATE TO SEE THE BOY COME TO HARM, AS HAREBRAINED A MOVE AS THIS WAS.
IT'S SETTLED, THEN!
WE'LL FIND CILIA'S YOUNG MAN, REPLACE THE JEWEL, SEND THE JUDOON PACKING, AND HAVE EVERYTHING CALMED DOWN IN TIME FOR A CELEBRATORY FEAST!
WAIT! WAIT FOR ME! YOU'LL NEED MY HELP!
I HOPE IT'S AS EASY AS YOU MAKE IT SOUND, DOCTOR...
IT VERY SELDOM IS...

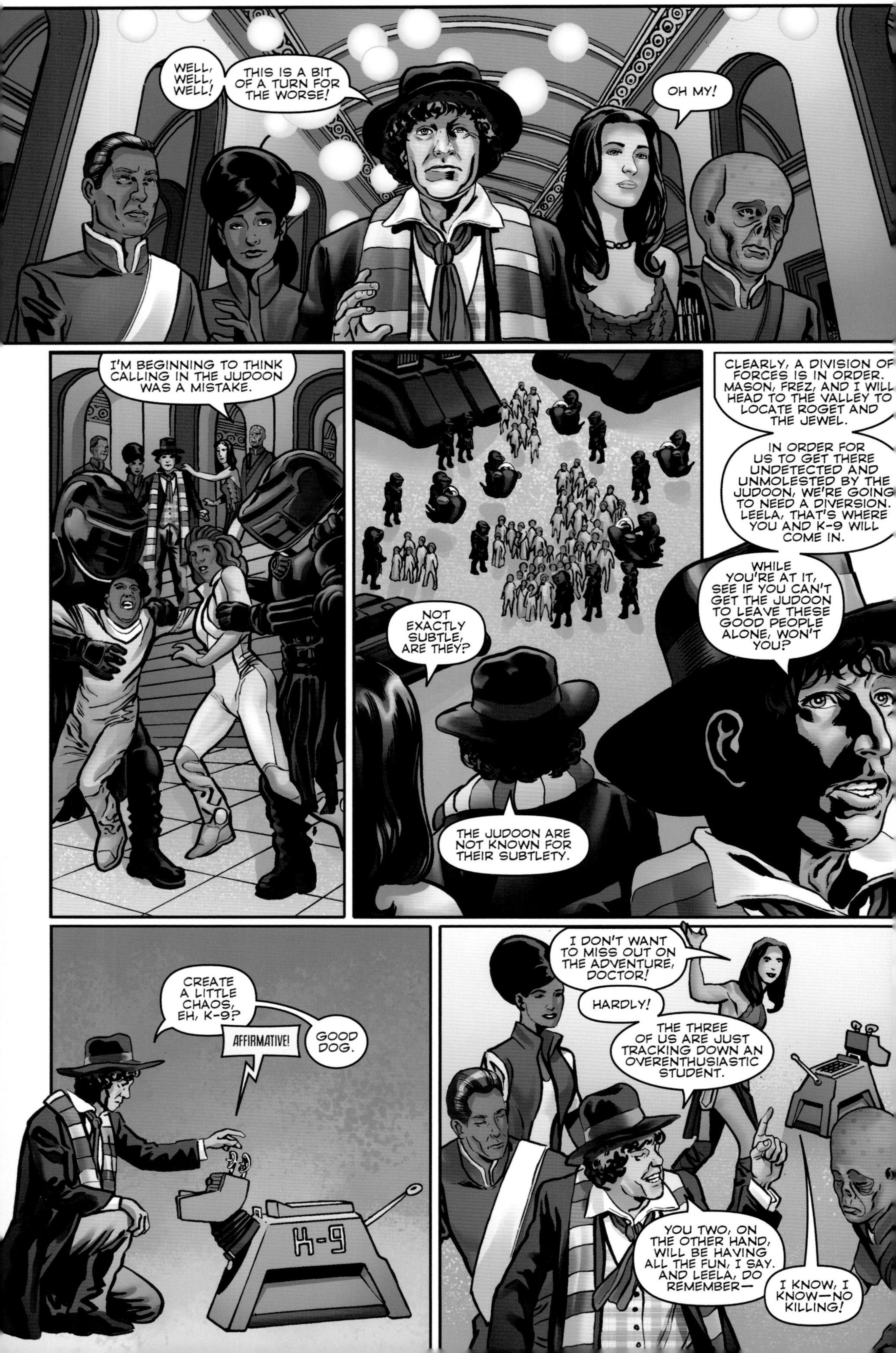
WELL, WELL, WELL!
THIS IS A BIT OF A TURN FOR THE WORSE!
OH MY!
I'M BEGINNING TO THINK CALLING IN THE JUDOON WAS A MISTAKE.
NOT EXACTLY SUBTLE, ARE THEY?
THE JUDOON ARE NOT KNOWN FOR THEIR SUBTLETY.
CLEARLY, A DIVISION OF FORCES IS IN ORDER. MASON, FREZ, AND I WILL HEAD TO THE VALLEY TO LOCATE ROGET AND THE JEWEL.
IN ORDER FOR US TO GET THERE UNDETECTED AND UNMOLESTED BY THE JUDOON, WE'RE GOING TO NEED A DIVERSION. LEELA, THAT'S WHERE YOU AND K-9 WILL COME IN.
WHILE YOU'RE AT IT, SEE IF YOU CAN'T GET THE JUDOON TO LEAVE THESE GOOD PEOPLE ALONE, WON'T YOU?
CREATE A LITTLE CHAOS, EH, K-9?
AFFIRMATIVE!
GOOD DOG.
K-9
I DON'T WANT TO MISS OUT ON THE ADVENTURE, DOCTOR!
HARDLY!
THE THREE OF US ARE JUST TRACKING DOWN AN OVERENTHUSIASTIC STUDENT.
YOU TWO, ON THE OTHER HAND, WILL BE HAVING ALL THE FUN, I SAY. AND LEELA, DO REMEMBER—
I KNOW, I KNOW—NO KILLING!

WELL, THEN. COME ALONG, GENTLEMEN.

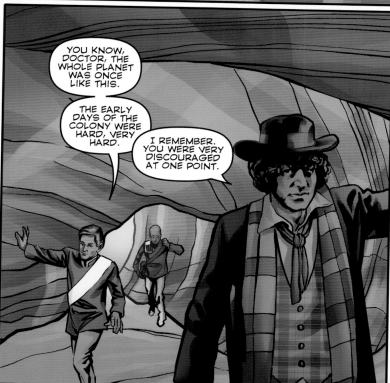

YOU KNOW, DOCTOR, THE WHOLE PLANET WAS ONCE LIKE THIS.

THE EARLY DAYS OF THE COLONY WERE HARD, VERY HARD.

I REMEMBER. YOU WERE VERY DISCOURAGED AT ONE POINT.

BUT ONCE WE DISCOVERED THE JEWEL, THE TOURISTS CAME!

THE WORD SPREAD THROUGH-OUT THE GALAXY OF ITS ASTONISHING BEAUTY, BRINGING VISITORS AND THEIR WEALTH TO AGRATIS.

THEN WE WERE ABLE TO BUILD CANALS AND RESERVOIRS AND IRRIGATE THE VAST TRACTS OF FARMLAND!

THIS WAY, DOCTOR.

WE WERE ON THE VERGE OF ABANDONING THE SETTLEMENT WHEN FREZ AND HIS FELLOW ARCHAEOLOGISTS FOUND THE JEWEL IN THIS CAVERN UP AHEAD.

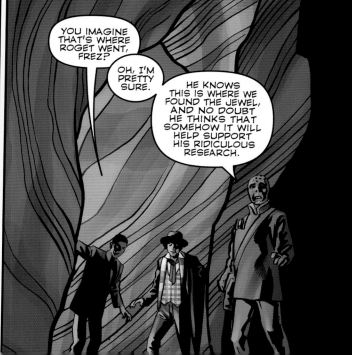

YOU IMAGINE THAT'S WHERE ROGET WENT, FREZ?

OH, I'M PRETTY SURE.

HE KNOWS THIS IS WHERE WE FOUND THE JEWEL, AND NO DOUBT HE THINKS THAT SOMEHOW IT WILL HELP SUPPORT HIS RIDICULOUS RESEARCH.

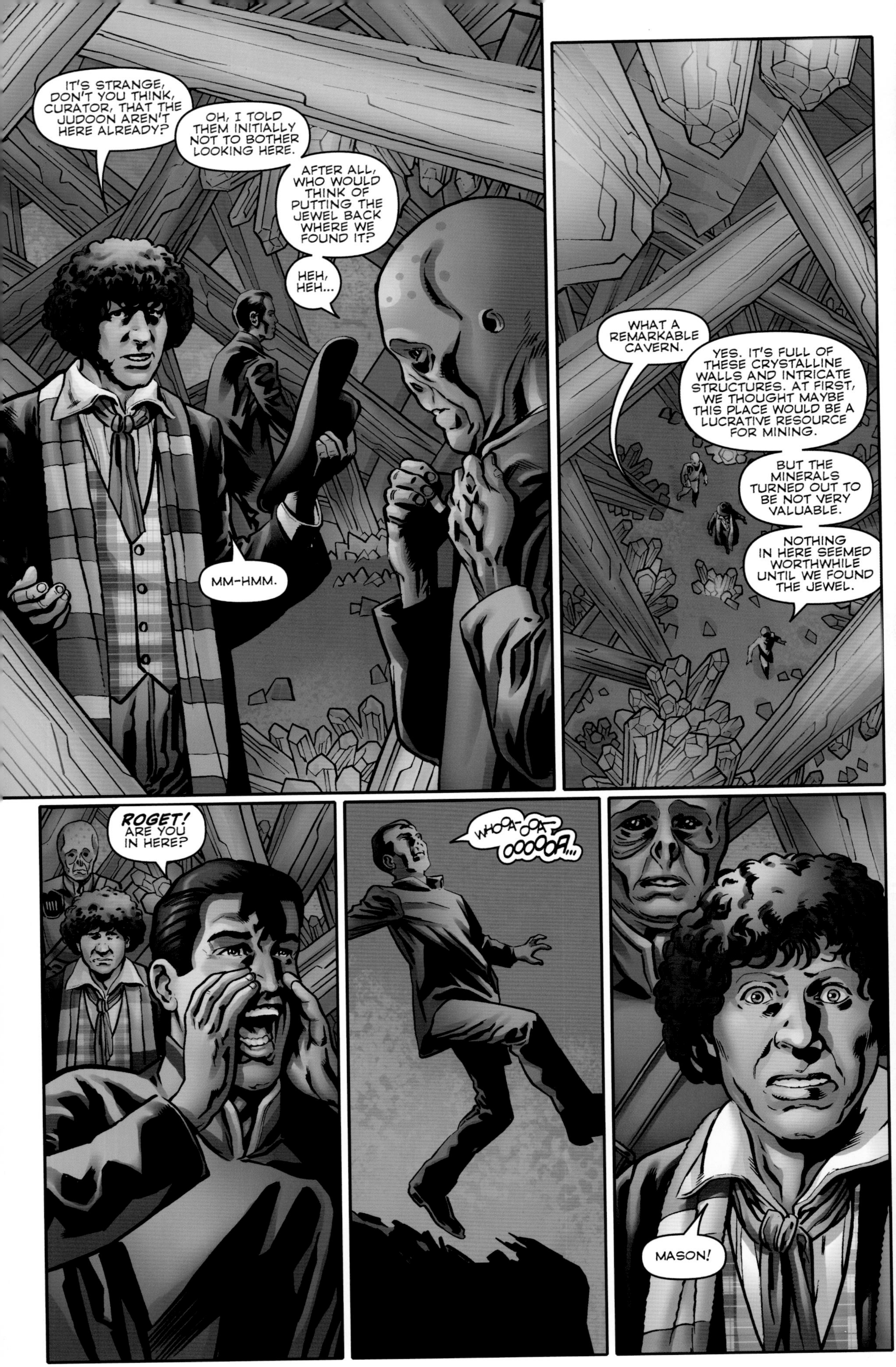
IT'S STRANGE, DON'T YOU THINK, CURATOR, THAT THE JUDOON AREN'T HERE ALREADY?
OH, I TOLD THEM INITIALLY NOT TO BOTHER LOOKING HERE.
AFTER ALL, WHO WOULD THINK OF PUTTING THE JEWEL BACK WHERE WE FOUND IT?
HEH, HEH...
MM-HMM.
WHAT A REMARKABLE CAVERN.
YES. IT'S FULL OF THESE CRYSTALLINE WALLS AND INTRICATE STRUCTURES. AT FIRST, WE THOUGHT MAYBE THIS PLACE WOULD BE A LUCRATIVE RESOURCE FOR MINING.
BUT THE MINERALS TURNED OUT TO BE NOT VERY VALUABLE.
NOTHING IN HERE SEEMED WORTHWHILE UNTIL WE FOUND THE JEWEL.
ROGET! ARE YOU IN HERE?
WHOA-OOA-OOOOOA!...
MASON!

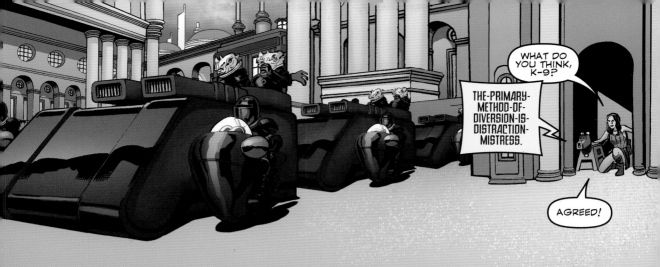

WHAT DO YOU THINK, K-9?

THE-PRIMARY-METHOD-OF-DIVERSION-IS-DISTRACTION-MISTRESS.

AGREED!

THE FIRST THING WE'LL NEED IS SUPPLIES! STAY, K-9! STAY!

HELLO!

SHO-NO-FO-RO-GO-MO!*

* 'WHAT THE–'

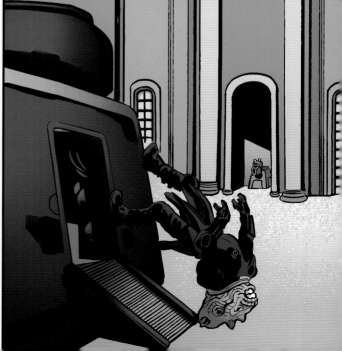

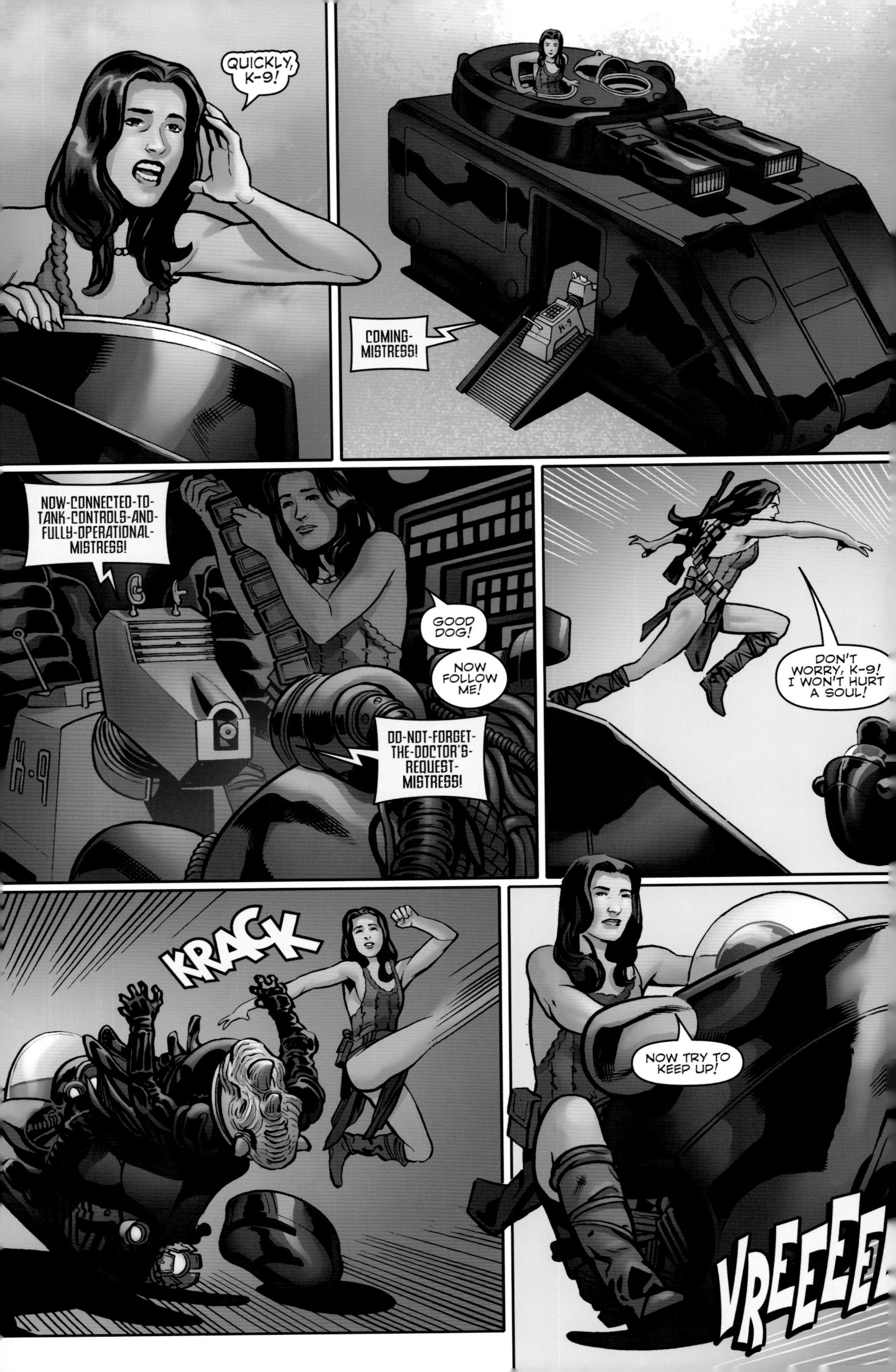
QUICKLY, K-9!
COMING-MISTRESS!
NOW-CONNECTED-TO-TANK-CONTROLS-AND-FULLY-OPERATIONAL-MISTRESS!
GOOD DOG!
NOW FOLLOW ME!
DO-NOT-FORGET-THE-DOCTOR'S-REQUEST-MISTRESS!
DON'T WORRY, K-9! I WON'T HURT A SOUL!
KRACK
NOW TRY TO KEEP UP!
VREEEEE

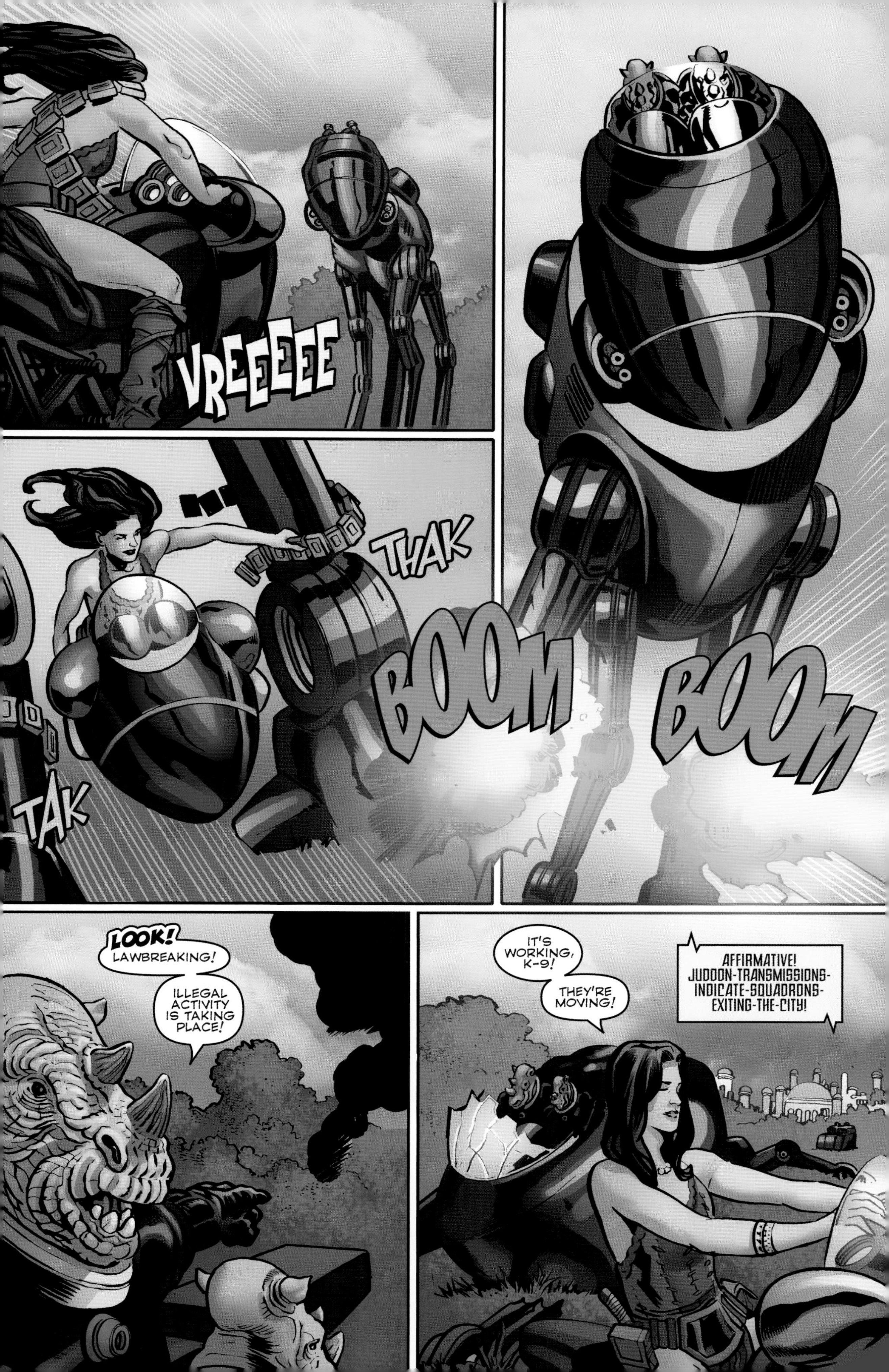
VREEEEE
THAK
TAK
BOOM
BOOM
LOOK! LAWBREAKING!
ILLEGAL ACTIVITY IS TAKING PLACE!
IT'S WORKING, K-9!
THEY'RE MOVING!
AFFIRMATIVE! JUDOON-TRANSMISSIONS-INDICATE-SQUADRONS-EXITING-THE-CITY!

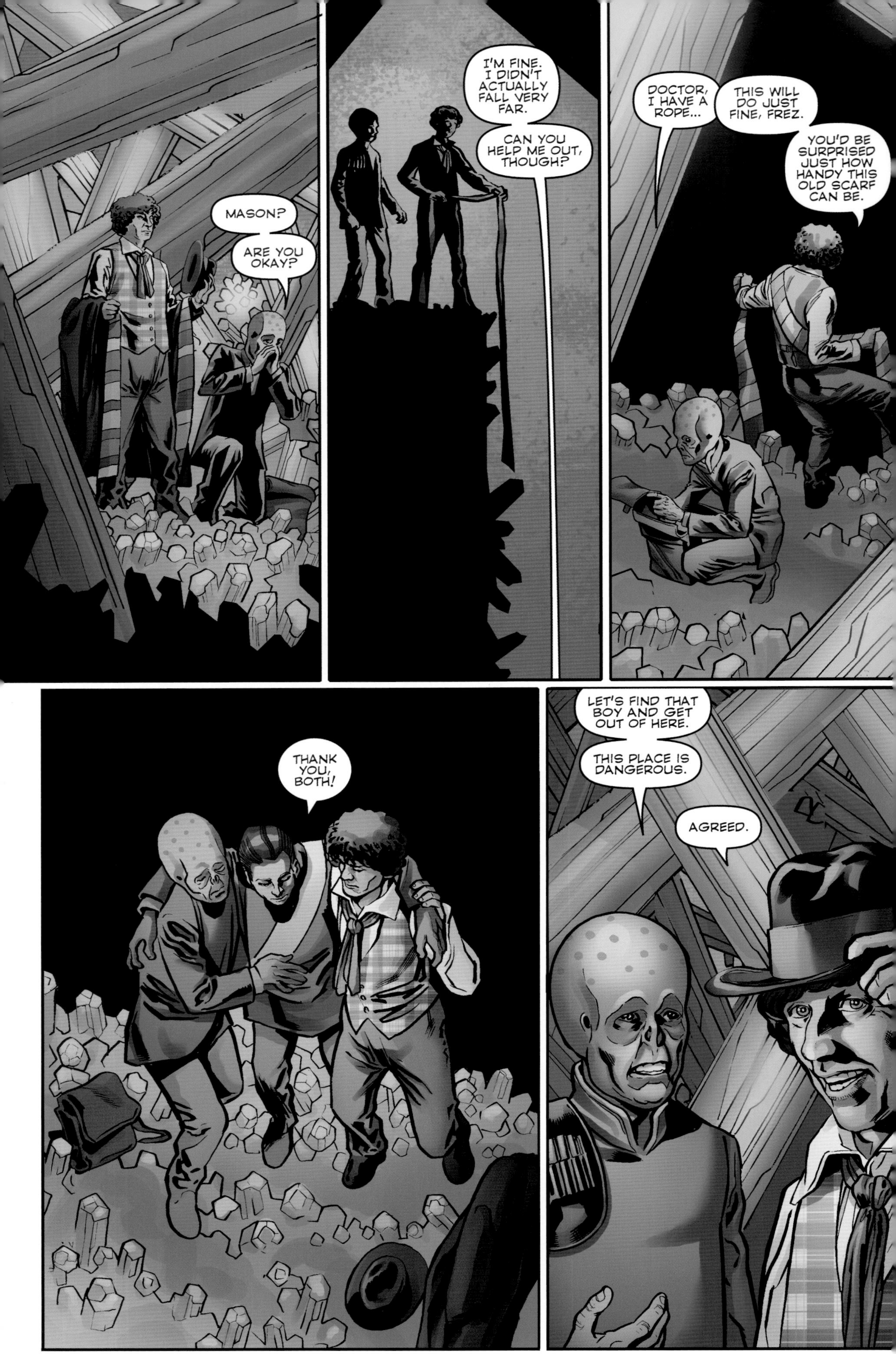

MASON?
ARE YOU OKAY?
I'M FINE. I DIDN'T ACTUALLY FALL VERY FAR.
CAN YOU HELP ME OUT, THOUGH?
DOCTOR, I HAVE A ROPE...
THIS WILL DO JUST FINE, FREZ.
YOU'D BE SURPRISED JUST HOW HANDY THIS OLD SCARF CAN BE.
THANK YOU, BOTH!
LET'S FIND THAT BOY AND GET OUT OF HERE.
THIS PLACE IS DANGEROUS.
AGREED.

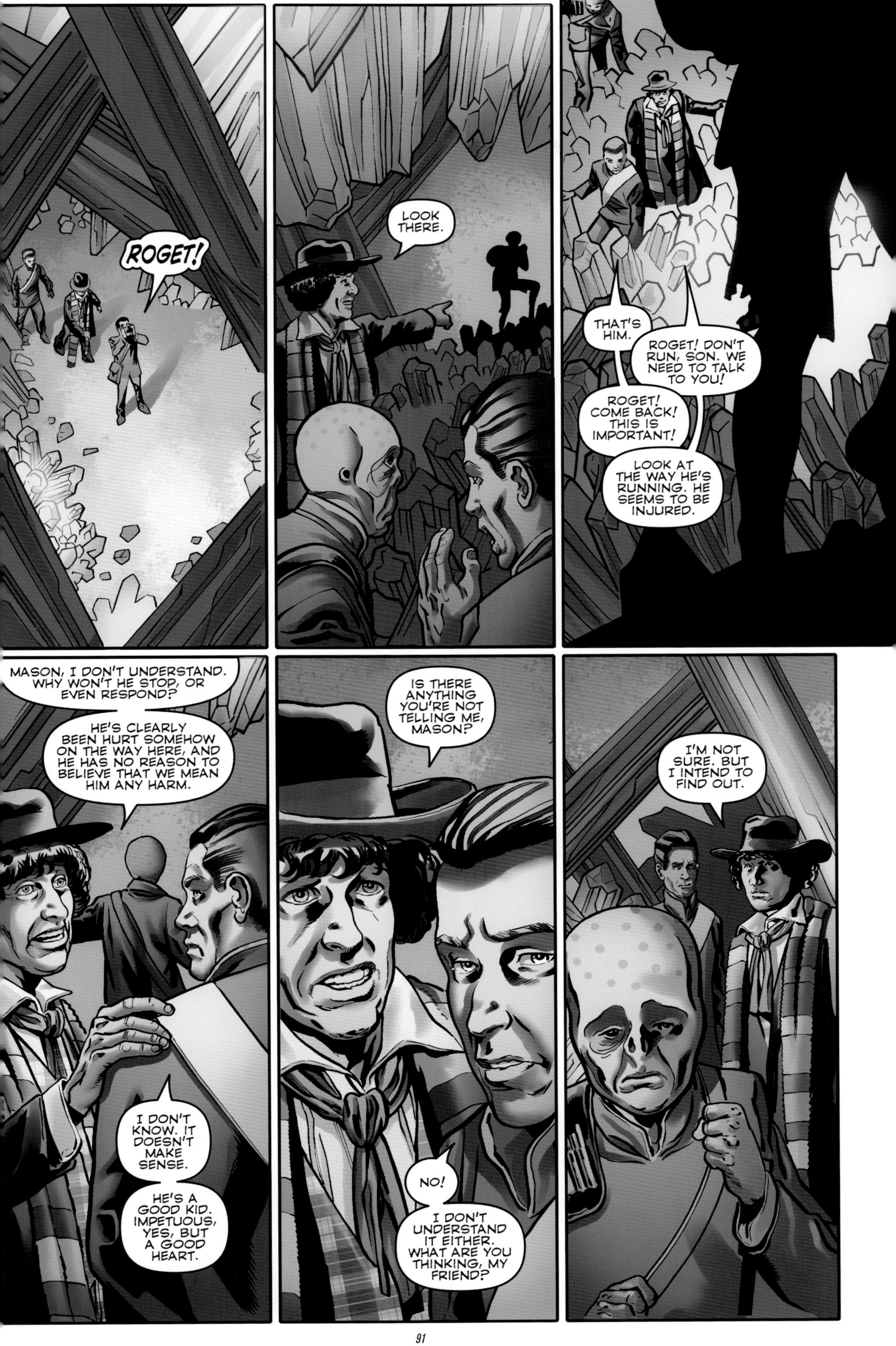
ROGET!
LOOK THERE.
THAT'S HIM.
ROGET! DON'T RUN, SON. WE NEED TO TALK TO YOU!
ROGET! COME BACK! THIS IS IMPORTANT!
LOOK AT THE WAY HE'S RUNNING. HE SEEMS TO BE INJURED.
MASON, I DON'T UNDERSTAND. WHY WON'T HE STOP, OR EVEN RESPOND?
HE'S CLEARLY BEEN HURT SOMEHOW ON THE WAY HERE, AND HE HAS NO REASON TO BELIEVE THAT WE MEAN HIM ANY HARM.
I DON'T KNOW. IT DOESN'T MAKE SENSE.
HE'S A GOOD KID. IMPETUOUS, YES, BUT A GOOD HEART.
IS THERE ANYTHING YOU'RE NOT TELLING ME, MASON?
NO!
I DON'T UNDERSTAND IT EITHER. WHAT ARE YOU THINKING, MY FRIEND?
I'M NOT SURE. BUT I INTEND TO FIND OUT.

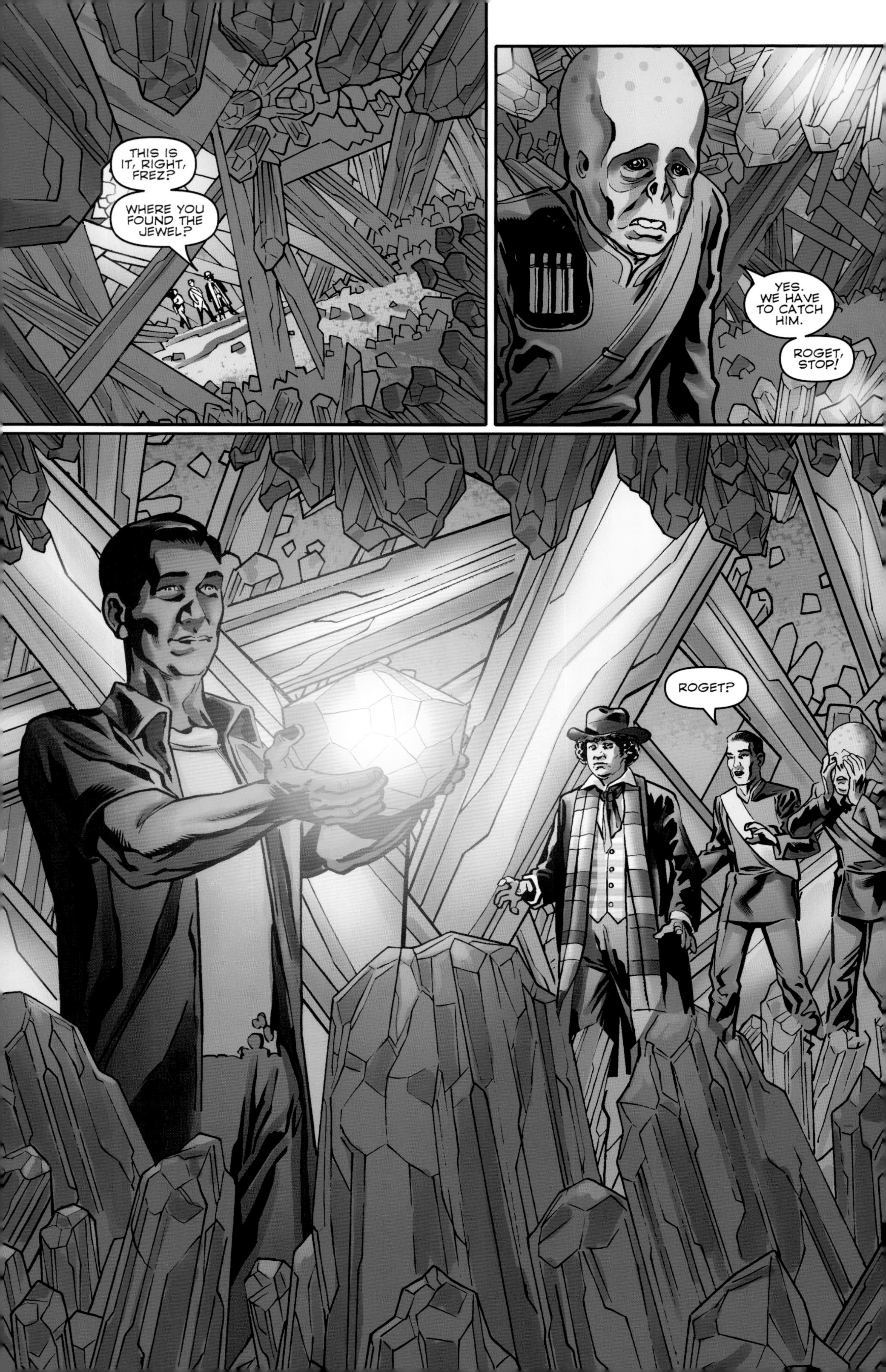
THIS IS IT, RIGHT, FREZ?
WHERE YOU FOUND THE JEWEL?
YES. WE HAVE TO CATCH HIM.
ROGET, STOP!
ROGET?

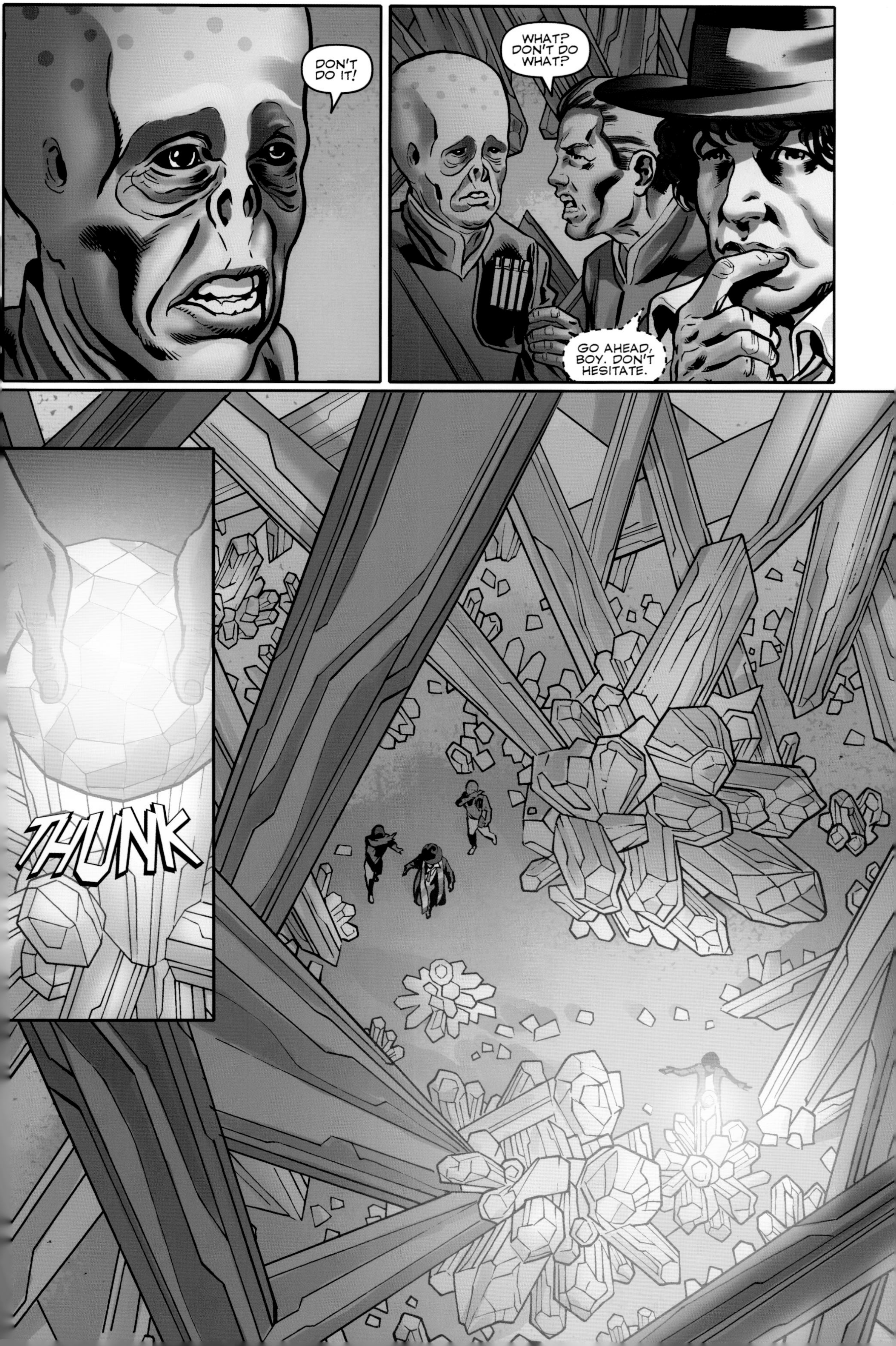
DON'T DO IT!
WHAT? DON'T DO WHAT?
GO AHEAD, BOY. DON'T HESITATE.
THUNK

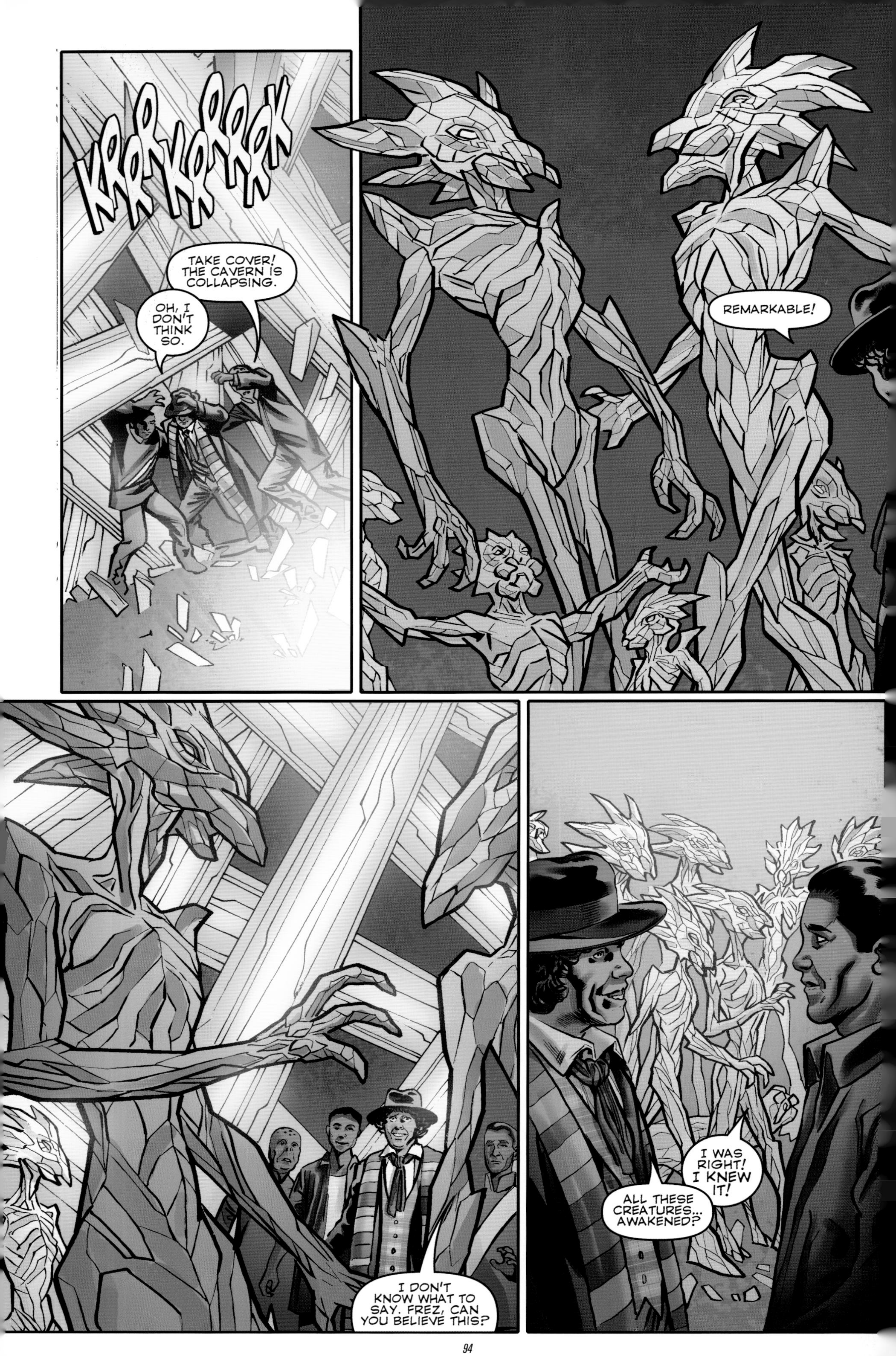
KRRKRRRK
TAKE COVER! THE CAVERN IS COLLAPSING.
OH, I DON'T THINK SO.
REMARKABLE!
I DON'T KNOW WHAT TO SAY. FREZ, CAN YOU BELIEVE THIS?
I WAS RIGHT! I KNEW IT!
ALL THESE CREATURES... AWAKENED?

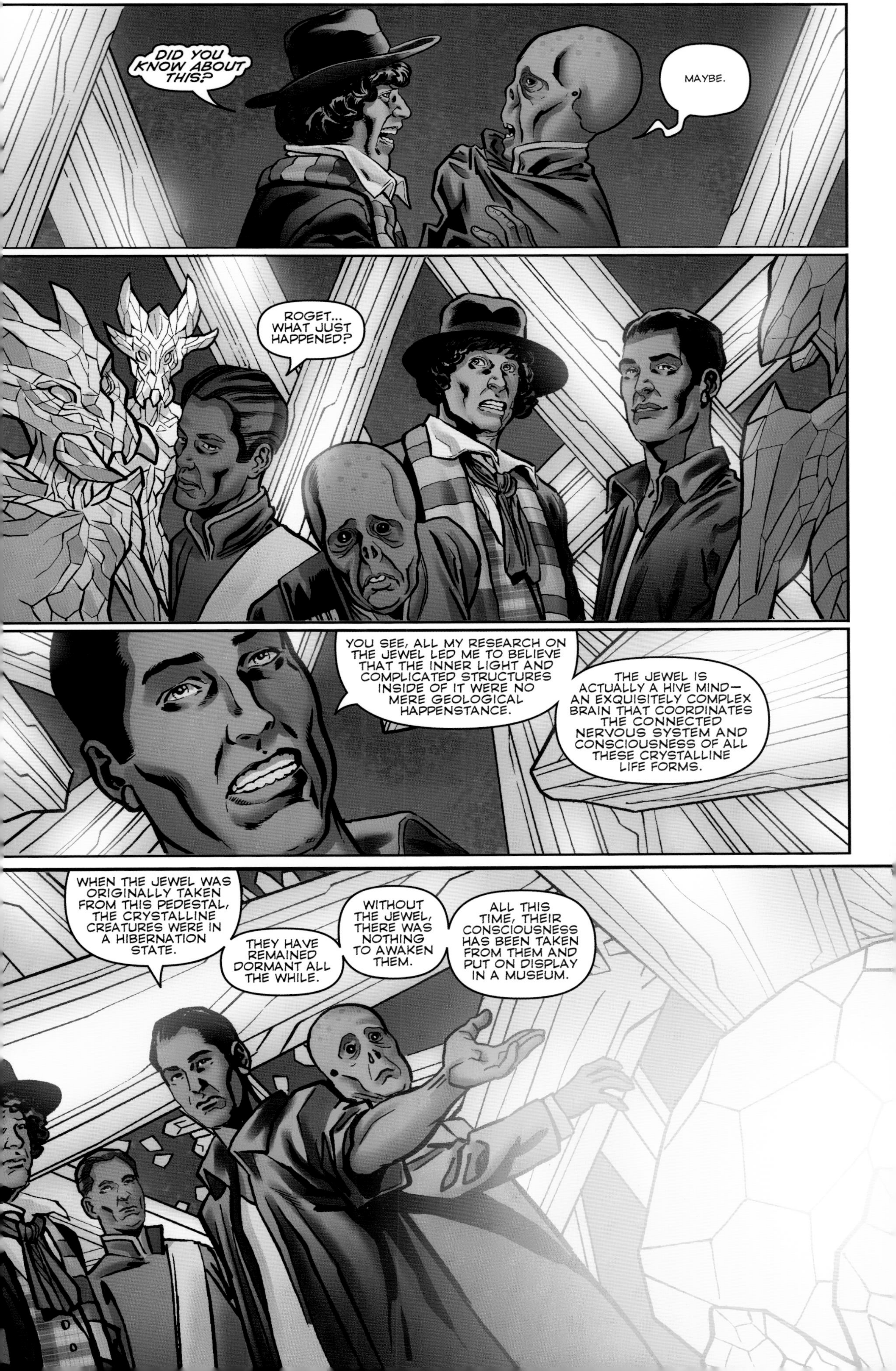

DID YOU KNOW ABOUT THIS?
MAYBE.
ROGET... WHAT JUST HAPPENED?
YOU SEE, ALL MY RESEARCH ON THE JEWEL LED ME TO BELIEVE THAT THE INNER LIGHT AND COMPLICATED STRUCTURES INSIDE OF IT WERE NO MERE GEOLOGICAL HAPPENSTANCE.
THE JEWEL IS ACTUALLY A HIVE MIND— AN EXQUISITELY COMPLEX BRAIN THAT COORDINATES THE CONNECTED NERVOUS SYSTEM AND CONSCIOUSNESS OF ALL THESE CRYSTALLINE LIFE FORMS.
WHEN THE JEWEL WAS ORIGINALLY TAKEN FROM THIS PEDESTAL, THE CRYSTALLINE CREATURES WERE IN A HIBERNATION STATE.
THEY HAVE REMAINED DORMANT ALL THE WHILE.
WITHOUT THE JEWEL, THERE WAS NOTHING TO AWAKEN THEM.
ALL THIS TIME, THEIR CONSCIOUSNESS HAS BEEN TAKEN FROM THEM AND PUT ON DISPLAY IN A MUSEUM.

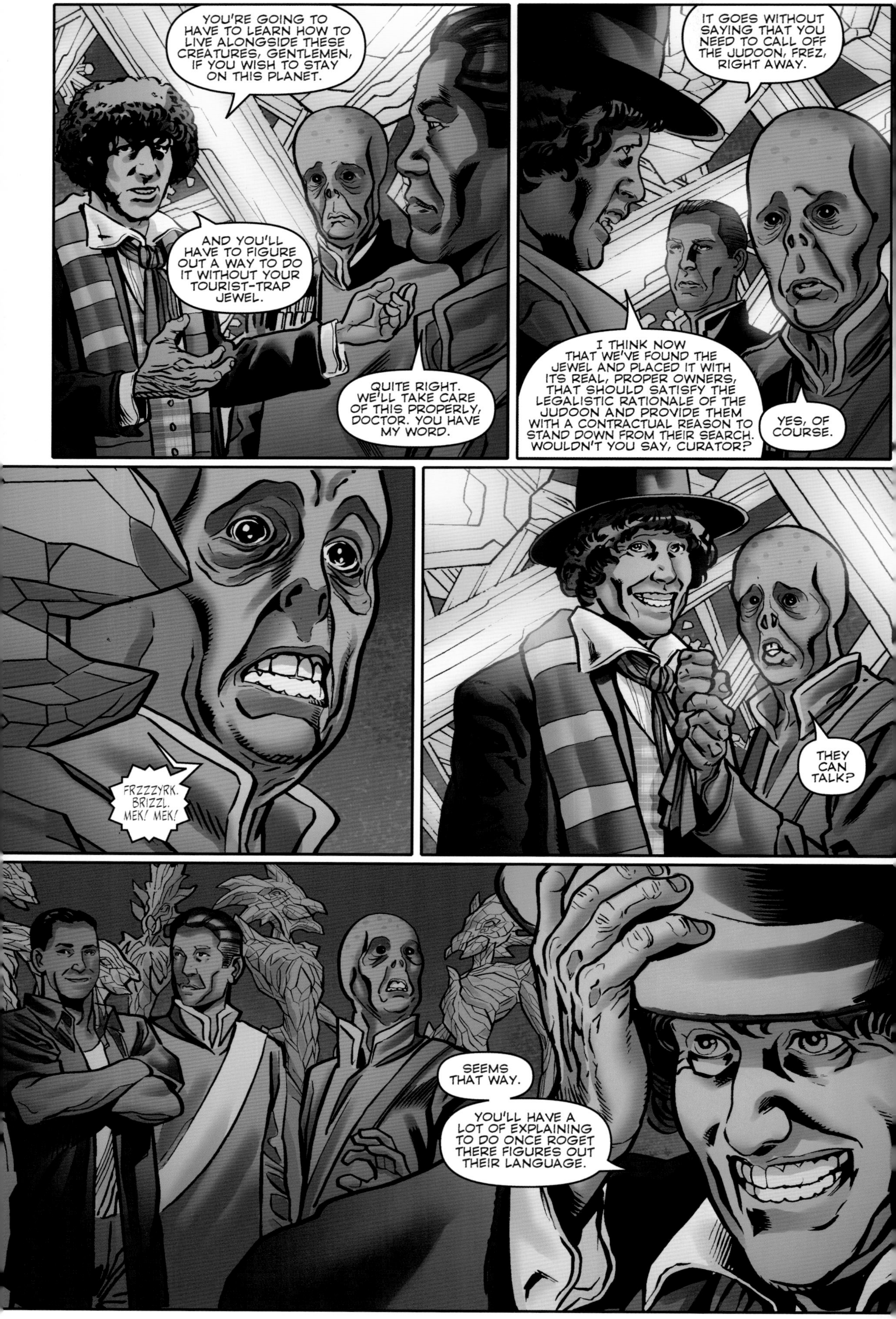
YOU'RE GOING TO HAVE TO LEARN HOW TO LIVE ALONGSIDE THESE CREATURES, GENTLEMEN, IF YOU WISH TO STAY ON THIS PLANET.
AND YOU'LL HAVE TO FIGURE OUT A WAY TO DO IT WITHOUT YOUR TOURIST-TRAP JEWEL.
QUITE RIGHT. WE'LL TAKE CARE OF THIS PROPERLY, DOCTOR. YOU HAVE MY WORD.
IT GOES WITHOUT SAYING THAT YOU NEED TO CALL OFF THE JUDOON, FREZ, RIGHT AWAY.
I THINK NOW THAT WE'VE FOUND THE JEWEL AND PLACED IT WITH ITS REAL, PROPER OWNERS, THAT SHOULD SATISFY THE LEGALISTIC RATIONALE OF THE JUDOON AND PROVIDE THEM WITH A CONTRACTUAL REASON TO STAND DOWN FROM THEIR SEARCH. WOULDN'T YOU SAY, CURATOR?
YES, OF COURSE.
FRZZZYRK. BRIZZL. MEK! MEK!
THEY CAN TALK?
SEEMS THAT WAY.
YOU'LL HAVE A LOT OF EXPLAINING TO DO ONCE ROGET THERE FIGURES OUT THEIR LANGUAGE.

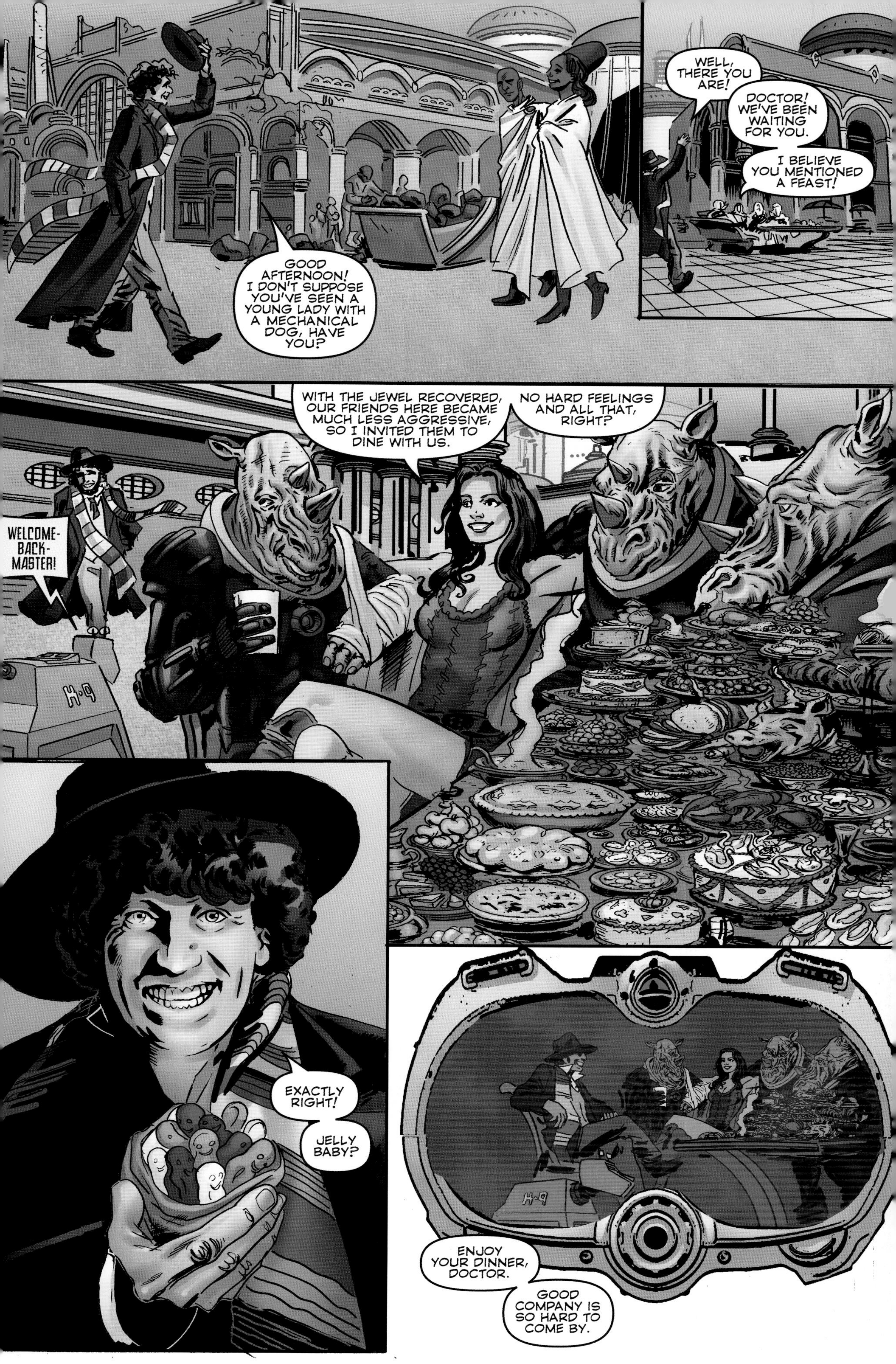
GOOD AFTERNOON! I DON'T SUPPOSE YOU'VE SEEN A YOUNG LADY WITH A MECHANICAL DOG, HAVE YOU?
WELL, THERE YOU ARE!
DOCTOR! WE'VE BEEN WAITING FOR YOU.
I BELIEVE YOU MENTIONED A FEAST!
WELCOME-BACK-MASTER!
WITH THE JEWEL RECOVERED, OUR FRIENDS HERE BECAME MUCH LESS AGGRESSIVE, SO I INVITED THEM TO DINE WITH US.
NO HARD FEELINGS AND ALL THAT, RIGHT?
EXACTLY RIGHT!
JELLY BABY?
ENJOY YOUR DINNER, DOCTOR.
GOOD COMPANY IS SO HARD TO COME BY.

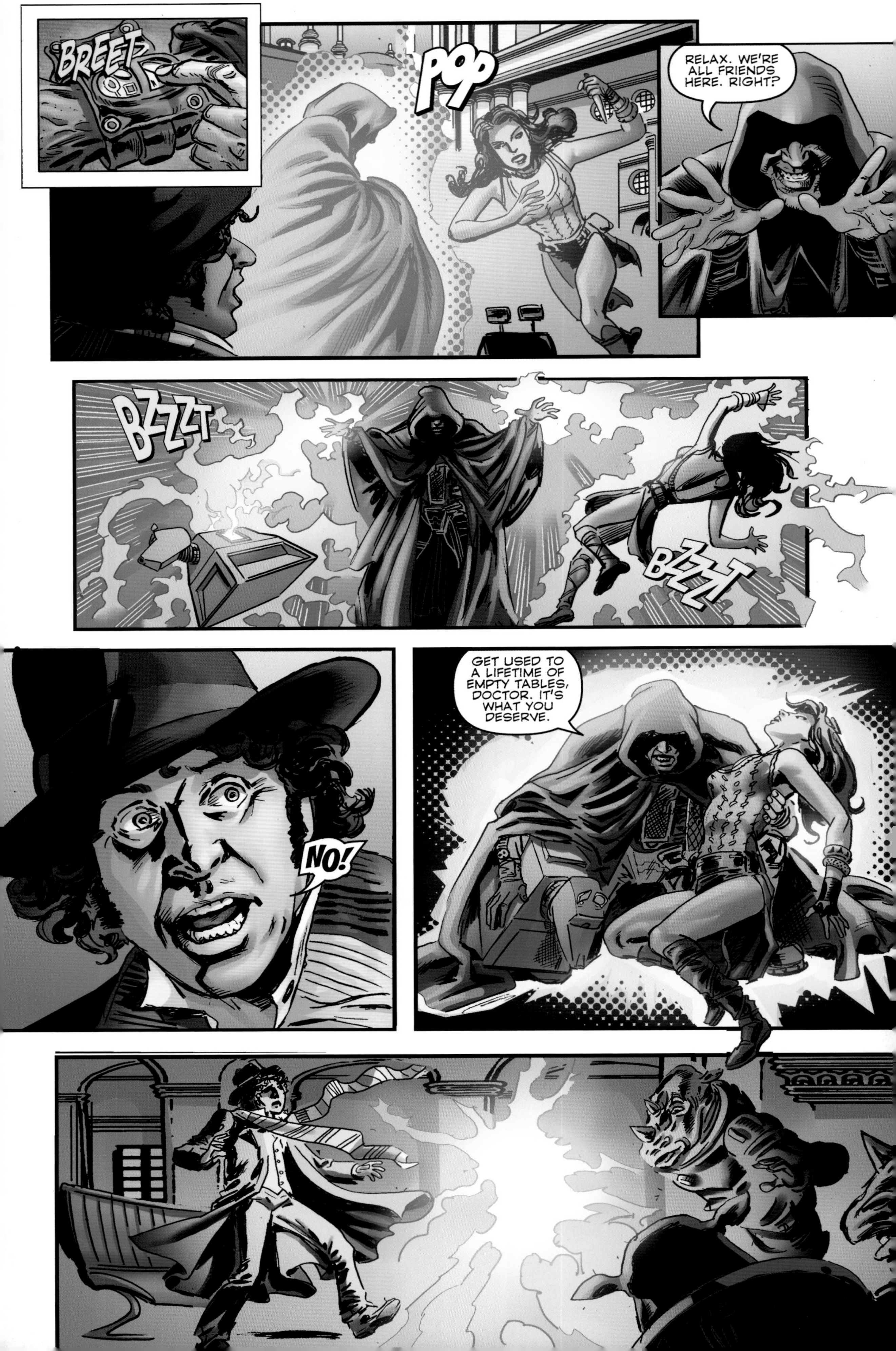
BREET
POP
RELAX. WE'RE ALL FRIENDS HERE. RIGHT?
BZZZT
BZZZT
NO!
GET USED TO A LIFETIME OF EMPTY TABLES, DOCTOR. IT'S WHAT YOU DESERVE.

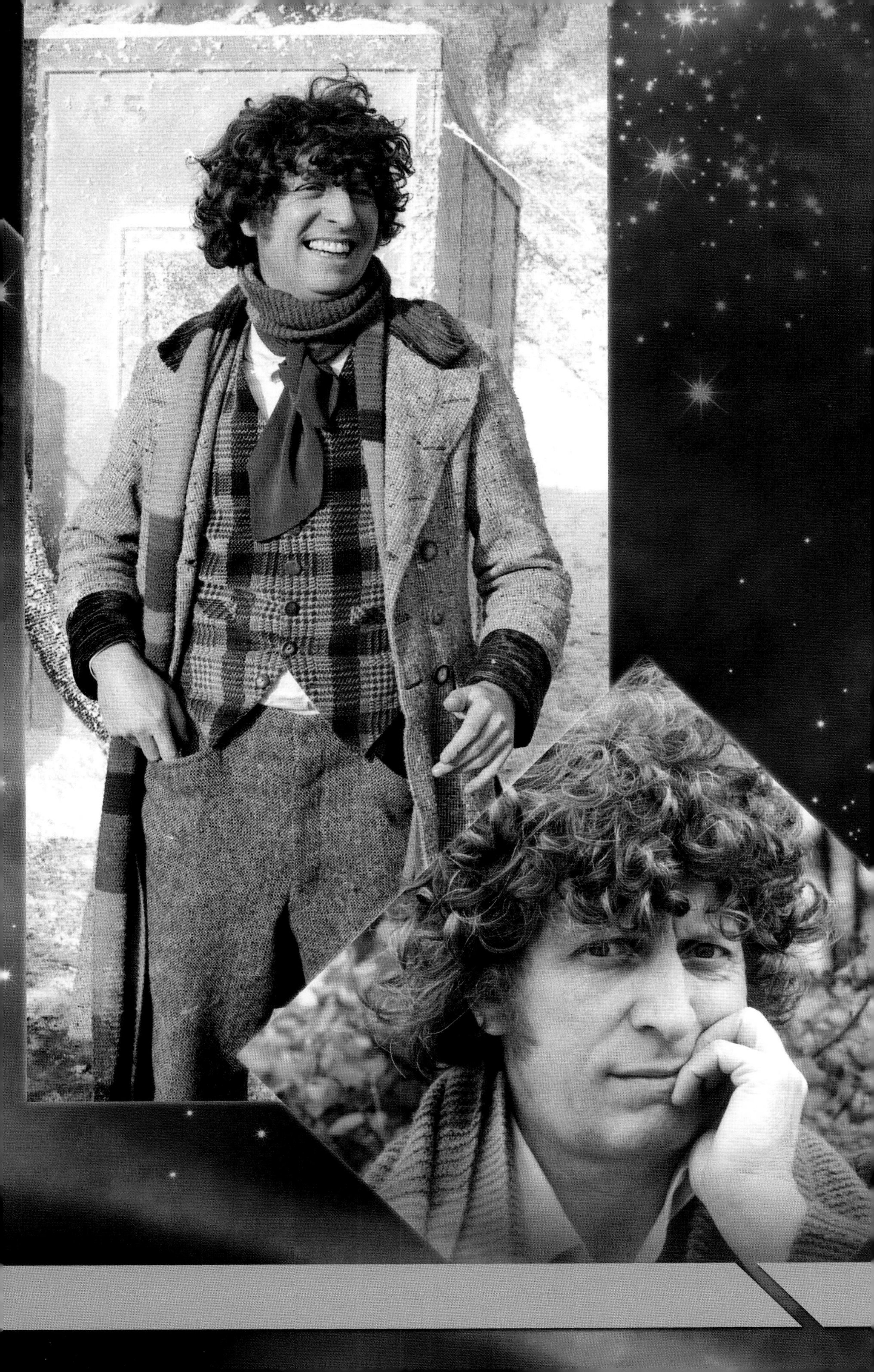

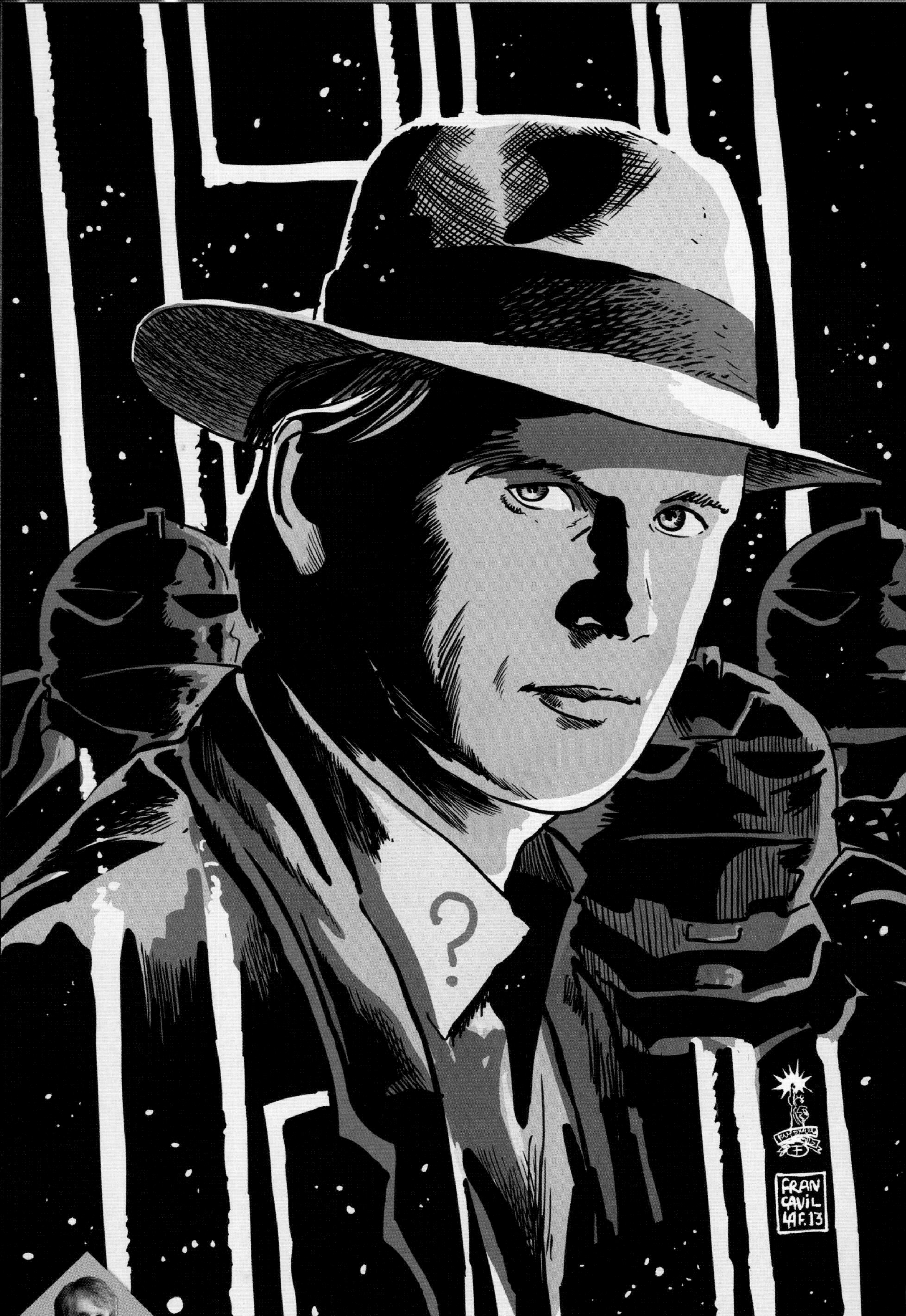
FRAN
CAVIL
LA F. 13

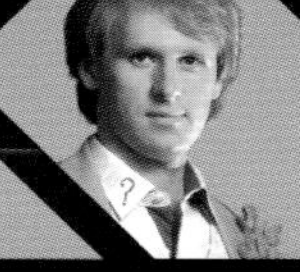

5TH DOCTOR
1981 - 1984

CHAPTER 5 "IN THEIR NATURE"

Cover Art by Francesco Francavilla

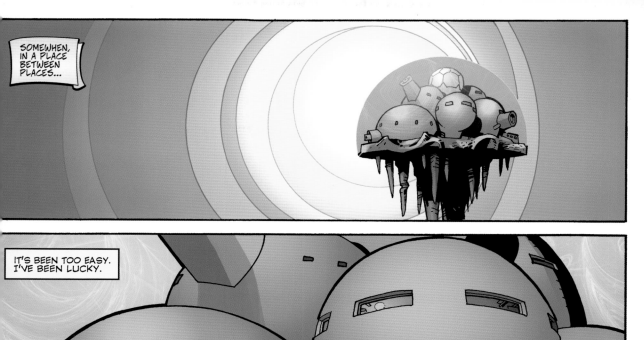

SOMEWHEN, IN A PLACE BETWEEN PLACES...

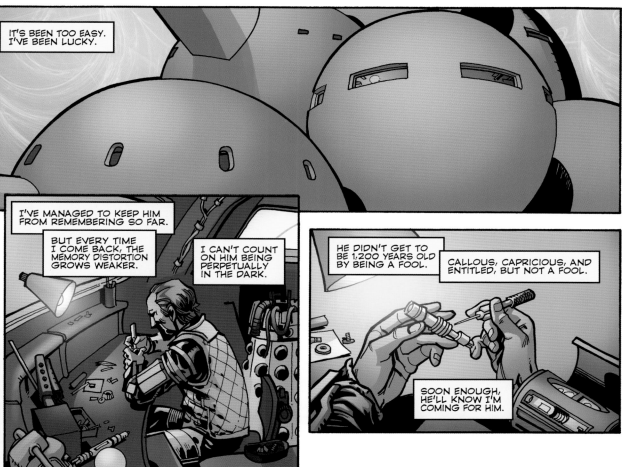

IT'S BEEN TOO EASY. I'VE BEEN LUCKY.

I'VE MANAGED TO KEEP HIM FROM REMEMBERING SO FAR.

BUT EVERY TIME I COME BACK, THE MEMORY DISTORTION GROWS WEAKER.

I CAN'T COUNT ON HIM BEING PERPETUALLY IN THE DARK.

HE DIDN'T GET TO BE 1,200 YEARS OLD BY BEING A FOOL.

CALLOUS, CAPRICIOUS, AND ENTITLED, BUT NOT A FOOL.

SOON ENOUGH, HE'LL KNOW I'M COMING FOR HIM.

VRMMMMMMM

WHEN THE TIME COMES, I'M GOING TO HAVE TO BE FASTER.

SHKOW

KABOOM

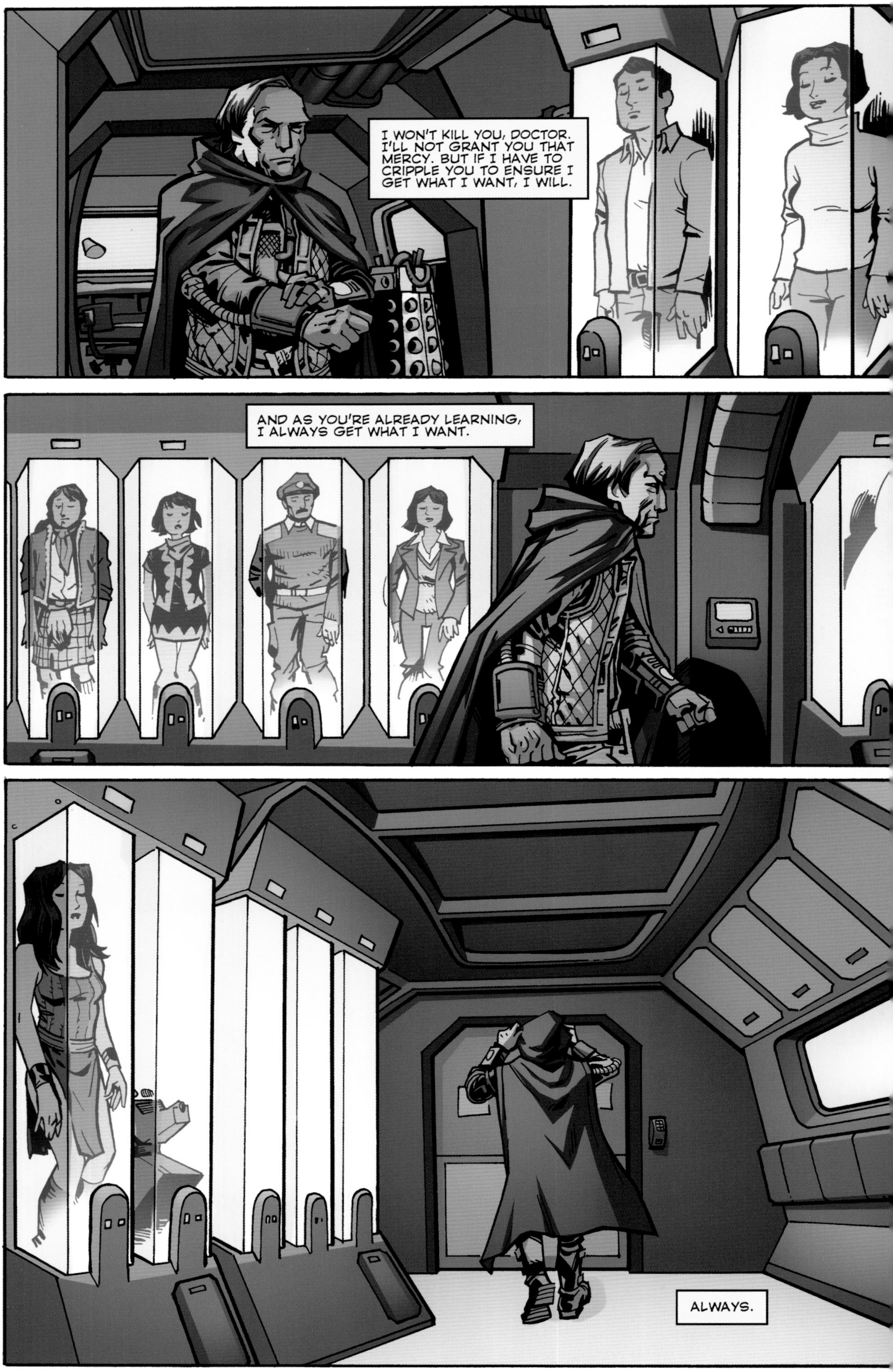

I WON'T KILL YOU, DOCTOR. I'LL NOT GRANT YOU THAT MERCY. BUT IF I HAVE TO CRIPPLE YOU TO ENSURE I GET WHAT I WANT, I WILL.
AND AS YOU'RE ALREADY LEARNING, I ALWAYS GET WHAT I WANT.
ALWAYS.

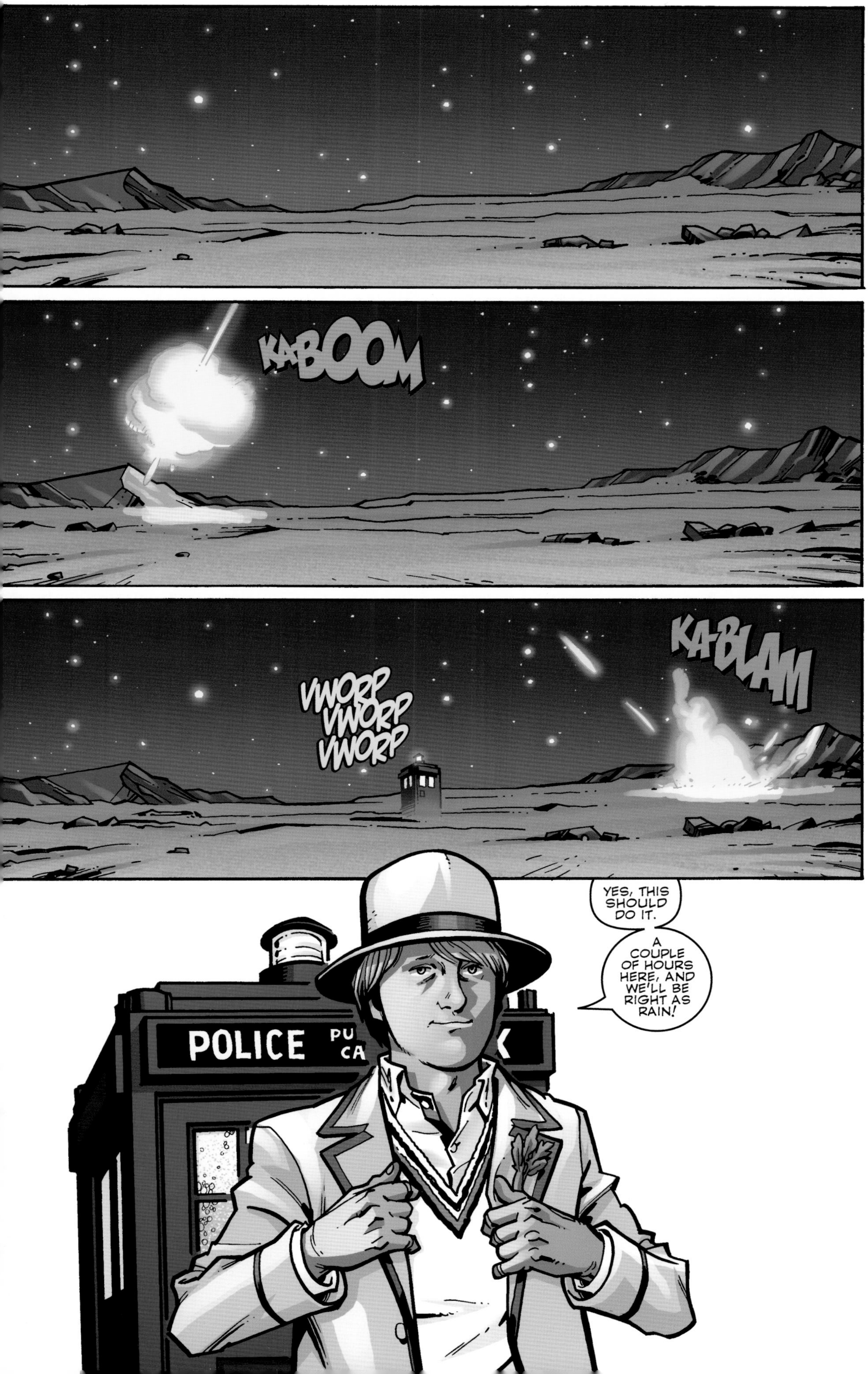
KA-BOOM
VWORP VWORP VWORP
KA-BLAM
YES, THIS SHOULD DO IT.
A COUPLE OF HOURS HERE, AND WE'LL BE RIGHT AS RAIN!
POLICE

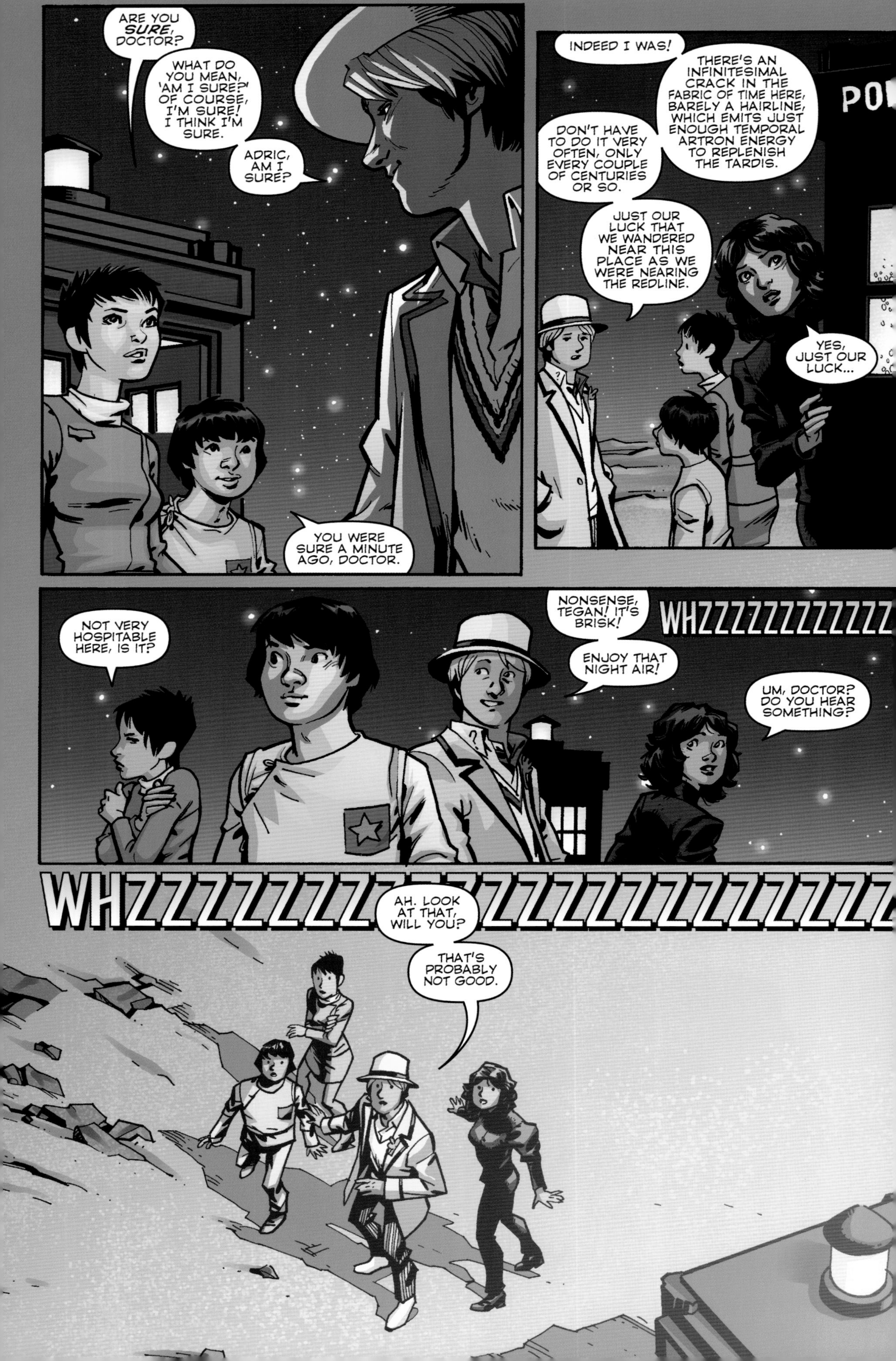
ARE YOU *SURE*, DOCTOR?
WHAT DO YOU MEAN, 'AM I SURE?' OF COURSE, I'M SURE! I THINK I'M SURE.
ADRIC, AM I SURE?
YOU WERE SURE A MINUTE AGO, DOCTOR.
INDEED I WAS!
THERE'S AN INFINITESIMAL CRACK IN THE FABRIC OF TIME HERE, BARELY A HAIRLINE, WHICH EMITS JUST ENOUGH TEMPORAL ARTRON ENERGY TO REPLENISH THE TARDIS.
DON'T HAVE TO DO IT VERY OFTEN, ONLY EVERY COUPLE OF CENTURIES OR SO.
JUST OUR LUCK THAT WE WANDERED NEAR THIS PLACE AS WE WERE NEARING THE REDLINE.
YES, JUST OUR LUCK...
NOT VERY HOSPITABLE HERE, IS IT?
NONSENSE, TEGAN! IT'S BRISK!
ENJOY THAT NIGHT AIR!
WHZZZZZZZZZZZZ
UM, DOCTOR? DO YOU HEAR SOMETHING?
WHZZZZZZZZZZZZZZZZZZZZZZZZZZZZ
AH. LOOK AT THAT, WILL YOU?
THAT'S PROBABLY NOT GOOD.

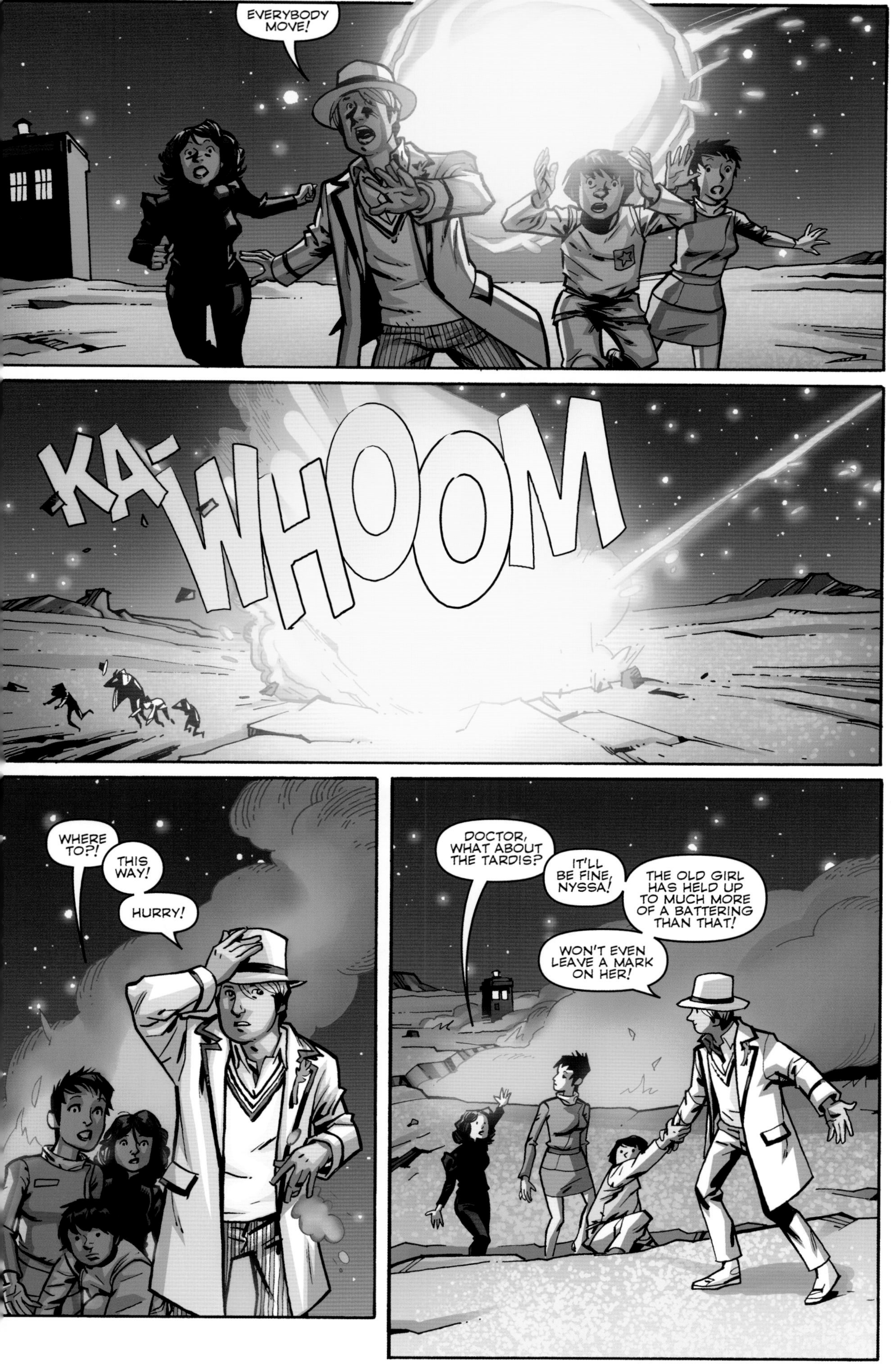
EVERYBODY MOVE!
KA-WHOOM
WHERE TO?!
THIS WAY!
HURRY!
DOCTOR, WHAT ABOUT THE TARDIS?
IT'LL BE FINE, NYSSA!
THE OLD GIRL HAS HELD UP TO MUCH MORE OF A BATTERING THAN THAT!
WON'T EVEN LEAVE A MARK ON HER!

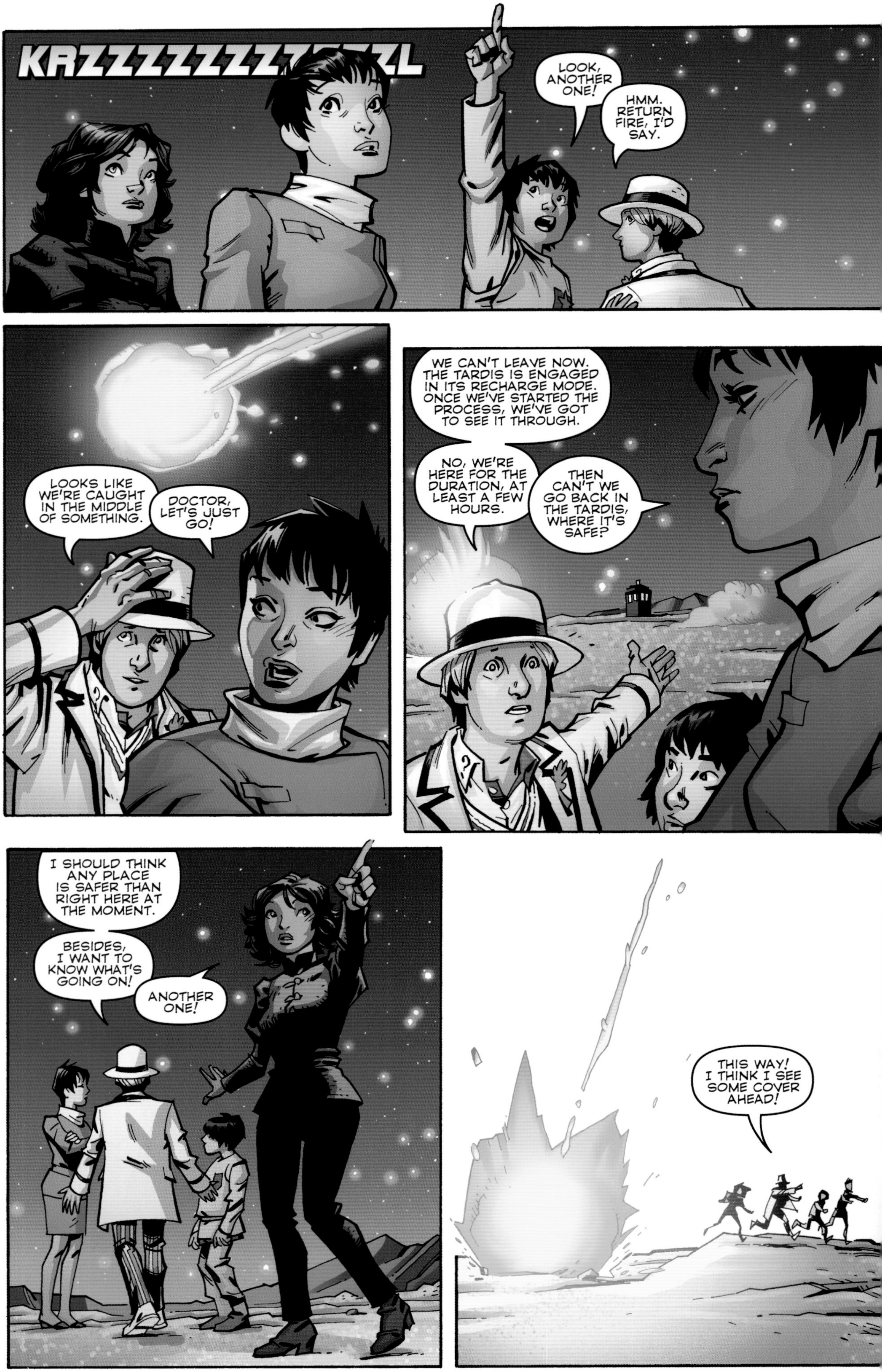
KRZZZZZZZZZZZL
LOOK, ANOTHER ONE!
HMM. RETURN FIRE, I'D SAY.
LOOKS LIKE WE'RE CAUGHT IN THE MIDDLE OF SOMETHING.
DOCTOR, LET'S JUST GO!
WE CAN'T LEAVE NOW. THE TARDIS IS ENGAGED IN ITS RECHARGE MODE. ONCE WE'VE STARTED THE PROCESS, WE'VE GOT TO SEE IT THROUGH.
THEN CAN'T WE GO BACK IN THE TARDIS, WHERE IT'S SAFE?
NO, WE'RE HERE FOR THE DURATION, AT LEAST A FEW HOURS.
I SHOULD THINK ANY PLACE IS SAFER THAN RIGHT HERE AT THE MOMENT.
BESIDES, I WANT TO KNOW WHAT'S GOING ON!
ANOTHER ONE!
THIS WAY! I THINK I SEE SOME COVER AHEAD!

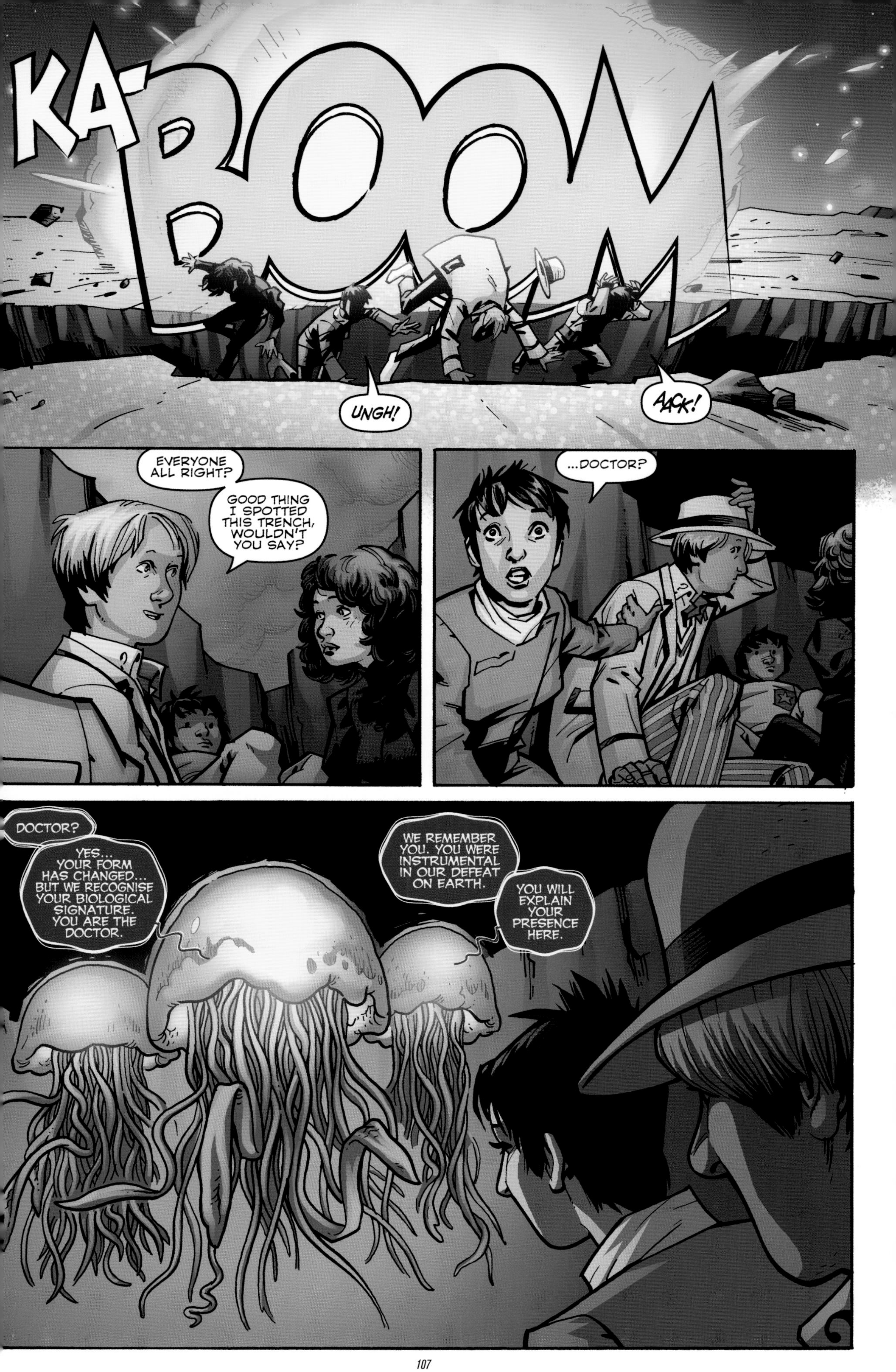
KA-BOOM
UNGH!
AACK!
EVERYONE ALL RIGHT?
GOOD THING I SPOTTED THIS TRENCH, WOULDN'T YOU SAY?
...DOCTOR?
DOCTOR?
YES... YOUR FORM HAS CHANGED... BUT WE RECOGNISE YOUR BIOLOGICAL SIGNATURE. YOU ARE THE DOCTOR.
WE REMEMBER YOU. YOU WERE INSTRUMENTAL IN OUR DEFEAT ON EARTH.
YOU WILL EXPLAIN YOUR PRESENCE HERE.

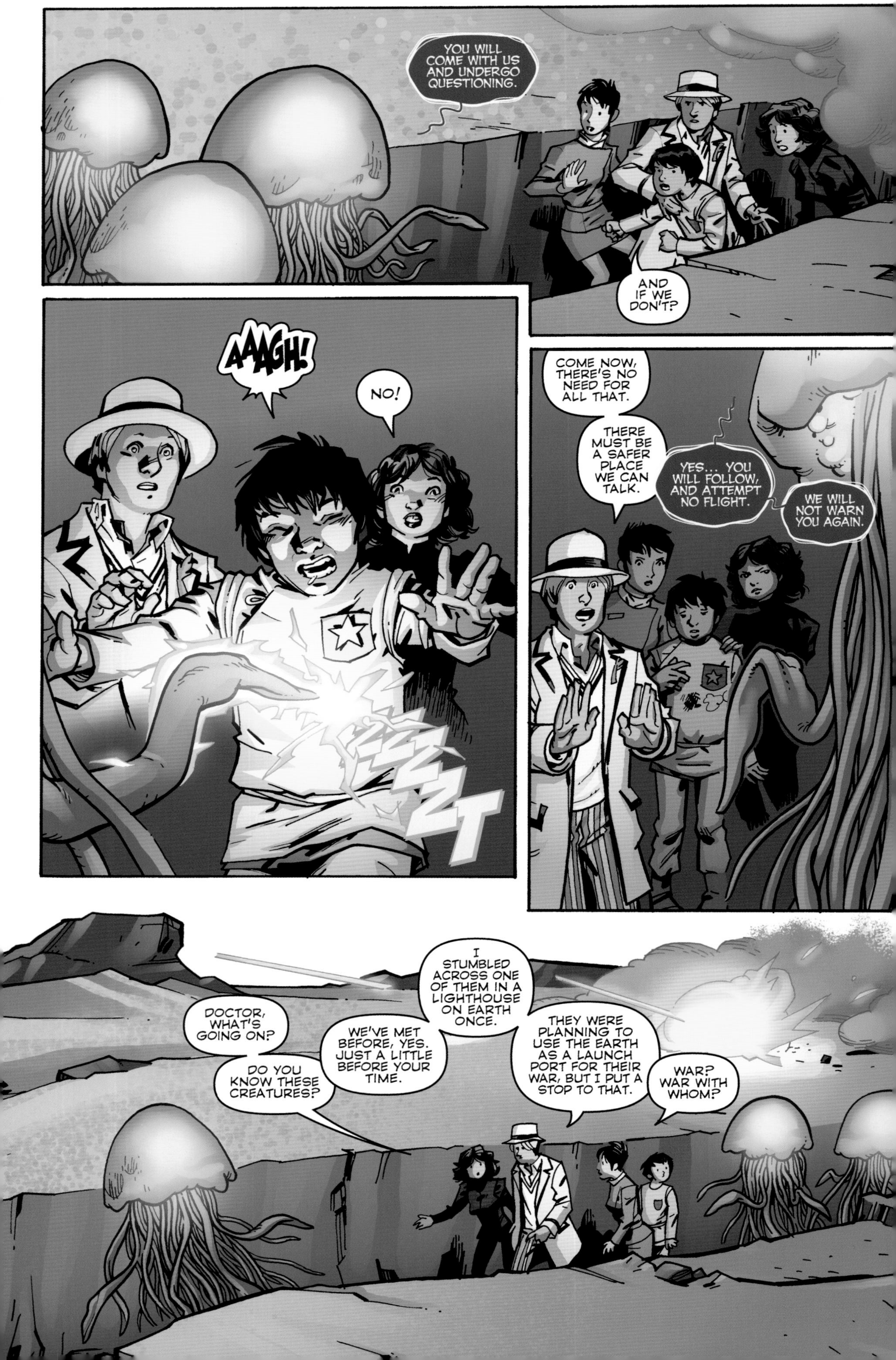
YOU WILL COME WITH US AND UNDERGO QUESTIONING.
AND IF WE DON'T?
AAAGH!
NO!
ZZZZZT
COME NOW, THERE'S NO NEED FOR ALL THAT.
THERE MUST BE A SAFER PLACE WE CAN TALK.
YES... YOU WILL FOLLOW, AND ATTEMPT NO FLIGHT.
WE WILL NOT WARN YOU AGAIN.
DOCTOR, WHAT'S GOING ON?
DO YOU KNOW THESE CREATURES?
WE'VE MET BEFORE, YES. JUST A LITTLE BEFORE YOUR TIME.
I STUMBLED ACROSS ONE OF THEM IN A LIGHTHOUSE ON EARTH ONCE.
THEY WERE PLANNING TO USE THE EARTH AS A LAUNCH PORT FOR THEIR WAR, BUT I PUT A STOP TO THAT.
WAR? WAR WITH WHOM?

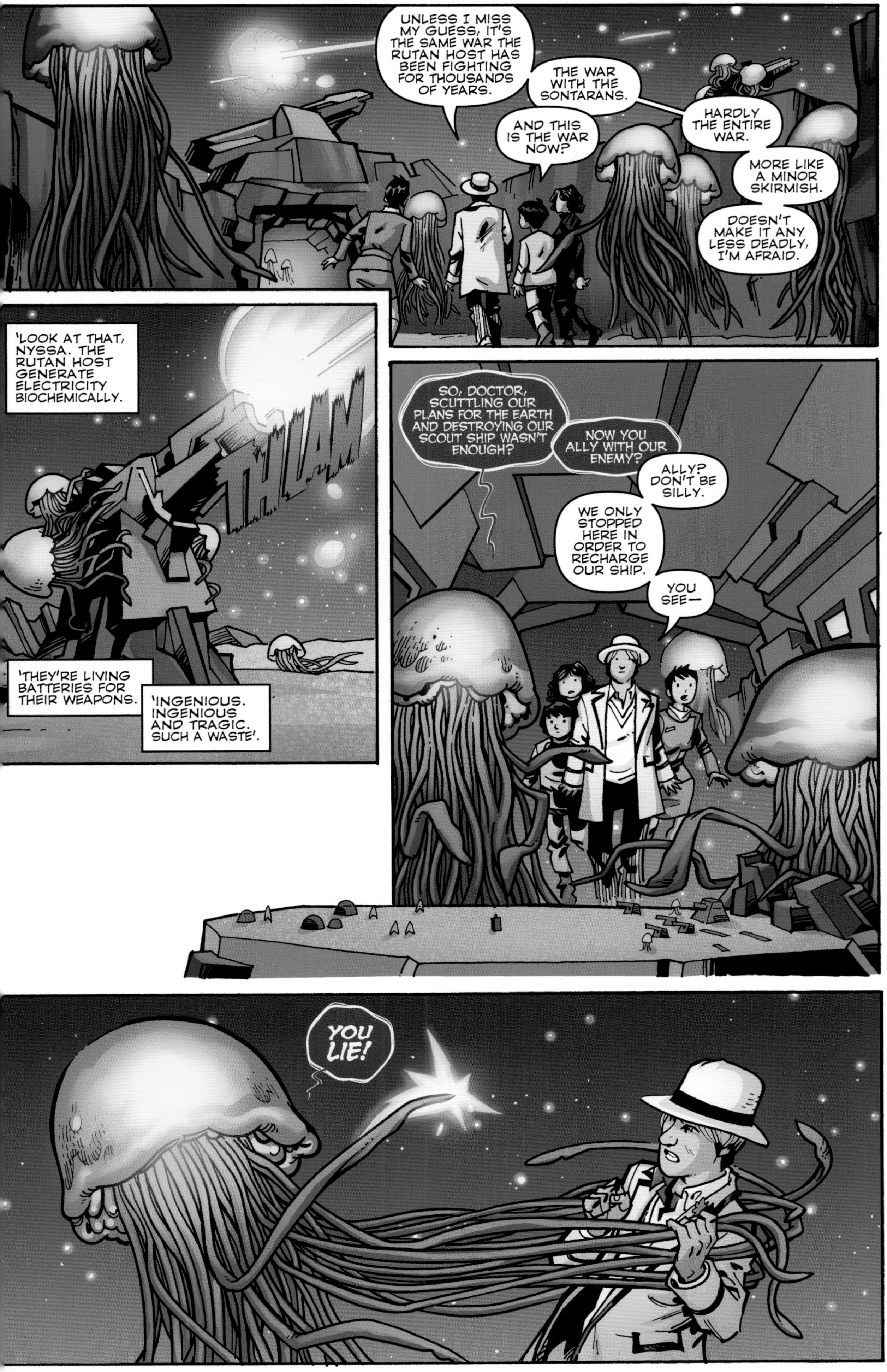
UNLESS I MISS MY GUESS, IT'S THE SAME WAR THE RUTAN HOST HAS BEEN FIGHTING FOR THOUSANDS OF YEARS.
THE WAR WITH THE SONTARANS.
AND THIS IS THE WAR NOW?
HARDLY THE ENTIRE WAR.
MORE LIKE A MINOR SKIRMISH.
DOESN'T MAKE IT ANY LESS DEADLY, I'M AFRAID.
'LOOK AT THAT, NYSSA. THE RUTAN HOST GENERATE ELECTRICITY BIOCHEMICALLY.
THLAM
'THEY'RE LIVING BATTERIES FOR THEIR WEAPONS.
'INGENIOUS. INGENIOUS AND TRAGIC. SUCH A WASTE'.
SO, DOCTOR, SCUTTLING OUR PLANS FOR THE EARTH AND DESTROYING OUR SCOUT SHIP WASN'T ENOUGH?
NOW YOU ALLY WITH OUR ENEMY?
ALLY? DON'T BE SILLY.
WE ONLY STOPPED HERE IN ORDER TO RECHARGE OUR SHIP.
YOU SEE—
YOU LIE!

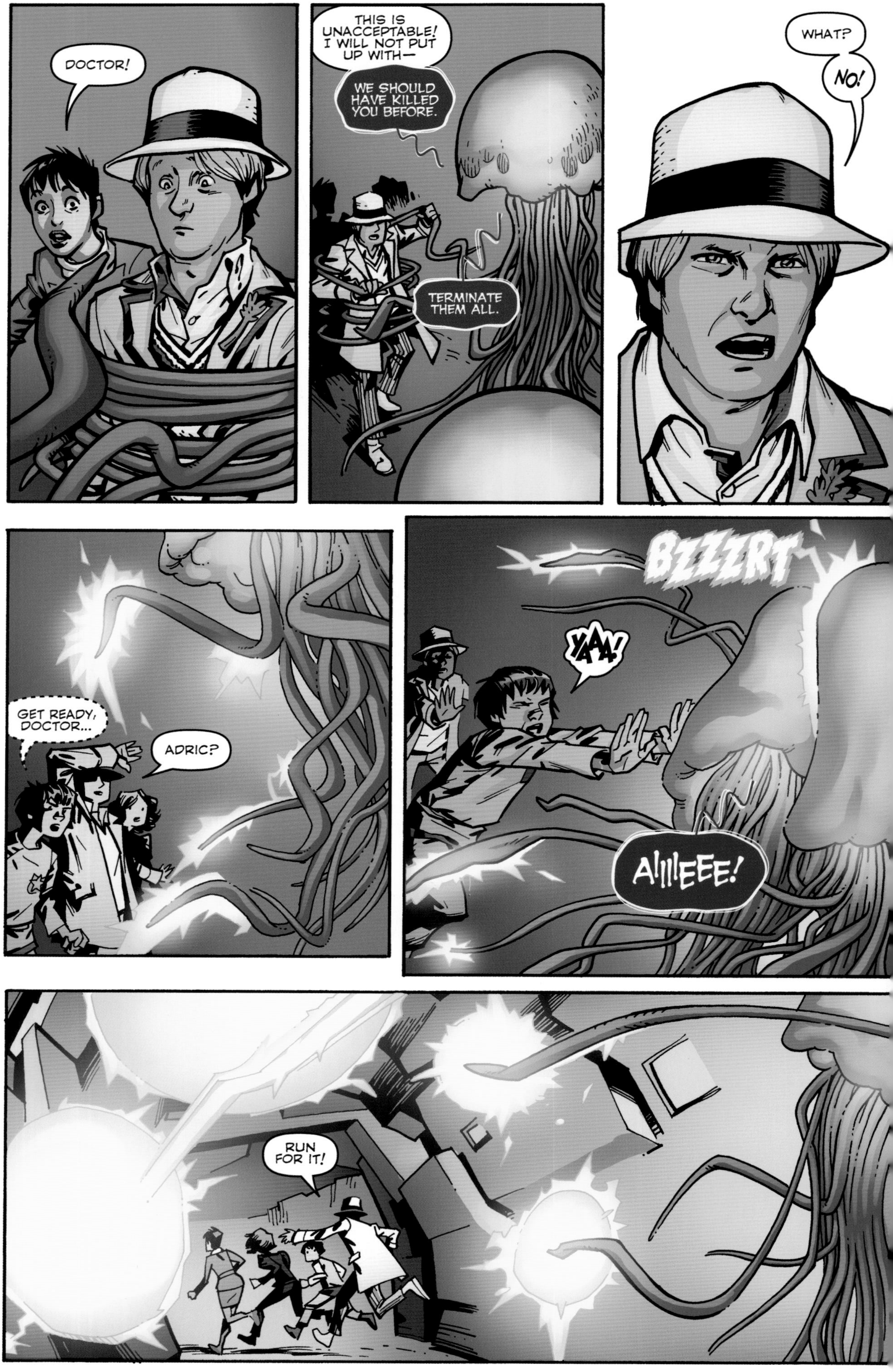
DOCTOR!
THIS IS UNACCEPTABLE! I WILL NOT PUT UP WITH—
WE SHOULD HAVE KILLED YOU BEFORE.
TERMINATE THEM ALL.
WHAT?
NO!
GET READY, DOCTOR...
ADRIC?
BZZZRT
YAAA!
AIIIIEEE!
RUN FOR IT!

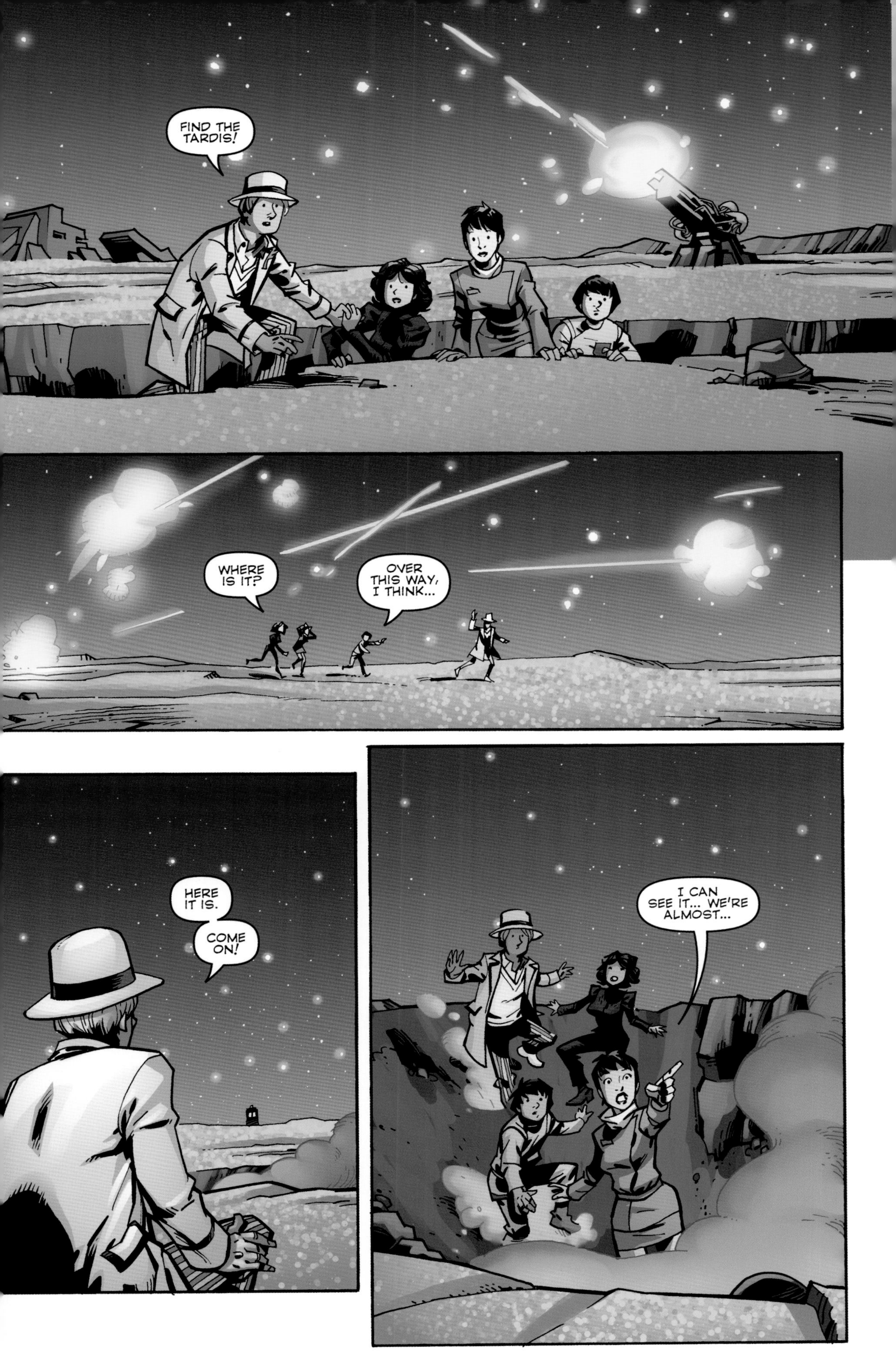
FIND THE TARDIS!
WHERE IS IT?
OVER THIS WAY, I THINK...
HERE IT IS.
COME ON!
I CAN SEE IT... WE'RE ALMOST...

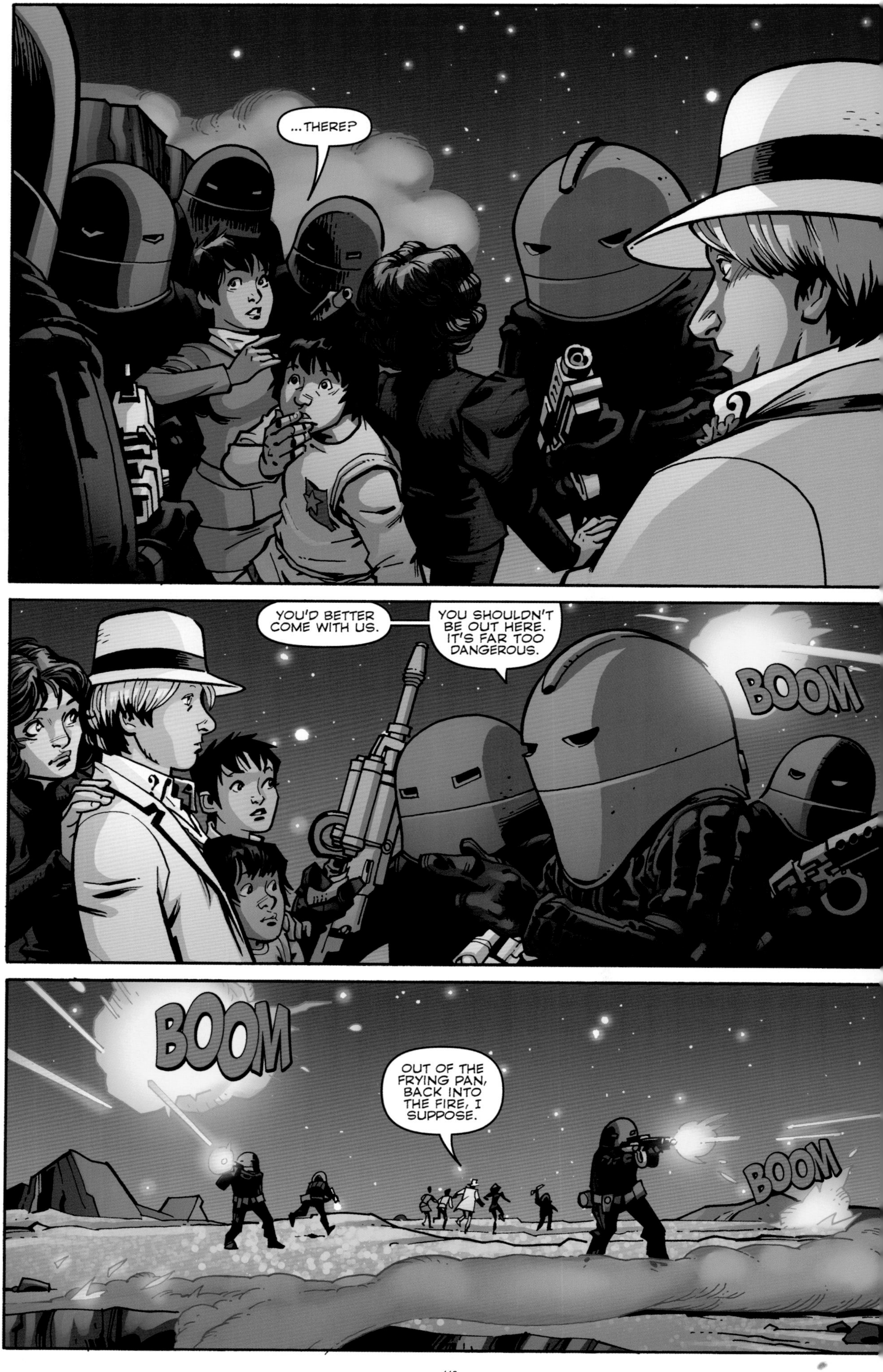
...THERE?
YOU'D BETTER COME WITH US.
YOU SHOULDN'T BE OUT HERE. IT'S FAR TOO DANGEROUS.
BOOM
BOOM
OUT OF THE FRYING PAN, BACK INTO THE FIRE, I SUPPOSE.
BOOM

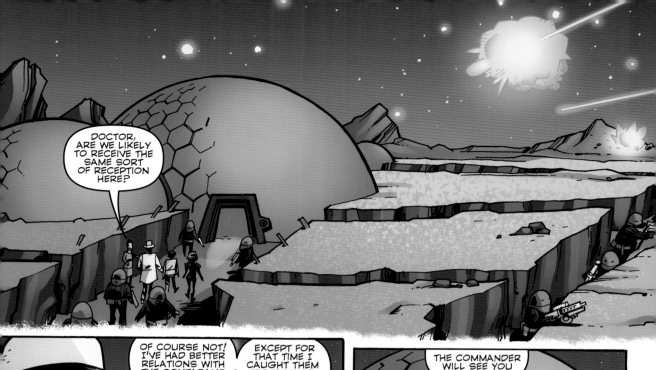

DOCTOR, ARE WE LIKELY TO RECEIVE THE SAME SORT OF RECEPTION HERE?

OF COURSE NOT! I'VE HAD BETTER RELATIONS WITH THE SONTARANS IN THE PAST.

EXCEPT FOR THAT TIME I CAUGHT THEM KIDNAPPING SCIENTISTS FROM EARTH.

AND I'M TOLD I FOILED THEIR INVASION OF GALLIFREY ONCE, BUT I'M A LITTLE HAZY ON THAT ONE...

THE COMMANDER WILL SEE YOU NOW.

WOW.

YES, THE SONTARANS ARE NO MERE DABBLERS IN THE ART OF WAR.

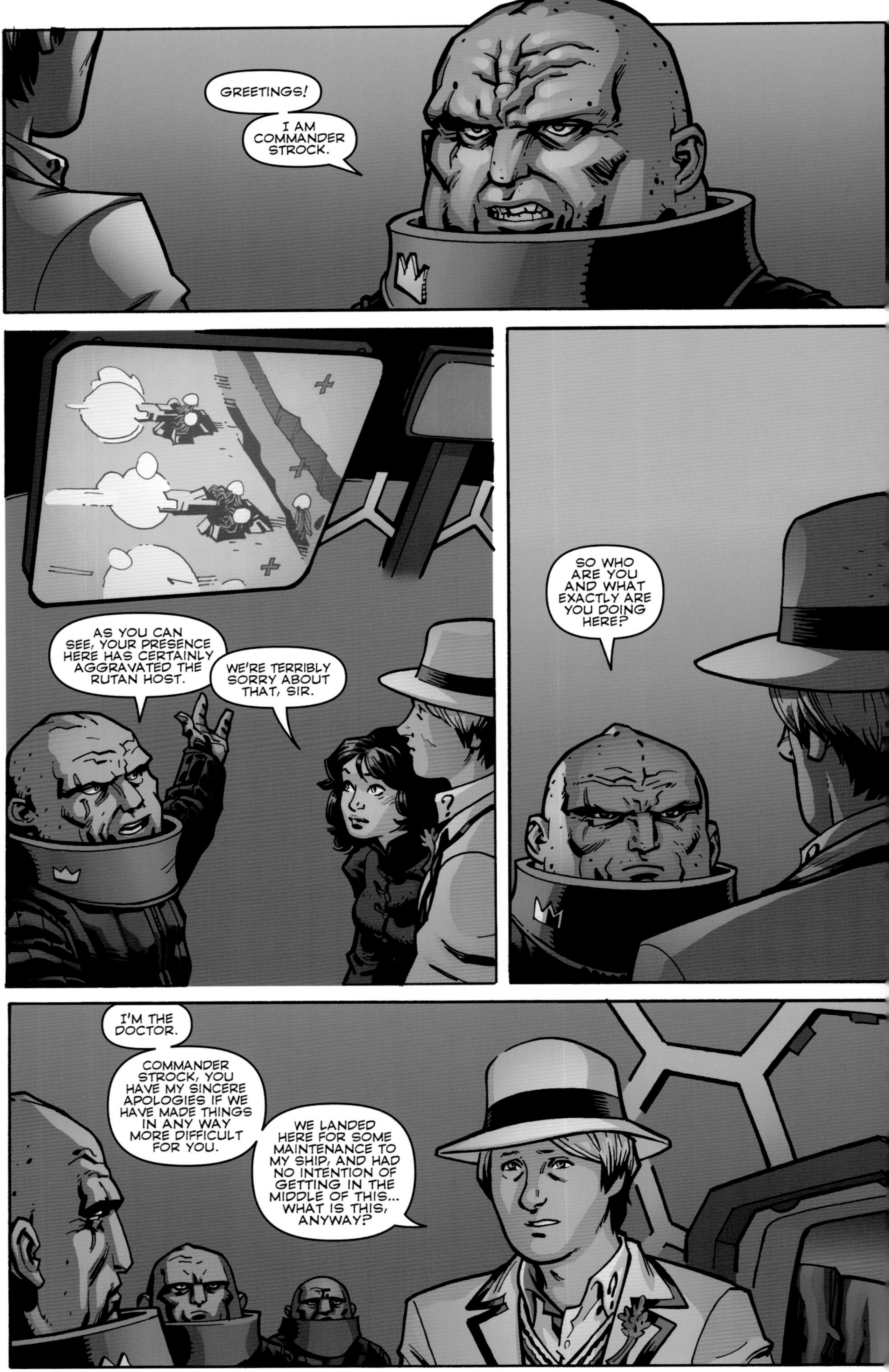

GREETINGS!
I AM COMMANDER STROCK.
AS YOU CAN SEE, YOUR PRESENCE HERE HAS CERTAINLY AGGRAVATED THE RUTAN HOST.
WE'RE TERRIBLY SORRY ABOUT THAT, SIR.
SO WHO ARE YOU AND WHAT EXACTLY ARE YOU DOING HERE?
I'M THE DOCTOR.
COMMANDER STROCK, YOU HAVE MY SINCERE APOLOGIES IF WE HAVE MADE THINGS IN ANY WAY MORE DIFFICULT FOR YOU.
WE LANDED HERE FOR SOME MAINTENANCE TO MY SHIP, AND HAD NO INTENTION OF GETTING IN THE MIDDLE OF THIS... WHAT IS THIS, ANYWAY?

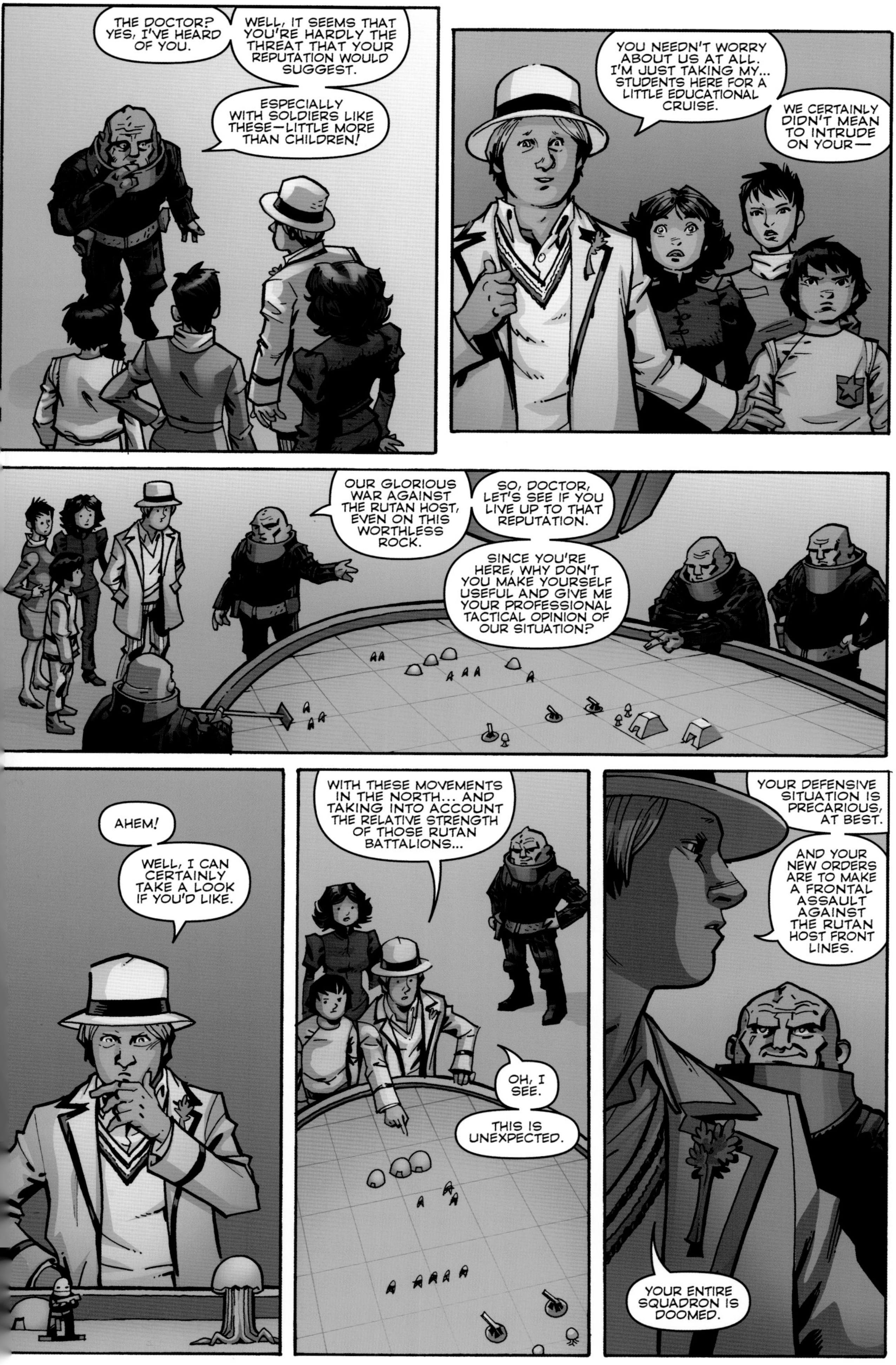
THE DOCTOR? YES, I'VE HEARD OF YOU.
WELL, IT SEEMS THAT YOU'RE HARDLY THE THREAT THAT YOUR REPUTATION WOULD SUGGEST.
ESPECIALLY WITH SOLDIERS LIKE THESE—LITTLE MORE THAN CHILDREN!
YOU NEEDN'T WORRY ABOUT US AT ALL. I'M JUST TAKING MY... STUDENTS HERE FOR A LITTLE EDUCATIONAL CRUISE.
WE CERTAINLY DIDN'T MEAN TO INTRUDE ON YOUR—
OUR GLORIOUS WAR AGAINST THE RUTAN HOST, EVEN ON THIS WORTHLESS ROCK.
SO, DOCTOR, LET'S SEE IF YOU LIVE UP TO THAT REPUTATION.
SINCE YOU'RE HERE, WHY DON'T YOU MAKE YOURSELF USEFUL AND GIVE ME YOUR PROFESSIONAL TACTICAL OPINION OF OUR SITUATION?
AHEM!
WELL, I CAN CERTAINLY TAKE A LOOK IF YOU'D LIKE.
WITH THESE MOVEMENTS IN THE NORTH... AND TAKING INTO ACCOUNT THE RELATIVE STRENGTH OF THOSE RUTAN BATTALIONS...
OH, I SEE.
THIS IS UNEXPECTED.
YOUR DEFENSIVE SITUATION IS PRECARIOUS, AT BEST.
AND YOUR NEW ORDERS ARE TO MAKE A FRONTAL ASSAULT AGAINST THE RUTAN HOST FRONT LINES.
YOUR ENTIRE SQUADRON IS DOOMED.

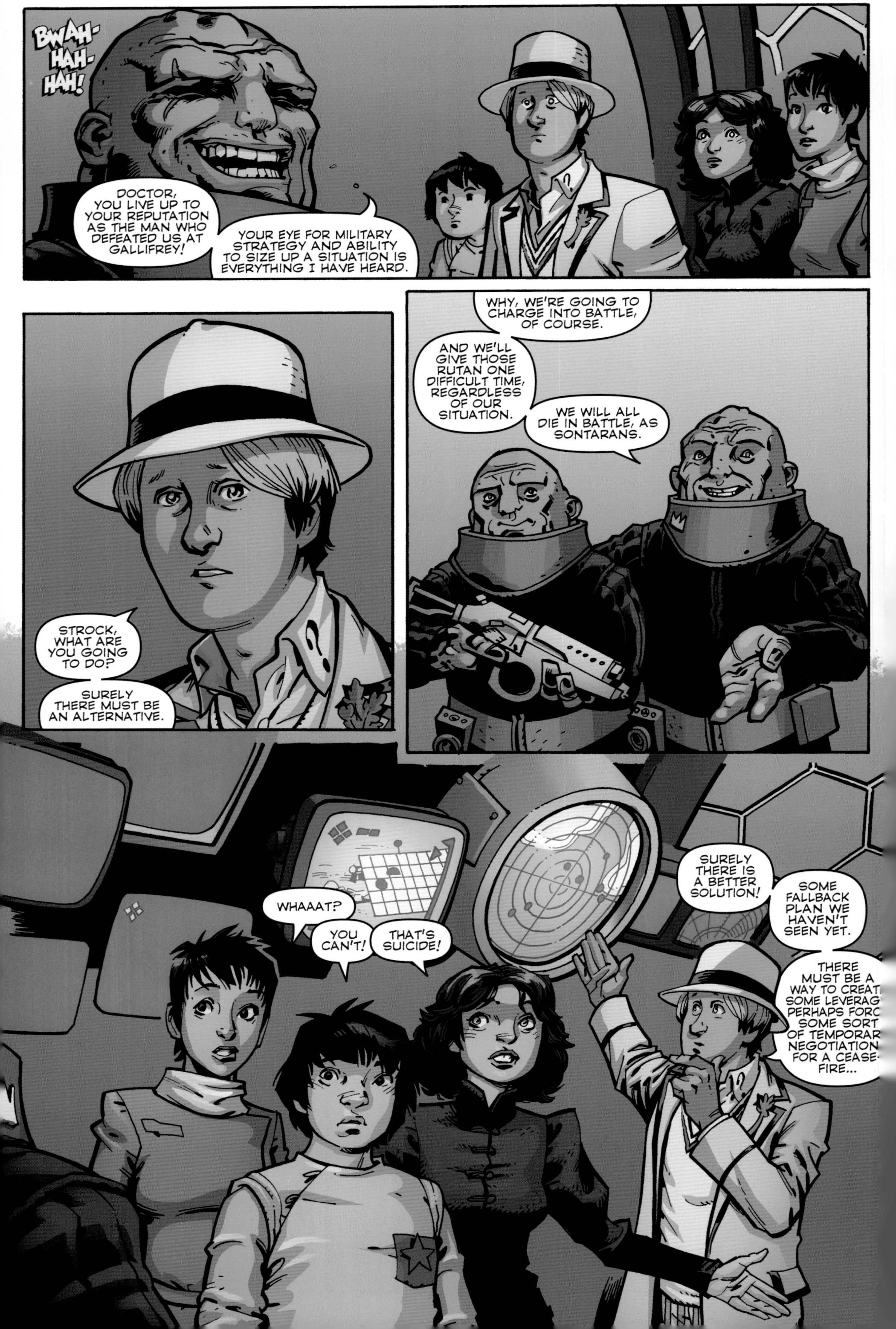
BWAH-HAH-HAH!
DOCTOR, YOU LIVE UP TO YOUR REPUTATION AS THE MAN WHO DEFEATED US AT GALLIFREY!
YOUR EYE FOR MILITARY STRATEGY AND ABILITY TO SIZE UP A SITUATION IS EVERYTHING I HAVE HEARD.
STROCK, WHAT ARE YOU GOING TO DO?
SURELY THERE MUST BE AN ALTERNATIVE.
WHY, WE'RE GOING TO CHARGE INTO BATTLE, OF COURSE.
AND WE'LL GIVE THOSE RUTAN ONE DIFFICULT TIME, REGARDLESS OF OUR SITUATION.
WE WILL ALL DIE IN BATTLE, AS SONTARANS.
WHAAAT?
YOU CAN'T!
THAT'S SUICIDE!
SURELY THERE IS A BETTER SOLUTION!
SOME FALLBACK PLAN WE HAVEN'T SEEN YET.
THERE MUST BE A WAY TO CREAT SOME LEVERAG PERHAPS FORC SOME SORT OF TEMPORAR NEGOTIATION FOR A CEASE-FIRE...

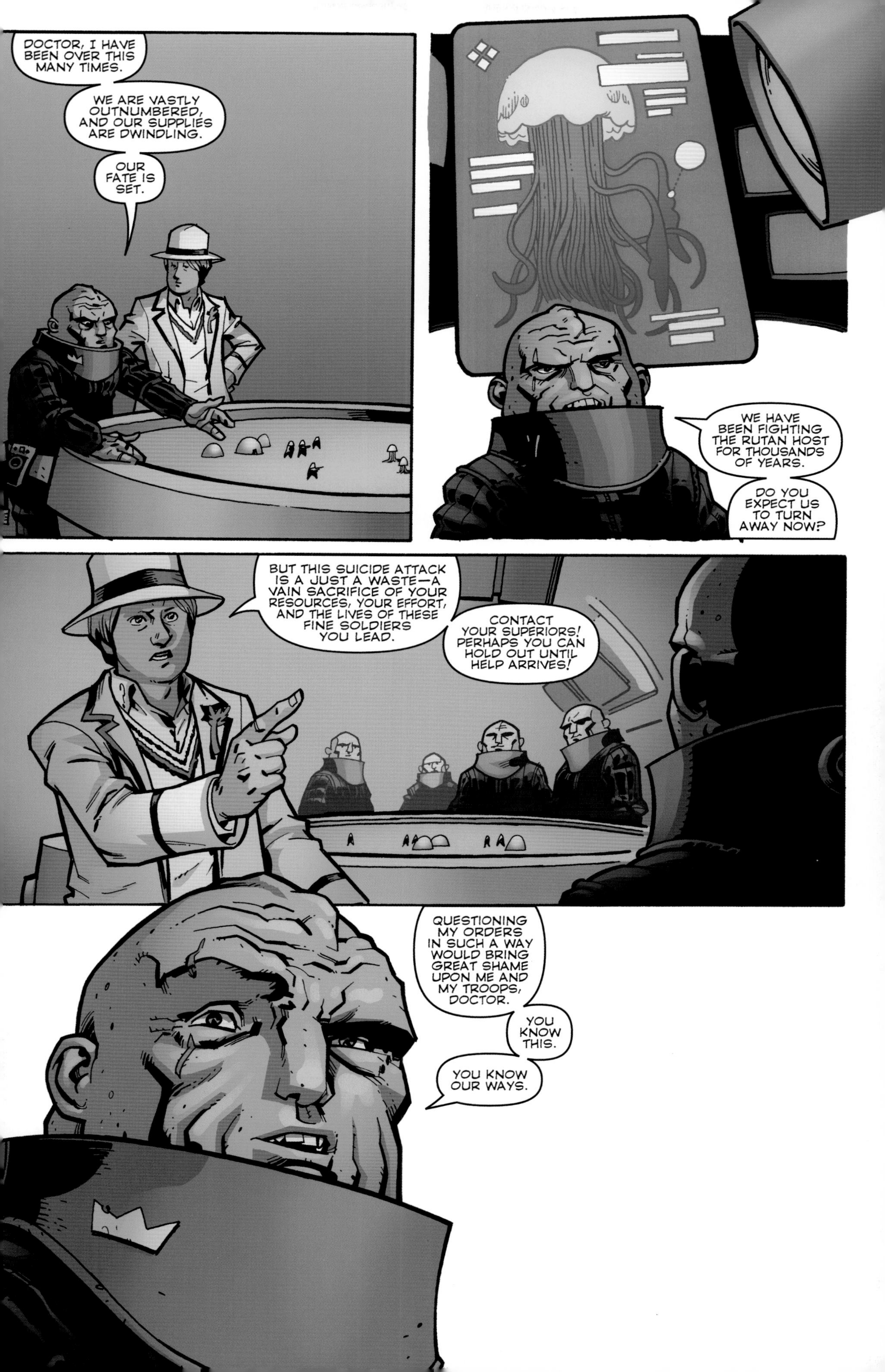
DOCTOR, I HAVE BEEN OVER THIS MANY TIMES.
WE ARE VASTLY OUTNUMBERED, AND OUR SUPPLIES ARE DWINDLING.
OUR FATE IS SET.
WE HAVE BEEN FIGHTING THE RUTAN HOST FOR THOUSANDS OF YEARS.
DO YOU EXPECT US TO TURN AWAY NOW?
BUT THIS SUICIDE ATTACK IS A JUST A WASTE—A VAIN SACRIFICE OF YOUR RESOURCES, YOUR EFFORT, AND THE LIVES OF THESE FINE SOLDIERS YOU LEAD.
CONTACT YOUR SUPERIORS! PERHAPS YOU CAN HOLD OUT UNTIL HELP ARRIVES!
QUESTIONING MY ORDERS IN SUCH A WAY WOULD BRING GREAT SHAME UPON ME AND MY TROOPS, DOCTOR.
YOU KNOW THIS.
YOU KNOW OUR WAYS.

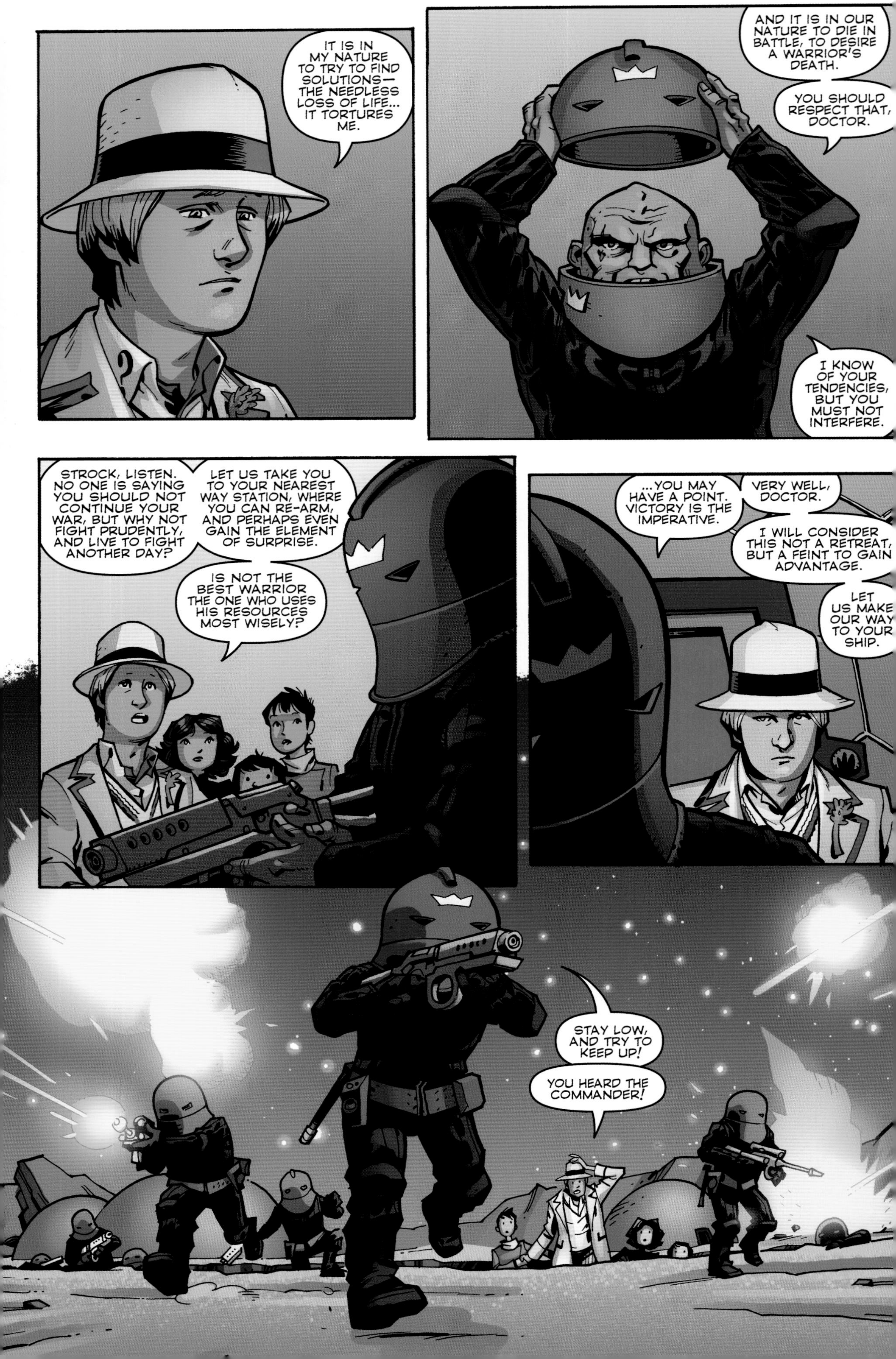

IT IS IN MY NATURE TO TRY TO FIND SOLUTIONS— THE NEEDLESS LOSS OF LIFE... IT TORTURES ME.
AND IT IS IN OUR NATURE TO DIE IN BATTLE, TO DESIRE A WARRIOR'S DEATH.
YOU SHOULD RESPECT THAT, DOCTOR.
I KNOW OF YOUR TENDENCIES, BUT YOU MUST NOT INTERFERE.
STROCK, LISTEN. NO ONE IS SAYING YOU SHOULD NOT CONTINUE YOUR WAR, BUT WHY NOT FIGHT PRUDENTLY, AND LIVE TO FIGHT ANOTHER DAY?
LET US TAKE YOU TO YOUR NEAREST WAY STATION, WHERE YOU CAN RE-ARM, AND PERHAPS EVEN GAIN THE ELEMENT OF SURPRISE.
IS NOT THE BEST WARRIOR THE ONE WHO USES HIS RESOURCES MOST WISELY?
...YOU MAY HAVE A POINT. VICTORY IS THE IMPERATIVE.
VERY WELL, DOCTOR.
I WILL CONSIDER THIS NOT A RETREAT, BUT A FEINT TO GAIN ADVANTAGE.
LET US MAKE OUR WAY TO YOUR SHIP.
STAY LOW, AND TRY TO KEEP UP!
YOU HEARD THE COMMANDER!

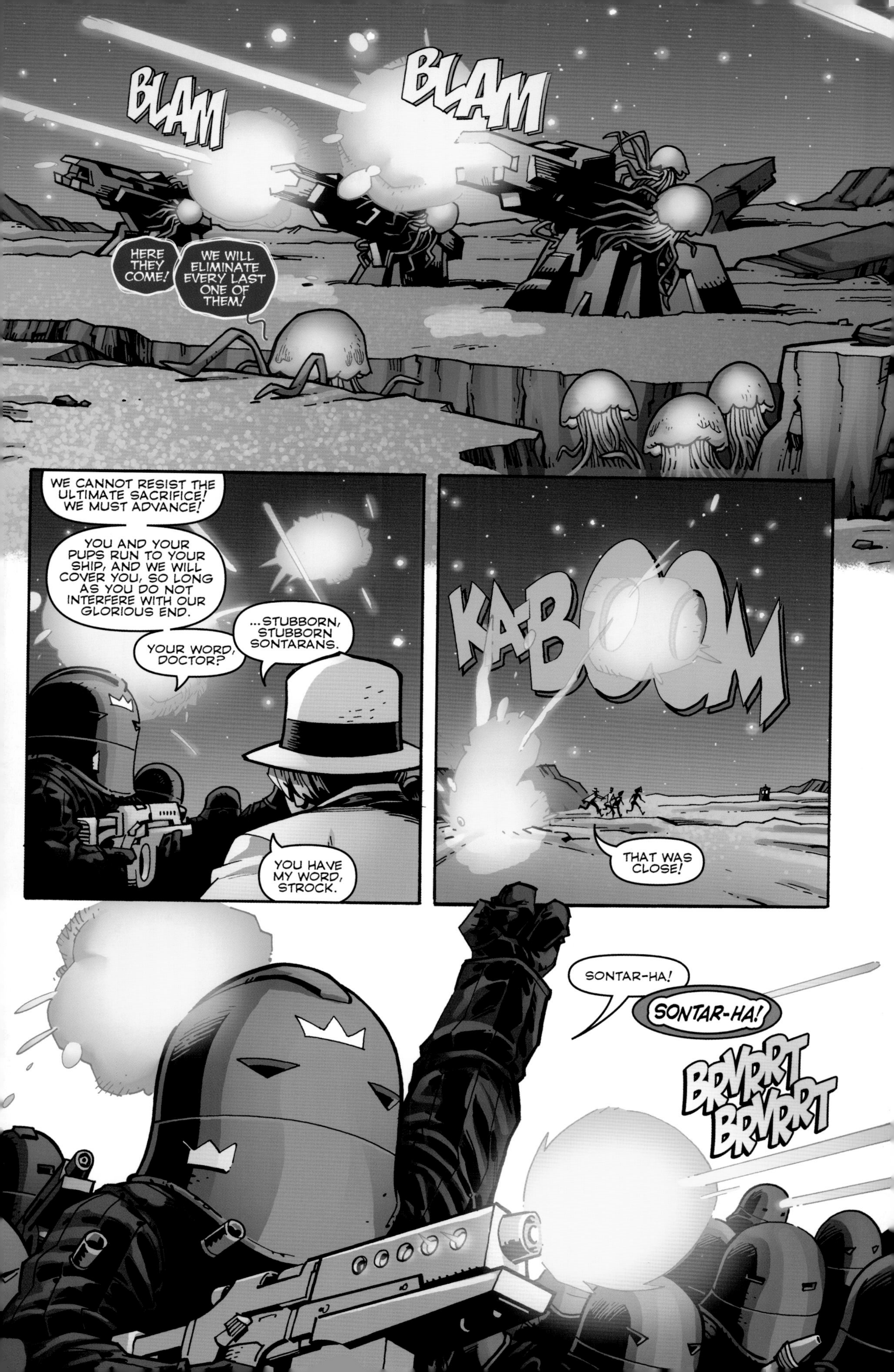
BLAM
BLAM
HERE THEY COME!
WE WILL ELIMINATE EVERY LAST ONE OF THEM!
WE CANNOT RESIST THE ULTIMATE SACRIFICE! WE MUST ADVANCE!
YOU AND YOUR PUPS RUN TO YOUR SHIP, AND WE WILL COVER YOU, SO LONG AS YOU DO NOT INTERFERE WITH OUR GLORIOUS END.
...STUBBORN, STUBBORN SONTARANS.
YOUR WORD, DOCTOR?
YOU HAVE MY WORD, STROCK.
KA-BOOOM
THAT WAS CLOSE!
SONTAR-HA!
SONTAR-HA!
BRVRRT
BRVRRT

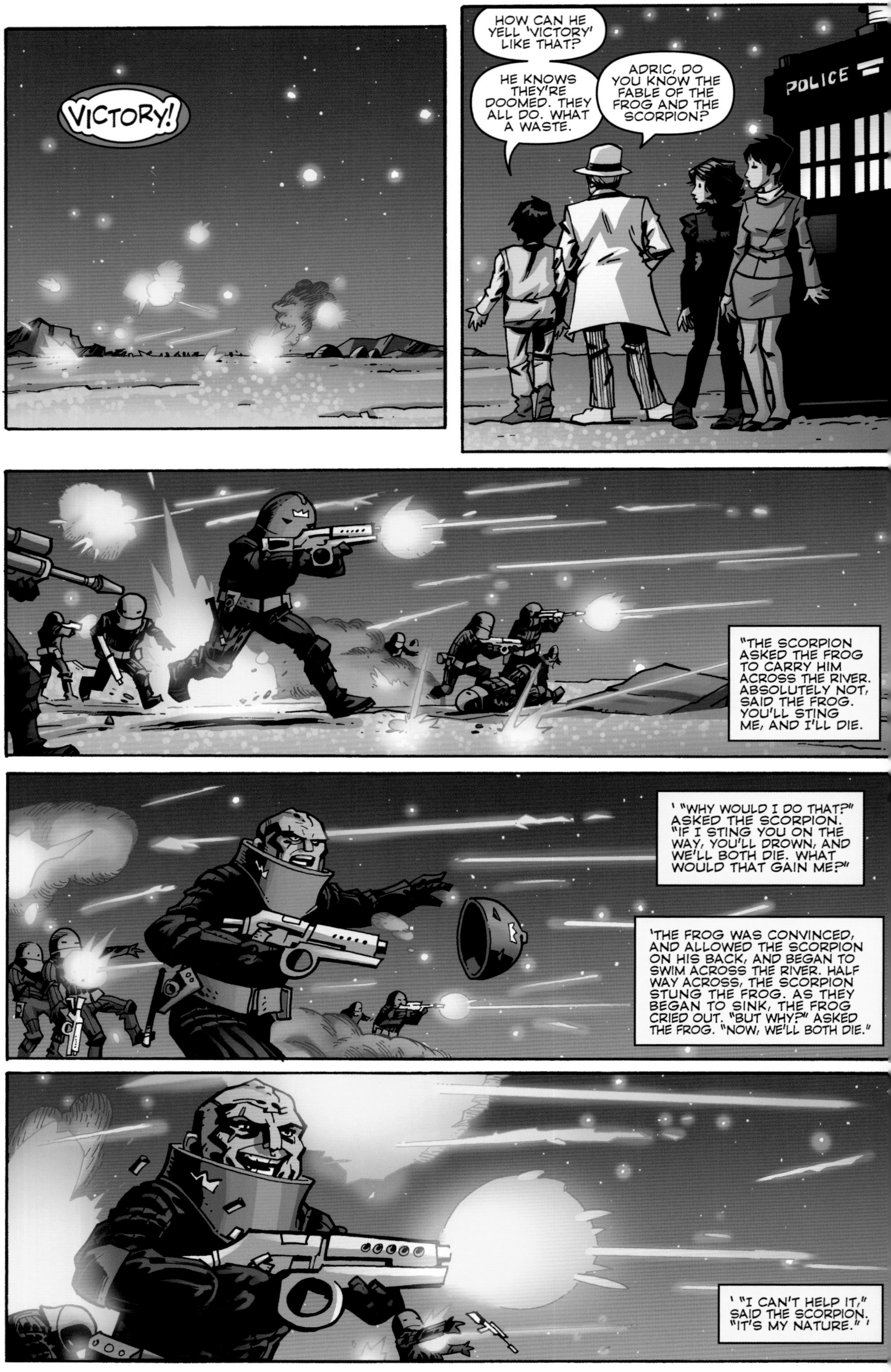
VICTORY!
HOW CAN HE YELL 'VICTORY' LIKE THAT?
HE KNOWS THEY'RE DOOMED. THEY ALL DO. WHAT A WASTE.
ADRIC, DO YOU KNOW THE FABLE OF THE FROG AND THE SCORPION?
POLICE
"THE SCORPION ASKED THE FROG TO CARRY HIM ACROSS THE RIVER. ABSOLUTELY NOT, SAID THE FROG. YOU'LL STING ME, AND I'LL DIE.
' "WHY WOULD I DO THAT?" ASKED THE SCORPION. "IF I STING YOU ON THE WAY, YOU'LL DROWN, AND WE'LL BOTH DIE. WHAT WOULD THAT GAIN ME?"
'THE FROG WAS CONVINCED, AND ALLOWED THE SCORPION ON HIS BACK, AND BEGAN TO SWIM ACROSS THE RIVER. HALF WAY ACROSS, THE SCORPION STUNG THE FROG. AS THEY BEGAN TO SINK, THE FROG CRIED OUT. "BUT WHY?" ASKED THE FROG. "NOW, WE'LL BOTH DIE."
' "I CAN'T HELP IT," SAID THE SCORPION. "IT'S MY NATURE." '

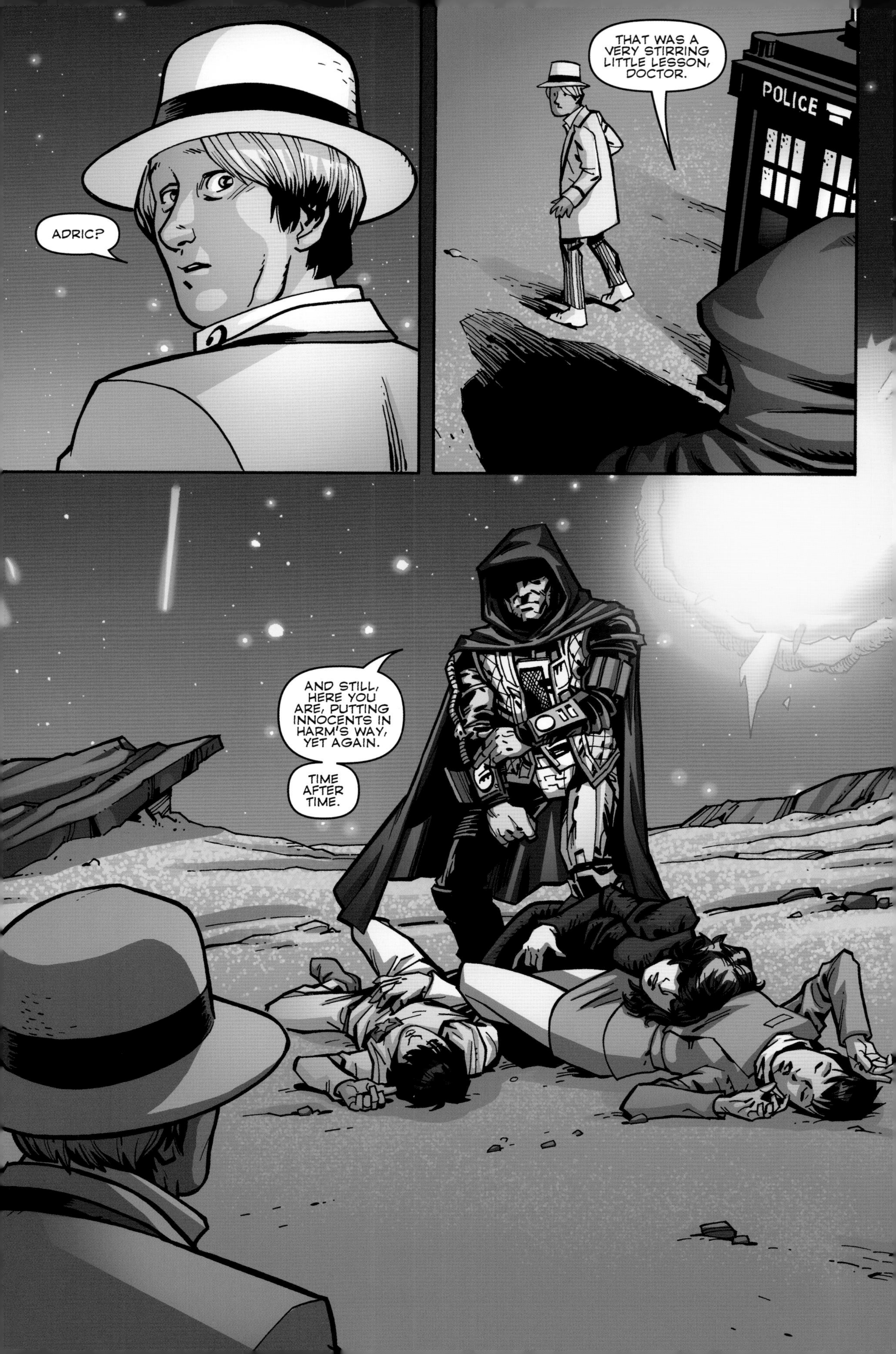

ADRIC?
THAT WAS A VERY STIRRING LITTLE LESSON, DOCTOR.
POLICE
AND STILL, HERE YOU ARE, PUTTING INNOCENTS IN HARM'S WAY, YET AGAIN.
TIME AFTER TIME.

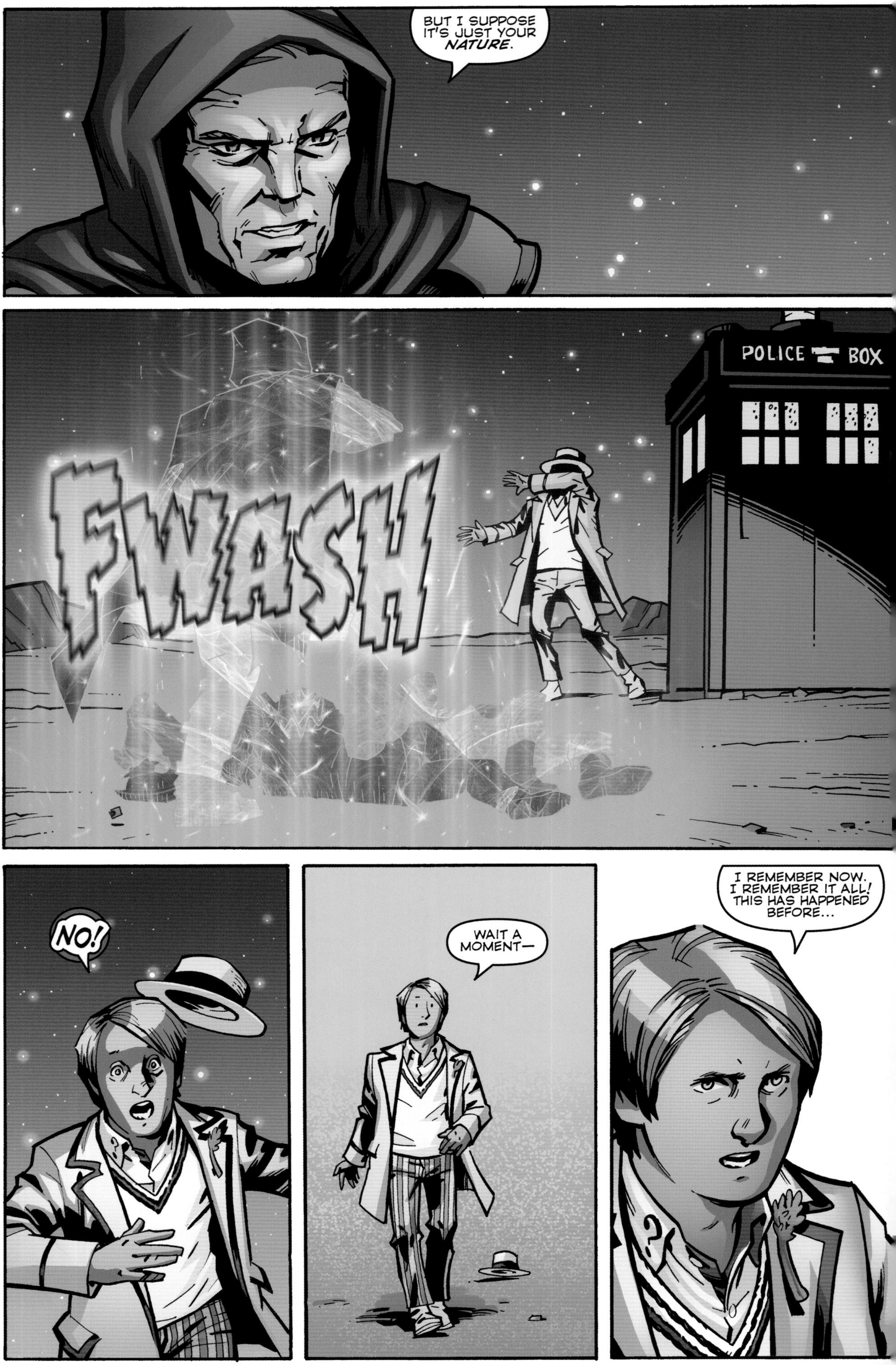

BUT I SUPPOSE IT'S JUST YOUR NATURE.
FWASH
POLICE BOX
NO!
WAIT A MOMENT—
I REMEMBER NOW. I REMEMBER IT ALL! THIS HAS HAPPENED BEFORE...

REFLECTIONS OF TIME

Wherein prominent Whovians past and present muse upon the Doctor's history in comic form.

While I had enjoyed the *Doctor Who* TV show as a child—I still remember the terror the Daleks instilled in me at the age of 9—I hadn't followed the show after the Second Doctor left. Then, many years later, I had been hired as the editor on Marvel UK's line of monthly magazines. At the time, the company was publishing *Doctor Who Weekly,* a comic very much aimed at the traditional UK comics audience, boys aged 8-12.

By 1981, the magazine was floundering to retain its audience, and the comic switched to a monthly schedule with beefed-up text content. The incumbent editor, Paul Neary, was struggling with the feature articles, which were taking up 75 percent of the magazine, and suggested that I trade him my *Marvel Super-Heroes, Rampage,* and *Savage Sword of Conan* monthly reprint magazines for *Doctor Who Monthly.* I had no real ambitions to edit a comic strip, as I was much more interested in being a magazine editor at the time, but I figured if I was going to do it, I was going to do it right.

Looking at the comic strip during that period, I figured it was still being aimed at that same traditional UK comic strip market. But the audience for the magazine was, in my opinion, older—specifically fans of the TV show. And I thought the strip (small in page count, but still the most expensive feature in the mag) should reflect that.

A well-respected British scripter, Steve Moore, was writing the main Doctor Who stories at that time, but I felt his take on The Doctor didn't really have much in common with TV's character. So I spent a lot of time with the writer, trying to help him re-align the feeling of the comic-strip stories to something that resembled the peculiar magic of the show. After a couple of re-writes of the "Spider-God" script, Steve lost patience with my meddling and decided he didn't want to do that any more. Looking back, I was pretty unfair to Steve, as he did struggle bravely to capture the mood I was after, but he'd had enough and I couldn't blame him.

So I turned to another writer I'd worked successfully with in the past, Steve Parkhouse, and asked him if he'd be interested in having a try at writing Doctor Who. He wasn't. Emphatically no. But we were kicking it back and forth a while when I hit on what the missing ingredient was. I told Steve that he should think of Doctor Who as having the same British eccentricity as the famous UK daily newspaper strip *Rupert the Bear.* That seemed to strike a chord with Steve, and he set to work and produced a magnificent run of stories—a sort of wide-screen epic version of The Doctor that dwarfed anything being done by the TV show at the time.

When I quit the Marvel UK staff in 1985, Steve Parkhouse felt he didn't want to write the strip for another editor. But with his encouragement, I stepped in and wrote the strip myself for almost a year, finding my feet as a writer in a very public way, even though I knew going in that I couldn't hope to replicate the glory years of Parkhouse. Brave or stupid... you decide.

It wouldn't be the last time we worked together, but it was one of my more successful collaborations with the brilliant Mr. Parkhouse.

—Alan McKenzie,
former *Doctor Who Magazine* editor
and writer

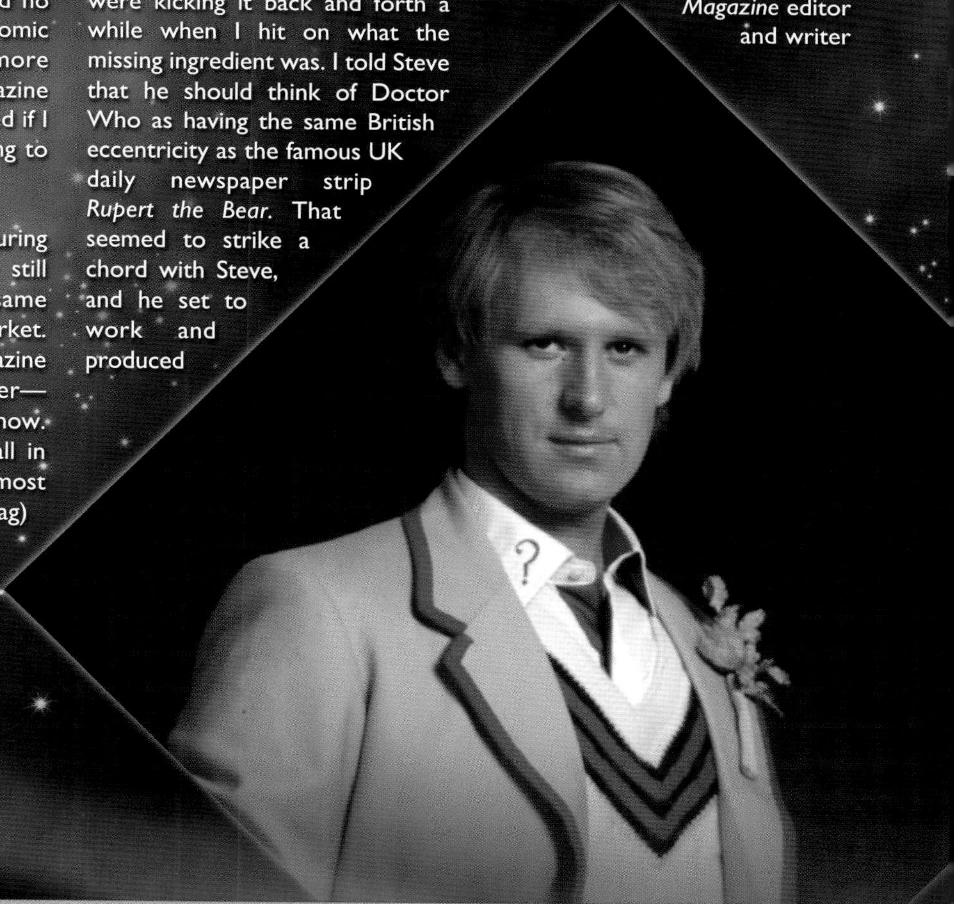

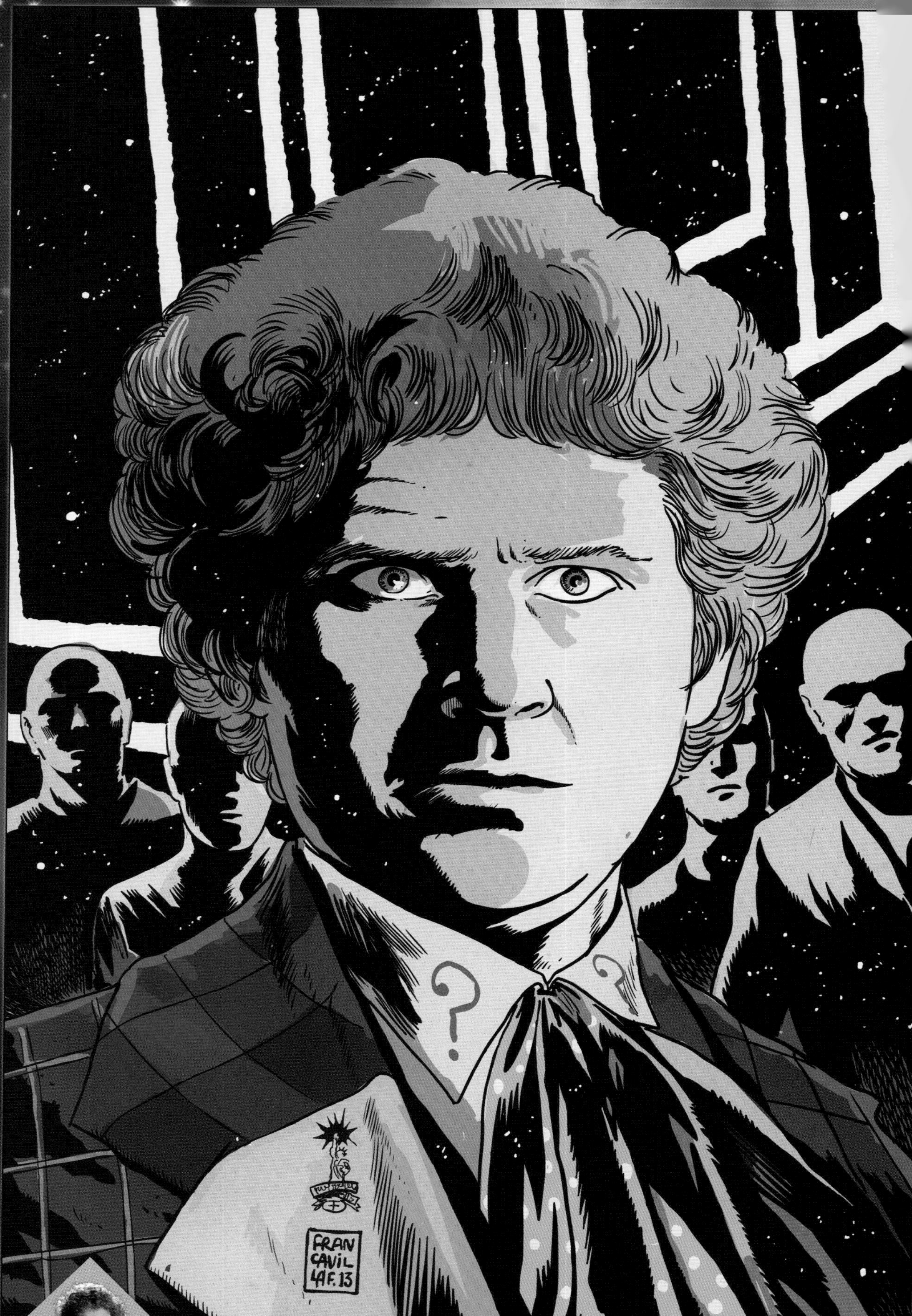
FRAN CAVIL LA F. 13

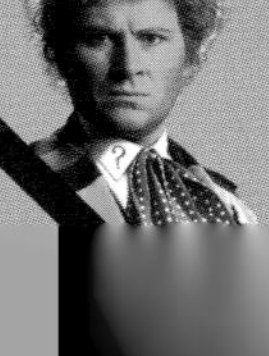

6TH DOCTOR
1984 - 1986

CHAPTER 6 "FAÇADES"
Cover Art by Francesco Francavilla

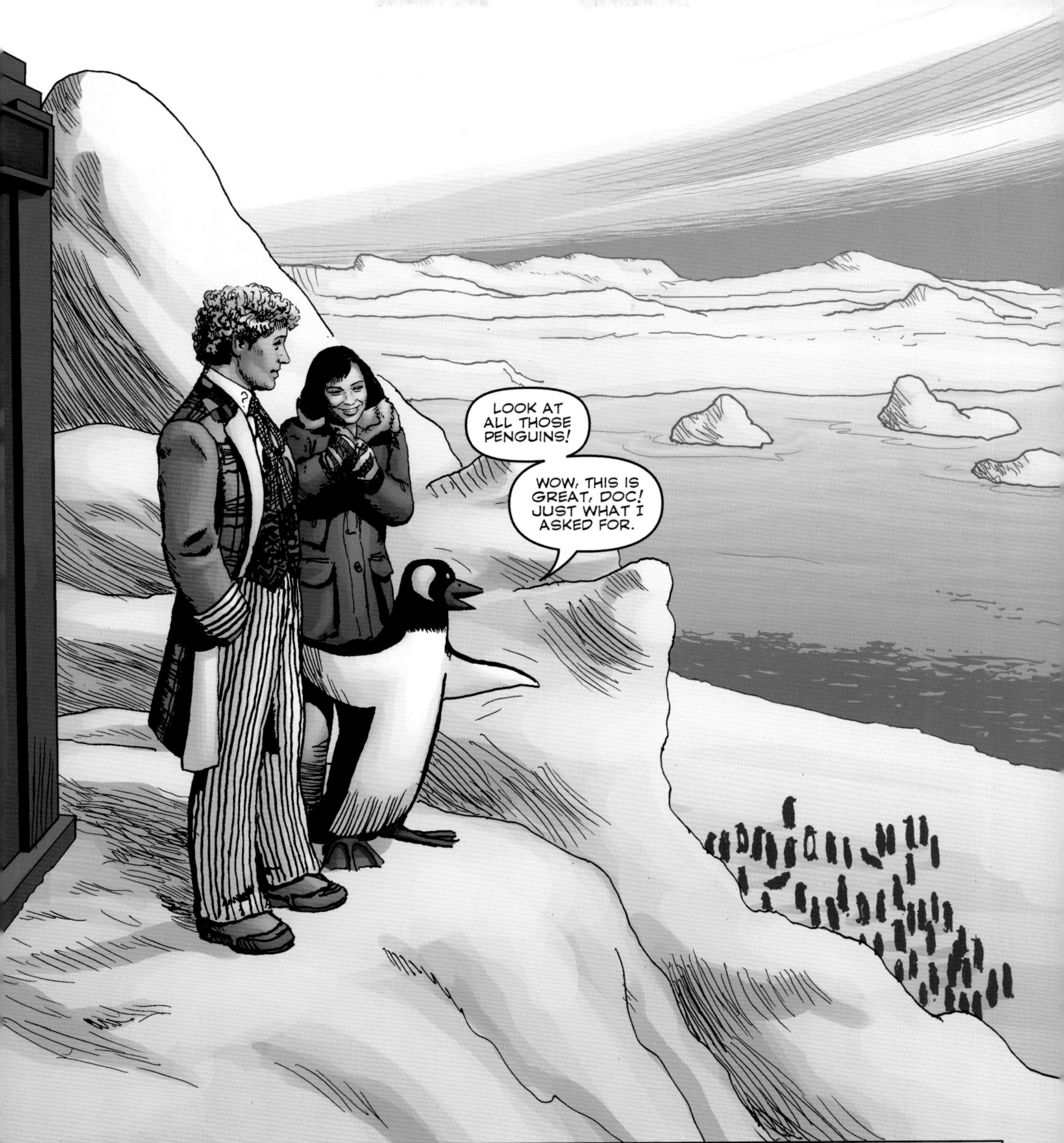
LOOK AT ALL THOSE PENGUINS!
WOW, THIS IS GREAT, DOC! JUST WHAT I ASKED FOR.

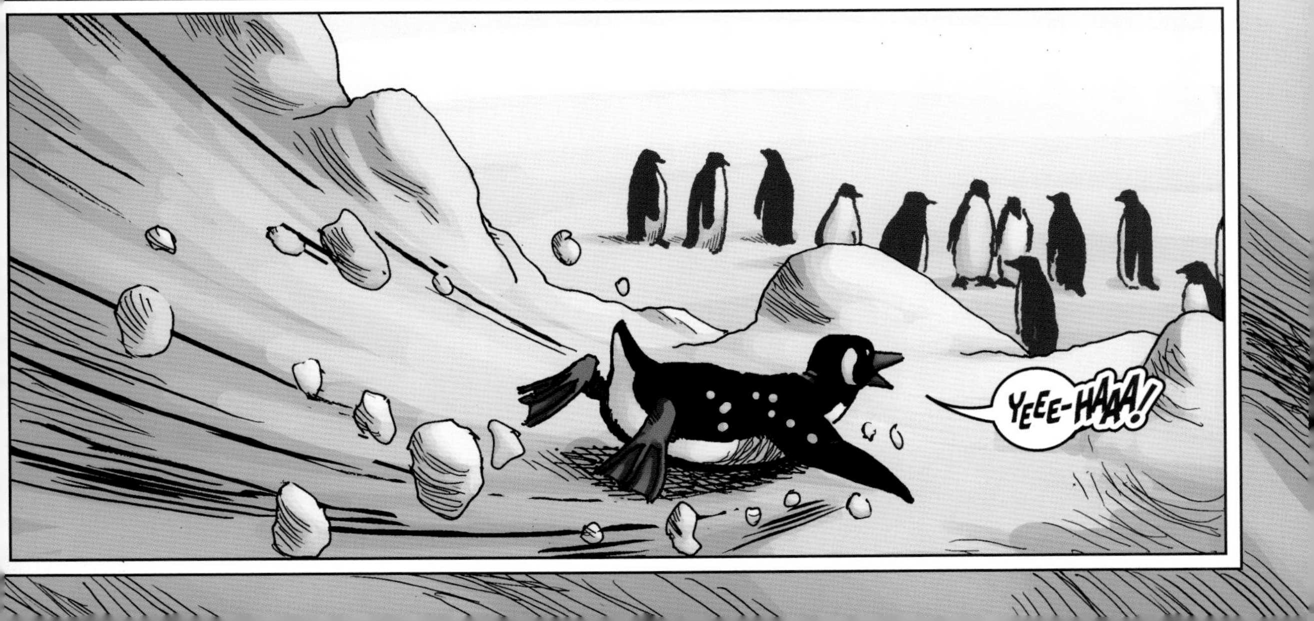
YEEE-HAAA!

JUST LOOK AT HIM GO.

I'VE RARELY SEEN HIM SO EXCITED.

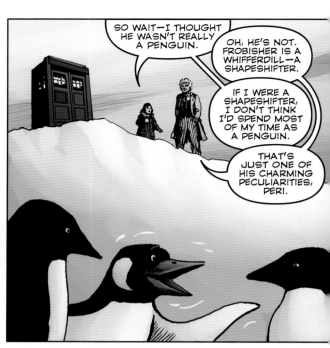

SO WAIT—I THOUGHT HE WASN'T REALLY A PENGUIN.

OH, HE'S NOT. FROBISHER IS A WHIFFERDILL—A SHAPESHIFTER.

IF I WERE A SHAPESHIFTER, I DON'T THINK I'D SPEND MOST OF MY TIME AS A PENGUIN.

THAT'S JUST ONE OF HIS CHARMING PECULIARITIES, PERI.

HOW DID YOU MEET FROBISHER, ANYWAY?

OH, IT'S QUITE A LONG STORY.

TO SUM UP, SOMEONE ONCE HAD THE TEMERITY TO PUT A BOUNTY ON MY HEAD.

A QUARTER OF A MILLION MAZUMAS!

CAN YOU BELIEVE THAT?

HE WAS WORKING AS A PRIVATE INVESTIGATOR WHEN HE TRIED TO COLLECT THE BOUNTY ON ME.

AS IT TURNED OUT, WE BECAME FAST FRIENDS.

AND WE SPLIT THE BOUNTY MONEY.

WE'VE OFTEN TRAVELLED TOGETHER SINCE THEN.

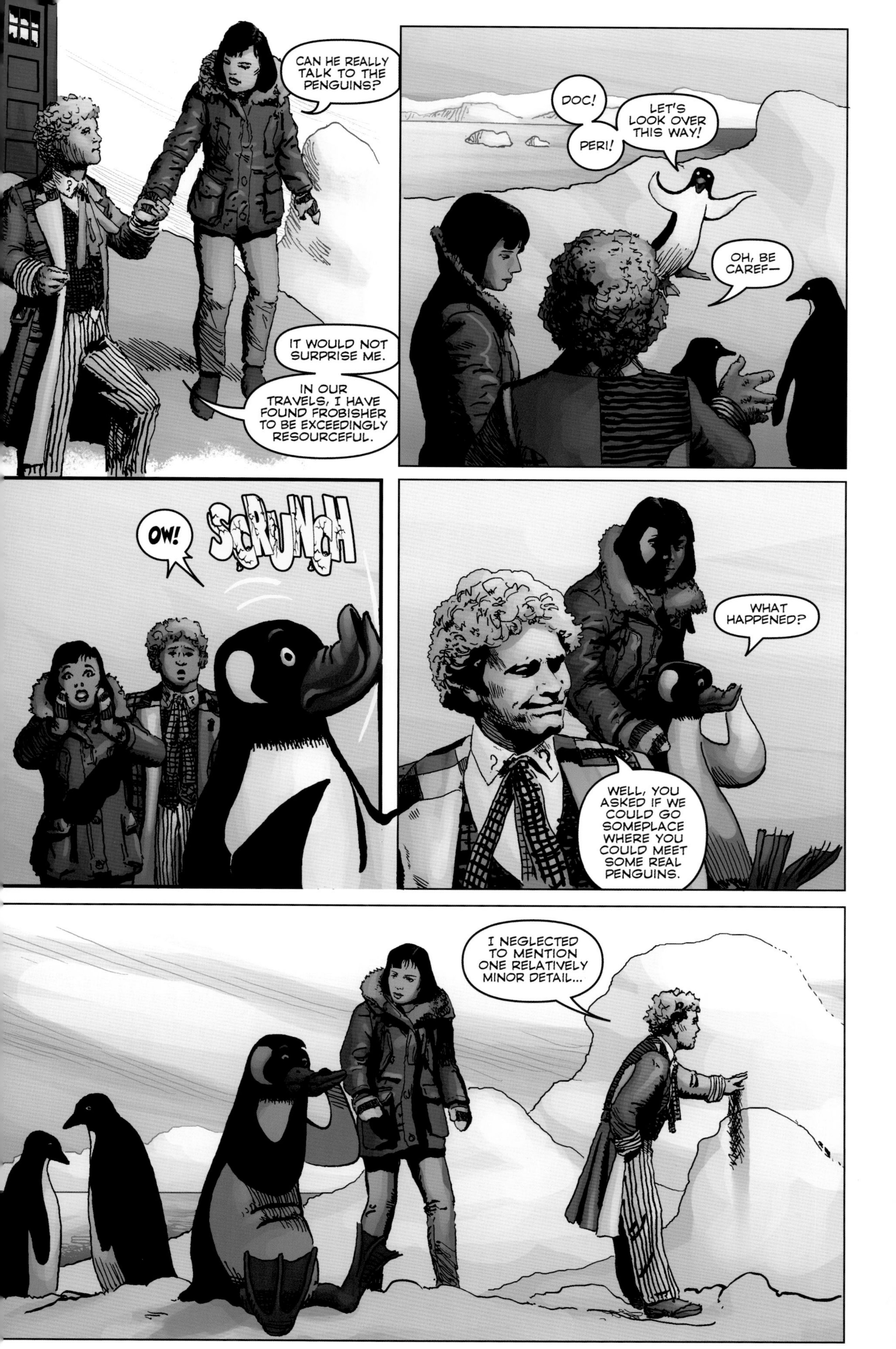
CAN HE REALLY TALK TO THE PENGUINS?
IT WOULD NOT SURPRISE ME.
IN OUR TRAVELS, I HAVE FOUND FROBISHER TO BE EXCEEDINGLY RESOURCEFUL.
DOC!
PERI!
LET'S LOOK OVER THIS WAY!
OH, BE CAREF—
OW!
SCRUNCH
WHAT HAPPENED?
WELL, YOU ASKED IF WE COULD GO SOMEPLACE WHERE YOU COULD MEET SOME REAL PENGUINS.
I NEGLECTED TO MENTION ONE RELATIVELY MINOR DETAIL...

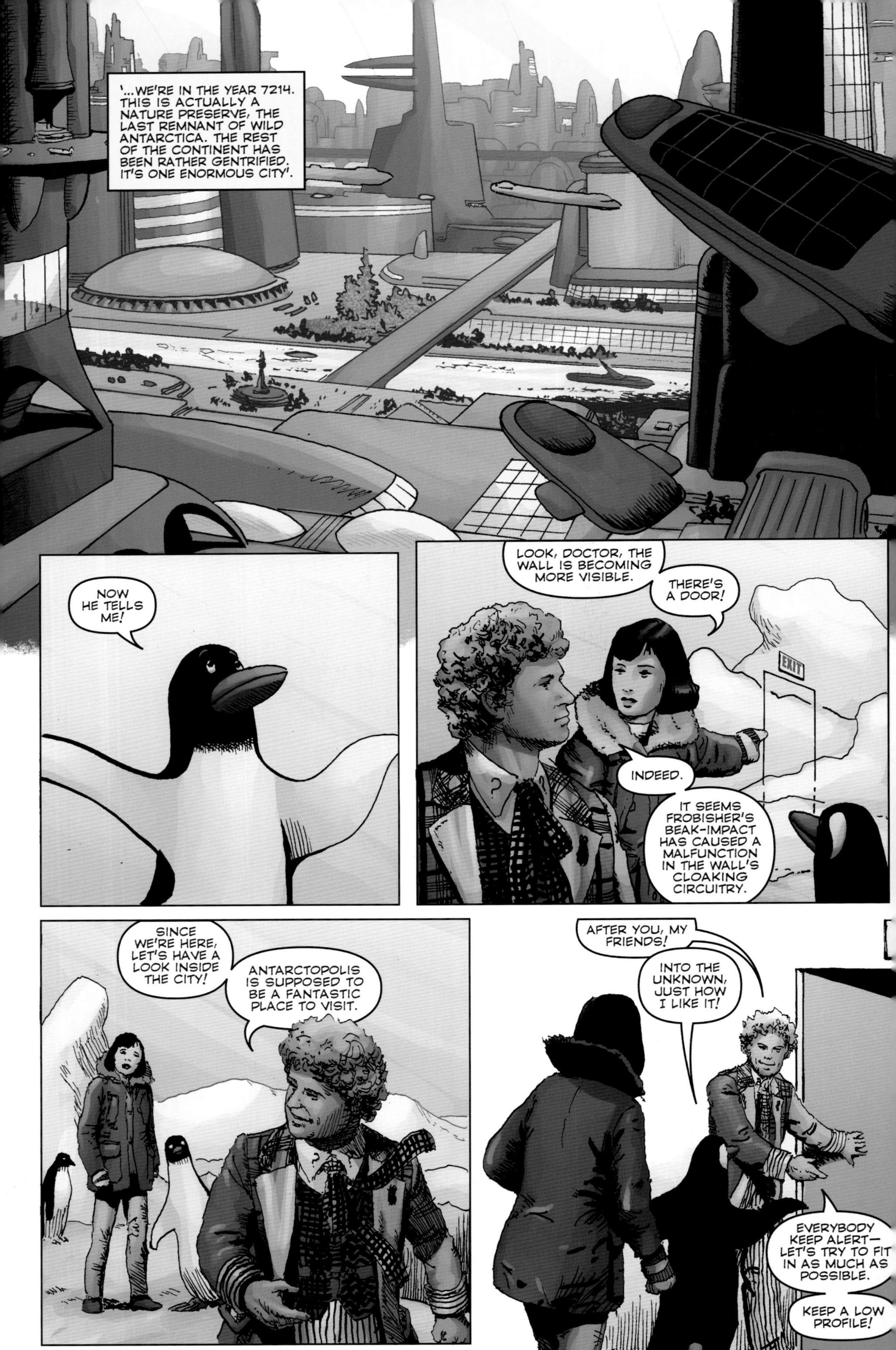
'...WE'RE IN THE YEAR 7214. THIS IS ACTUALLY A NATURE PRESERVE, THE LAST REMNANT OF WILD ANTARCTICA. THE REST OF THE CONTINENT HAS BEEN RATHER GENTRIFIED. IT'S ONE ENORMOUS CITY'.
NOW HE TELLS ME!
LOOK, DOCTOR, THE WALL IS BECOMING MORE VISIBLE.
THERE'S A DOOR!
EXIT
INDEED.
IT SEEMS FROBISHER'S BEAK-IMPACT HAS CAUSED A MALFUNCTION IN THE WALL'S CLOAKING CIRCUITRY.
SINCE WE'RE HERE, LET'S HAVE A LOOK INSIDE THE CITY!
ANTARCTOPOLIS IS SUPPOSED TO BE A FANTASTIC PLACE TO VISIT.
AFTER YOU, MY FRIENDS!
INTO THE UNKNOWN, JUST HOW I LIKE IT!
EVERYBODY KEEP ALERT— LET'S TRY TO FIT IN AS MUCH AS POSSIBLE.
KEEP A LOW PROFILE!

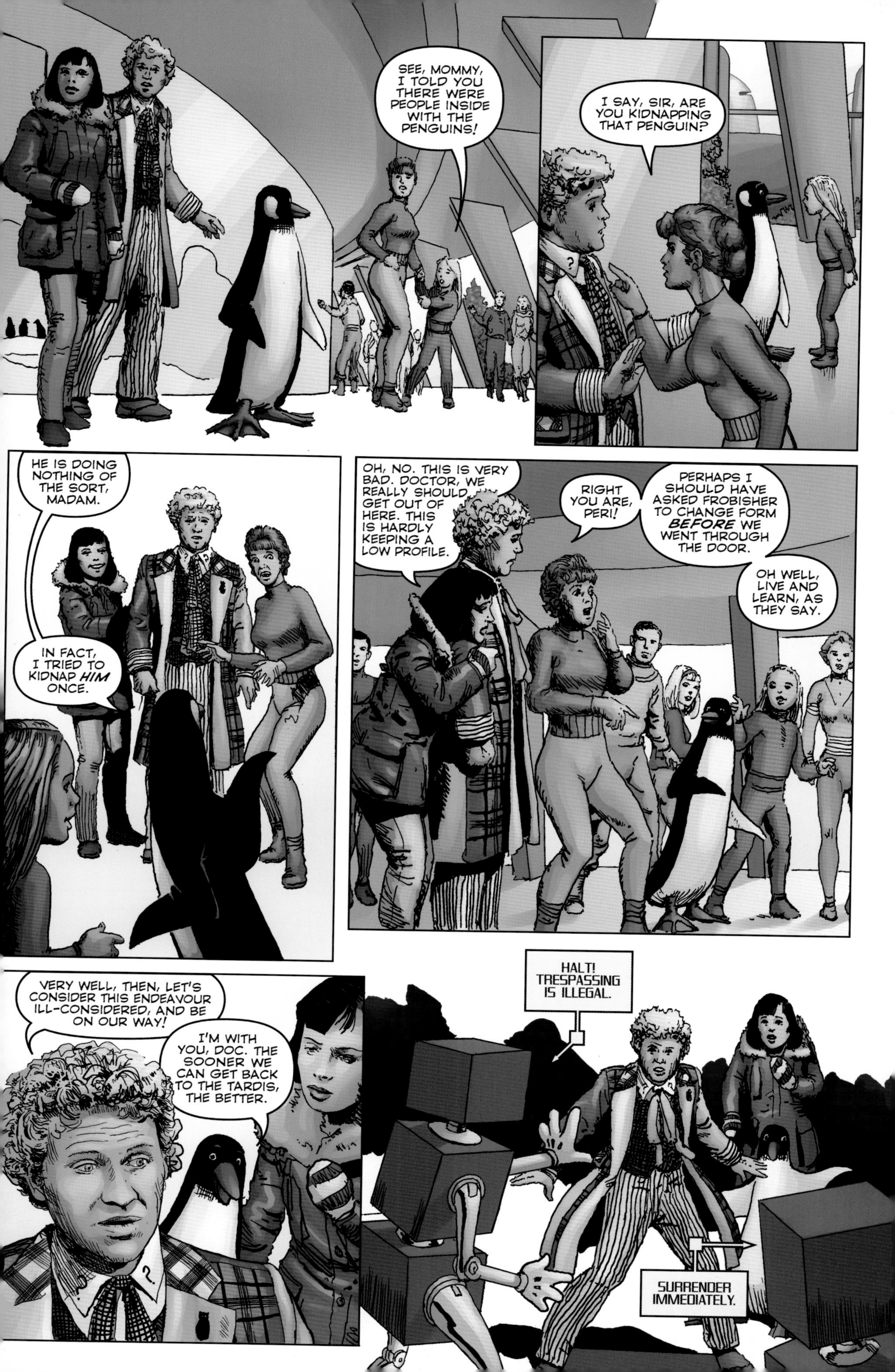
SEE, MOMMY, I TOLD YOU THERE WERE PEOPLE INSIDE WITH THE PENGUINS!
I SAY, SIR, ARE YOU KIDNAPPING THAT PENGUIN?
HE IS DOING NOTHING OF THE SORT, MADAM.
IN FACT, I TRIED TO KIDNAP HIM ONCE.
OH, NO. THIS IS VERY BAD. DOCTOR, WE REALLY SHOULD GET OUT OF HERE. THIS IS HARDLY KEEPING A LOW PROFILE.
RIGHT YOU ARE, PERI!
PERHAPS I SHOULD HAVE ASKED FROBISHER TO CHANGE FORM BEFORE WE WENT THROUGH THE DOOR.
OH WELL, LIVE AND LEARN, AS THEY SAY.
VERY WELL, THEN, LET'S CONSIDER THIS ENDEAVOUR ILL-CONSIDERED, AND BE ON OUR WAY!
I'M WITH YOU, DOC. THE SOONER WE CAN GET BACK TO THE TARDIS, THE BETTER.
HALT! TRESPASSING IS ILLEGAL.
SURRENDER IMMEDIATELY.

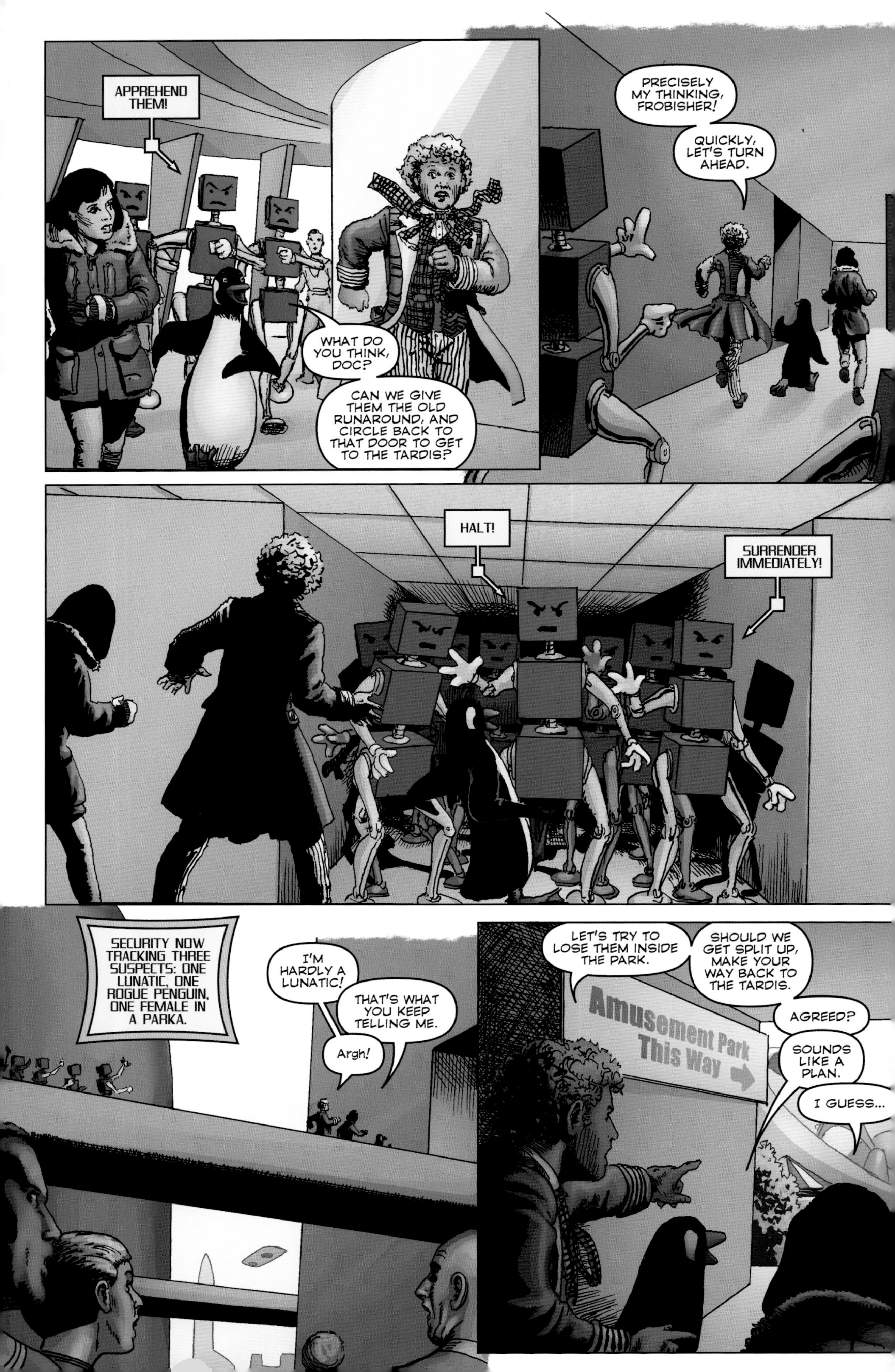
APPREHEND THEM!
WHAT DO YOU THINK, DOC?
CAN WE GIVE THEM THE OLD RUNAROUND, AND CIRCLE BACK TO THAT DOOR TO GET TO THE TARDIS?
PRECISELY MY THINKING, FROBISHER!
QUICKLY, LET'S TURN AHEAD.
HALT!
SURRENDER IMMEDIATELY!
SECURITY NOW TRACKING THREE SUSPECTS: ONE LUNATIC, ONE ROGUE PENGUIN, ONE FEMALE IN A PARKA.
I'M HARDLY A LUNATIC!
THAT'S WHAT YOU KEEP TELLING ME.
Argh!
LET'S TRY TO LOSE THEM INSIDE THE PARK.
SHOULD WE GET SPLIT UP, MAKE YOUR WAY BACK TO THE TARDIS.
AGREED?
Amusement Park This Way
SOUNDS LIKE A PLAN.
I GUESS...

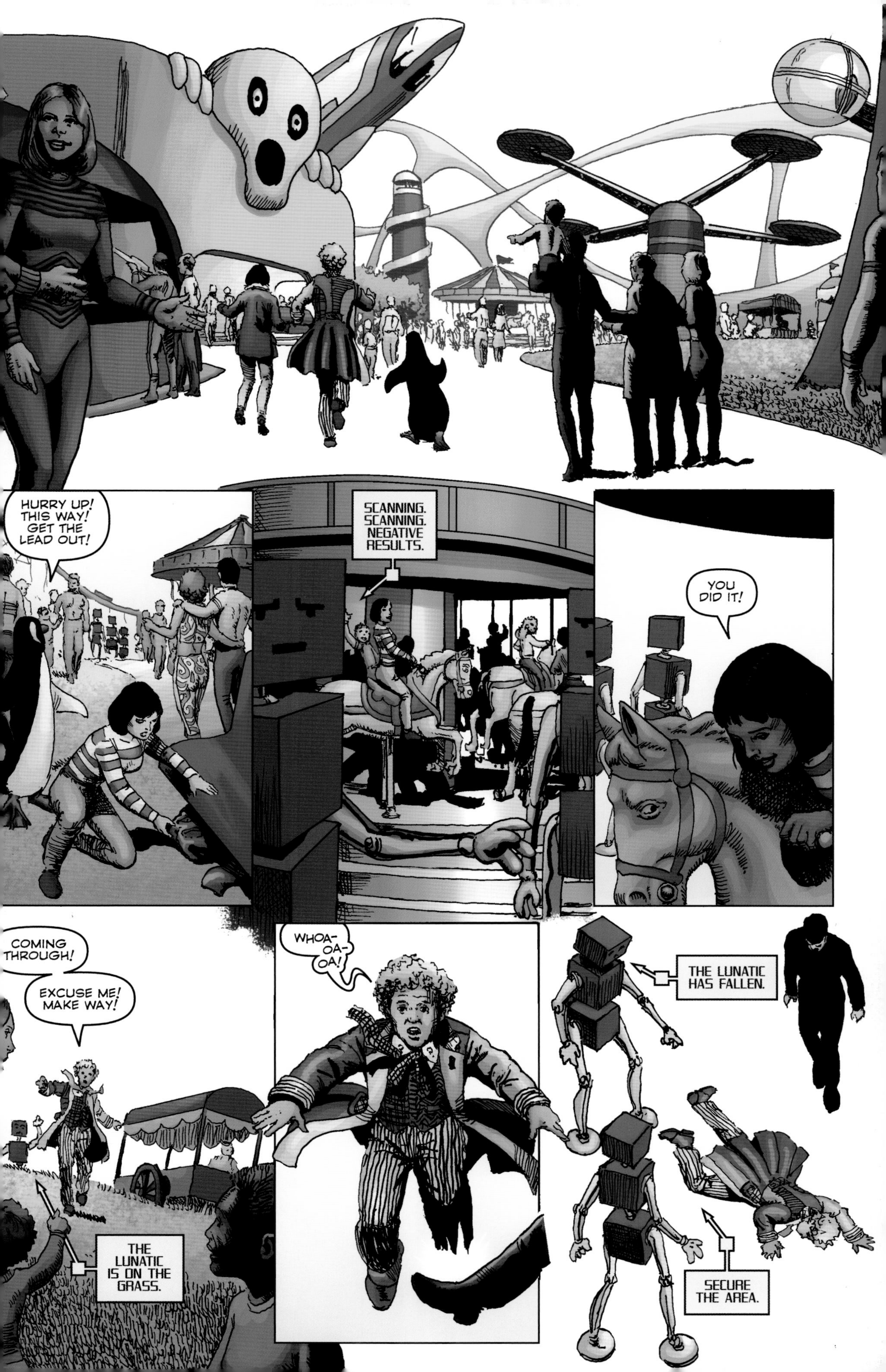
HURRY UP! THIS WAY! GET THE LEAD OUT!
SCANNING. SCANNING. NEGATIVE RESULTS.
YOU DID IT!
COMING THROUGH!
EXCUSE ME! MAKE WAY!
THE LUNATIC IS ON THE GRASS.
WHOA-OA-OA!
THE LUNATIC HAS FALLEN.
SECURE THE AREA.

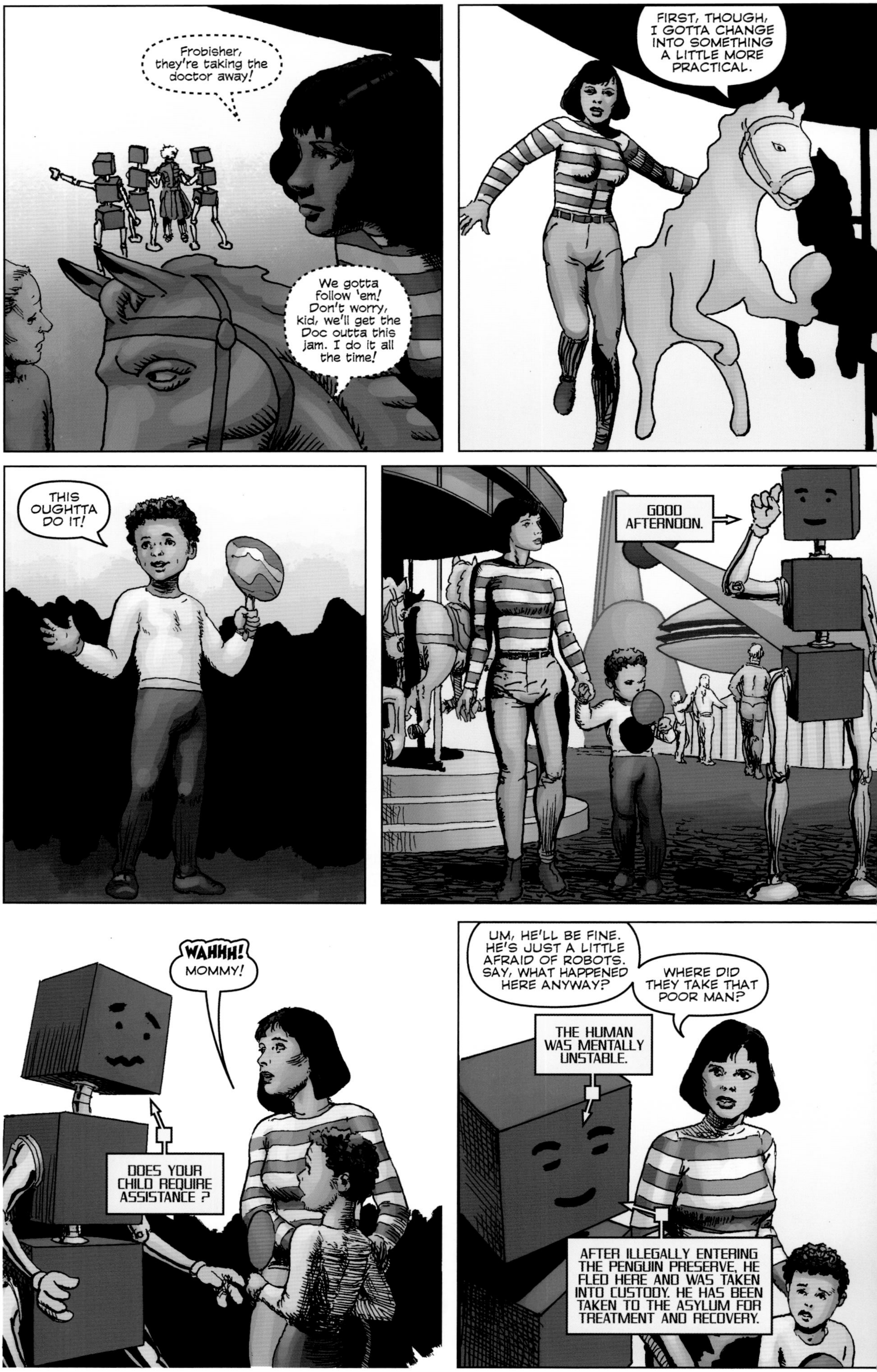

Frobisher, they're taking the doctor away!
We gotta follow 'em! Don't worry, kid, we'll get the Doc outta this jam. I do it all the time!
FIRST, THOUGH, I GOTTA CHANGE INTO SOMETHING A LITTLE MORE PRACTICAL.
THIS OUGHTTA DO IT!
GOOD AFTERNOON.
WAHHH! MOMMY!
DOES YOUR CHILD REQUIRE ASSISTANCE ?
UM, HE'LL BE FINE. HE'S JUST A LITTLE AFRAID OF ROBOTS. SAY, WHAT HAPPENED HERE ANYWAY?
WHERE DID THEY TAKE THAT POOR MAN?
THE HUMAN WAS MENTALLY UNSTABLE.
AFTER ILLEGALLY ENTERING THE PENGUIN PRESERVE, HE FLED HERE AND WAS TAKEN INTO CUSTODY. HE HAS BEEN TAKEN TO THE ASYLUM FOR TREATMENT AND RECOVERY.

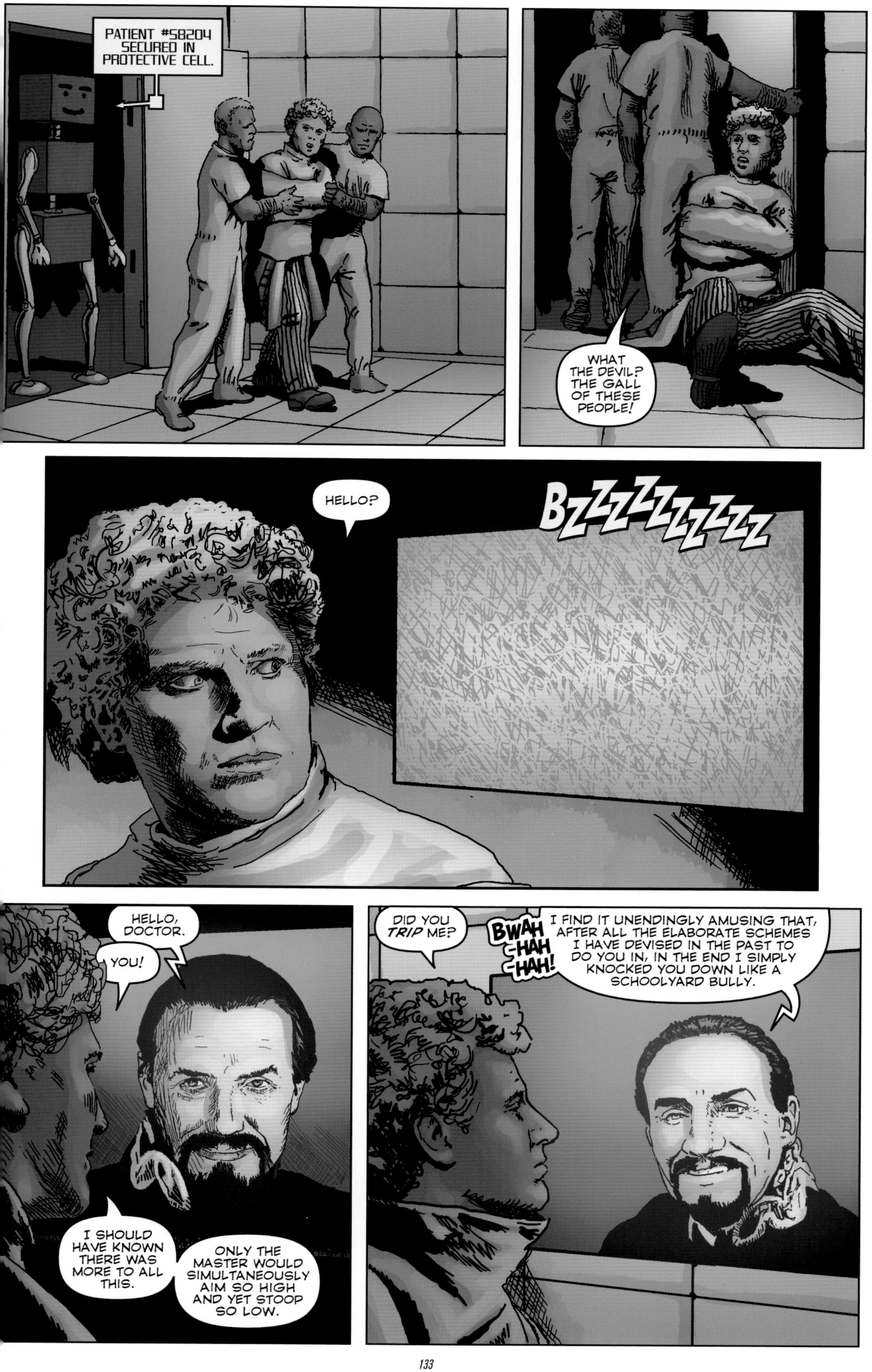
PATIENT #58204 SECURED IN PROTECTIVE CELL.
WHAT THE DEVIL? THE GALL OF THESE PEOPLE!
HELLO?
BZZZZZZZZZ
HELLO, DOCTOR.
YOU!
I SHOULD HAVE KNOWN THERE WAS MORE TO ALL THIS.
ONLY THE MASTER WOULD SIMULTANEOUSLY AIM SO HIGH AND YET STOOP SO LOW.
DID YOU TRIP ME?
BWAH-HAH-HAH!
I FIND IT UNENDINGLY AMUSING THAT, AFTER ALL THE ELABORATE SCHEMES I HAVE DEVISED IN THE PAST TO DO YOU IN, IN THE END I SIMPLY KNOCKED YOU DOWN LIKE A SCHOOLYARD BULLY.

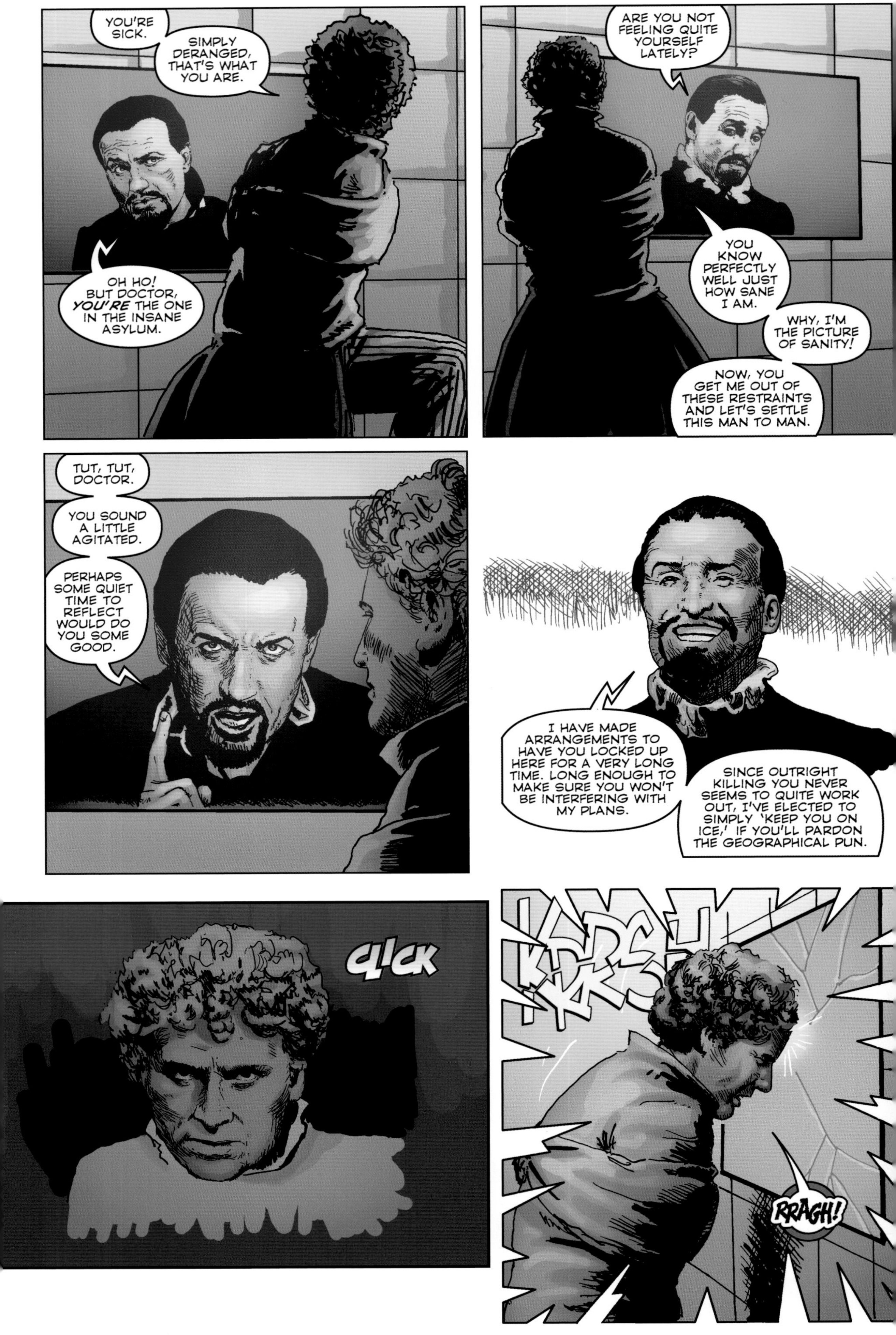
YOU'RE SICK.
SIMPLY DERANGED, THAT'S WHAT YOU ARE.
OH HO! BUT DOCTOR, *YOU'RE* THE ONE IN THE INSANE ASYLUM.
ARE YOU NOT FEELING QUITE YOURSELF LATELY?
YOU KNOW PERFECTLY WELL JUST HOW SANE I AM.
WHY, I'M THE PICTURE OF SANITY!
NOW, YOU GET ME OUT OF THESE RESTRAINTS AND LET'S SETTLE THIS MAN TO MAN.
TUT, TUT, DOCTOR.
YOU SOUND A LITTLE AGITATED.
PERHAPS SOME QUIET TIME TO REFLECT WOULD DO YOU SOME GOOD.
I HAVE MADE ARRANGEMENTS TO HAVE YOU LOCKED UP HERE FOR A VERY LONG TIME. LONG ENOUGH TO MAKE SURE YOU WON'T BE INTERFERING WITH MY PLANS.
SINCE OUTRIGHT KILLING YOU NEVER SEEMS TO QUITE WORK OUT, I'VE ELECTED TO SIMPLY 'KEEP YOU ON ICE,' IF YOU'LL PARDON THE GEOGRAPHICAL PUN.
CLICK
KRRSH
RRAGH!

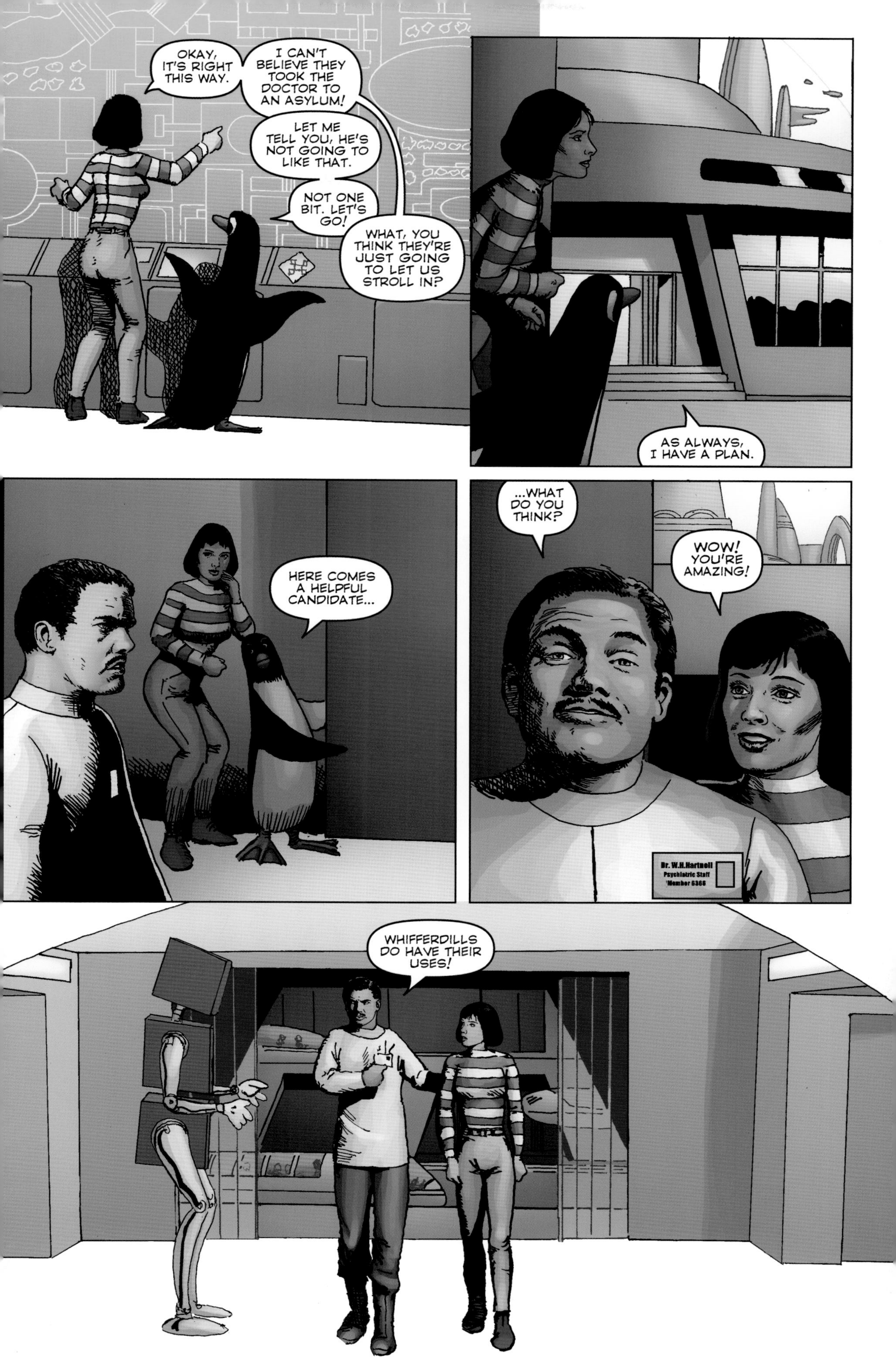

OKAY, IT'S RIGHT THIS WAY.
I CAN'T BELIEVE THEY TOOK THE DOCTOR TO AN ASYLUM!
LET ME TELL YOU, HE'S NOT GOING TO LIKE THAT.
NOT ONE BIT. LET'S GO!
WHAT, YOU THINK THEY'RE JUST GOING TO LET US STROLL IN?
AS ALWAYS, I HAVE A PLAN.
HERE COMES A HELPFUL CANDIDATE...
...WHAT DO YOU THINK?
WOW! YOU'RE AMAZING!
Dr. W.H.Hartnell
Psychiatric Staff
Member 6366
WHIFFERDILLS DO HAVE THEIR USES!

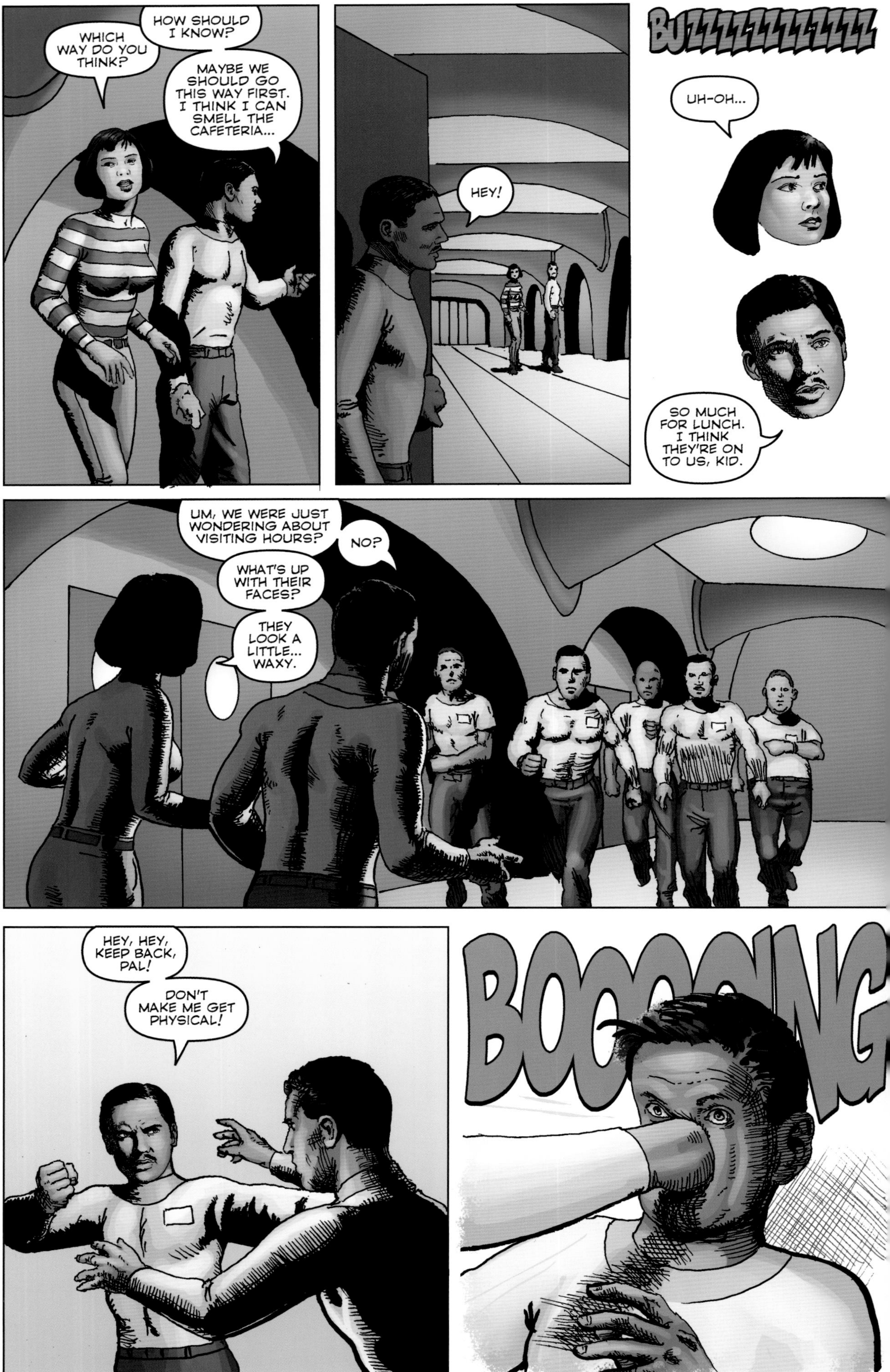
WHICH WAY DO YOU THINK?
HOW SHOULD I KNOW?
MAYBE WE SHOULD GO THIS WAY FIRST. I THINK I CAN SMELL THE CAFETERIA...
HEY!
BUZZZZZZZZZZZ
UH-OH...
SO MUCH FOR LUNCH. I THINK THEY'RE ON TO US, KID.
UM, WE WERE JUST WONDERING ABOUT VISITING HOURS?
NO?
WHAT'S UP WITH THEIR FACES?
THEY LOOK A LITTLE... WAXY.
HEY, HEY, KEEP BACK, PAL!
DON'T MAKE ME GET PHYSICAL!
BOOOOING

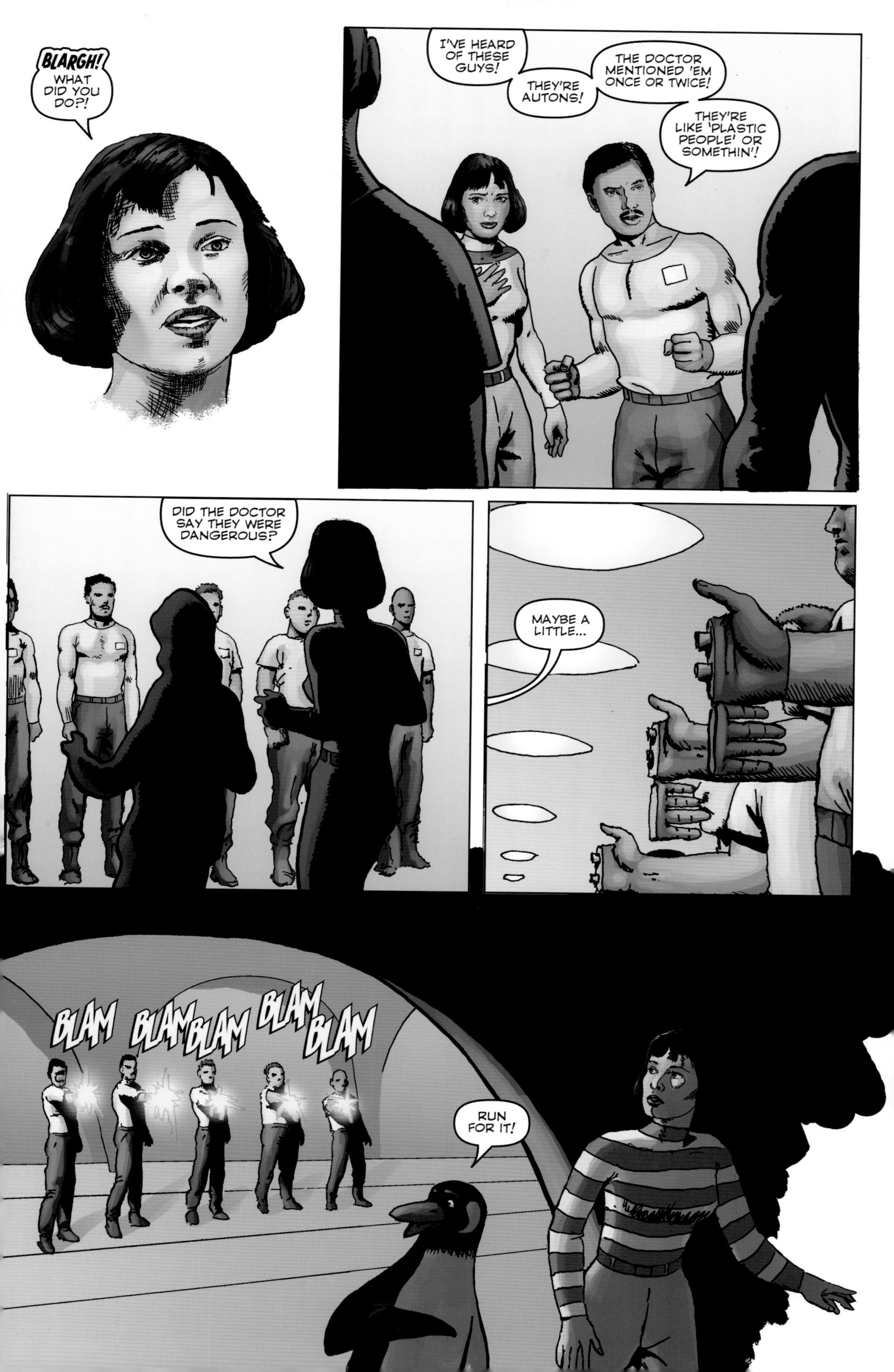
BLARGH! WHAT DID YOU DO?!
I'VE HEARD OF THESE GUYS!
THEY'RE AUTONS!
THE DOCTOR MENTIONED 'EM ONCE OR TWICE!
THEY'RE LIKE 'PLASTIC PEOPLE' OR SOMETHIN'!
DID THE DOCTOR SAY THEY WERE DANGEROUS?
MAYBE A LITTLE...
BLAM BLAM BLAM BLAM BLAM
RUN FOR IT!

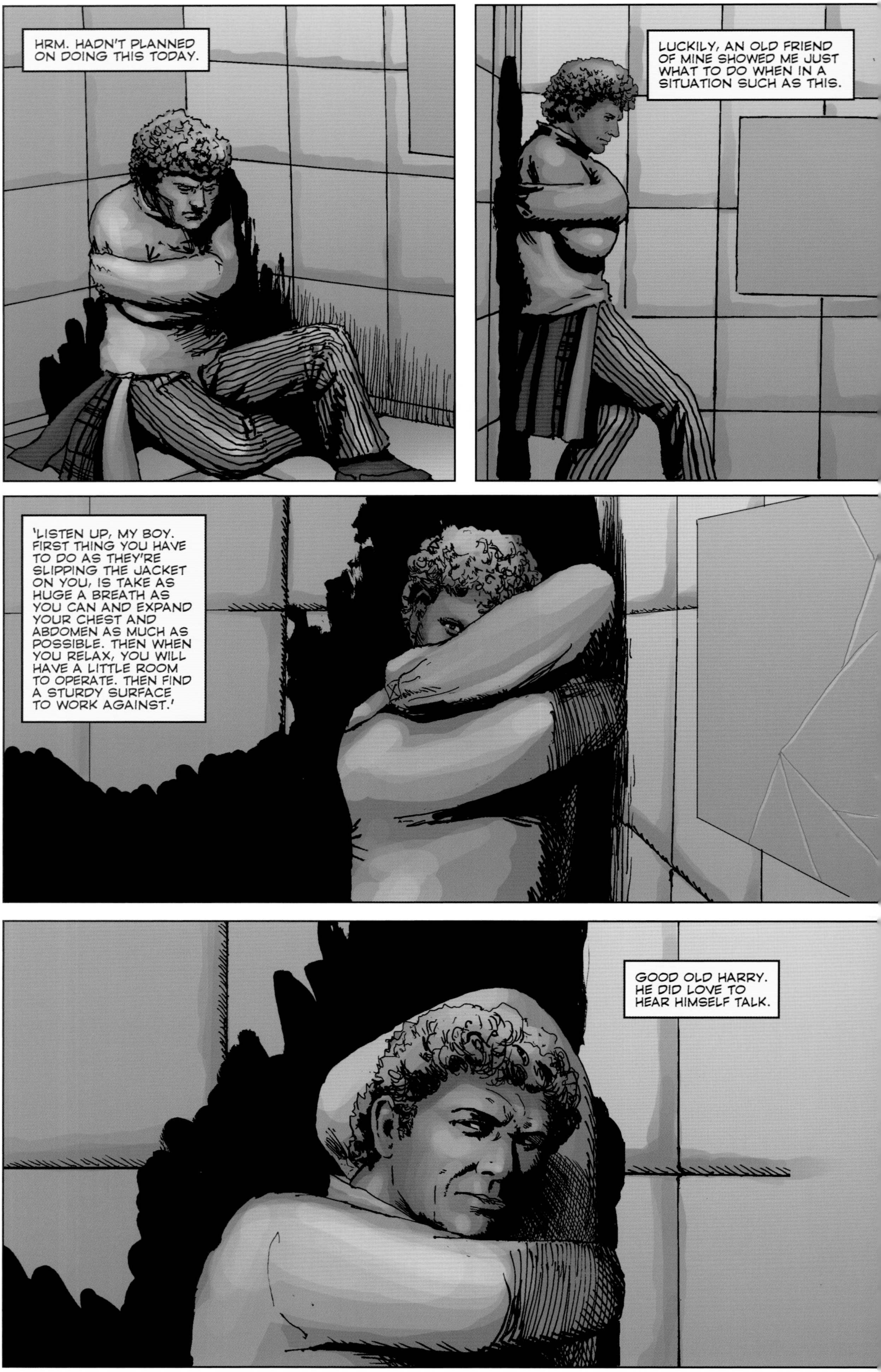
HRM. HADN'T PLANNED ON DOING THIS TODAY.
LUCKILY, AN OLD FRIEND OF MINE SHOWED ME JUST WHAT TO DO WHEN IN A SITUATION SUCH AS THIS.
'LISTEN UP, MY BOY. FIRST THING YOU HAVE TO DO AS THEY'RE SLIPPING THE JACKET ON YOU, IS TAKE AS HUGE A BREATH AS YOU CAN AND EXPAND YOUR CHEST AND ABDOMEN AS MUCH AS POSSIBLE. THEN WHEN YOU RELAX, YOU WILL HAVE A LITTLE ROOM TO OPERATE. THEN FIND A STURDY SURFACE TO WORK AGAINST.'
GOOD OLD HARRY. HE DID LOVE TO HEAR HIMSELF TALK.

A LITTLE OBSESSED WITH HIS MOTHER, BUT A GOOD EGG NONETHELESS.

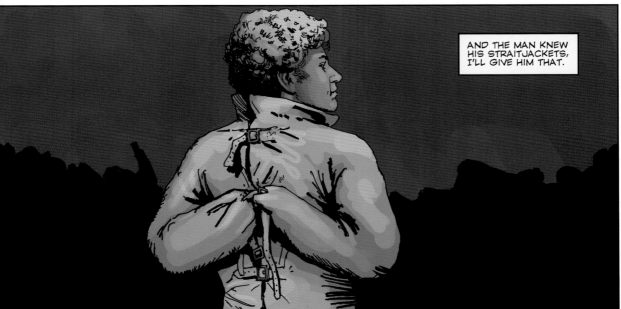

AND THE MAN KNEW HIS STRAITJACKETS, I'LL GIVE HIM THAT.

NOW HOPEFULLY NO ONE'S SEEN MY LITTLE FLOOR SHOW...

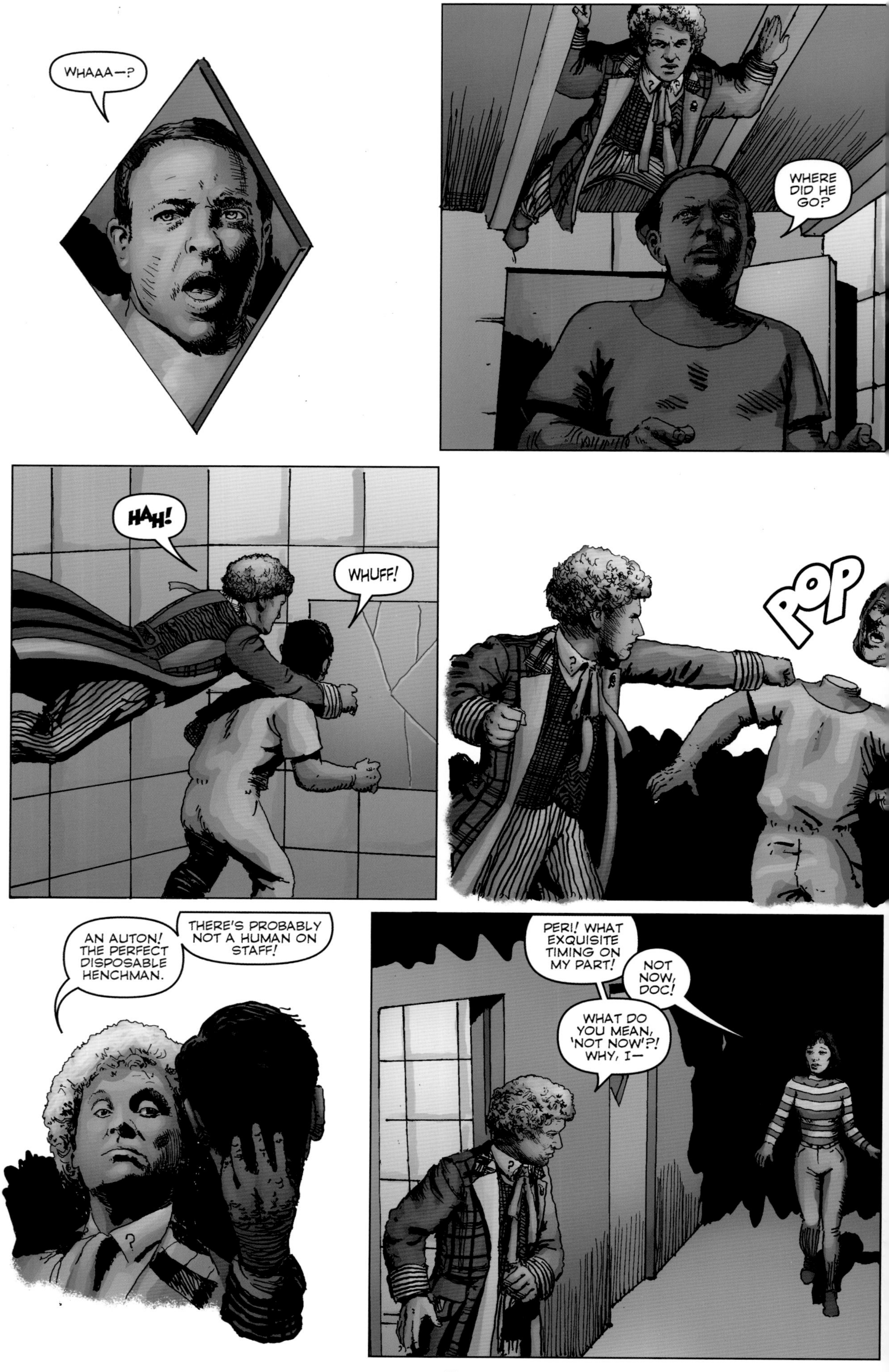
WHAAA—?
WHERE DID HE GO?
HAH!
WHUFF!
POP
AN AUTON! THE PERFECT DISPOSABLE HENCHMAN.
THERE'S PROBABLY NOT A HUMAN ON STAFF!
PERI! WHAT EXQUISITE TIMING ON MY PART!
NOT NOW, DOC!
WHAT DO YOU MEAN, 'NOT NOW'?! WHY, I—

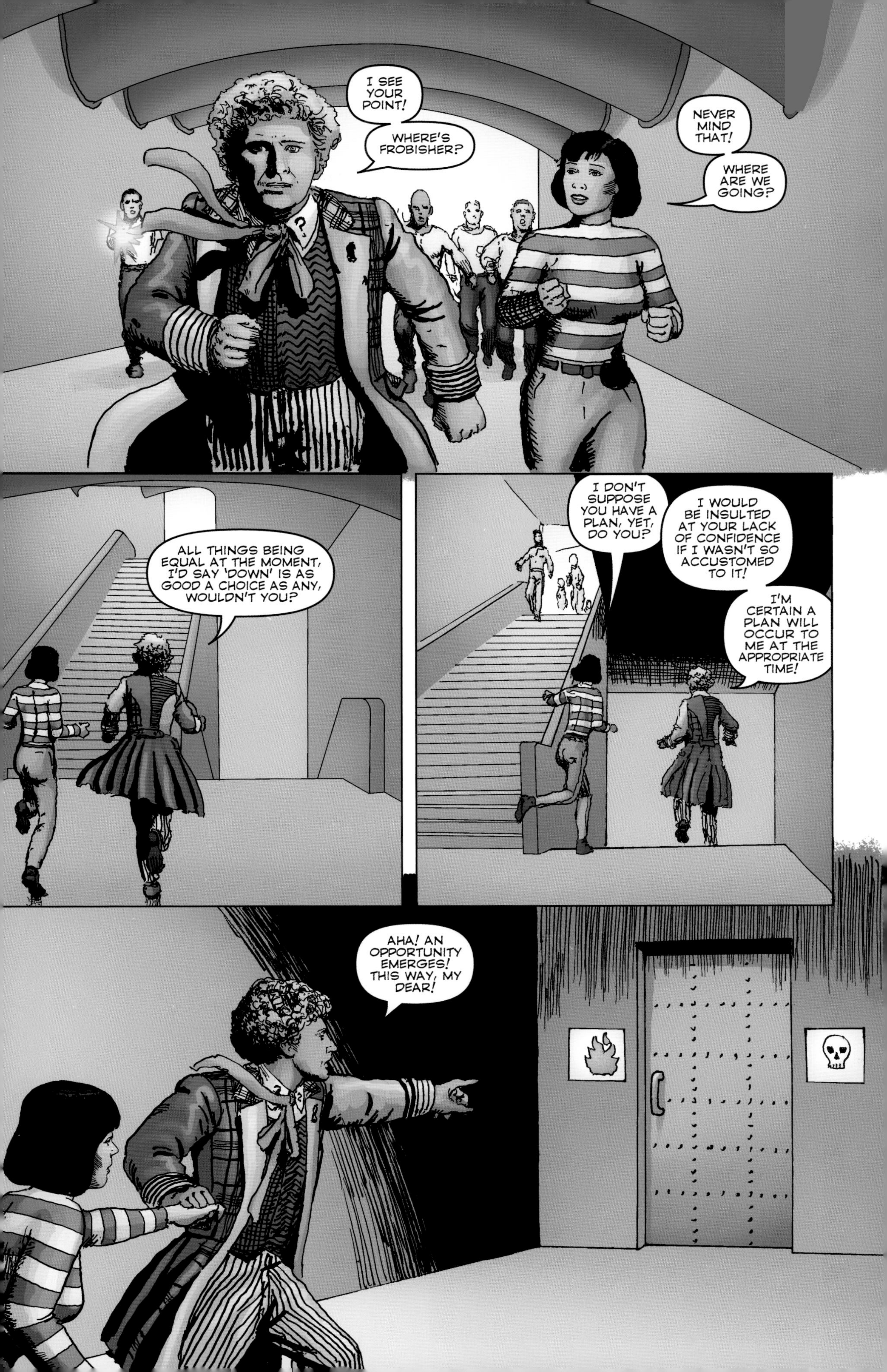
I SEE YOUR POINT!
WHERE'S FROBISHER?
NEVER MIND THAT!
WHERE ARE WE GOING?
ALL THINGS BEING EQUAL AT THE MOMENT, I'D SAY 'DOWN' IS AS GOOD A CHOICE AS ANY, WOULDN'T YOU?
I DON'T SUPPOSE YOU HAVE A PLAN, YET, DO YOU?
I WOULD BE INSULTED AT YOUR LACK OF CONFIDENCE IF I WASN'T SO ACCUSTOMED TO IT!
I'M CERTAIN A PLAN WILL OCCUR TO ME AT THE APPROPRIATE TIME!
AHA! AN OPPORTUNITY EMERGES! THIS WAY, MY DEAR!

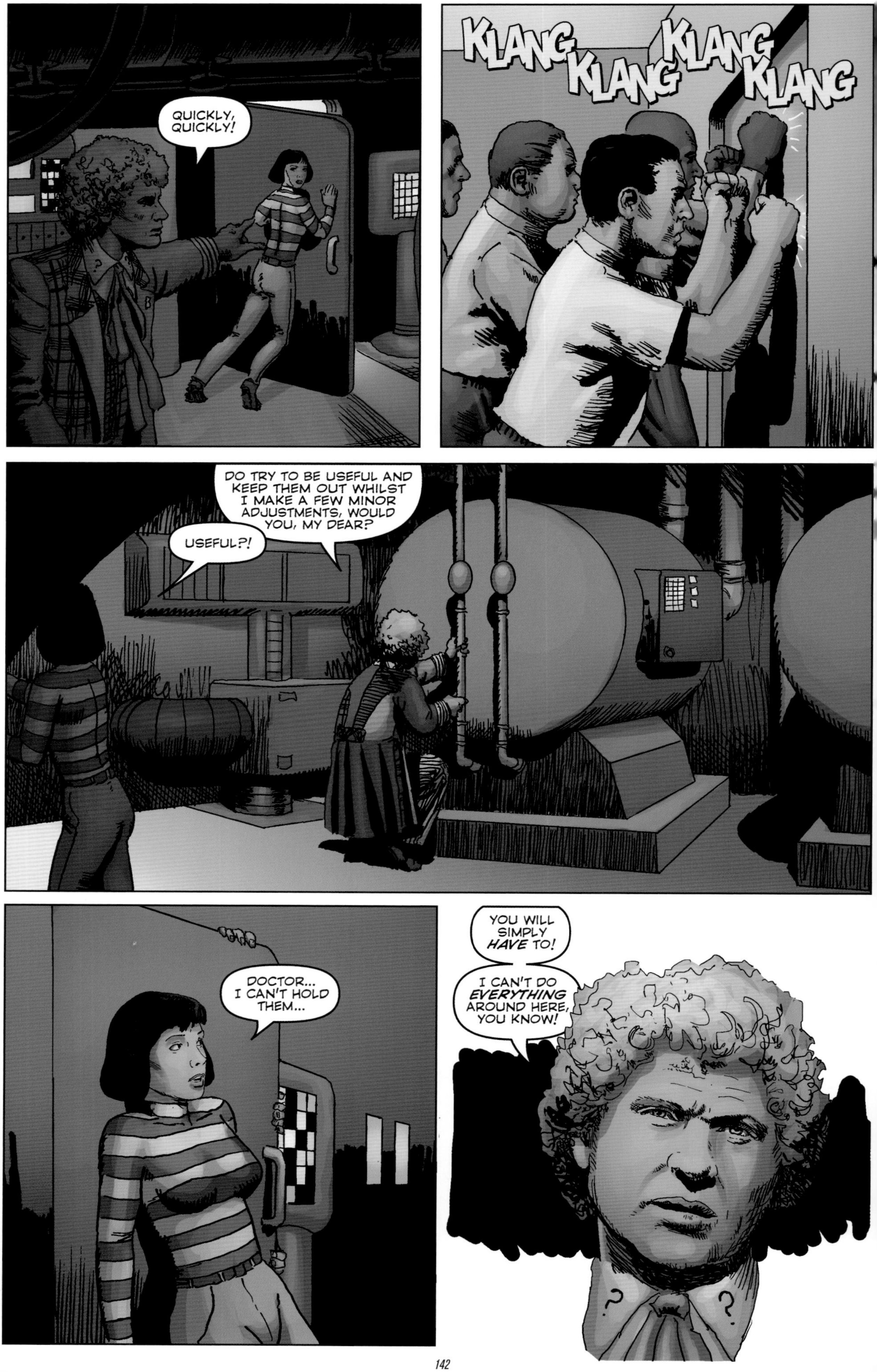
QUICKLY, QUICKLY!
KLANG KLANG KLANG KLANG
DO TRY TO BE USEFUL AND KEEP THEM OUT WHILST I MAKE A FEW MINOR ADJUSTMENTS, WOULD YOU, MY DEAR?
USEFUL?!
DOCTOR... I CAN'T HOLD THEM...
YOU WILL SIMPLY *HAVE* TO!
I CAN'T DO *EVERYTHING* AROUND HERE, YOU KNOW!

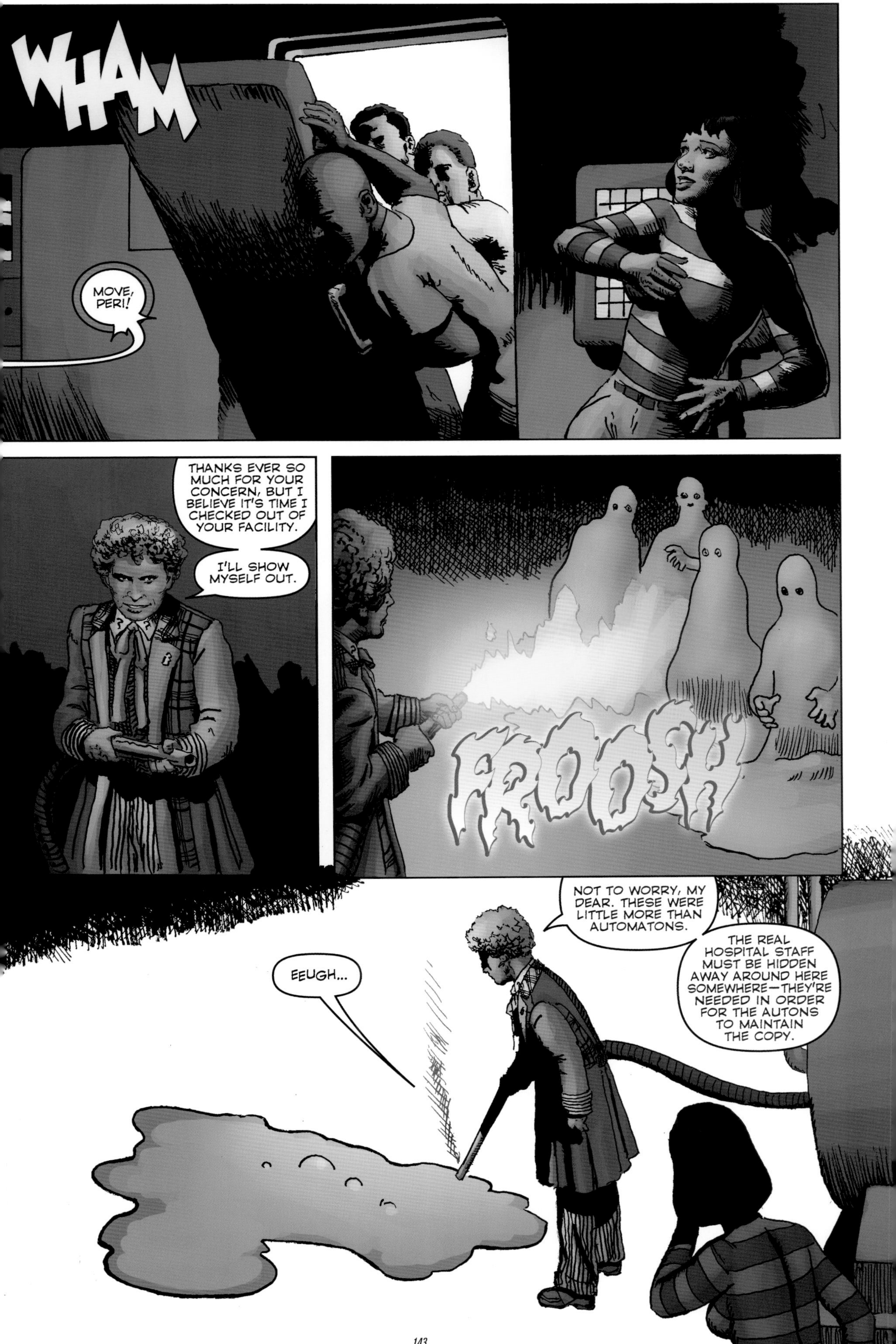
WHAM
MOVE, PERI!
THANKS EVER SO MUCH FOR YOUR CONCERN, BUT I BELIEVE IT'S TIME I CHECKED OUT OF YOUR FACILITY.
I'LL SHOW MYSELF OUT.
FROOSH
NOT TO WORRY, MY DEAR. THESE WERE LITTLE MORE THAN AUTOMATONS.
THE REAL HOSPITAL STAFF MUST BE HIDDEN AWAY AROUND HERE SOMEWHERE—THEY'RE NEEDED IN ORDER FOR THE AUTONS TO MAINTAIN THE COPY.
EEUGH...

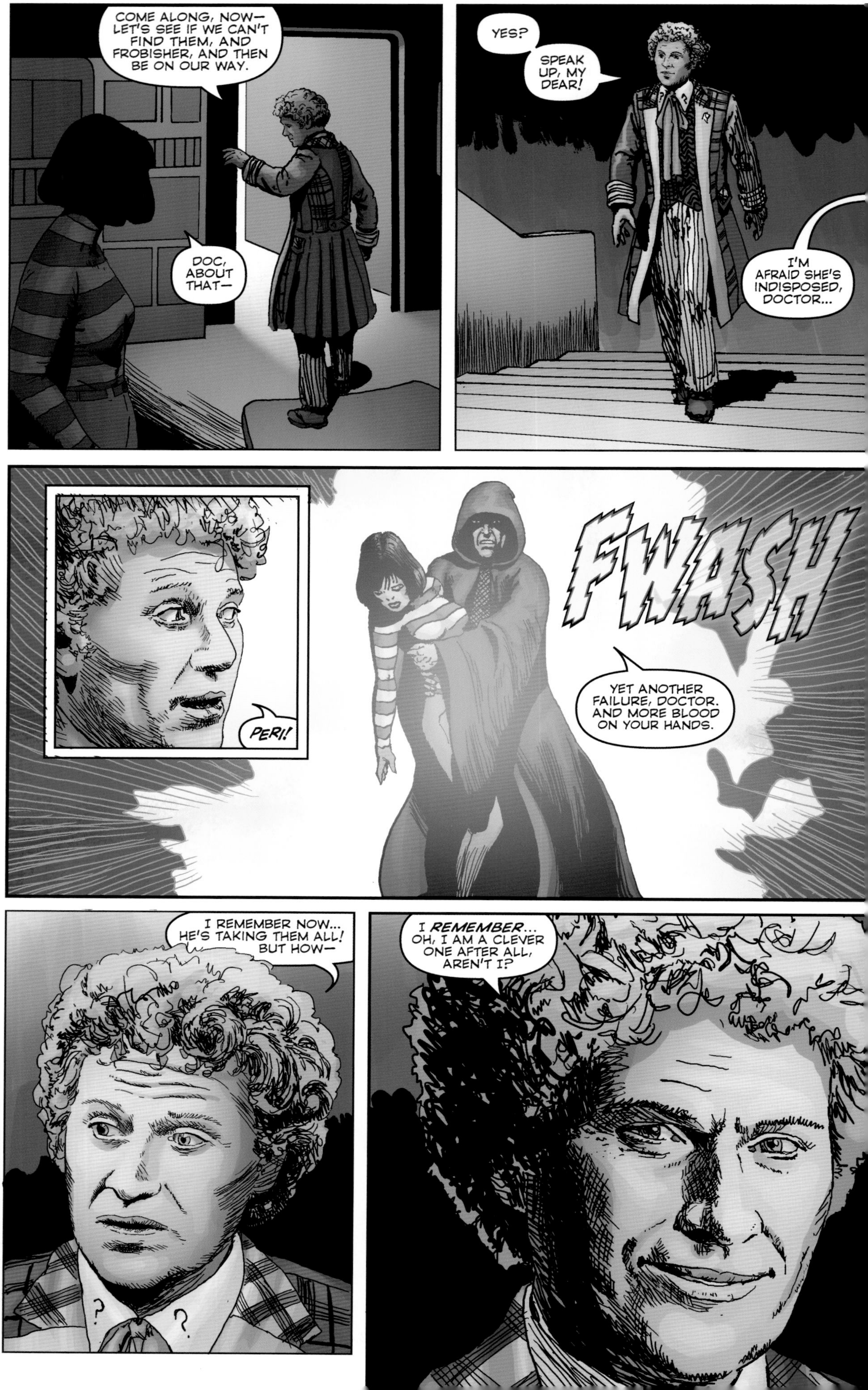
COME ALONG, NOW— LET'S SEE IF WE CAN'T FIND THEM, AND FROBISHER, AND THEN BE ON OUR WAY.
DOC, ABOUT THAT—
YES?
SPEAK UP, MY DEAR!
I'M AFRAID SHE'S INDISPOSED, DOCTOR...
PERI!
FWASH
YET ANOTHER FAILURE, DOCTOR. AND MORE BLOOD ON YOUR HANDS.
I REMEMBER NOW... HE'S TAKING THEM ALL! BUT HOW—
I *REMEMBER*... OH, I AM A CLEVER ONE AFTER ALL, AREN'T I?

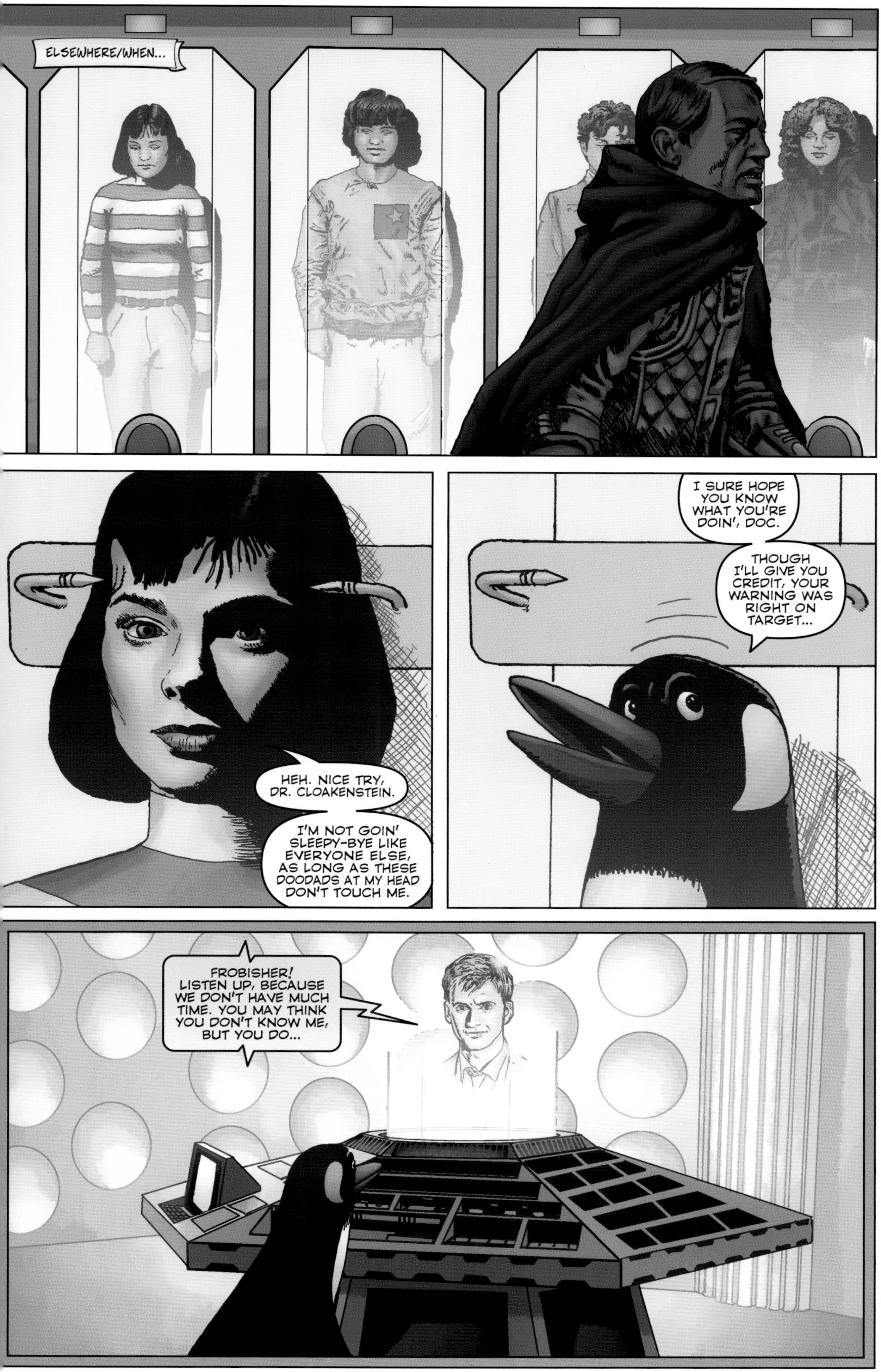
ELSEWHERE/WHEN...
HEH. NICE TRY, DR. CLOAKENSTEIN.
I'M NOT GOIN' SLEEPY-BYE LIKE EVERYONE ELSE, AS LONG AS THESE DOODADS AT MY HEAD DON'T TOUCH ME.
I SURE HOPE YOU KNOW WHAT YOU'RE DOIN', DOC.
THOUGH I'LL GIVE YOU CREDIT, YOUR WARNING WAS RIGHT ON TARGET...
FROBISHER! LISTEN UP, BECAUSE WE DON'T HAVE MUCH TIME. YOU MAY THINK YOU DON'T KNOW ME, BUT YOU DO...

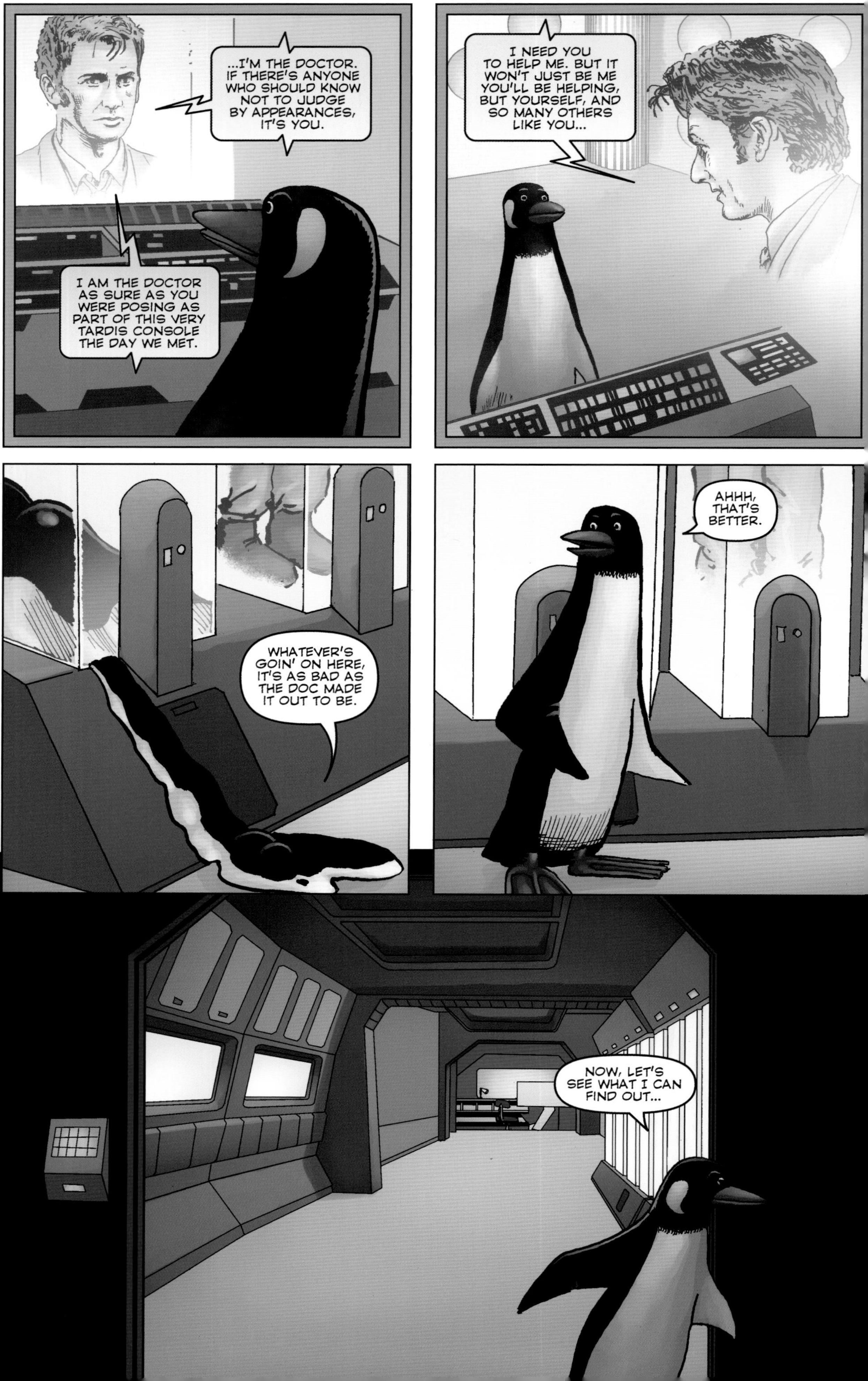
...I'M THE DOCTOR. IF THERE'S ANYONE WHO SHOULD KNOW NOT TO JUDGE BY APPEARANCES, IT'S YOU.
I AM THE DOCTOR AS SURE AS YOU WERE POSING AS PART OF THIS VERY TARDIS CONSOLE THE DAY WE MET.
I NEED YOU TO HELP ME. BUT IT WON'T JUST BE ME YOU'LL BE HELPING, BUT YOURSELF, AND SO MANY OTHERS LIKE YOU...
WHATEVER'S GOIN' ON HERE, IT'S AS BAD AS THE DOC MADE IT OUT TO BE.
AHHH, THAT'S BETTER.
NOW, LET'S SEE WHAT I CAN FIND OUT...

REFLECTIONS OF TIME

Wherein prominent Whovians past and present muse upon the Doctor's history in comic form.

It's no real secret that Colin Baker, the actor who portrayed the Sixth Doctor on television, wasn't entirely satisfied by the way he was asked to play the character, feeling too much time was spent being unpleasant and shouty—he enjoyed exploring the darker side of the Doctor, but still wanted to retain something of the Doctor's joy at the universe, rather than yelling at it.

It is therefore no surprise to learn that he was a huge fan of the concurrent run of comic strips featuring his Doctor—and this pleasure can be laid squarely at the feet of three people: writer Steve Parkhouse, editor/writer Alan McKenzie, and, most of all, the gorgeous black-and-white artwork of John Ridgway, quite possibly the finest artist and storyteller ever to work on the *Doctor Who* comic strips.

Parkhouse and McKenzie constructed clever, post-modern stories that stretched and flowed over many issues, predicting the 'season arcs' that would dominate fantasy television years later. Each time a particular story seemed to end, there were enough running threads and arcs that kept you hanging on for more, and brilliant as they were in each installment, re-reading the whole run enabled fans to see the most intricate and beautiful and complex-without-being-unfathomable storytelling that the strip had ever been fortunate enough to print.

From 'The Shape-Shifter' right through to 'Frobisher's Story' (more about whom later), in what collectively is known as 'Voyager', these three creators wove magic, elevating both the strip and the Sixth Doctor to heights the TV producers could only dream of, unrestricted by budget or imagination.

Even when 'Voyager' was over, the effect could be felt over the remaining Sixth Doctor stories and beyond, into those of the Seventh, when Frobisher finally departed. And what of Frobisher? Finally a companion created for the comic strip who simply couldn't work on television and yet sits aside the Doctor so perfectly. A shape-changing alien Whifferdill, a lame PI from Xenon, who gets stuck as a penguin (although it was more probably by choice). Caustic, smart, comical, and passionately loyal, Frobisher was both the most memorable and the most recognisable companion ever created purely for the comic strips (his subsequent appearances in novels and audio plays accentuates this). For a while, the Doctor and Frobisher were also joined by TV companion Peri Brown (the first human one to do so since Sarah Jane Smith in *TV Comic*) and Frobisher and Peri had a delightful brotherly/sisterly relationship, playful and cheeky. When Peri left the strip, Frobisher was left despondent by this.

But there's more to the Sixth Doctor strips than the 'Voyager' run—after Parkhouse and McKenzie (the latter's swan song was a superbly dark story about humans being converted into Cybermen, into which Ridgway drew himself as one of their victims), writers such as Grant Morrison, Jamie Delano, Simon Furman, and Mike Collins took the reins, but the one constant, the one benchmark of quality was always John Ridgway's artwork. The writers gave the strip some of their best work, as if never wanting to let the artist down. The *Doctor Who* strip had had many highlights before (the *Countdown/TV Action* years of the Third Doctor, the early Fourth Doctor strips by Pat Mills and John Wagner, and the Fifth Doctor's amazing 'The Tides of Time'), but never before had the mix of writers and one superb artist created a flawless run of adventures for the entirety of one Doctor's run.

—Gary Russell,
author, former BBC Drama script editor, former *Doctor Who Magazine* editor, and producer for Big Finish Productions

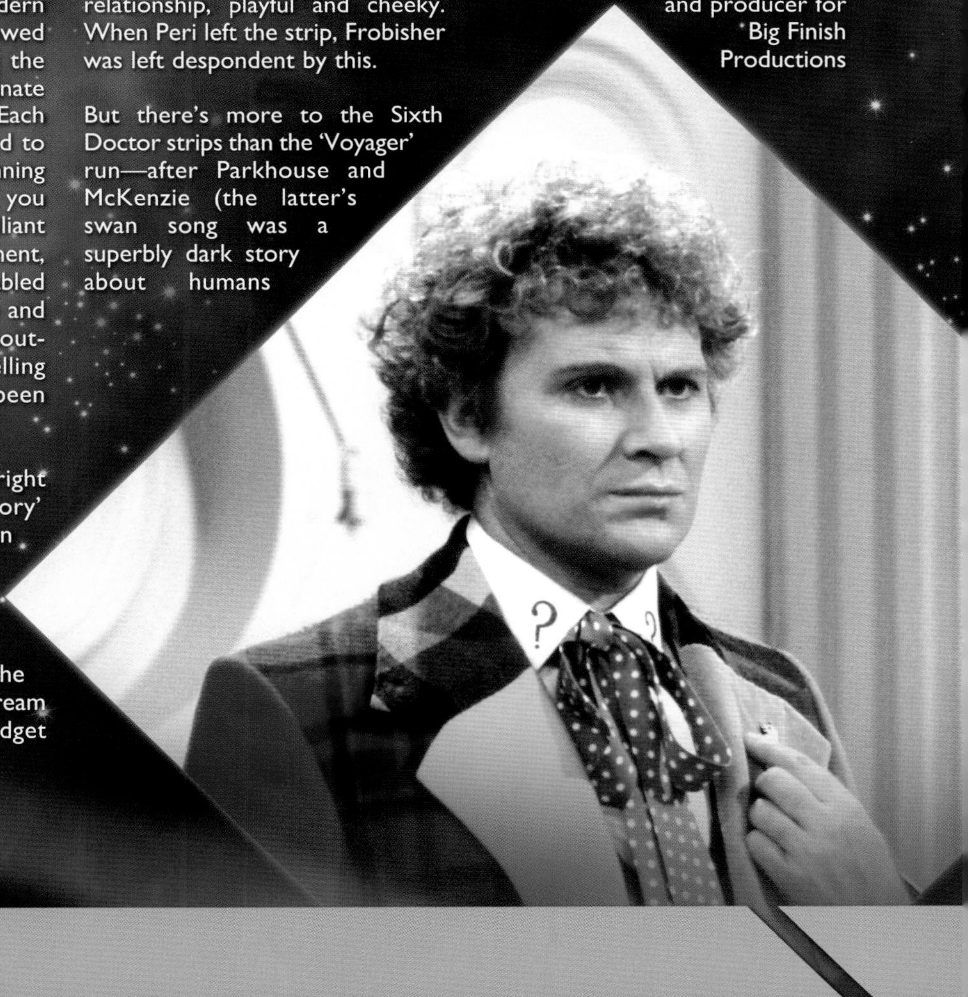

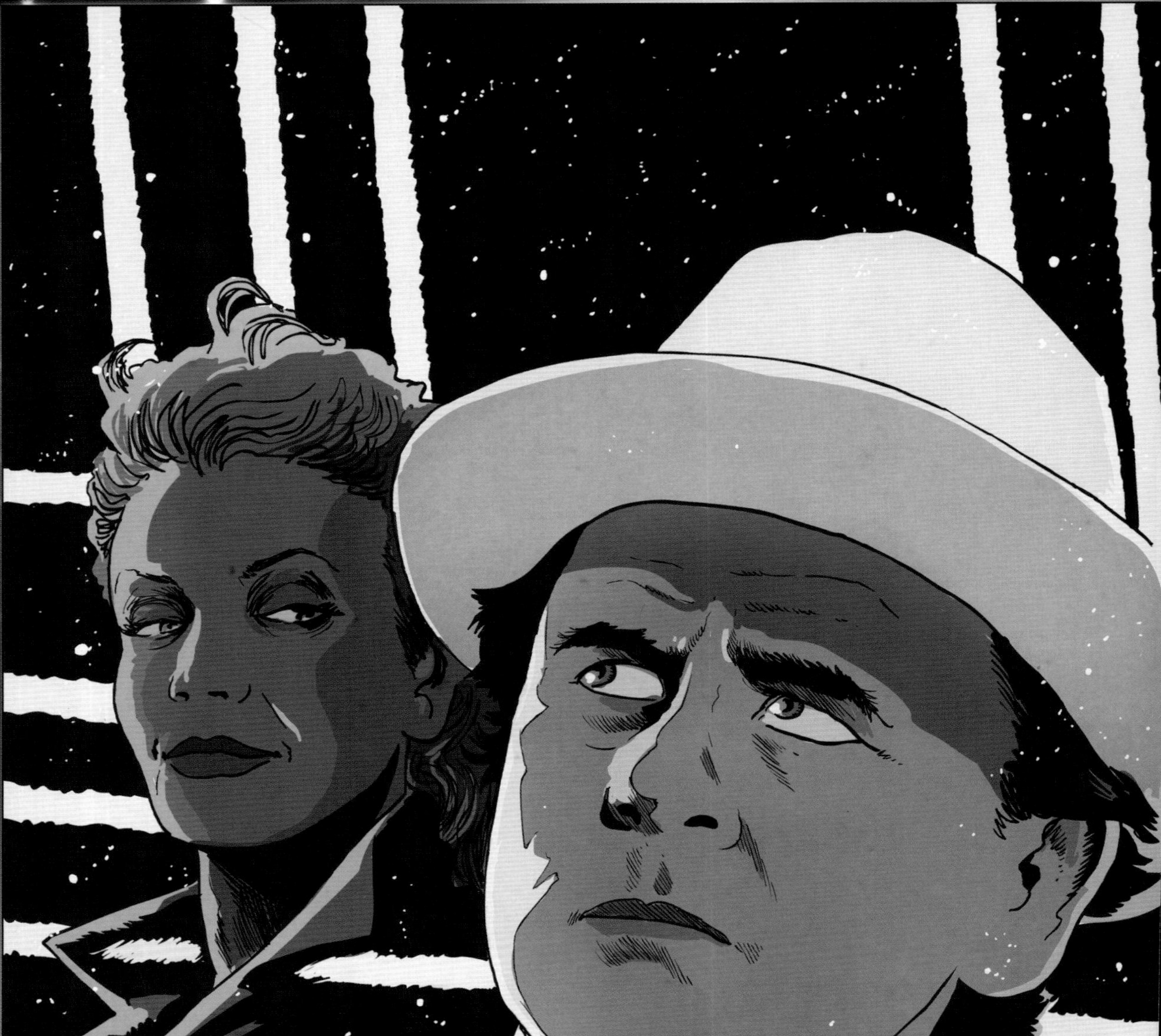
FRAN
CAVIL
LA F. 13

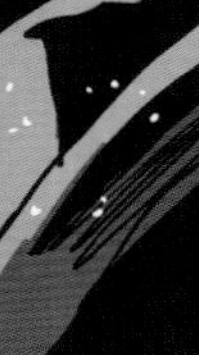

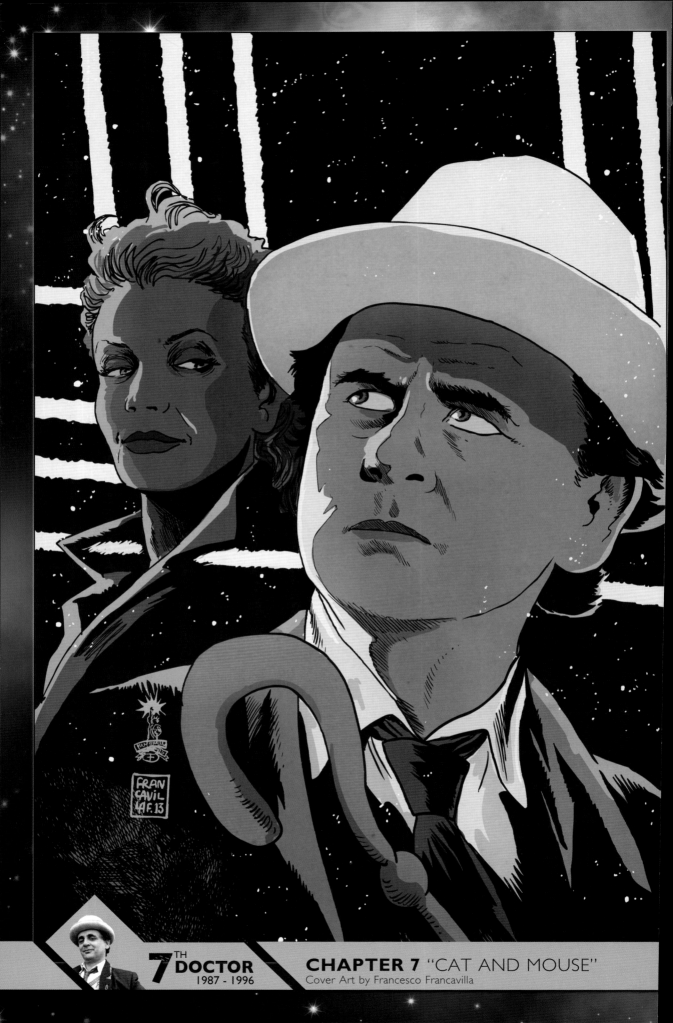

7TH DOCTOR
1987 - 1996

CHAPTER 7 "CAT AND MOUSE"

Cover Art by Francesco Francavilla

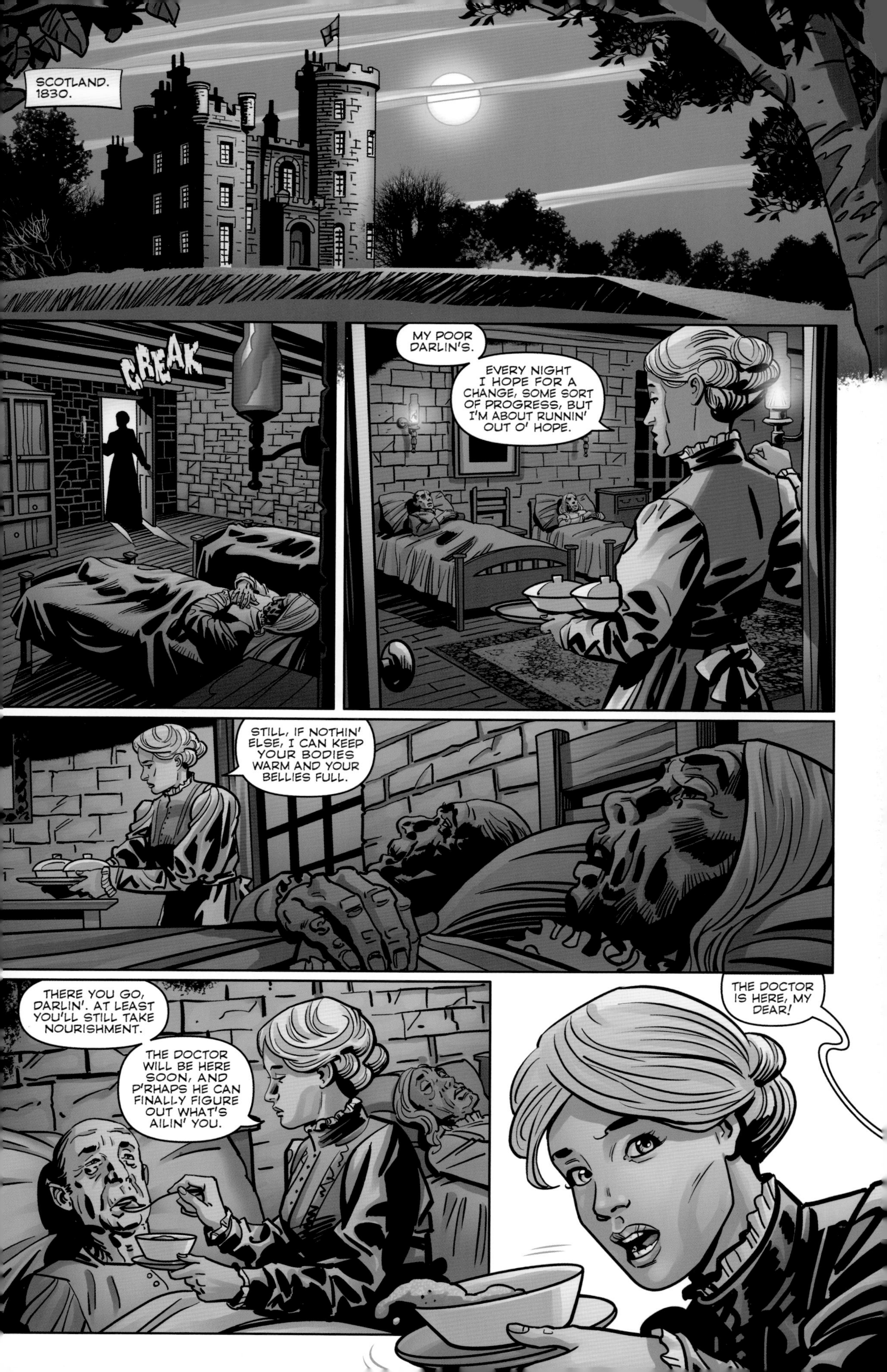
SCOTLAND. 1830.
CREAK
MY POOR DARLIN'S.
EVERY NIGHT I HOPE FOR A CHANGE, SOME SORT OF PROGRESS, BUT I'M ABOUT RUNNIN' OUT O' HOPE.
STILL, IF NOTHIN' ELSE, I CAN KEEP YOUR BODIES WARM AND YOUR BELLIES FULL.
THERE YOU GO, DARLIN'. AT LEAST YOU'LL STILL TAKE NOURISHMENT.
THE DOCTOR WILL BE HERE SOON, AND P'RHAPS HE CAN FINALLY FIGURE OUT WHAT'S AILIN' YOU.
THE DOCTOR IS HERE, MY DEAR!

AND I DARESAY, IF I CAN'T FIGURE OUT WHAT'S WRONG WITH YOUR PATIENTS, NO ONE CAN.

MODEST AS ALWAYS, EH, PROFESSOR?

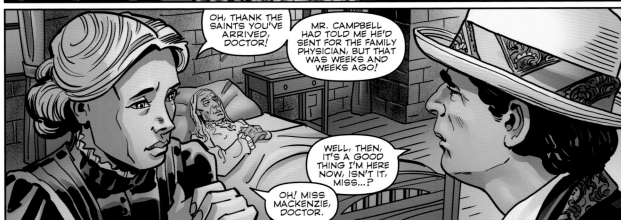

OH, THANK THE SAINTS YOU'VE ARRIVED, DOCTOR!

MR. CAMPBELL HAD TOLD ME HE'D SENT FOR THE FAMILY PHYSICIAN, BUT THAT WAS WEEKS AND WEEKS AGO!

WELL, THEN, IT'S A GOOD THING I'M HERE NOW, ISN'T IT, MISS...?

OH! MISS MACKENZIE, DOCTOR.

A PLEASURE. THIS IS MY ASSISTANT, ACE.

HIYA!

UM... HELLO.

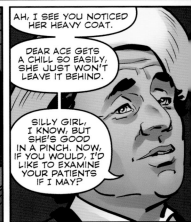

AH, I SEE YOU NOTICED HER HEAVY COAT.

DEAR ACE GETS A CHILL SO EASILY, SHE JUST WON'T LEAVE IT BEHIND.

SILLY GIRL, I KNOW, BUT SHE'S GOOD IN A PINCH. NOW, IF YOU WOULD, I'D LIKE TO EXAMINE YOUR PATIENTS IF I MAY?

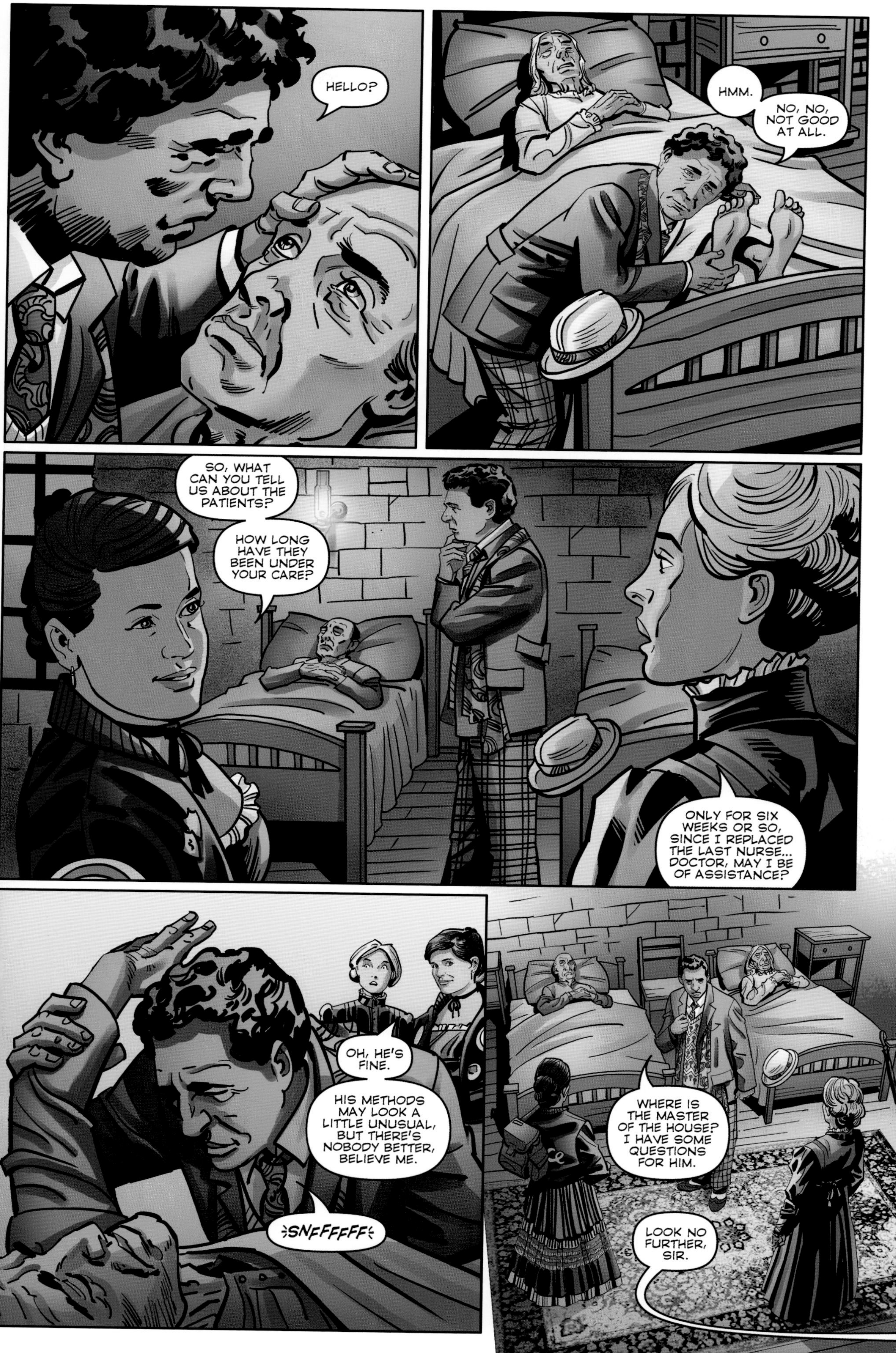
HELLO?
HMM.
NO, NO, NOT GOOD AT ALL.
SO, WHAT CAN YOU TELL US ABOUT THE PATIENTS?
HOW LONG HAVE THEY BEEN UNDER YOUR CARE?
ONLY FOR SIX WEEKS OR SO, SINCE I REPLACED THE LAST NURSE... DOCTOR, MAY I BE OF ASSISTANCE?
OH, HE'S FINE.
HIS METHODS MAY LOOK A LITTLE UNUSUAL, BUT THERE'S NOBODY BETTER, BELIEVE ME.
SNFFFFFF
WHERE IS THE MASTER OF THE HOUSE? I HAVE SOME QUESTIONS FOR HIM.
LOOK NO FURTHER, SIR.

ALAN CAMPBELL, AT YOUR SERVICE.

AND WE'VE NOT MET, DOCTOR...

NOT MET?

BUT I THOUGHT YOU WERE THE FAMILY PHYSICIAN!

I NEVER SAID I WAS, MISS MACKENZIE!

NO, HE WAS UNABLE TO ATTEND, SO HE SENT ME IN HIS PLACE.

I HOPE THAT'S NOT A PROBLEM, MR. CAMPBELL.

NOT AT ALL. ANYONE RECOMMENDED BY DR. LEWIS CERTAINLY HAS GAINED MY TRUST.

I STILL DIDN'T CATCH YOUR NAME, SIR.

SMITH. DR. JOHN SMITH.

AND YES, DR. LEWIS SENDS HIS APOLOGIES THAT HE WAS UNABLE TO MAKE THE JOURNEY FROM EDINBURGH.

OF COURSE HE DOES. HOW FORTUNATE YOU WERE FREE.

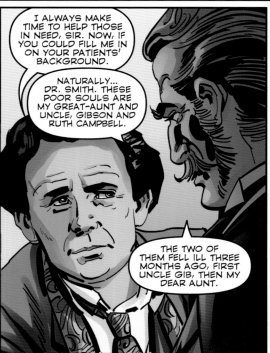

I ALWAYS MAKE TIME TO HELP THOSE IN NEED, SIR. NOW, IF YOU COULD FILL ME IN ON YOUR PATIENTS' BACKGROUND.

NATURALLY... DR. SMITH. THESE POOR SOULS ARE MY GREAT-AUNT AND UNCLE, GIBSON AND RUTH CAMPBELL.

THE TWO OF THEM FELL ILL THREE MONTHS AGO, FIRST UNCLE GIB, THEN MY DEAR AUNT.

IT WAS SLOW AT FIRST, A WORSENING FATIGUE UNTIL EVENTUALLY THEY WERE AS Y' SEE THEM HERE, BARELY MOVING, ALMOST FROZEN ALIVE.

I SEE, YES, YES, QUITE A PUZZLEMENT.

AND FORGIVE ME IF I INTRUDE TOO MUCH INTO THE PERSONAL, MR. CAMPBELL, BUT THIS ESTATE, THE CASTLE, THE GROUNDS... IS IT THEIRS?

THIS IS THE CAMPBELL ANCESTRAL HOME, SIR!

YES, YES, IT IS, NO DOUBT.

BUT AS IT STANDS TODAY, IS IT YOURS... OR THEIRS?

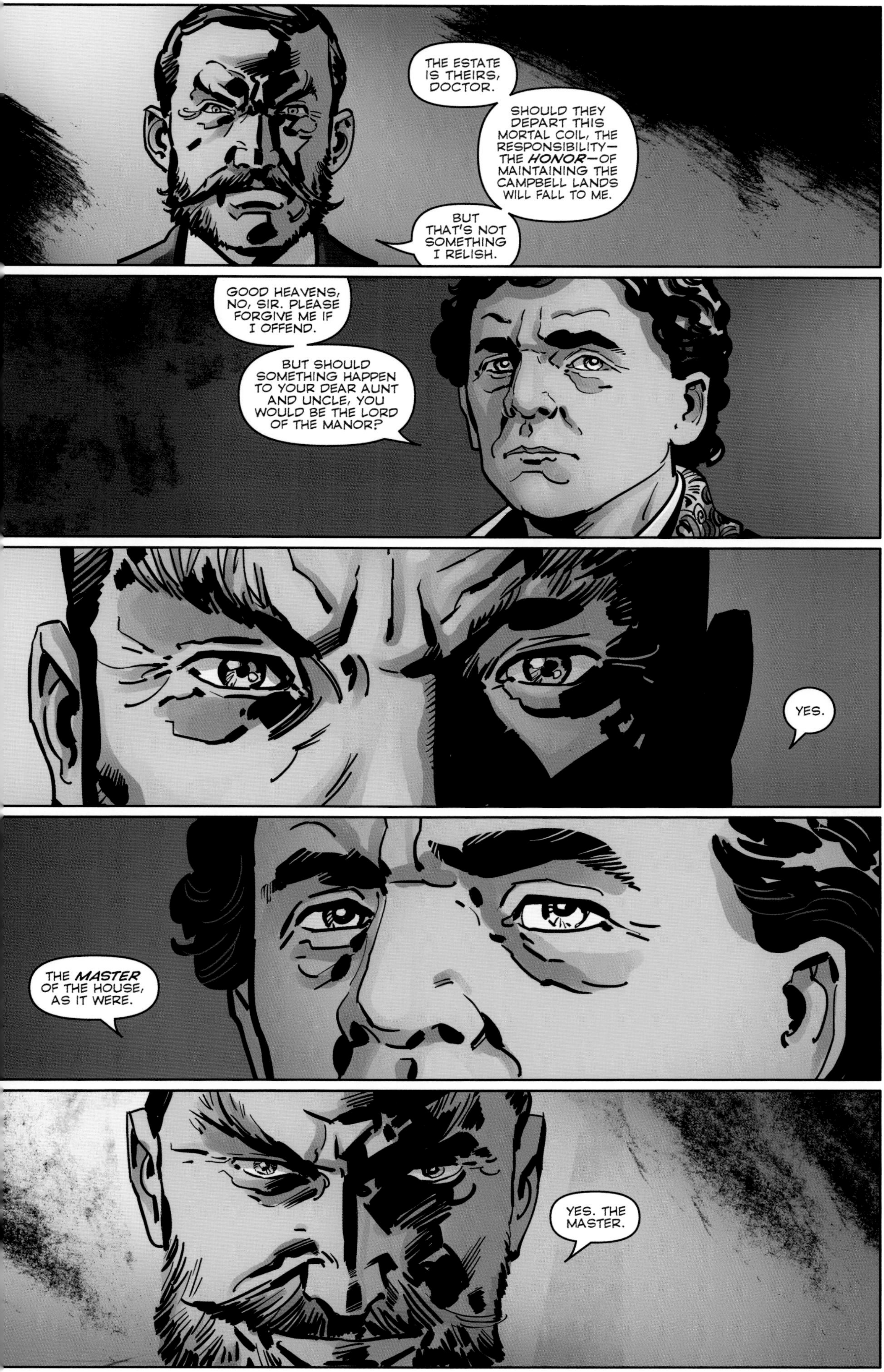
THE ESTATE IS THEIRS, DOCTOR.
SHOULD THEY DEPART THIS MORTAL COIL, THE RESPONSIBILITY—THE *HONOR*—OF MAINTAINING THE CAMPBELL LANDS WILL FALL TO ME.
BUT THAT'S NOT SOMETHING I RELISH.
GOOD HEAVENS, NO, SIR. PLEASE FORGIVE ME IF I OFFEND.
BUT SHOULD SOMETHING HAPPEN TO YOUR DEAR AUNT AND UNCLE, YOU WOULD BE THE LORD OF THE MANOR?
YES.
THE *MASTER* OF THE HOUSE, AS IT WERE.
YES. THE MASTER.

WELL, THEN, I JUST NEED TO CONSULT A FEW TEXTS I BROUGHT ALONG IN MY CARRIAGE, AND I CAN BEGIN A MORE THOROUGH EXAMINATION AND TREATMENT.

WITH YOUR PERMISSION, MR. CAMPBELL?

BY ALL MEANS, *DOCTOR* SMITH.

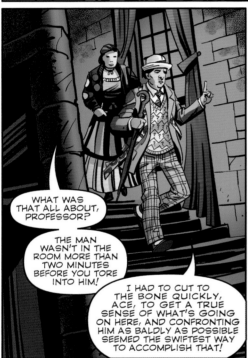

WHAT WAS THAT ALL ABOUT, PROFESSOR?

THE MAN WASN'T IN THE ROOM MORE THAN TWO MINUTES BEFORE YOU TORE INTO HIM!

I HAD TO CUT TO THE BONE QUICKLY, ACE, TO GET A TRUE SENSE OF WHAT'S GOING ON HERE, AND CONFRONTING HIM AS BALDLY AS POSSIBLE SEEMED THE SWIFTEST WAY TO ACCOMPLISH THAT!

AND WHAT DID YOU ACCOMPLISH BY ATTACKING THAT FELLA?

THAT NURSE LOOKED LIKE SHE'D SEEN A GHOST!

OH, I ACCOMPLISHED QUITE A BIT.

I LEARNED FOR A FACT THAT WHOEVER HE MAY BE, THAT IS NOT ALAN CAMPBELL.

AND HOW DO YOU KNOW THAT?

BECAUSE WHOEVER HIS 'UNCLE' AND 'AUNT' ARE, THEY'RE NOT HUMAN.

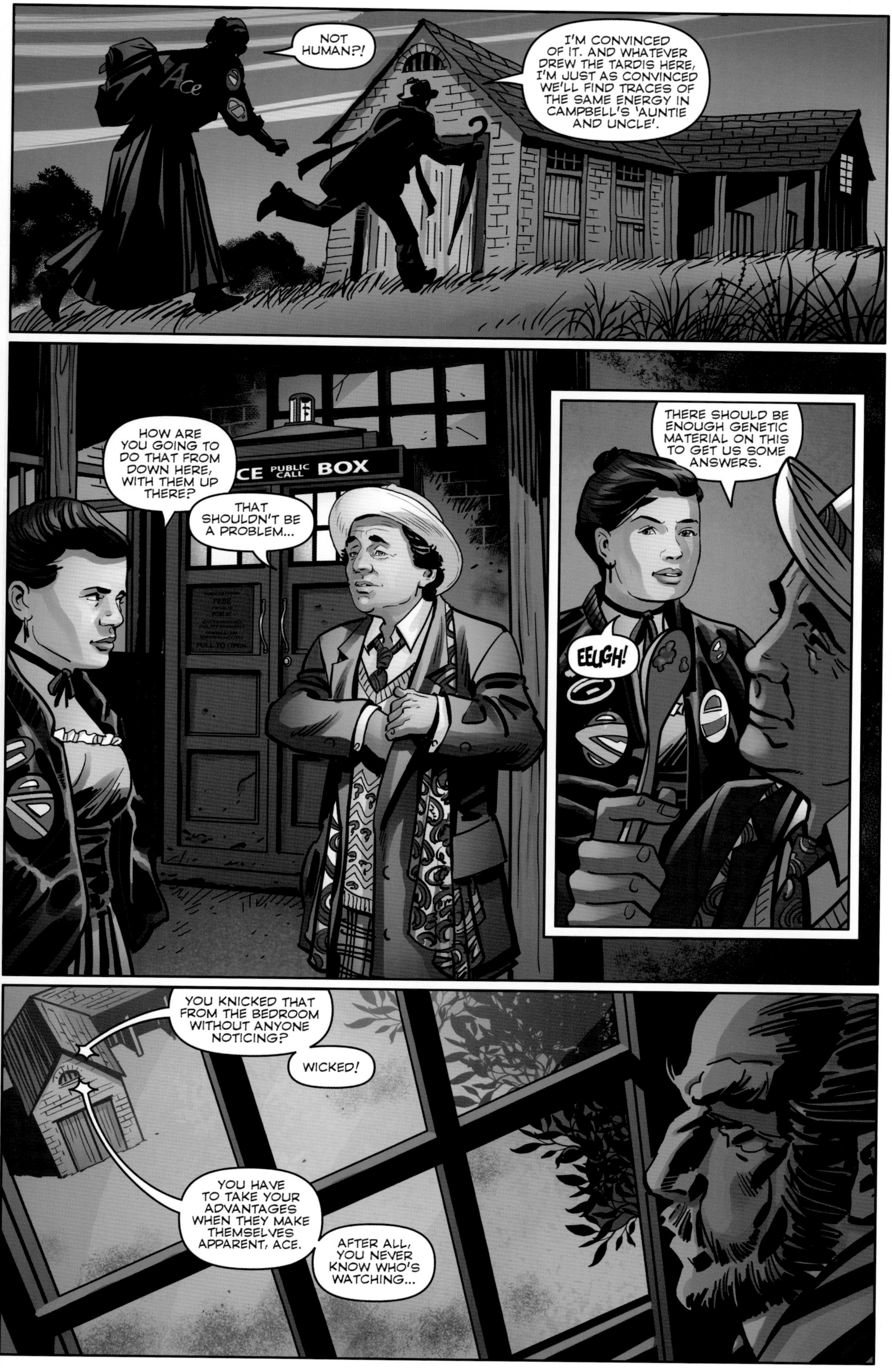
NOT HUMAN?!
I'M CONVINCED OF IT. AND WHATEVER DREW THE TARDIS HERE, I'M JUST AS CONVINCED WE'LL FIND TRACES OF THE SAME ENERGY IN CAMPBELL'S 'AUNTIE AND UNCLE'.
ACE
CE PUBLIC CALL BOX
HOW ARE YOU GOING TO DO THAT FROM DOWN HERE, WITH THEM UP THERE?
THAT SHOULDN'T BE A PROBLEM...
PULL TO OPEN
THERE SHOULD BE ENOUGH GENETIC MATERIAL ON THIS TO GET US SOME ANSWERS.
EEUGH!
YOU KNICKED THAT FROM THE BEDROOM WITHOUT ANYONE NOTICING?
WICKED!
YOU HAVE TO TAKE YOUR ADVANTAGES WHEN THEY MAKE THEMSELVES APPARENT, ACE.
AFTER ALL, YOU NEVER KNOW WHO'S WATCHING...

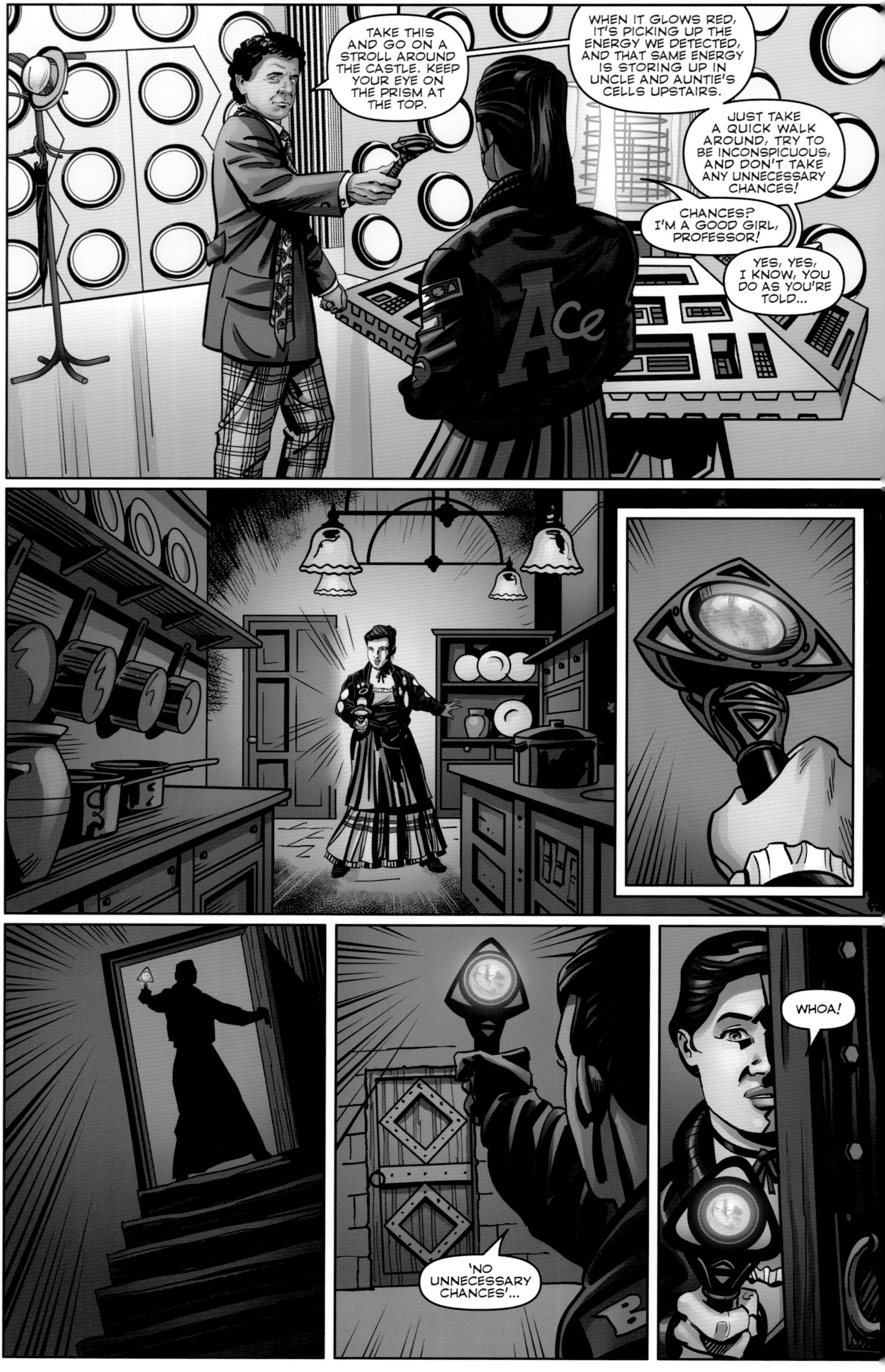

TAKE THIS AND GO ON A STROLL AROUND THE CASTLE. KEEP YOUR EYE ON THE PRISM AT THE TOP.
WHEN IT GLOWS RED, IT'S PICKING UP THE ENERGY WE DETECTED, AND THAT SAME ENERGY IS STORING UP IN UNCLE AND AUNTIE'S CELLS UPSTAIRS.
JUST TAKE A QUICK WALK AROUND, TRY TO BE INCONSPICUOUS, AND DON'T TAKE ANY UNNECESSARY CHANCES!
CHANCES? I'M A GOOD GIRL, PROFESSOR!
YES, YES, I KNOW, YOU DO AS YOU'RE TOLD...
'NO UNNECESSARY CHANCES'...
WHOA!

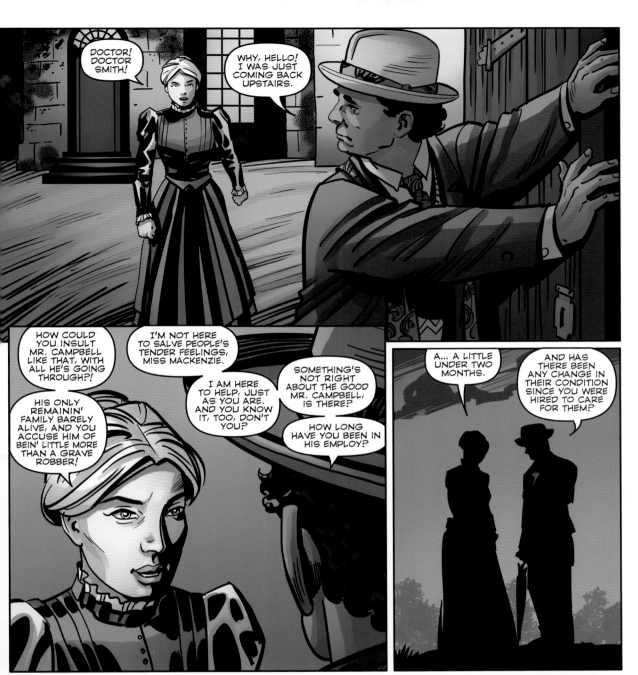

DOCTOR! DOCTOR SMITH!

WHY, HELLO! I WAS JUST COMING BACK UPSTAIRS.

HOW COULD YOU INSULT MR. CAMPBELL LIKE THAT, WITH ALL HE'S GOING THROUGH?!

I'M NOT HERE TO SALVE PEOPLE'S TENDER FEELINGS, MISS MACKENZIE.

I AM HERE TO HELP, JUST AS YOU ARE. AND YOU KNOW IT, TOO, DON'T YOU?

SOMETHING'S NOT RIGHT ABOUT THE GOOD MR. CAMPBELL, IS THERE? HOW LONG HAVE YOU BEEN IN HIS EMPLOY?

HIS ONLY REMAININ' FAMILY BARELY ALIVE, AND YOU ACCUSE HIM OF BEIN' LITTLE MORE THAN A GRAVE ROBBER!

A... A LITTLE UNDER TWO MONTHS.

AND HAS THERE BEEN ANY CHANGE IN THEIR CONDITION SINCE YOU WERE HIRED TO CARE FOR THEM?

...NO. NO, THEY'VE NOT CHANGED A WHIT IN ALL THE TIME I'VE BEEN HERE.

AND YOU'VE BEEN TERRIBLY WORRIED, HAVEN'T YOU?

THAT'S WHY YOU DIDN'T EVEN QUESTION WHO I WAS WHEN I ARRIVED, SO LONG AS SOMEONE, ANYONE, MIGHT BE ABLE TO HELP.

THERE IS SOMETHING ABOUT MR. CAMPBELL, DOCTOR.

I CAN'T EXPLAIN IT, BUT... IT JUST DOESN'T FEEL RIGHT.

YOU WILL HELP ME, WON'T YOU?

I'M THE DOCTOR. I'M HERE TO HELP.

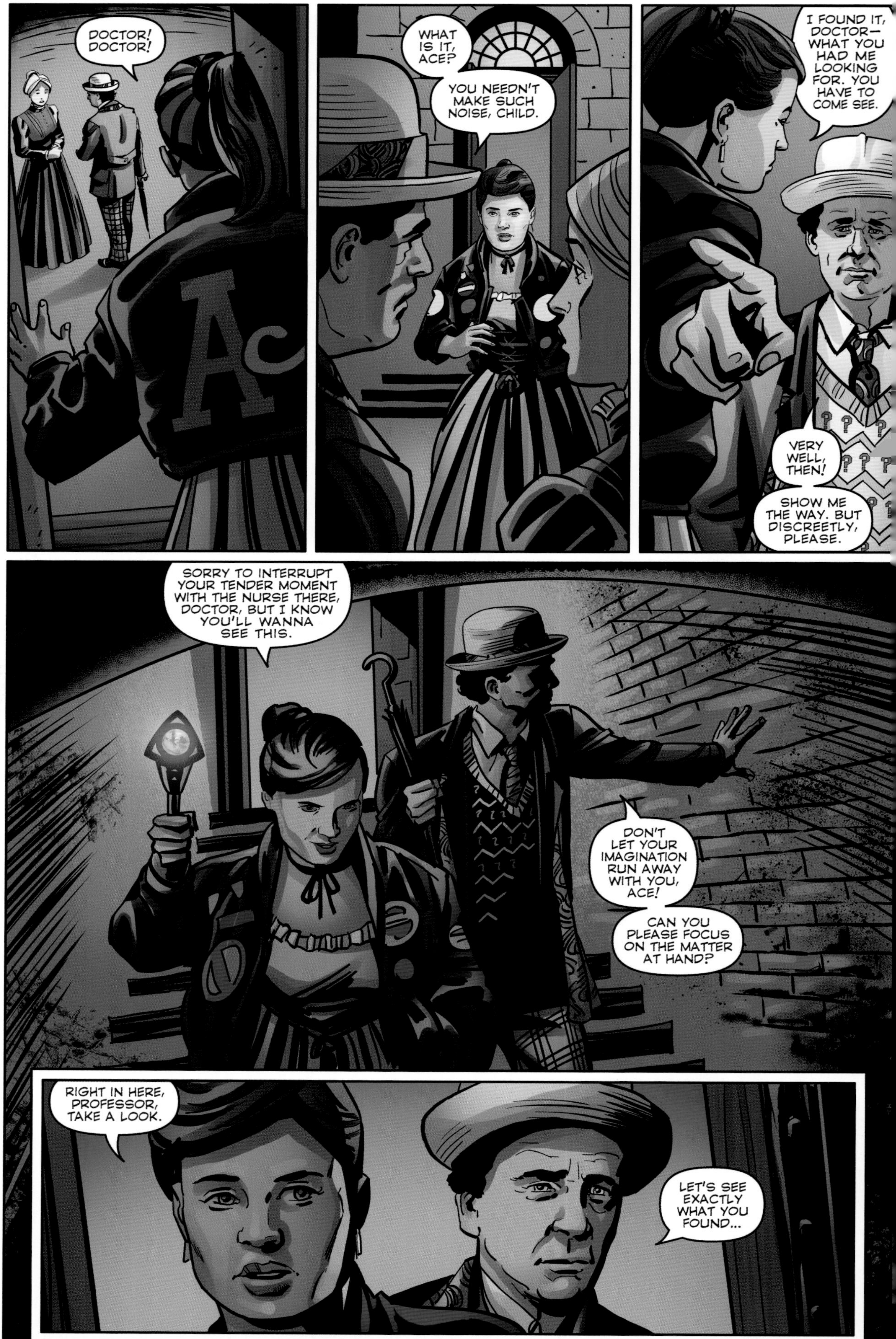
DOCTOR! DOCTOR!
WHAT IS IT, ACE?
YOU NEEDN'T MAKE SUCH NOISE, CHILD.
I FOUND IT, DOCTOR— WHAT YOU HAD ME LOOKING FOR. YOU HAVE TO COME SEE.
VERY WELL, THEN!
SHOW ME THE WAY. BUT DISCREETLY, PLEASE.
SORRY TO INTERRUPT YOUR TENDER MOMENT WITH THE NURSE THERE, DOCTOR, BUT I KNOW YOU'LL WANNA SEE THIS.
DON'T LET YOUR IMAGINATION RUN AWAY WITH YOU, ACE!
CAN YOU PLEASE FOCUS ON THE MATTER AT HAND?
RIGHT IN HERE, PROFESSOR, TAKE A LOOK.
LET'S SEE EXACTLY WHAT YOU FOUND...

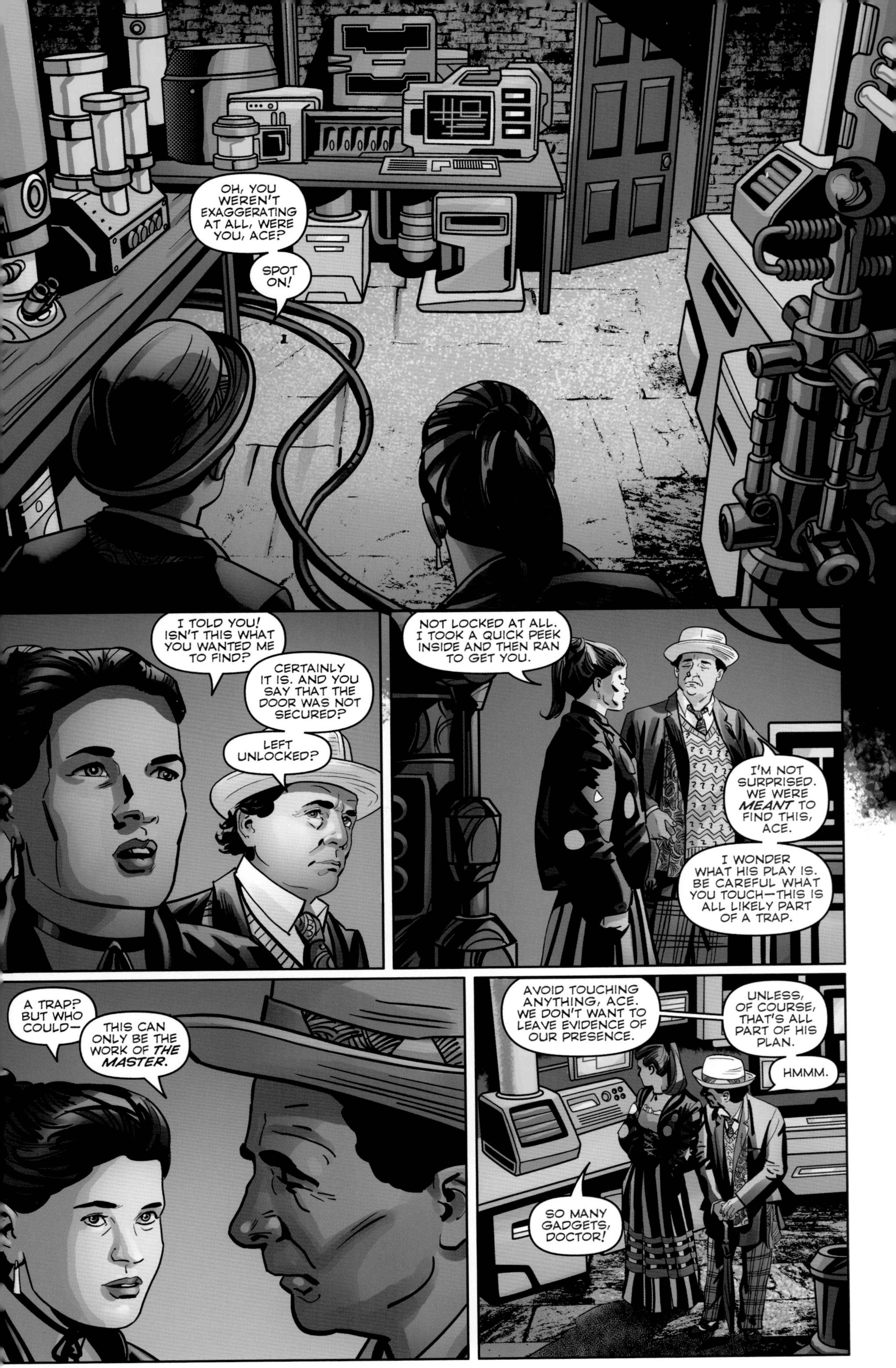
OH, YOU WEREN'T EXAGGERATING AT ALL, WERE YOU, ACE?
SPOT ON!
I TOLD YOU! ISN'T THIS WHAT YOU WANTED ME TO FIND?
CERTAINLY IT IS. AND YOU SAY THAT THE DOOR WAS NOT SECURED?
LEFT UNLOCKED?
NOT LOCKED AT ALL. I TOOK A QUICK PEEK INSIDE AND THEN RAN TO GET YOU.
I'M NOT SURPRISED. WE WERE *MEANT* TO FIND THIS, ACE.
I WONDER WHAT HIS PLAY IS. BE CAREFUL WHAT YOU TOUCH—THIS IS ALL LIKELY PART OF A TRAP.
A TRAP? BUT WHO COULD—
THIS CAN ONLY BE THE WORK OF ***THE MASTER***.
AVOID TOUCHING ANYTHING, ACE. WE DON'T WANT TO LEAVE EVIDENCE OF OUR PRESENCE.
UNLESS, OF COURSE, THAT'S ALL PART OF HIS PLAN.
HMMM.
SO MANY GADGETS, DOCTOR!

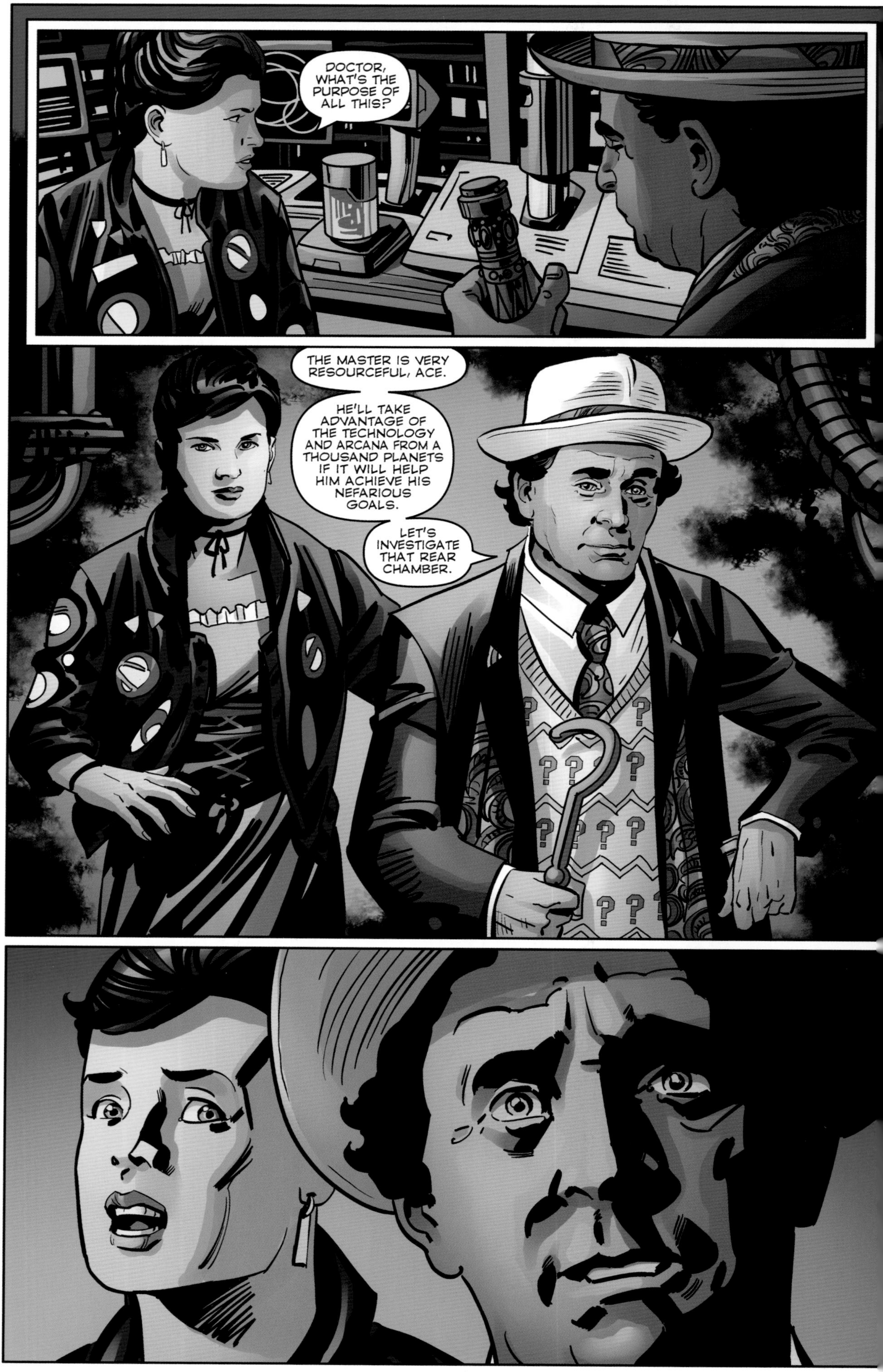
DOCTOR, WHAT'S THE PURPOSE OF ALL THIS?
THE MASTER IS VERY RESOURCEFUL, ACE.
HE'LL TAKE ADVANTAGE OF THE TECHNOLOGY AND ARCANA FROM A THOUSAND PLANETS IF IT WILL HELP HIM ACHIEVE HIS NEFARIOUS GOALS.
LET'S INVESTIGATE THAT REAR CHAMBER.

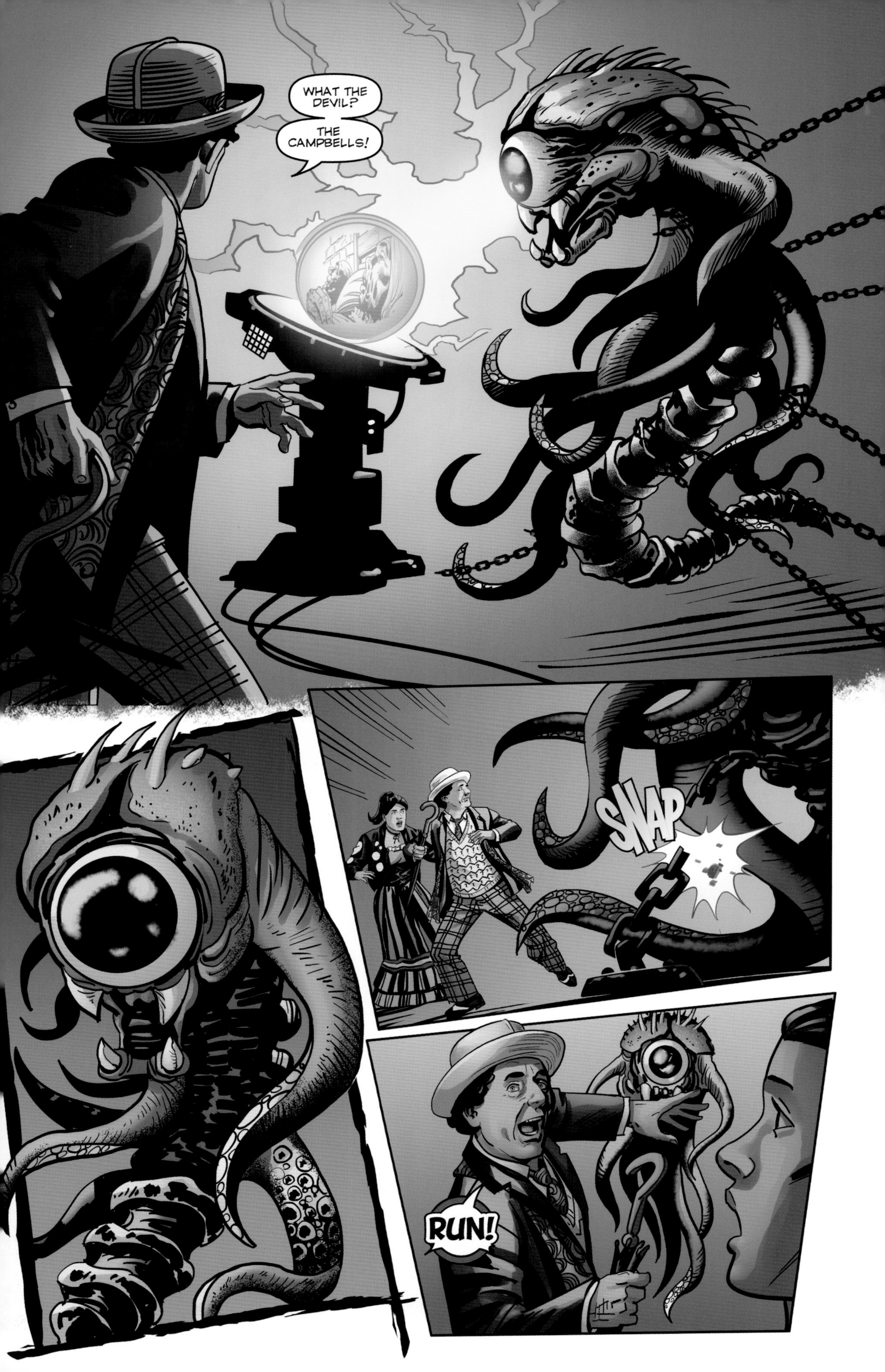
WHAT THE DEVIL?
THE CAMPBELLS!
SNAP
RUN!

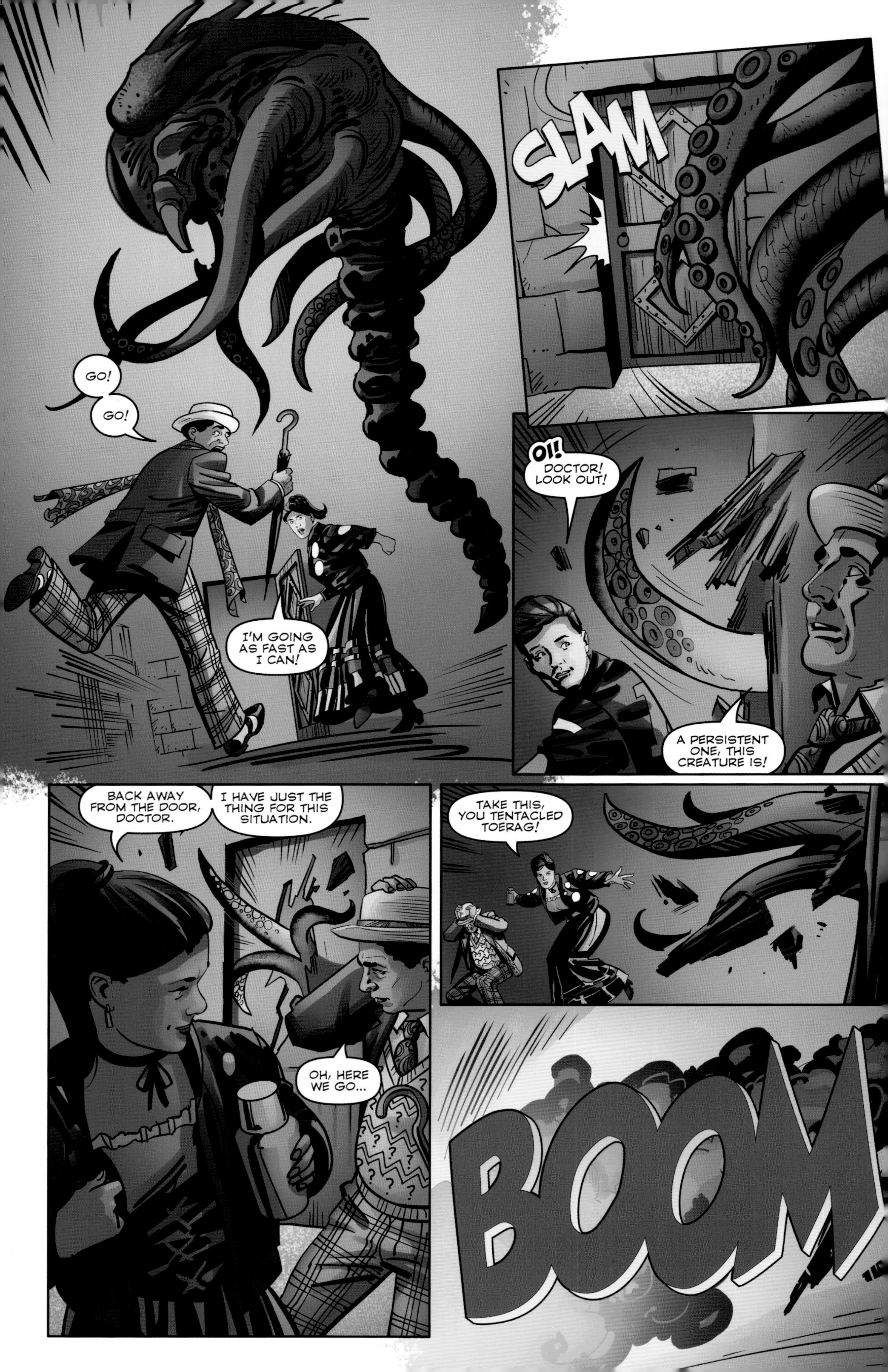
GO!
GO!
I'M GOING AS FAST AS I CAN!
SLAM
OI! DOCTOR! LOOK OUT!
A PERSISTENT ONE, THIS CREATURE IS!
BACK AWAY FROM THE DOOR, DOCTOR.
I HAVE JUST THE THING FOR THIS SITUATION.
OH, HERE WE GO...
TAKE THIS, YOU TENTACLED TOERAG!
BOOM

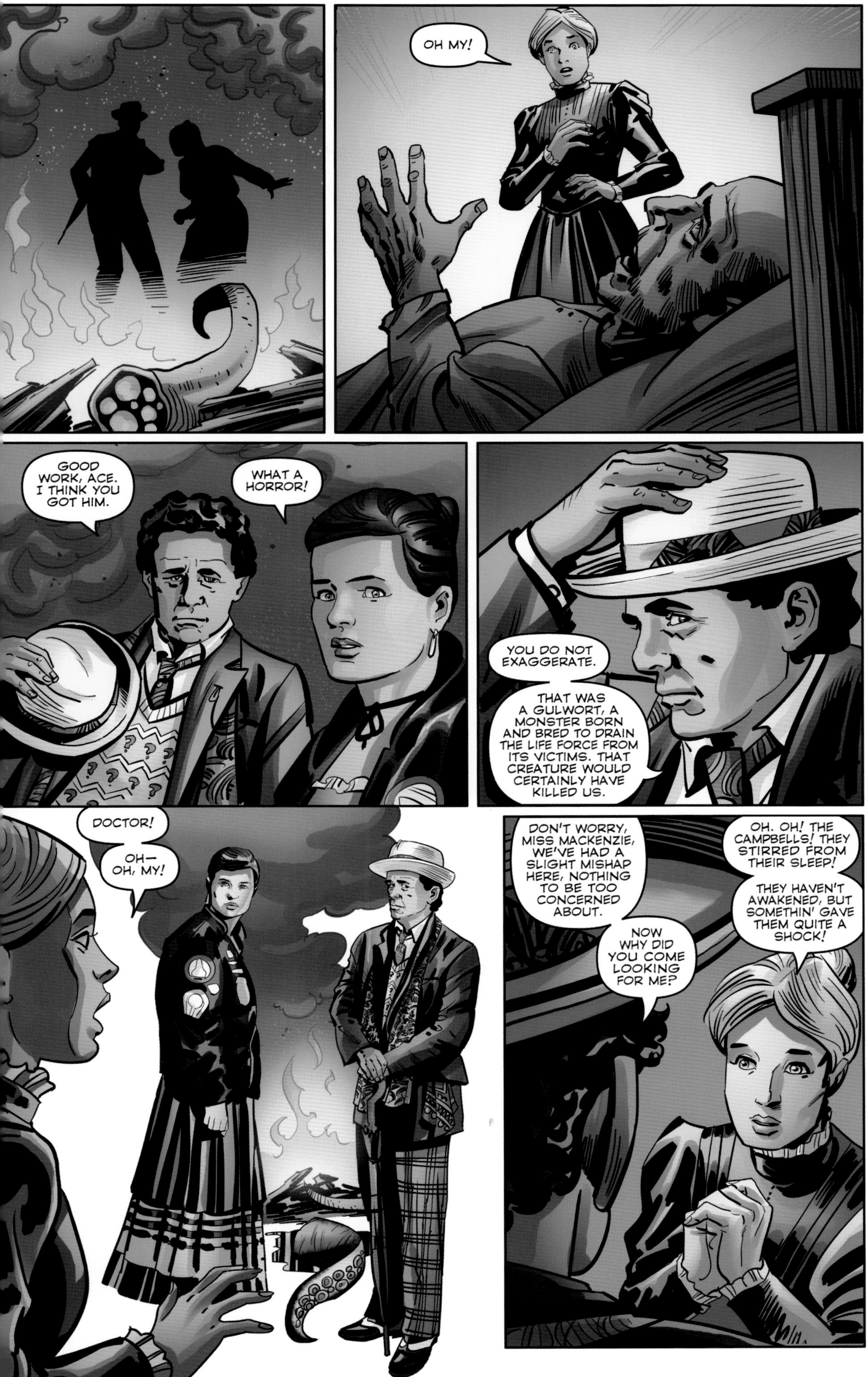
OH MY!
GOOD WORK, ACE. I THINK YOU GOT HIM.
WHAT A HORROR!
YOU DO NOT EXAGGERATE.
THAT WAS A GULWORT, A MONSTER BORN AND BRED TO DRAIN THE LIFE FORCE FROM ITS VICTIMS. THAT CREATURE WOULD CERTAINLY HAVE KILLED US.
DOCTOR!
OH— OH, MY!
DON'T WORRY, MISS MACKENZIE, WE'VE HAD A SLIGHT MISHAP HERE, NOTHING TO BE TOO CONCERNED ABOUT.
NOW WHY DID YOU COME LOOKING FOR ME?
OH. OH! THE CAMPBELLS! THEY STIRRED FROM THEIR SLEEP!
THEY HAVEN'T AWAKENED, BUT SOMETHIN' GAVE THEM QUITE A SHOCK!

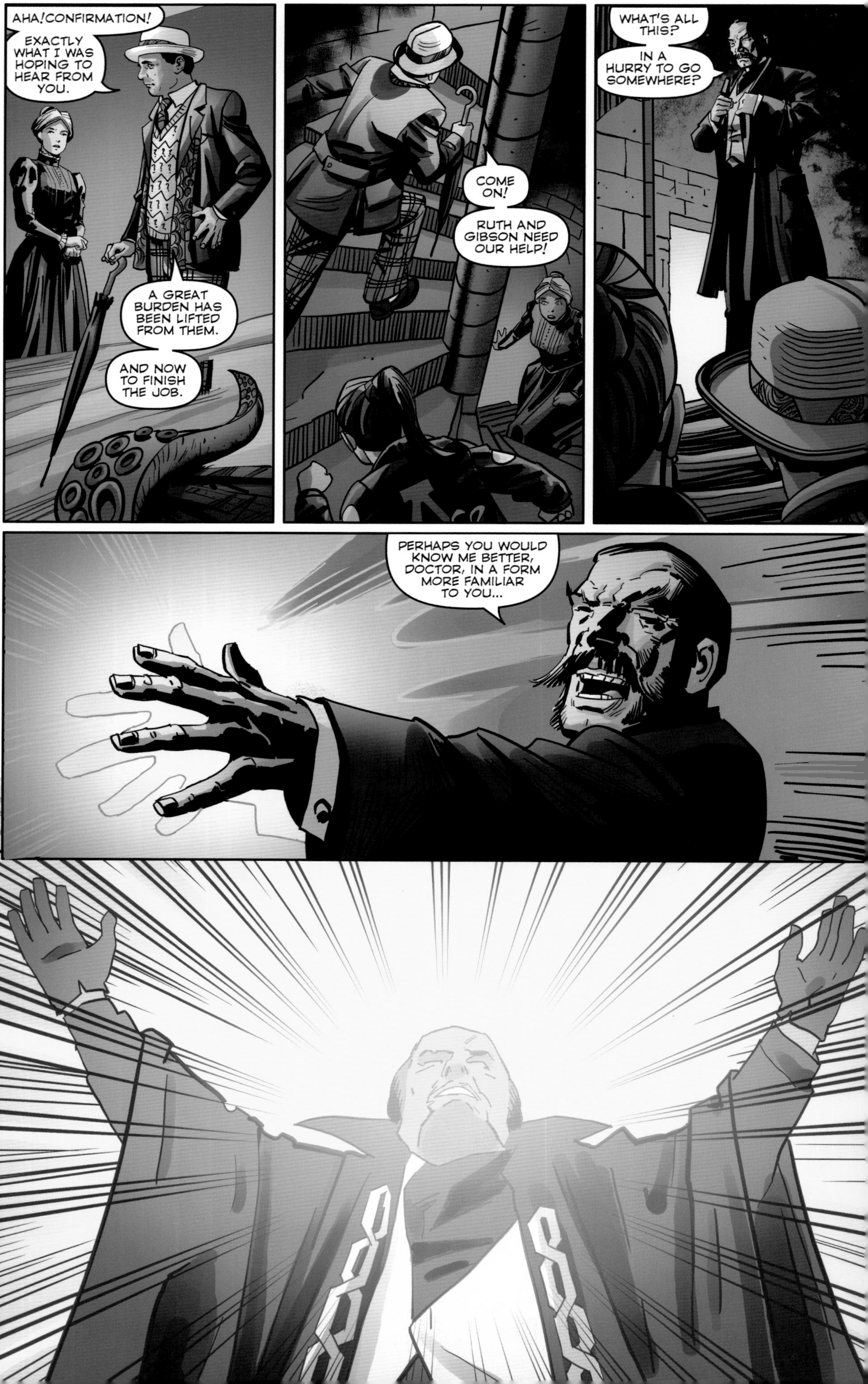
AHA! CONFIRMATION!
EXACTLY WHAT I WAS HOPING TO HEAR FROM YOU.
A GREAT BURDEN HAS BEEN LIFTED FROM THEM.
AND NOW TO FINISH THE JOB.
COME ON!
RUTH AND GIBSON NEED OUR HELP!
WHAT'S ALL THIS?
IN A HURRY TO GO SOMEWHERE?
PERHAPS YOU WOULD KNOW ME BETTER, DOCTOR, IN A FORM MORE FAMILIAR TO YOU...

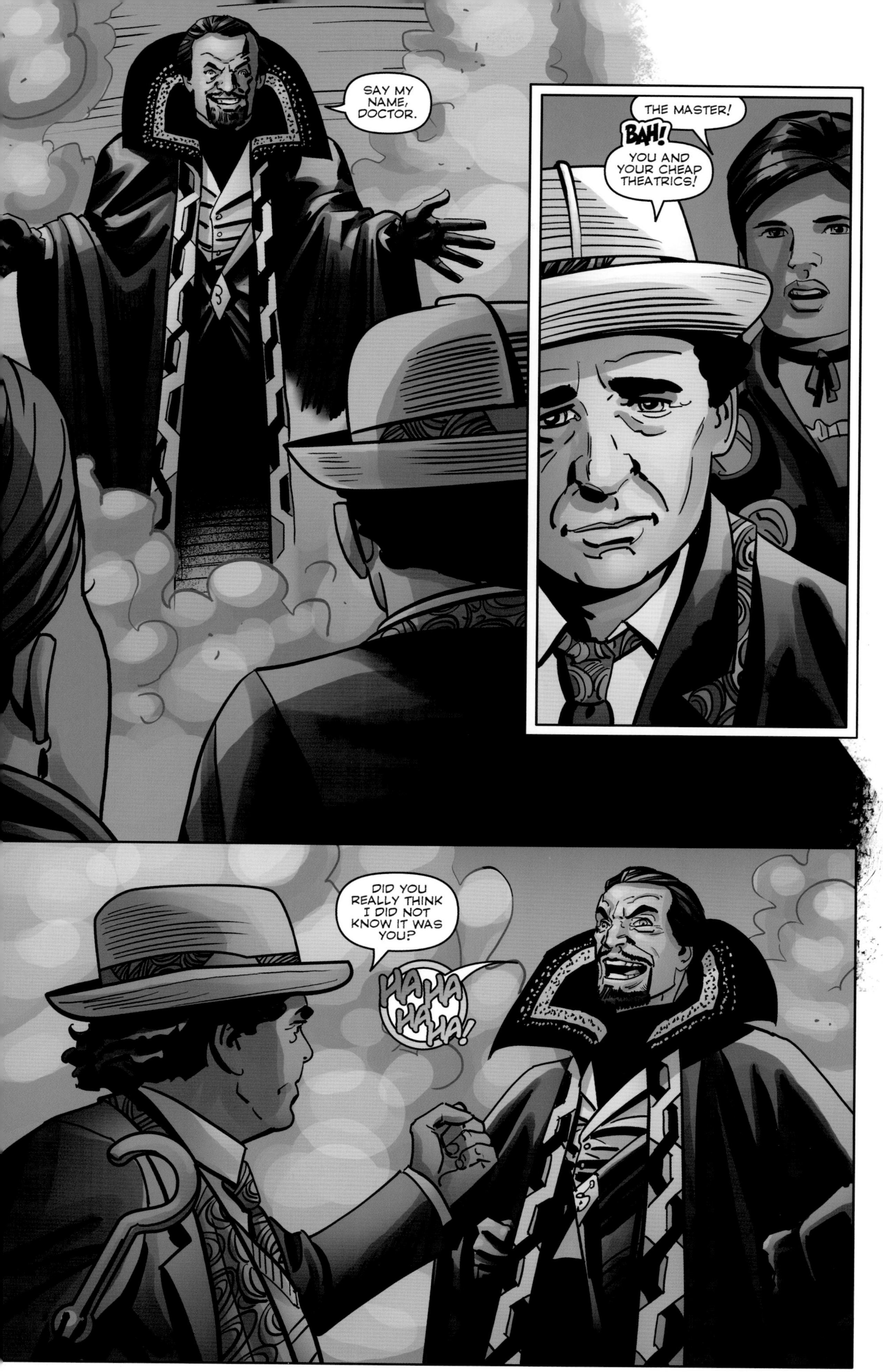
SAY MY NAME, DOCTOR.
THE MASTER!
BAH!
YOU AND YOUR CHEAP THEATRICS!
DID YOU REALLY THINK I DID NOT KNOW IT WAS YOU?
HA HA HA HA!

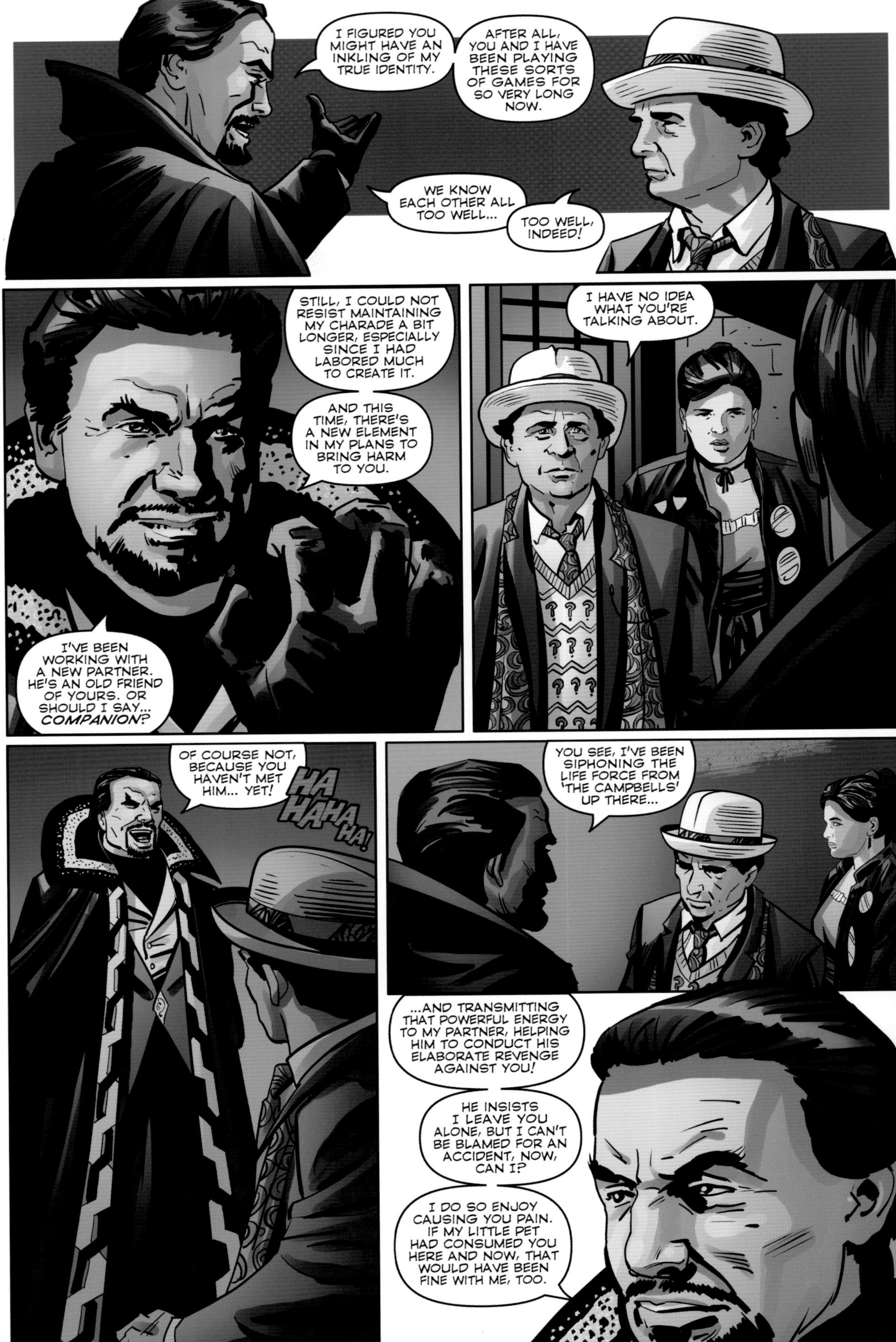
I FIGURED YOU MIGHT HAVE AN INKLING OF MY TRUE IDENTITY.
AFTER ALL, YOU AND I HAVE BEEN PLAYING THESE SORTS OF GAMES FOR SO VERY LONG NOW.
WE KNOW EACH OTHER ALL TOO WELL...
TOO WELL, INDEED!
STILL, I COULD NOT RESIST MAINTAINING MY CHARADE A BIT LONGER, ESPECIALLY SINCE I HAD LABORED MUCH TO CREATE IT.
AND THIS TIME, THERE'S A NEW ELEMENT IN MY PLANS TO BRING HARM TO YOU.
I'VE BEEN WORKING WITH A NEW PARTNER. HE'S AN OLD FRIEND OF YOURS. OR SHOULD I SAY... *COMPANION*?
I HAVE NO IDEA WHAT YOU'RE TALKING ABOUT.
OF COURSE NOT, BECAUSE YOU HAVEN'T MET HIM... YET!
HA HA HA HA HA!
YOU SEE, I'VE BEEN SIPHONING THE LIFE FORCE FROM 'THE CAMPBELLS' UP THERE...
...AND TRANSMITTING THAT POWERFUL ENERGY TO MY PARTNER, HELPING HIM TO CONDUCT HIS ELABORATE REVENGE AGAINST YOU!
HE INSISTS I LEAVE YOU ALONE, BUT I CAN'T BE BLAMED FOR AN ACCIDENT, NOW, CAN I?
I DO SO ENJOY CAUSING YOU PAIN. IF MY LITTLE PET HAD CONSUMED YOU HERE AND NOW, THAT WOULD HAVE BEEN FINE WITH ME, TOO.

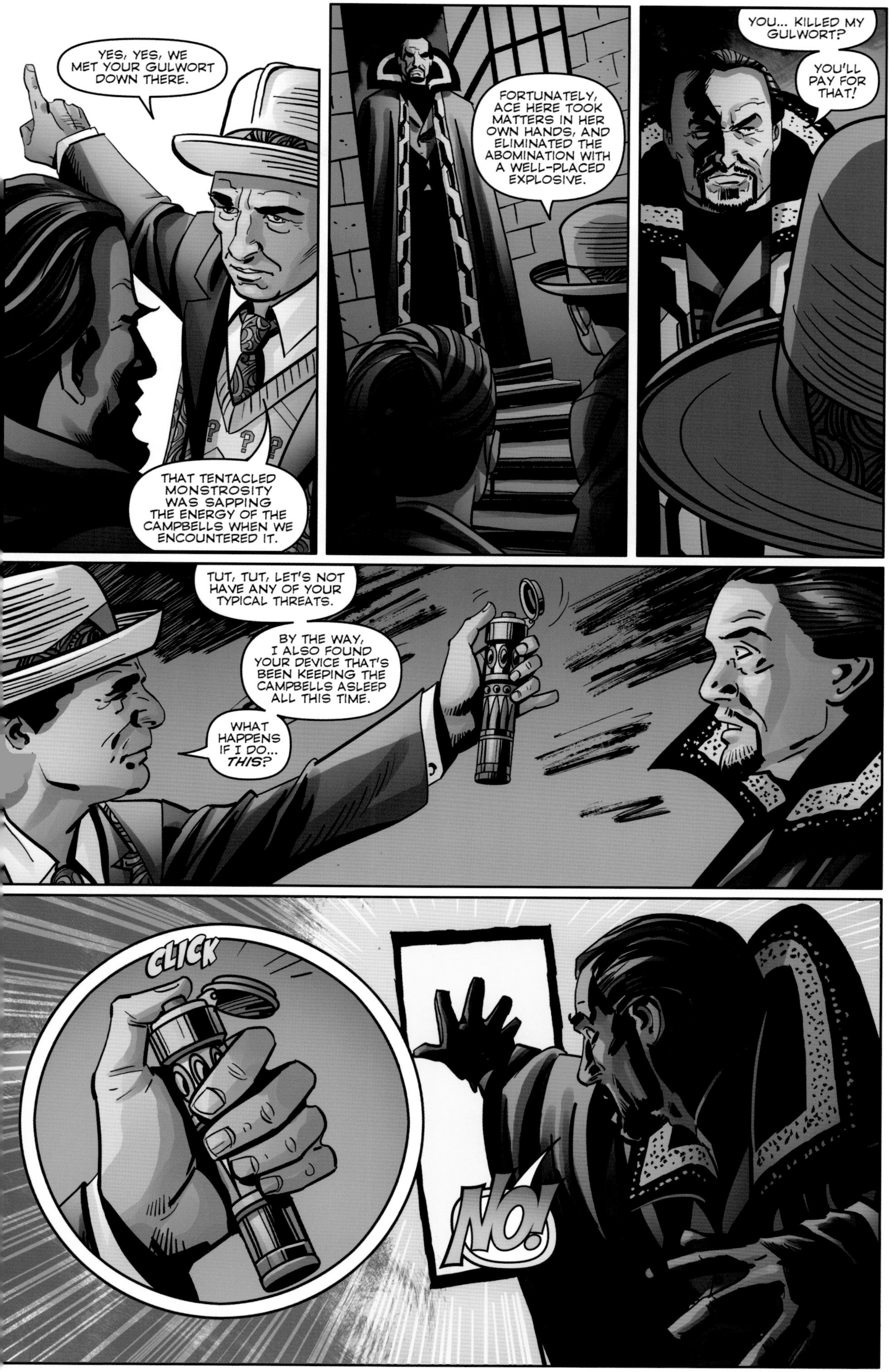
YES, YES, WE MET YOUR GULWORT DOWN THERE.
THAT TENTACLED MONSTROSITY WAS SAPPING THE ENERGY OF THE CAMPBELLS WHEN WE ENCOUNTERED IT.
FORTUNATELY, ACE HERE TOOK MATTERS IN HER OWN HANDS, AND ELIMINATED THE ABOMINATION WITH A WELL-PLACED EXPLOSIVE.
YOU... KILLED MY GULWORT?
YOU'LL PAY FOR THAT!
TUT, TUT, LET'S NOT HAVE ANY OF YOUR TYPICAL THREATS.
BY THE WAY, I ALSO FOUND YOUR DEVICE THAT'S BEEN KEEPING THE CAMPBELLS ASLEEP ALL THIS TIME.
WHAT HAPPENS IF I DO... *THIS*?
CLICK
NO!

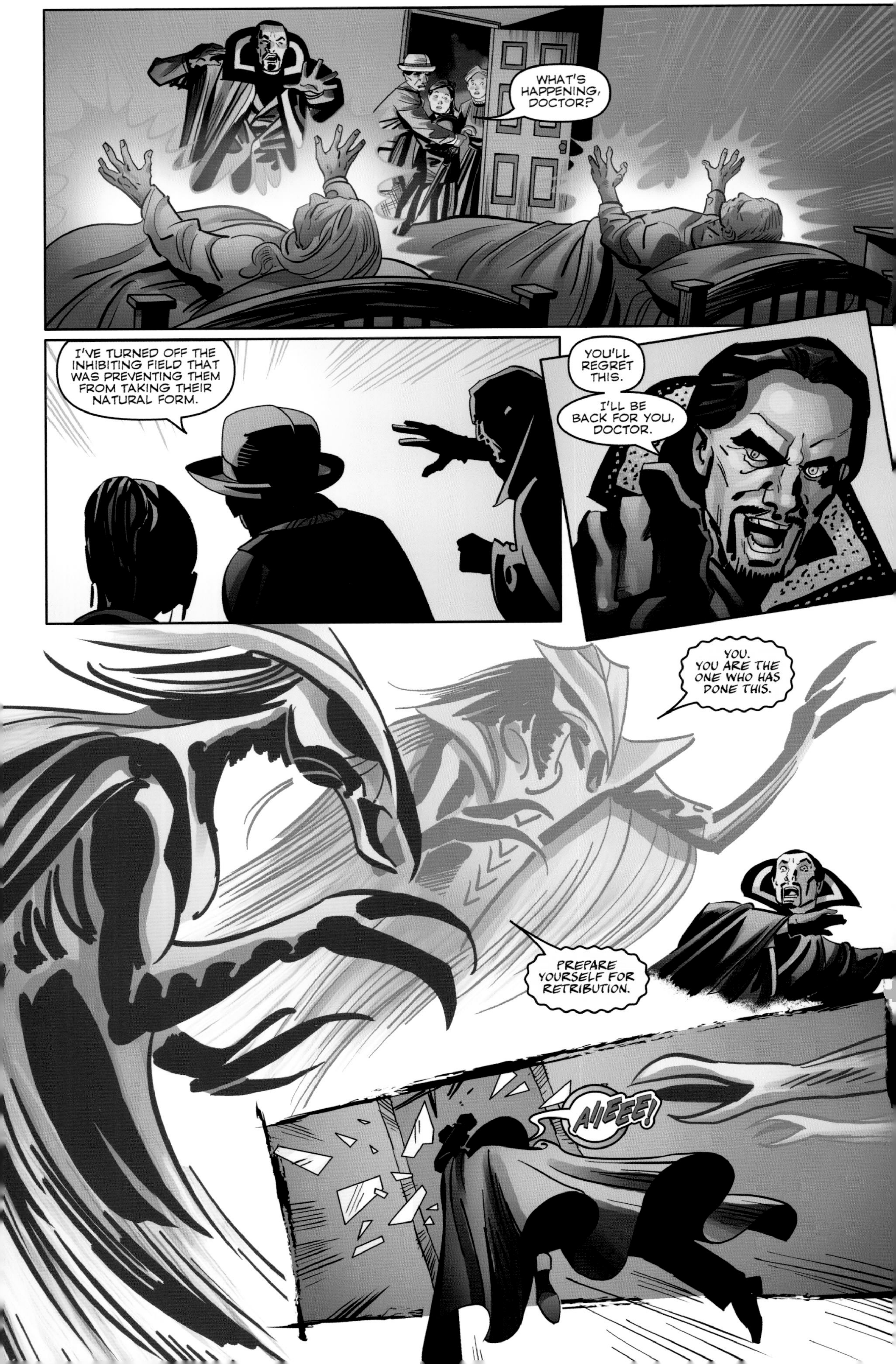
WHAT'S HAPPENING, DOCTOR?
I'VE TURNED OFF THE INHIBITING FIELD THAT WAS PREVENTING THEM FROM TAKING THEIR NATURAL FORM.
YOU'LL REGRET THIS.
I'LL BE BACK FOR YOU, DOCTOR.
YOU. YOU ARE THE ONE WHO HAS DONE THIS.
PREPARE YOURSELF FOR RETRIBUTION.
AIIEEE!

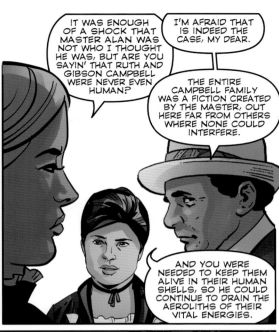

WHO ARE THEY, DOCTOR?

THEY ARE CALLED AEROLITHS, ACE—CREATURES OF LIGHT AND WIND, FOUND ONLY ON A PLANET MANY, MANY LIGHT YEARS FROM HERE.

IT MUST HAVE TAKEN GREAT EFFORT ON THE PART OF THE MASTER TO CAPTURE AND INCAPACITATE THEM IN SUCH A MANNER.

IT WAS ENOUGH OF A SHOCK THAT MASTER ALAN WAS NOT WHO I THOUGHT HE WAS, BUT ARE YOU SAYIN' THAT RUTH AND GIBSON CAMPBELL WERE NEVER EVEN HUMAN?

I'M AFRAID THAT IS INDEED THE CASE, MY DEAR.

THE ENTIRE CAMPBELL FAMILY WAS A FICTION CREATED BY THE MASTER, OUT HERE FAR FROM OTHERS WHERE NONE COULD INTERFERE.

AND YOU WERE NEEDED TO KEEP THEM ALIVE IN THEIR HUMAN SHELLS, SO HE COULD CONTINUE TO DRAIN THE AEROLITHS OF THEIR VITAL ENERGIES.

'IN HIS ARROGANCE, THE MASTER WOULD NEVER "LOWER HIMSELF" TO SERVING AS A NURSEMAID'.

'THEY SEEMED QUITE ANGRY. WHAT WILL HAPPEN IF THEY CATCH HIM, DOCTOR?'

'OH, THEY *WILL* CATCH HIM, ACE. THEY ARE MORE THAN ANGRY, AND THEY HAVE VERY LONG MEMORIES AND A VENGEFUL DISPOSITION.

'THEY WILL VISIT UPON HIM TORTURES AND PAIN BEYOND EVEN THE SLIGHTEST UNDERSTANDING OF YOU AND I'.

ONCE AGAIN HE HAS MADE NEW ENEMIES FOR HIMSELF.

THE ANGUISH THE AEROLITHS WILL VISIT UPON HIM WILL ONLY FURTHER WARP HIS PERVERTED, MALEVOLENT SOUL.

HIS DESCENT INTO THE ABYSS WILL ONLY INTENSIFY AS A RESULT OF THIS.

AND WITH IT, THE MASTER'S VENDETTA AGAINST ME WILL ONLY INTENSIFY AS WELL, AND HE WILL NOW BE A DEADLIER FOE THAN EVER.

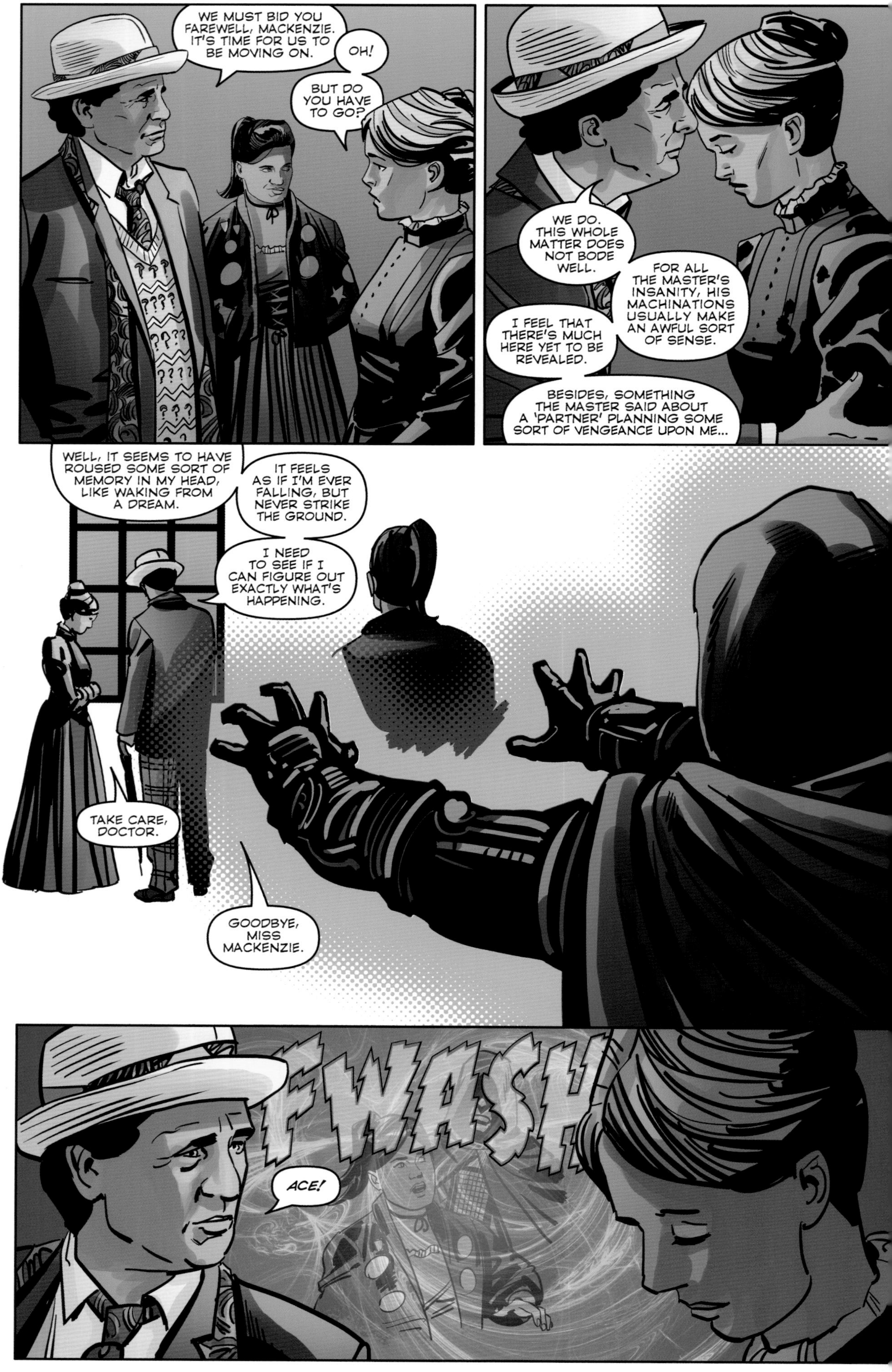
WE MUST BID YOU FAREWELL, MACKENZIE. IT'S TIME FOR US TO BE MOVING ON.
OH!
BUT DO YOU HAVE TO GO?
WE DO. THIS WHOLE MATTER DOES NOT BODE WELL.
FOR ALL THE MASTER'S INSANITY, HIS MACHINATIONS USUALLY MAKE AN AWFUL SORT OF SENSE.
I FEEL THAT THERE'S MUCH HERE YET TO BE REVEALED.
BESIDES, SOMETHING THE MASTER SAID ABOUT A 'PARTNER' PLANNING SOME SORT OF VENGEANCE UPON ME...
WELL, IT SEEMS TO HAVE ROUSED SOME SORT OF MEMORY IN MY HEAD, LIKE WAKING FROM A DREAM.
IT FEELS AS IF I'M EVER FALLING, BUT NEVER STRIKE THE GROUND.
I NEED TO SEE IF I CAN FIGURE OUT EXACTLY WHAT'S HAPPENING.
TAKE CARE, DOCTOR.
GOODBYE, MISS MACKENZIE.
FWASH
ACE!

REFLECTIONS OF TIME
Wherein prominent Whovians past and present muse upon the Doctor's history in comic form.

Incredibly, there was a time when there almost wasn't an ongoing *Doctor Who* comic strip—and the future of the Seventh Doctor looked as grim on paper as it did when he and Ace walked off our TV screen to unknown adventures at the end of "Survival" in 1989.

Falling ratings for the show in part led to the BBC's decision to put the show on hiatus until the 1996 TV movie featuring Paul McGann as a new incarnation of the character. Which rather left Marvel UK, then publishers of *Doctor Who Magazine*, wondering—should they continue to publish the title?

The declining popularity of the show had impacted sales and then-comics editor Richard Starkings—now perhaps best known as the creator of *Elephantmen*—instituted format changes to save on production costs. He also dropped the long-running 'saga'-like stories penned by the likes of Steve Parkhouse, perhaps in part just in case the magazine was cancelled, which would have left fans disappointed; but also to open the strip to a huge range of talents such as Dan Abnett, John Higgins, and Doug Braithwaite, to see what they could bring to the *Who* mythos.

Thankfully, a number of editorial changes to *DWM* helped ensure the title's continuation, despite the lack of an ongoing TV show, meaning the Seventh Doctor's continuing comic adventures were, for a short time before new novels began,

the *only* new professionally produced *Doctor Who* stories available to fans.

Creators included some involved with the original TV series, such as script editor Andrew Cartmel and "Ghost Light" writer Marc Platt, keen to continue their mission to bring a sense of mystery back to the character that had been largely stripped away down the years. That mission included the arrival of companion Ace (actress Sophie Aldred obligingly providing new cover shoots to mark her debut). Also brought on board were creators such as Paul Cornell (making his professional comics debut on the title), Mike Collins (then well known for his work for DC Comics), John Ridgway (*Hellblazer*), John Higgins (*Watchmen*), Doug Braithwaite (*Storm Dogs*), Arthur Ranson (*2000 AD*), Richard Piers Rayner (*Road to Perdition*), Warwick Gray (whose ongoing contributions to the Doctor's comic-strip life has made him one of the most respected teller of Time Lord tales), and Lee Sullivan, who also designed the look of Virgin's New

Adventures companion Bernice Summerfield, created by Cornell, a character who also joined the comic strip.

Despite a shaky start in the face of the TV show's cancellation, in the end the Seventh Doctor enjoyed a longer run in comics than any TV Doctor thanks to an amazing range of creative talent—and *Doctor Who*'s many fans that would not let their fictional hero die…

—John Freeman is the former editor of *Doctor Who Magazine*, currently writing the creator-owned science-fiction adventure *Crucible* for Britain's *STRIP Magazine* and editor at *ROK Comics*. Find him online: downthetubes.net

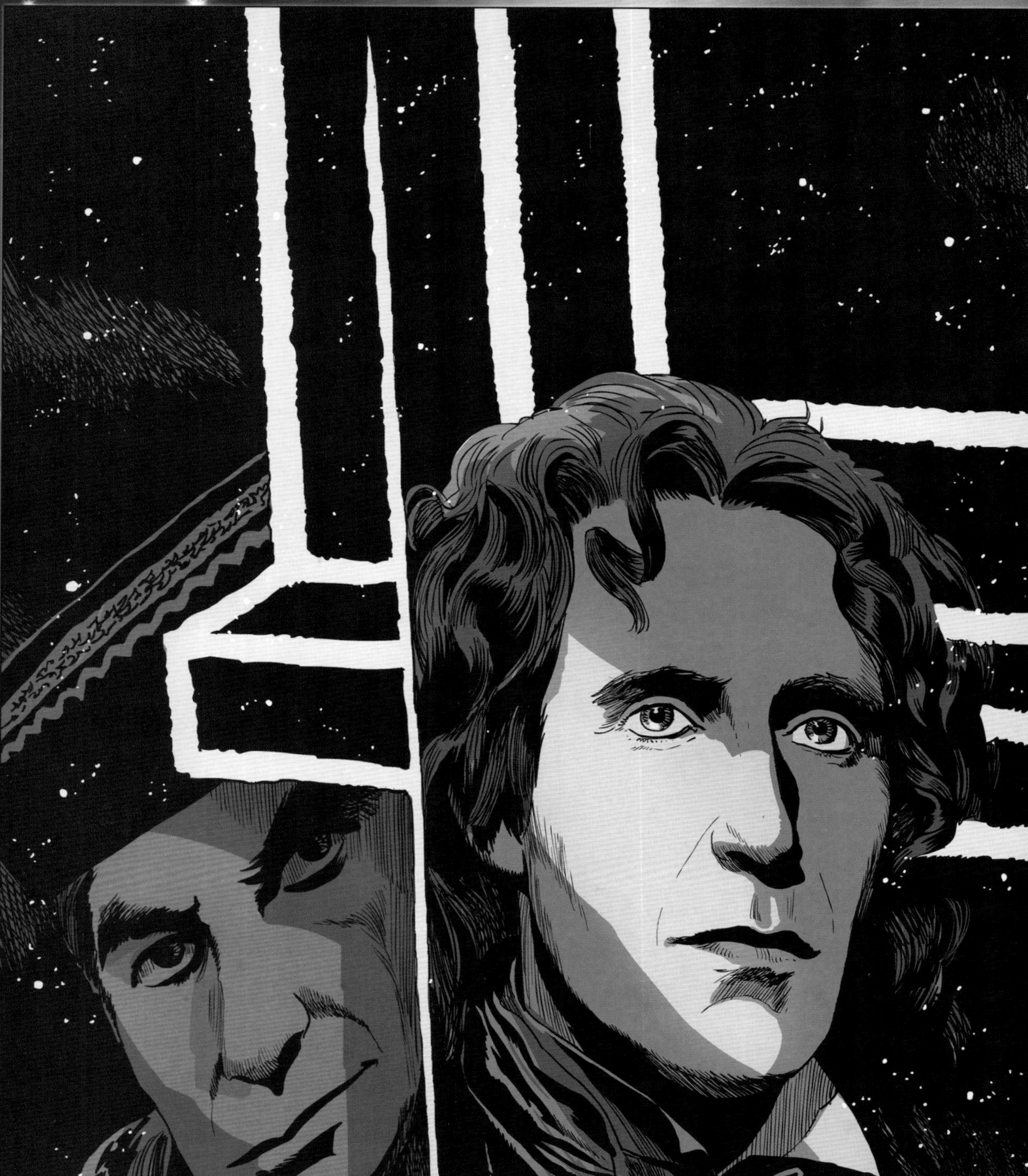

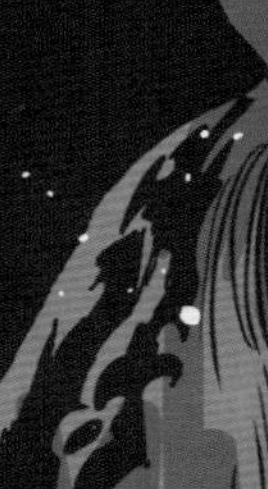

8TH DOCTOR 1996

CHAPTER 8 "THE BODY POLITIC"

Cover Art by Francesco Francavilla

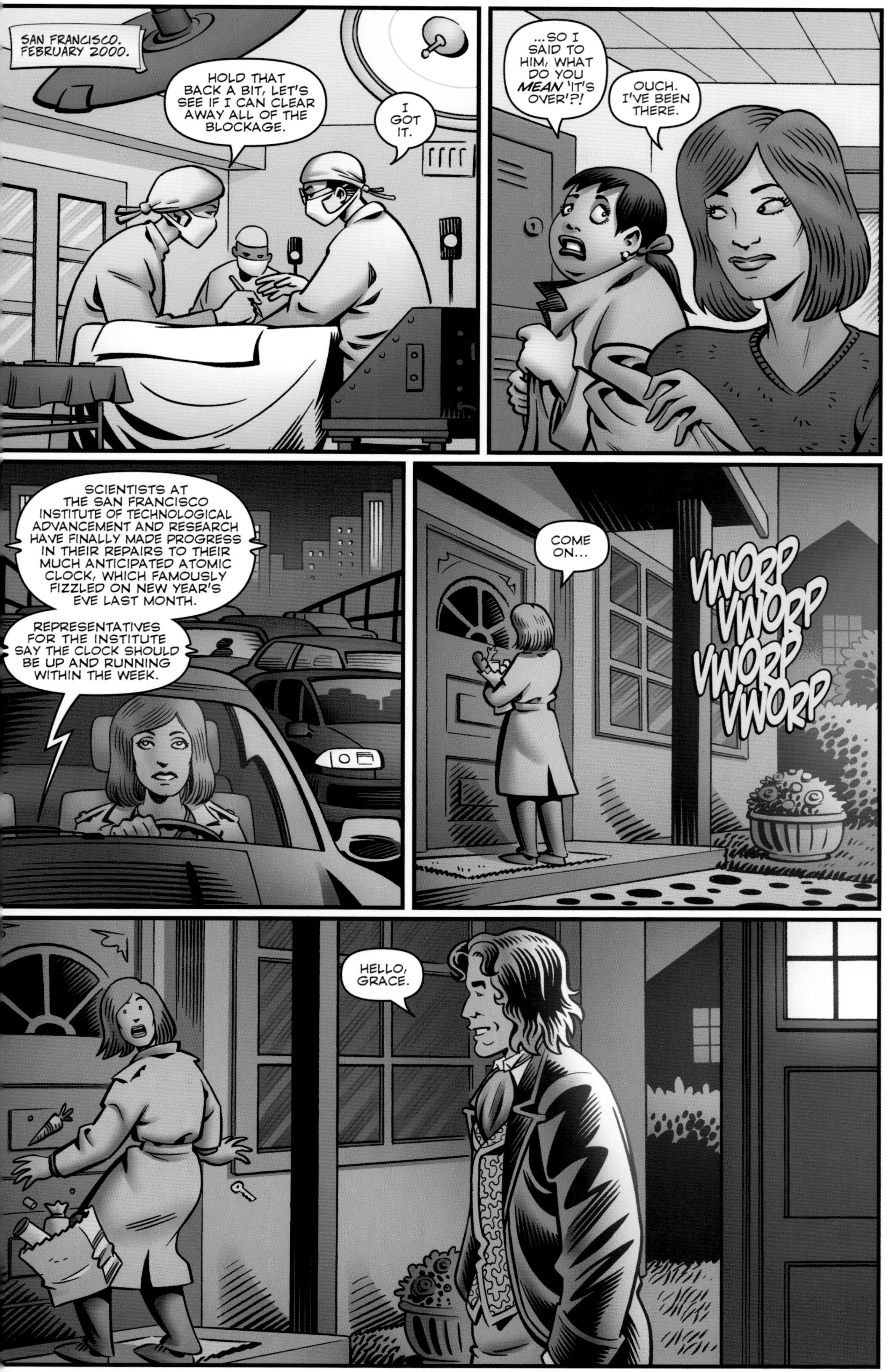
SAN FRANCISCO. FEBRUARY 2000.
HOLD THAT BACK A BIT, LET'S SEE IF I CAN CLEAR AWAY ALL OF THE BLOCKAGE.
I GOT IT.
...SO I SAID TO HIM, WHAT DO YOU *MEAN* 'IT'S OVER'?!
OUCH. I'VE BEEN THERE.
SCIENTISTS AT THE SAN FRANCISCO INSTITUTE OF TECHNOLOGICAL ADVANCEMENT AND RESEARCH HAVE FINALLY MADE PROGRESS IN THEIR REPAIRS TO THEIR MUCH ANTICIPATED ATOMIC CLOCK, WHICH FAMOUSLY FIZZLED ON NEW YEAR'S EVE LAST MONTH.
REPRESENTATIVES FOR THE INSTITUTE SAY THE CLOCK SHOULD BE UP AND RUNNING WITHIN THE WEEK.
COME ON...
VWORP VWORP VWORP VWORP
HELLO, GRACE.

DOCTOR! YOU'RE BACK!

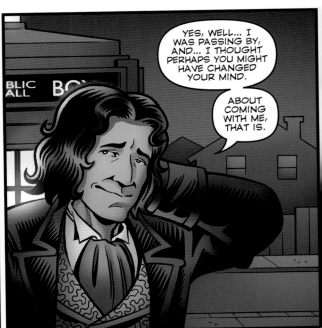

YES, WELL... I WAS PASSING BY, AND... I THOUGHT PERHAPS YOU MIGHT HAVE CHANGED YOUR MIND.

ABOUT COMING WITH ME, THAT IS.

NO, THANK YOU, DOCTOR, BUT I TOLD YOU BEFORE. I DON'T THINK I'M CUT OUT FOR YOUR LIFE.

I'M HAPPY. I'M SAFE. I'M—

BORED?

WHAT DO YOU SAY, GRACE? JUST ONE TRIP.

JUST ONE TRIP.

SPLENDID...

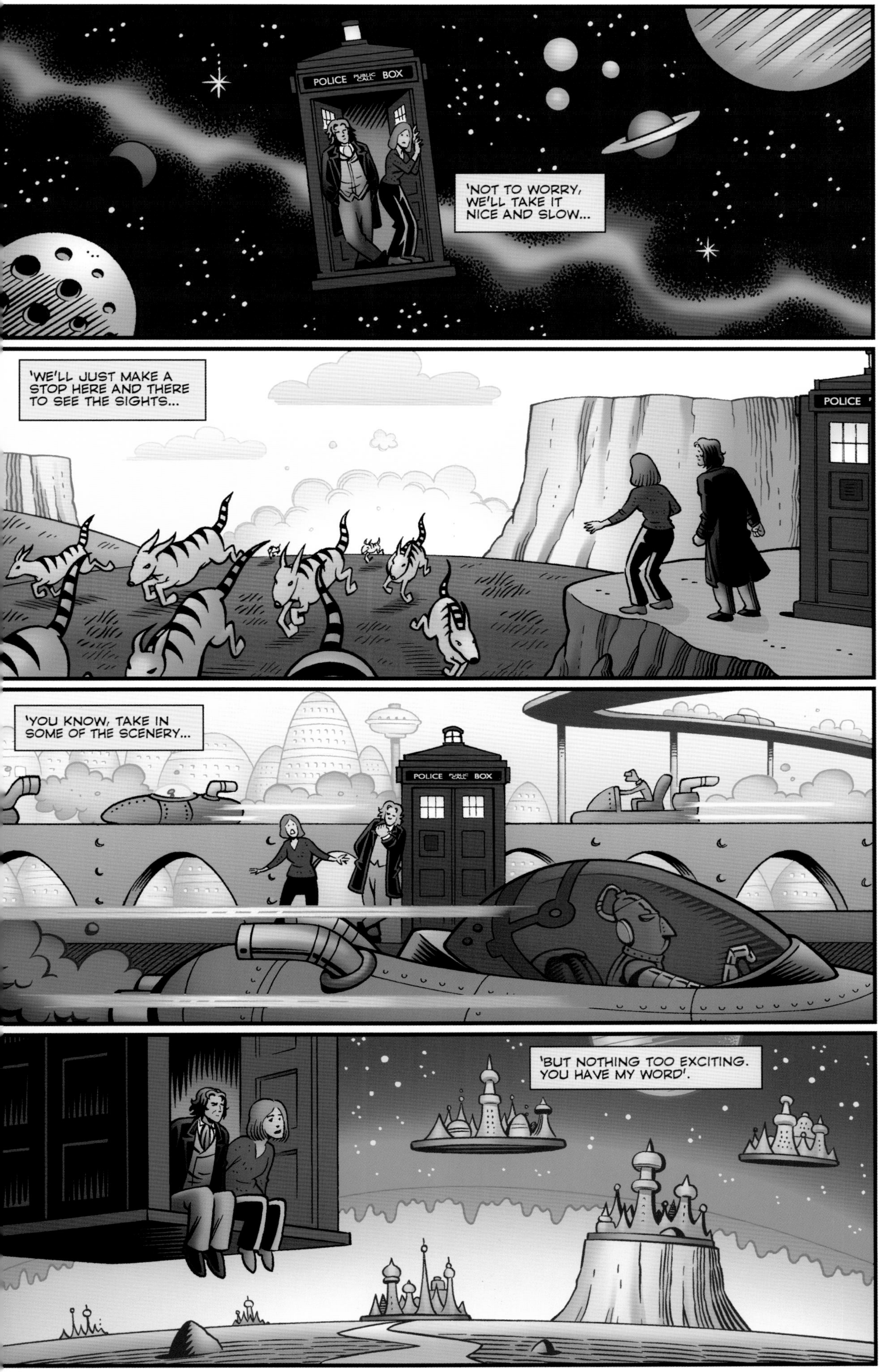

POLICE PUBLIC CALL BOX
'NOT TO WORRY, WE'LL TAKE IT NICE AND SLOW...
'WE'LL JUST MAKE A STOP HERE AND THERE TO SEE THE SIGHTS...
POLICE
'YOU KNOW, TAKE IN SOME OF THE SCENERY...
POLICE PUBLIC CALL BOX
'BUT NOTHING TOO EXCITING. YOU HAVE MY WORD'.

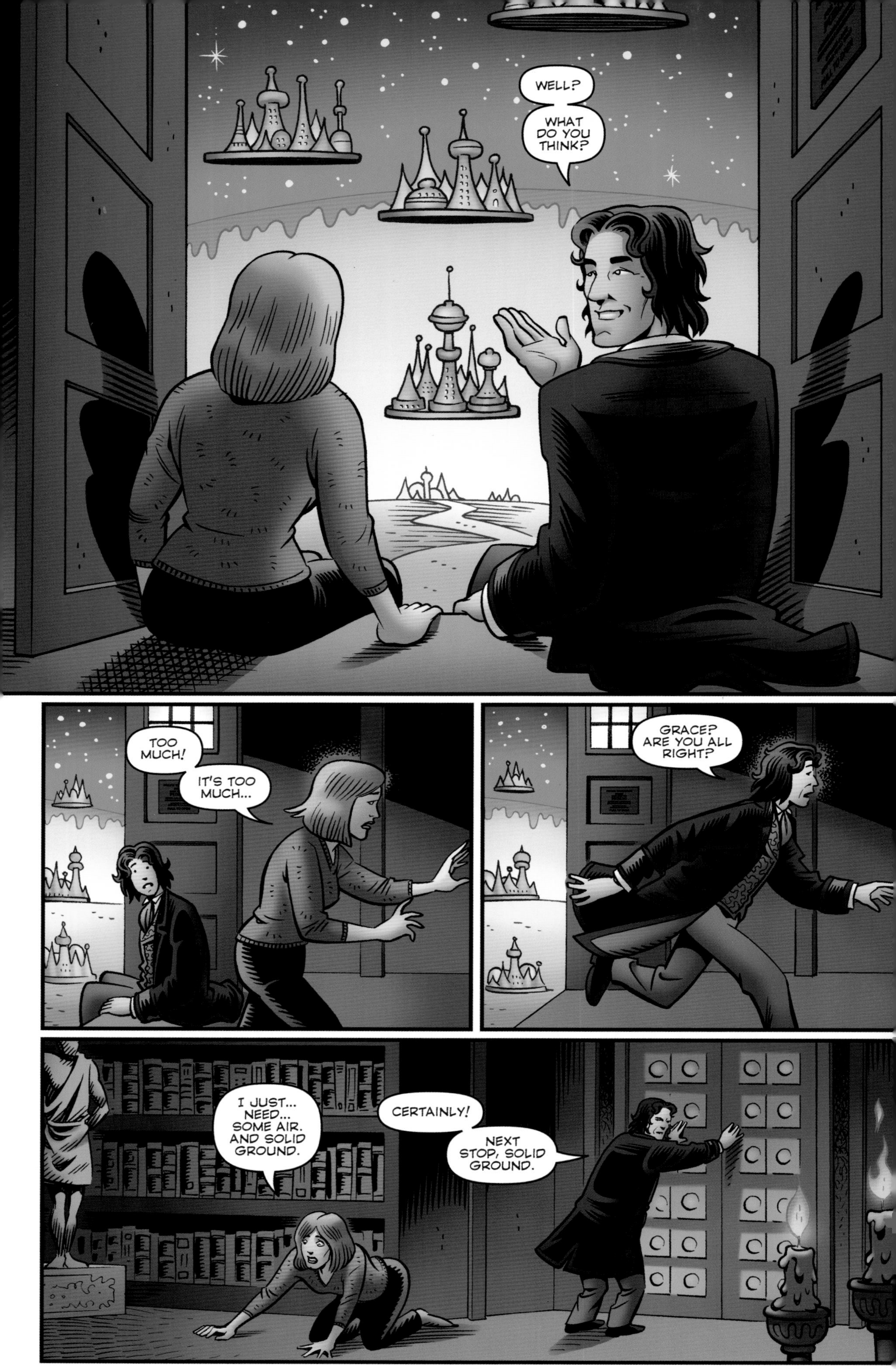
WELL?
WHAT DO YOU THINK?
TOO MUCH!
IT'S TOO MUCH...
GRACE? ARE YOU ALL RIGHT?
I JUST... NEED... SOME AIR. AND SOLID GROUND.
CERTAINLY!
NEXT STOP, SOLID GROUND.

VWORP VWORP VWORP

POLICE PUBLIC CALL BOX

HANG ON, ALMOST THERE...

HERE WE ARE!

COMING THROUGH!

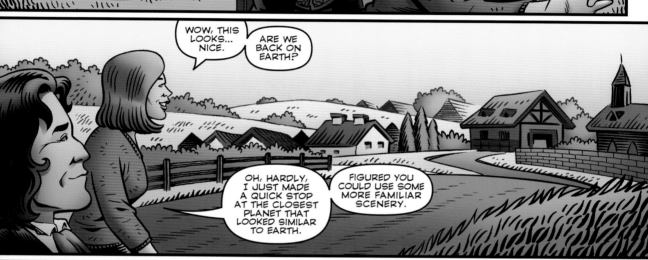

WOW, THIS LOOKS... NICE.

ARE WE BACK ON EARTH?

OH, HARDLY, I JUST MADE A QUICK STOP AT THE CLOSEST PLANET THAT LOOKED SIMILAR TO EARTH.

FIGURED YOU COULD USE SOME MORE FAMILIAR SCENERY.

HELLO THERE!

WHY IS HE SPEAKING ENGLISH? I THOUGHT WE WEREN'T ON EARTH.

OH, THAT'S NOT ENGLISH.

THE TARDIS TAKES CARE OF THAT FOR YOU. AS LONG AS YOU'RE TRAVELING WITH ME, IT AUTOMATICALLY TRANSLATES WHAT-EVER LANGUAGE YOU HEAR.

CONVENIENT, NO? ANYWAY, WE'RE BEING RUDE...

HELLO BACK! I AM THE DOCTOR, AND THIS IS MY FRIEND GRACE HOLLOWAY. ALSO A DOCTOR, NOW THAT I THINK ABOUT IT! BUT NOT THE DOCTOR.

WHICH IS ME. ANYWAY, WE'RE JUST PASSING THROUGH AND THOUGHT WE'D STOP AND ENJOY THE SCENERY.

HI. I'M OREN.

YOU'RE NOT FROM THE CITY, ARE YOU?

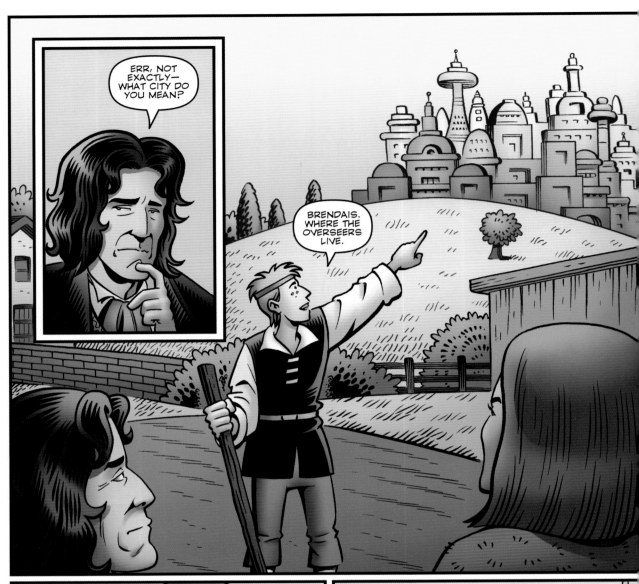

ERR, NOT EXACTLY— WHAT CITY DO YOU MEAN?

BRENDAIS. WHERE THE OVERSEERS LIVE.

OH, NO, NO. GRACE AND I ARE TRAVELLING FROM MUCH FARTHER AWAY.

WOW. WE RARELY HAVE VISITORS HERE. NO ONE EVER GETS TO TRAVEL, EITHER.

I DON'T WANT TO PRY, BUT PERHAPS YOU COULD TELL ME MORE...

BUT IT LOOKS LIKE YOU HAVE HAD A LONG JOURNEY. COME, LET'S GO TO MY FAMILY'S HOME.

WE'LL HAVE A MEAL AND YOU CAN GET A LITTLE REST.

THAT SOUNDS LIKE A GREAT IDEA.

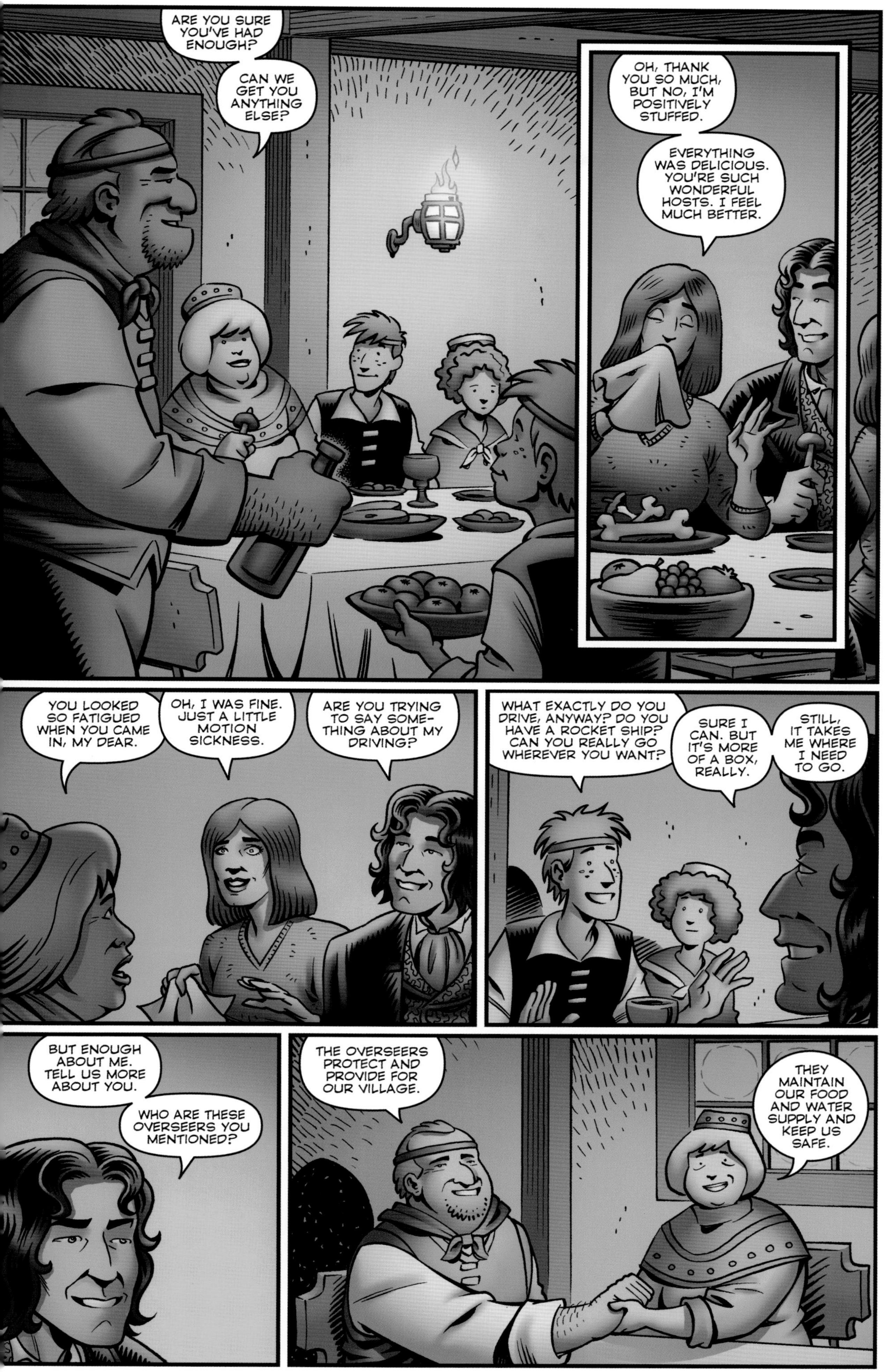
ARE YOU SURE YOU'VE HAD ENOUGH?
CAN WE GET YOU ANYTHING ELSE?
OH, THANK YOU SO MUCH, BUT NO, I'M POSITIVELY STUFFED.
EVERYTHING WAS DELICIOUS. YOU'RE SUCH WONDERFUL HOSTS. I FEEL MUCH BETTER.
YOU LOOKED SO FATIGUED WHEN YOU CAME IN, MY DEAR.
OH, I WAS FINE. JUST A LITTLE MOTION SICKNESS.
ARE YOU TRYING TO SAY SOMETHING ABOUT MY DRIVING?
WHAT EXACTLY DO YOU DRIVE, ANYWAY? DO YOU HAVE A ROCKET SHIP? CAN YOU REALLY GO WHEREVER YOU WANT?
SURE I CAN. BUT IT'S MORE OF A BOX, REALLY.
STILL, IT TAKES ME WHERE I NEED TO GO.
BUT ENOUGH ABOUT ME. TELL US MORE ABOUT YOU.
WHO ARE THESE OVERSEERS YOU MENTIONED?
THE OVERSEERS PROTECT AND PROVIDE FOR OUR VILLAGE.
THEY MAINTAIN OUR FOOD AND WATER SUPPLY AND KEEP US SAFE.

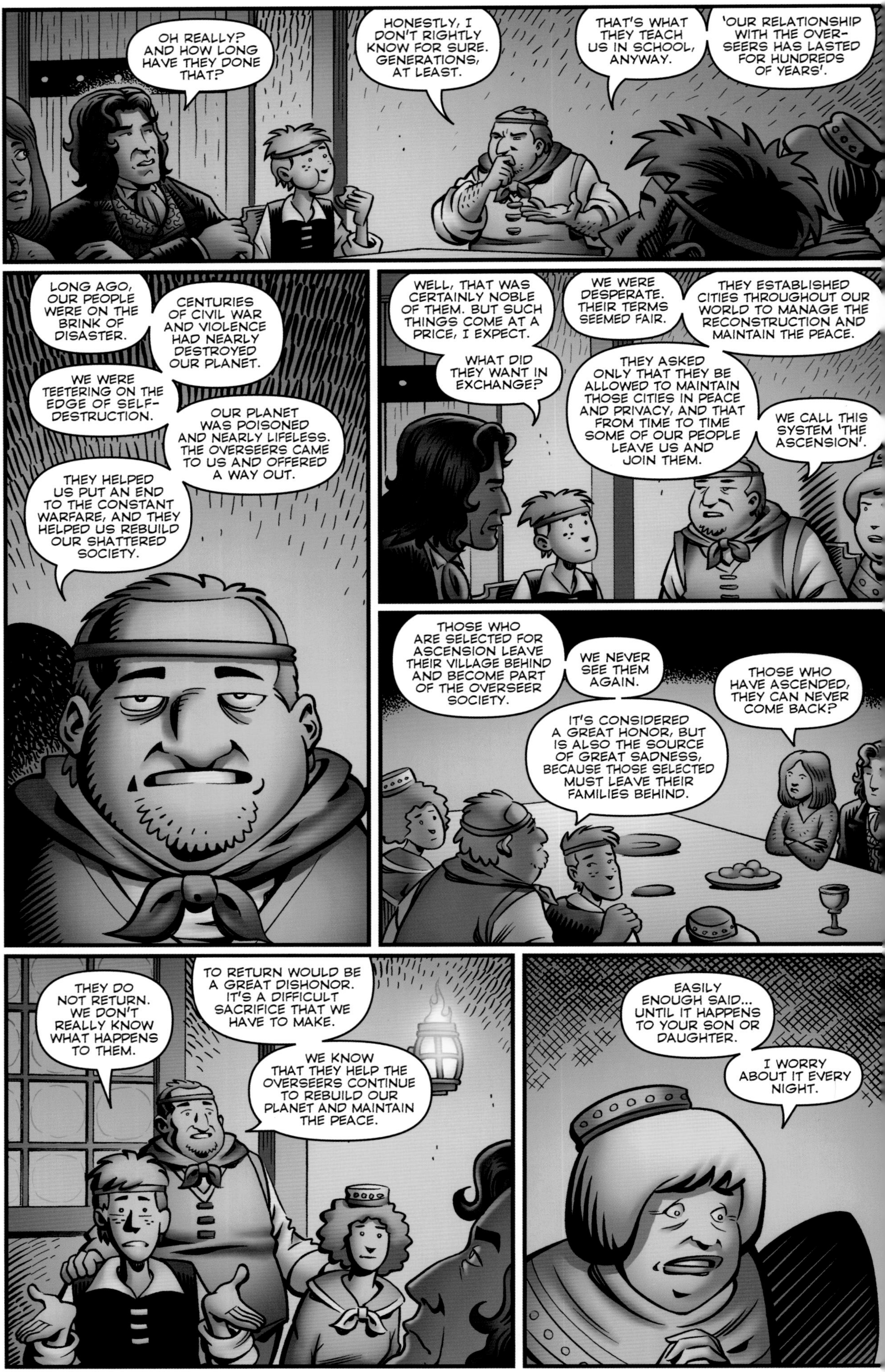
OH REALLY? AND HOW LONG HAVE THEY DONE THAT?
HONESTLY, I DON'T RIGHTLY KNOW FOR SURE. GENERATIONS, AT LEAST.
THAT'S WHAT THEY TEACH US IN SCHOOL, ANYWAY.
'OUR RELATIONSHIP WITH THE OVER-SEERS HAS LASTED FOR HUNDREDS OF YEARS'.
LONG AGO, OUR PEOPLE WERE ON THE BRINK OF DISASTER.
CENTURIES OF CIVIL WAR AND VIOLENCE HAD NEARLY DESTROYED OUR PLANET.
WE WERE TEETERING ON THE EDGE OF SELF-DESTRUCTION.
OUR PLANET WAS POISONED AND NEARLY LIFELESS. THE OVERSEERS CAME TO US AND OFFERED A WAY OUT.
THEY HELPED US PUT AN END TO THE CONSTANT WARFARE, AND THEY HELPED US REBUILD OUR SHATTERED SOCIETY.
WELL, THAT WAS CERTAINLY NOBLE OF THEM. BUT SUCH THINGS COME AT A PRICE, I EXPECT.
WHAT DID THEY WANT IN EXCHANGE?
WE WERE DESPERATE. THEIR TERMS SEEMED FAIR.
THEY ESTABLISHED CITIES THROUGHOUT OUR WORLD TO MANAGE THE RECONSTRUCTION AND MAINTAIN THE PEACE.
THEY ASKED ONLY THAT THEY BE ALLOWED TO MAINTAIN THOSE CITIES IN PEACE AND PRIVACY, AND THAT FROM TIME TO TIME SOME OF OUR PEOPLE LEAVE US AND JOIN THEM.
WE CALL THIS SYSTEM 'THE ASCENSION'.
THOSE WHO ARE SELECTED FOR ASCENSION LEAVE THEIR VILLAGE BEHIND AND BECOME PART OF THE OVERSEER SOCIETY.
WE NEVER SEE THEM AGAIN.
IT'S CONSIDERED A GREAT HONOR, BUT IS ALSO THE SOURCE OF GREAT SADNESS, BECAUSE THOSE SELECTED MUST LEAVE THEIR FAMILIES BEHIND.
THOSE WHO HAVE ASCENDED, THEY CAN NEVER COME BACK?
THEY DO NOT RETURN. WE DON'T REALLY KNOW WHAT HAPPENS TO THEM.
TO RETURN WOULD BE A GREAT DISHONOR. IT'S A DIFFICULT SACRIFICE THAT WE HAVE TO MAKE.
WE KNOW THAT THEY HELP THE OVERSEERS CONTINUE TO REBUILD OUR PLANET AND MAINTAIN THE PEACE.
EASILY ENOUGH SAID... UNTIL IT HAPPENS TO YOUR SON OR DAUGHTER.
I WORRY ABOUT IT EVERY NIGHT.

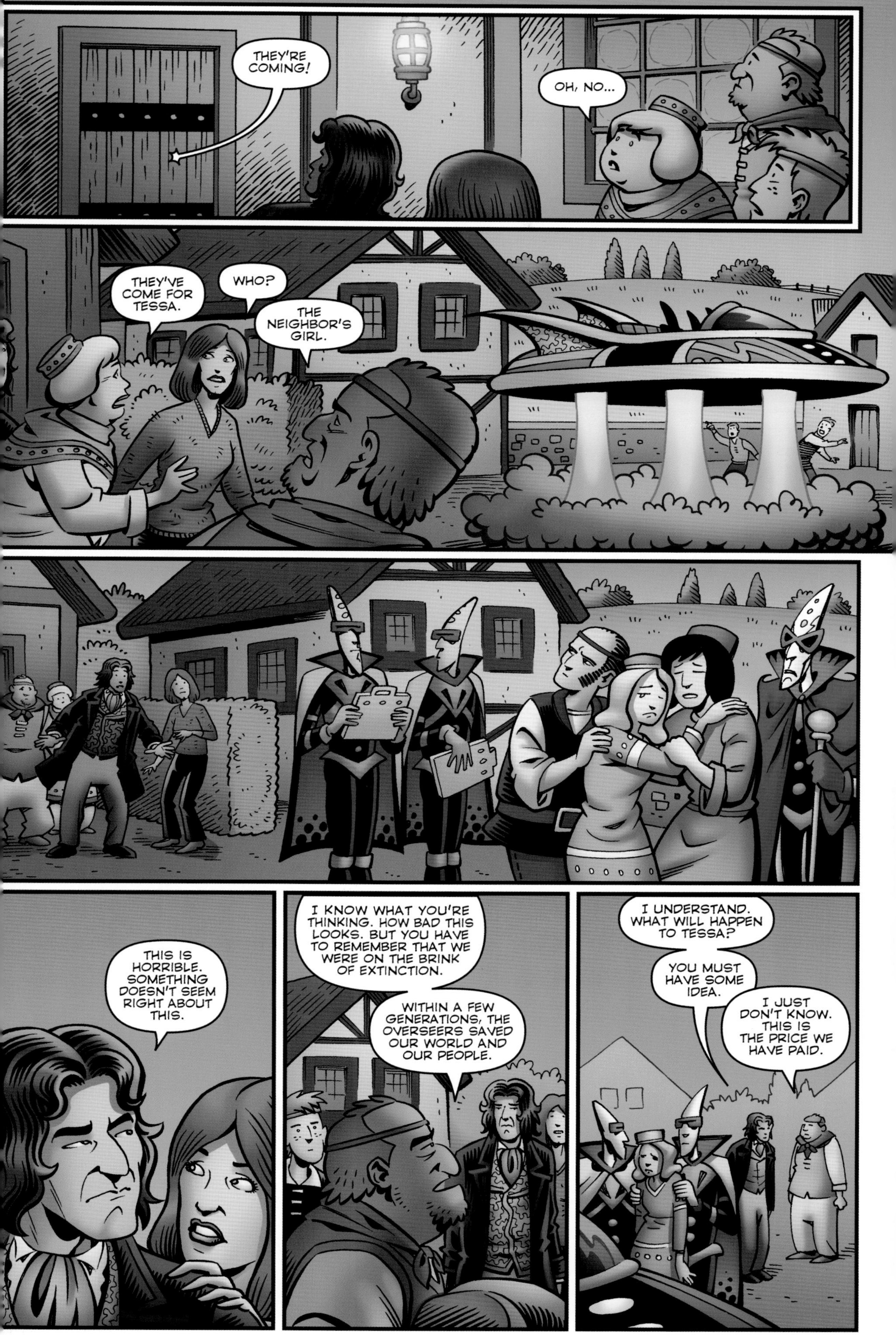
THEY'RE COMING!
OH, NO...
THEY'VE COME FOR TESSA.
WHO?
THE NEIGHBOR'S GIRL.
THIS IS HORRIBLE. SOMETHING DOESN'T SEEM RIGHT ABOUT THIS.
I KNOW WHAT YOU'RE THINKING. HOW BAD THIS LOOKS. BUT YOU HAVE TO REMEMBER THAT WE WERE ON THE BRINK OF EXTINCTION.
WITHIN A FEW GENERATIONS, THE OVERSEERS SAVED OUR WORLD AND OUR PEOPLE.
I UNDERSTAND. WHAT WILL HAPPEN TO TESSA?
YOU MUST HAVE SOME IDEA.
I JUST DON'T KNOW. THIS IS THE PRICE WE HAVE PAID.

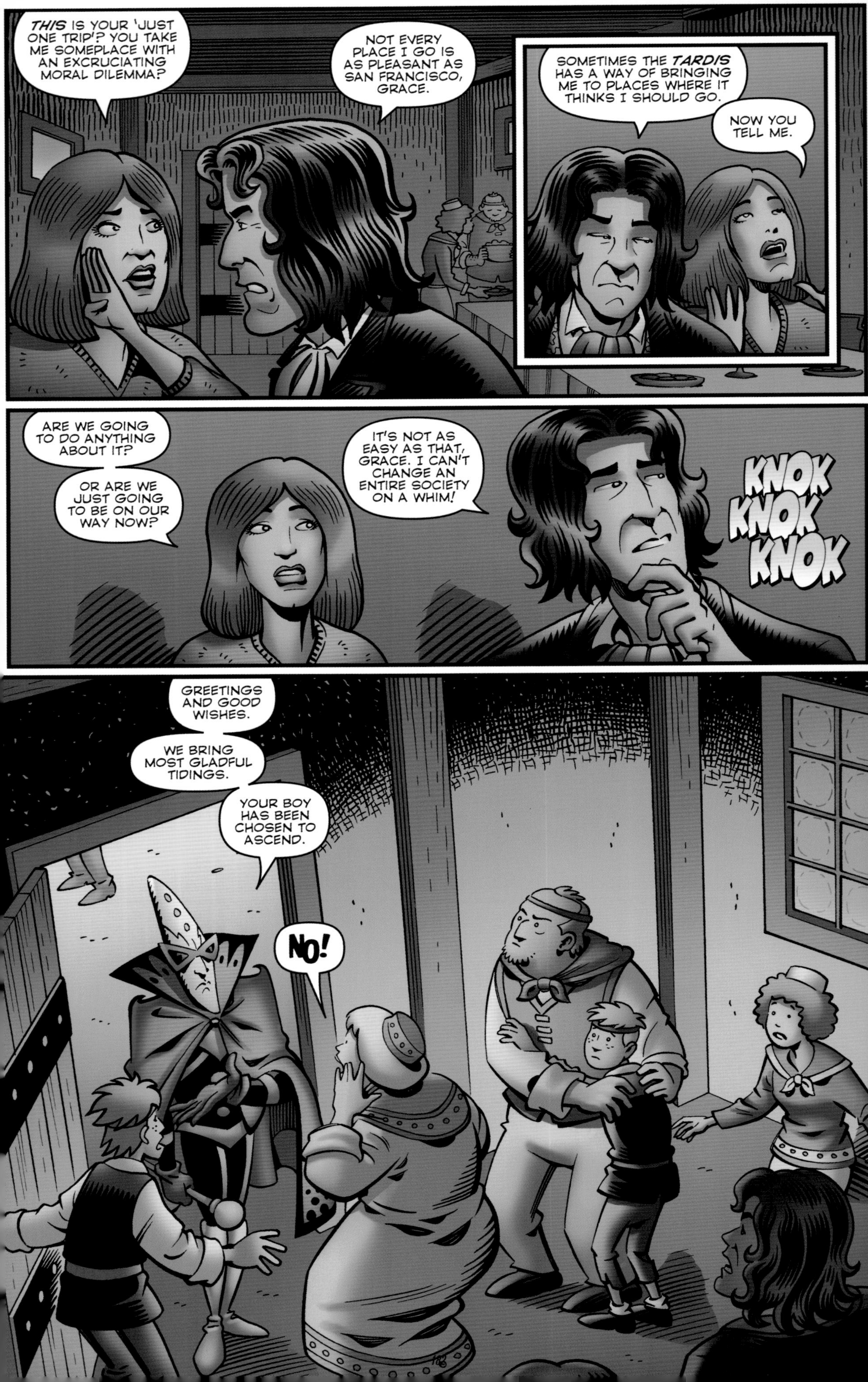
THIS IS YOUR 'JUST ONE TRIP'? YOU TAKE ME SOMEPLACE WITH AN EXCRUCIATING MORAL DILEMMA?
NOT EVERY PLACE I GO IS AS PLEASANT AS SAN FRANCISCO, GRACE.
SOMETIMES THE TARDIS HAS A WAY OF BRINGING ME TO PLACES WHERE IT THINKS I SHOULD GO.
NOW YOU TELL ME.
ARE WE GOING TO DO ANYTHING ABOUT IT?
OR ARE WE JUST GOING TO BE ON OUR WAY NOW?
IT'S NOT AS EASY AS THAT, GRACE. I CAN'T CHANGE AN ENTIRE SOCIETY ON A WHIM!
KNOK KNOK KNOK
GREETINGS AND GOOD WISHES.
WE BRING MOST GLADFUL TIDINGS.
YOUR BOY HAS BEEN CHOSEN TO ASCEND.
NO!

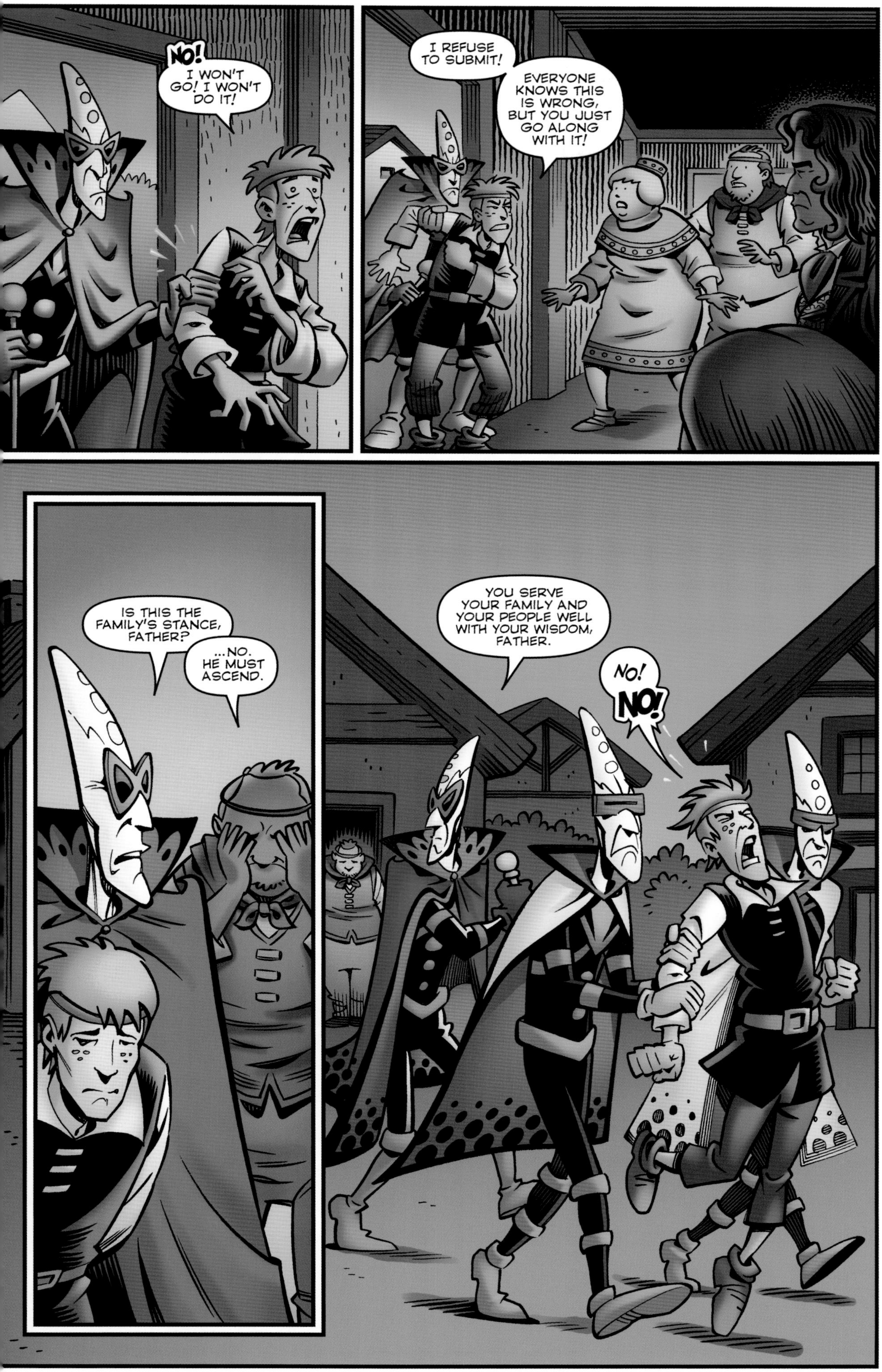
NO! I WON'T GO! I WON'T DO IT!
I REFUSE TO SUBMIT!
EVERYONE KNOWS THIS IS WRONG, BUT YOU JUST GO ALONG WITH IT!
IS THIS THE FAMILY'S STANCE, FATHER?
...NO. HE MUST ASCEND.
YOU SERVE YOUR FAMILY AND YOUR PEOPLE WELL WITH YOUR WISDOM, FATHER.
NO! NO!

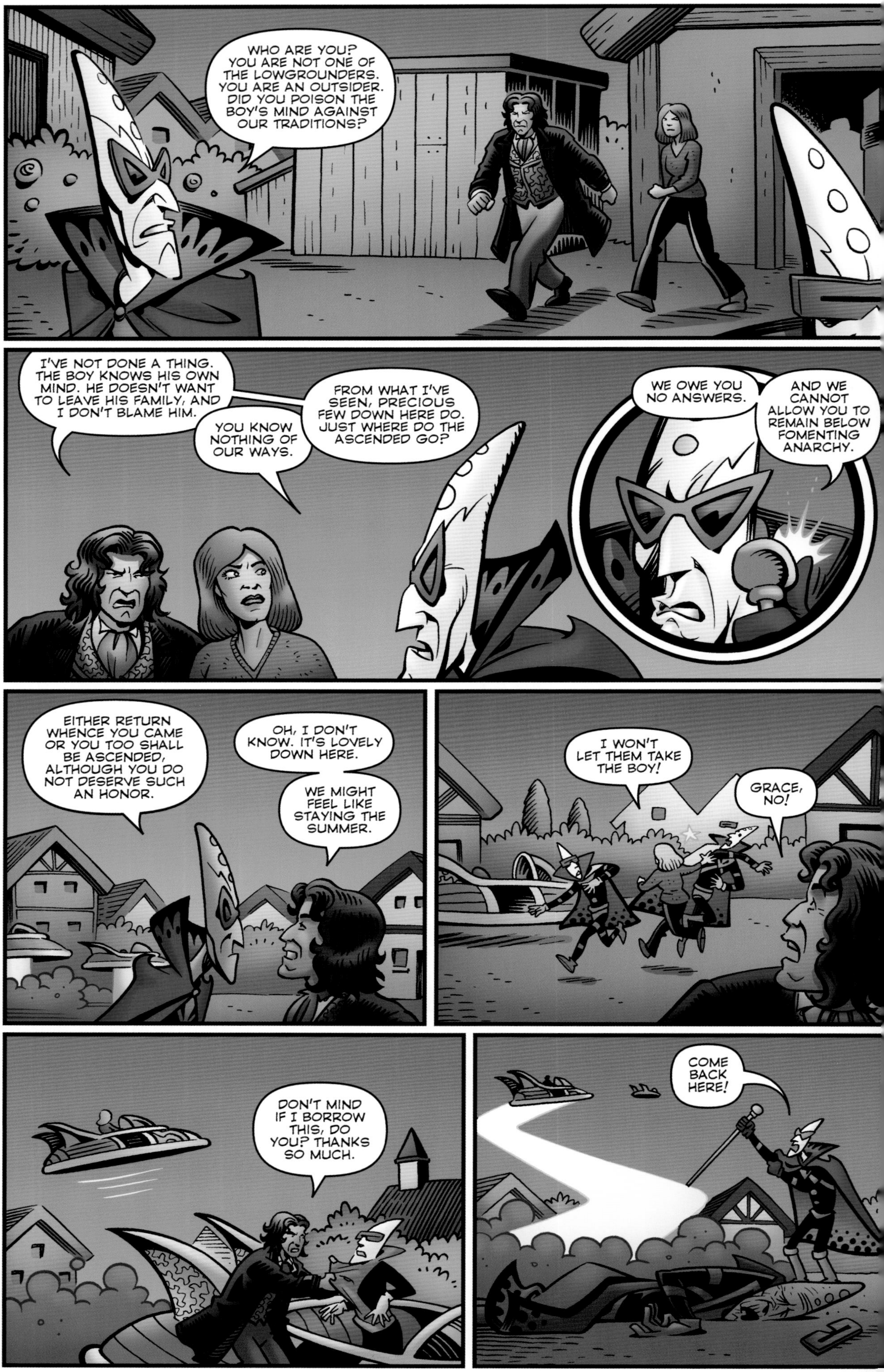
WHO ARE YOU? YOU ARE NOT ONE OF THE LOWGROUNDERS. YOU ARE AN OUTSIDER. DID YOU POISON THE BOY'S MIND AGAINST OUR TRADITIONS?
I'VE NOT DONE A THING. THE BOY KNOWS HIS OWN MIND. HE DOESN'T WANT TO LEAVE HIS FAMILY, AND I DON'T BLAME HIM.
FROM WHAT I'VE SEEN, PRECIOUS FEW DOWN HERE DO. JUST WHERE DO THE ASCENDED GO?
YOU KNOW NOTHING OF OUR WAYS.
WE OWE YOU NO ANSWERS.
AND WE CANNOT ALLOW YOU TO REMAIN BELOW FOMENTING ANARCHY.
EITHER RETURN WHENCE YOU CAME OR YOU TOO SHALL BE ASCENDED, ALTHOUGH YOU DO NOT DESERVE SUCH AN HONOR.
OH, I DON'T KNOW. IT'S LOVELY DOWN HERE.
WE MIGHT FEEL LIKE STAYING THE SUMMER.
I WON'T LET THEM TAKE THE BOY!
GRACE, NO!
DON'T MIND IF I BORROW THIS, DO YOU? THANKS SO MUCH.
COME BACK HERE!

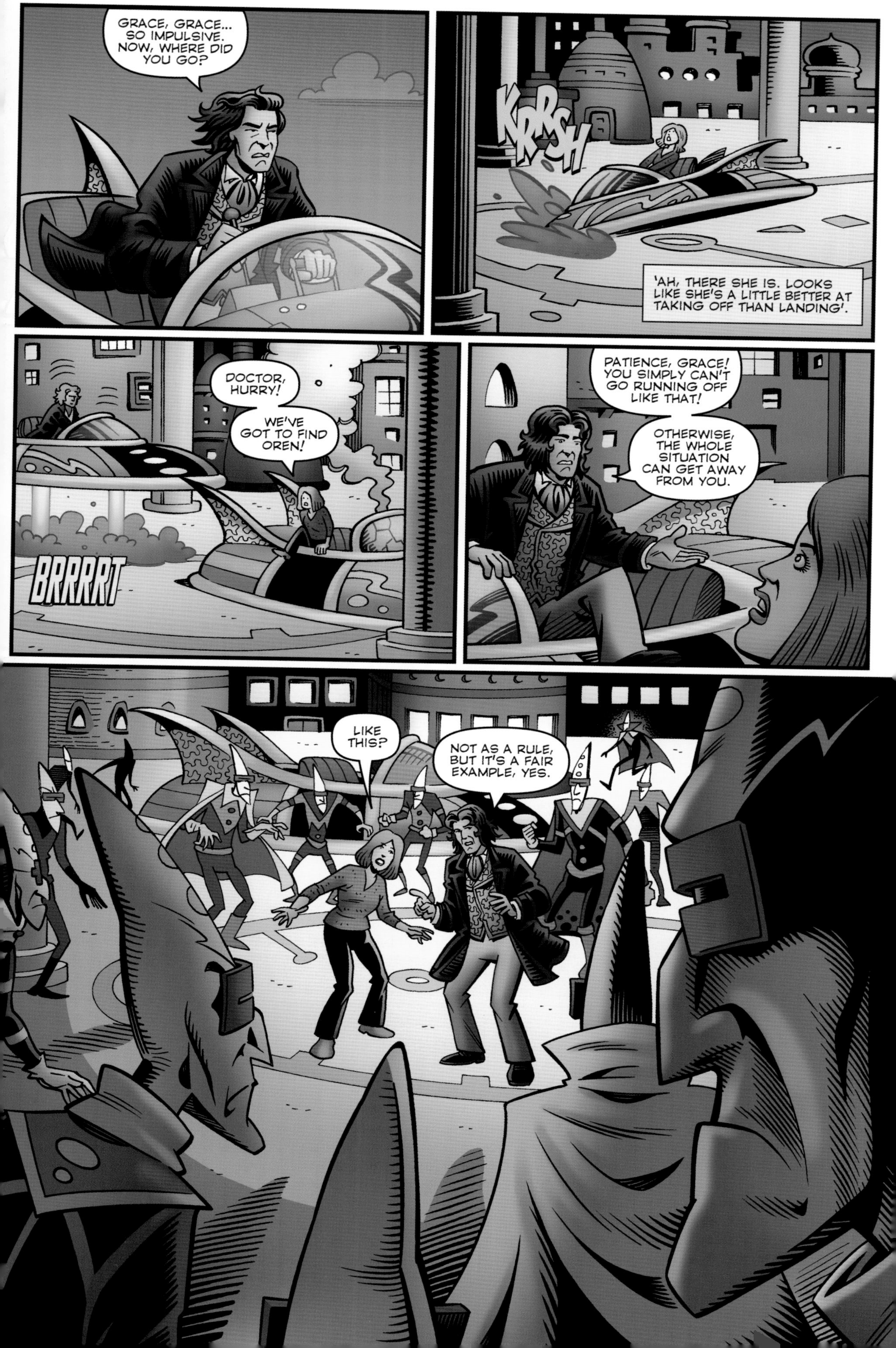
GRACE, GRACE... SO IMPULSIVE. NOW, WHERE DID YOU GO?
KRRSH
'AH, THERE SHE IS. LOOKS LIKE SHE'S A LITTLE BETTER AT TAKING OFF THAN LANDING'.
DOCTOR, HURRY!
WE'VE GOT TO FIND OREN!
BRRRRT
PATIENCE, GRACE! YOU SIMPLY CAN'T GO RUNNING OFF LIKE THAT!
OTHERWISE, THE WHOLE SITUATION CAN GET AWAY FROM YOU.
LIKE THIS?
NOT AS A RULE, BUT IT'S A FAIR EXAMPLE, YES.

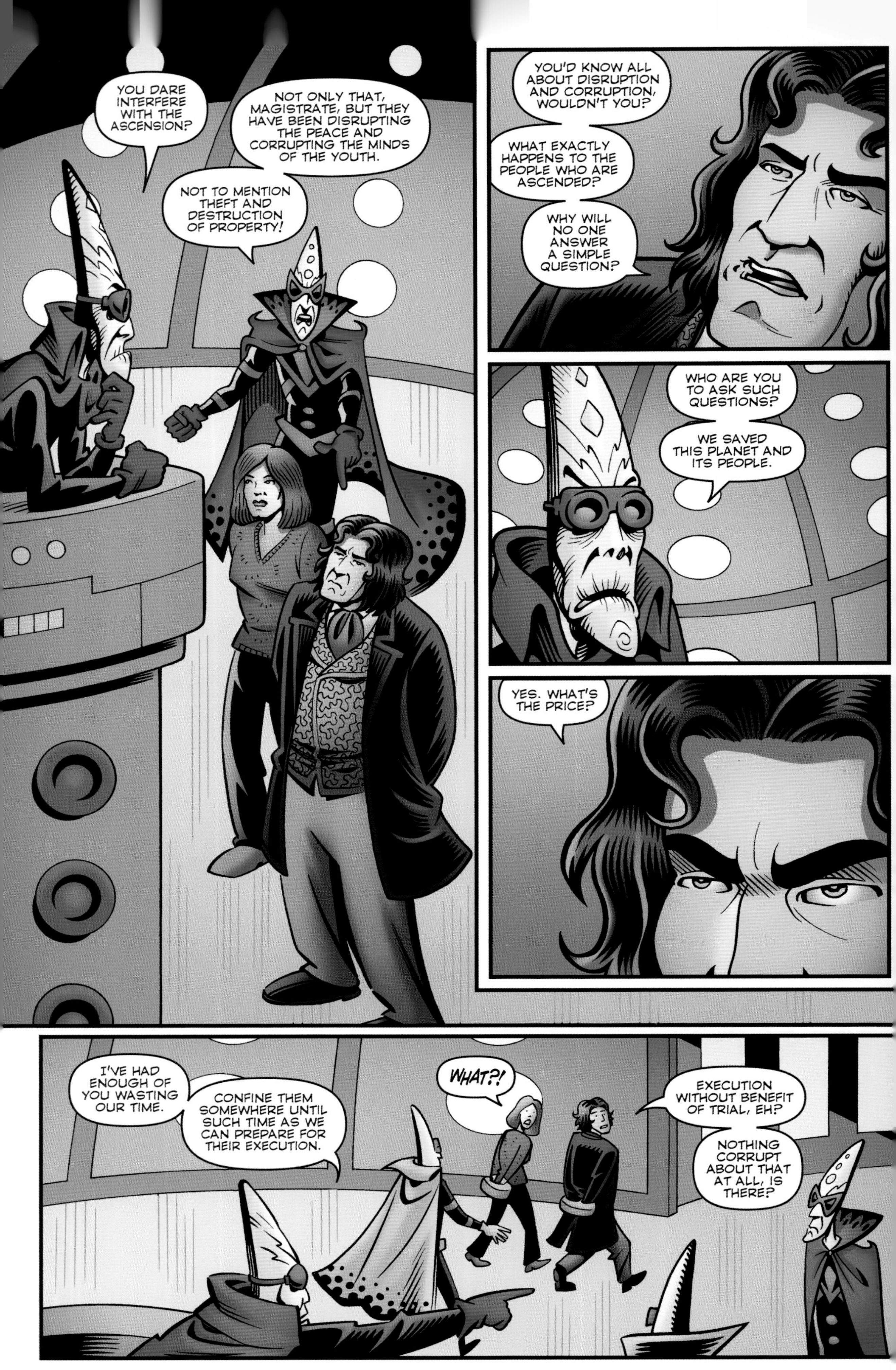
YOU DARE INTERFERE WITH THE ASCENSION?
NOT ONLY THAT, MAGISTRATE, BUT THEY HAVE BEEN DISRUPTING THE PEACE AND CORRUPTING THE MINDS OF THE YOUTH.
NOT TO MENTION THEFT AND DESTRUCTION OF PROPERTY!
YOU'D KNOW ALL ABOUT DISRUPTION AND CORRUPTION, WOULDN'T YOU?
WHAT EXACTLY HAPPENS TO THE PEOPLE WHO ARE ASCENDED?
WHY WILL NO ONE ANSWER A SIMPLE QUESTION?
WHO ARE YOU TO ASK SUCH QUESTIONS?
WE SAVED THIS PLANET AND ITS PEOPLE.
YES. WHAT'S THE PRICE?
I'VE HAD ENOUGH OF YOU WASTING OUR TIME.
CONFINE THEM SOMEWHERE UNTIL SUCH TIME AS WE CAN PREPARE FOR THEIR EXECUTION.
WHAT?!
EXECUTION WITHOUT BENEFIT OF TRIAL, EH?
NOTHING CORRUPT ABOUT THAT AT ALL, IS THERE?

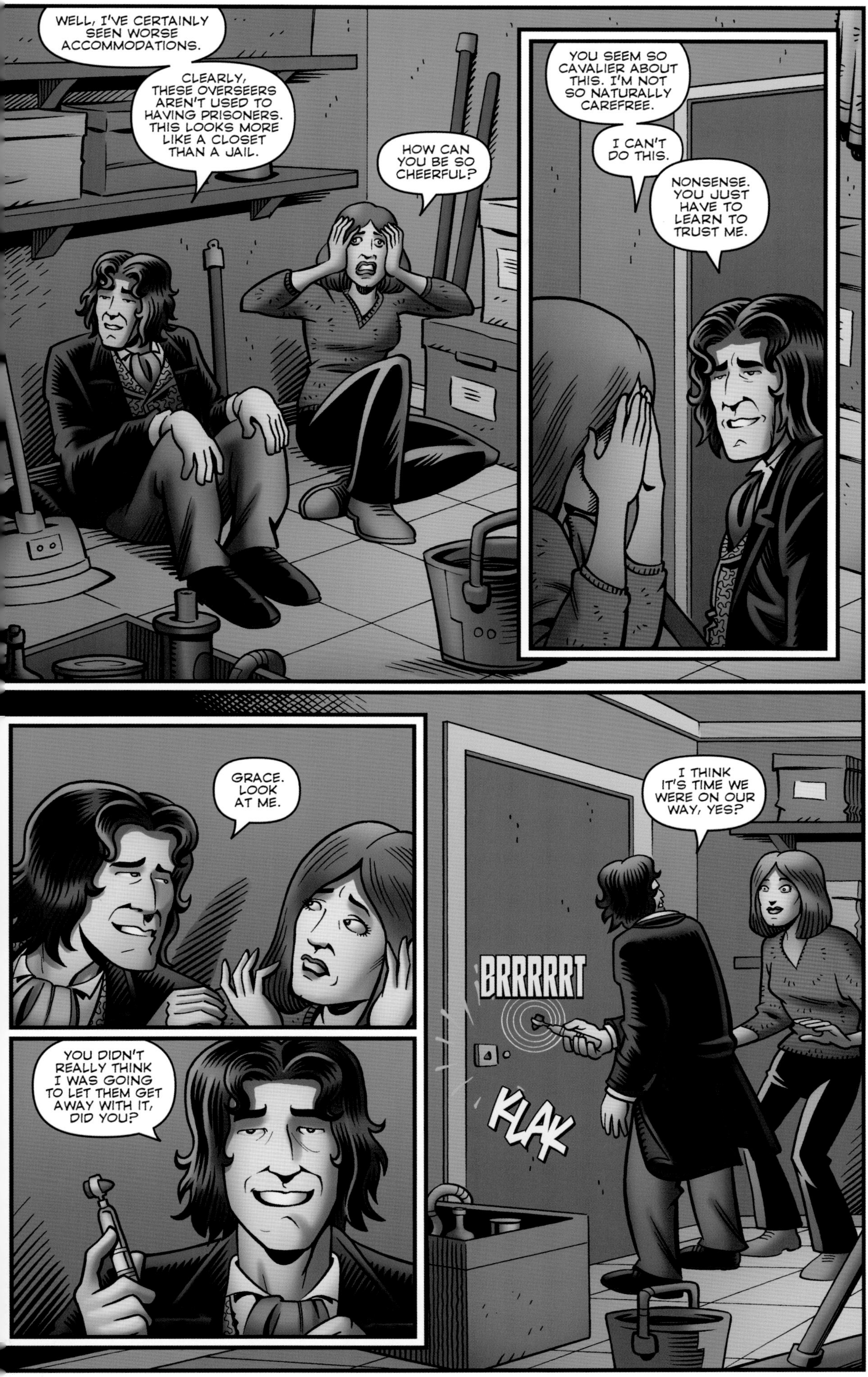
WELL, I'VE CERTAINLY SEEN WORSE ACCOMMODATIONS.
CLEARLY, THESE OVERSEERS AREN'T USED TO HAVING PRISONERS. THIS LOOKS MORE LIKE A CLOSET THAN A JAIL.
HOW CAN YOU BE SO CHEERFUL?
YOU SEEM SO CAVALIER ABOUT THIS. I'M NOT SO NATURALLY CAREFREE.
I CAN'T DO THIS.
NONSENSE. YOU JUST HAVE TO LEARN TO TRUST ME.
GRACE. LOOK AT ME.
YOU DIDN'T REALLY THINK I WAS GOING TO LET THEM GET AWAY WITH IT, DID YOU?
I THINK IT'S TIME WE WERE ON OUR WAY, YES?
BRRRRRT
KLAK

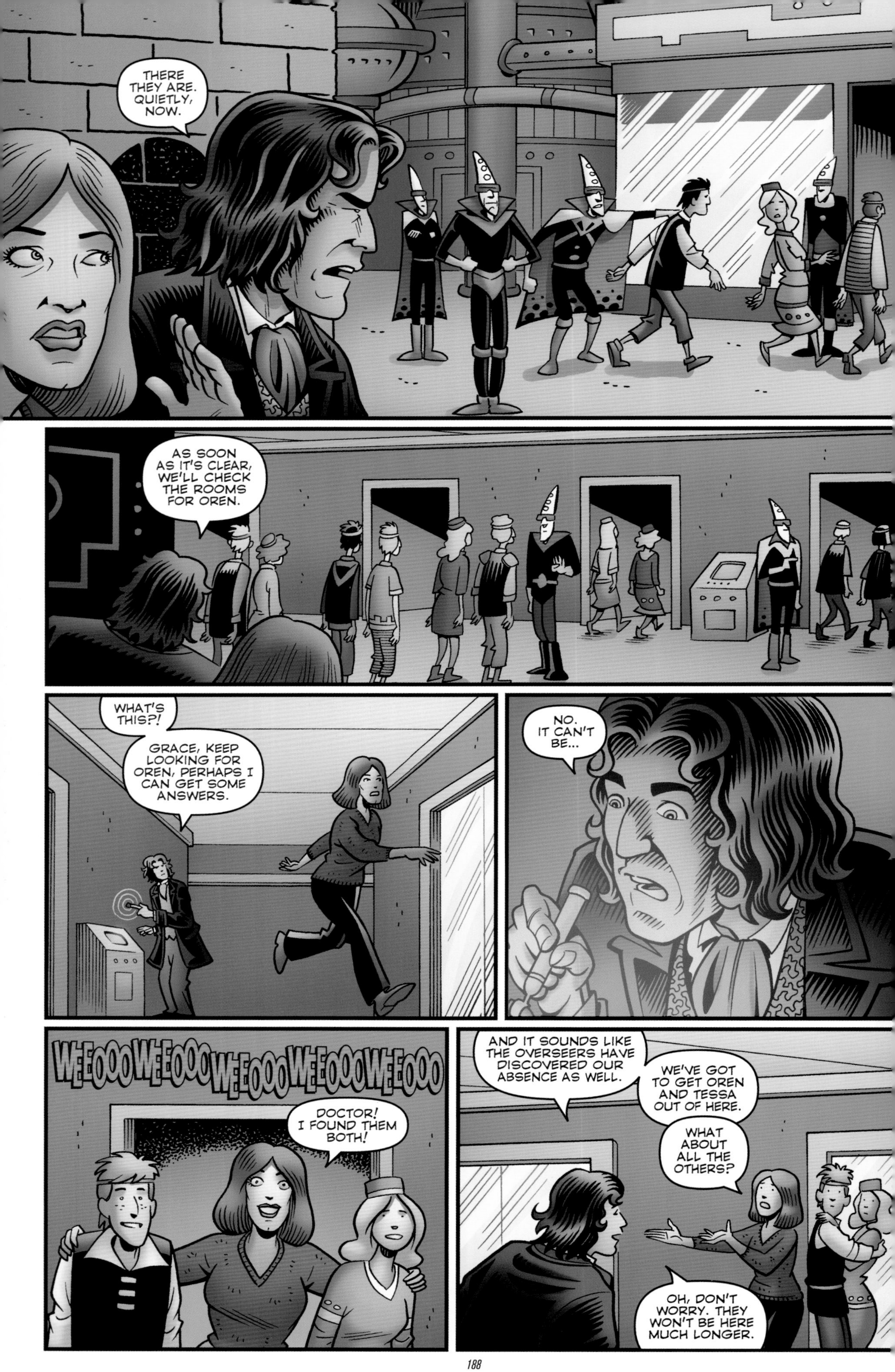

THERE THEY ARE. QUIETLY, NOW.
AS SOON AS IT'S CLEAR, WE'LL CHECK THE ROOMS FOR OREN.
WHAT'S THIS?!
GRACE, KEEP LOOKING FOR OREN, PERHAPS I CAN GET SOME ANSWERS.
NO. IT CAN'T BE...
WEEOOOWEEOOOWEEOOOWEEOOOWEEOOO
DOCTOR! I FOUND THEM BOTH!
AND IT SOUNDS LIKE THE OVERSEERS HAVE DISCOVERED OUR ABSENCE AS WELL.
WE'VE GOT TO GET OREN AND TESSA OUT OF HERE.
WHAT ABOUT ALL THE OTHERS?
OH, DON'T WORRY. THEY WON'T BE HERE MUCH LONGER.

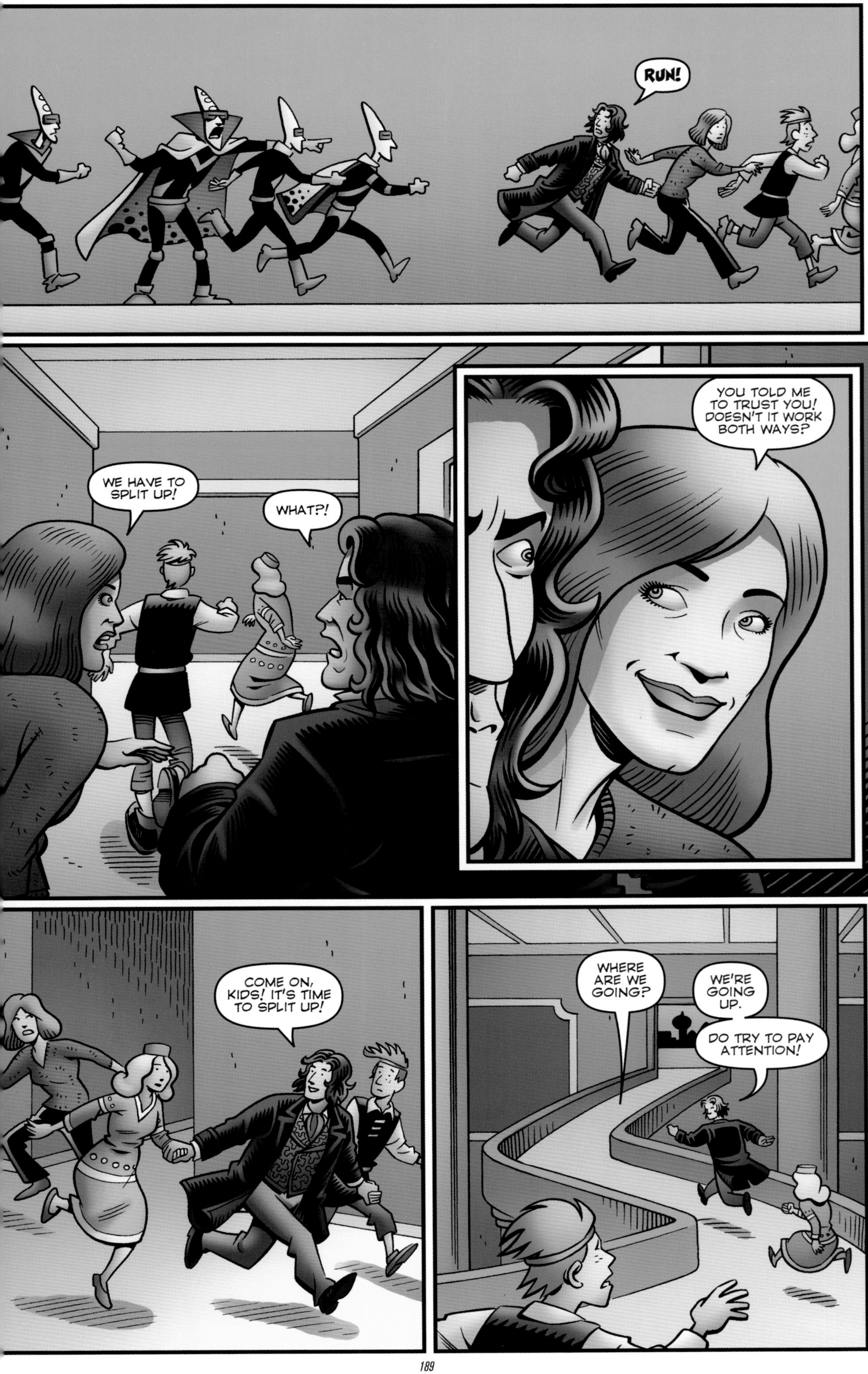
RUN!
WE HAVE TO SPLIT UP!
WHAT?!
YOU TOLD ME TO TRUST YOU! DOESN'T IT WORK BOTH WAYS?
COME ON, KIDS! IT'S TIME TO SPLIT UP!
WHERE ARE WE GOING?
WE'RE GOING UP.
DO TRY TO PAY ATTENTION!

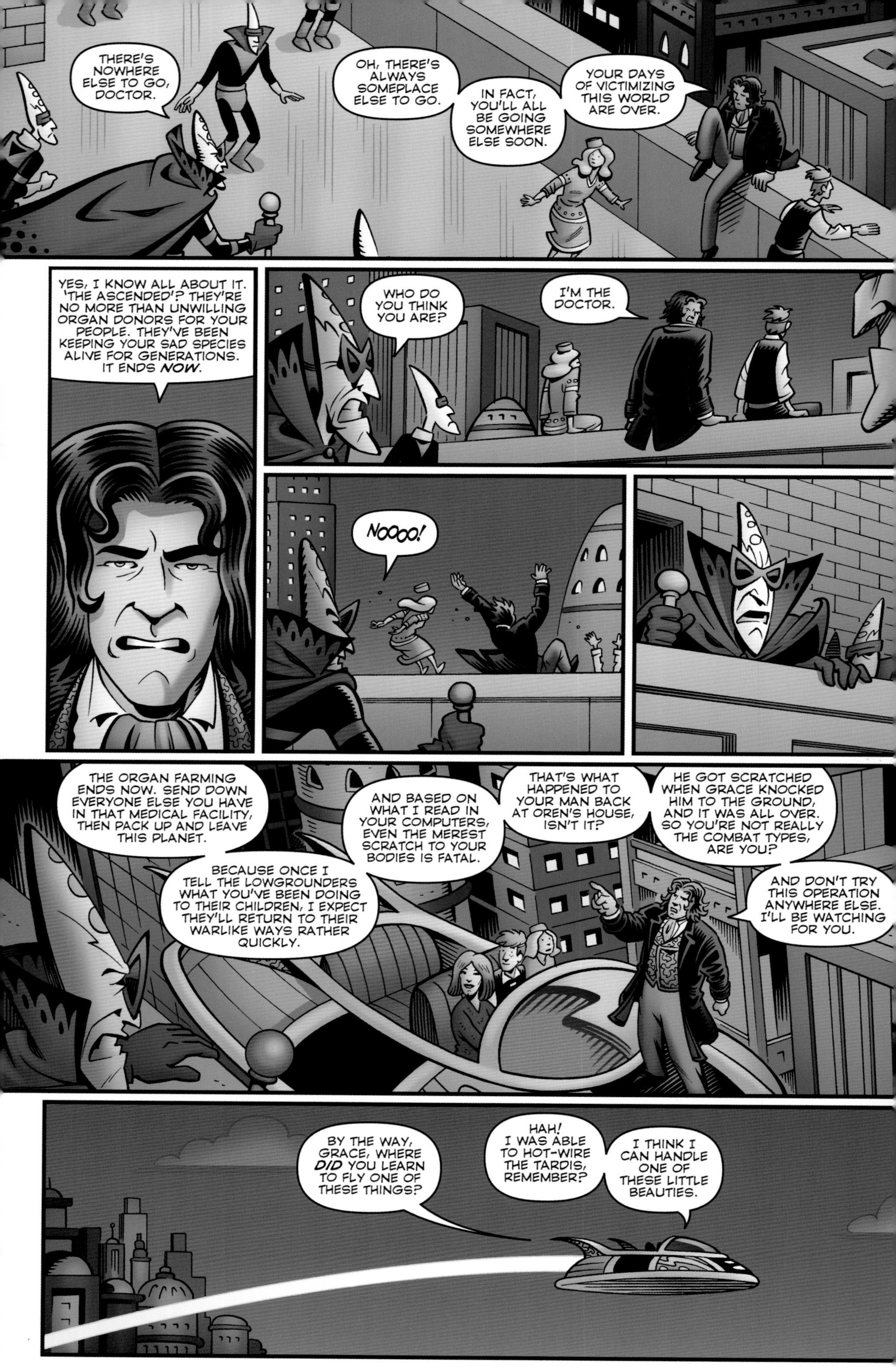
THERE'S NOWHERE ELSE TO GO, DOCTOR.
OH, THERE'S ALWAYS SOMEPLACE ELSE TO GO.
IN FACT, YOU'LL ALL BE GOING SOMEWHERE ELSE SOON.
YOUR DAYS OF VICTIMIZING THIS WORLD ARE OVER.
YES, I KNOW ALL ABOUT IT. 'THE ASCENDED'? THEY'RE NO MORE THAN UNWILLING ORGAN DONORS FOR YOUR PEOPLE. THEY'VE BEEN KEEPING YOUR SAD SPECIES ALIVE FOR GENERATIONS. IT ENDS NOW.
WHO DO YOU THINK YOU ARE?
I'M THE DOCTOR.
NOOOO!
THE ORGAN FARMING ENDS NOW. SEND DOWN EVERYONE ELSE YOU HAVE IN THAT MEDICAL FACILITY, THEN PACK UP AND LEAVE THIS PLANET.
BECAUSE ONCE I TELL THE LOWGROUNDERS WHAT YOU'VE BEEN DOING TO THEIR CHILDREN, I EXPECT THEY'LL RETURN TO THEIR WARLIKE WAYS RATHER QUICKLY.
AND BASED ON WHAT I READ IN YOUR COMPUTERS, EVEN THE MEREST SCRATCH TO YOUR BODIES IS FATAL.
THAT'S WHAT HAPPENED TO YOUR MAN BACK AT OREN'S HOUSE, ISN'T IT?
HE GOT SCRATCHED WHEN GRACE KNOCKED HIM TO THE GROUND, AND IT WAS ALL OVER. SO YOU'RE NOT REALLY THE COMBAT TYPES, ARE YOU?
AND DON'T TRY THIS OPERATION ANYWHERE ELSE. I'LL BE WATCHING FOR YOU.
BY THE WAY, GRACE, WHERE DID YOU LEARN TO FLY ONE OF THESE THINGS?
HAH! I WAS ABLE TO HOT-WIRE THE TARDIS, REMEMBER?
I THINK I CAN HANDLE ONE OF THESE LITTLE BEAUTIES.

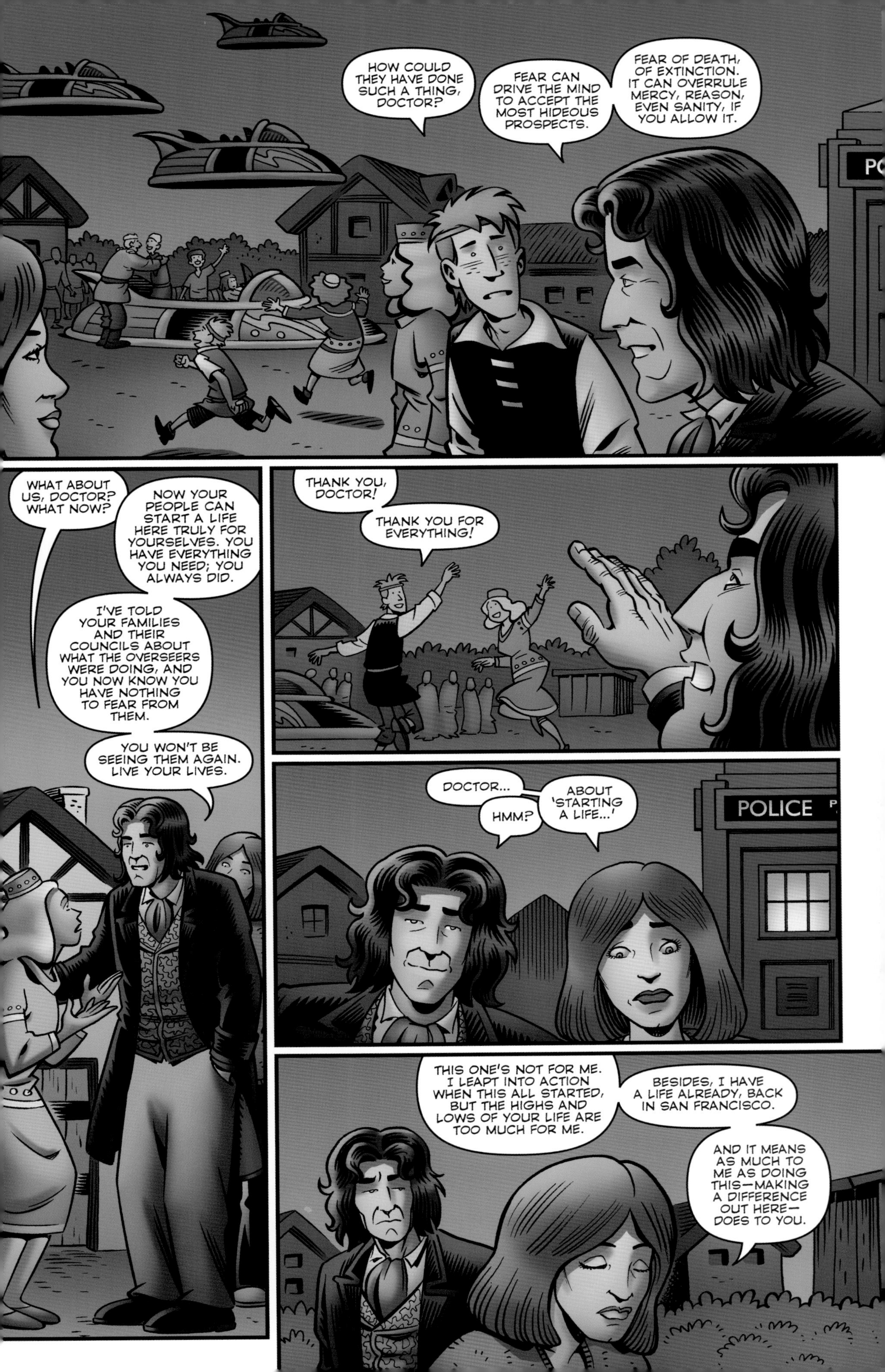
HOW COULD THEY HAVE DONE SUCH A THING, DOCTOR?
FEAR CAN DRIVE THE MIND TO ACCEPT THE MOST HIDEOUS PROSPECTS.
FEAR OF DEATH, OF EXTINCTION. IT CAN OVERRULE MERCY, REASON, EVEN SANITY, IF YOU ALLOW IT.
PO
WHAT ABOUT US, DOCTOR? WHAT NOW?
NOW YOUR PEOPLE CAN START A LIFE HERE TRULY FOR YOURSELVES. YOU HAVE EVERYTHING YOU NEED; YOU ALWAYS DID.
I'VE TOLD YOUR FAMILIES AND THEIR COUNCILS ABOUT WHAT THE OVERSEERS WERE DOING, AND YOU NOW KNOW YOU HAVE NOTHING TO FEAR FROM THEM.
YOU WON'T BE SEEING THEM AGAIN. LIVE YOUR LIVES.
THANK YOU, DOCTOR!
THANK YOU FOR EVERYTHING!
DOCTOR...
HMM?
ABOUT 'STARTING A LIFE...'
POLICE
THIS ONE'S NOT FOR ME. I LEAPT INTO ACTION WHEN THIS ALL STARTED, BUT THE HIGHS AND LOWS OF YOUR LIFE ARE TOO MUCH FOR ME.
BESIDES, I HAVE A LIFE ALREADY, BACK IN SAN FRANCISCO.
AND IT MEANS AS MUCH TO ME AS DOING THIS—MAKING A DIFFERENCE OUT HERE—DOES TO YOU.

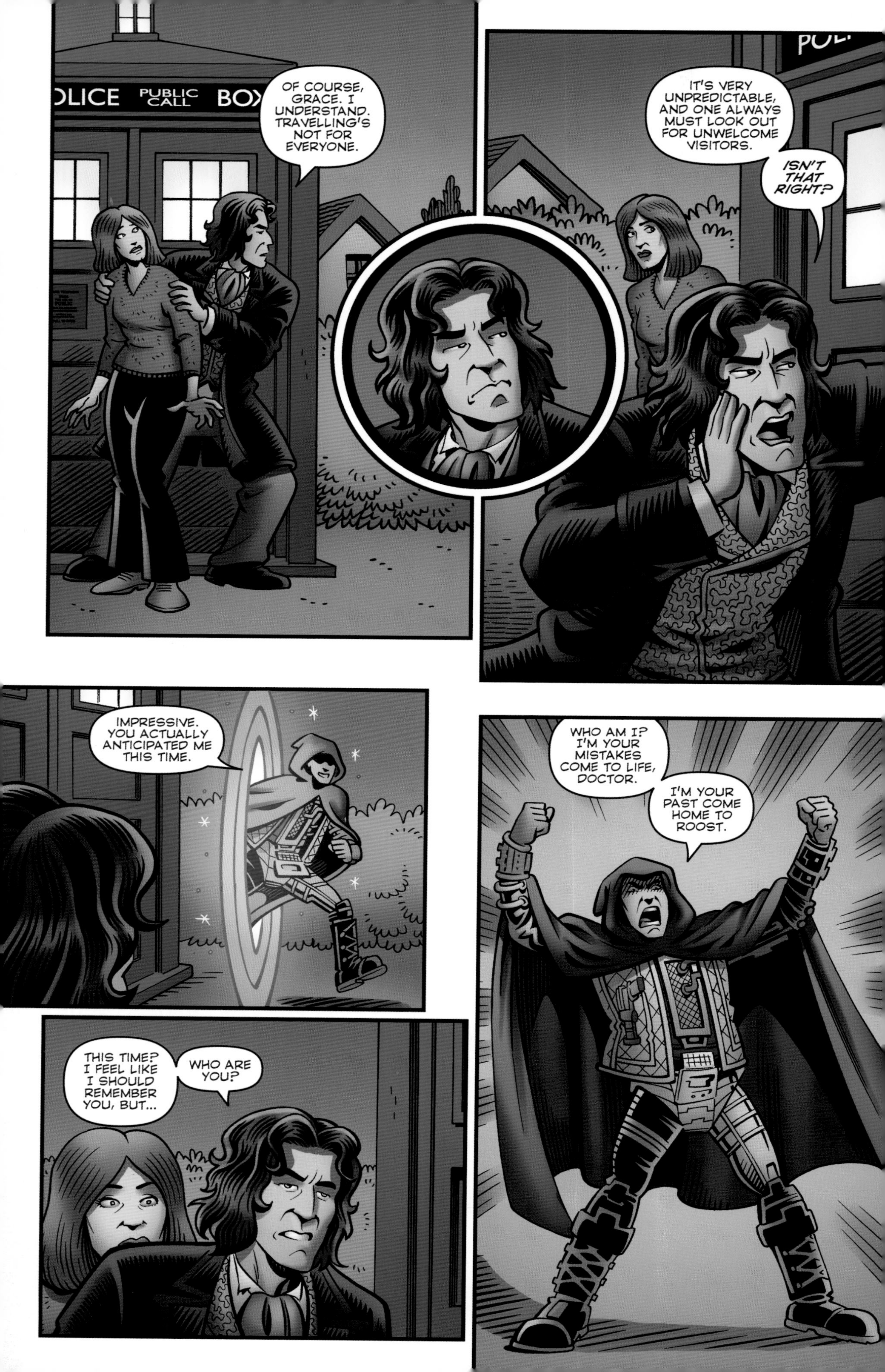
POLICE PUBLIC CALL BOX
OF COURSE, GRACE. I UNDERSTAND. TRAVELLING'S NOT FOR EVERYONE.
IT'S VERY UNPREDICTABLE, AND ONE ALWAYS MUST LOOK OUT FOR UNWELCOME VISITORS.
ISN'T THAT RIGHT?
IMPRESSIVE. YOU ACTUALLY ANTICIPATED ME THIS TIME.
THIS TIME? I FEEL LIKE I SHOULD REMEMBER YOU, BUT...
WHO ARE YOU?
WHO AM I? I'M YOUR MISTAKES COME TO LIFE, DOCTOR.
I'M YOUR PAST COME HOME TO ROOST.

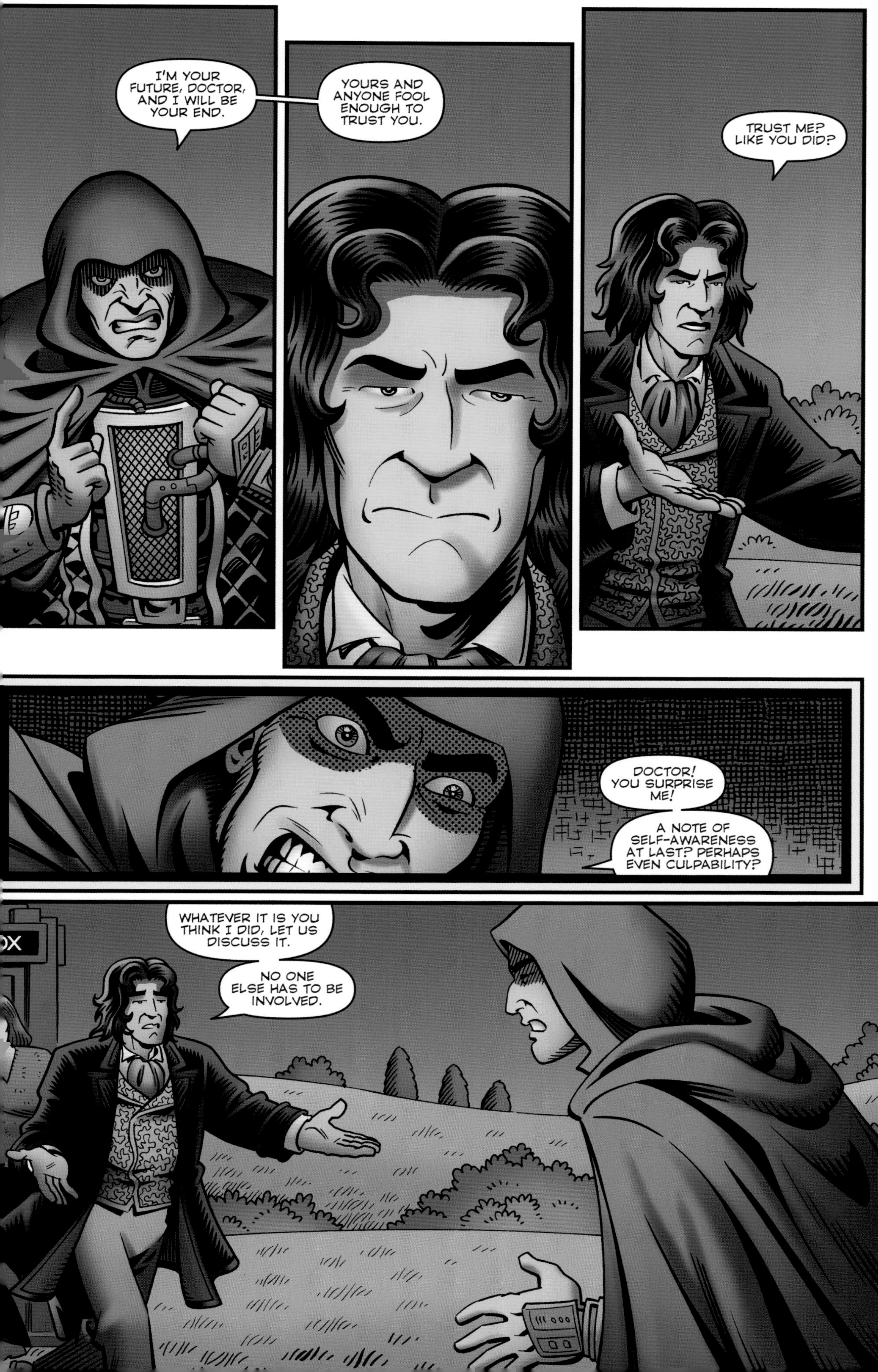

I'M YOUR FUTURE, DOCTOR, AND I WILL BE YOUR END.
YOURS AND ANYONE FOOL ENOUGH TO TRUST YOU.
TRUST ME? LIKE YOU DID?
DOCTOR! YOU SURPRISE ME!
A NOTE OF SELF-AWARENESS AT LAST? PERHAPS EVEN CULPABILITY?
OX
WHATEVER IT IS YOU THINK I DID, LET US DISCUSS IT.
NO ONE ELSE HAS TO BE INVOLVED.

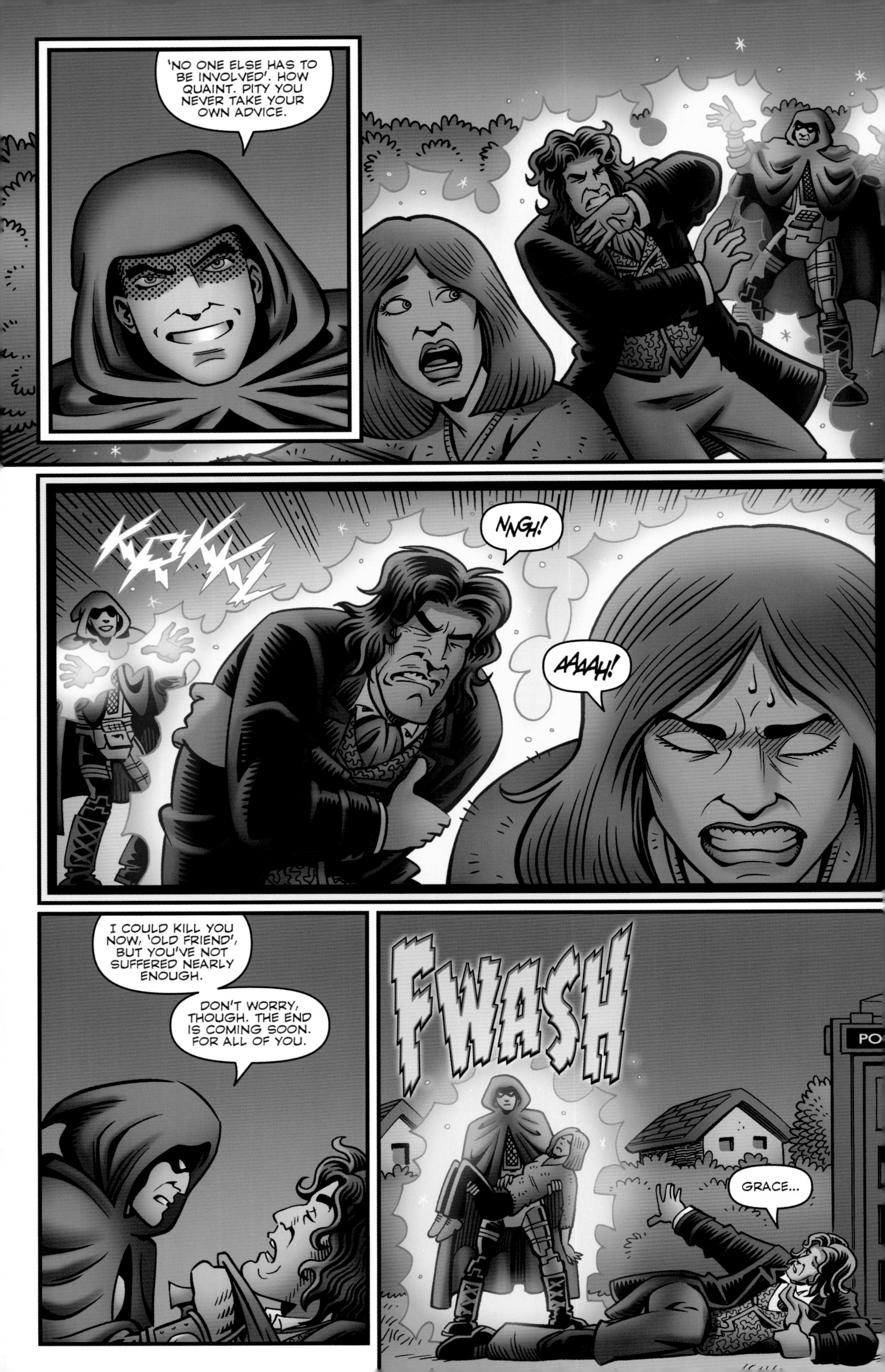
'NO ONE ELSE HAS TO BE INVOLVED'. HOW QUAINT. PITY YOU NEVER TAKE YOUR OWN ADVICE.
KZZKKZ
NNGH!
AAAAH!
I COULD KILL YOU NOW, 'OLD FRIEND', BUT YOU'VE NOT SUFFERED NEARLY ENOUGH.
DON'T WORRY, THOUGH. THE END IS COMING SOON. FOR ALL OF YOU.
FWASH
GRACE...

REFLECTIONS OF TIME

Wherein prominent Whovians past and present muse upon the Doctor's history in comic form.

It was 1996. The Fugees' *Killing Me Softly* was No. 1. Bill Clinton was president. No one you've ever heard of was prime minister. The Internet was steam-powered.

And *Doctor Who* was coming back to life on TV after a seven-year drought! I have to confess, I wasn't expecting to like the Paul McGann TV movie. I had read the script a few weeks earlier and had been a tad underwhelmed. But Geoff Sax's direction was so much more sophisticated than anything the show had seen before and the production values were fantastic. Best of all, McGann's performance was a perfect blend of charm, danger, silliness, and genius—he simply was the Doctor, effortlessly, brilliantly.

And 90 minutes later he was gone. The TV movie went up against the 'Dan's heart attack' episode of *Roseanne* in the U.S. and was clobbered in the ratings. It was all over. There was no ongoing series, no further specials, nothing. At least on TV...

Ah, but the comics were a different story! At *Doctor Who Magazine,* we immediately got to work on new Eighth Doctor adventures for our regular comic-strip section. It was an exciting time—we had been handed a fantastic new Doctor who had proven instantly popular with the fans. He had a distinct visual style that easily translated into illustration. Most important, he came without any restrictions—we could do whatever we liked with him. Total freedom!

Alan Barnes came aboard as the regular writer and was

joined by artist Martin Geraghty, then a rising star at Marvel UK. Alan and Martin created a new companion: Izzy S, a sci-fi 'geekette' who became an instant hit with the readership. The Doctor and Izzy battled the Celestial Toymaker, the Daleks, alien vampires, rogue Time Lords, and the sinister mercenaries called the Threshold. People sat up, took notice, and got excited!

Alan moved on to great things as the editor of *The Judge Dredd Megazine* and later became the script editor for Big Finish's *Doctor Who* audio range. I took over writing the comic strip. Martin and I sent the Doctor and Izzy to London for a reunion with Grace Holloway, then to an adventure in 10th-century Japan. Our heroes encountered a figure from the *DWM* strip's past: Kroton, a Cyberman with emotions, and the trio took on the Master in an epic 10-part story, *The Glorious Dead.*

The comic strip shifted to full-colour. An amoral fish-girl called Destrii muscled her way into the stories, making life very difficult for the Doctor and Izzy. They faced Necrotists, the Horde, the Mobox, and a unique tribe of benevolent Daleks. Izzy went home and Destrii gained a conscience. It was a brilliant,

creative time for everyone involved. In addition to Martin Geraghty, I had the pleasure of working with stellar artists Adrian Salmon, Lee Sullivan, Roger Langridge, Anthony Williams, and John Ross.

The final story, *The Flood,* saw Cybermen from the future laying claim to Earth. It arrived on the eve of *Doctor Who*'s return to British TV screens in 2005 and, I'm happy to report, turned out to be the most popular story Martin and I produced. The Doctor and Destrii walked off into the sunset, happy and triumphant. We were sorry to see them go. From 90 minutes of television, the Eighth Doctor had gone on to enjoy a solid nine years as the resident hero of *Doctor Who Magazine.* Happy times!

—Scott Gray,
former *Doctor Who Magazine*
assistant editor and
writer

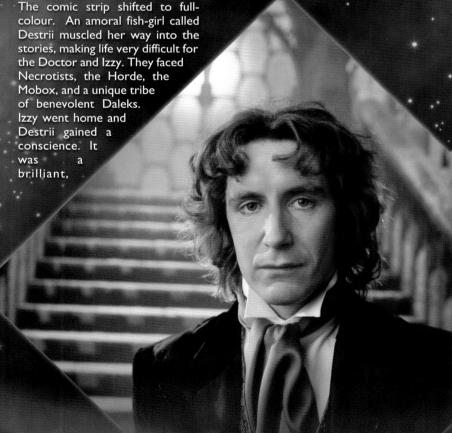

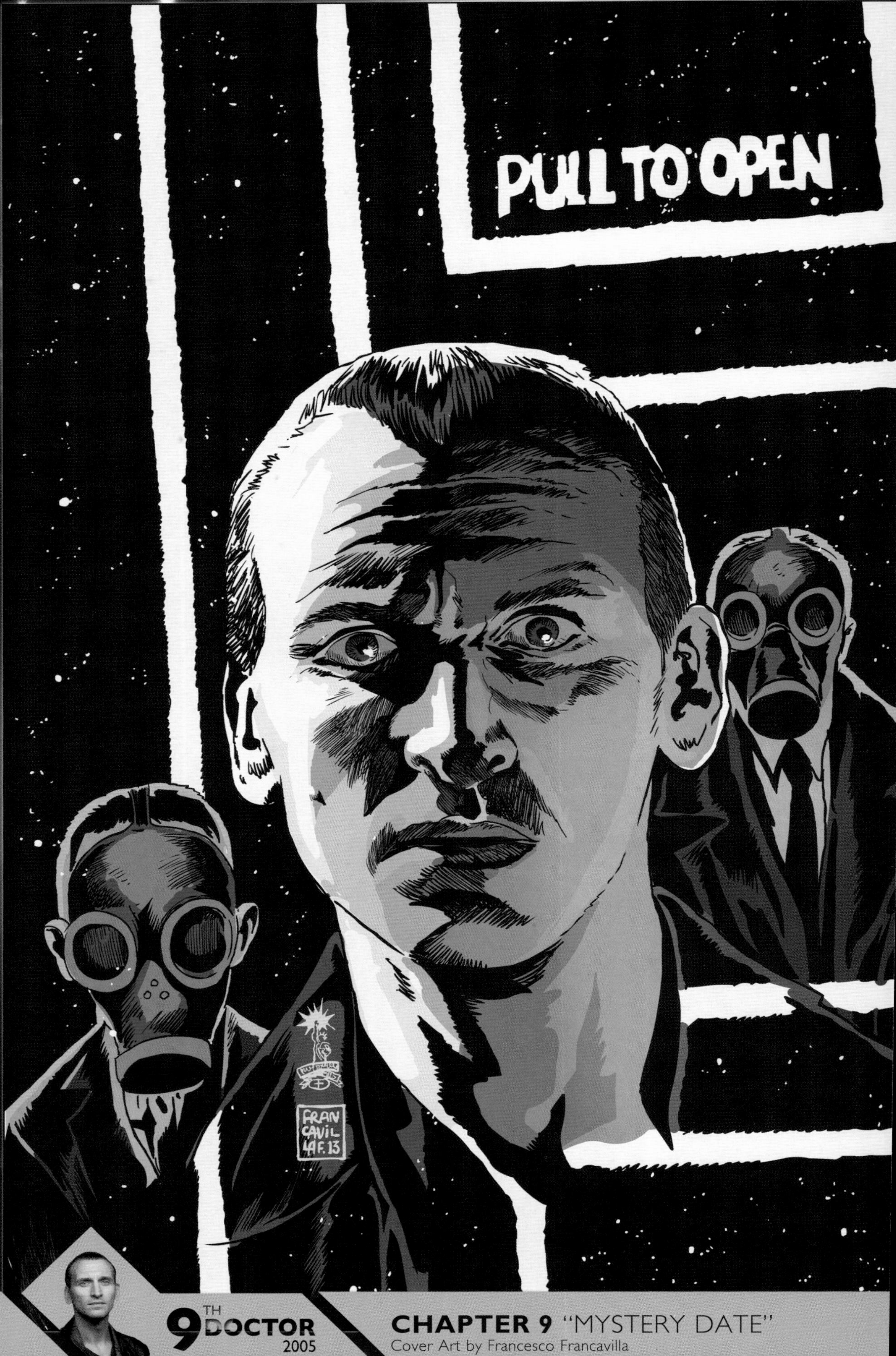
PULL TO OPEN
FRAN
CAVIL
LAF. 13

9TH DOCTOR 2005

CHAPTER 9 "MYSTERY DATE"
Cover Art by Francesco Francavilla

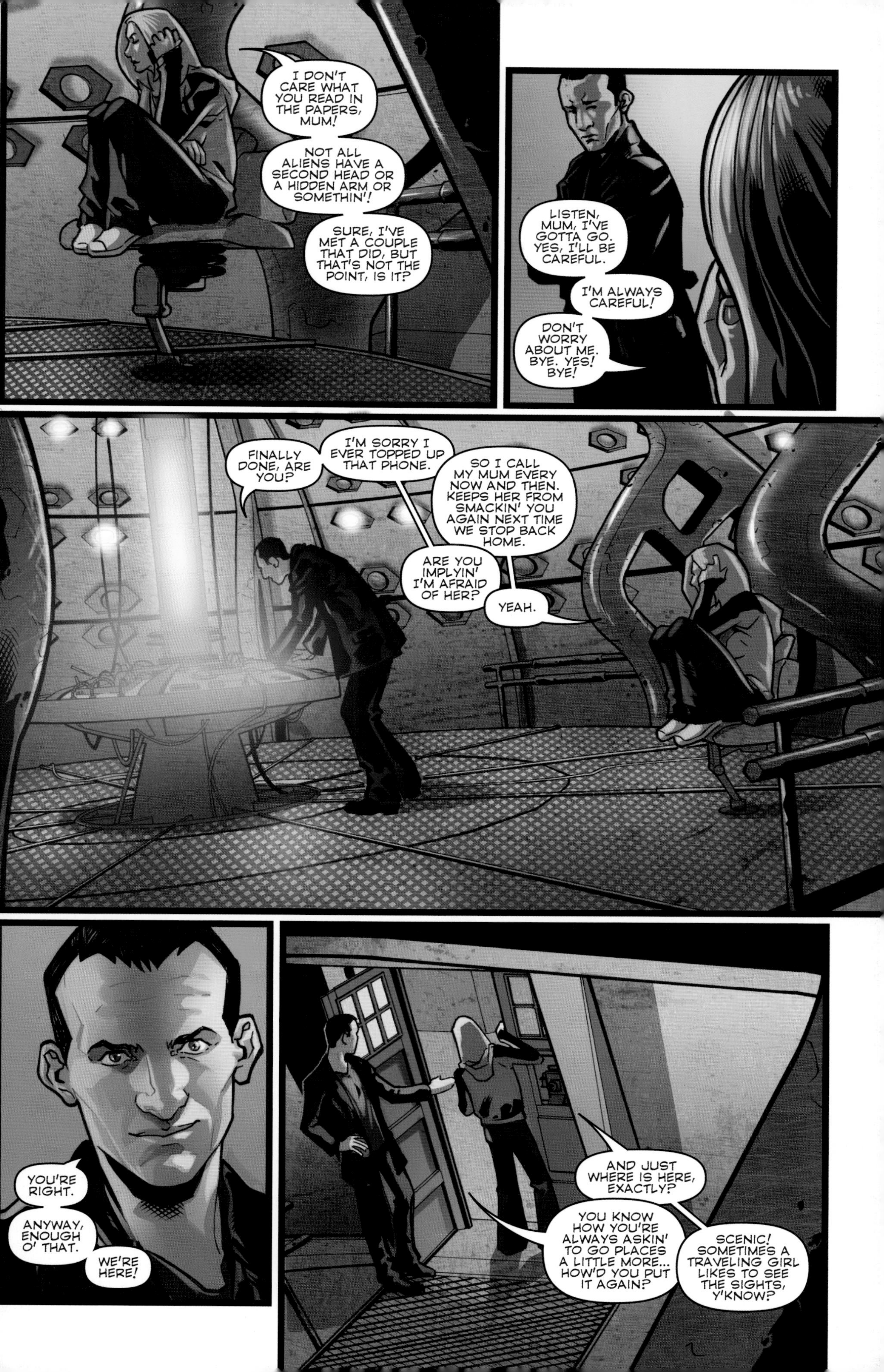
I DON'T CARE WHAT YOU READ IN THE PAPERS, MUM!
NOT ALL ALIENS HAVE A SECOND HEAD OR A HIDDEN ARM OR SOMETHIN'!
SURE, I'VE MET A COUPLE THAT DID, BUT THAT'S NOT THE POINT, IS IT?
LISTEN, MUM, I'VE GOTTA GO. YES, I'LL BE CAREFUL.
I'M ALWAYS CAREFUL!
DON'T WORRY ABOUT ME. BYE. YES! BYE!
FINALLY DONE, ARE YOU?
I'M SORRY I EVER TOPPED UP THAT PHONE.
SO I CALL MY MUM EVERY NOW AND THEN. KEEPS HER FROM SMACKIN' YOU AGAIN NEXT TIME WE STOP BACK HOME.
ARE YOU IMPLYIN' I'M AFRAID OF HER?
YEAH.
YOU'RE RIGHT.
ANYWAY, ENOUGH O' THAT.
WE'RE HERE!
AND JUST WHERE IS HERE, EXACTLY?
YOU KNOW HOW YOU'RE ALWAYS ASKIN' TO GO PLACES A LITTLE MORE... HOW'D YOU PUT IT AGAIN?
SCENIC! SOMETIMES A TRAVELING GIRL LIKES TO SEE THE SIGHTS, Y'KNOW?

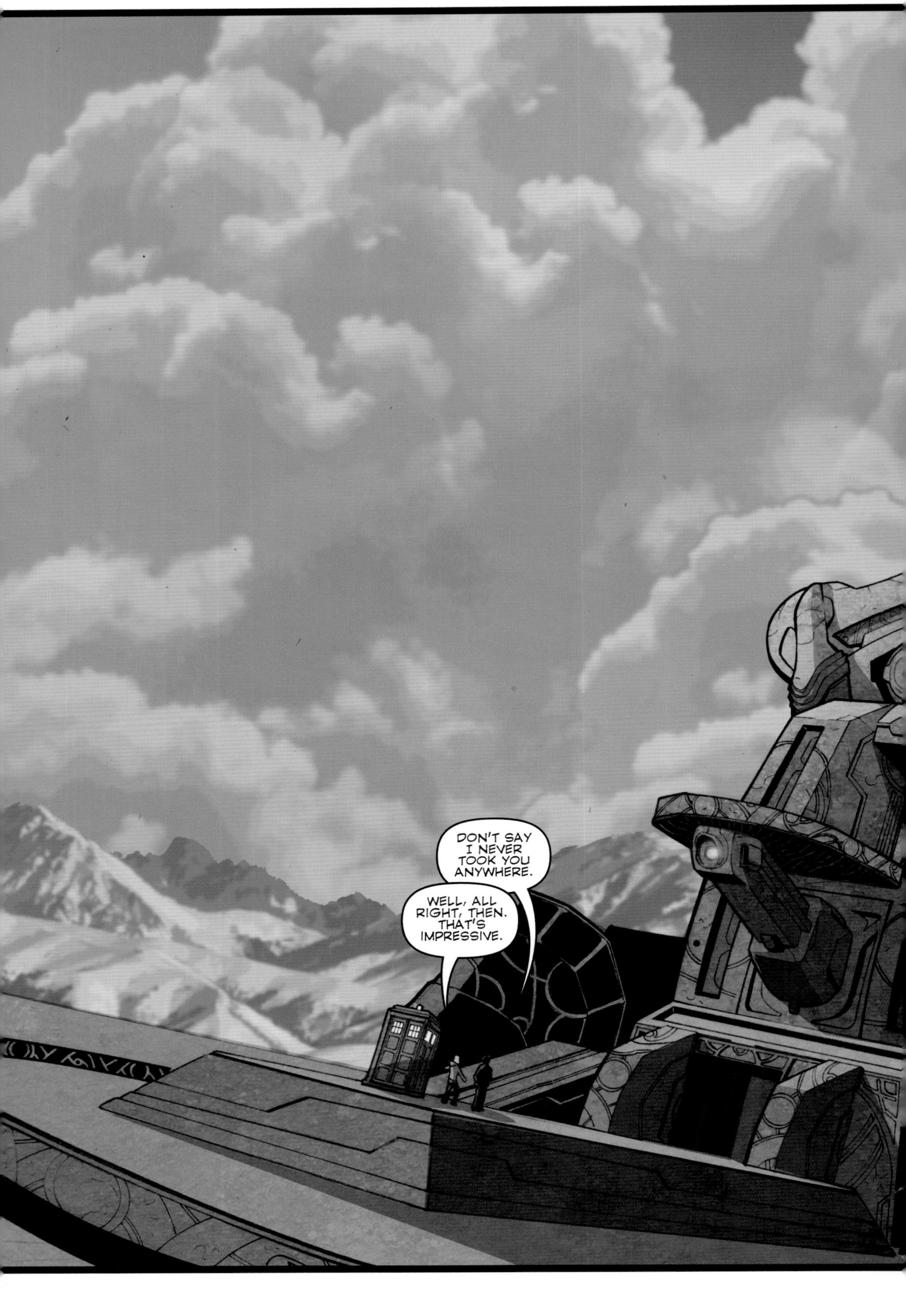
DON'T SAY I NEVER TOOK YOU ANYWHERE.
WELL, ALL RIGHT, THEN. THAT'S IMPRESSIVE.

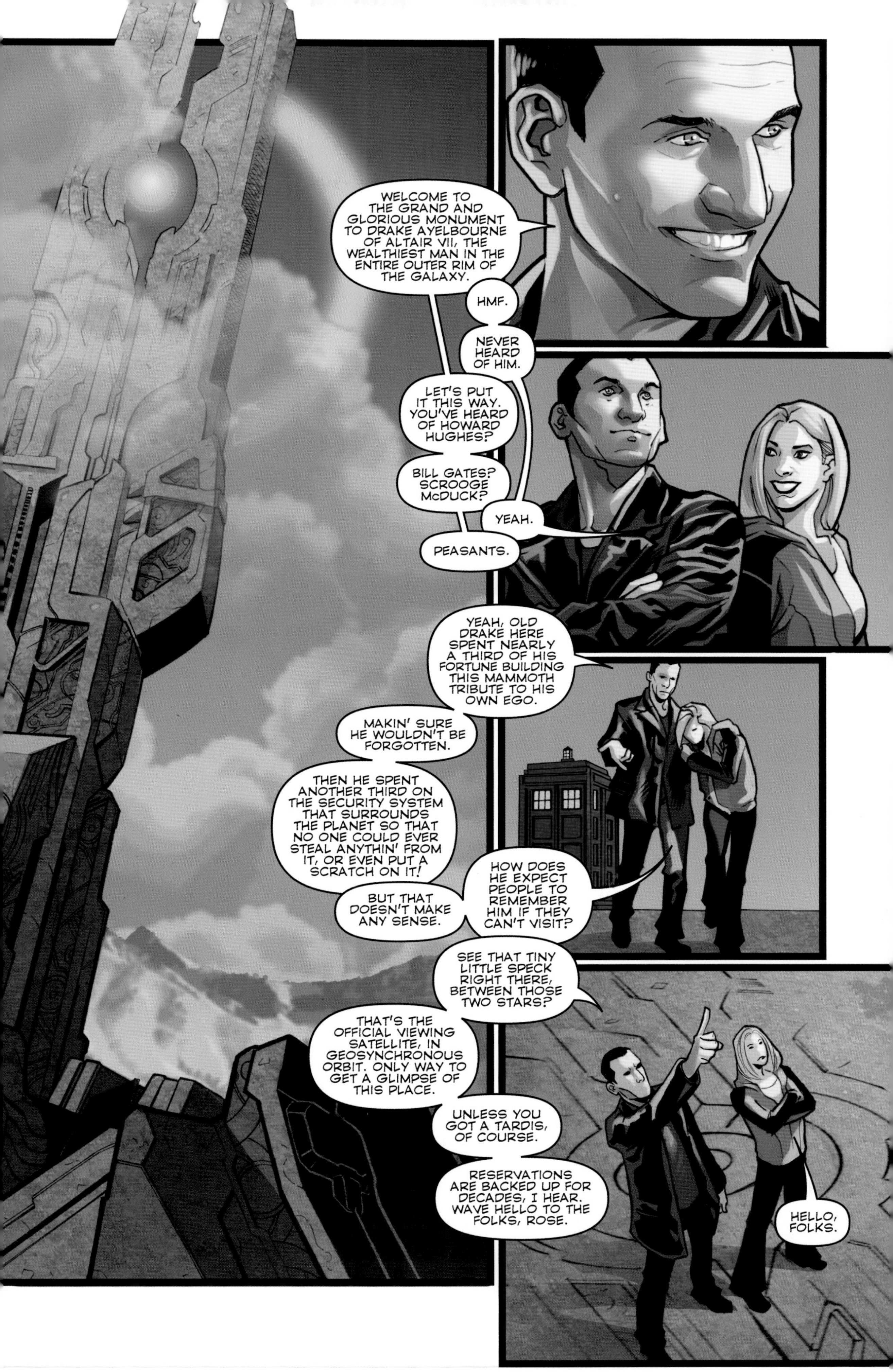
WELCOME TO THE GRAND AND GLORIOUS MONUMENT TO DRAKE AYELBOURNE OF ALTAIR VII, THE WEALTHIEST MAN IN THE ENTIRE OUTER RIM OF THE GALAXY.
HMF.
NEVER HEARD OF HIM.
LET'S PUT IT THIS WAY. YOU'VE HEARD OF HOWARD HUGHES?
BILL GATES? SCROOGE McDUCK?
YEAH.
PEASANTS.
YEAH, OLD DRAKE HERE SPENT NEARLY A THIRD OF HIS FORTUNE BUILDING THIS MAMMOTH TRIBUTE TO HIS OWN EGO.
MAKIN' SURE HE WOULDN'T BE FORGOTTEN.
THEN HE SPENT ANOTHER THIRD ON THE SECURITY SYSTEM THAT SURROUNDS THE PLANET SO THAT NO ONE COULD EVER STEAL ANYTHIN' FROM IT, OR EVEN PUT A SCRATCH ON IT!
BUT THAT DOESN'T MAKE ANY SENSE.
HOW DOES HE EXPECT PEOPLE TO REMEMBER HIM IF THEY CAN'T VISIT?
SEE THAT TINY LITTLE SPECK RIGHT THERE, BETWEEN THOSE TWO STARS?
THAT'S THE OFFICIAL VIEWING SATELLITE, IN GEOSYNCHRONOUS ORBIT. ONLY WAY TO GET A GLIMPSE OF THIS PLACE.
UNLESS YOU GOT A TARDIS, OF COURSE.
RESERVATIONS ARE BACKED UP FOR DECADES, I HEAR. WAVE HELLO TO THE FOLKS, ROSE.
HELLO, FOLKS.

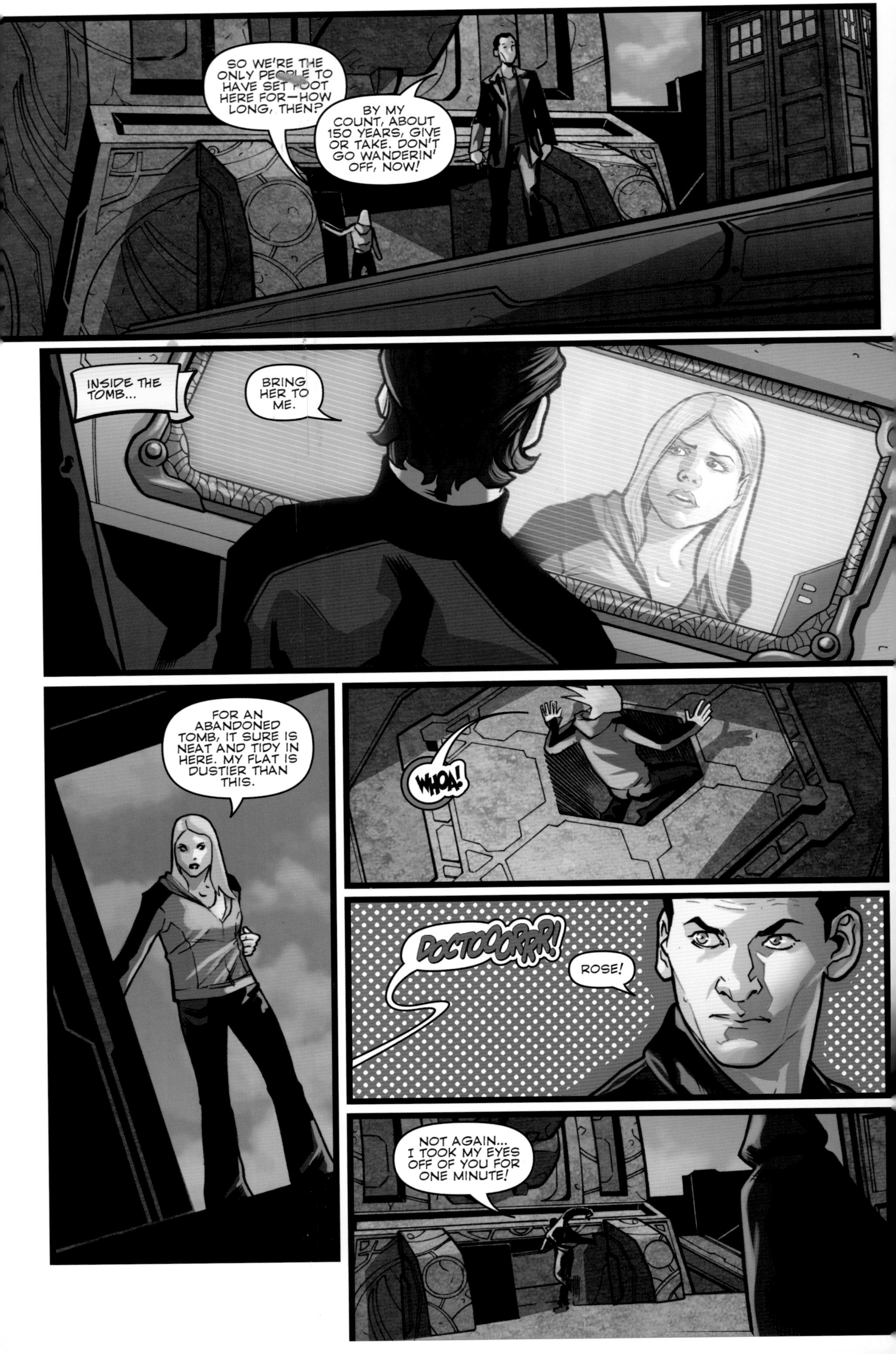
SO WE'RE THE ONLY PEOPLE TO HAVE SET FOOT HERE FOR—HOW LONG, THEN?
BY MY COUNT, ABOUT 150 YEARS, GIVE OR TAKE. DON'T GO WANDERIN' OFF, NOW!
INSIDE THE TOMB...
BRING HER TO ME.
FOR AN ABANDONED TOMB, IT SURE IS NEAT AND TIDY IN HERE. MY FLAT IS DUSTIER THAN THIS.
WHOA!
DOCTOOORRR!
ROSE!
NOT AGAIN... I TOOK MY EYES OFF OF YOU FOR ONE MINUTE!

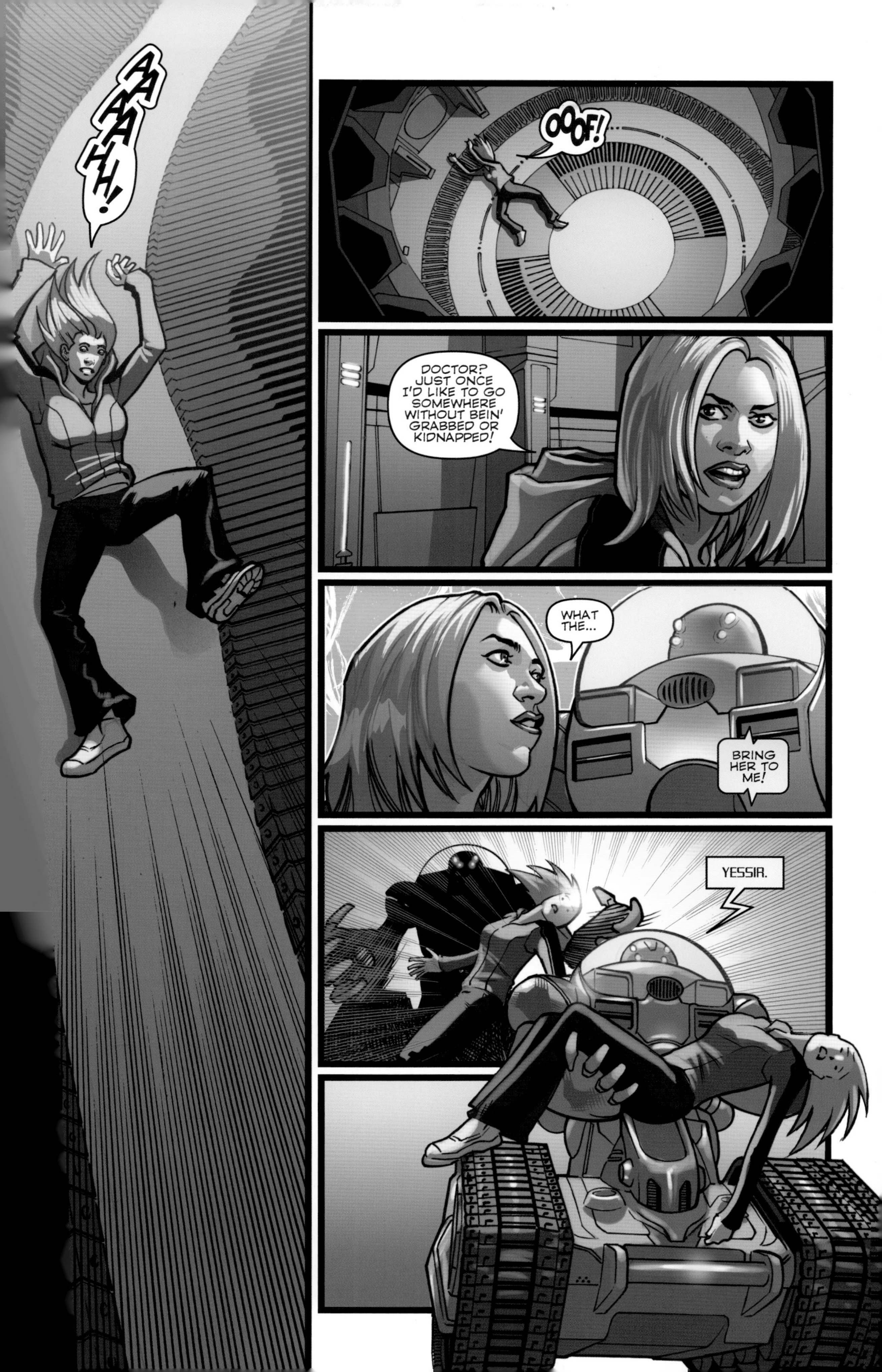
AAAAHH!
OOOF!
DOCTOR? JUST ONCE I'D LIKE TO GO SOMEWHERE WITHOUT BEIN' GRABBED OR KIDNAPPED!
WHAT THE...
BRING HER TO ME!
YESSIR.

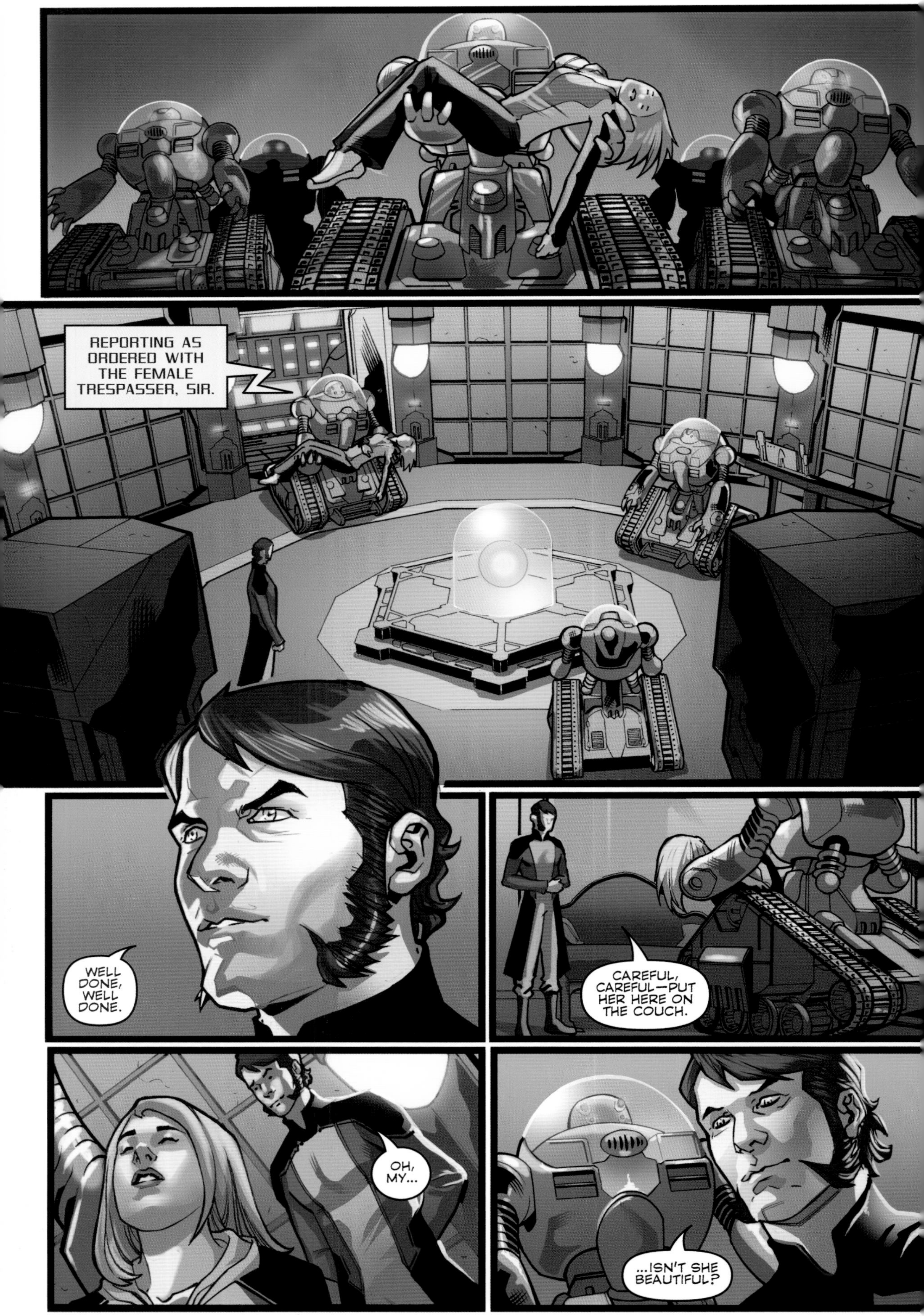
REPORTING AS ORDERED WITH THE FEMALE TRESPASSER, SIR.
WELL DONE, WELL DONE.
CAREFUL, CAREFUL—PUT HER HERE ON THE COUCH.
OH, MY...
...ISN'T SHE BEAUTIFUL?

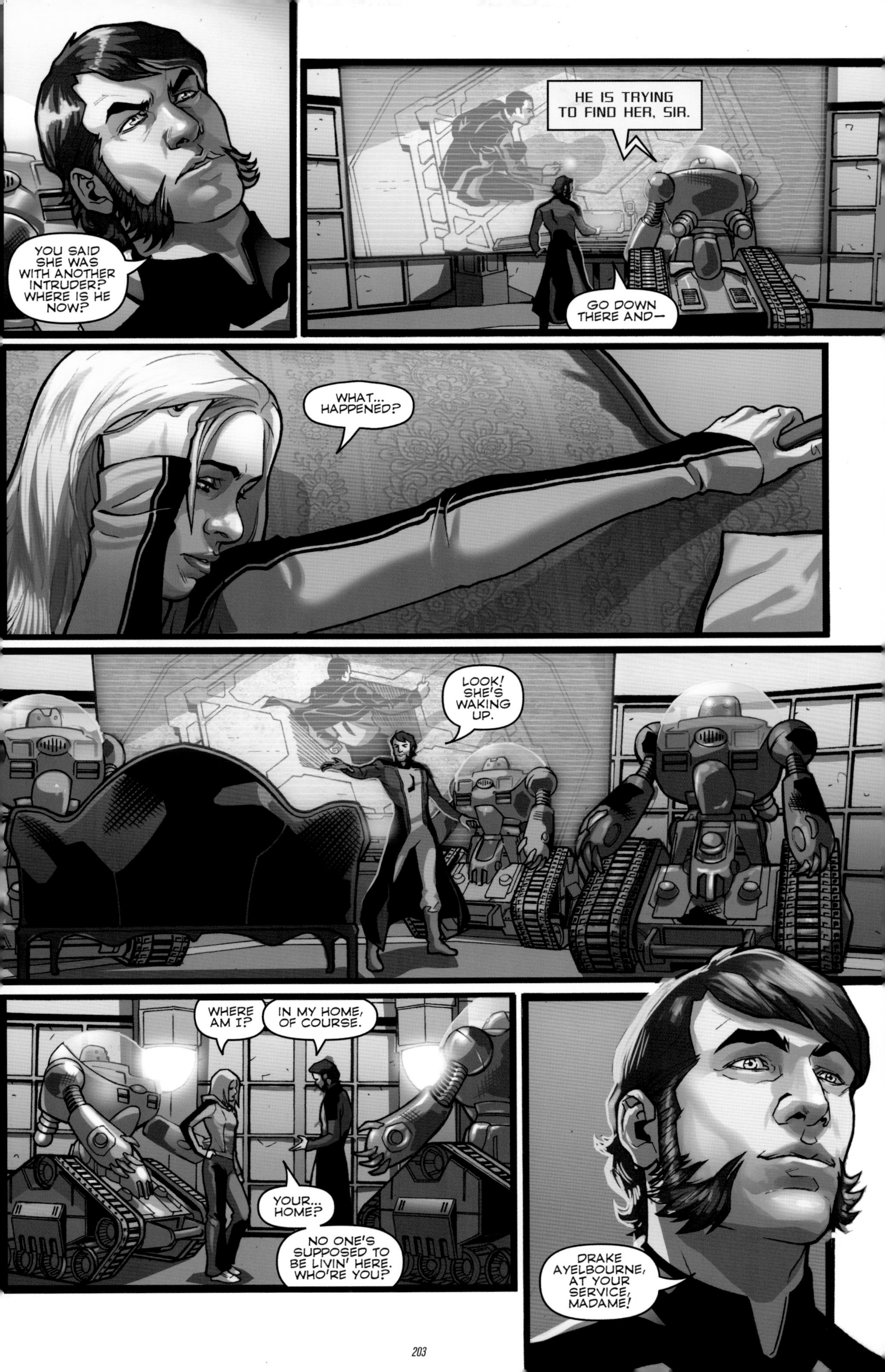
YOU SAID SHE WAS WITH ANOTHER INTRUDER? WHERE IS HE NOW?
HE IS TRYING TO FIND HER, SIR.
GO DOWN THERE AND—
WHAT... HAPPENED?
LOOK! SHE'S WAKING UP.
WHERE AM I?
IN MY HOME, OF COURSE.
YOUR... HOME?
NO ONE'S SUPPOSED TO BE LIVIN' HERE. WHO'RE YOU?
DRAKE AYELBOURNE, AT YOUR SERVICE, MADAME!

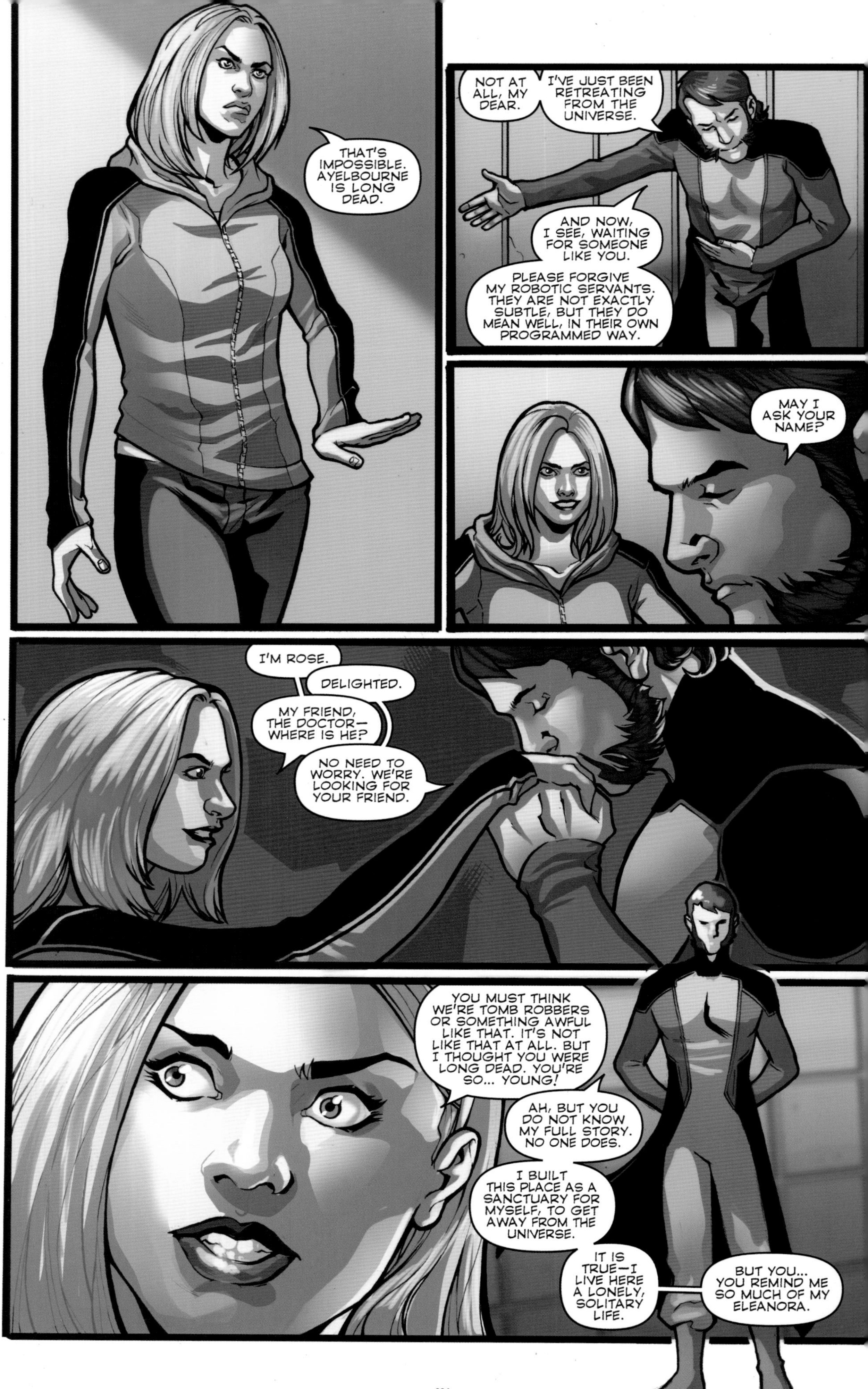
THAT'S IMPOSSIBLE. AYELBOURNE IS LONG DEAD.
NOT AT ALL, MY DEAR.
I'VE JUST BEEN RETREATING FROM THE UNIVERSE.
AND NOW, I SEE, WAITING FOR SOMEONE LIKE YOU.
PLEASE FORGIVE MY ROBOTIC SERVANTS. THEY ARE NOT EXACTLY SUBTLE, BUT THEY DO MEAN WELL, IN THEIR OWN PROGRAMMED WAY.
MAY I ASK YOUR NAME?
I'M ROSE.
DELIGHTED.
MY FRIEND, THE DOCTOR—WHERE IS HE?
NO NEED TO WORRY. WE'RE LOOKING FOR YOUR FRIEND.
YOU MUST THINK WE'RE TOMB ROBBERS OR SOMETHING AWFUL LIKE THAT. IT'S NOT LIKE THAT AT ALL. BUT I THOUGHT YOU WERE LONG DEAD. YOU'RE SO... YOUNG!
AH, BUT YOU DO NOT KNOW MY FULL STORY. NO ONE DOES.
I BUILT THIS PLACE AS A SANCTUARY FOR MYSELF, TO GET AWAY FROM THE UNIVERSE.
IT IS TRUE—I LIVE HERE A LONELY, SOLITARY LIFE.
BUT YOU... YOU REMIND ME SO MUCH OF MY ELEANORA.

ME?

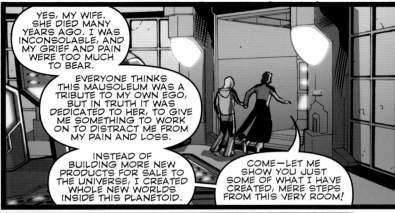

YES, MY WIFE. SHE DIED MANY YEARS AGO. I WAS INCONSOLABLE, AND MY GRIEF AND PAIN WERE TOO MUCH TO BEAR.

EVERYONE THINKS THIS MAUSOLEUM WAS A TRIBUTE TO MY OWN EGO, BUT IN TRUTH IT WAS DEDICATED TO HER, TO GIVE ME SOMETHING TO WORK ON TO DISTRACT ME FROM MY PAIN AND LOSS.

INSTEAD OF BUILDING MORE NEW PRODUCTS FOR SALE TO THE UNIVERSE, I CREATED WHOLE NEW WORLDS INSIDE THIS PLANETOID.

COME—LET ME SHOW YOU JUST SOME OF WHAT I HAVE CREATED, MERE STEPS FROM THIS VERY ROOM!

I'VE LEARNED HOW TO CREATE ENTIRE ECOSYSTEMS FROM SCRATCH... ENCLOSED ENVIRONMENTS OF MY OWN DESIGN THAT GROW AND MAINTAIN THEMSELVES.

YEARS I HAVE SPENT DEVELOPING AND FINESSING THESE TECHNIQUES, LEARNING HOW TO CREATE ENTIRE WORLDS AT MY VERY WHIM.

I'VE NEVER SEEN ANYTHING LIKE THIS!

ALL THIS TIME, I HAVE DISTRACTED MYSELF WITH MY WORK.

BUT WHEN I SAW YOU UP THERE, I COULD NOT HELP BUT THINK THAT MAYBE... MAYBE I HAVE BEEN LONELY FOR TOO LONG.

THIS IS AMAZING, AND I AM FLATTERED, BUT...

DOCTOR!

I'VE BEEN LOOKIN' FOR YOU.

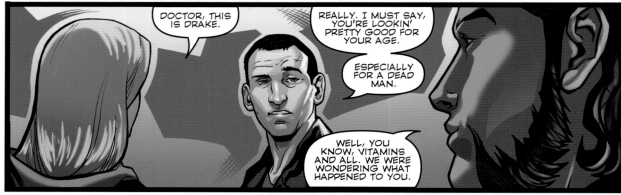

DOCTOR, THIS IS DRAKE.

REALLY. I MUST SAY, YOU'RE LOOKIN' PRETTY GOOD FOR YOUR AGE.

ESPECIALLY FOR A DEAD MAN.

WELL, YOU KNOW, VITAMINS AND ALL. WE WERE WONDERING WHAT HAPPENED TO YOU.

OH, I'M JUST FINE. RAN INTO QUITE A FEW ROBOTS ON THE WAY HERE, THOUGH.

PESKY THINGS. ARE THOSE YOURS?

AH, YES, WELL, I WAS JUST SHOWING ROSE HERE MY HOME.

ARE YOU OKAY?

IF YOU HAVE HARMED HER...

DOCTOR, I'M FINE!

DRAKE HAS BEEN TELLING ME HIS STORY. COME ON, HEAR HIM OUT. HE'S A BIT OF A CHARMER.

I HAVE TO ADMIT THAT WHAT YOU HAVE DONE HERE IS PHENOMENAL.

WELL, THANK YOU INDEED— HIGH PRAISE FROM ONE SO CLEARLY DISTRUSTFUL OF ME.

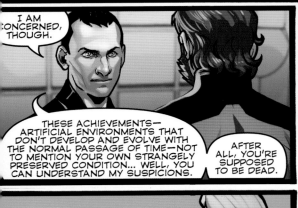

I AM CONCERNED, THOUGH.

THESE ACHIEVEMENTS— ARTIFICIAL ENVIRONMENTS THAT DON'T DEVELOP AND EVOLVE WITH THE NORMAL PASSAGE OF TIME—NOT TO MENTION YOUR OWN STRANGELY PRESERVED CONDITION... WELL, YOU CAN UNDERSTAND MY SUSPICIONS.

AFTER ALL, YOU'RE SUPPOSED TO BE DEAD.

BAH! THAT'S JEALOUSY TALKING.

YOU ENVY MY ABILITIES. AND PERHAPS JEALOUS FOR OTHER REASONS?

ROSE, WON'T YOU STAY HERE WITH ME?

REALLY, I'M FLATTERED, BUT I'M NOT MUCH FOR SETTLIN' DOWN...

I ALWAYS GET WHAT I WANT.

ROBOTS! TAKE HIM!

DOCTOR!

DRAKE, DON'T DO THIS!

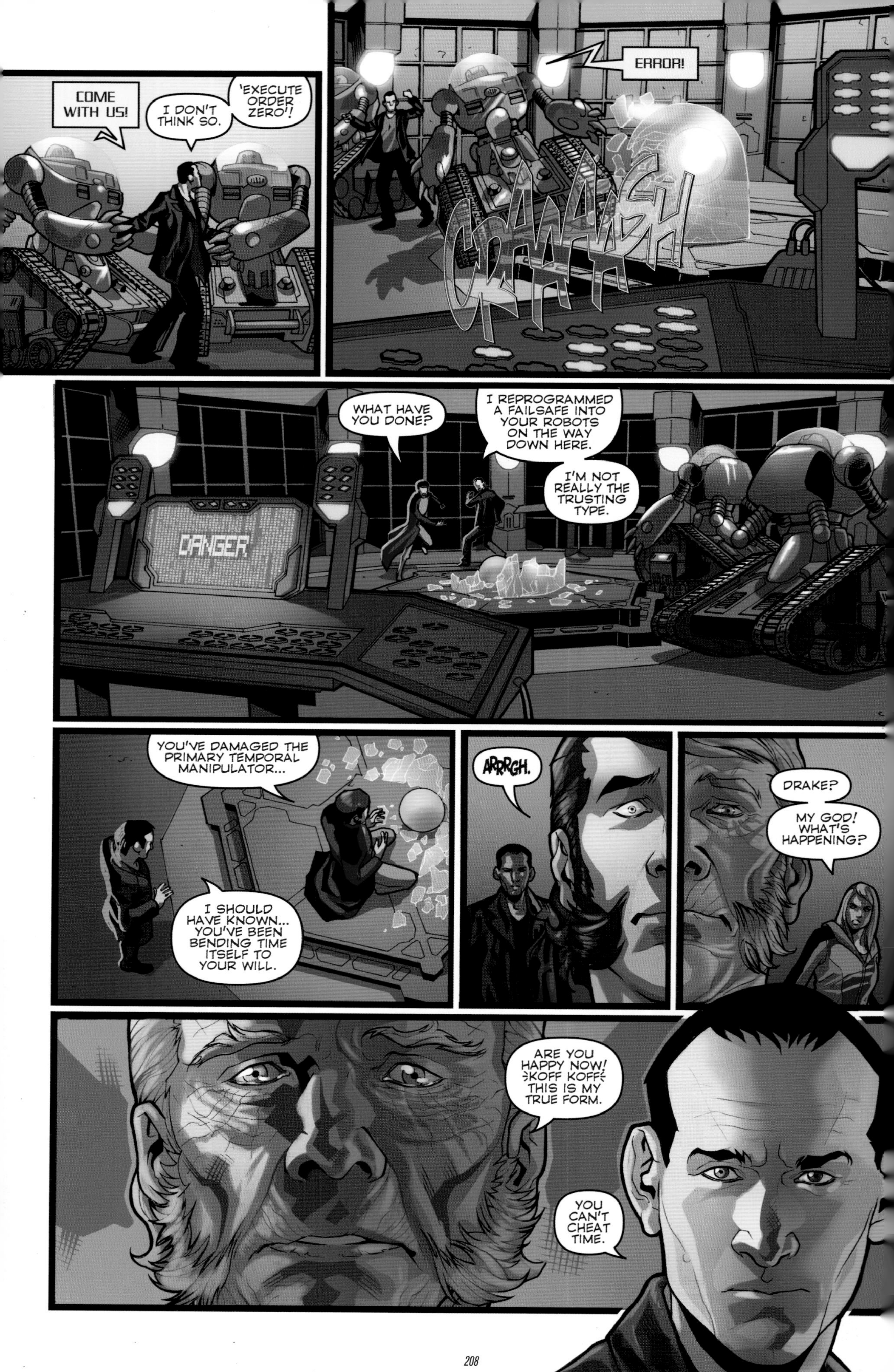
COME WITH US!
I DON'T THINK SO.
'EXECUTE ORDER ZERO'!
ERROR!
CRAAASH
WHAT HAVE YOU DONE?
I REPROGRAMMED A FAILSAFE INTO YOUR ROBOTS ON THE WAY DOWN HERE.
I'M NOT REALLY THE TRUSTING TYPE.
DANGER
YOU'VE DAMAGED THE PRIMARY TEMPORAL MANIPULATOR...
I SHOULD HAVE KNOWN... YOU'VE BEEN BENDING TIME ITSELF TO YOUR WILL.
ARRRGH.
DRAKE?
MY GOD! WHAT'S HAPPENING?
ARE YOU HAPPY NOW! *KOFF KOFF* THIS IS MY TRUE FORM.
YOU CAN'T CHEAT TIME.

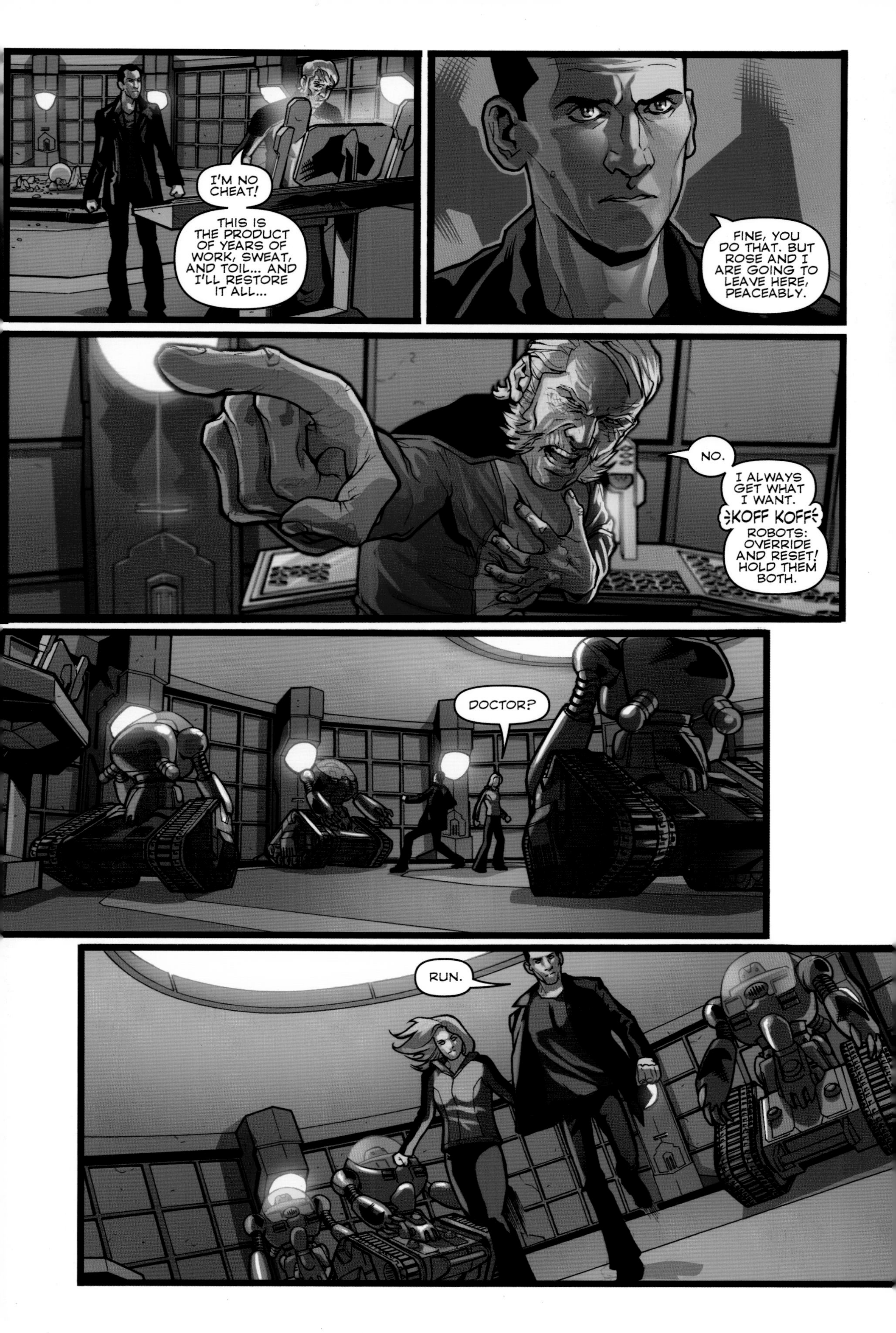
I'M NO CHEAT!
THIS IS THE PRODUCT OF YEARS OF WORK, SWEAT, AND TOIL... AND I'LL RESTORE IT ALL...
FINE, YOU DO THAT. BUT ROSE AND I ARE GOING TO LEAVE HERE, PEACEABLY.
NO.
I ALWAYS GET WHAT I WANT.
KOFF KOFF
ROBOTS: OVERRIDE AND RESET! HOLD THEM BOTH.
DOCTOR?
RUN.

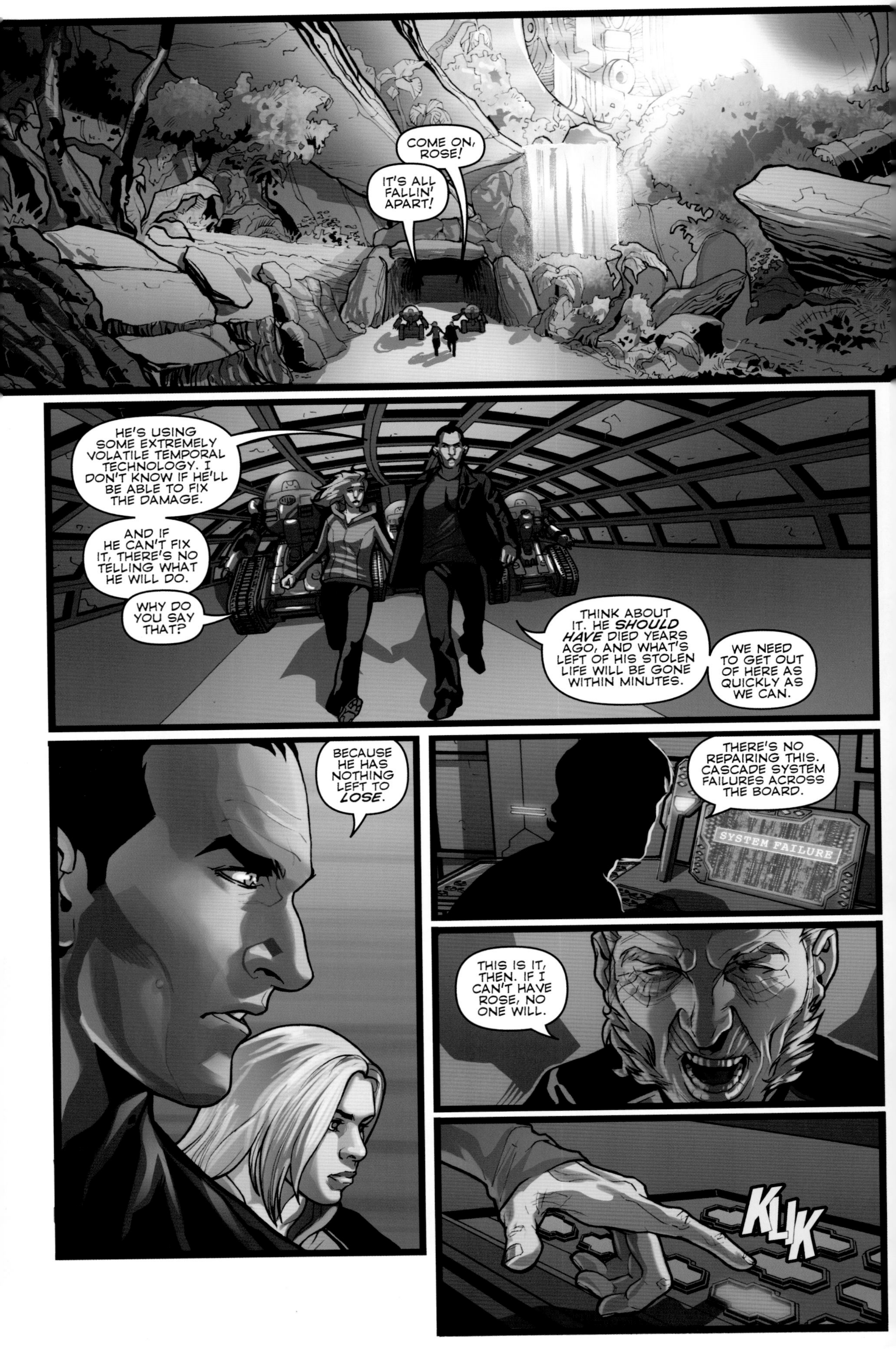
COME ON, ROSE!
IT'S ALL FALLIN' APART!
HE'S USING SOME EXTREMELY VOLATILE TEMPORAL TECHNOLOGY. I DON'T KNOW IF HE'LL BE ABLE TO FIX THE DAMAGE.
AND IF HE CAN'T FIX IT, THERE'S NO TELLING WHAT HE WILL DO.
WHY DO YOU SAY THAT?
THINK ABOUT IT. HE SHOULD HAVE DIED YEARS AGO, AND WHAT'S LEFT OF HIS STOLEN LIFE WILL BE GONE WITHIN MINUTES.
WE NEED TO GET OUT OF HERE AS QUICKLY AS WE CAN.
BECAUSE HE HAS NOTHING LEFT TO LOSE.
THERE'S NO REPAIRING THIS. CASCADE SYSTEM FAILURES ACROSS THE BOARD.
SYSTEM FAILURE
THIS IS IT, THEN. IF I CAN'T HAVE ROSE, NO ONE WILL.
KLIK

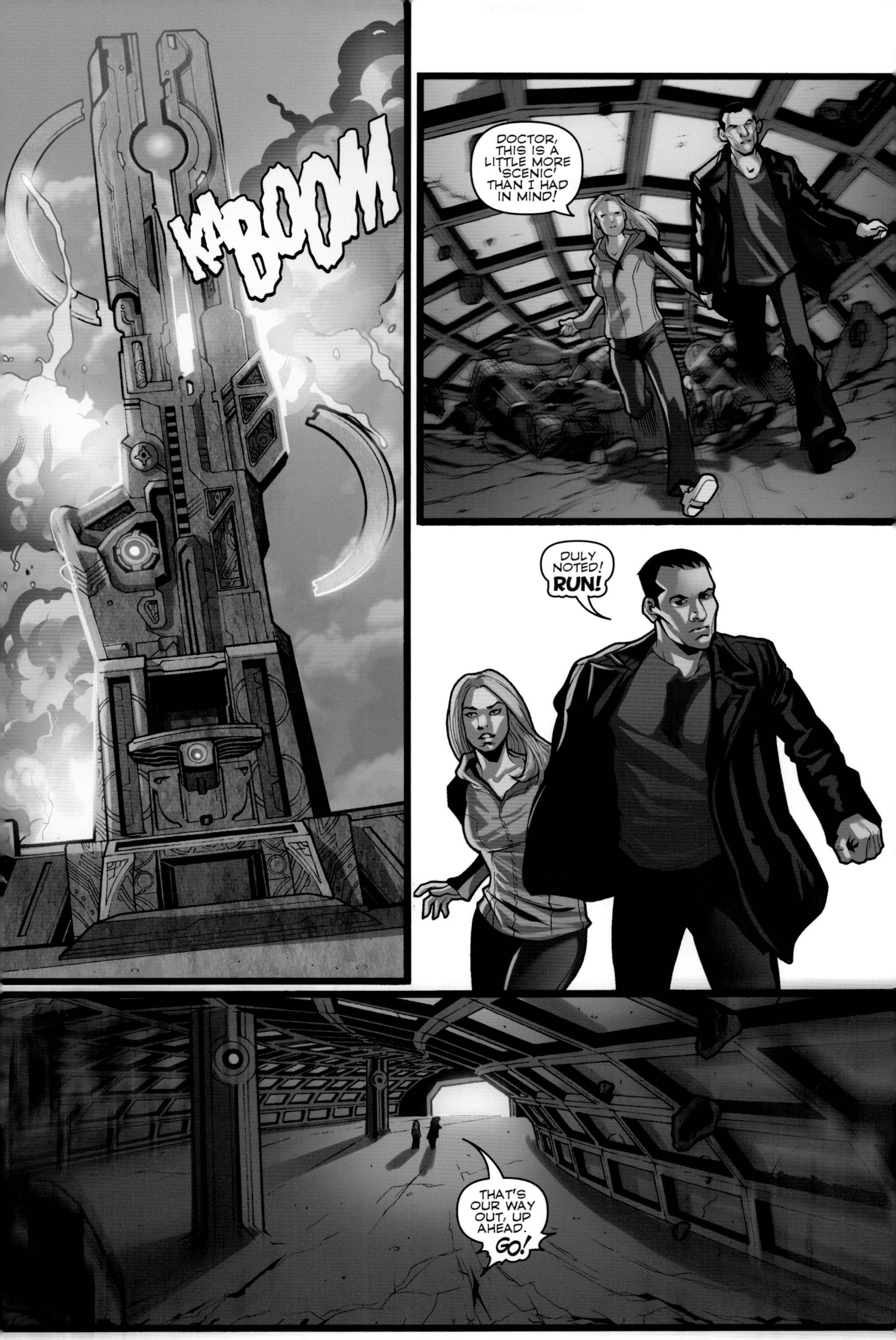
KABOOM
DOCTOR, THIS IS A LITTLE MORE 'SCENIC' THAN I HAD IN MIND!
DULY NOTED! RUN!
THAT'S OUR WAY OUT, UP AHEAD. GO!

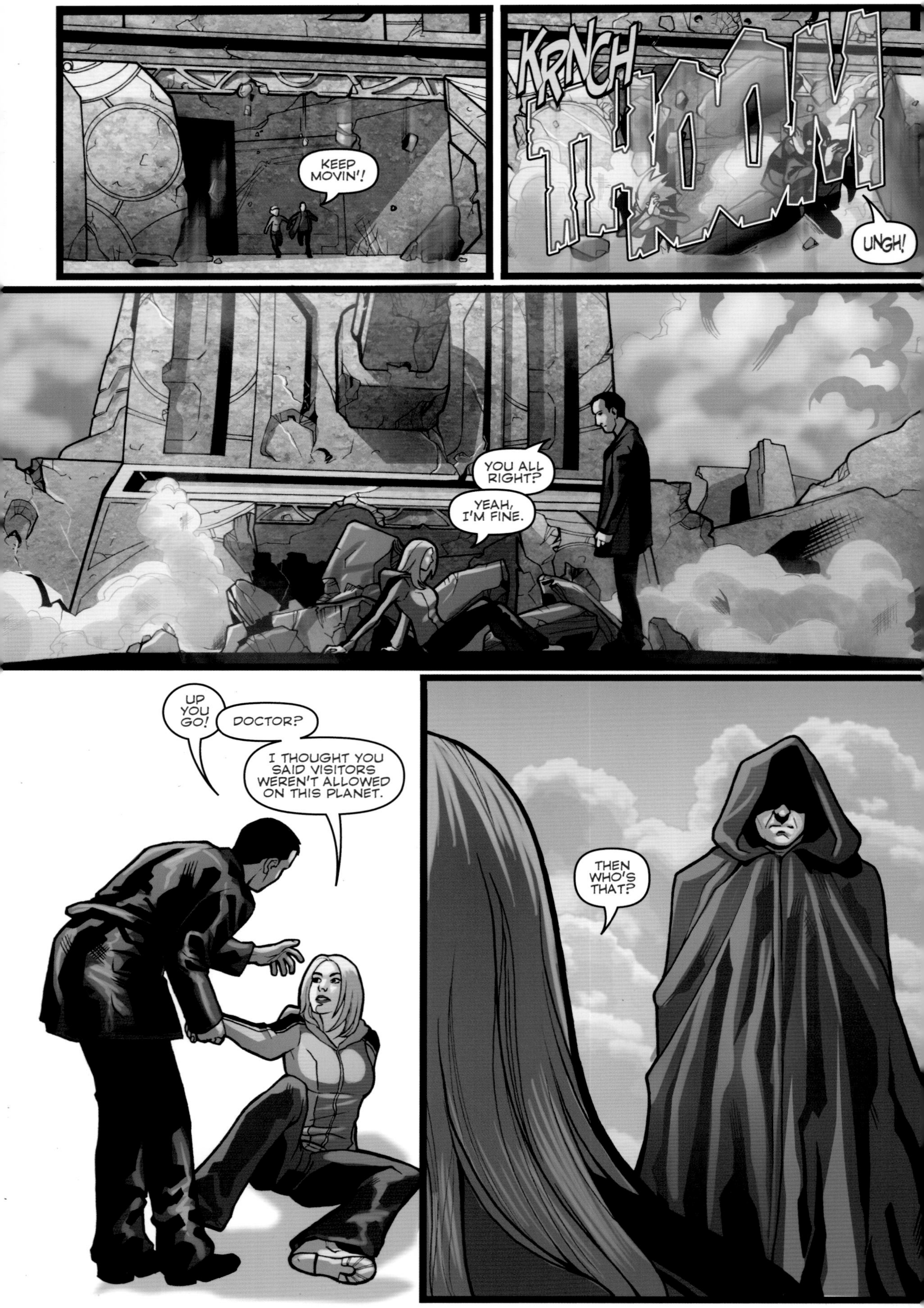
KEEP MOVIN'!
KRNCH
THOOM
UNGH!
YOU ALL RIGHT?
YEAH, I'M FINE.
UP YOU GO!
DOCTOR?
I THOUGHT YOU SAID VISITORS WEREN'T ALLOWED ON THIS PLANET.
THEN WHO'S THAT?

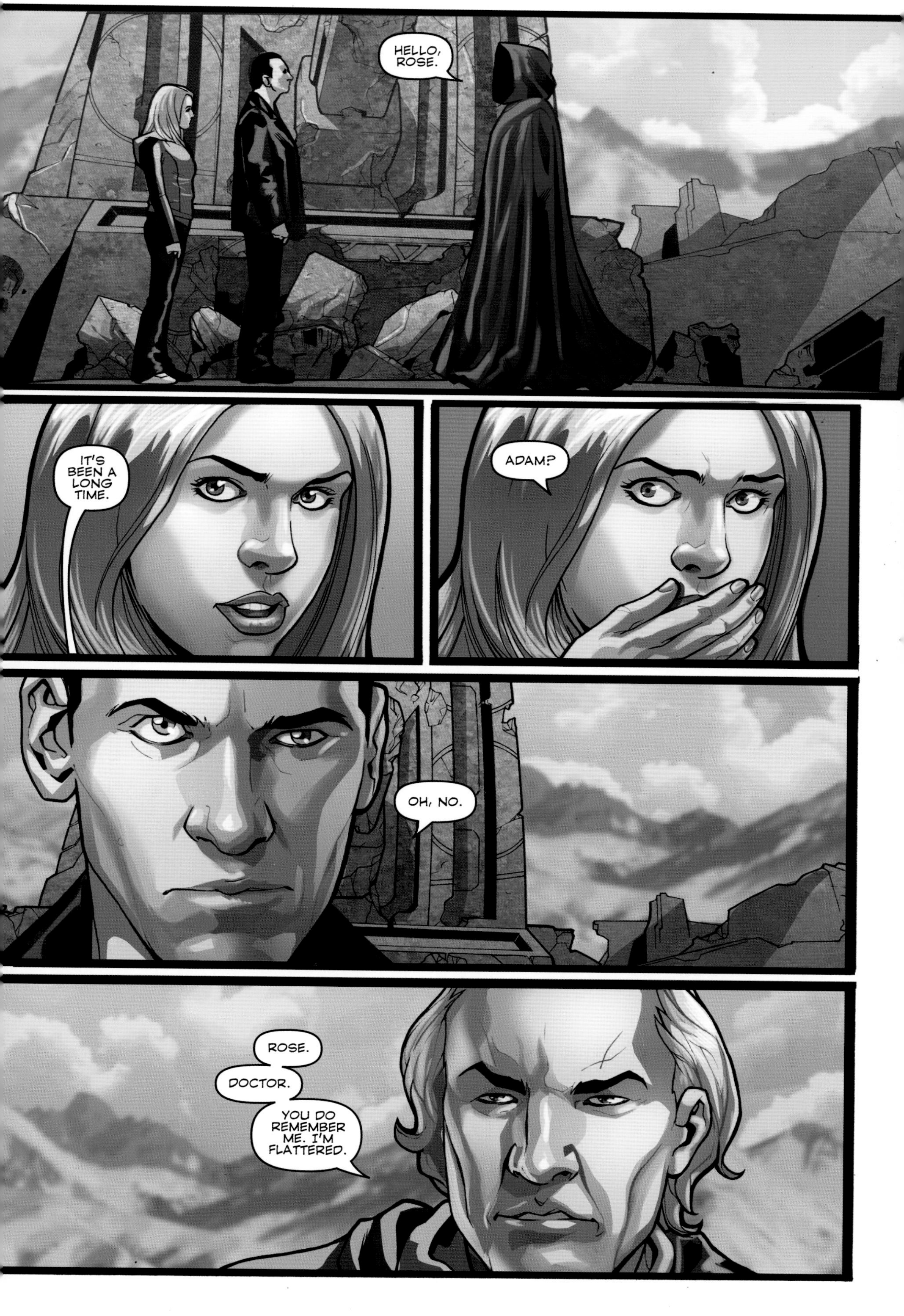
HELLO, ROSE.
IT'S BEEN A LONG TIME.
ADAM?
OH, NO.
ROSE.
DOCTOR.
YOU DO REMEMBER ME. I'M FLATTERED.

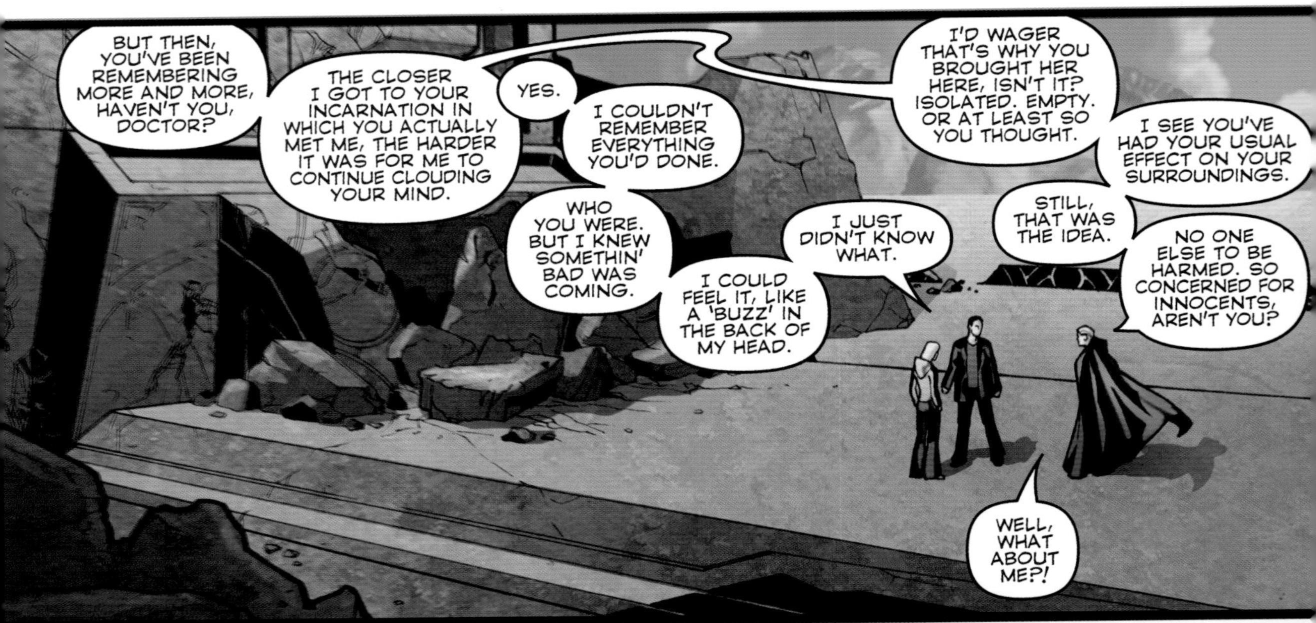
BUT THEN, YOU'VE BEEN REMEMBERING MORE AND MORE, HAVEN'T YOU, DOCTOR?
THE CLOSER I GOT TO YOUR INCARNATION IN WHICH YOU ACTUALLY MET ME, THE HARDER IT WAS FOR ME TO CONTINUE CLOUDING YOUR MIND.
YES.
I COULDN'T REMEMBER EVERYTHING YOU'D DONE.
WHO YOU WERE. BUT I KNEW SOMETHIN' BAD WAS COMING.
I COULD FEEL IT, LIKE A 'BUZZ' IN THE BACK OF MY HEAD.
I JUST DIDN'T KNOW WHAT.
I'D WAGER THAT'S WHY YOU BROUGHT HER HERE, ISN'T IT? ISOLATED. EMPTY. OR AT LEAST SO YOU THOUGHT.
I SEE YOU'VE HAD YOUR USUAL EFFECT ON YOUR SURROUNDINGS.
STILL, THAT WAS THE IDEA.
NO ONE ELSE TO BE HARMED. SO CONCERNED FOR INNOCENTS, AREN'T YOU?
WELL, WHAT ABOUT ME?!

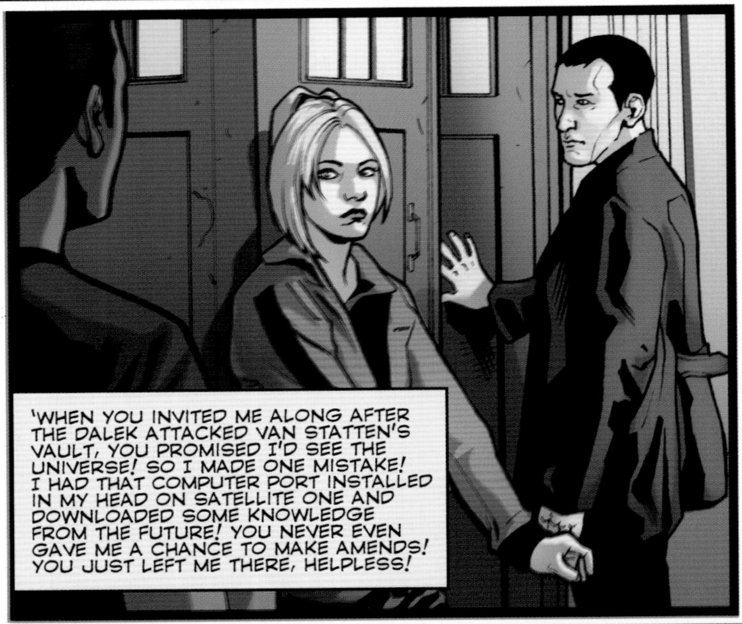
'WHEN YOU INVITED ME ALONG AFTER THE DALEK ATTACKED VAN STATTEN'S VAULT, YOU PROMISED I'D SEE THE UNIVERSE! SO I MADE ONE MISTAKE! I HAD THAT COMPUTER PORT INSTALLED IN MY HEAD ON SATELLITE ONE AND DOWNLOADED SOME KNOWLEDGE FROM THE FUTURE! YOU NEVER EVEN GAVE ME A CHANCE TO MAKE AMENDS! YOU JUST LEFT ME THERE, HELPLESS!

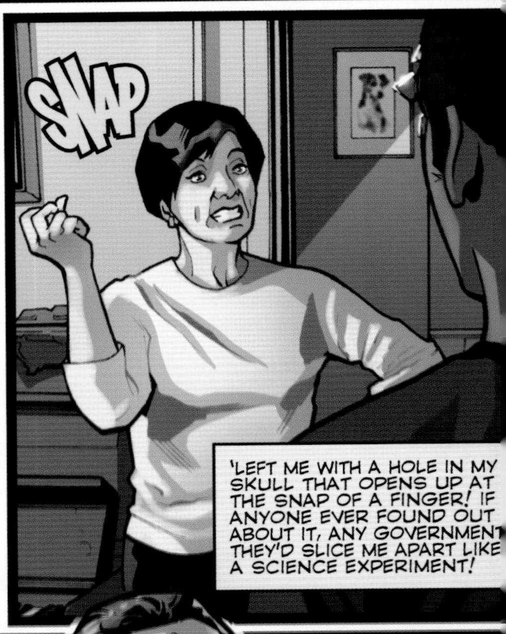
SNAP
'LEFT ME WITH A HOLE IN MY SKULL THAT OPENS UP AT THE SNAP OF A FINGER! IF ANYONE EVER FOUND OUT ABOUT IT, ANY GOVERNMENT THEY'D SLICE ME APART LIKE A SCIENCE EXPERIMENT!

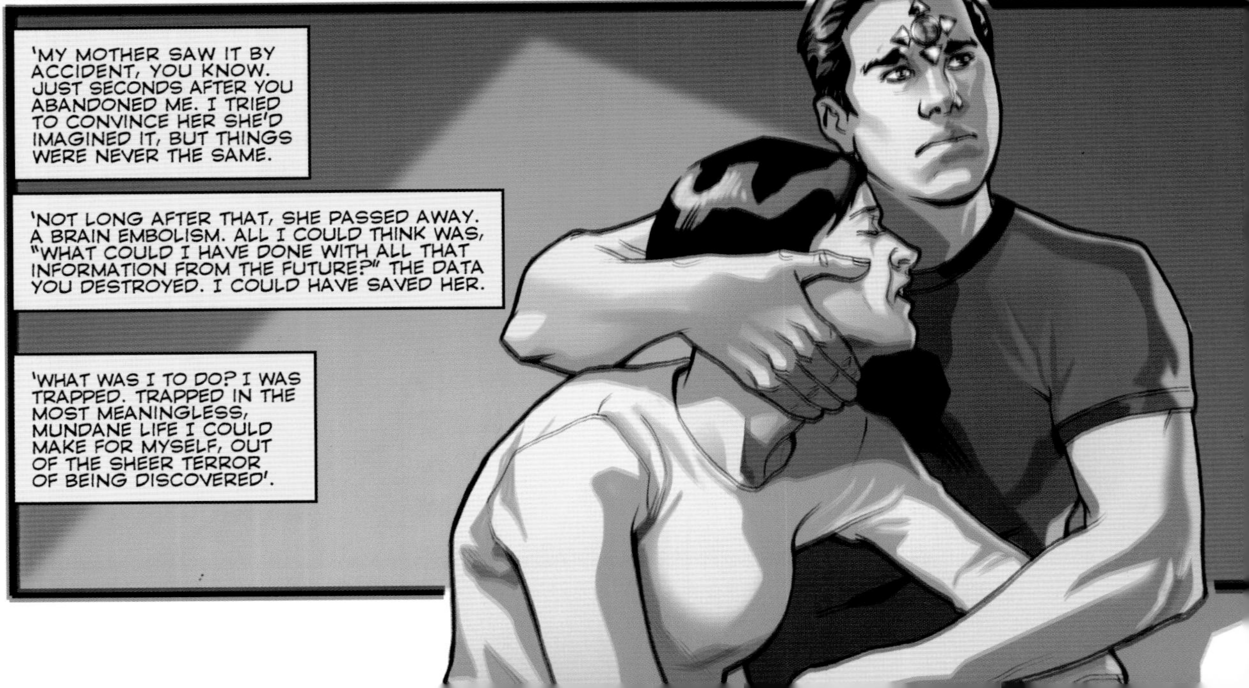
'MY MOTHER SAW IT BY ACCIDENT, YOU KNOW. JUST SECONDS AFTER YOU ABANDONED ME. I TRIED TO CONVINCE HER SHE'D IMAGINED IT, BUT THINGS WERE NEVER THE SAME.
'NOT LONG AFTER THAT, SHE PASSED AWAY. A BRAIN EMBOLISM. ALL I COULD THINK WAS, "WHAT COULD I HAVE DONE WITH ALL THAT INFORMATION FROM THE FUTURE?" THE DATA YOU DESTROYED. I COULD HAVE SAVED HER.
'WHAT WAS I TO DO? I WAS TRAPPED. TRAPPED IN THE MOST MEANINGLESS, MUNDANE LIFE I COULD MAKE FOR MYSELF, OUT OF THE SHEER TERROR OF BEING DISCOVERED'.

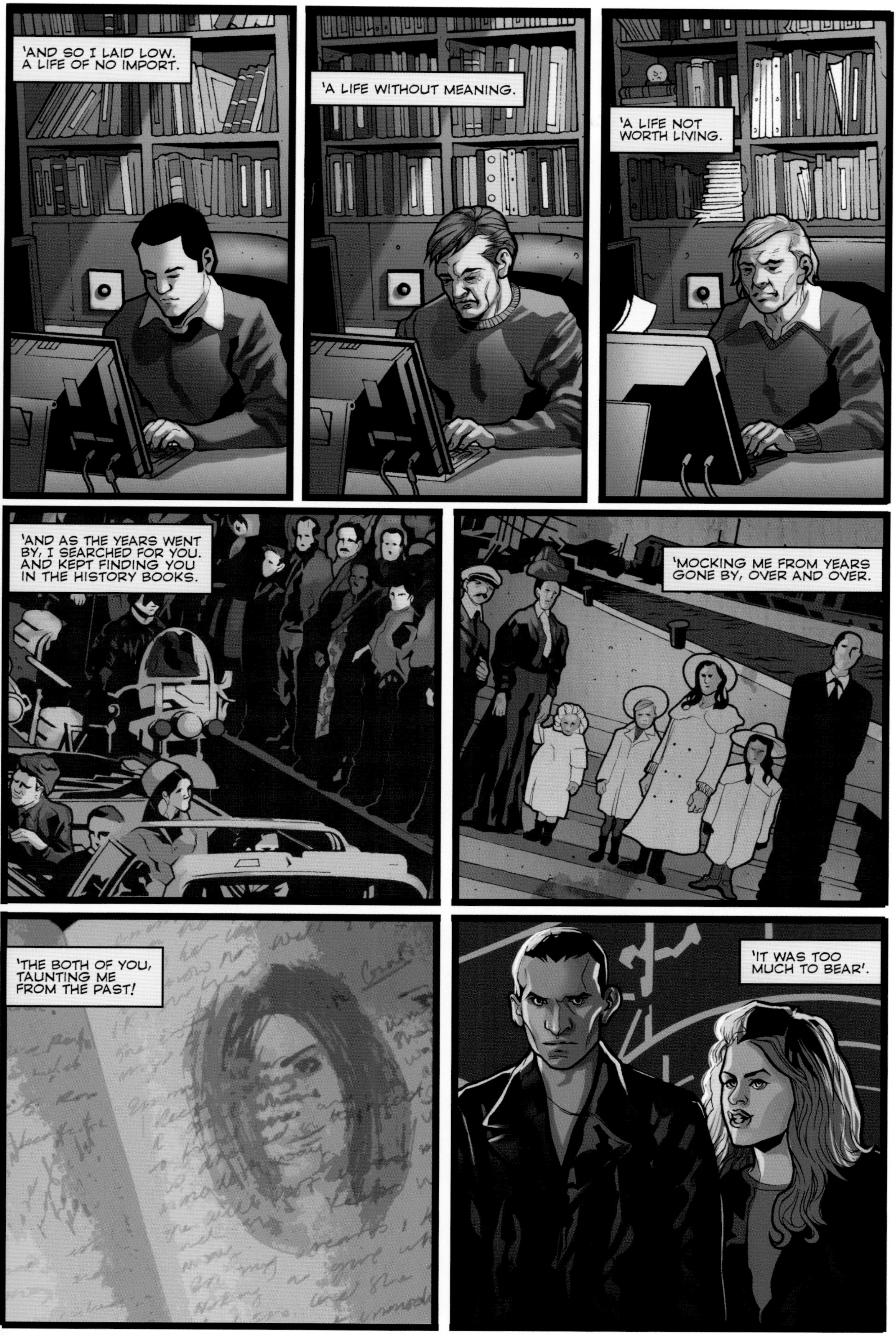
'AND SO I LAID LOW. A LIFE OF NO IMPORT.
'A LIFE WITHOUT MEANING.
'A LIFE NOT WORTH LIVING.
'AND AS THE YEARS WENT BY, I SEARCHED FOR YOU. AND KEPT FINDING YOU IN THE HISTORY BOOKS.
'MOCKING ME FROM YEARS GONE BY, OVER AND OVER.
'THE BOTH OF YOU, TAUNTING ME FROM THE PAST!
'IT WAS TOO MUCH TO BEAR'.

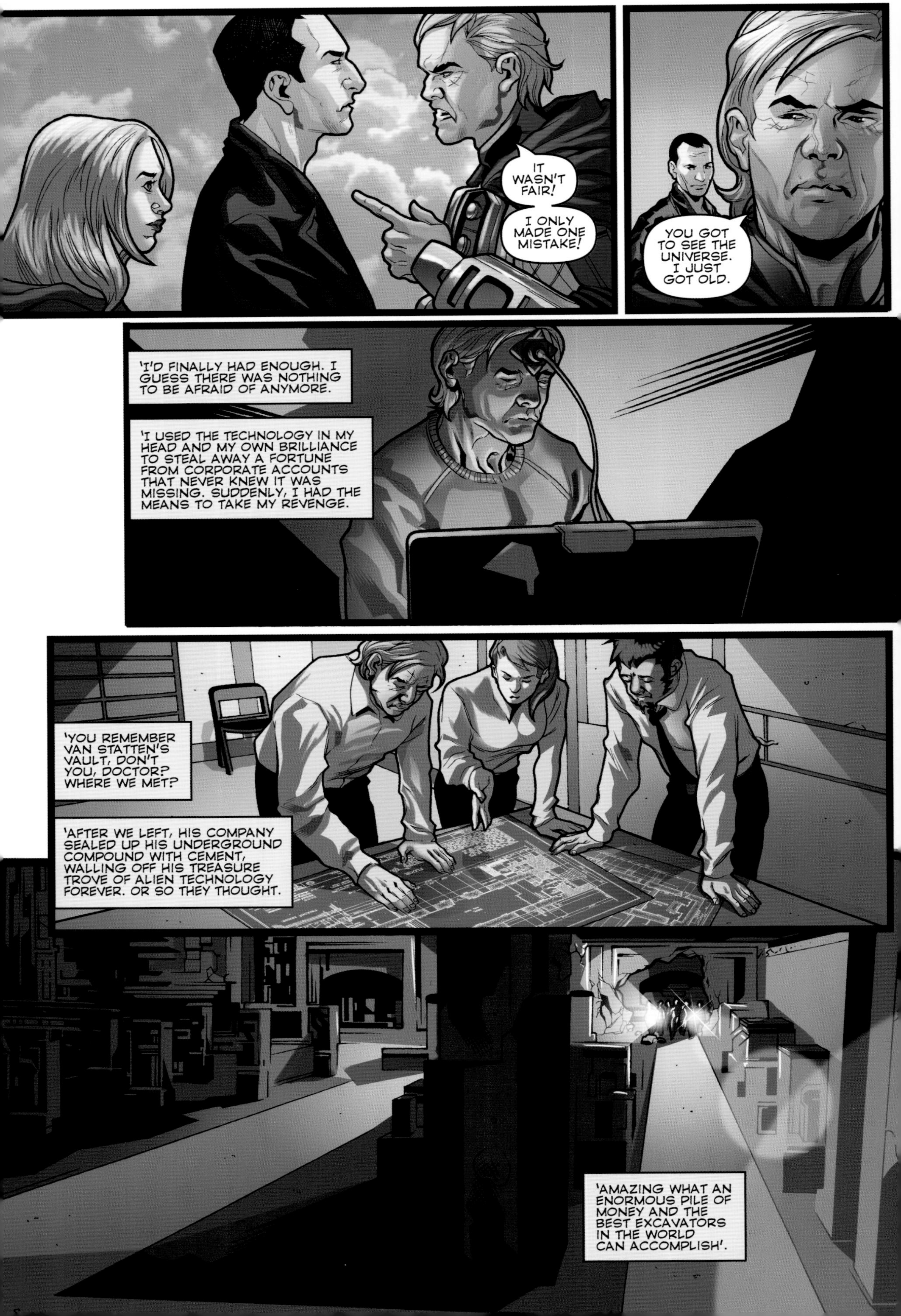
IT WASN'T FAIR!
I ONLY MADE ONE MISTAKE!
YOU GOT TO SEE THE UNIVERSE. I JUST GOT OLD.
'I'D FINALLY HAD ENOUGH. I GUESS THERE WAS NOTHING TO BE AFRAID OF ANYMORE.
'I USED THE TECHNOLOGY IN MY HEAD AND MY OWN BRILLIANCE TO STEAL AWAY A FORTUNE FROM CORPORATE ACCOUNTS THAT NEVER KNEW IT WAS MISSING. SUDDENLY, I HAD THE MEANS TO TAKE MY REVENGE.
'YOU REMEMBER VAN STATTEN'S VAULT, DON'T YOU, DOCTOR? WHERE WE MET?
'AFTER WE LEFT, HIS COMPANY SEALED UP HIS UNDERGROUND COMPOUND WITH CEMENT, WALLING OFF HIS TREASURE TROVE OF ALIEN TECHNOLOGY FOREVER. OR SO THEY THOUGHT.
'AMAZING WHAT AN ENORMOUS PILE OF MONEY AND THE BEST EXCAVATORS IN THE WORLD CAN ACCOMPLISH'.

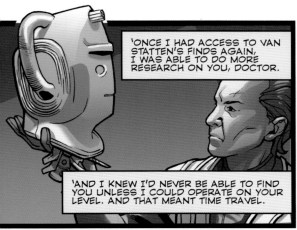

'ONCE I HAD ACCESS TO VAN STATTEN'S FINDS AGAIN, I WAS ABLE TO DO MORE RESEARCH ON YOU, DOCTOR.

'AND I KNEW I'D NEVER BE ABLE TO FIND YOU UNLESS I COULD OPERATE ON YOUR LEVEL. AND THAT MEANT TIME TRAVEL.

'USING THE ALIEN TECHNOLOGY, I WAS ABLE TO SEND OUT A SUB-ETHER SIGNAL TO LURE IN SOMEONE ELSE I FOUND RECORD OF...

'I GUESS YOU CALL THEM "TIME AGENTS".

FWASH

'NOT THAT IT MATTERED. HE DIDN'T HAVE TIME TO INTRODUCE HIMSELF.

FSSSSSSSSS

'WITH THE VORTEX MANIPULATOR, I COULD TRULY BEGIN. BEGIN TO SEARCH OUT THE KNOWLEDGE AND WEAPONS I NEEDED TO FIND YOU, DOCTOR. FIND YOU AND REPAY YOU FOR MY WASTED LIFE'.

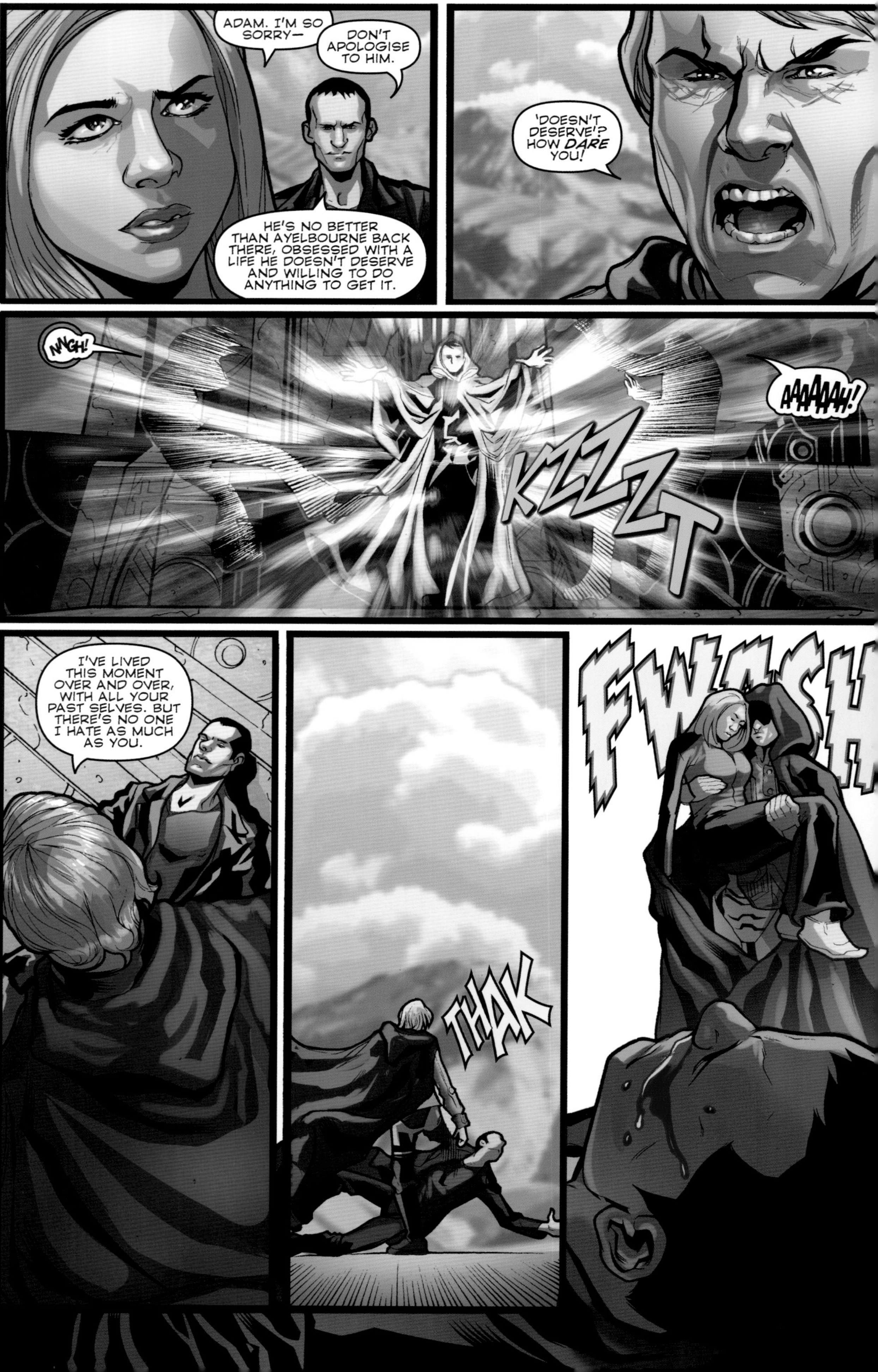

ADAM. I'M SO SORRY—
DON'T APOLOGISE TO HIM.
HE'S NO BETTER THAN AYELBOURNE BACK THERE, OBSESSED WITH A LIFE HE DOESN'T DESERVE AND WILLING TO DO ANYTHING TO GET IT.
'DOESN'T DESERVE'? HOW DARE YOU!
NNGH!
AAAAAAH!
KZZZT
I'VE LIVED THIS MOMENT OVER AND OVER, WITH ALL YOUR PAST SELVES. BUT THERE'S NO ONE I HATE AS MUCH AS YOU.
THAK
FWASH

REFLECTIONS OF TIME
Wherein prominent Whovians past and present muse upon the Doctor's history in comic form.

Change was afoot at *Doctor Who Magazine* in 2004. Well, change was afoot *everywhere* in the wide world of *Who*, because, against all the odds, the new TV series we fans had dreamed of for 16 long years was about to become a reality. I'd taken over as *DWM* editor in 2002, and one of my favourite parts of the job was working with writer Scott Gray on his frankly stunning run of Eighth Doctor comic strips. With a new Doctor on the horizon, we planned a big 'season finale' for McGann's Doctor in an epic Cyberman tale called *The Flood*.

Now it's pretty common knowledge that, as a fan of the *DWM* strip and a very, very nice man, *Doctor Who* showrunner Russell T Davies made Scott and me a completely unprecedented offer: Would we like to show the regeneration between the Eighth and Ninth Doctors in our comic strip? Uh... yes. Yes, we would. Thank you! Wow.

Sadly, things didn't work out due to licensing issues, which meant we couldn't show the new Doctor before he appeared on TV, and couldn't show McGann's Doctor once the new series began—hence the one-to-the-other transformation so vital to a regeneration story was impossible to depict. Russell suggested we get around this with a strip where the new Doctor kept regenerating for the entire story—depicted as a figure formed from blazing energy. But very soon we realized that, as an adjunct to a huge new flagship BBC show, our strip needed to reflect what was soon to be seen on the nation's screens: the Ninth Doctor and Rose Tyler having fantastic adventures.

Not really knowing how much of a new, young readership the show would bring to *DWM* (children's comic *Doctor Who Adventures*, with its own comic strip, didn't arrive until 2006), we initially decided to skew our stories a little younger. In practice, however, that doesn't show very much as Russell, Scott, and I were all such fans of the old Pat Mills & John Wagner/Dave Gibbons strips from *Doctor Who Weekly* (which never talked down to their young readers) so we attempted to echo those. And to be quite honest that's what we'd already been doing with the McGann strips! We even tried to get Gibbons back for a Ninth Doctor strip that Russell himself would have written. It wasn't possible given Dave's work schedule, but the basic story Russell had worked out ended up

on TV later as *Love & Monsters*. Fact, fans! Russell offered to personally check over our scripts to make sure they reflected the TV show, which was amazing given the insane amount he had on his plate. It was a huge help, though, especially with the early strips where we had little to go on in terms of performances.

Just as he burned brightly but briefly on TV, so Christopher Eccleston's Doctor notched up a short but sweet run of five *DWM* strips. But in those adventures he packed in trips to Earth in the 1600s, the 1960s, and the 21st century, an art gallery in space, a devastated planet, a Martian cruise ship, and a sinister dream world.

Regular writer Scott Gray and our go-to artist Martin Geraghty needed a break after the hectic schedule we'd been working to with *The Flood*, so for art duties I approached Mike Collins, whose work on Seventh Doctor strip *The Good Soldier* I'd always admired. Mike's dazzling visuals saw the Ninth Doctor through the whole of his comic strip run, with a brief detour for the *Doctor Who Annual* 2006 when Scott Gray and artist John Ross (soon destined for *Doctor Who Adventures*) teamed up for *Mr Nobody*. On the writing side I turned to soon-to-be TV writer Gareth Roberts, already-been TV writer Robert Shearman, and, showing sickening versatility, Mike Collins who doubled up as writer and penciller for *Art Attack*. Rob delivered a twisted, nightmarish *tour-de-force* in *The Cruel Sea*, while I worked with Gareth on the first Ninth Doctor strip, *The Love Invasion*, a fun romp

through the swinging Sixties. Gareth flew solo for the final Ninth Doctor strip, *A Groatsworth of Wit*, which saw the Doctor meet Shakespeare. It must be noted that Gareth's work on these strips, along with his excellent novel *Only Human*, impressed Russell and helped him onto the writing team for the TV show, and *Groatsworth* heavily influenced his first *Doctor Who* script, *The Shakespeare Code*. Later, another of Gareth's *DWM* strips, *The Lodger*, was adapted for TV featuring Matt Smith's Doctor, but even *The Love Invasion* provided a scene for Gareth's 2008 story *The Unicorn and the Wasp*, where the Doctor cures himself of poisoning with a bizarre range of foodstuffs.

Short as the Ninth Doctor's comic strip tenure in *Doctor Who Magazine* was, I don't think anyone could claim it wasn't influential. Plus, I was told by Billie Piper that she loved being a comic-strip hero. And you can't argue with Rose Tyler, can you?

—Clayton Hickman
former *Doctor Who Magazine* editor, writer for CBBC's *The Sarah Jane Adventures* and *Wizards vs Aliens*, *Doctor Who* book and DVD designer, editor of *The Brilliant Book of Doctor Who*

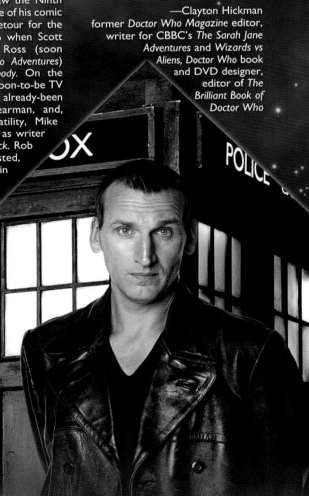

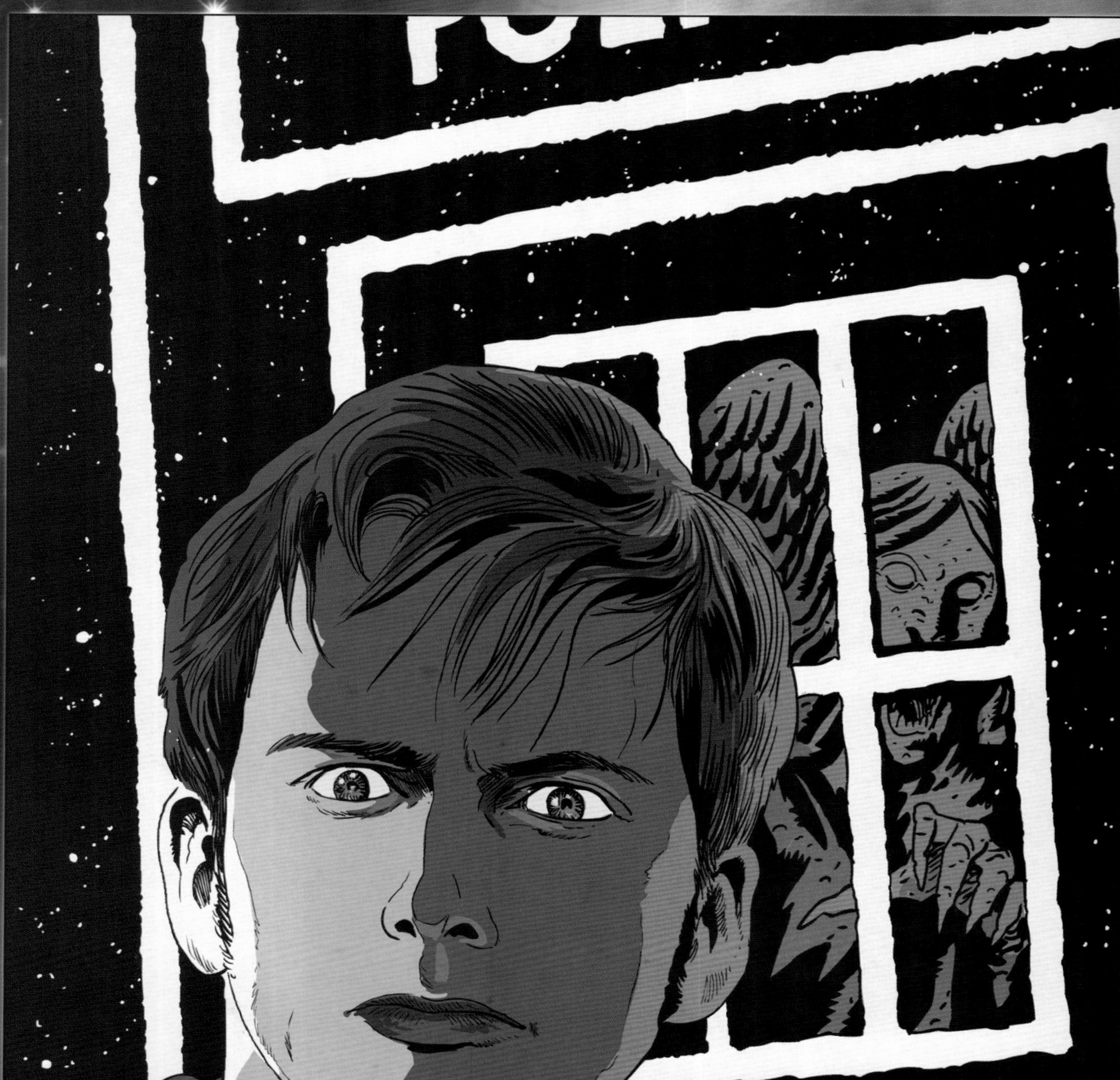
ICE TELEPHONE
REE
CE OF
IC
FRAN CAVIL LAF. 13

10TH DOCTOR
2005 - 2010

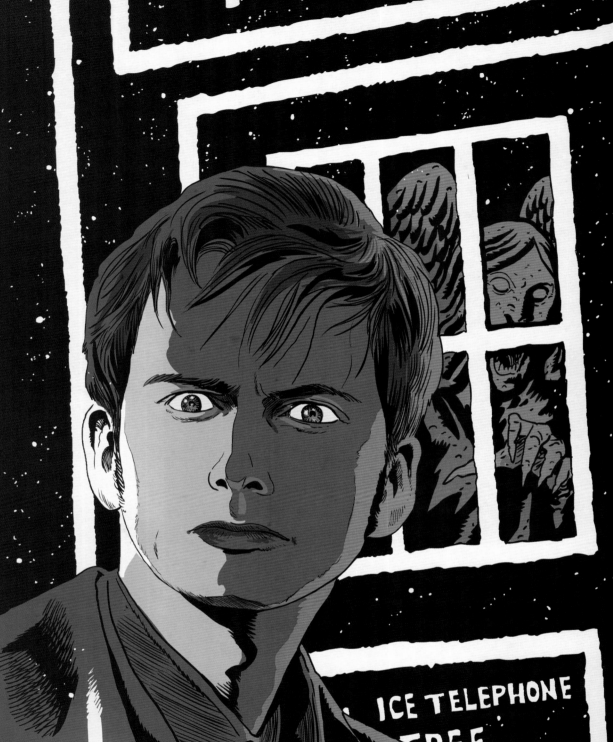

CHAPTER 10 "QUIET ON THE SET"
Cover Art by Francesco Francavilla

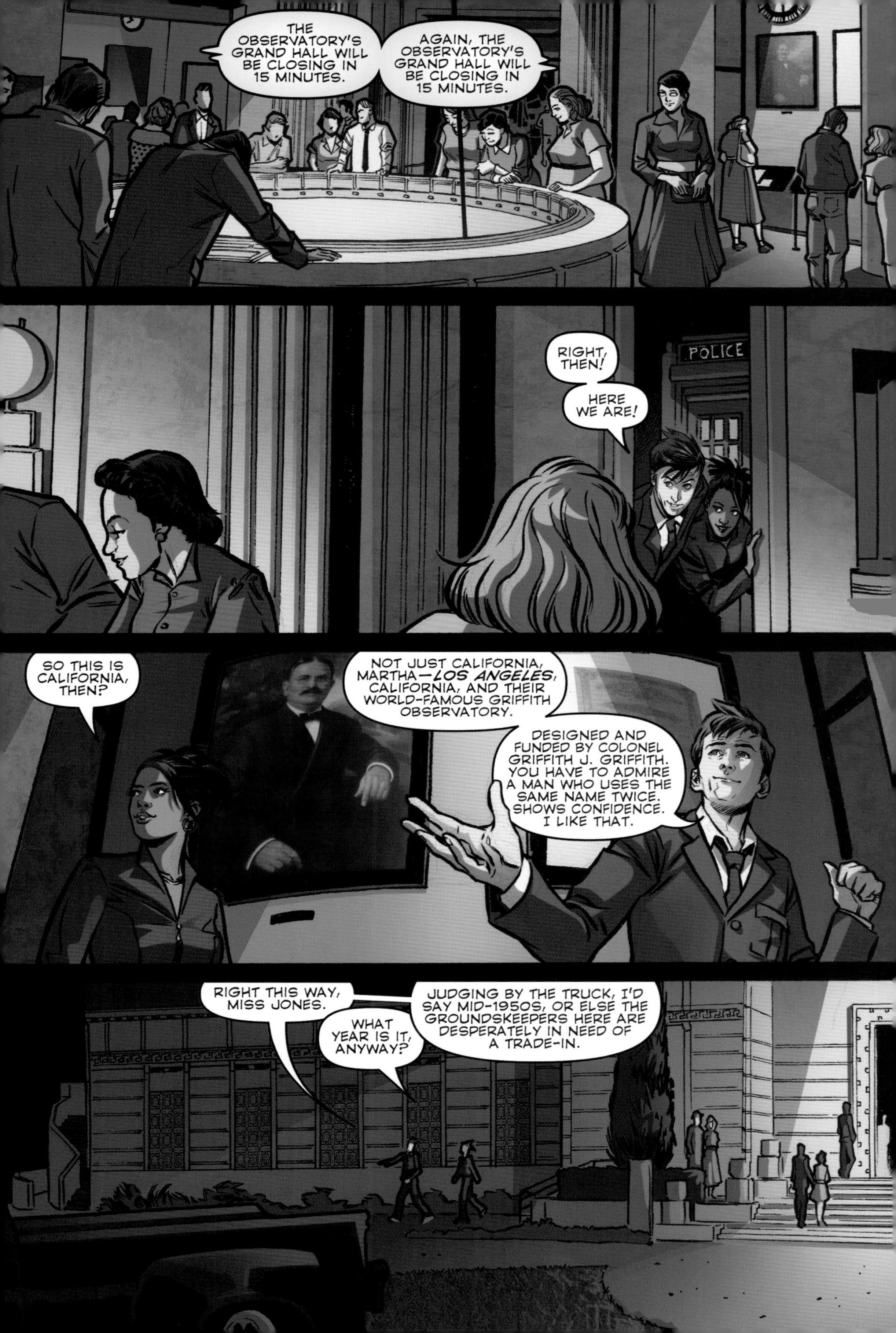
THE OBSERVATORY'S GRAND HALL WILL BE CLOSING IN 15 MINUTES.
AGAIN, THE OBSERVATORY'S GRAND HALL WILL BE CLOSING IN 15 MINUTES.
POLICE
RIGHT, THEN!
HERE WE ARE!
SO THIS IS CALIFORNIA, THEN?
NOT JUST CALIFORNIA, MARTHA—LOS ANGELES, CALIFORNIA, AND THEIR WORLD-FAMOUS GRIFFITH OBSERVATORY.
DESIGNED AND FUNDED BY COLONEL GRIFFITH J. GRIFFITH. YOU HAVE TO ADMIRE A MAN WHO USES THE SAME NAME TWICE. SHOWS CONFIDENCE. I LIKE THAT.
RIGHT THIS WAY, MISS JONES.
WHAT YEAR IS IT, ANYWAY?
JUDGING BY THE TRUCK, I'D SAY MID-1950S, OR ELSE THE GROUNDSKEEPERS HERE ARE DESPERATELY IN NEED OF A TRADE-IN.

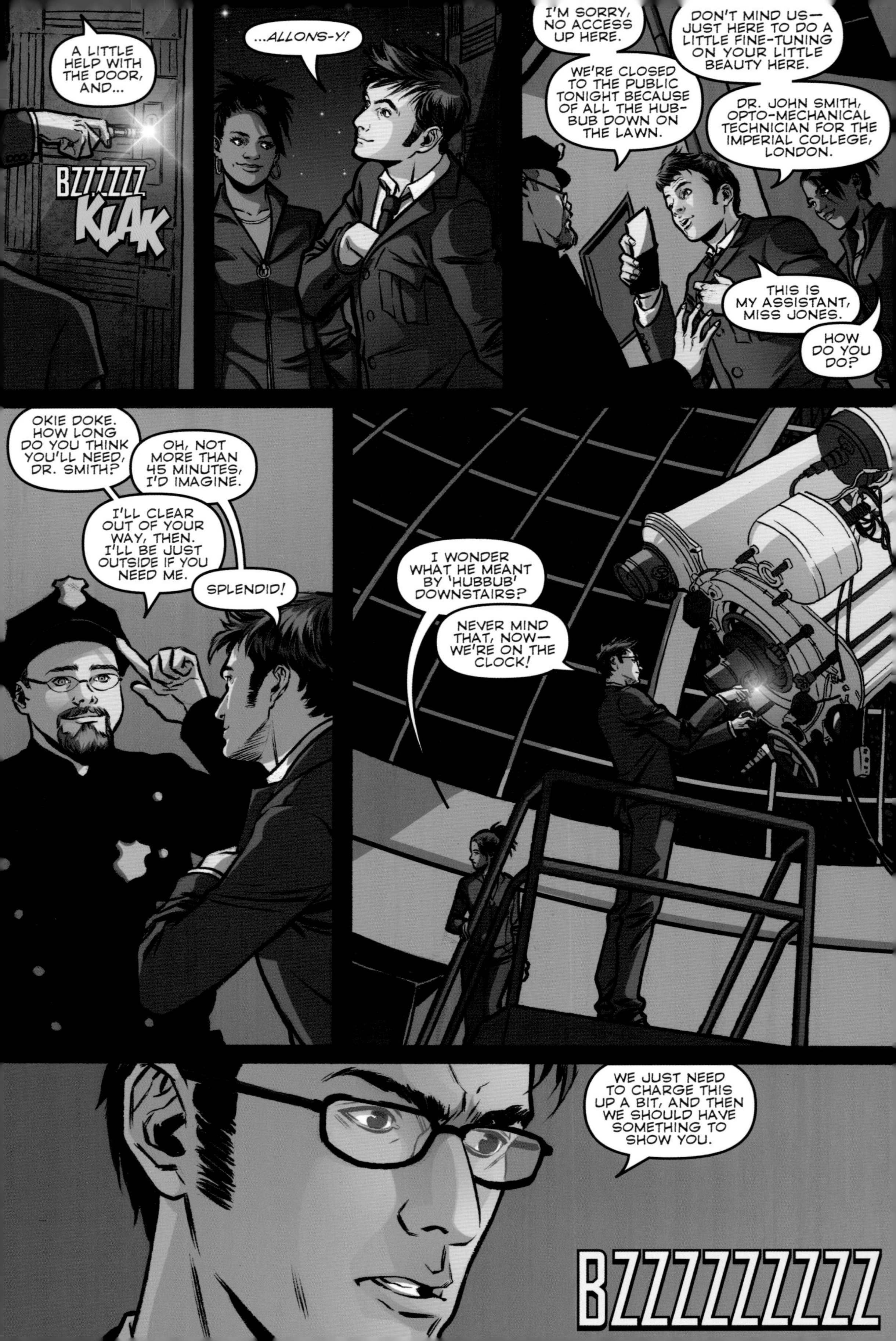
A LITTLE HELP WITH THE DOOR, AND...
BZZZZZZ
KLAK
...ALLONS-Y!
I'M SORRY, NO ACCESS UP HERE.
WE'RE CLOSED TO THE PUBLIC TONIGHT BECAUSE OF ALL THE HUB-BUB DOWN ON THE LAWN.
DON'T MIND US— JUST HERE TO DO A LITTLE FINE-TUNING ON YOUR LITTLE BEAUTY HERE.
DR. JOHN SMITH, OPTO-MECHANICAL TECHNICIAN FOR THE IMPERIAL COLLEGE, LONDON.
THIS IS MY ASSISTANT, MISS JONES.
HOW DO YOU DO?
OKIE DOKE. HOW LONG DO YOU THINK YOU'LL NEED, DR. SMITH?
OH, NOT MORE THAN 45 MINUTES, I'D IMAGINE.
I'LL CLEAR OUT OF YOUR WAY, THEN. I'LL BE JUST OUTSIDE IF YOU NEED ME.
SPLENDID!
I WONDER WHAT HE MEANT BY 'HUBBUB' DOWNSTAIRS?
NEVER MIND THAT, NOW— WE'RE ON THE CLOCK!
WE JUST NEED TO CHARGE THIS UP A BIT, AND THEN WE SHOULD HAVE SOMETHING TO SHOW YOU.
BZZZZZZZZZZ

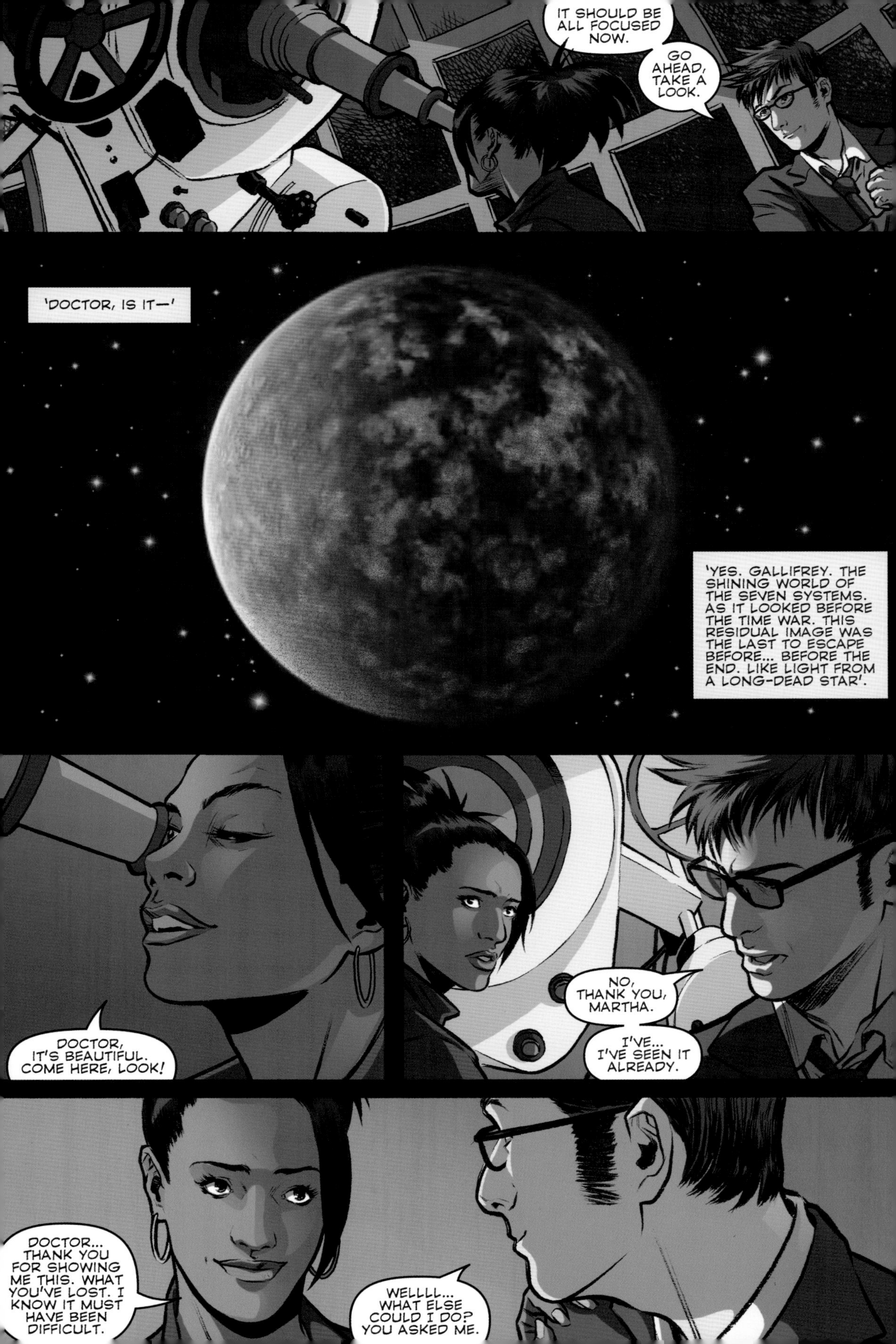
IT SHOULD BE ALL FOCUSED NOW.
GO AHEAD, TAKE A LOOK.
'DOCTOR, IS IT—'
'YES. GALLIFREY. THE SHINING WORLD OF THE SEVEN SYSTEMS. AS IT LOOKED BEFORE THE TIME WAR. THIS RESIDUAL IMAGE WAS THE LAST TO ESCAPE BEFORE... BEFORE THE END. LIKE LIGHT FROM A LONG-DEAD STAR'.
DOCTOR, IT'S BEAUTIFUL. COME HERE, LOOK!
NO, THANK YOU, MARTHA.
I'VE... I'VE SEEN IT ALREADY.
DOCTOR... THANK YOU FOR SHOWING ME THIS. WHAT YOU'VE LOST. I KNOW IT MUST HAVE BEEN DIFFICULT.
WELLLL... WHAT ELSE COULD I DO? YOU ASKED ME.

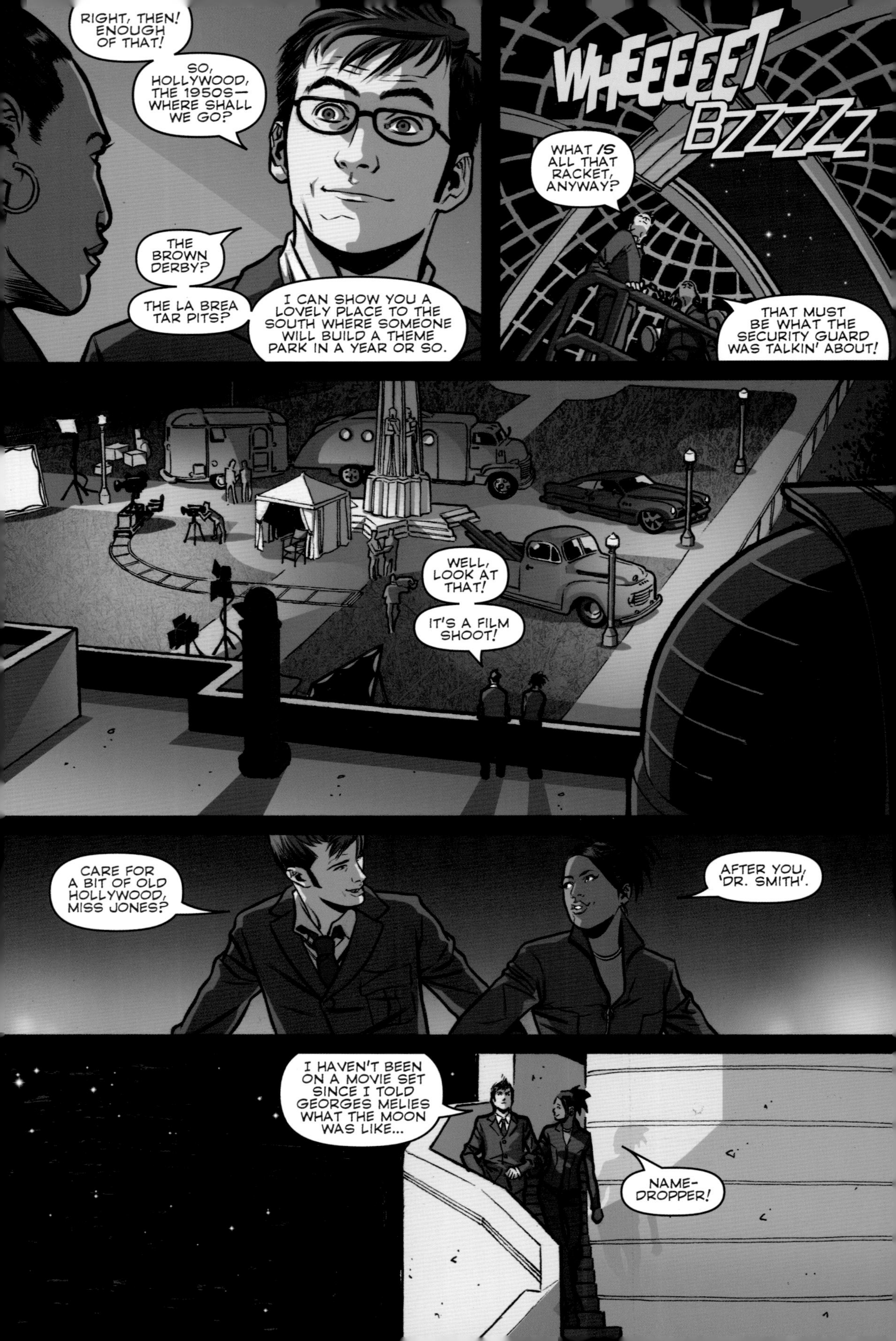
RIGHT, THEN! ENOUGH OF THAT!
SO, HOLLYWOOD, THE 1950S— WHERE SHALL WE GO?
THE BROWN DERBY?
THE LA BREA TAR PITS?
I CAN SHOW YOU A LOVELY PLACE TO THE SOUTH WHERE SOMEONE WILL BUILD A THEME PARK IN A YEAR OR SO.
WHEEEEET
BZZZZZ
WHAT *IS* ALL THAT RACKET, ANYWAY?
THAT MUST BE WHAT THE SECURITY GUARD WAS TALKIN' ABOUT!
WELL, LOOK AT THAT!
IT'S A FILM SHOOT!
CARE FOR A BIT OF OLD HOLLYWOOD, MISS JONES?
AFTER YOU, 'DR. SMITH'.
I HAVEN'T BEEN ON A MOVIE SET SINCE I TOLD GEORGES MELIES WHAT THE MOON WAS LIKE...
NAME-DROPPER!

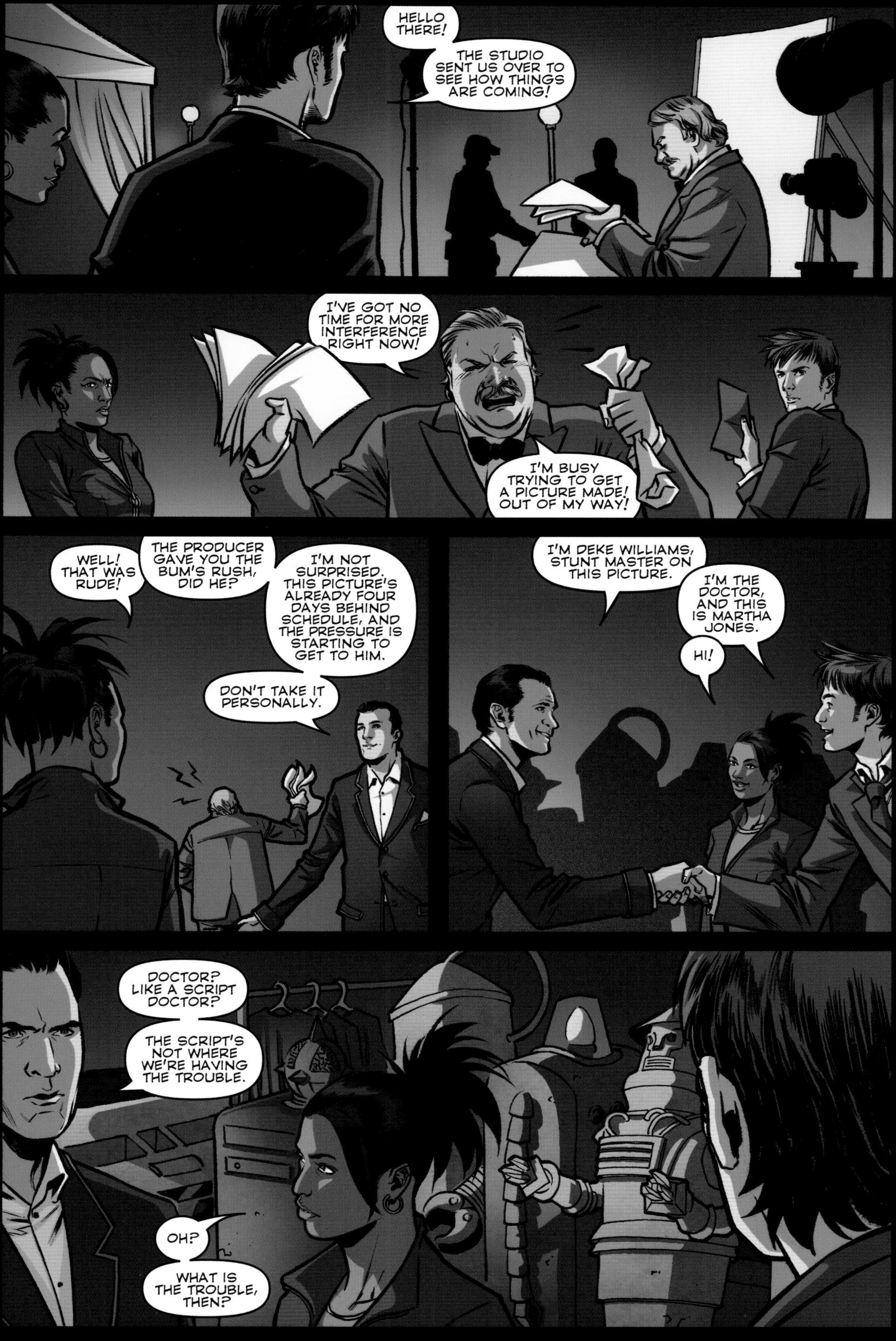
HELLO THERE!
THE STUDIO SENT US OVER TO SEE HOW THINGS ARE COMING!
I'VE GOT NO TIME FOR MORE INTERFERENCE RIGHT NOW!
I'M BUSY TRYING TO GET A PICTURE MADE! OUT OF MY WAY!
WELL! THAT WAS RUDE!
THE PRODUCER GAVE YOU THE BUM'S RUSH, DID HE?
I'M NOT SURPRISED. THIS PICTURE'S ALREADY FOUR DAYS BEHIND SCHEDULE, AND THE PRESSURE IS STARTING TO GET TO HIM.
DON'T TAKE IT PERSONALLY.
I'M DEKE WILLIAMS, STUNT MASTER ON THIS PICTURE.
I'M THE DOCTOR, AND THIS IS MARTHA JONES.
HI!
DOCTOR? LIKE A SCRIPT DOCTOR?
THE SCRIPT'S NOT WHERE WE'RE HAVING THE TROUBLE.
OH?
WHAT IS THE TROUBLE, THEN?

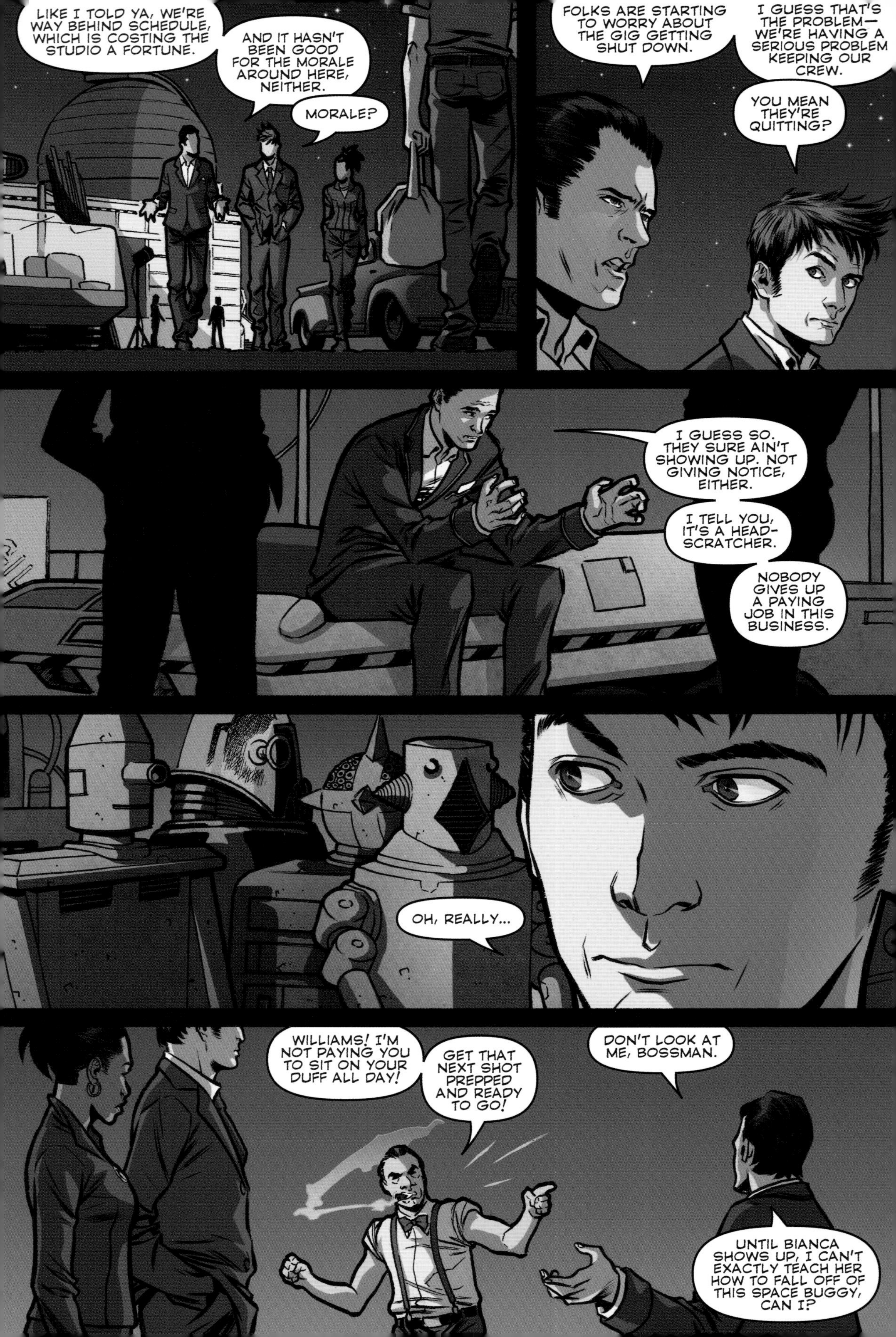
LIKE I TOLD YA, WE'RE WAY BEHIND SCHEDULE, WHICH IS COSTING THE STUDIO A FORTUNE.
AND IT HASN'T BEEN GOOD FOR THE MORALE AROUND HERE, NEITHER.
MORALE?
FOLKS ARE STARTING TO WORRY ABOUT THE GIG GETTING SHUT DOWN.
I GUESS THAT'S THE PROBLEM— WE'RE HAVING A SERIOUS PROBLEM KEEPING OUR CREW.
YOU MEAN THEY'RE QUITTING?
I GUESS SO. THEY SURE AIN'T SHOWING UP. NOT GIVING NOTICE, EITHER.
I TELL YOU, IT'S A HEAD-SCRATCHER.
NOBODY GIVES UP A PAYING JOB IN THIS BUSINESS.
OH, REALLY...
WILLIAMS! I'M NOT PAYING YOU TO SIT ON YOUR DUFF ALL DAY!
GET THAT NEXT SHOT PREPPED AND READY TO GO!
DON'T LOOK AT ME, BOSSMAN.
UNTIL BIANCA SHOWS UP, I CAN'T EXACTLY TEACH HER HOW TO FALL OFF OF THIS SPACE BUGGY, CAN I?

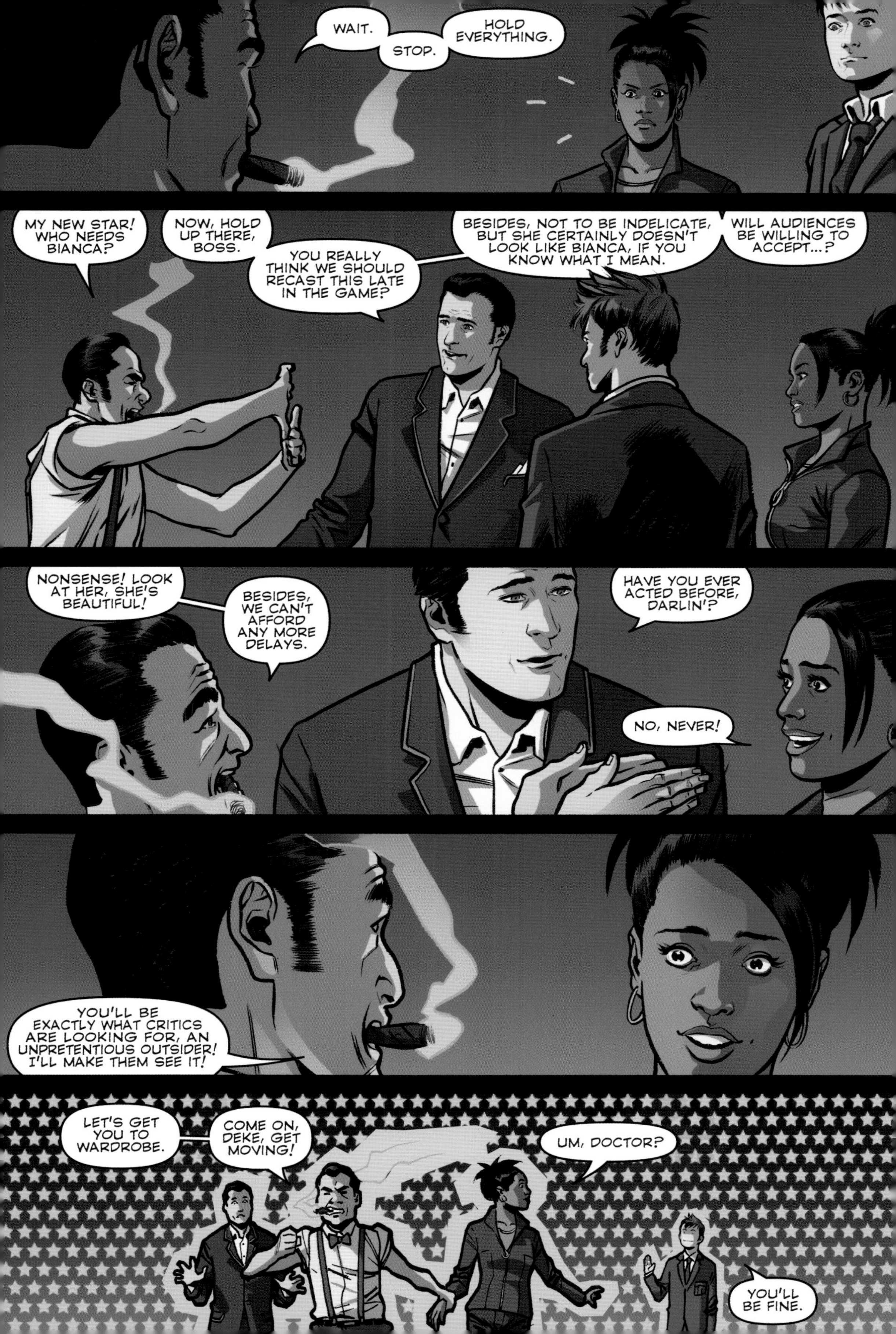
WAIT.
STOP.
HOLD EVERYTHING.
MY NEW STAR! WHO NEEDS BIANCA?
NOW, HOLD UP THERE, BOSS.
YOU REALLY THINK WE SHOULD RECAST THIS LATE IN THE GAME?
BESIDES, NOT TO BE INDELICATE, BUT SHE CERTAINLY DOESN'T LOOK LIKE BIANCA, IF YOU KNOW WHAT I MEAN.
WILL AUDIENCES BE WILLING TO ACCEPT...?
NONSENSE! LOOK AT HER, SHE'S BEAUTIFUL!
BESIDES, WE CAN'T AFFORD ANY MORE DELAYS.
HAVE YOU EVER ACTED BEFORE, DARLIN'?
NO, NEVER!
YOU'LL BE EXACTLY WHAT CRITICS ARE LOOKING FOR, AN UNPRETENTIOUS OUTSIDER! I'LL MAKE THEM SEE IT!
LET'S GET YOU TO WARDROBE.
COME ON, DEKE, GET MOVING!
UM, DOCTOR?
YOU'LL BE FINE.

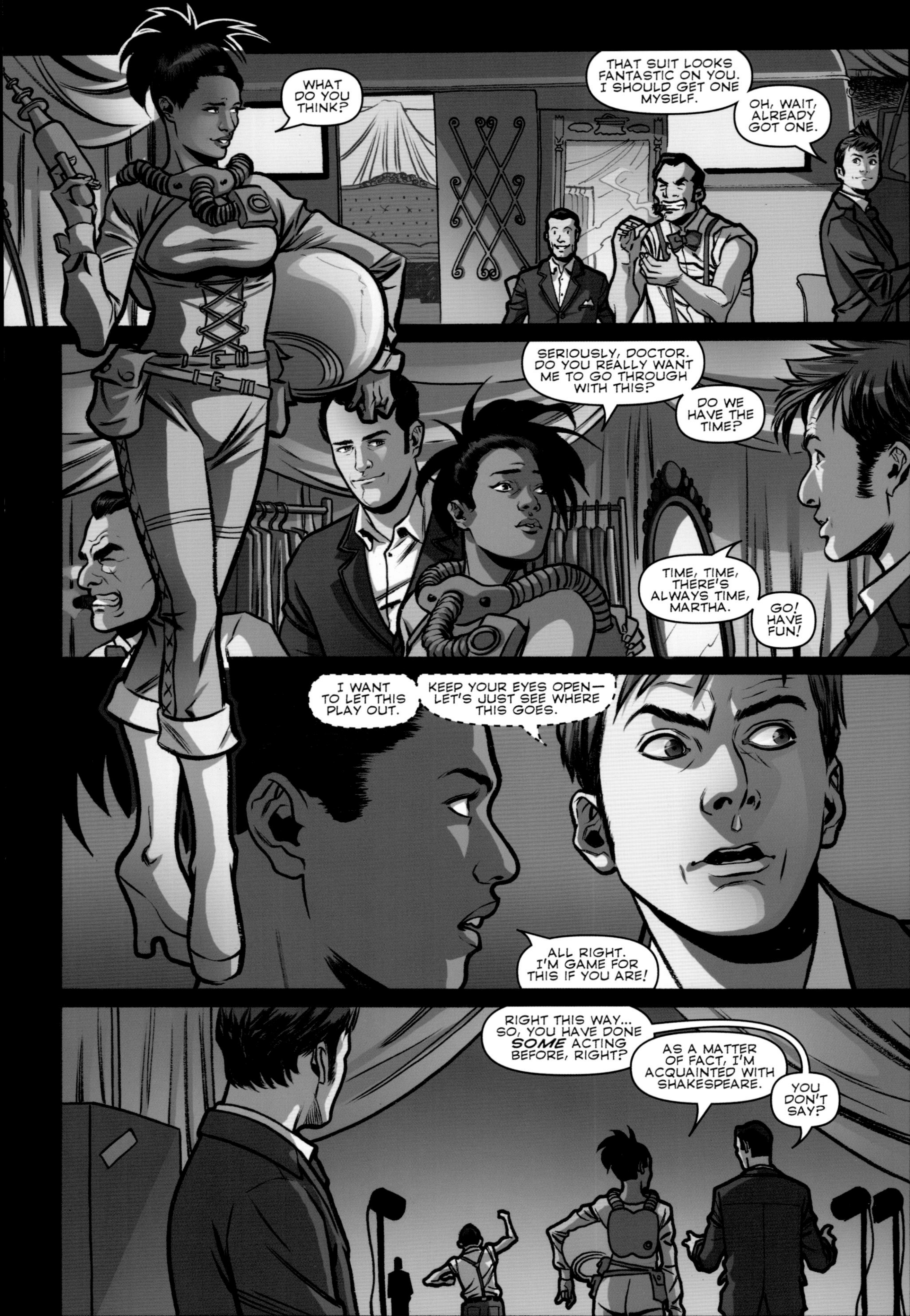
WHAT DO YOU THINK?
THAT SUIT LOOKS FANTASTIC ON YOU. I SHOULD GET ONE MYSELF.
OH, WAIT, ALREADY GOT ONE.
SERIOUSLY, DOCTOR. DO YOU REALLY WANT ME TO GO THROUGH WITH THIS?
DO WE HAVE THE TIME?
TIME, TIME, THERE'S ALWAYS TIME, MARTHA.
GO! HAVE FUN!
I WANT TO LET THIS PLAY OUT.
KEEP YOUR EYES OPEN— LET'S JUST SEE WHERE THIS GOES.
ALL RIGHT. I'M GAME FOR THIS IF YOU ARE!
RIGHT THIS WAY... SO, YOU HAVE DONE SOME ACTING BEFORE, RIGHT?
AS A MATTER OF FACT, I'M ACQUAINTED WITH SHAKESPEARE.
YOU DON'T SAY?

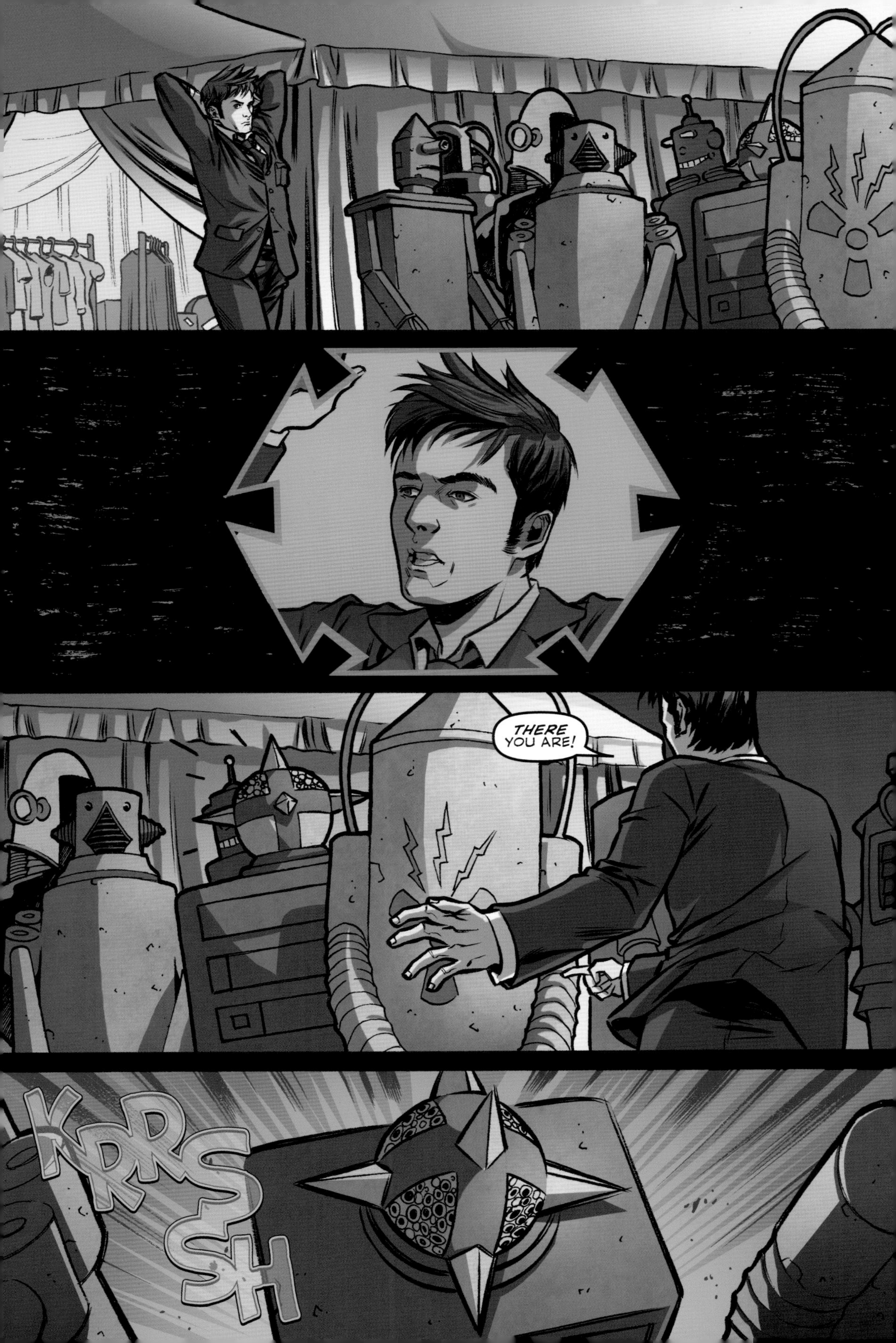
THERE YOU ARE!
KRRSSH

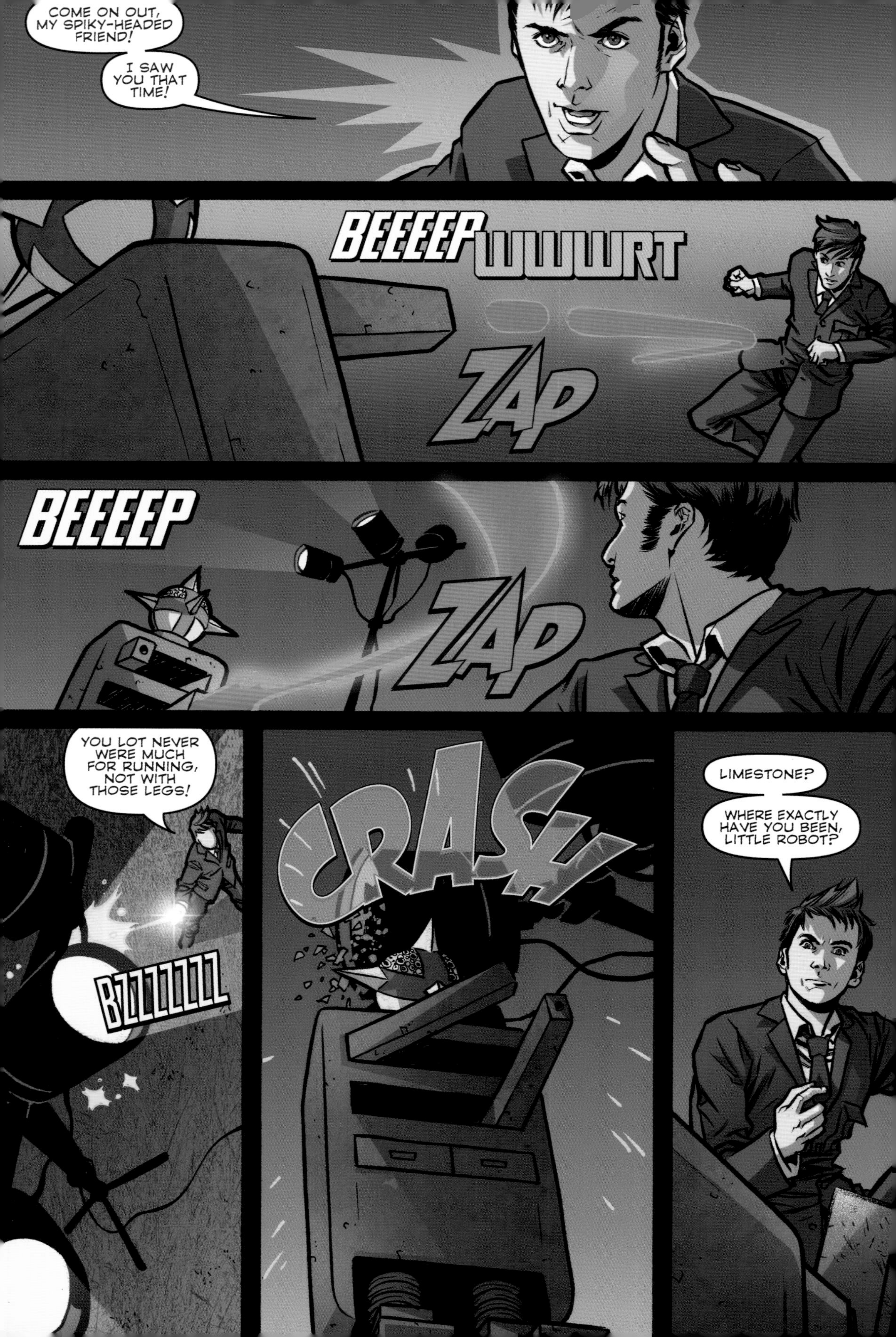
COME ON OUT, MY SPIKY-HEADED FRIEND!
I SAW YOU THAT TIME!
BEEEEP
WWWRT
ZAP
BEEEEP
ZAP
YOU LOT NEVER WERE MUCH FOR RUNNING, NOT WITH THOSE LEGS!
BZZZZZZZ
CRASH
LIMESTONE?
WHERE EXACTLY HAVE YOU BEEN, LITTLE ROBOT?

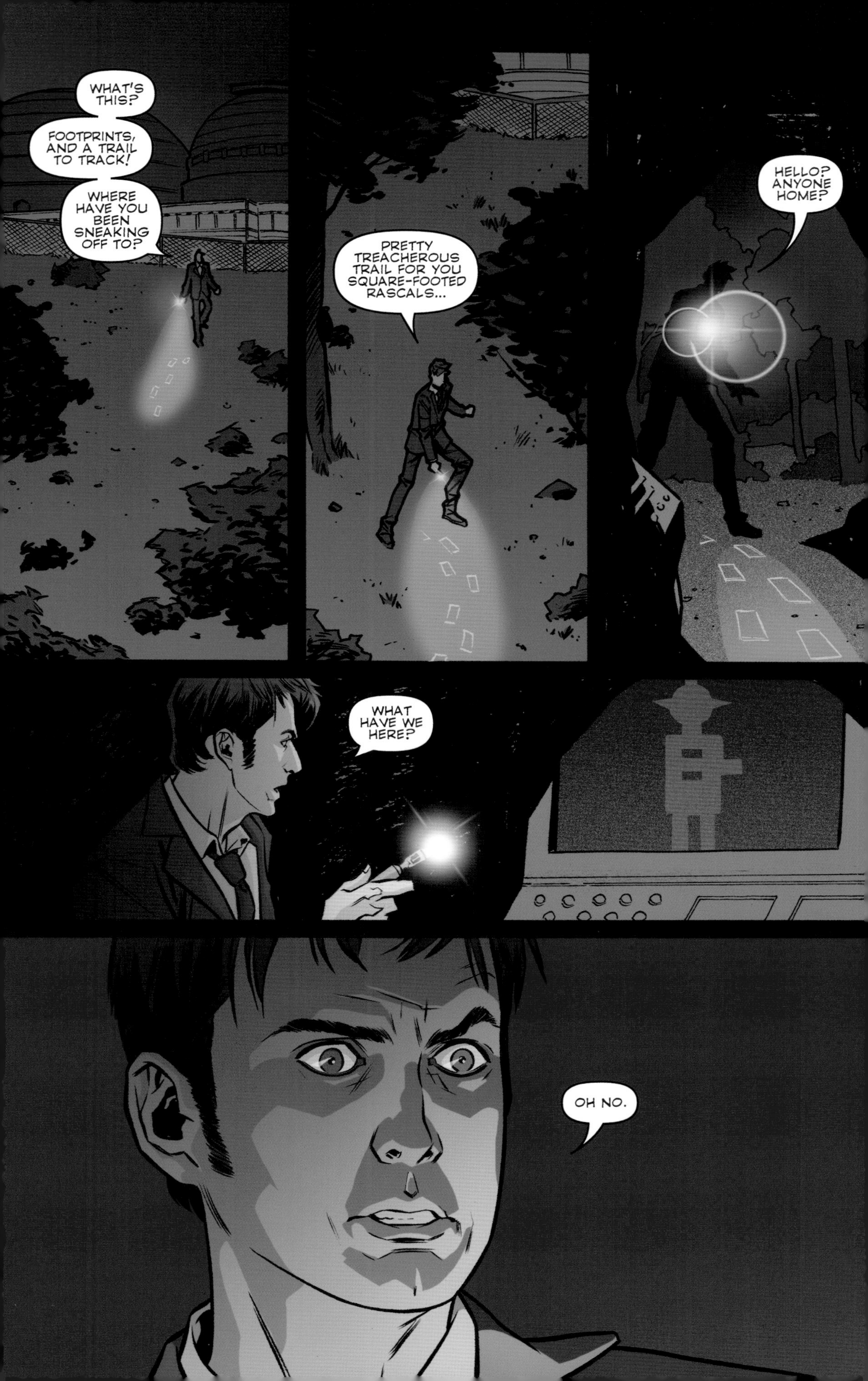
WHAT'S THIS?
FOOTPRINTS, AND A TRAIL TO TRACK!
WHERE HAVE YOU BEEN SNEAKING OFF TO?
PRETTY TREACHEROUS TRAIL FOR YOU SQUARE-FOOTED RASCALS...
HELLO? ANYONE HOME?
WHAT HAVE WE HERE?
OH NO.

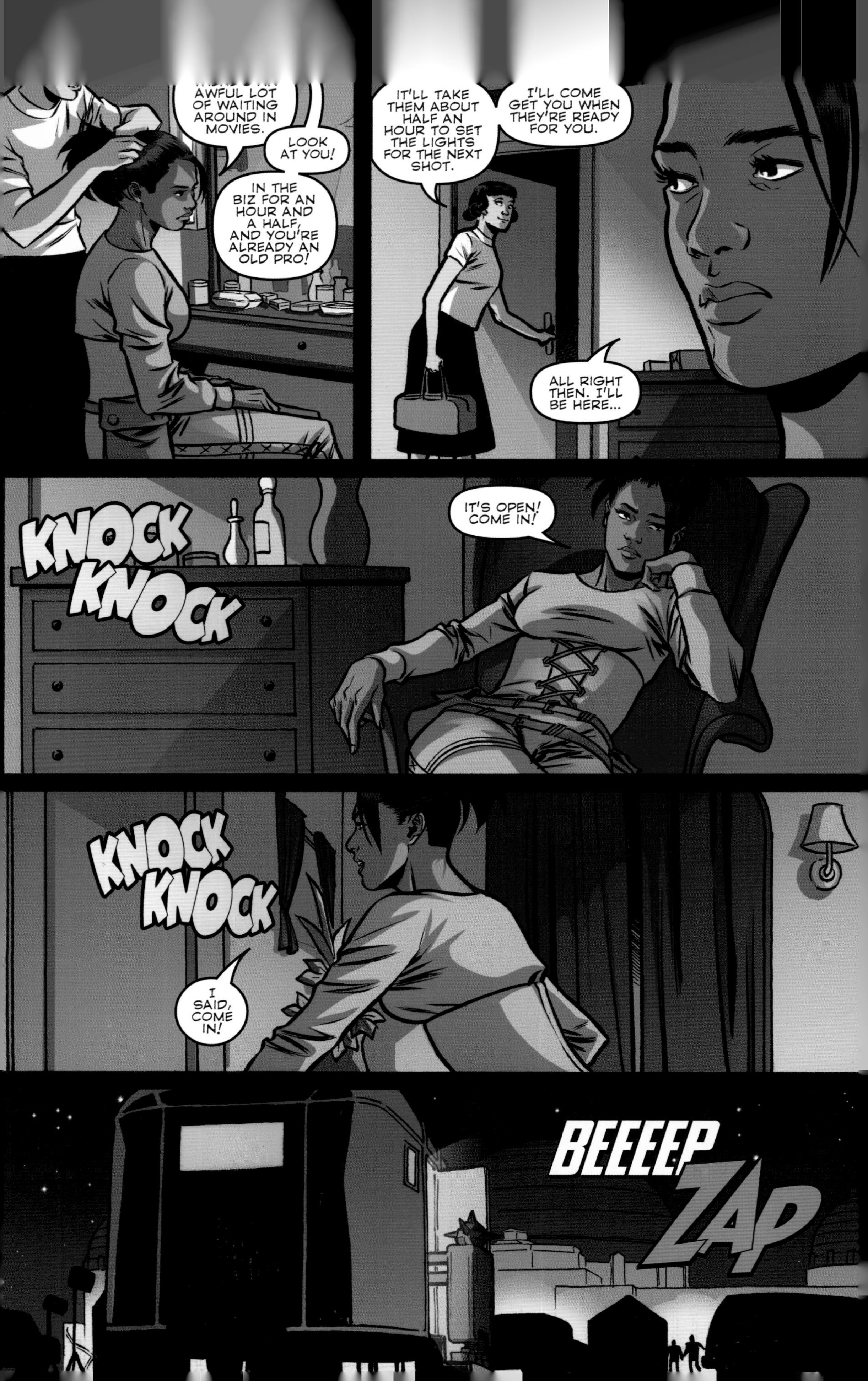
AWFUL LOT OF WAITING AROUND IN MOVIES.
LOOK AT YOU!
IN THE BIZ FOR AN HOUR AND A HALF, AND YOU'RE ALREADY AN OLD PRO!
IT'LL TAKE THEM ABOUT HALF AN HOUR TO SET THE LIGHTS FOR THE NEXT SHOT.
I'LL COME GET YOU WHEN THEY'RE READY FOR YOU.
ALL RIGHT THEN. I'LL BE HERE...
KNOCK KNOCK
IT'S OPEN! COME IN!
KNOCK KNOCK
I SAID, COME IN!
BEEEEP
ZAP

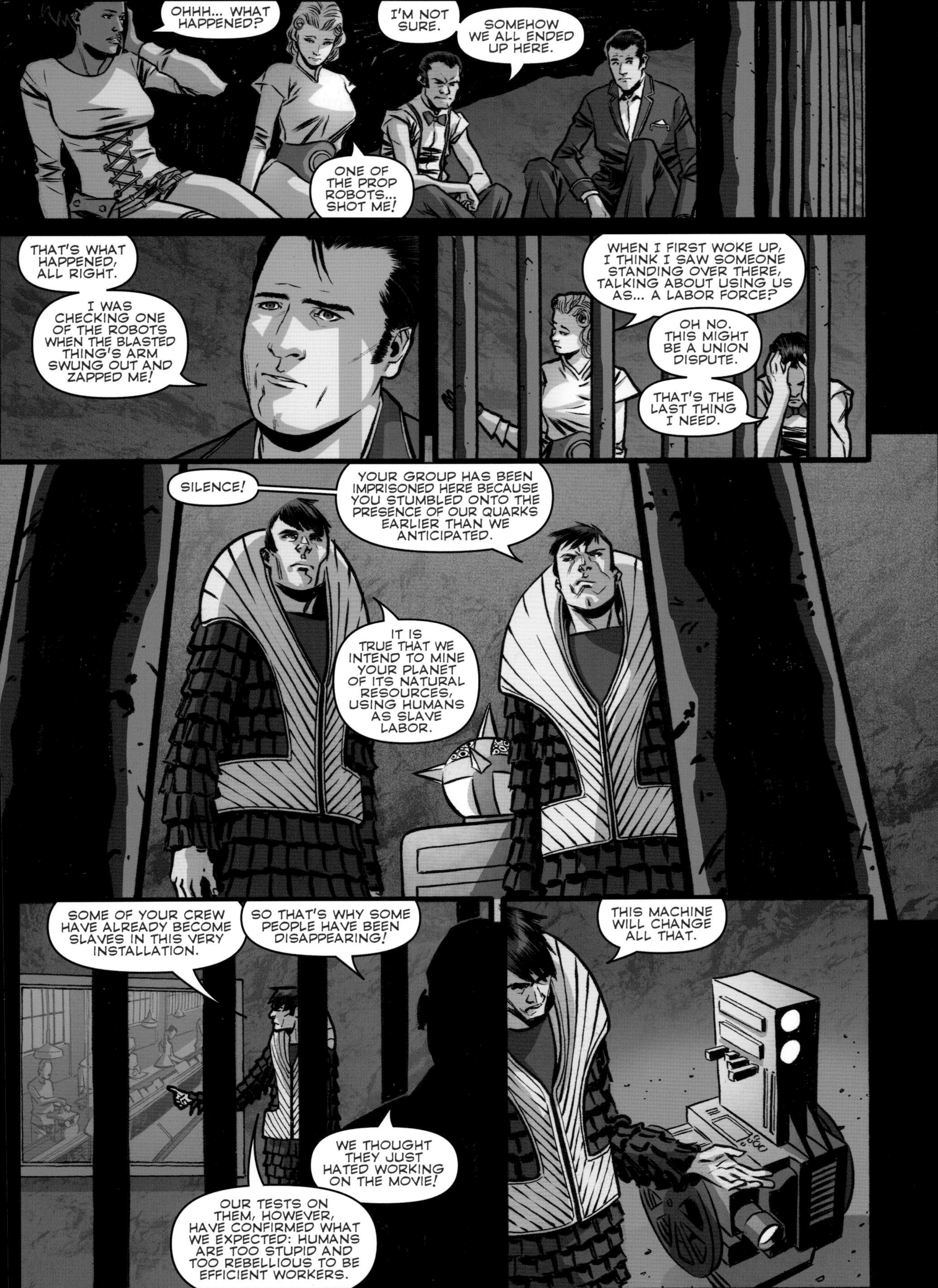
OHHH... WHAT HAPPENED?
I'M NOT SURE.
SOMEHOW WE ALL ENDED UP HERE.
ONE OF THE PROP ROBOTS... SHOT ME!
THAT'S WHAT HAPPENED, ALL RIGHT.
I WAS CHECKING ONE OF THE ROBOTS WHEN THE BLASTED THING'S ARM SWUNG OUT AND ZAPPED ME!
WHEN I FIRST WOKE UP, I THINK I SAW SOMEONE STANDING OVER THERE, TALKING ABOUT USING US AS... A LABOR FORCE?
OH NO. THIS MIGHT BE A UNION DISPUTE.
THAT'S THE LAST THING I NEED.
SILENCE!
YOUR GROUP HAS BEEN IMPRISONED HERE BECAUSE YOU STUMBLED ONTO THE PRESENCE OF OUR QUARKS EARLIER THAN WE ANTICIPATED.
IT IS TRUE THAT WE INTEND TO MINE YOUR PLANET OF ITS NATURAL RESOURCES, USING HUMANS AS SLAVE LABOR.
SOME OF YOUR CREW HAVE ALREADY BECOME SLAVES IN THIS VERY INSTALLATION.
SO THAT'S WHY SOME PEOPLE HAVE BEEN DISAPPEARING!
WE THOUGHT THEY JUST HATED WORKING ON THE MOVIE!
OUR TESTS ON THEM, HOWEVER, HAVE CONFIRMED WHAT WE EXPECTED: HUMANS ARE TOO STUPID AND TOO REBELLIOUS TO BE EFFICIENT WORKERS.
THIS MACHINE WILL CHANGE ALL THAT.

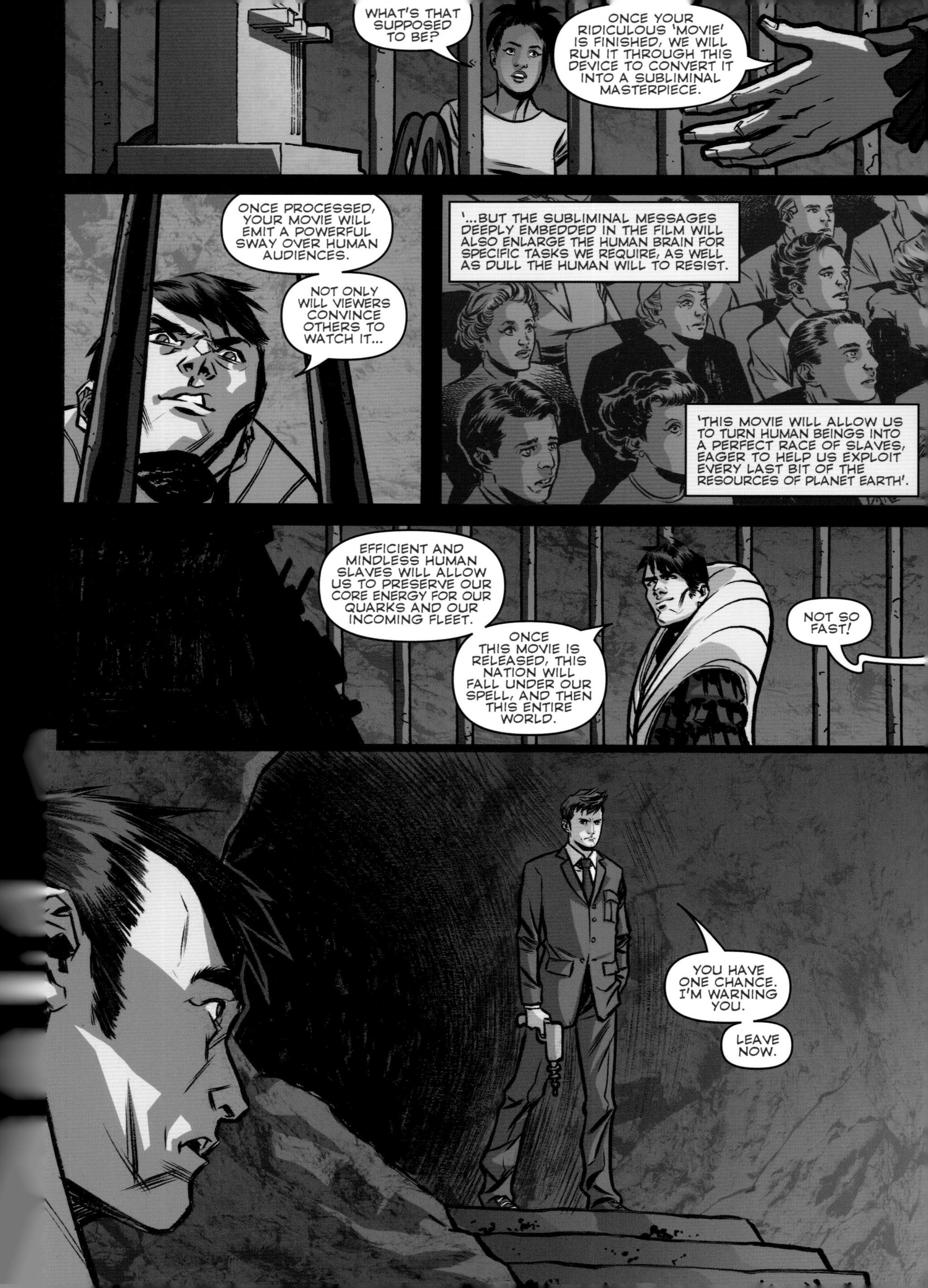
WHAT'S THAT SUPPOSED TO BE?
ONCE YOUR RIDICULOUS 'MOVIE' IS FINISHED, WE WILL RUN IT THROUGH THIS DEVICE TO CONVERT IT INTO A SUBLIMINAL MASTERPIECE.
ONCE PROCESSED, YOUR MOVIE WILL EMIT A POWERFUL SWAY OVER HUMAN AUDIENCES.
NOT ONLY WILL VIEWERS CONVINCE OTHERS TO WATCH IT...
'...BUT THE SUBLIMINAL MESSAGES DEEPLY EMBEDDED IN THE FILM WILL ALSO ENLARGE THE HUMAN BRAIN FOR SPECIFIC TASKS WE REQUIRE, AS WELL AS DULL THE HUMAN WILL TO RESIST.
'THIS MOVIE WILL ALLOW US TO TURN HUMAN BEINGS INTO A PERFECT RACE OF SLAVES, EAGER TO HELP US EXPLOIT EVERY LAST BIT OF THE RESOURCES OF PLANET EARTH'.
EFFICIENT AND MINDLESS HUMAN SLAVES WILL ALLOW US TO PRESERVE OUR CORE ENERGY FOR OUR QUARKS AND OUR INCOMING FLEET.
ONCE THIS MOVIE IS RELEASED, THIS NATION WILL FALL UNDER OUR SPELL, AND THEN THIS ENTIRE WORLD.
NOT SO FAST!
YOU HAVE ONE CHANCE. I'M WARNING YOU.
LEAVE NOW.

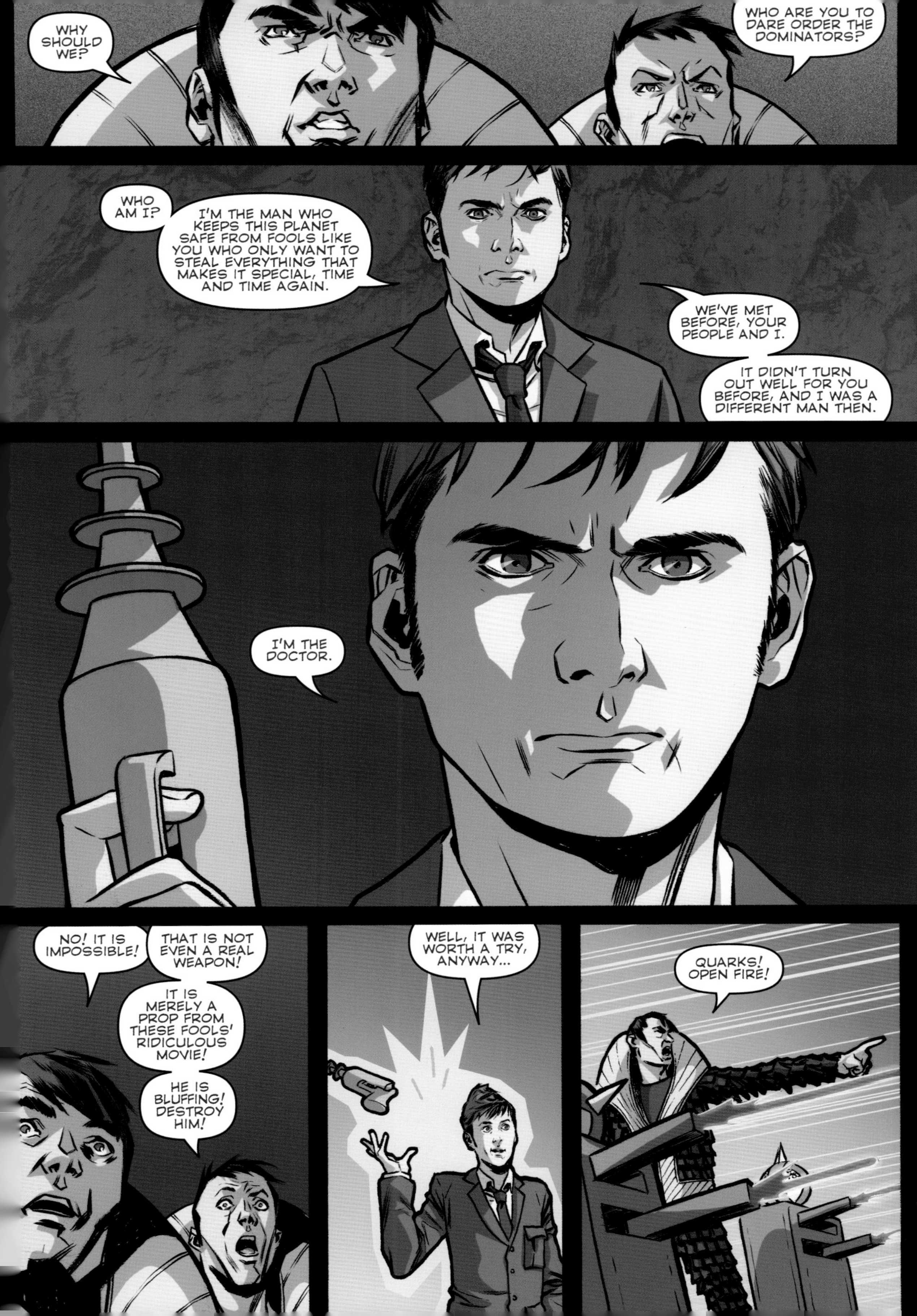
WHY SHOULD WE?
WHO ARE YOU TO DARE ORDER THE DOMINATORS?
WHO AM I?
I'M THE MAN WHO KEEPS THIS PLANET SAFE FROM FOOLS LIKE YOU WHO ONLY WANT TO STEAL EVERYTHING THAT MAKES IT SPECIAL, TIME AND TIME AGAIN.
WE'VE MET BEFORE, YOUR PEOPLE AND I.
IT DIDN'T TURN OUT WELL FOR YOU BEFORE, AND I WAS A DIFFERENT MAN THEN.
I'M THE DOCTOR.
NO! IT IS IMPOSSIBLE!
THAT IS NOT EVEN A REAL WEAPON!
IT IS MERELY A PROP FROM THESE FOOLS' RIDICULOUS MOVIE!
HE IS BLUFFING! DESTROY HIM!
WELL, IT WAS WORTH A TRY, ANYWAY...
QUARKS! OPEN FIRE!

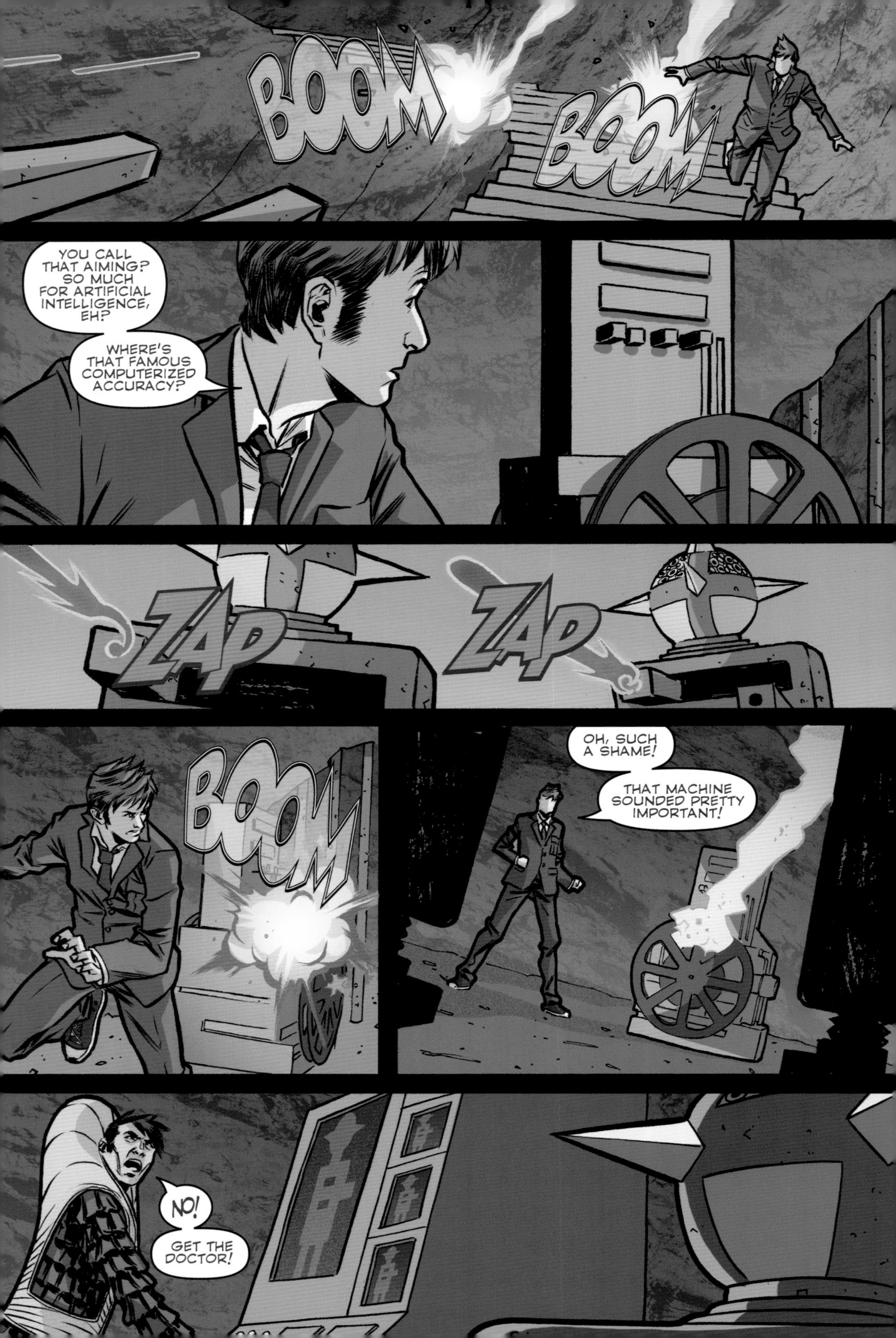
BOOM
BOOM
YOU CALL THAT AIMING? SO MUCH FOR ARTIFICIAL INTELLIGENCE, EH?
WHERE'S THAT FAMOUS COMPUTERIZED ACCURACY?
ZAP
ZAP
BOOM
OH, SUCH A SHAME!
THAT MACHINE SOUNDED PRETTY IMPORTANT!
NO!
GET THE DOCTOR!

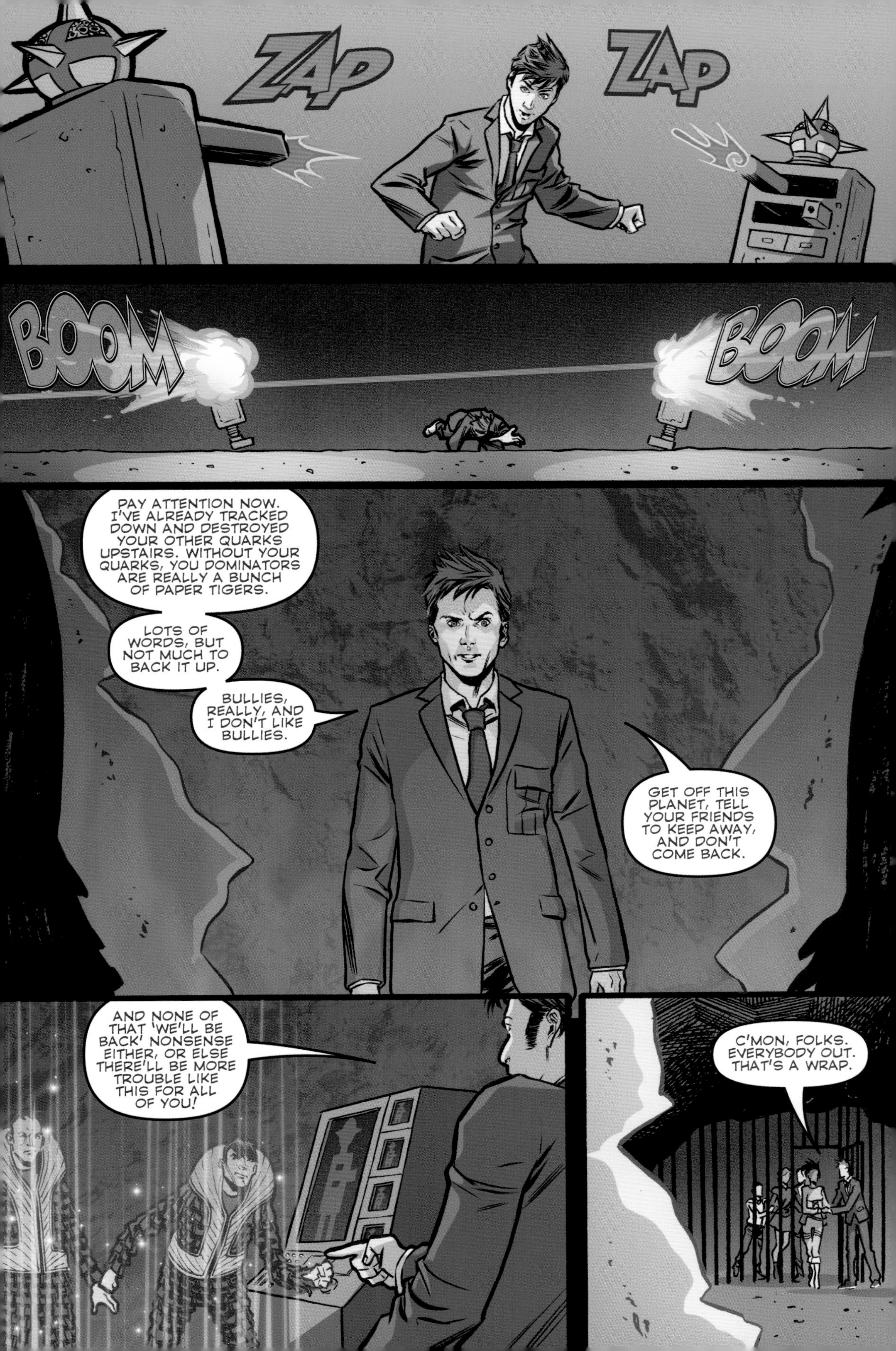
ZAP
ZAP
BOOM
BOOM
PAY ATTENTION NOW. I'VE ALREADY TRACKED DOWN AND DESTROYED YOUR OTHER QUARKS UPSTAIRS. WITHOUT YOUR QUARKS, YOU DOMINATORS ARE REALLY A BUNCH OF PAPER TIGERS.
LOTS OF WORDS, BUT NOT MUCH TO BACK IT UP.
BULLIES, REALLY, AND I DON'T LIKE BULLIES.
GET OFF THIS PLANET, TELL YOUR FRIENDS TO KEEP AWAY, AND DON'T COME BACK.
AND NONE OF THAT 'WE'LL BE BACK' NONSENSE EITHER, OR ELSE THERE'LL BE MORE TROUBLE LIKE THIS FOR ALL OF YOU!
C'MON, FOLKS. EVERYBODY OUT. THAT'S A WRAP.

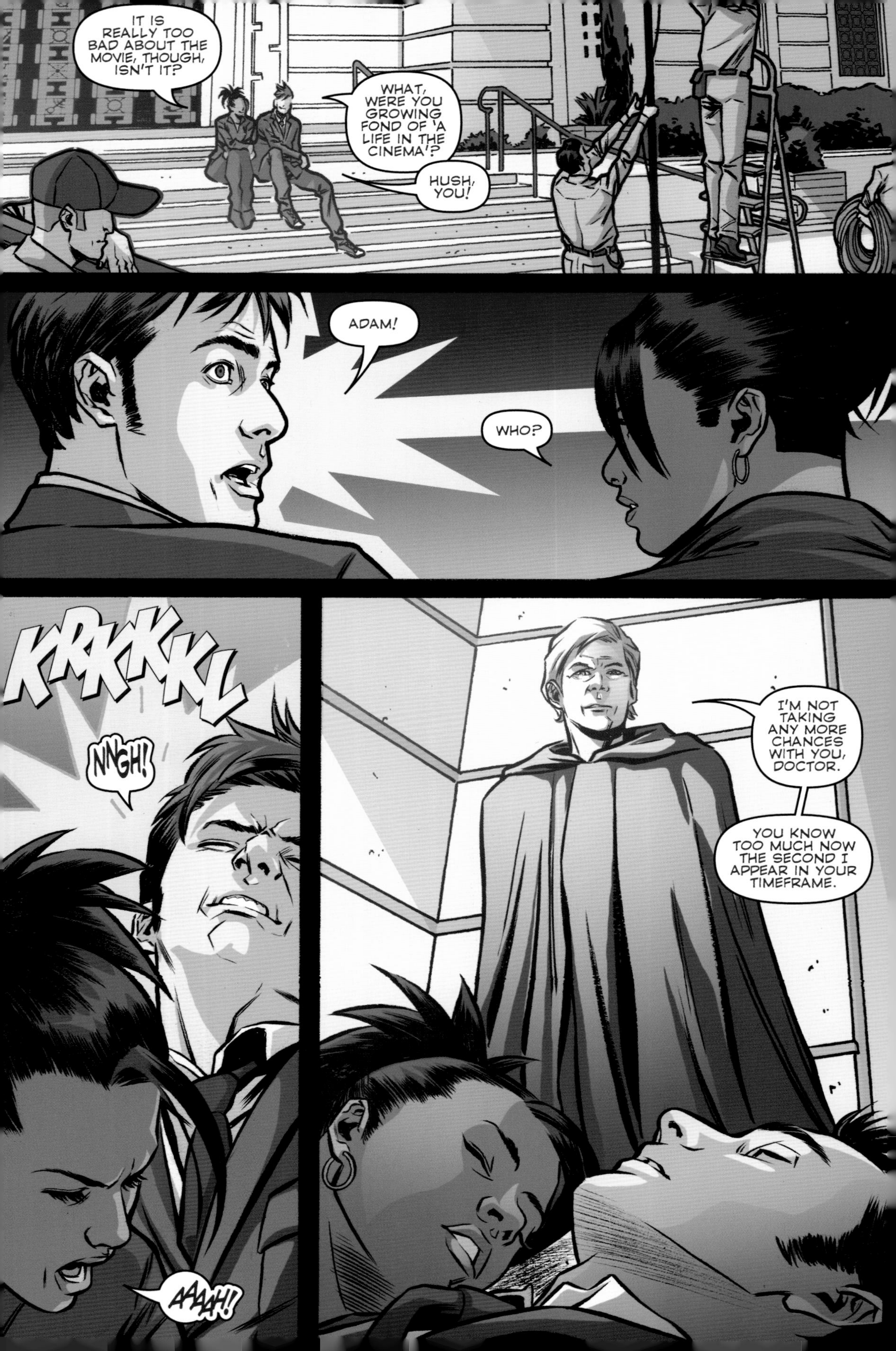
IT IS REALLY TOO BAD ABOUT THE MOVIE, THOUGH, ISN'T IT?
WHAT, WERE YOU GROWING FOND OF 'A LIFE IN THE CINEMA'?
HUSH, YOU!
ADAM!
WHO?
KRKKKL
NNGH!
AAAAH!
I'M NOT TAKING ANY MORE CHANCES WITH YOU, DOCTOR.
YOU KNOW TOO MUCH NOW THE SECOND I APPEAR IN YOUR TIMEFRAME.

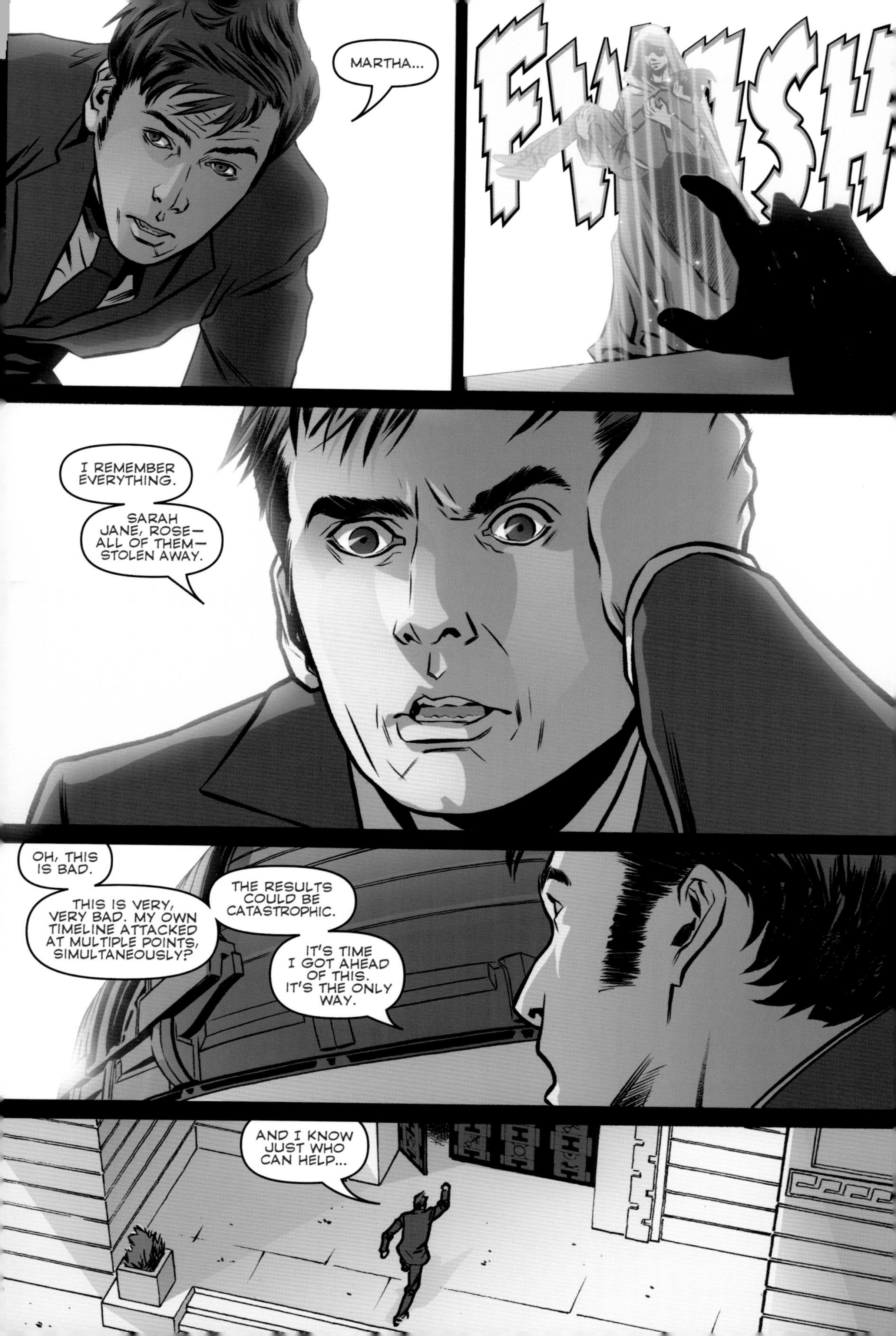
MARTHA...
FWASH
I REMEMBER EVERYTHING.
SARAH JANE, ROSE— ALL OF THEM— STOLEN AWAY.
OH, THIS IS BAD.
THIS IS VERY, VERY BAD. MY OWN TIMELINE ATTACKED AT MULTIPLE POINTS, SIMULTANEOUSLY?
THE RESULTS COULD BE CATASTROPHIC.
IT'S TIME I GOT AHEAD OF THIS. IT'S THE ONLY WAY.
AND I KNOW JUST WHO CAN HELP...

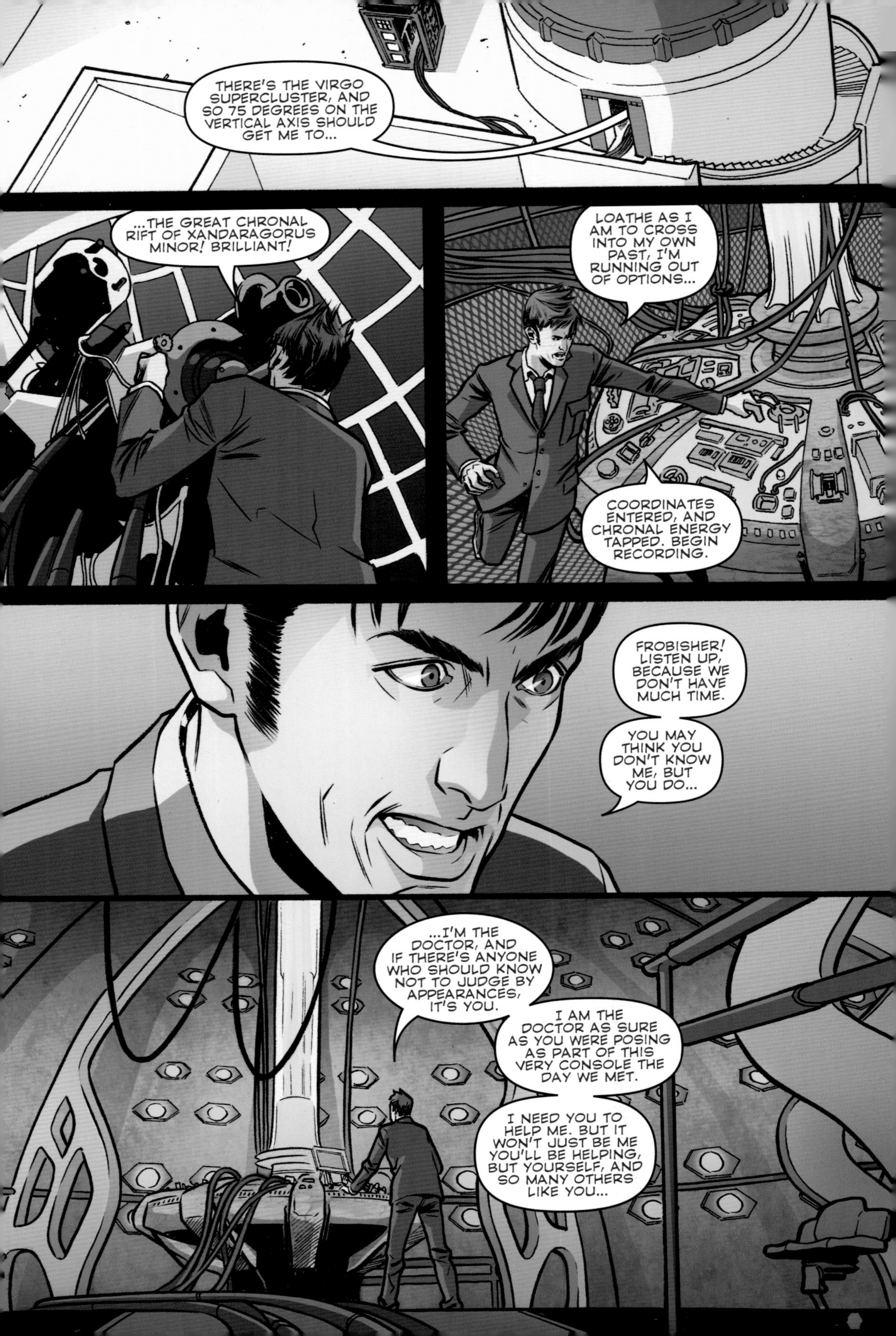
THERE'S THE VIRGO SUPERCLUSTER, AND SO 75 DEGREES ON THE VERTICAL AXIS SHOULD GET ME TO...
...THE GREAT CHRONAL RIFT OF XANDARAGORUS MINOR! BRILLIANT!
LOATHE AS I AM TO CROSS INTO MY OWN PAST, I'M RUNNING OUT OF OPTIONS...
COORDINATES ENTERED, AND CHRONAL ENERGY TAPPED. BEGIN RECORDING.
FROBISHER! LISTEN UP, BECAUSE WE DON'T HAVE MUCH TIME.
YOU MAY THINK YOU DON'T KNOW ME, BUT YOU DO...
...I'M THE DOCTOR, AND IF THERE'S ANYONE WHO SHOULD KNOW NOT TO JUDGE BY APPEARANCES, IT'S YOU.
I AM THE DOCTOR AS SURE AS YOU WERE POSING AS PART OF THIS VERY CONSOLE THE DAY WE MET.
I NEED YOU TO HELP ME. BUT IT WON'T JUST BE ME YOU'LL BE HELPING, BUT YOURSELF, AND SO MANY OTHERS LIKE YOU...

REFLECTIONS OF TIME
Wherein prominent Whovians past and present muse upon the Doctor's history in comic form.

In the late '90s and early '00s, *Doctor Who Magazine* was the go-to place for *Doctor Who* comics, a place where the long-term fan could read continuing stories of Paul McGann's Eighth Doctor, who—like Colin Baker's Sixth Doctor—gained new life (and fans) in the comic strips and audio adventures. But then everything changed when Russell T Davies and the BBC brought the show back. It was under the scrutinizing eye of BBC again, and suddenly, things were that little bit more complicated.

The *DWM* strips were now Rose-and-Doctor-centric, nine pages every month. The future looked good for the reader, until Christopher Eccleston suddenly quit the role. Whether he'd always intended to do one season, whether he decided he wasn't happy with the role, it didn't matter. A new Doctor was coming to play, and his name was Tennant.

I had the dubious honour of writing one of the Tenth Doctor's first comic-strip adventures. I wasn't the first choice for editor Clayton Hickman; in fact, I believe that my phone call was simply 'right place, right time' more than 'right person'. Following on from both John Tomlinson and Nick Abadzis

and Gareth Roberts, we had to create stories for the Tenth Doctor that character-wise revolved around the last 20 minutes of 'The Christmas Invasion', as that was all we'd seen of Tennant's portrayal. Because of this, some of the early stories have massive variances in character, but they still keep to the basic tenet of a solid *Who* story.

At this point, something new happened. American comic publishers took note of *Doctor Who*, and they liked what they saw. This wasn't the first time the Doctor had been in U.S. comics—Marvel reprinted *DWM* stories in the '80s and even had him drop off the mercenary Death's Head at the Baxter Building in one issue, but they were short-lived.

In 2006, IDW Publishing pitched for and received the rights to not only reprint the *DWM* stories, but to create new, ongoing storylines. With Script Editor Gary Russell writing the first arc entitled 'Agent Provocateur', they timed it perfectly, moving the Tenth Doctor and Martha into comics at a time when young American fans were discovering the TV show for the first time.

Suddenly there were new options for the comic reader. No longer was *DWM* the only shop in town. But there was a problem—because of Panini's deal with the BBC, the IDW comics couldn't be sold in the U.K. The British fans could only purchase the books through 'grey channel' comic stores, online with Amazon, or through Comixology's digital platform. And they did, in droves. My first book, 'The Forgotten', is still a solid seller, five years on.

With two solid miniseries, a handful of one-shots from A–list creators and a successful ongoing series weaving an intricate story arc, IDW were on a Tenth Doctor roll.

Little did they know that waiting in the wings was an even bigger phenomenon named Smith...

—Tony Lee, writer at large

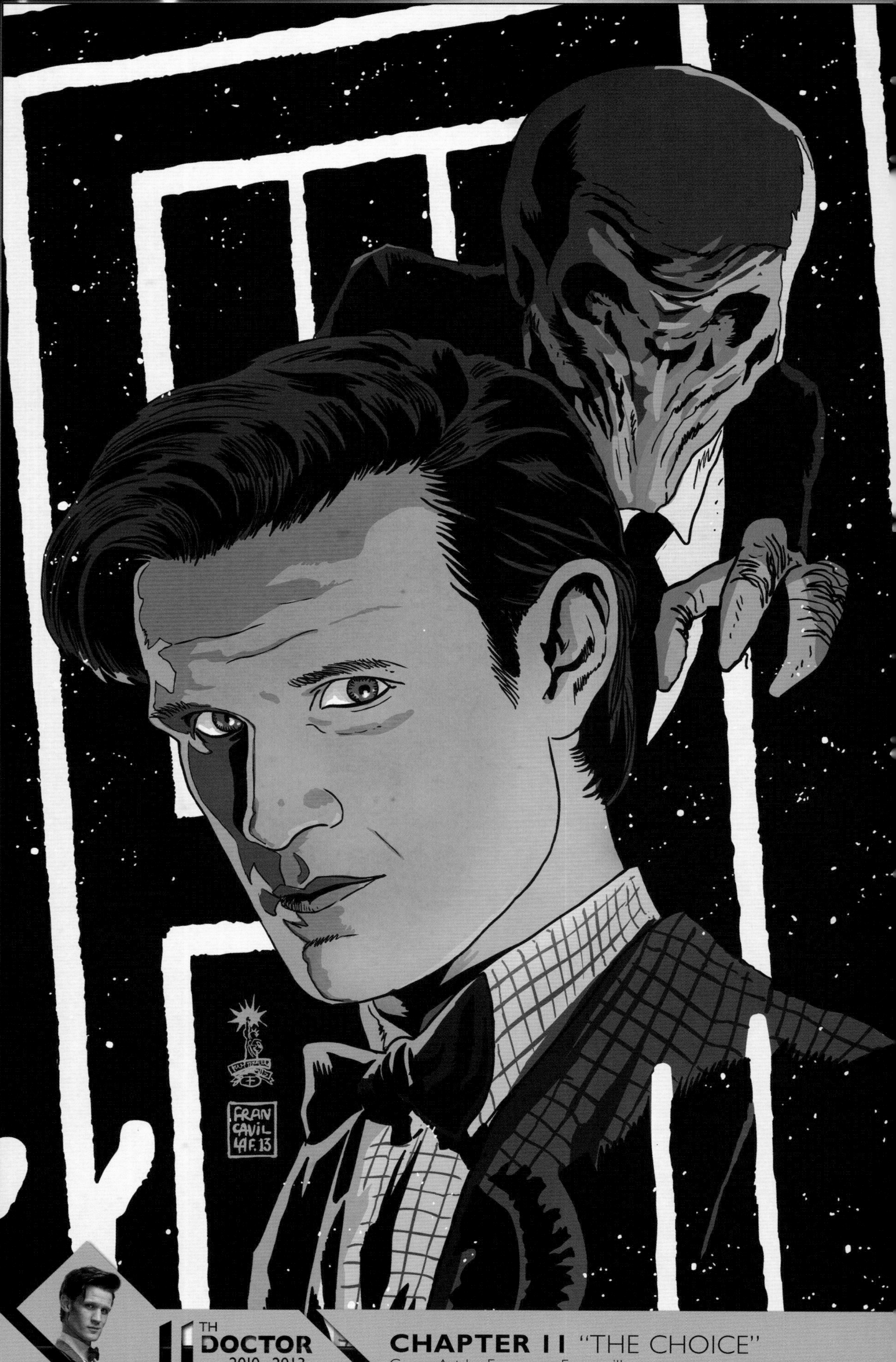
FRAN
CAVIL
LAF. 13

11TH DOCTOR 2010 - 2013

CHAPTER 11 "THE CHOICE"

Cover Art by Francesco Francavilla

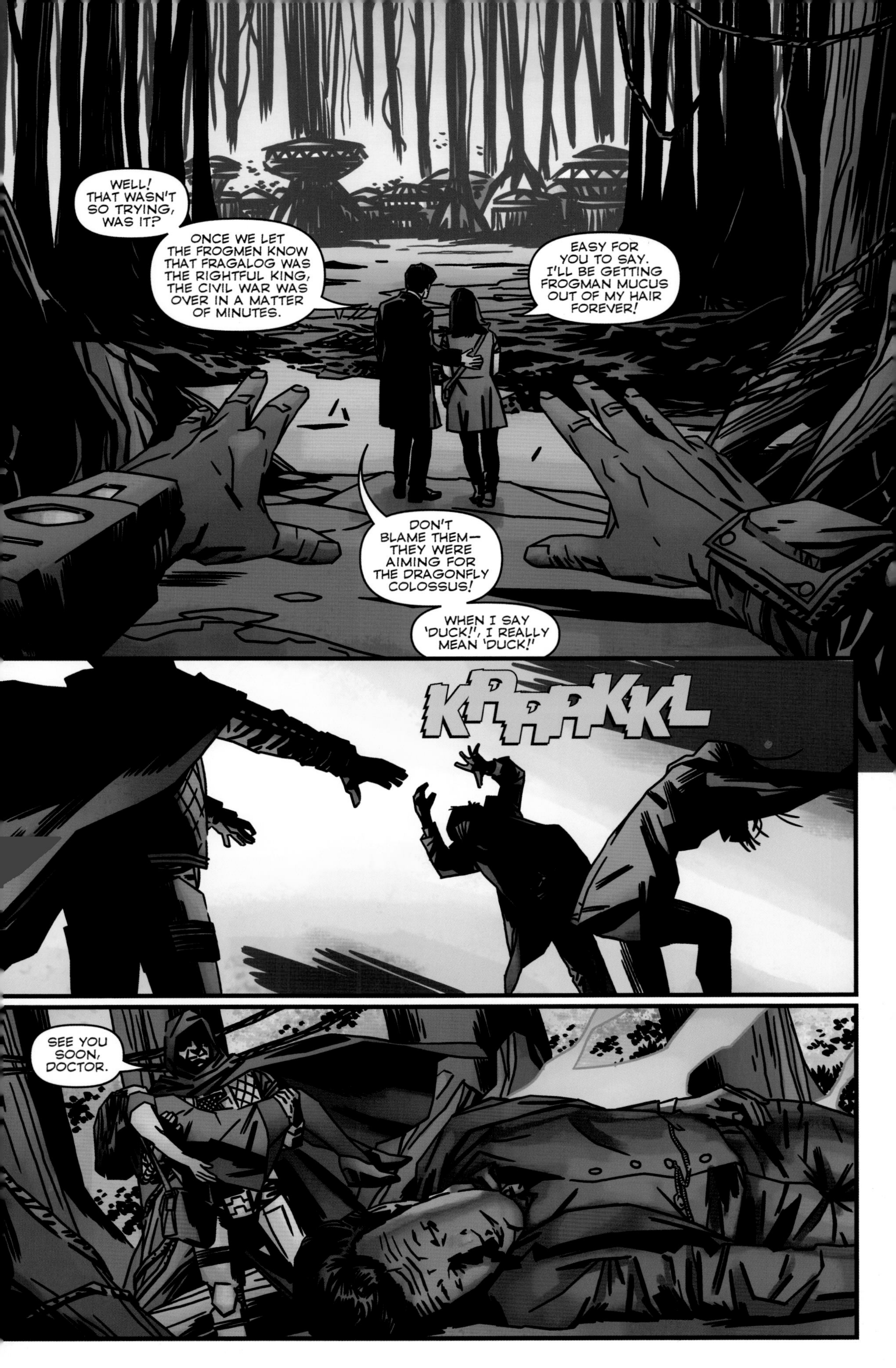
WELL! THAT WASN'T SO TRYING, WAS IT?
ONCE WE LET THE FROGMEN KNOW THAT FRAGALOG WAS THE RIGHTFUL KING, THE CIVIL WAR WAS OVER IN A MATTER OF MINUTES.
EASY FOR YOU TO SAY. I'LL BE GETTING FROGMAN MUCUS OUT OF MY HAIR FOREVER!
DON'T BLAME THEM— THEY WERE AIMING FOR THE DRAGONFLY COLOSSUS!
WHEN I SAY 'DUCK!', I REALLY MEAN 'DUCK!'
KRAAKKL
SEE YOU SOON, DOCTOR.

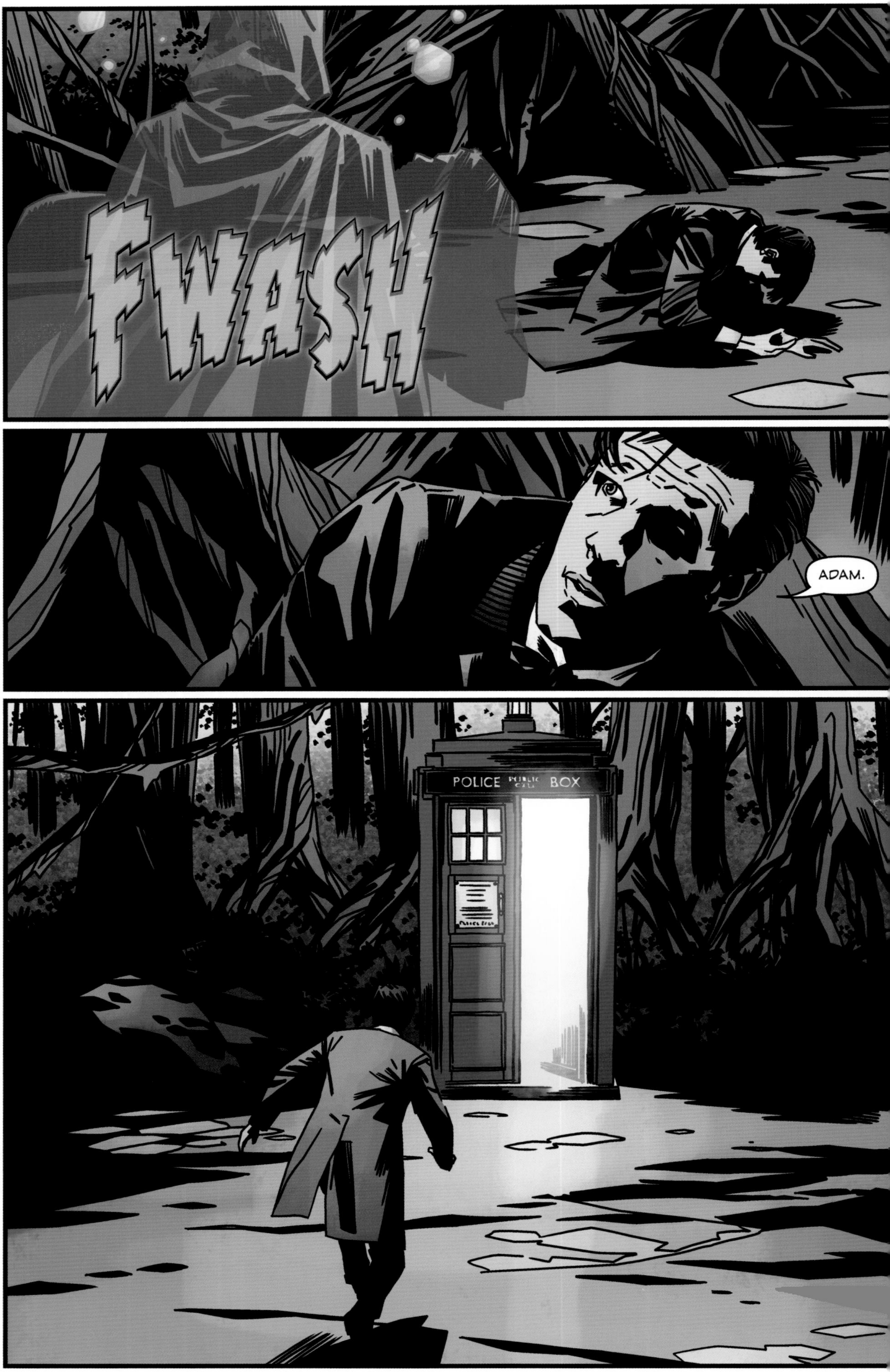
FWASH
ADAM.
POLICE BOX

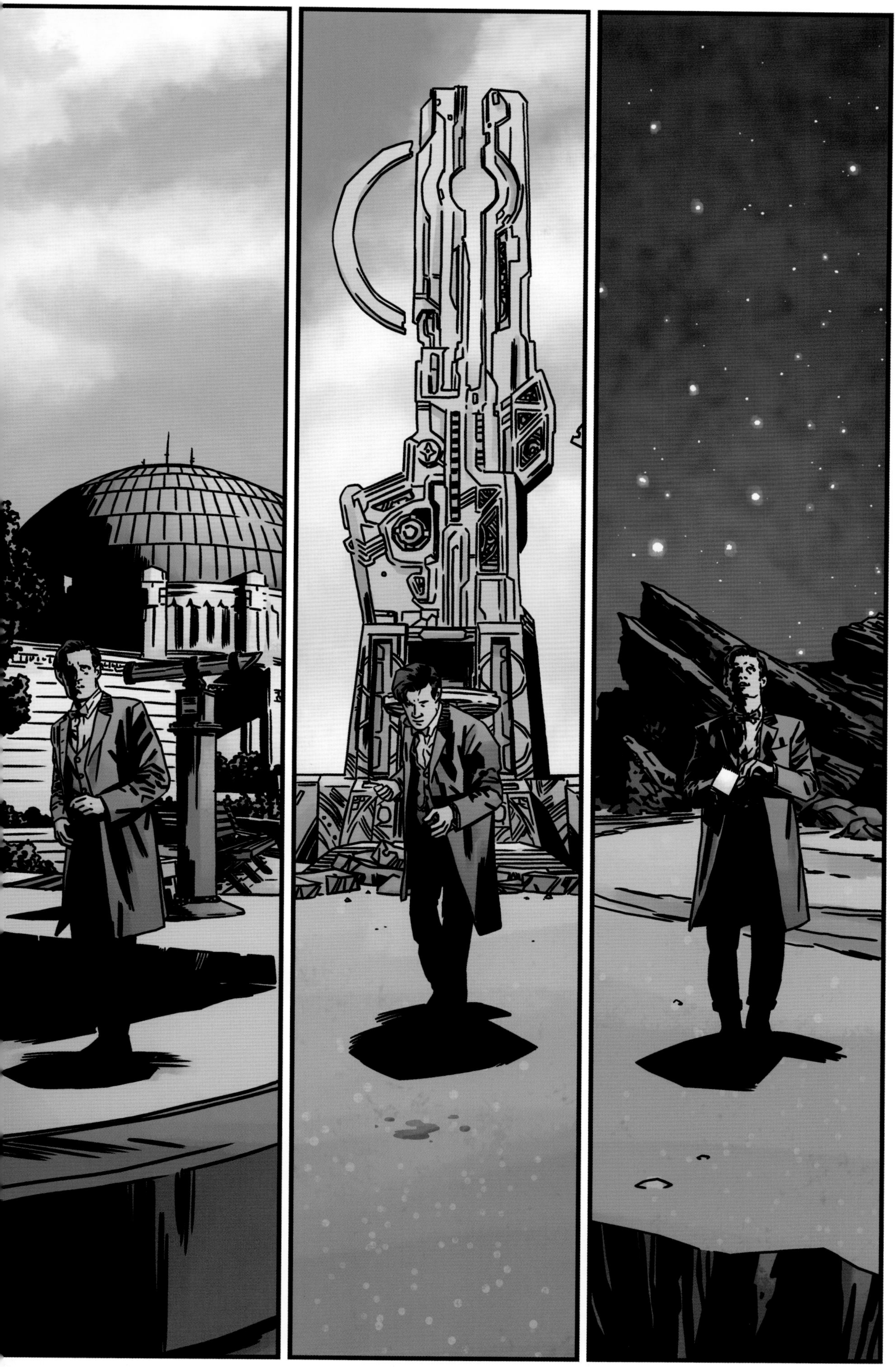

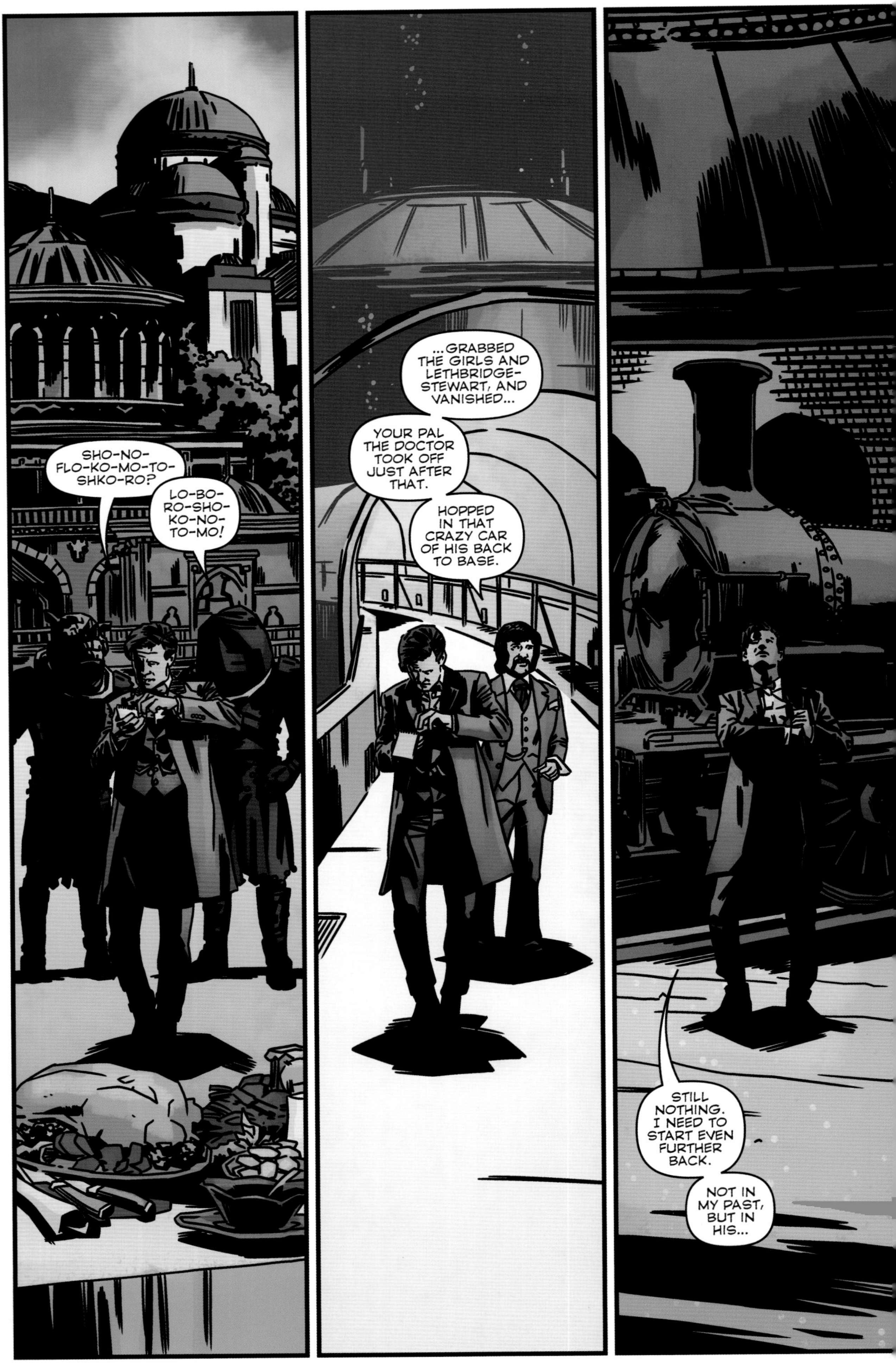
SHO-NO-FLO-KO-MO-TO-SHKO-RO?
LO-BO-RO-SHO-KO-NO-TO-MO!
...GRABBED THE GIRLS AND LETHBRIDGE-STEWART, AND VANISHED...
YOUR PAL THE DOCTOR TOOK OFF JUST AFTER THAT.
HOPPED IN THAT CRAZY CAR OF HIS BACK TO BASE.
STILL NOTHING. I NEED TO START EVEN FURTHER BACK.
NOT IN MY PAST, BUT IN HIS...

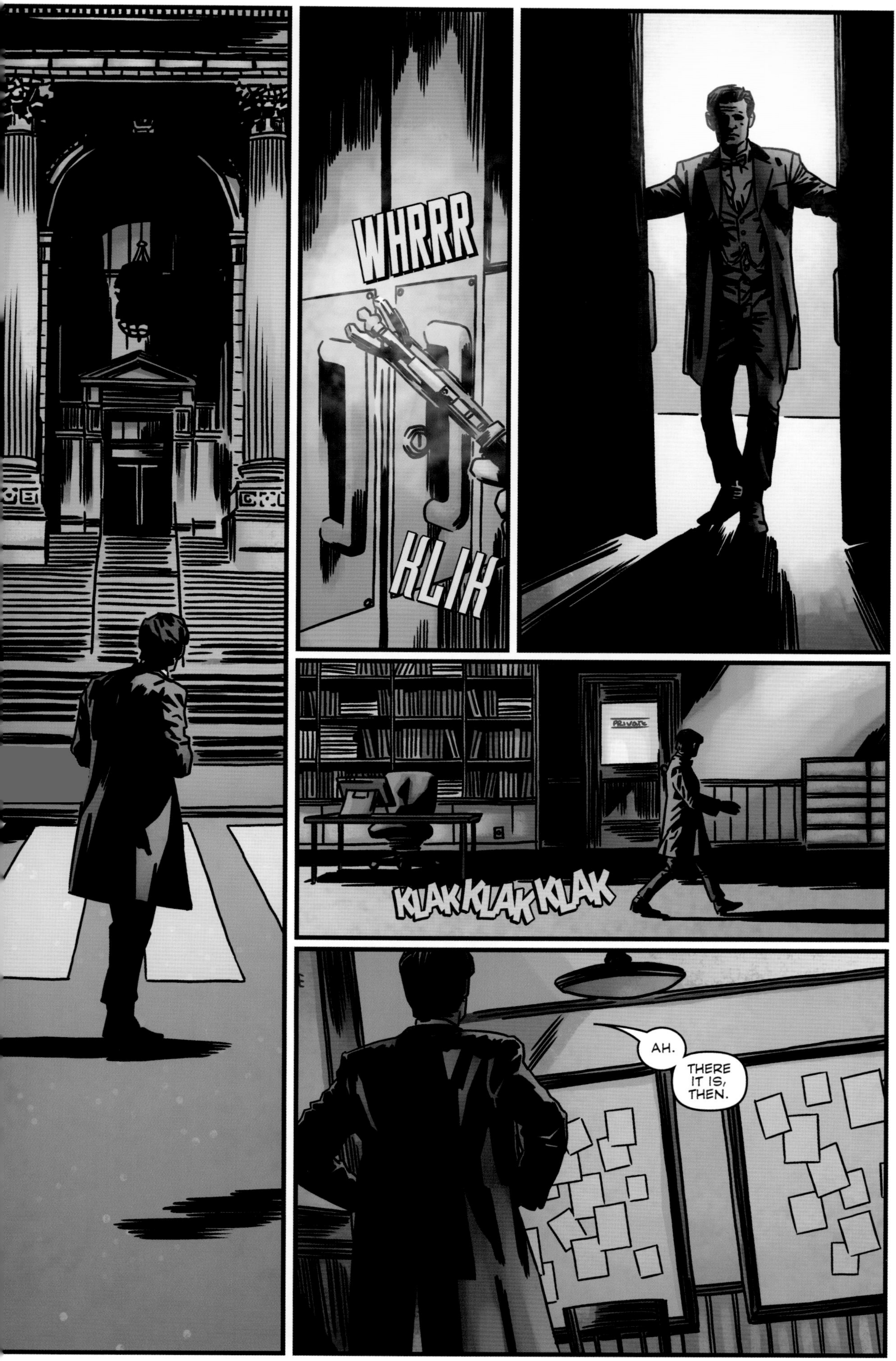
WHRRR
KLIK
Private
KLAK KLAK KLAK
AH.
THERE IT IS, THEN.

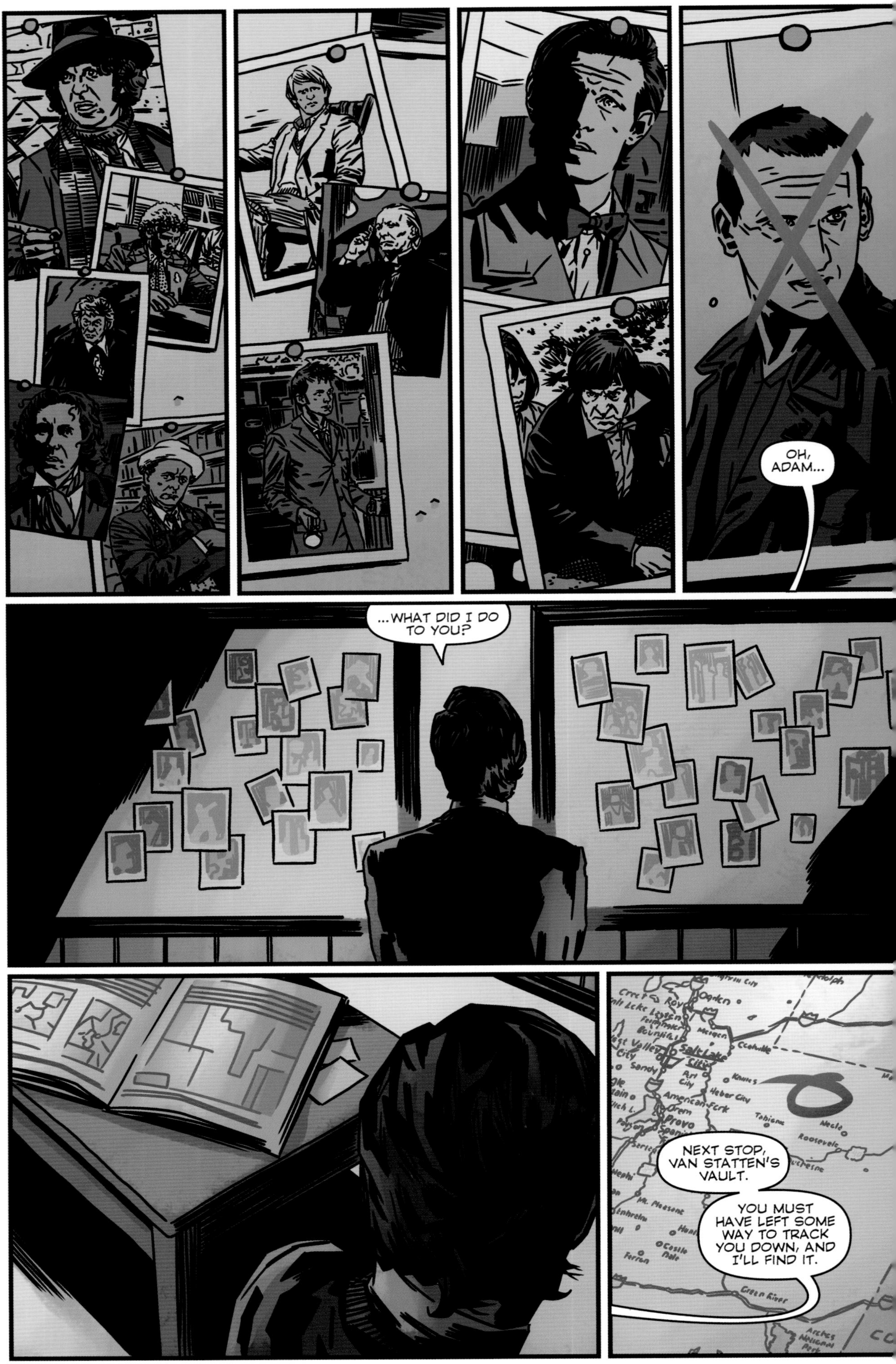
OH, ADAM...
...WHAT DID I DO TO YOU?
Ogden
Salt Lake City
American Fork
Orem
Provo
Heber City
Roosevelt
Mt. Pleasant
Castle Dale
Ferron
Green River
NEXT STOP, VAN STATTEN'S VAULT.
YOU MUST HAVE LEFT SOME WAY TO TRACK YOU DOWN, AND I'LL FIND IT.

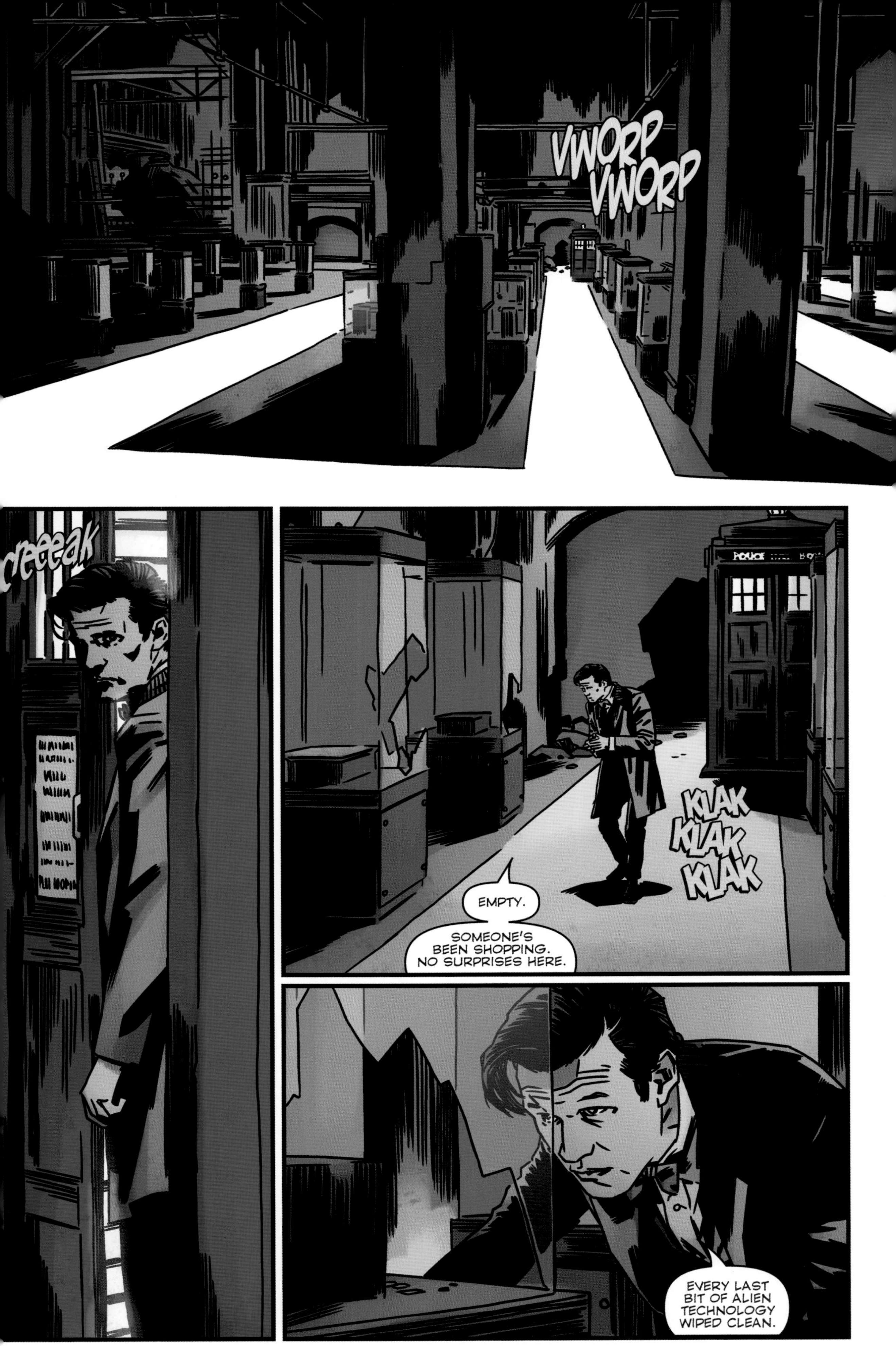
VWORP VWORP
creeak
EMPTY.
SOMEONE'S BEEN SHOPPING. NO SURPRISES HERE.
KLAK KLAK KLAK
EVERY LAST BIT OF ALIEN TECHNOLOGY WIPED CLEAN.

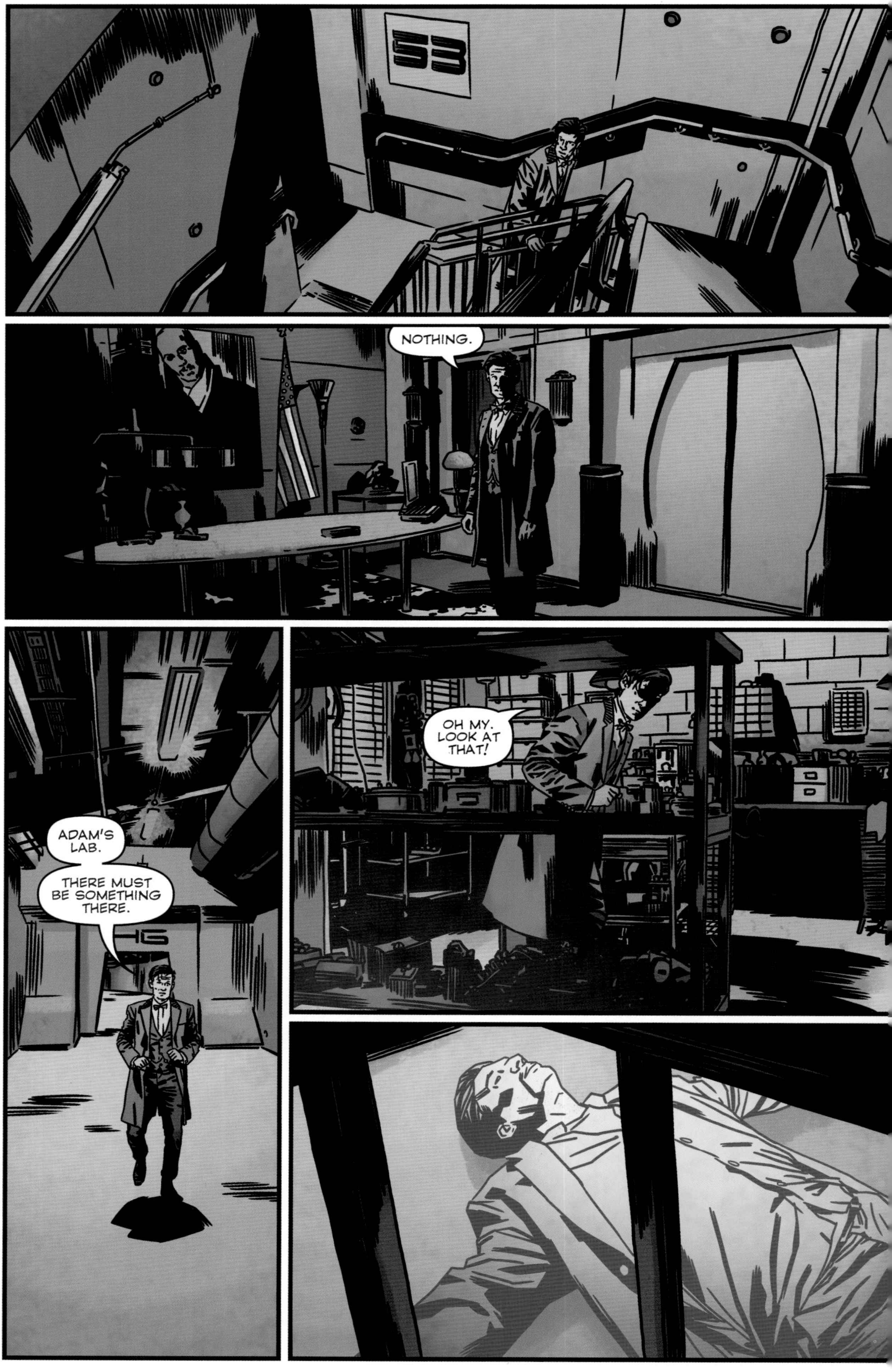
NOTHING.
ADAM'S LAB.
THERE MUST BE SOMETHING THERE.
OH MY. LOOK AT THAT!

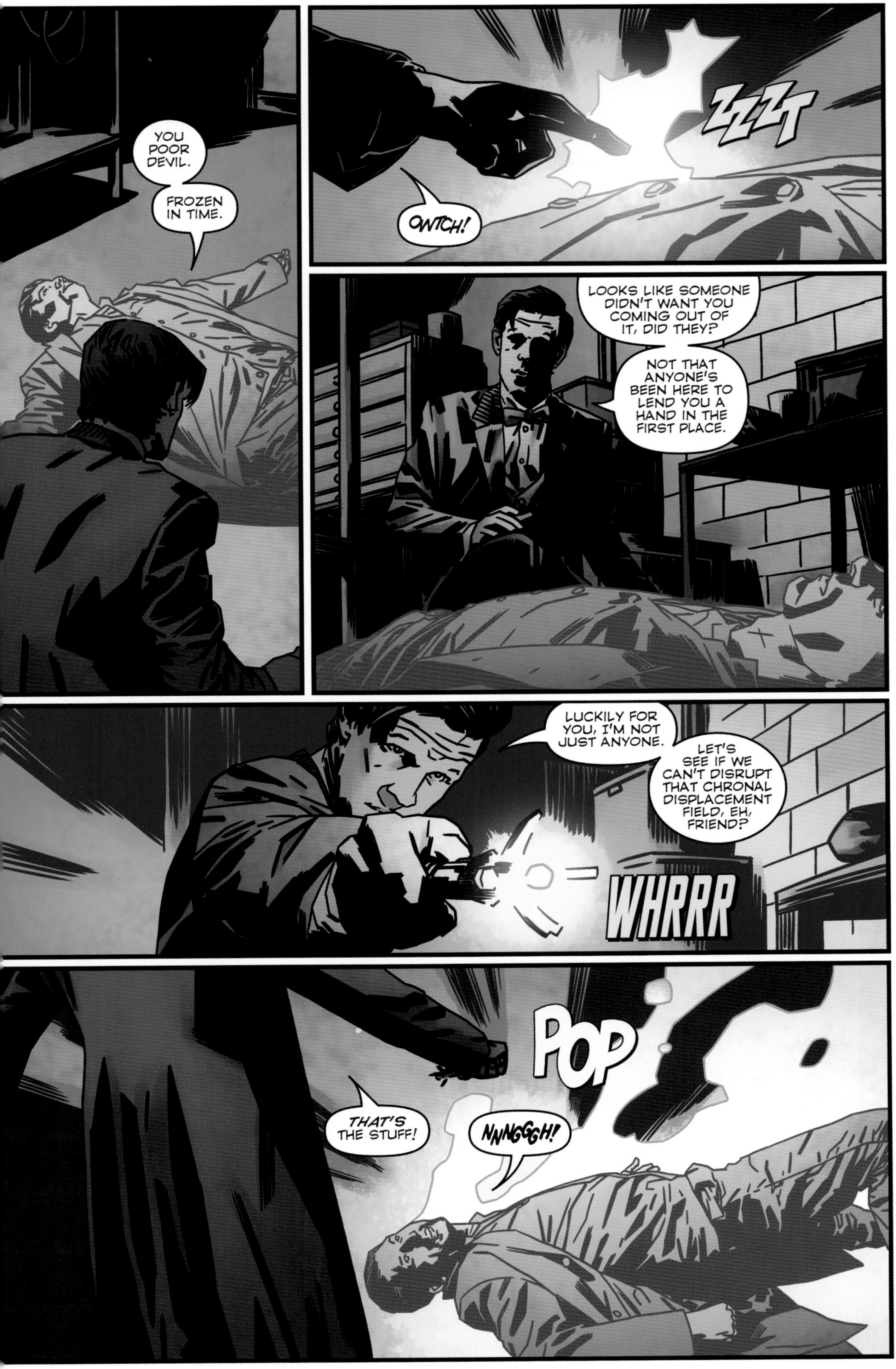
YOU POOR DEVIL.
FROZEN IN TIME.
ZZZT
OWTCH!
LOOKS LIKE SOMEONE DIDN'T WANT YOU COMING OUT OF IT, DID THEY?
NOT THAT ANYONE'S BEEN HERE TO LEND YOU A HAND IN THE FIRST PLACE.
LUCKILY FOR YOU, I'M NOT JUST ANYONE.
LET'S SEE IF WE CAN'T DISRUPT THAT CHRONAL DISPLACEMENT FIELD, EH, FRIEND?
WHRRR
POP
THAT'S THE STUFF!
NNNGGGH!

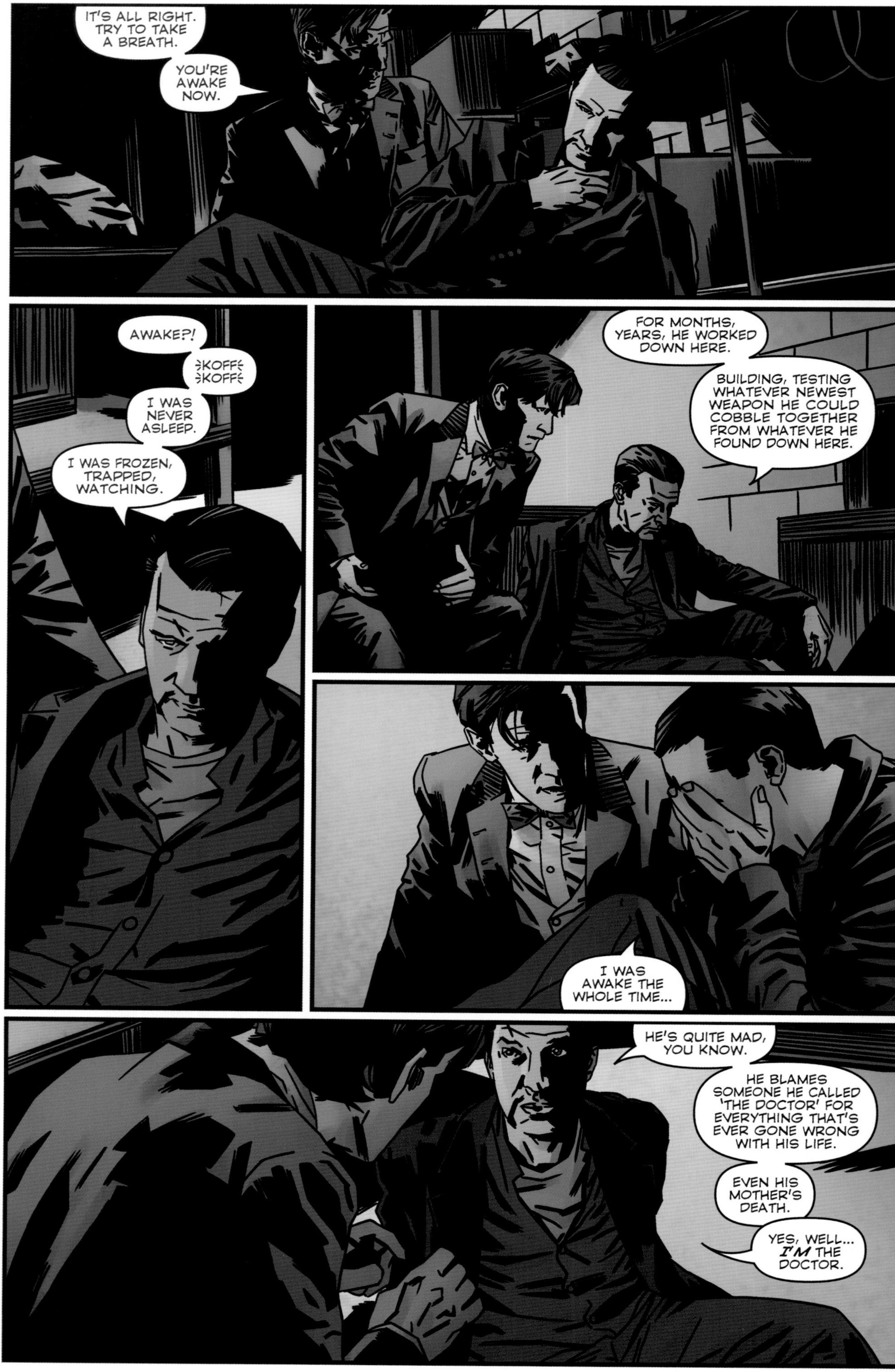
IT'S ALL RIGHT. TRY TO TAKE A BREATH.
YOU'RE AWAKE NOW.
AWAKE?!
KOFF KOFF
I WAS NEVER ASLEEP.
I WAS FROZEN, TRAPPED, WATCHING.
FOR MONTHS, YEARS, HE WORKED DOWN HERE.
BUILDING, TESTING WHATEVER NEWEST WEAPON HE COULD COBBLE TOGETHER FROM WHATEVER HE FOUND DOWN HERE.
I WAS AWAKE THE WHOLE TIME...
HE'S QUITE MAD, YOU KNOW.
HE BLAMES SOMEONE HE CALLED 'THE DOCTOR' FOR EVERYTHING THAT'S EVER GONE WRONG WITH HIS LIFE.
EVEN HIS MOTHER'S DEATH.
YES, WELL... *I'M* THE DOCTOR.

AHA! YOU LOOK DIFFERENT THAN I EXPECTED.

I'M CAPTAIN NEAL SHAW, TIME AGENT.

IT'S A PRIVILEGE TO MEET YOU, SIR!

YES, I KNOW ALL ABOUT THE TIME AGENCY.

YOUR VORTEX MANIPULATOR WRISTBAND. IT'S MISSING.

THAT DEVICE IS WHAT GIVES YOU AGENTS TIME-TRAVEL AND TRANSPORT ABILITIES.

A RATHER IMPORTANT PIECE OF HARDWARE TO HANG ON TO, IF YOU ASK ME. WHAT HAPPENED TO IT?

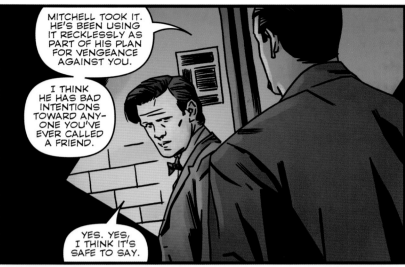

MITCHELL TOOK IT. HE'S BEEN USING IT RECKLESSLY AS PART OF HIS PLAN FOR VENGEANCE AGAINST YOU.

I THINK HE HAS BAD INTENTIONS TOWARD ANY- ONE YOU'VE EVER CALLED A FRIEND.

YES. YES, I THINK IT'S SAFE TO SAY.

YOU'RE A TIME LORD.

FINDING HIM SHOULD BE EASY FOR YOU, RIGHT?

NO.

IT'S NOT BEEN EASY AT ALL.

HE'S DONE A REMARKABLE JOB OF COVERING HIS TRACKS.

I HAVE SOMETHING HERE THAT MIGHT HELP YOU WITH THAT.

THIS DEVICE TRACKS THE UNIQUE CHRONAL FREQUENCY OF MY VORTEX MANIPULATOR. EVERY TIME AGENT HAS ONE IN CASE IT BECOMES NECESSARY TO TRACK DOWN AND RECOVER A STOLEN WRISTBAND.

THIS WILL LEAD US DIRECTLY TO MITCHELL. LET'S GO GET HIM.

YOU'RE NOT COMING WITH ME. YOU'RE IN NO SHAPE FOR A FIGHT, AND BESIDES, THIS IS BETWEEN ME AND ADAM.

I'LL NOT PUT ANY MORE INNOCENTS IN HARM'S WAY.

BUT—

WE'RE GETTING YOU TO A SAFE PLACE, AND THEN I'LL BRING BACK YOUR WRISTBAND, I PROMISE.

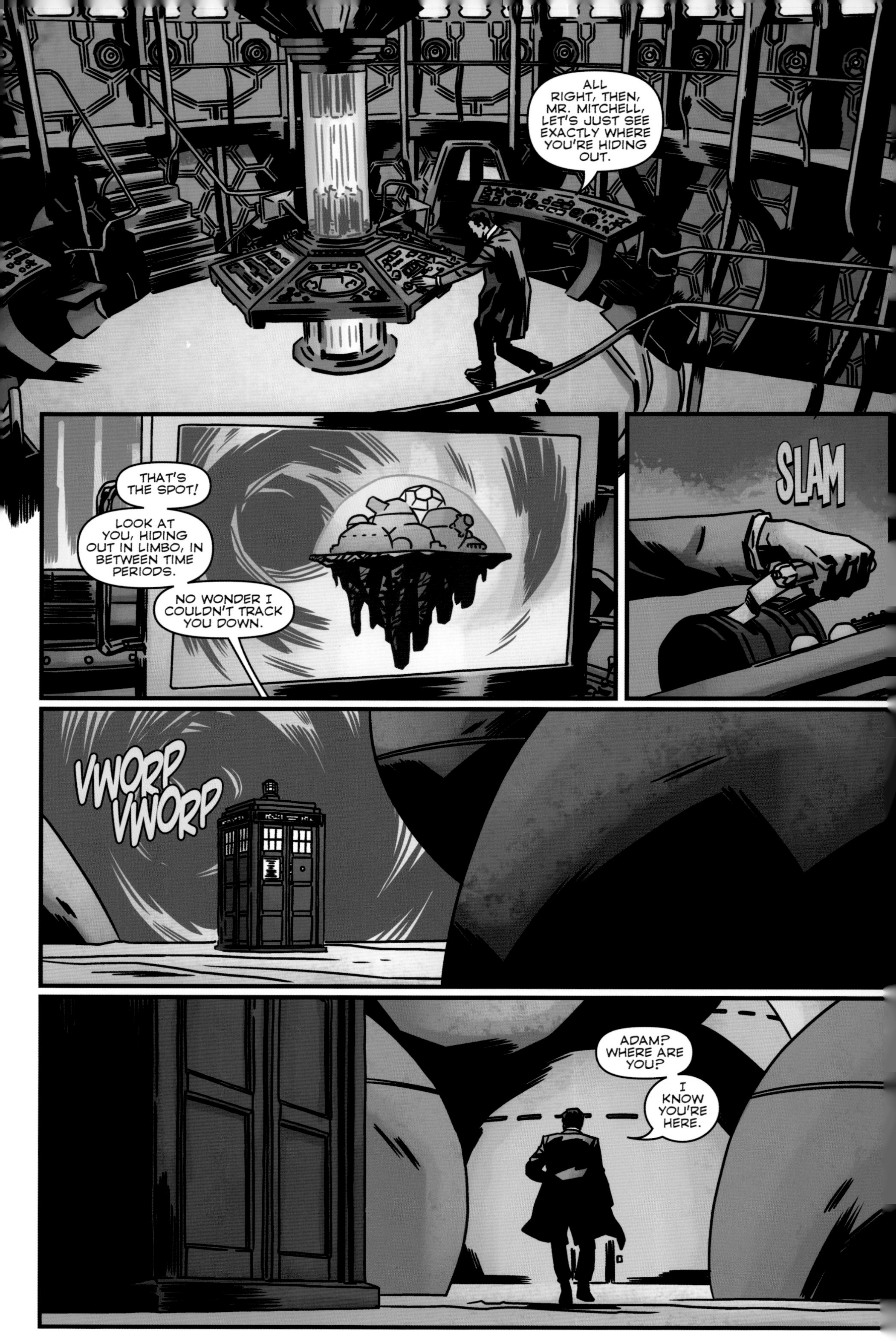
ALL RIGHT, THEN, MR. MITCHELL, LET'S JUST SEE EXACTLY WHERE YOU'RE HIDING OUT.
THAT'S THE SPOT!
LOOK AT YOU, HIDING OUT IN LIMBO, IN BETWEEN TIME PERIODS.
NO WONDER I COULDN'T TRACK YOU DOWN.
SLAM
VWORP VWORP
ADAM? WHERE ARE YOU?
I KNOW YOU'RE HERE.

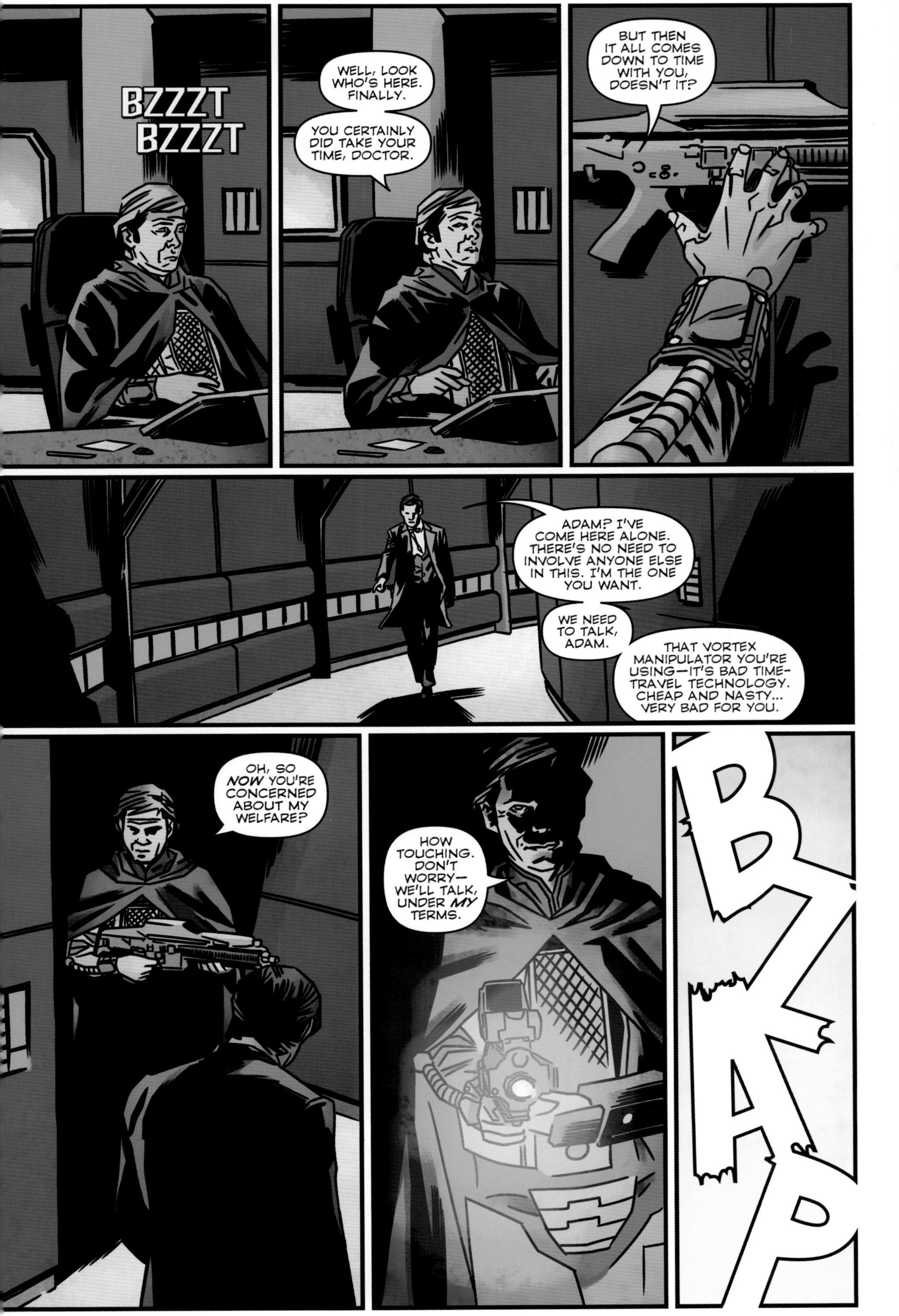
BZZZT
BZZZT
WELL, LOOK WHO'S HERE. FINALLY.
YOU CERTAINLY DID TAKE YOUR TIME, DOCTOR.
BUT THEN IT ALL COMES DOWN TO TIME WITH YOU, DOESN'T IT?
ADAM? I'VE COME HERE ALONE. THERE'S NO NEED TO INVOLVE ANYONE ELSE IN THIS. I'M THE ONE YOU WANT.
WE NEED TO TALK, ADAM.
THAT VORTEX MANIPULATOR YOU'RE USING—IT'S BAD TIME-TRAVEL TECHNOLOGY. CHEAP AND NASTY... VERY BAD FOR YOU.
OH, SO *NOW* YOU'RE CONCERNED ABOUT MY WELFARE?
HOW TOUCHING. DON'T WORRY—WE'LL TALK, UNDER *MY* TERMS.
BKAP

IT'S BEEN A LONG TIME, DOCTOR.

I KNOW WHAT YOU'VE BEEN DOING, ADAM.

I REMEMBER IT ALL NOW.

OF COURSE YOU DO. I KNEW I COULDN'T KEEP YOU IN THE DARK FOREVER. YOU'RE TOO SAVVY FOR THAT.

I TALKED TO THE TIME AGENT, THE ONE YOU AMBUSHED.

HE'S THE ONE WHO LED ME HERE. YOU SHOULDN'T BE USING HIS VORTEX MANIPULATOR.

YOU'RE NOT AS SHARP AS YOU USED TO BE, ARE YOU, DOCTOR?

COULDN'T EVEN SPOT BAIT WHEN LEFT IT FROZEN IN FRONT OF YOU.

OH COME ON, DON'T PRETEND YOU'RE SURPRISED AT MY CUNNING!

TURNS OUT THAT WHEN YOU GET AN INFOSPIKE INSTALLED, IT TENDS TO EXPONENTIALLY EXPAND YOUR MIND!

AND THAT'S WHAT THIS IS ALL ABOUT, DOCTOR. SOMEONE CLICKS THEIR FINGERS AND MY FOREHEAD OPENS UP LIKE A DOOR IN A CUCKOO CLOCK.

SNAP

BZZZ

YOU ABANDONED ME TO LIVE WITH THAT— AFRAID TO GO OUT, AFRAID TO HAVE A LIFE FOR FEAR OF BEING FOUND OUT.

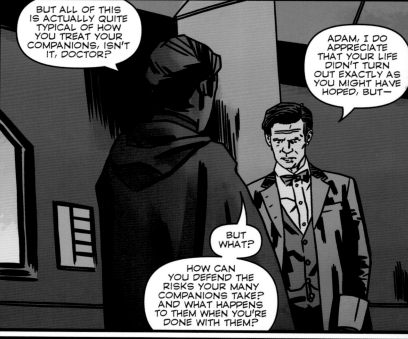

BUT ALL OF THIS IS ACTUALLY QUITE TYPICAL OF HOW YOU TREAT YOUR COMPANIONS, ISN'T IT, DOCTOR?

ADAM, I DO APPRECIATE THAT YOUR LIFE DIDN'T TURN OUT EXACTLY AS YOU MIGHT HAVE HOPED, BUT—

BUT WHAT?

HOW CAN YOU DEFEND THE RISKS YOUR MANY COMPANIONS TAKE? AND WHAT HAPPENS TO THEM WHEN YOU'RE DONE WITH THEM?

WE'RE LITTLE MORE THAN PETS TO YOU, AREN'T WE? THE LONELY ALIEN WHO PICKS UP A NEW HUMAN PUPPY WHEN HE GETS BORED OF THE LAST ONE.

SOMEONE TO FLATTER HIS EGO AND STEP ON THE TRAPDOORS.

YOU COULDN'T BE MORE WRONG, ADAM. THEY'RE MY FRIENDS—ALL OF THEM. THEY MAKE THE UNIVERSE WORTH SAVING.

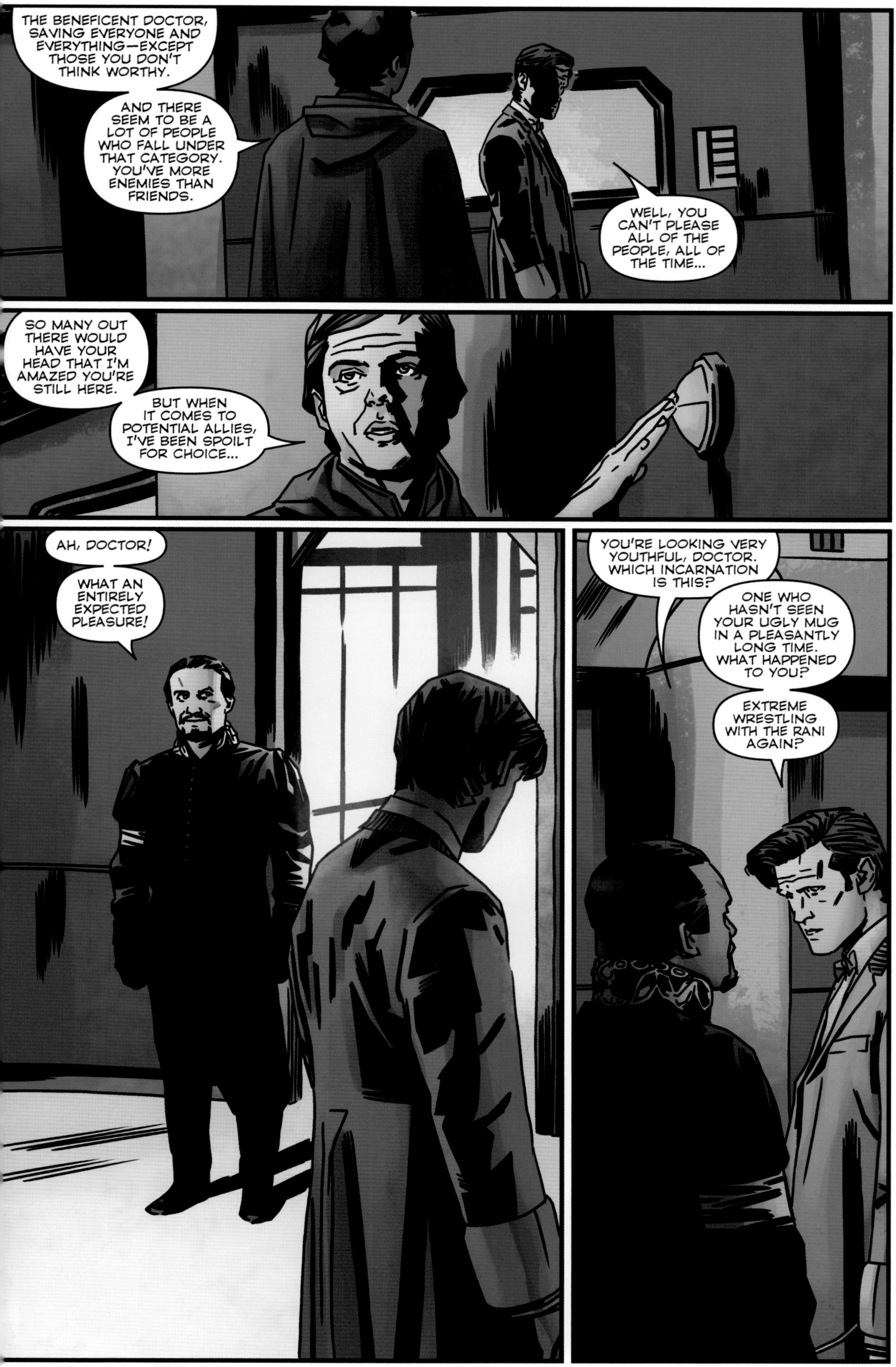
THE BENEFICENT DOCTOR, SAVING EVERYONE AND EVERYTHING—EXCEPT THOSE YOU DON'T THINK WORTHY.
AND THERE SEEM TO BE A LOT OF PEOPLE WHO FALL UNDER THAT CATEGORY. YOU'VE MORE ENEMIES THAN FRIENDS.
WELL, YOU CAN'T PLEASE ALL OF THE PEOPLE, ALL OF THE TIME...
SO MANY OUT THERE WOULD HAVE YOUR HEAD THAT I'M AMAZED YOU'RE STILL HERE.
BUT WHEN IT COMES TO POTENTIAL ALLIES, I'VE BEEN SPOILT FOR CHOICE...
AH, DOCTOR!
WHAT AN ENTIRELY EXPECTED PLEASURE!
YOU'RE LOOKING VERY YOUTHFUL, DOCTOR. WHICH INCARNATION IS THIS?
ONE WHO HASN'T SEEN YOUR UGLY MUG IN A PLEASANTLY LONG TIME. WHAT HAPPENED TO YOU?
EXTREME WRESTLING WITH THE RANI AGAIN?

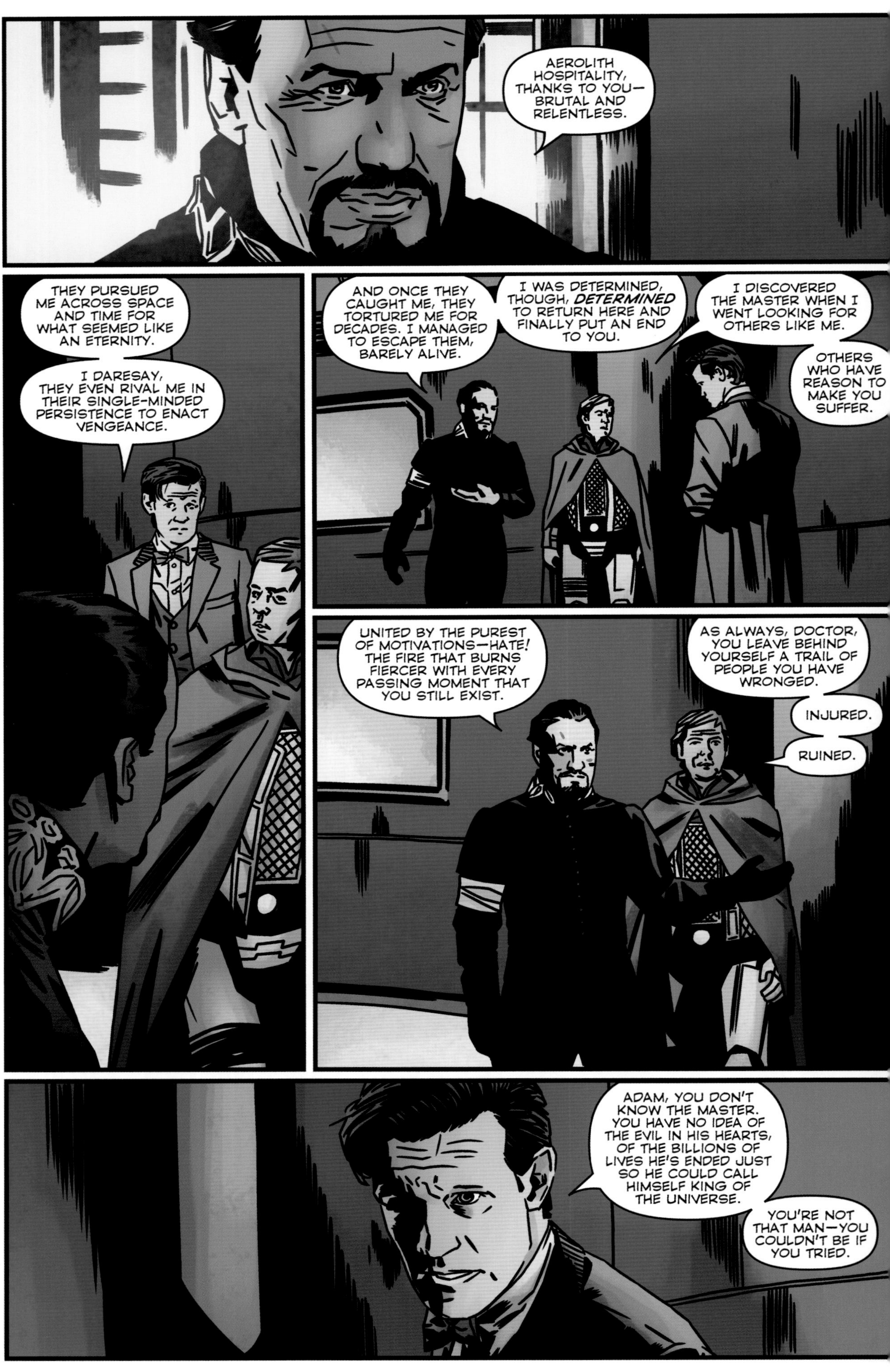
AEROLITH HOSPITALITY, THANKS TO YOU— BRUTAL AND RELENTLESS.
THEY PURSUED ME ACROSS SPACE AND TIME FOR WHAT SEEMED LIKE AN ETERNITY.
I DARESAY, THEY EVEN RIVAL ME IN THEIR SINGLE-MINDED PERSISTENCE TO ENACT VENGEANCE.
AND ONCE THEY CAUGHT ME, THEY TORTURED ME FOR DECADES. I MANAGED TO ESCAPE THEM, BARELY ALIVE.
I WAS DETERMINED, THOUGH, *DETERMINED* TO RETURN HERE AND FINALLY PUT AN END TO YOU.
I DISCOVERED THE MASTER WHEN I WENT LOOKING FOR OTHERS LIKE ME.
OTHERS WHO HAVE REASON TO MAKE YOU SUFFER.
UNITED BY THE PUREST OF MOTIVATIONS—HATE! THE FIRE THAT BURNS FIERCER WITH EVERY PASSING MOMENT THAT YOU STILL EXIST.
AS ALWAYS, DOCTOR, YOU LEAVE BEHIND YOURSELF A TRAIL OF PEOPLE YOU HAVE WRONGED.
INJURED.
RUINED.
ADAM, YOU DON'T KNOW THE MASTER. YOU HAVE NO IDEA OF THE EVIL IN HIS HEARTS, OF THE BILLIONS OF LIVES HE'S ENDED JUST SO HE COULD CALL HIMSELF KING OF THE UNIVERSE.
YOU'RE NOT THAT MAN—YOU COULDN'T BE IF YOU TRIED.

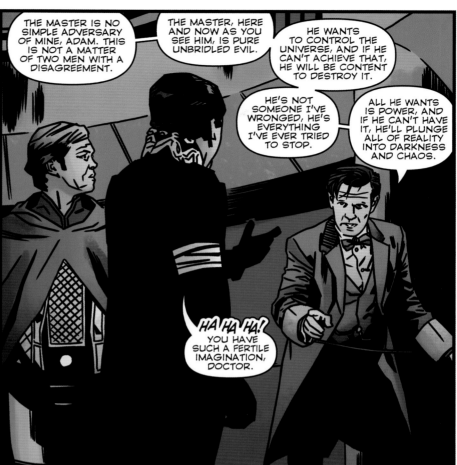

WHY, DOCTOR. YOU POSITIVELY FLATTER ME!

THE MASTER IS NO SIMPLE ADVERSARY OF MINE, ADAM. THIS IS NOT A MATTER OF TWO MEN WITH A DISAGREEMENT.

THE MASTER, HERE AND NOW AS YOU SEE HIM, IS PURE UNBRIDLED EVIL.

HE WANTS TO CONTROL THE UNIVERSE, AND IF HE CAN'T ACHIEVE THAT, HE WILL BE CONTENT TO DESTROY IT.

HE'S NOT SOMEONE I'VE WRONGED, HE'S EVERYTHING I'VE EVER TRIED TO STOP.

ALL HE WANTS IS POWER, AND IF HE CAN'T HAVE IT, HE'LL PLUNGE ALL OF REALITY INTO DARKNESS AND CHAOS.

HA HA HA! YOU HAVE SUCH A FERTILE IMAGINATION, DOCTOR.

COME NOW, ADAM, DON'T LET THE DOCTOR'S FICKLE, PETTY WORDS GET IN THE WAY OF YOUR PLANS.

PROCEED, PROCEED!

YES... YES, OF COURSE.

STEP RIGHT THIS WAY, DOCTOR, AND COME SEE THE RESULTS OF ALL MY EFFORTS.

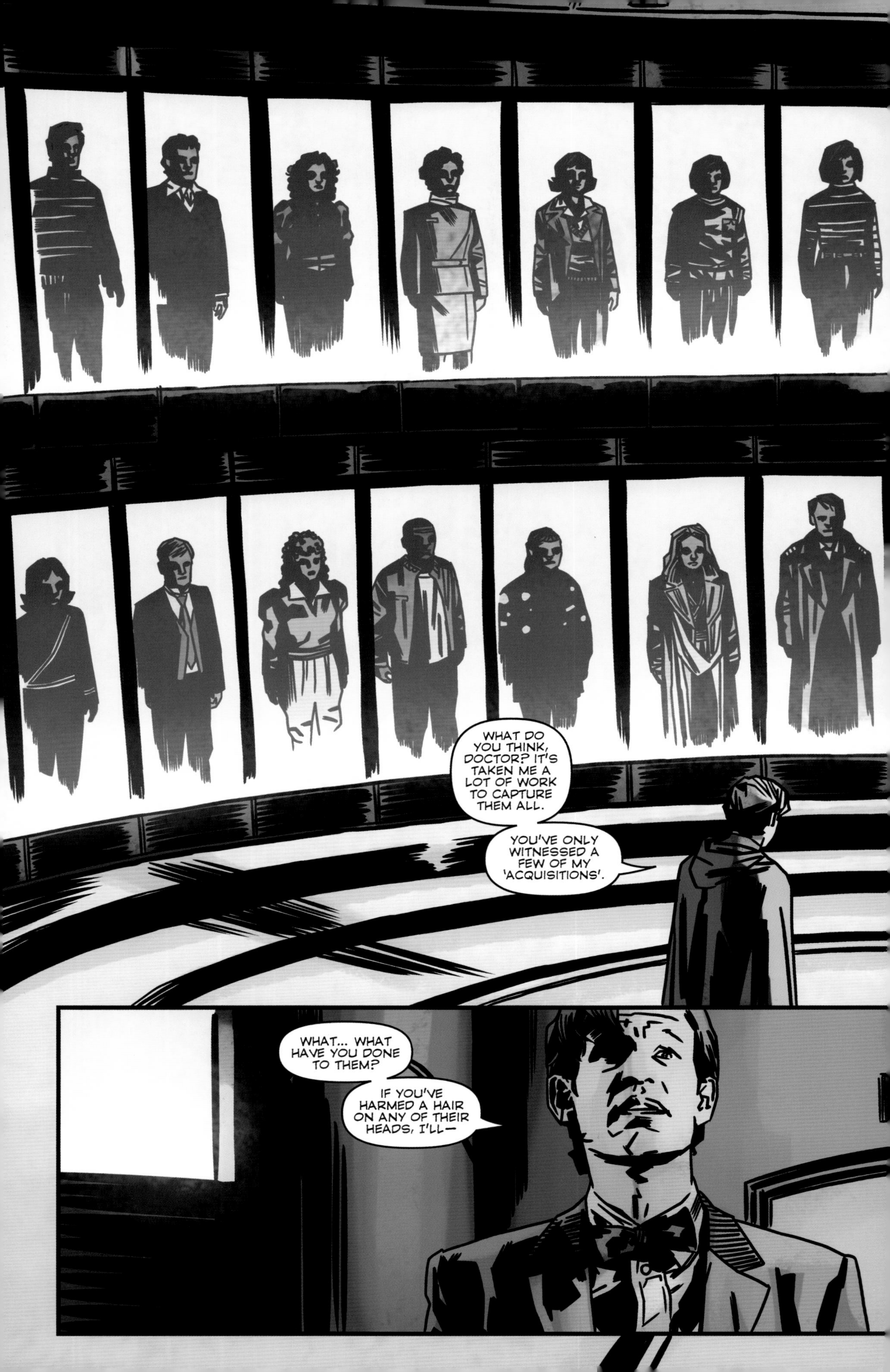

WHAT DO YOU THINK, DOCTOR? IT'S TAKEN ME A LOT OF WORK TO CAPTURE THEM ALL.
YOU'VE ONLY WITNESSED A FEW OF MY 'ACQUISITIONS'.
WHAT... WHAT HAVE YOU DONE TO THEM?
IF YOU'VE HARMED A HAIR ON ANY OF THEIR HEADS, I'LL—

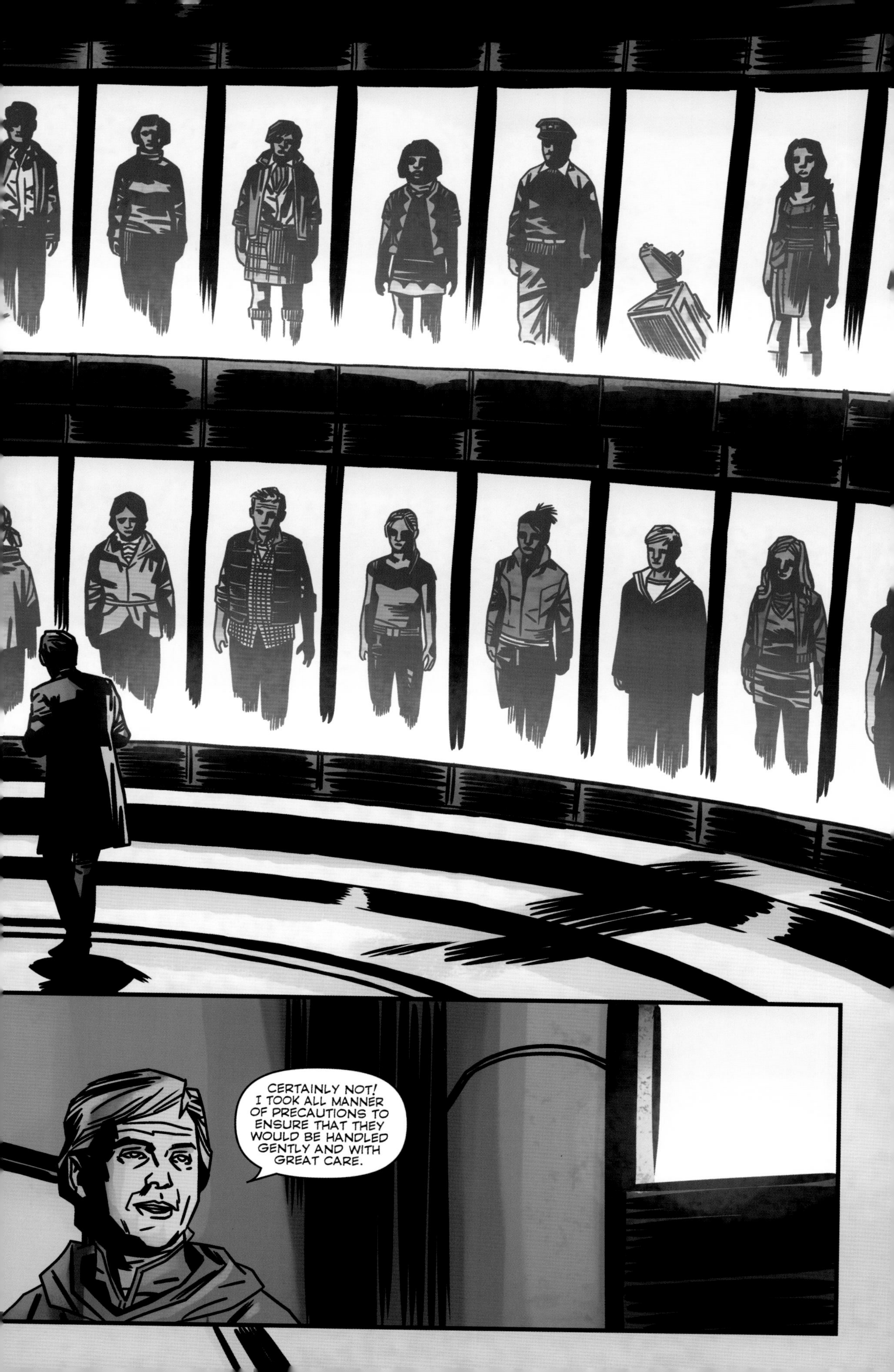
CERTAINLY NOT! I TOOK ALL MANNER OF PRECAUTIONS TO ENSURE THAT THEY WOULD BE HANDLED GENTLY AND WITH GREAT CARE.

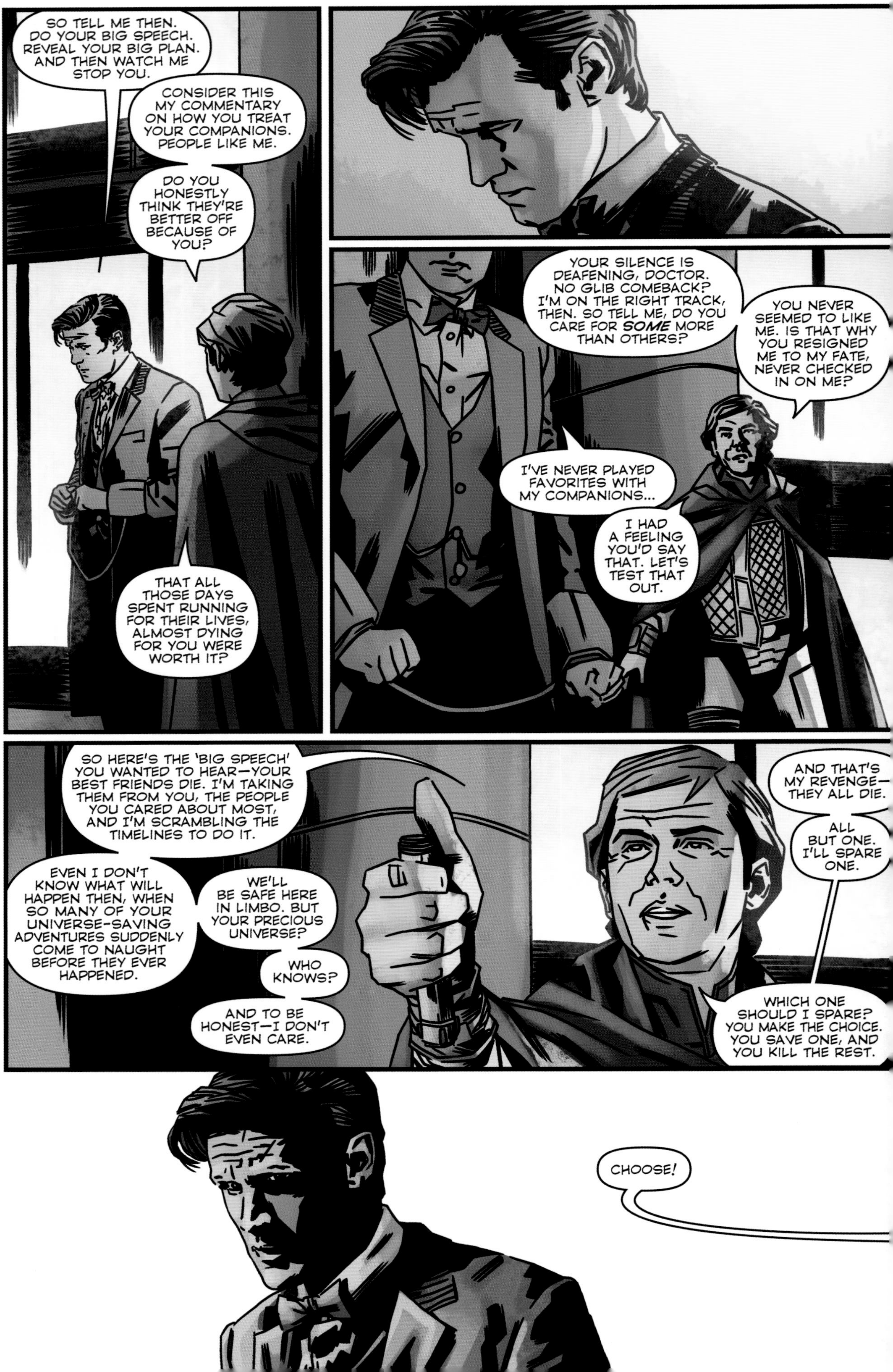
SO TELL ME THEN. DO YOUR BIG SPEECH. REVEAL YOUR BIG PLAN. AND THEN WATCH ME STOP YOU.
CONSIDER THIS MY COMMENTARY ON HOW YOU TREAT YOUR COMPANIONS. PEOPLE LIKE ME.
DO YOU HONESTLY THINK THEY'RE BETTER OFF BECAUSE OF YOU?
THAT ALL THOSE DAYS SPENT RUNNING FOR THEIR LIVES, ALMOST DYING FOR YOU WERE WORTH IT?
YOUR SILENCE IS DEAFENING, DOCTOR. NO GLIB COMEBACK? I'M ON THE RIGHT TRACK, THEN. SO TELL ME, DO YOU CARE FOR SOME MORE THAN OTHERS?
YOU NEVER SEEMED TO LIKE ME. IS THAT WHY YOU RESIGNED ME TO MY FATE, NEVER CHECKED IN ON ME?
I'VE NEVER PLAYED FAVORITES WITH MY COMPANIONS...
I HAD A FEELING YOU'D SAY THAT. LET'S TEST THAT OUT.
SO HERE'S THE 'BIG SPEECH' YOU WANTED TO HEAR—YOUR BEST FRIENDS DIE. I'M TAKING THEM FROM YOU, THE PEOPLE YOU CARED ABOUT MOST, AND I'M SCRAMBLING THE TIMELINES TO DO IT.
EVEN I DON'T KNOW WHAT WILL HAPPEN THEN, WHEN SO MANY OF YOUR UNIVERSE-SAVING ADVENTURES SUDDENLY COME TO NAUGHT BEFORE THEY EVER HAPPENED.
WE'LL BE SAFE HERE IN LIMBO. BUT YOUR PRECIOUS UNIVERSE?
WHO KNOWS?
AND TO BE HONEST—I DON'T EVEN CARE.
AND THAT'S MY REVENGE—THEY ALL DIE.
ALL BUT ONE. I'LL SPARE ONE.
WHICH ONE SHOULD I SPARE? YOU MAKE THE CHOICE. YOU SAVE ONE, AND YOU KILL THE REST.
CHOOSE!

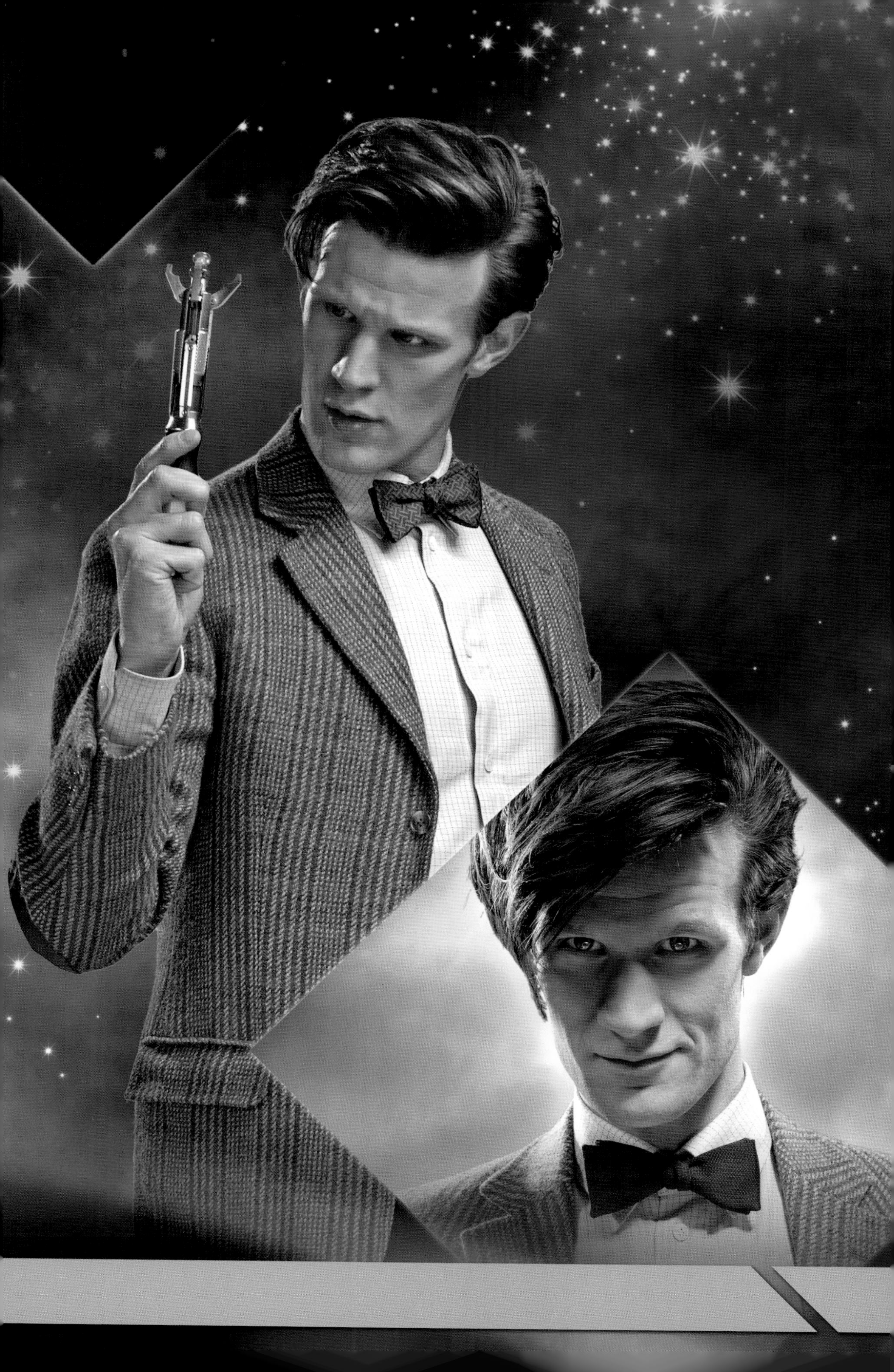

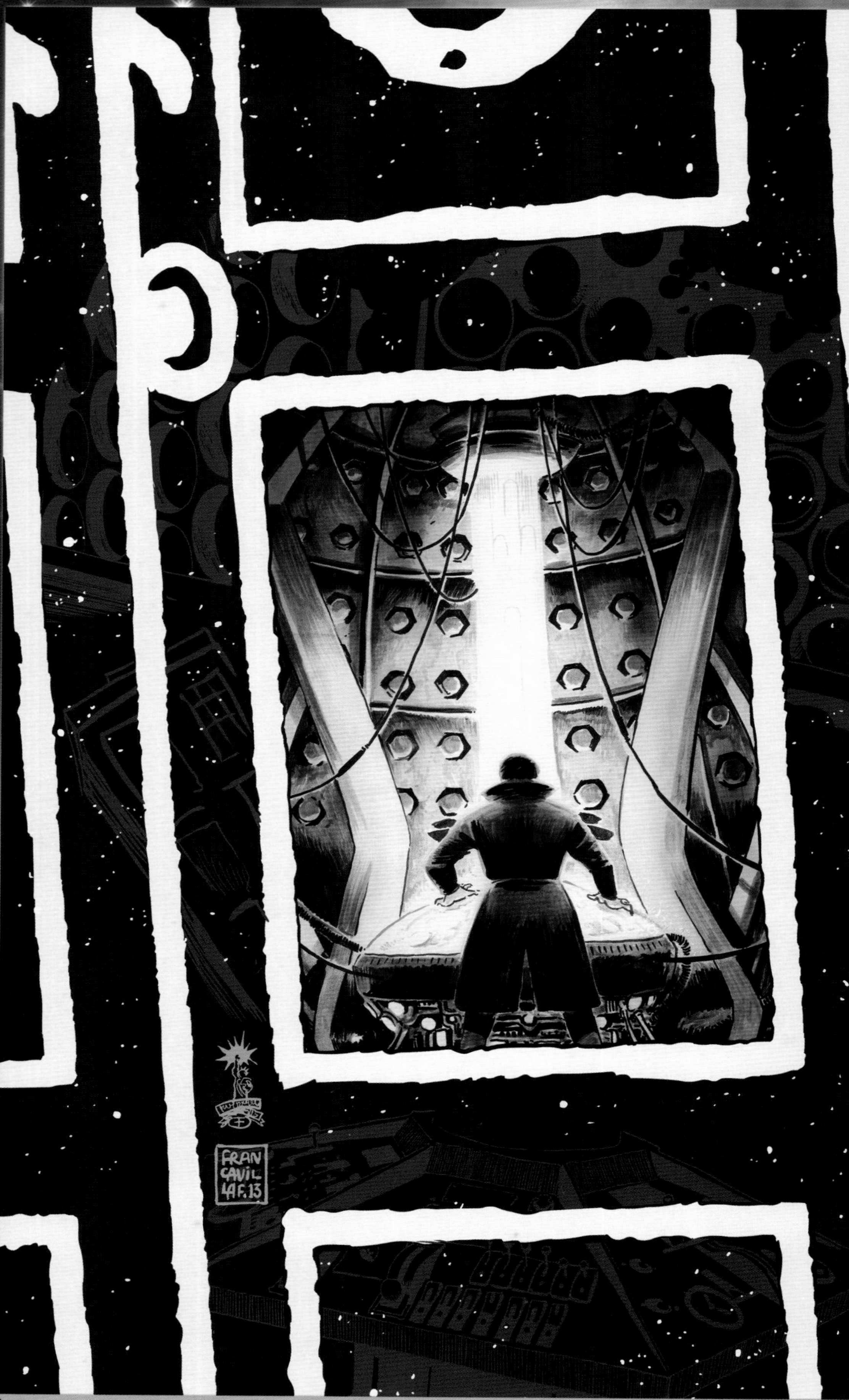
FRAN
CAVIL
LA F.13

CHAPTER 12 "ENDGAME"
Cover Art by Francesco Francavilla

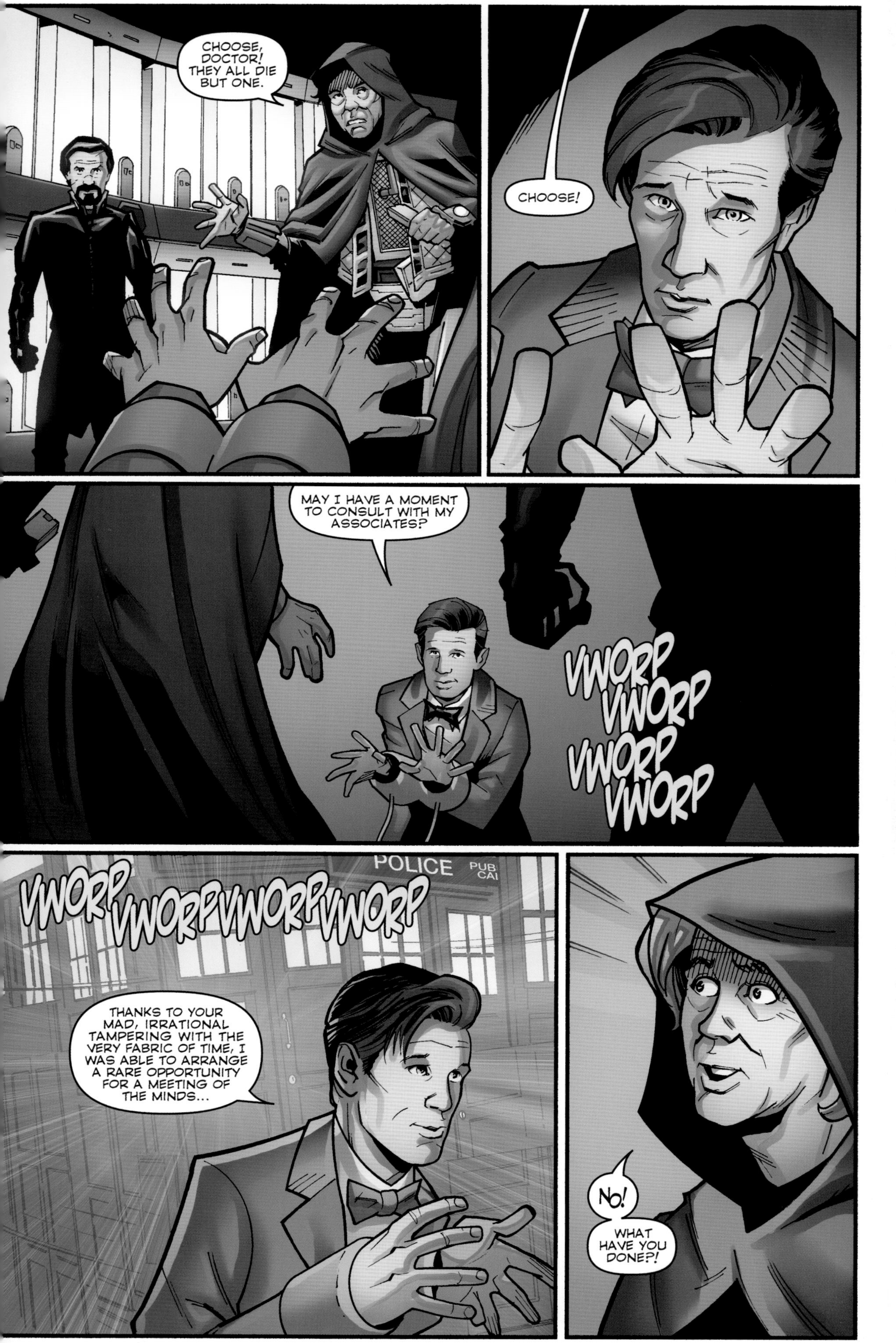
CHOOSE, DOCTOR! THEY ALL DIE BUT ONE.
CHOOSE!
MAY I HAVE A MOMENT TO CONSULT WITH MY ASSOCIATES?
VWORP VWORP VWORP VWORP
VWORP VWORP VWORP VWORP
POLICE PUB CAL
THANKS TO YOUR MAD, IRRATIONAL TAMPERING WITH THE VERY FABRIC OF TIME, I WAS ABLE TO ARRANGE A RARE OPPORTUNITY FOR A MEETING OF THE MINDS...
NO!
WHAT HAVE YOU DONE?!

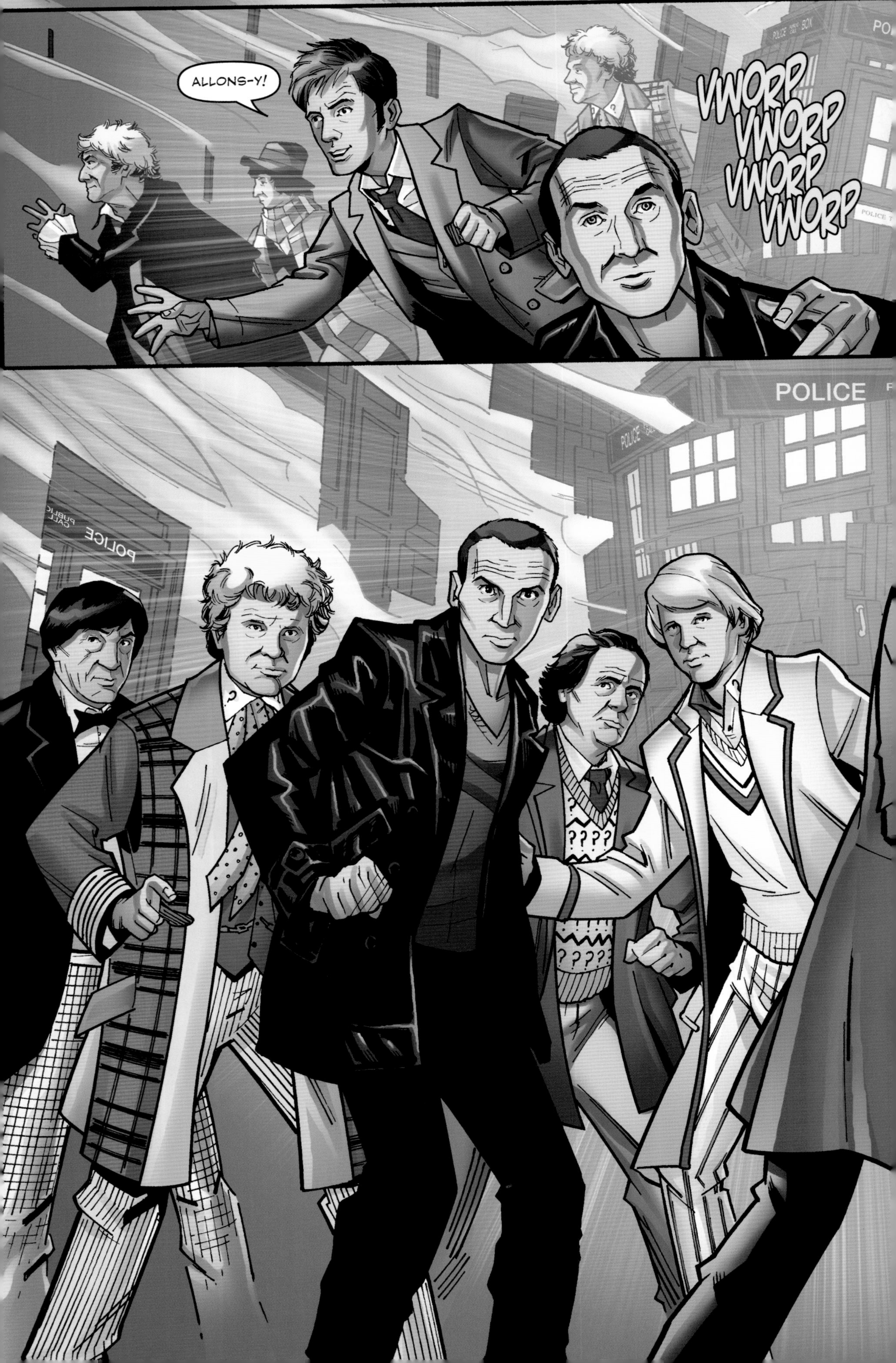
ALLONS-Y!
VWORP
VWORP
VWORP
VWORP
POLICE

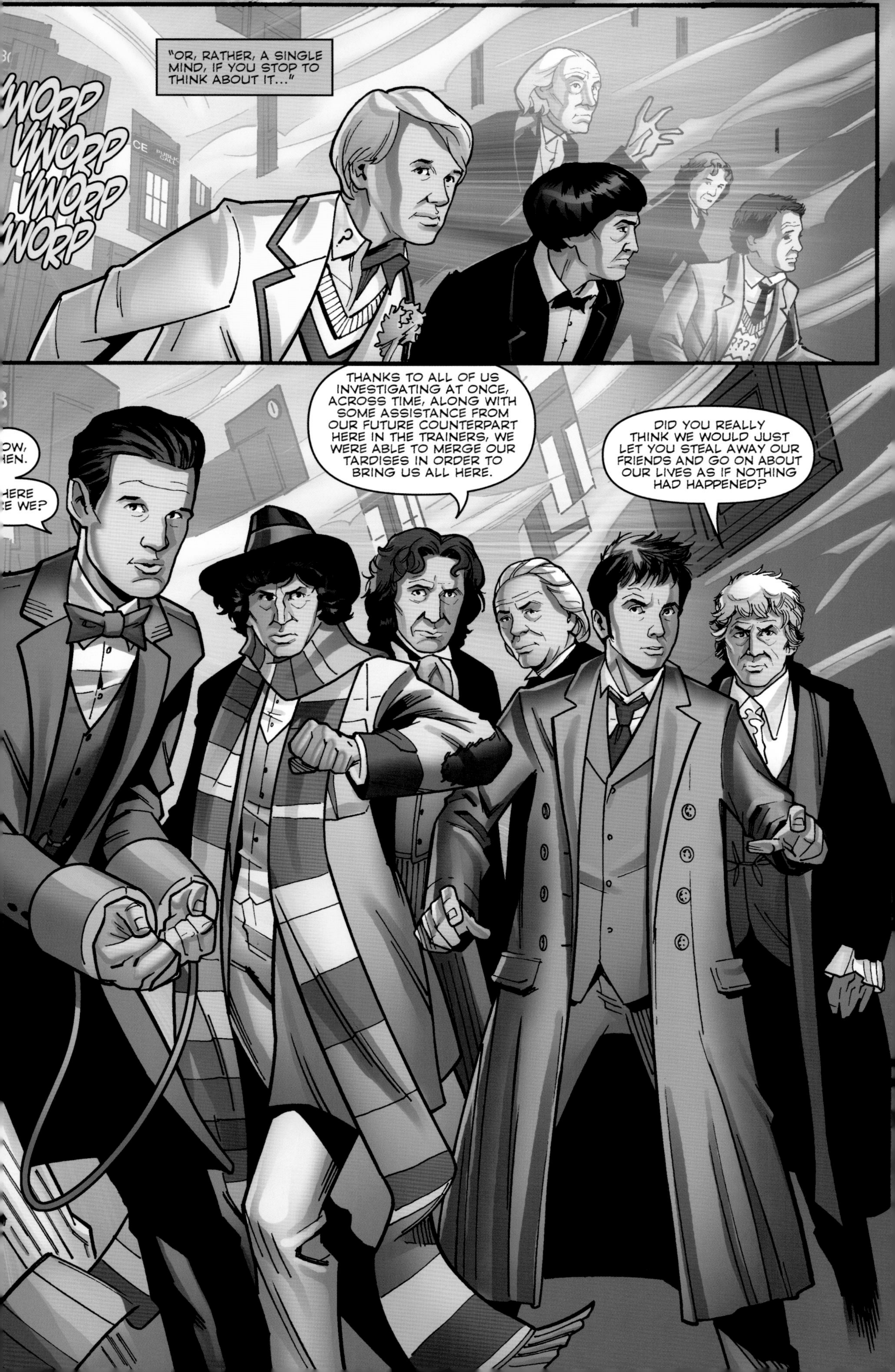
"OR, RATHER, A SINGLE MIND, IF YOU STOP TO THINK ABOUT IT..."
VWORP VWORP VWORP VWORP
THANKS TO ALL OF US INVESTIGATING AT ONCE, ACROSS TIME, ALONG WITH SOME ASSISTANCE FROM OUR FUTURE COUNTERPART HERE IN THE TRAINERS, WE WERE ABLE TO MERGE OUR TARDISES IN ORDER TO BRING US ALL HERE.
DID YOU REALLY THINK WE WOULD JUST LET YOU STEAL AWAY OUR FRIENDS AND GO ON ABOUT OUR LIVES AS IF NOTHING HAD HAPPENED?

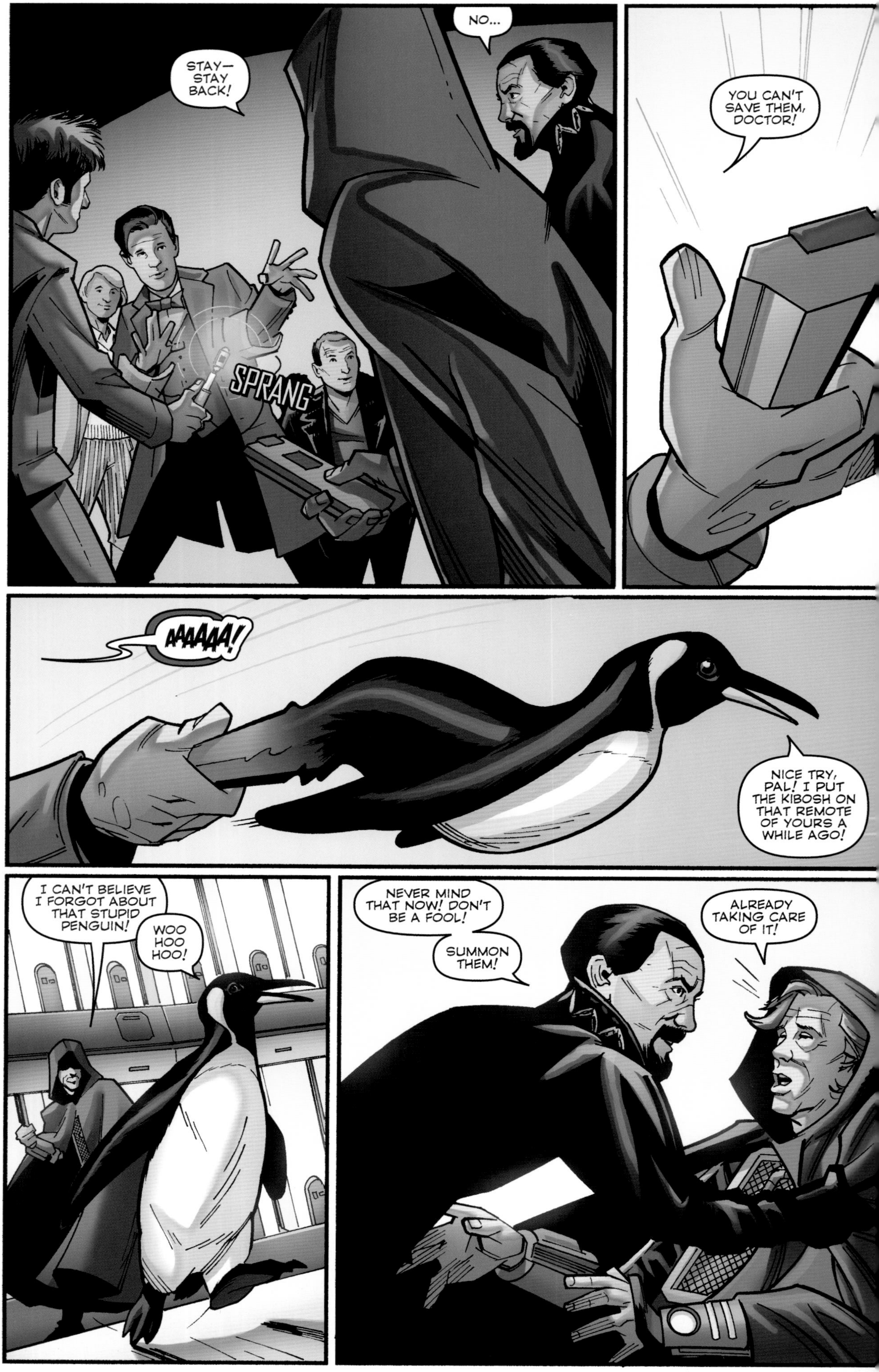
STAY—
STAY
BACK!
NO...
SPRANG
YOU CAN'T SAVE THEM, DOCTOR!
AAAAAA!
NICE TRY, PAL! I PUT THE KIBOSH ON THAT REMOTE OF YOURS A WHILE AGO!
I CAN'T BELIEVE I FORGOT ABOUT THAT STUPID PENGUIN!
WOO HOO HOO!
NEVER MIND THAT NOW! DON'T BE A FOOL!
SUMMON THEM!
ALREADY TAKING CARE OF IT!

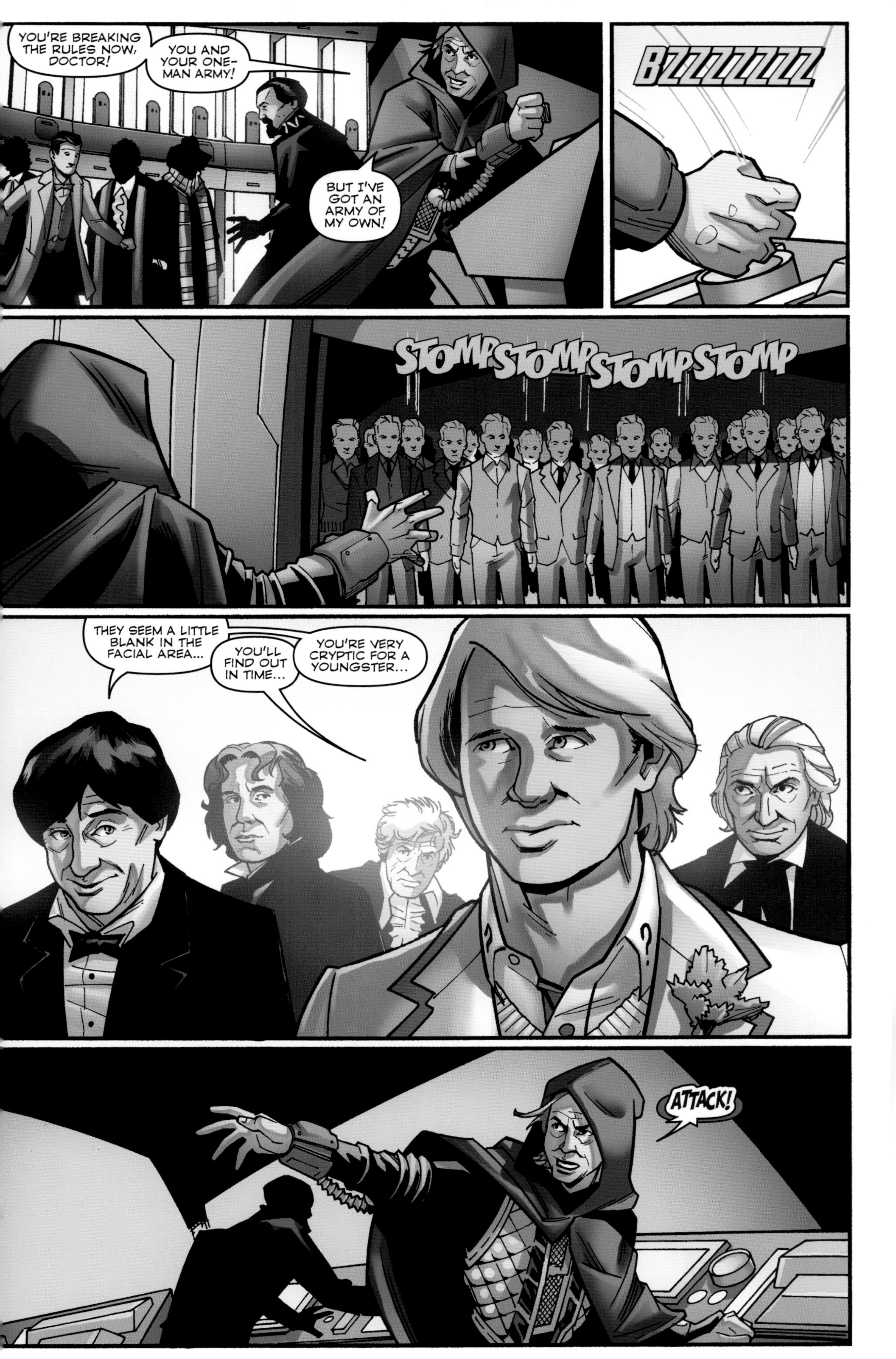
YOU'RE BREAKING THE RULES NOW, DOCTOR!
YOU AND YOUR ONE-MAN ARMY!
BUT I'VE GOT AN ARMY OF MY OWN!
BZZZZZZZ
STOMPSTOMPSTOMPSTOMP
THEY SEEM A LITTLE BLANK IN THE FACIAL AREA...
YOU'LL FIND OUT IN TIME...
YOU'RE VERY CRYPTIC FOR A YOUNGSTER...
ATTACK!

ANY SUGGESTIONS FROM YOU LOT?

WELL, I DID ARRANGE FOR FROBISHER TO GET HERE, ISN'T THAT ENOUGH?

AND I LEFT THE CHRONAL TRAIL THAT ALLOWED YOU TO MERGE YOUR TARDISES AND GET HERE.

WHAT HAVE YOU CONTRIBUTED LATELY?

MY WINNING SMILE, OF COURSE!

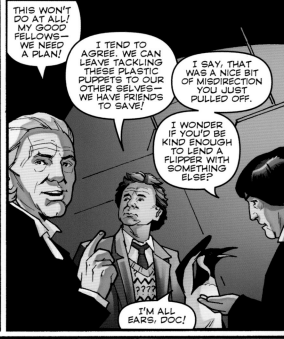

THIS WON'T DO AT ALL! MY GOOD FELLOWS— WE NEED A PLAN!

I TEND TO AGREE. WE CAN LEAVE TACKLING THESE PLASTIC PUPPETS TO OUR OTHER SELVES— WE HAVE FRIENDS TO SAVE!

I SAY, THAT WAS A NICE BIT OF MISDIRECTION YOU JUST PULLED OFF.

I WONDER IF YOU'D BE KIND ENOUGH TO LEND A FLIPPER WITH SOMETHING ELSE?

I'M ALL EARS, DOC!

WHAT DO YOU WANT?! GET BACK OUT THERE!

I CANNOT BELIEVE YOU JUST KEEP FALLING FOR THIS BIT!

NOW LET'S GET THE DOC A LITTLE HELP...

KLIK

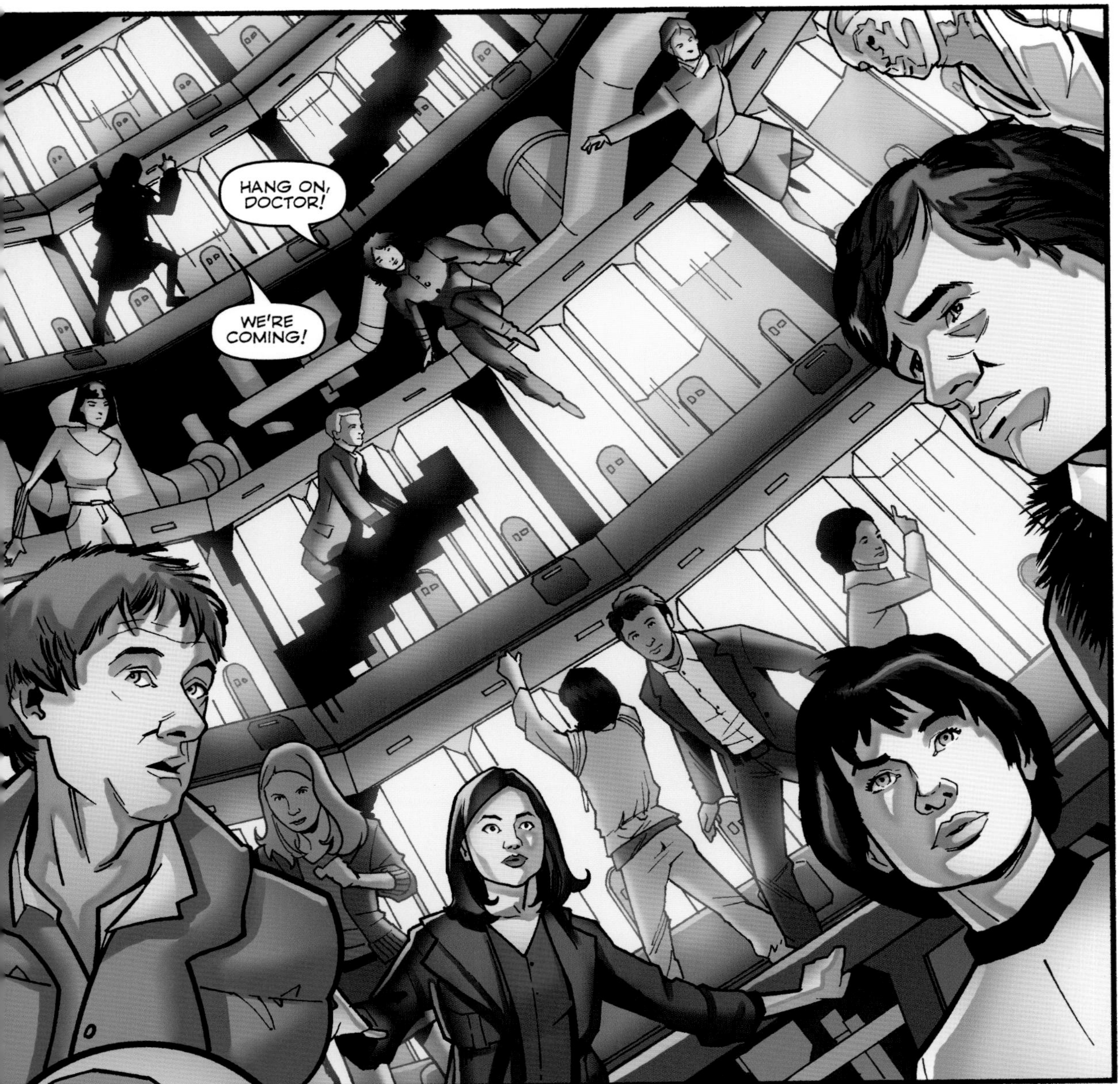
HANG ON, DOCTOR!
WE'RE COMING!
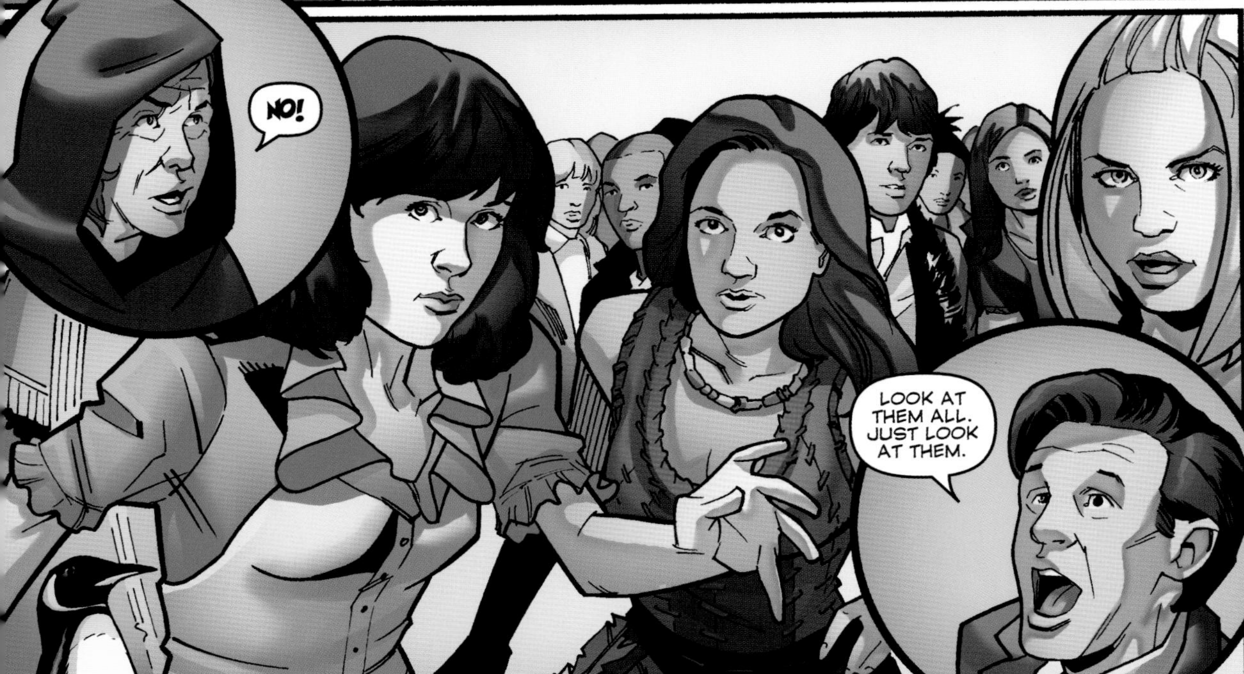
NO!
LOOK AT THEM ALL. JUST LOOK AT THEM.

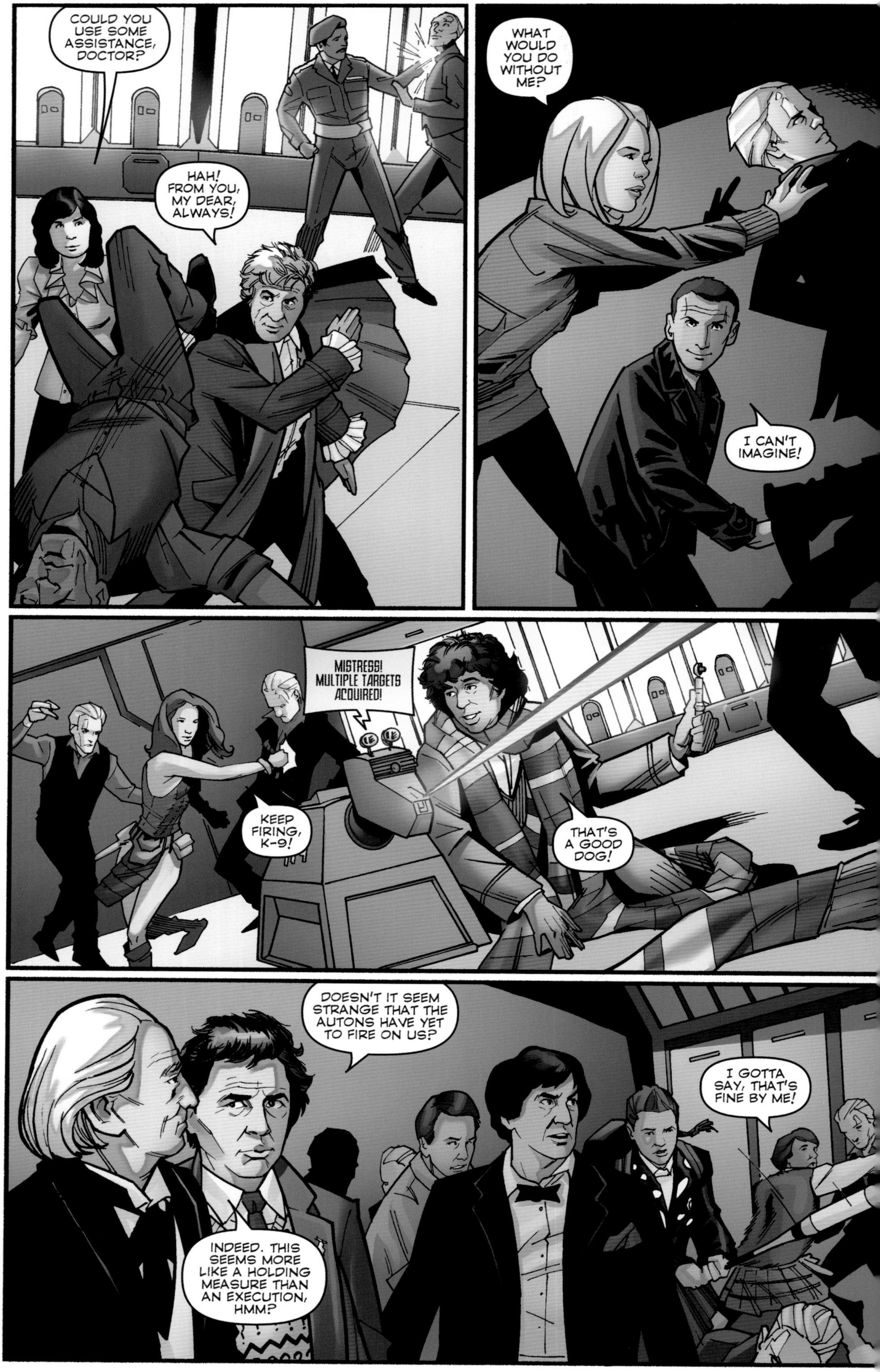
COULD YOU USE SOME ASSISTANCE, DOCTOR?
HAH! FROM YOU, MY DEAR, ALWAYS!
WHAT WOULD YOU DO WITHOUT ME?
I CAN'T IMAGINE!
MISTRESS! MULTIPLE TARGETS ACQUIRED!
KEEP FIRING, K-9!
THAT'S A GOOD DOG!
DOESN'T IT SEEM STRANGE THAT THE AUTONS HAVE YET TO FIRE ON US?
I GOTTA SAY, THAT'S FINE BY ME!
INDEED. THIS SEEMS MORE LIKE A HOLDING MEASURE THAN AN EXECUTION, HMM?

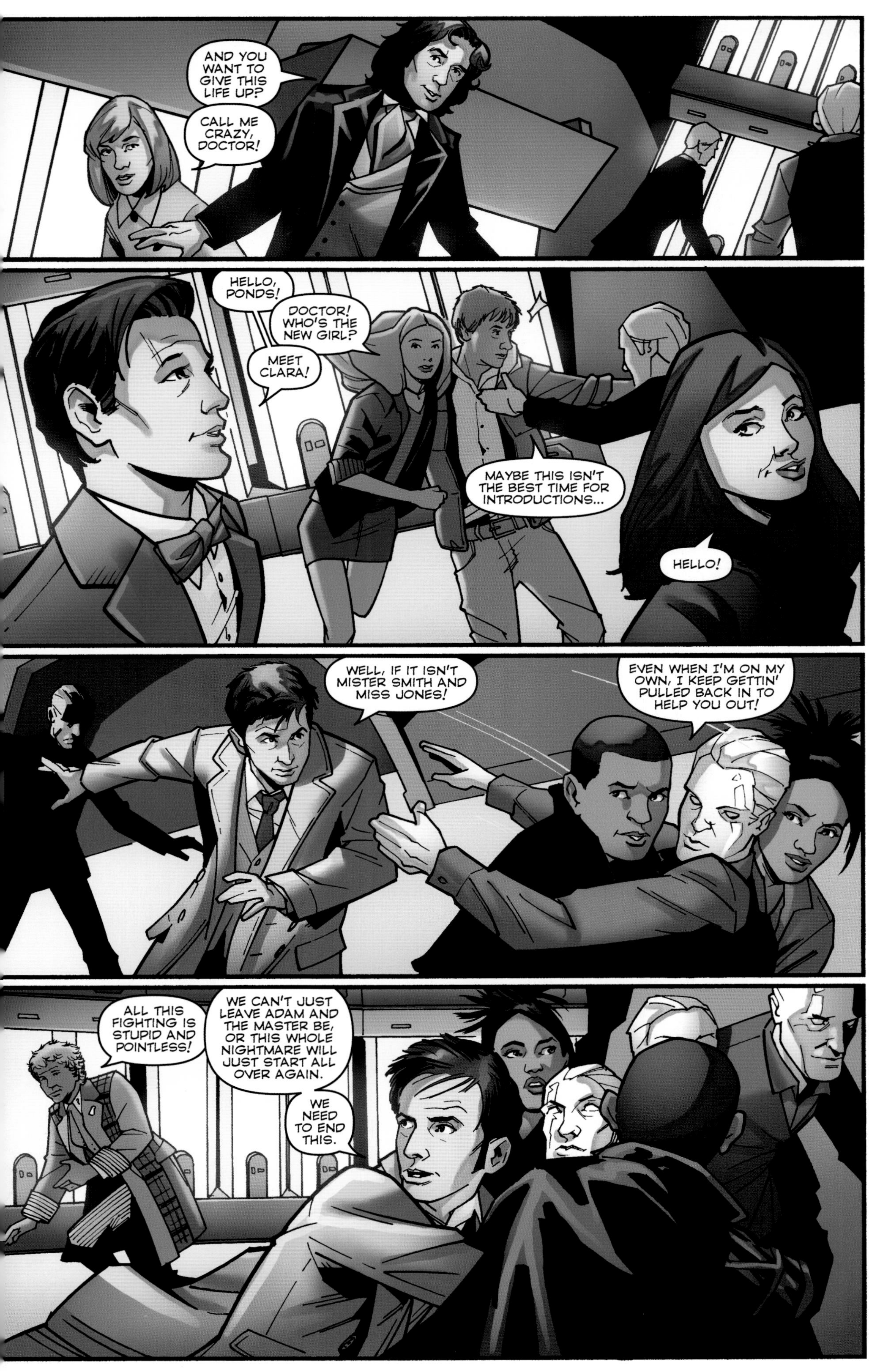
AND YOU WANT TO GIVE THIS LIFE UP?
CALL ME CRAZY, DOCTOR!
HELLO, PONDS!
DOCTOR! WHO'S THE NEW GIRL?
MEET CLARA!
MAYBE THIS ISN'T THE BEST TIME FOR INTRODUCTIONS...
HELLO!
WELL, IF IT ISN'T MISTER SMITH AND MISS JONES!
EVEN WHEN I'M ON MY OWN, I KEEP GETTIN' PULLED BACK IN TO HELP YOU OUT!
ALL THIS FIGHTING IS STUPID AND POINTLESS!
WE CAN'T JUST LEAVE ADAM AND THE MASTER BE, OR THIS WHOLE NIGHTMARE WILL JUST START ALL OVER AGAIN.
WE NEED TO END THIS.

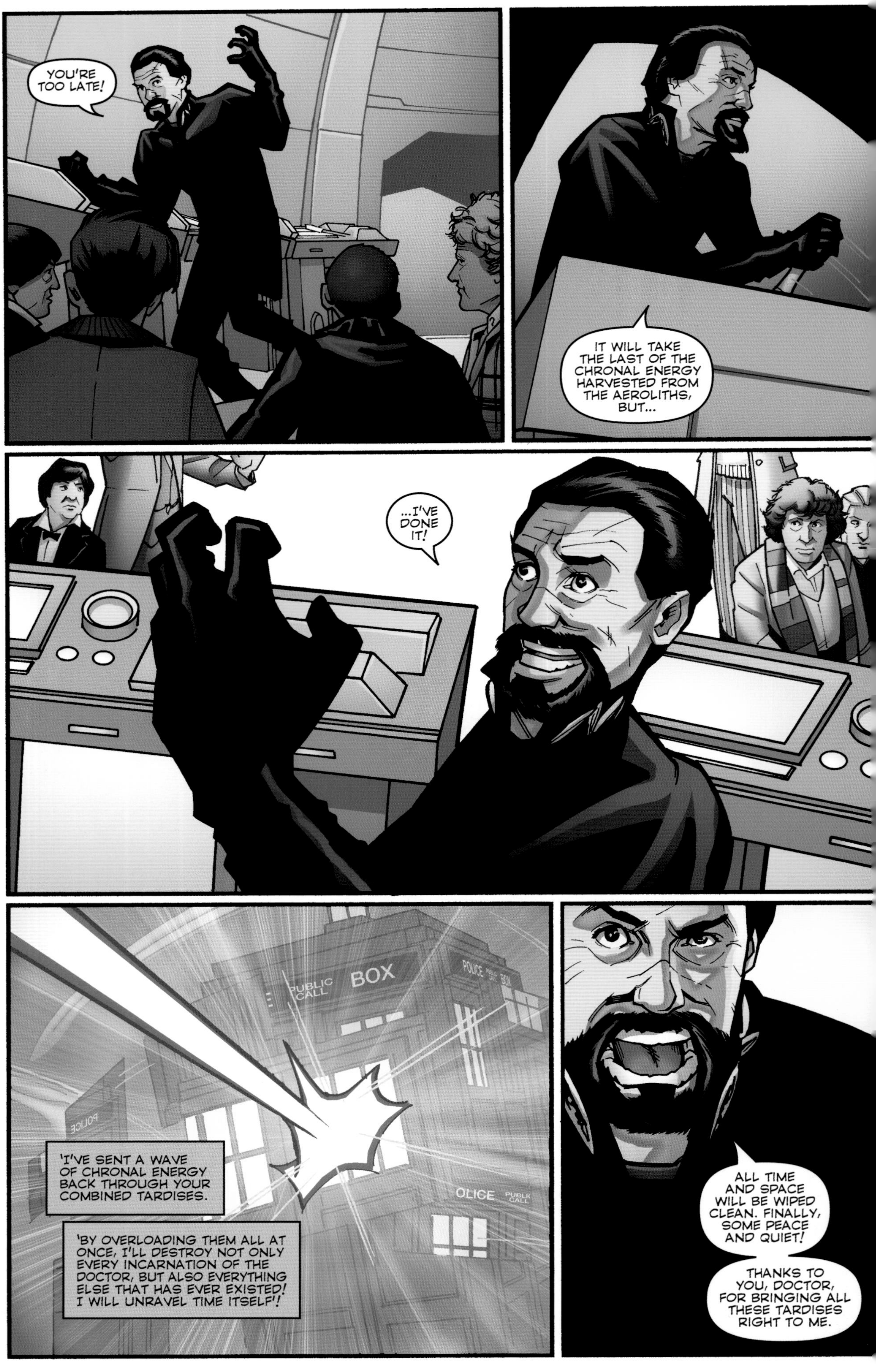
YOU'RE TOO LATE!
IT WILL TAKE THE LAST OF THE CHRONAL ENERGY HARVESTED FROM THE AEROLITHS, BUT...
...I'VE DONE IT!
'I'VE SENT A WAVE OF CHRONAL ENERGY BACK THROUGH YOUR COMBINED TARDISES.
'BY OVERLOADING THEM ALL AT ONCE, I'LL DESTROY NOT ONLY EVERY INCARNATION OF THE DOCTOR, BUT ALSO EVERYTHING ELSE THAT HAS EVER EXISTED! I WILL UNRAVEL TIME ITSELF'!
ALL TIME AND SPACE WILL BE WIPED CLEAN. FINALLY, SOME PEACE AND QUIET!
THANKS TO YOU, DOCTOR, FOR BRINGING ALL THESE TARDISES RIGHT TO ME.

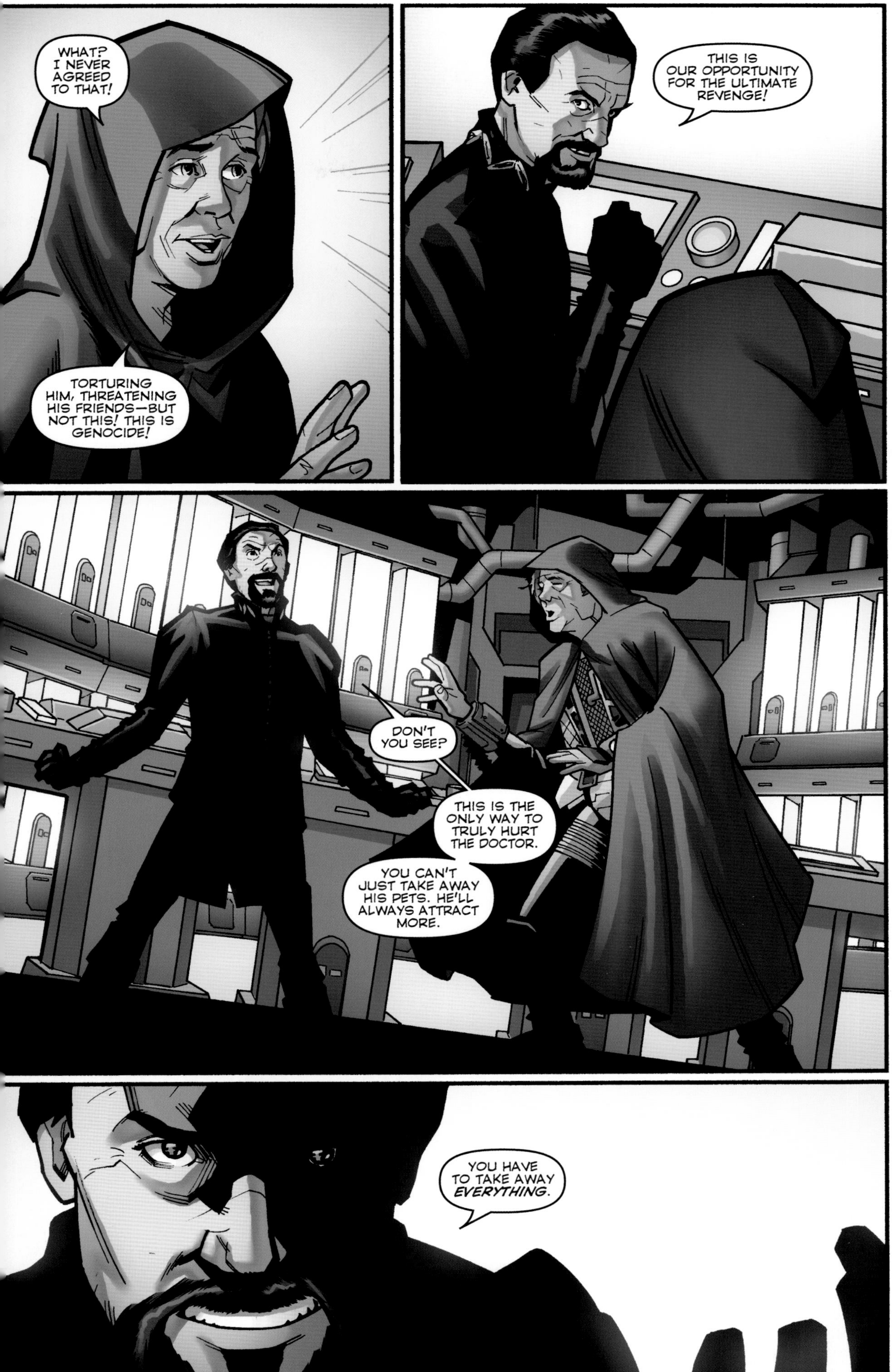
WHAT? I NEVER AGREED TO THAT!
TORTURING HIM, THREATENING HIS FRIENDS—BUT NOT THIS! THIS IS GENOCIDE!
THIS IS OUR OPPORTUNITY FOR THE ULTIMATE REVENGE!
DON'T YOU SEE?
THIS IS THE ONLY WAY TO TRULY HURT THE DOCTOR.
YOU CAN'T JUST TAKE AWAY HIS PETS. HE'LL ALWAYS ATTRACT MORE.
YOU HAVE TO TAKE AWAY *EVERYTHING*.

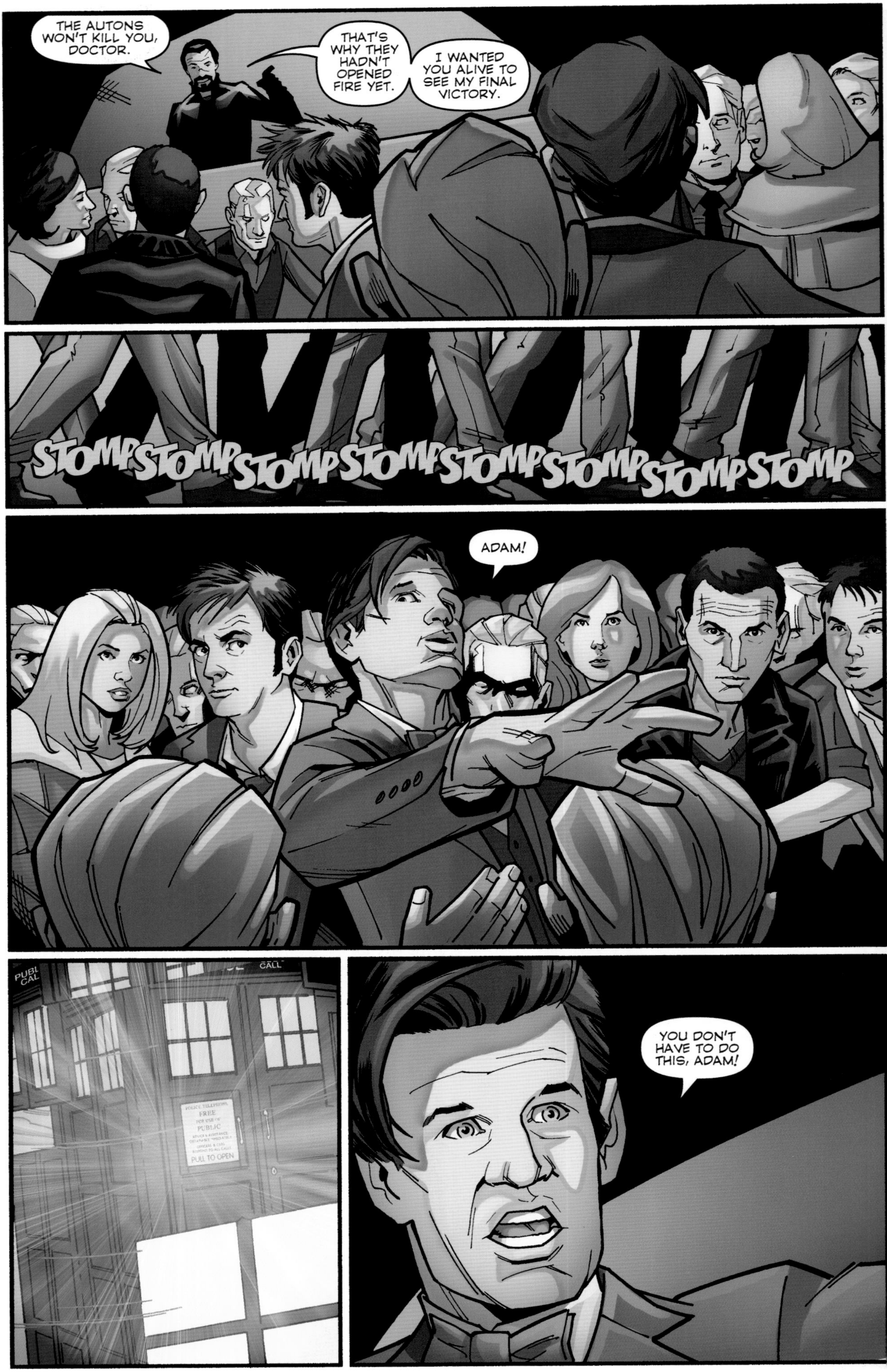
THE AUTONS WON'T KILL YOU, DOCTOR.
THAT'S WHY THEY HADN'T OPENED FIRE YET.
I WANTED YOU ALIVE TO SEE MY FINAL VICTORY.
STOMP STOMP STOMP STOMP STOMP STOMP STOMP STOMP STOMP
ADAM!
PUBLIC CALL
FREE
PUBLIC
PULL TO OPEN
YOU DON'T HAVE TO DO THIS, ADAM!

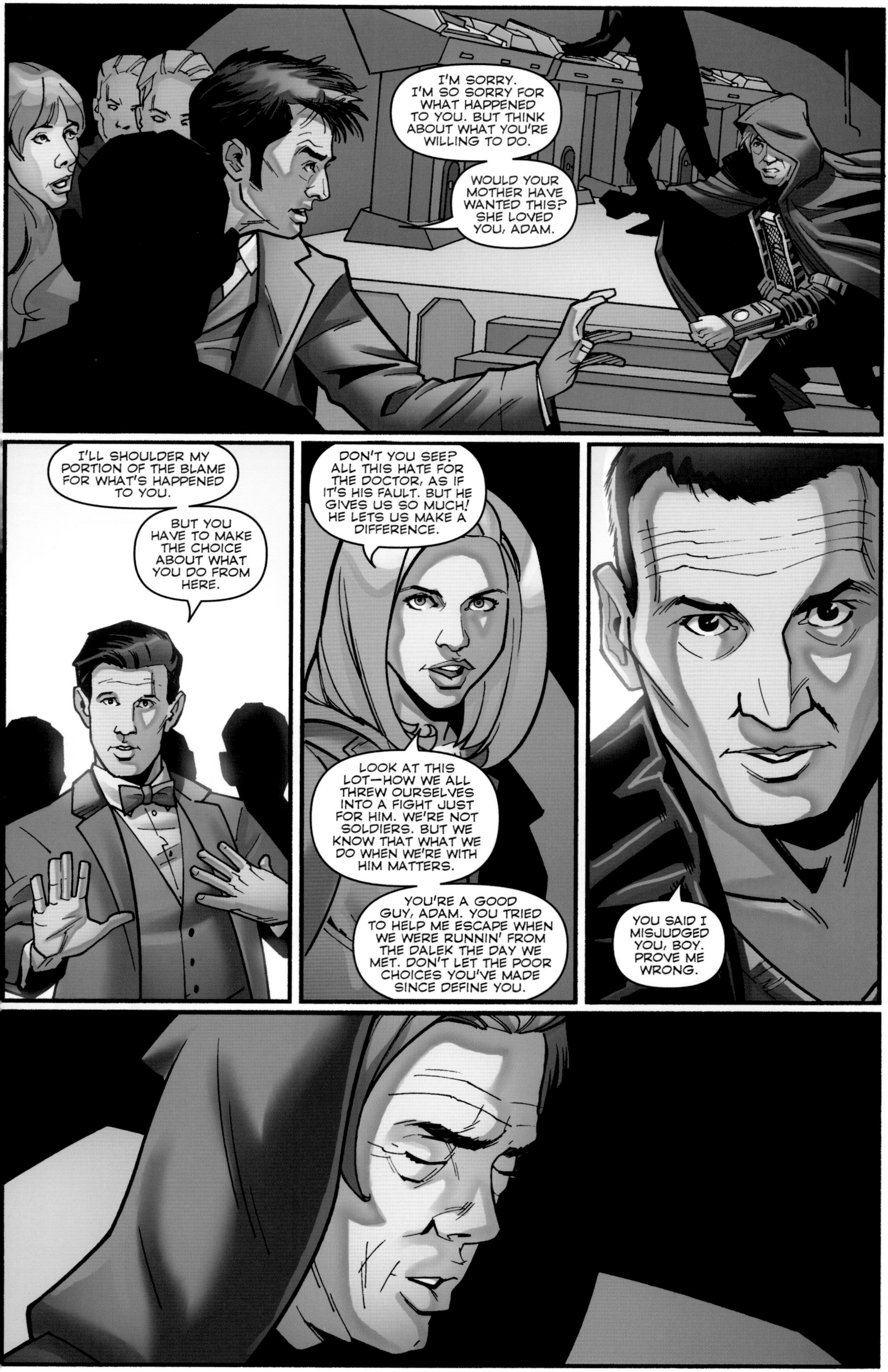
I'M SORRY. I'M SO SORRY FOR WHAT HAPPENED TO YOU. BUT THINK ABOUT WHAT YOU'RE WILLING TO DO.
WOULD YOUR MOTHER HAVE WANTED THIS? SHE LOVED YOU, ADAM.
I'LL SHOULDER MY PORTION OF THE BLAME FOR WHAT'S HAPPENED TO YOU.
BUT YOU HAVE TO MAKE THE CHOICE ABOUT WHAT YOU DO FROM HERE.
DON'T YOU SEE? ALL THIS HATE FOR THE DOCTOR, AS IF IT'S HIS FAULT. BUT HE GIVES US SO MUCH! HE LETS US MAKE A DIFFERENCE.
LOOK AT THIS LOT—HOW WE ALL THREW OURSELVES INTO A FIGHT JUST FOR HIM. WE'RE NOT SOLDIERS. BUT WE KNOW THAT WHAT WE DO WHEN WE'RE WITH HIM MATTERS.
YOU'RE A GOOD GUY, ADAM. YOU TRIED TO HELP ME ESCAPE WHEN WE WERE RUNNIN' FROM THE DALEK THE DAY WE MET. DON'T LET THE POOR CHOICES YOU'VE MADE SINCE DEFINE YOU.
YOU SAID I MISJUDGED YOU, BOY. PROVE ME WRONG.

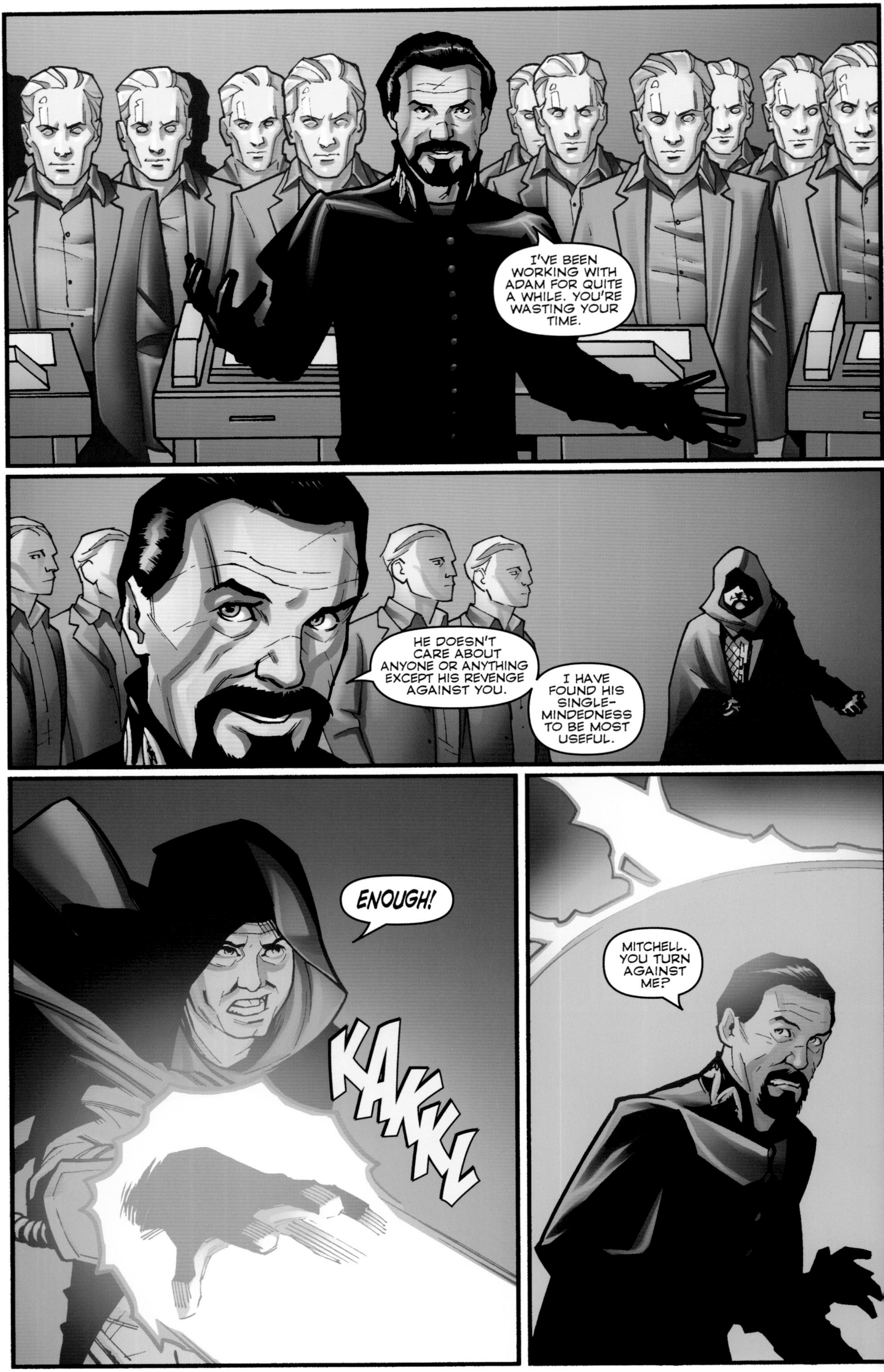
I'VE BEEN WORKING WITH ADAM FOR QUITE A WHILE. YOU'RE WASTING YOUR TIME.
HE DOESN'T CARE ABOUT ANYONE OR ANYTHING EXCEPT HIS REVENGE AGAINST YOU.
I HAVE FOUND HIS SINGLE-MINDEDNESS TO BE MOST USEFUL.
ENOUGH!
KAKKL
MITCHELL. YOU TURN AGAINST ME?

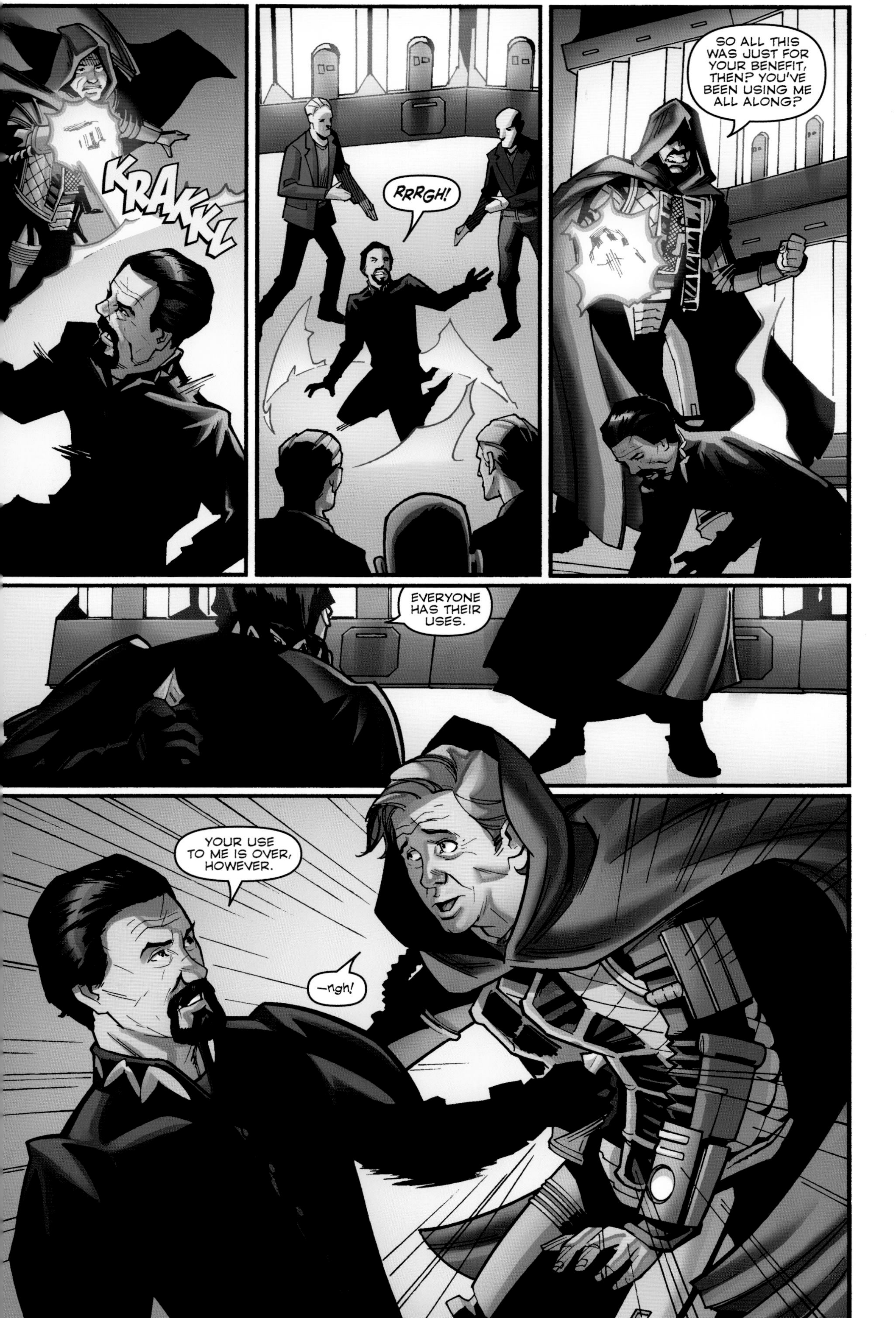
KRAKKL
RRRGH!
SO ALL THIS WAS JUST FOR YOUR BENEFIT, THEN? YOU'VE BEEN USING ME ALL ALONG?
EVERYONE HAS THEIR USES.
YOUR USE TO ME IS OVER, HOWEVER.
—ngh!

I'VE HAD TO LISTEN TO YOUR SIMPERING FOR DECADES.

MEWLING SELF-PITY.

BUT IT WAS ALL WORTH IT, TO ORCHESTRATE THIS LEVEL OF VENGEANCE AGAINST THE MAN WHO'S THWARTED ME TIME AND AGAIN.

AND NOW, WITH ALL TIME AND SPACE WIPED CLEAN, I CAN REMAKE REALITY TO MY DESIGN. A SHAME YOU WON'T BE AROUND TO SEE IT.

F'WASH

AND SO THE COWARD RUNS...

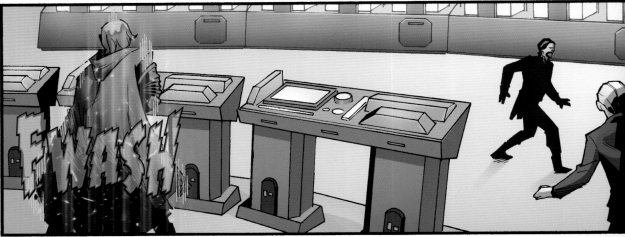

FWASH

I CAN'T LET YOU DO THIS. IT'S TOO MUCH.

DESTROYING THE UNIVERSE WAS NEVER WHAT I HAD IN MIND.

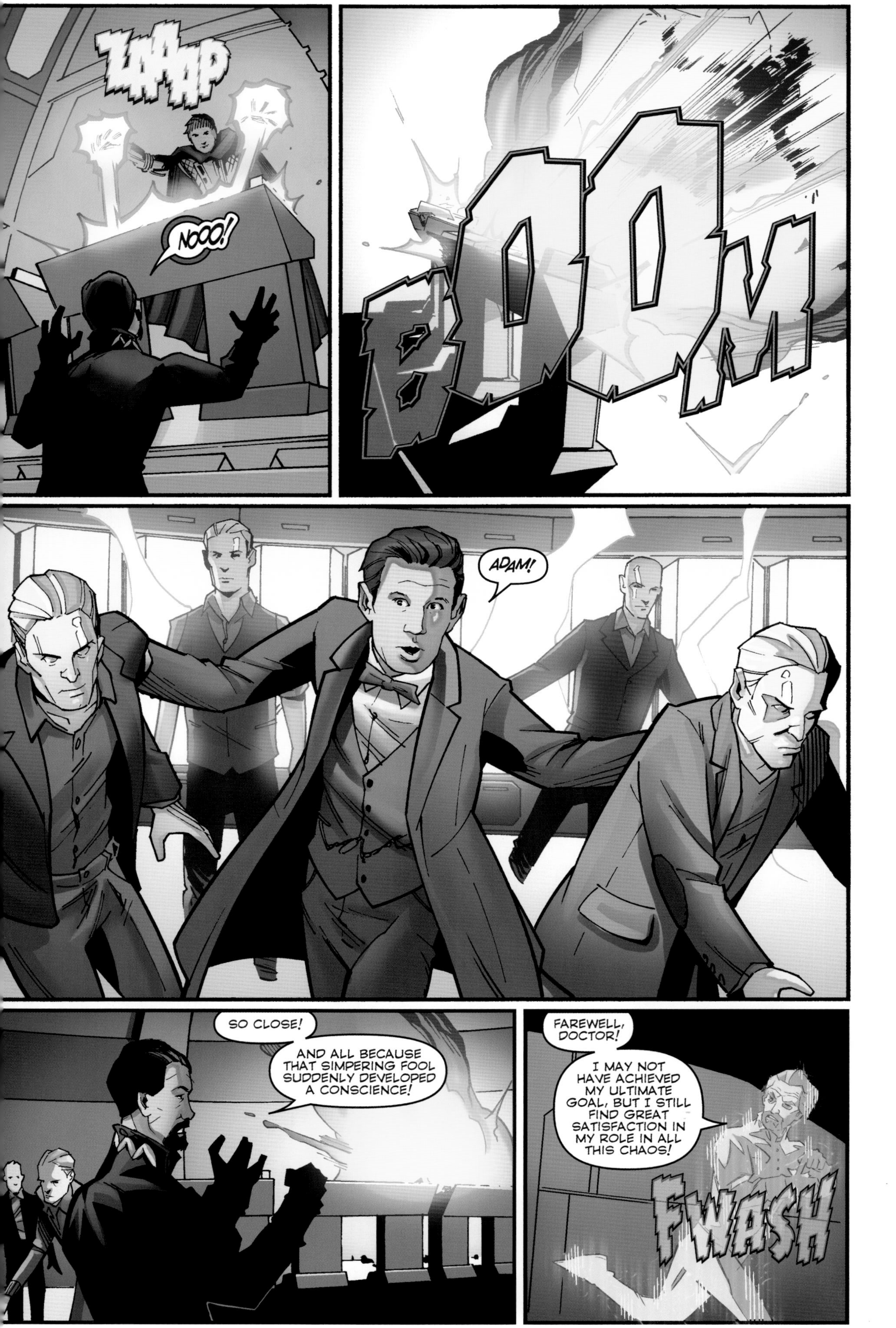

ZAAAP
NOOO!
BOOM
ADAM!
SO CLOSE!
AND ALL BECAUSE THAT SIMPERING FOOL SUDDENLY DEVELOPED A CONSCIENCE!
FAREWELL, DOCTOR!
I MAY NOT HAVE ACHIEVED MY ULTIMATE GOAL, BUT I STILL FIND GREAT SATISFACTION IN MY ROLE IN ALL THIS CHAOS!
FWASH

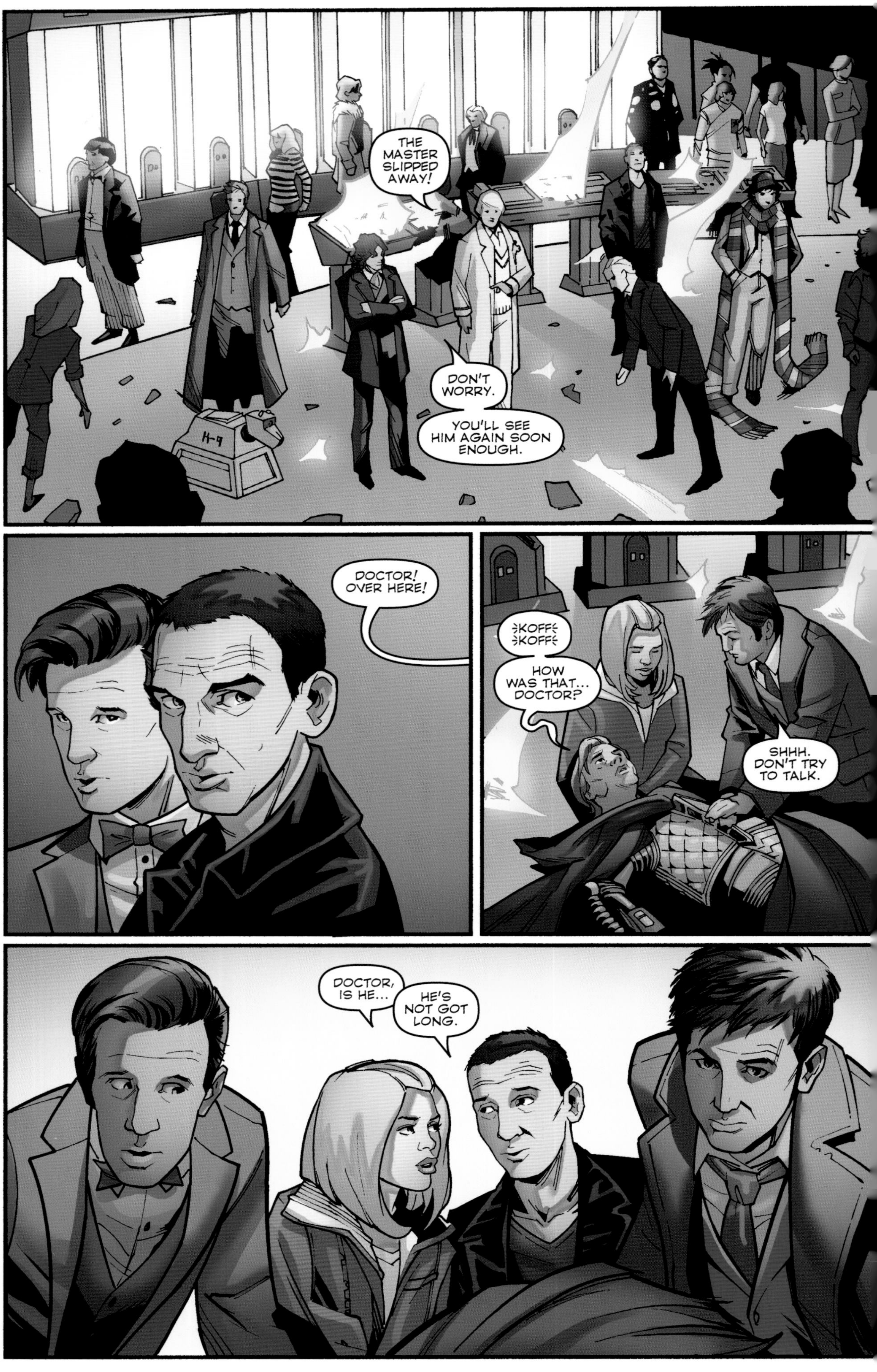
THE MASTER SLIPPED AWAY!
DON'T WORRY.
YOU'LL SEE HIM AGAIN SOON ENOUGH.
DOCTOR! OVER HERE!
KOFF KOFF
HOW WAS THAT... DOCTOR?
SHHH. DON'T TRY TO TALK.
DOCTOR, IS HE...
HE'S NOT GOT LONG.

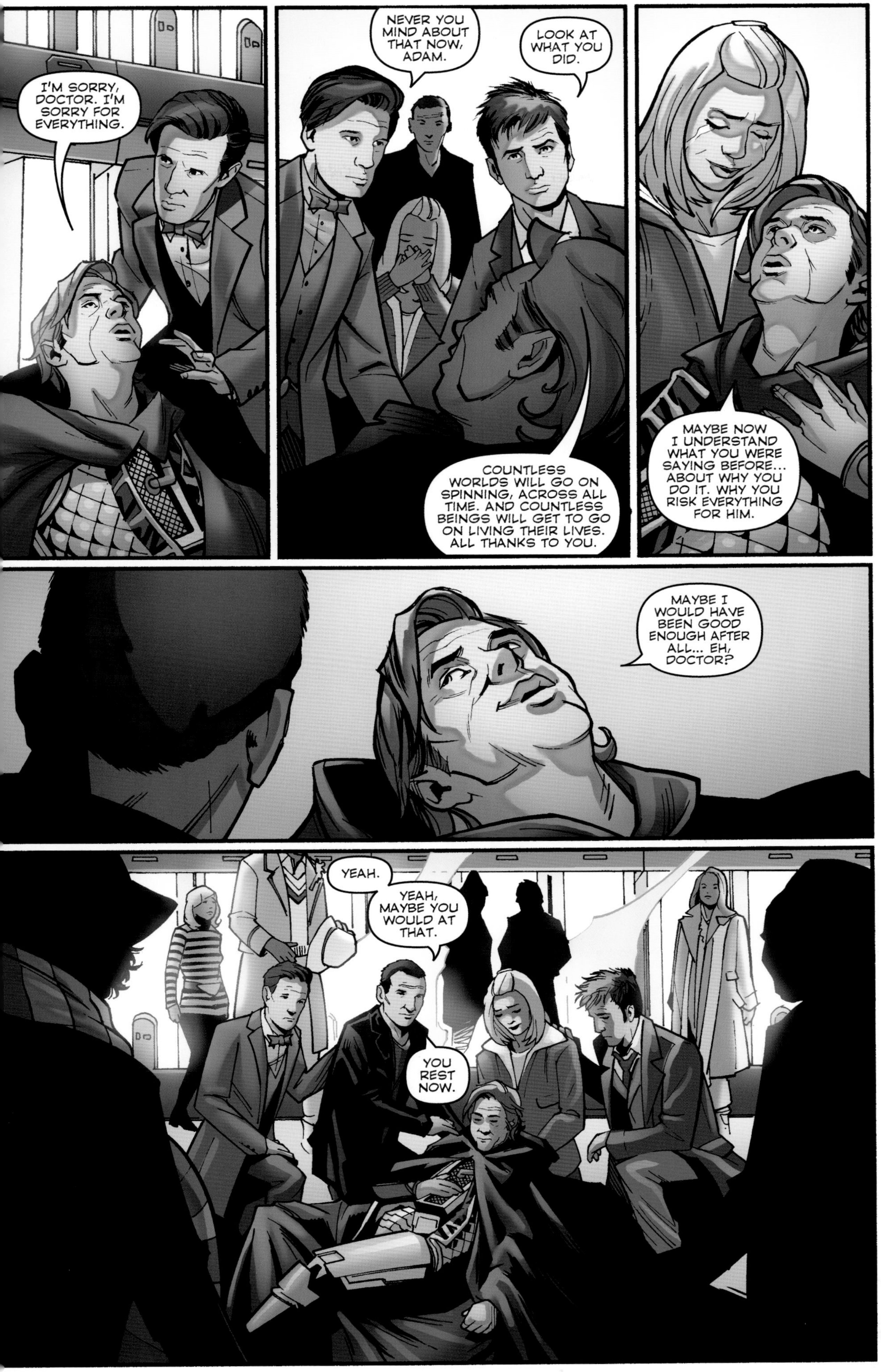
I'M SORRY, DOCTOR. I'M SORRY FOR EVERYTHING.
NEVER YOU MIND ABOUT THAT NOW, ADAM.
LOOK AT WHAT YOU DID.
COUNTLESS WORLDS WILL GO ON SPINNING, ACROSS ALL TIME. AND COUNTLESS BEINGS WILL GET TO GO ON LIVING THEIR LIVES. ALL THANKS TO YOU.
MAYBE NOW I UNDERSTAND WHAT YOU WERE SAYING BEFORE... ABOUT WHY YOU DO IT. WHY YOU RISK EVERYTHING FOR HIM.
MAYBE I WOULD HAVE BEEN GOOD ENOUGH AFTER ALL... EH, DOCTOR?
YEAH.
YEAH, MAYBE YOU WOULD AT THAT.
YOU REST NOW.

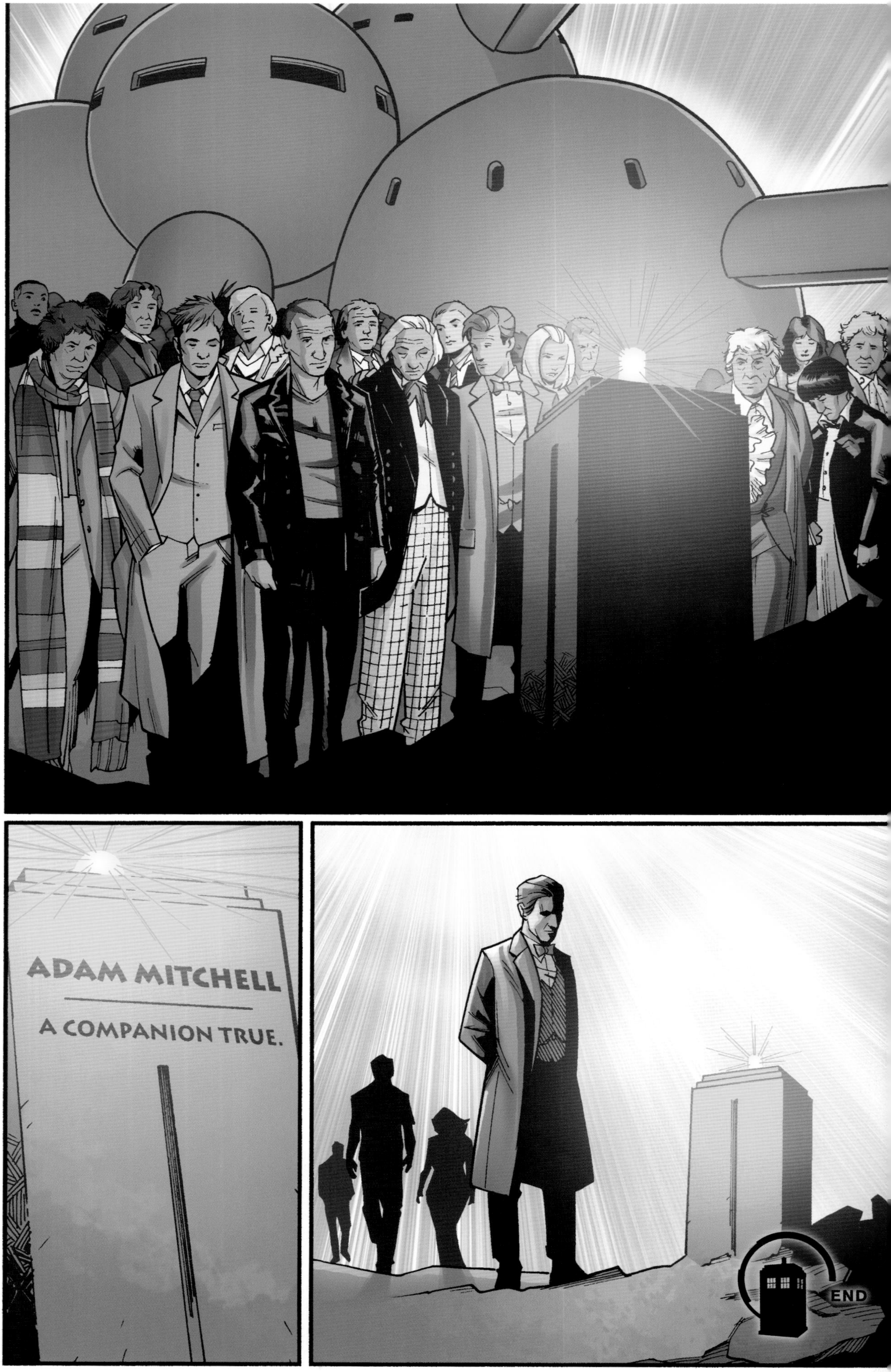
ADAM MITCHELL
A COMPANION TRUE.
END

REFLECTIONS OF TIME

Wherein prominent Whovians past and present muse upon the Doctor's history in comic form.

Fifty years of *Doctor Who*. It's amazing when you stop to think about it. How did they pull it off?

A mostly pacifist hero with no name. A continually shifting and changing cast. And a spaceship that looks like no other spaceship in all of science-fiction or popular culture (and that's putting it mildly). Elements that wouldn't work in any other television series. And yet, in the perfect example of the whole being greater than the sum of its parts, all this coalesced into the longest-running and most globally popular science-fiction franchise of all time.

What's the secret?

There's plenty of credit to go around, of course, beginning with the show's creators, folks like BBC's then-Head of Drama Sydney Newman, Head of Script Department Donald Wilson, and writer C.E. Webber, who incorporated the idea of time travel into the show with the idea of providing educational value by traveling to famous historical periods. The core time-travel concept opened up such a vista of possibilities for the series, allowing it to go anywhere and anywhen, giving it all the flexibility of an anthology while still providing the stability and comfort of a regular cast.

A veritable army of producers, writers, and directors have added to the *Doctor Who* mythology over the decades, from the show's inaugural producer Verity Lambert all the way to her current counterpart Steven Moffat—not to mention all the talented actors and actresses who have introduced viewers to eleven Doctors (going on twelve) and dozens of companions.

There's also that ingenious concept of "regeneration," allowing the series to change over the years and adapt to the times. Each regeneration lets the program survive the (repeated) departure of its leading man, while still retaining the continuity and respect for its own history that cultivates the kind of dedicated fan base for which *Doctor Who* has become famous. As each Doctor passes the TARDIS key to the next, viewers consistently find themselves going from "I miss the old Doctor" to "Yes, he's the Doctor" within a matter of weeks. What other show could pull that off time and time again?

And then we can't forget the Doctor's amazing rogues gallery of enemies, beginning with the most famous, the Daleks, which catapulted *Doctor Who* into the British consciousness in only the program's second month on the air, and made the phrase "watching from behind the couch" a household expression in the U.K. Whether it's the Cybermen and the Autons or the Silence and the Weeping Angels, there isn't another series around that has creepier villains than *Doctor Who*.

For me, I think it all comes down to a simple idea. It's a scary world. And we'd all like to believe there's someone out there looking out for us. Someone b r a v e. Someone smart. Someone kind. And someone who likes us enough to invite one of us to come along with him, running among the stars, helping people who need it.

So as I close the TARDIS door behind me, special thanks to IDW Publishing and the BBC for giving this kid from California an opportunity for something he never thought he'd get: the chance to run with the Doctor.

—Scott Tipton
Los Angeles, California
October 2013

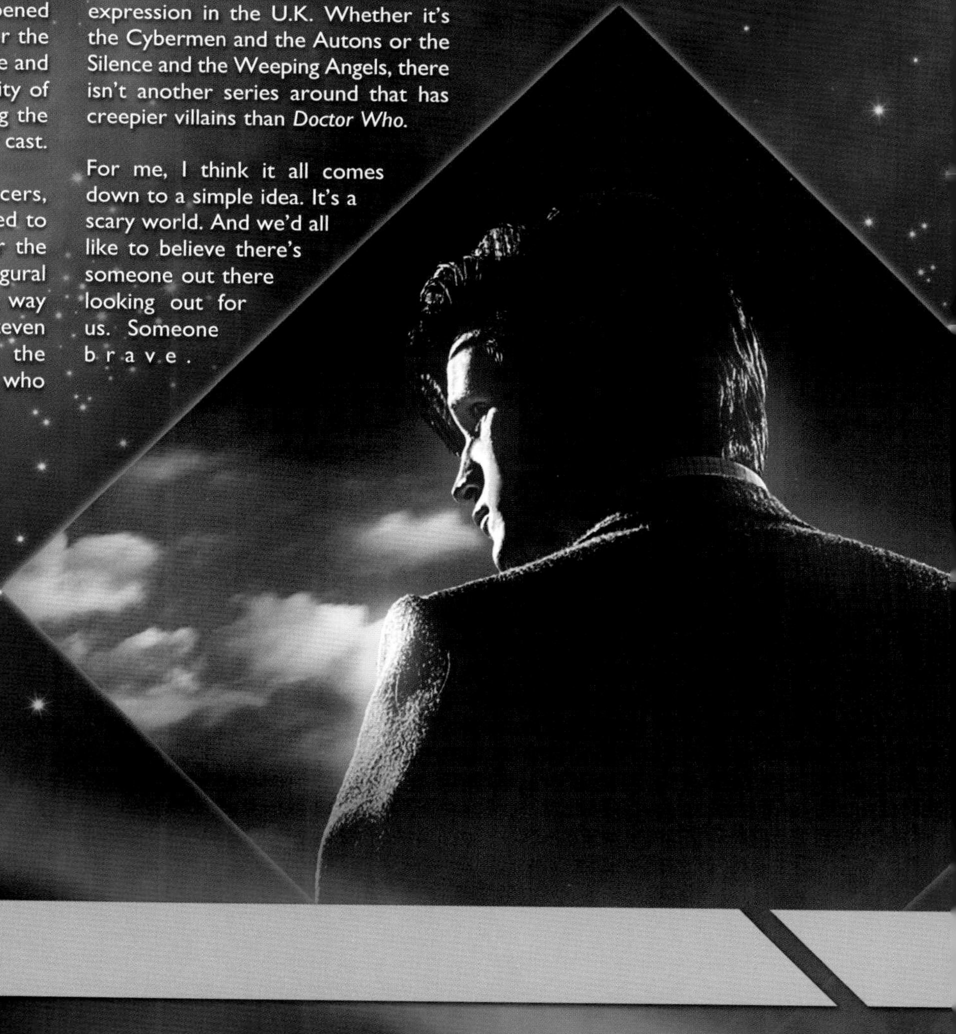

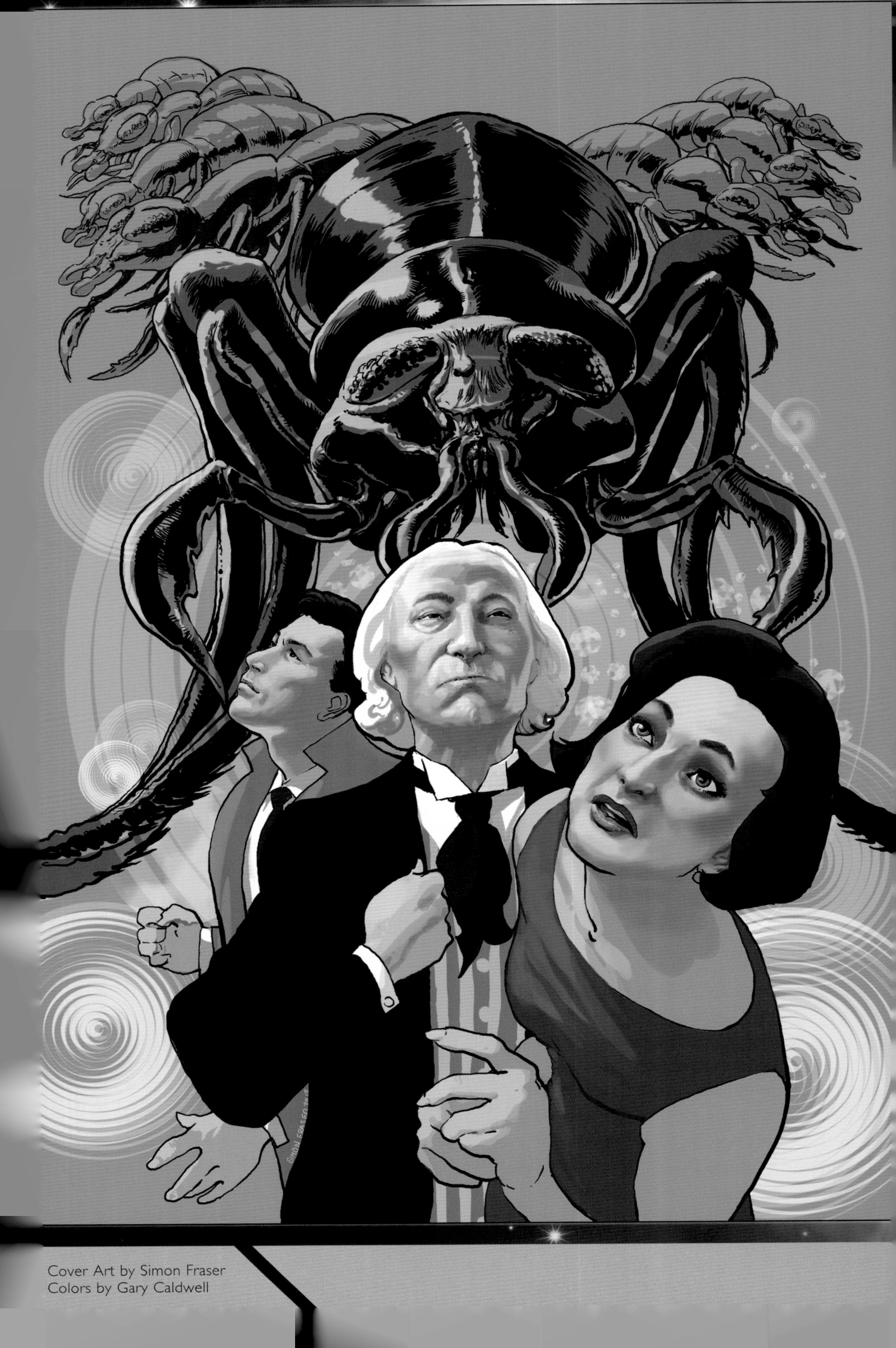
SIMON FRASER 2012

Cover Art by Simon Fraser
Colors by Gary Caldwell

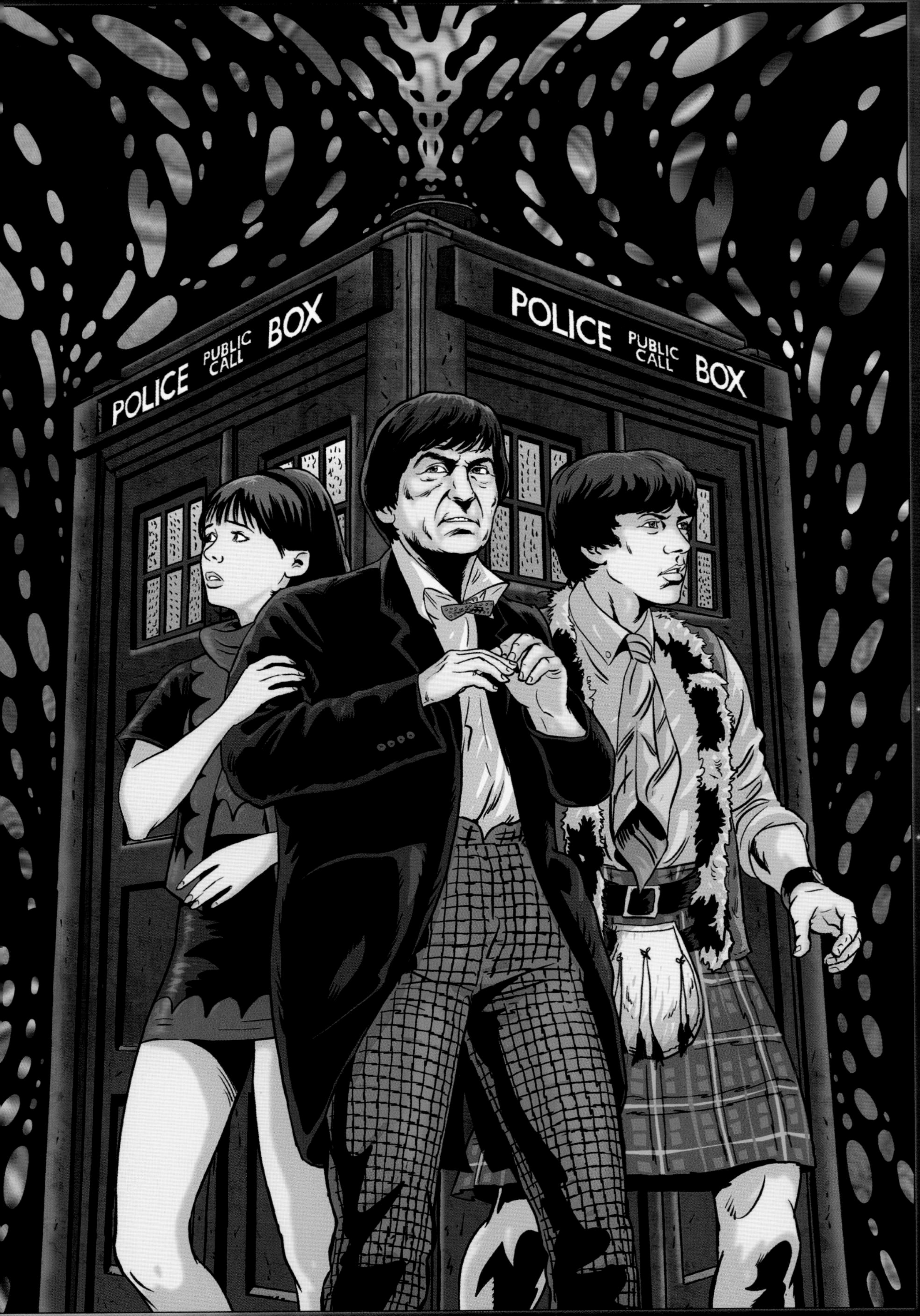
POLICE PUBLIC CALL BOX
POLICE PUBLIC CALL BOX

Cover Art by Lee Sullivan
Colors by Phil Elliott

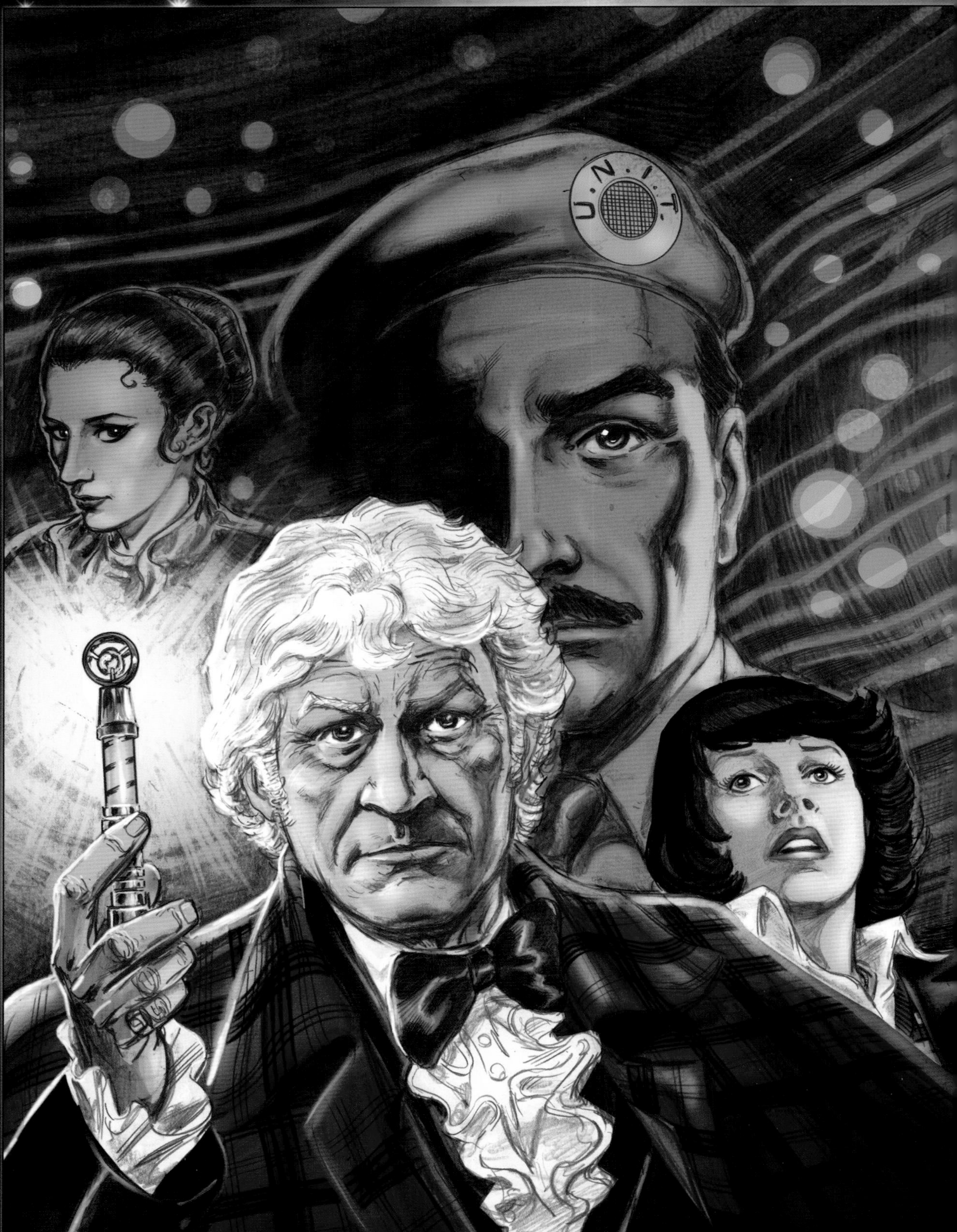
U.N.I.T.

Cover Art by Mike Collins

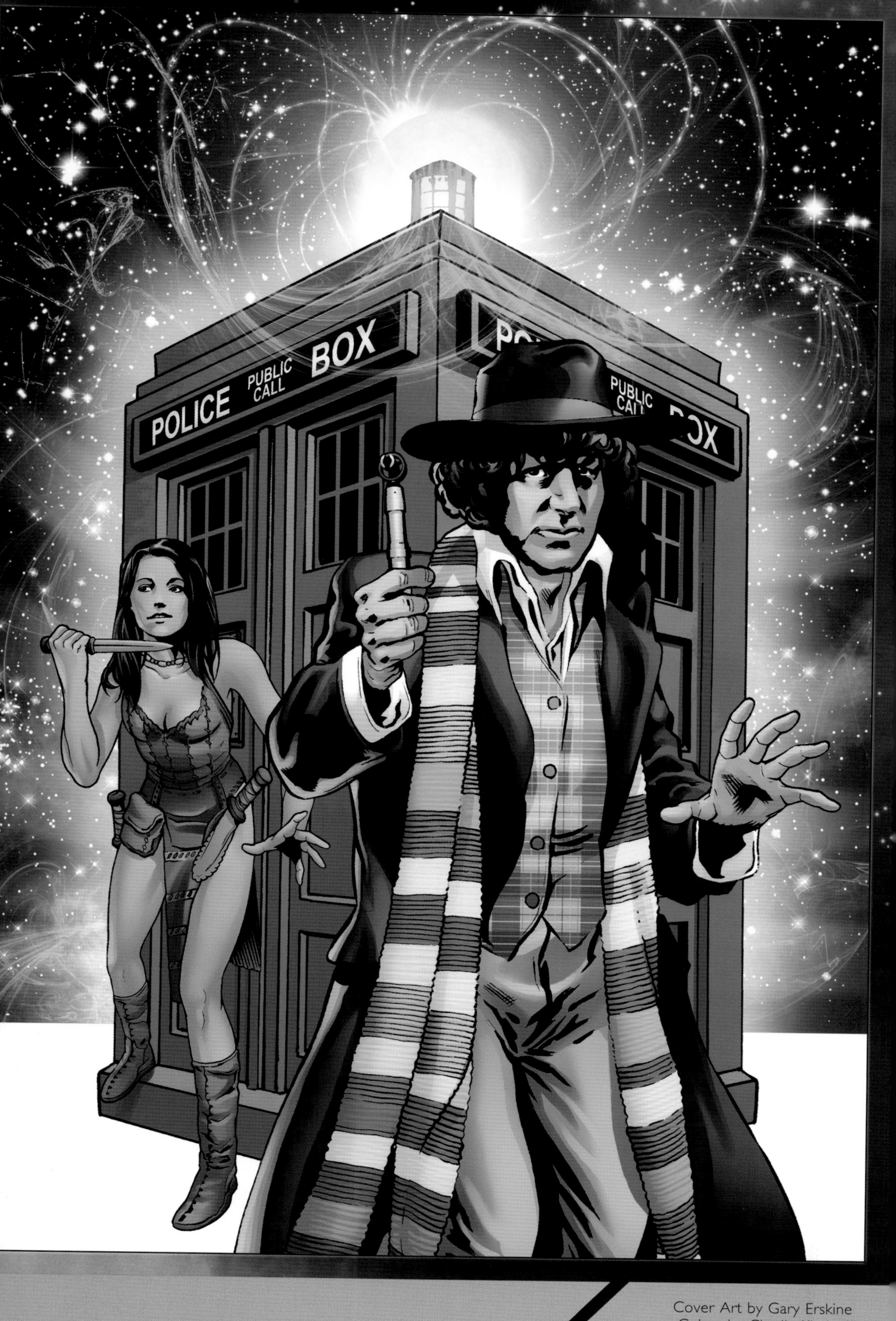
POLICE PUBLIC CALL BOX
PUBLIC CALL

Cover Art by Gary Erskine
Colors by Charlie Kirchoff

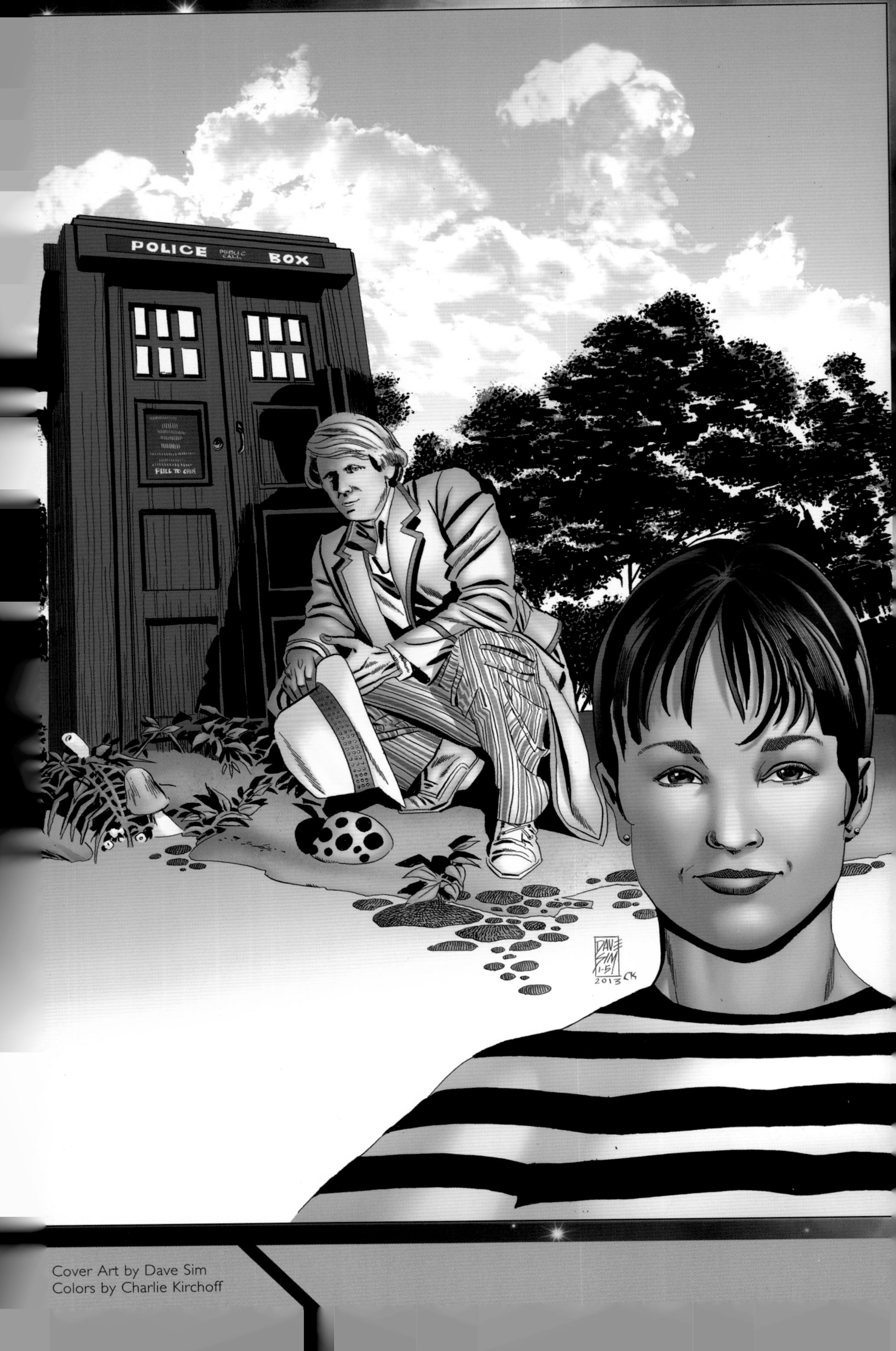
POLICE PUBLIC CALL BOX
PULL TO OPEN
DAVE SIM 1-5 2013
CK

Cover Art by Dave Sim
Colors by Charlie Kirchoff

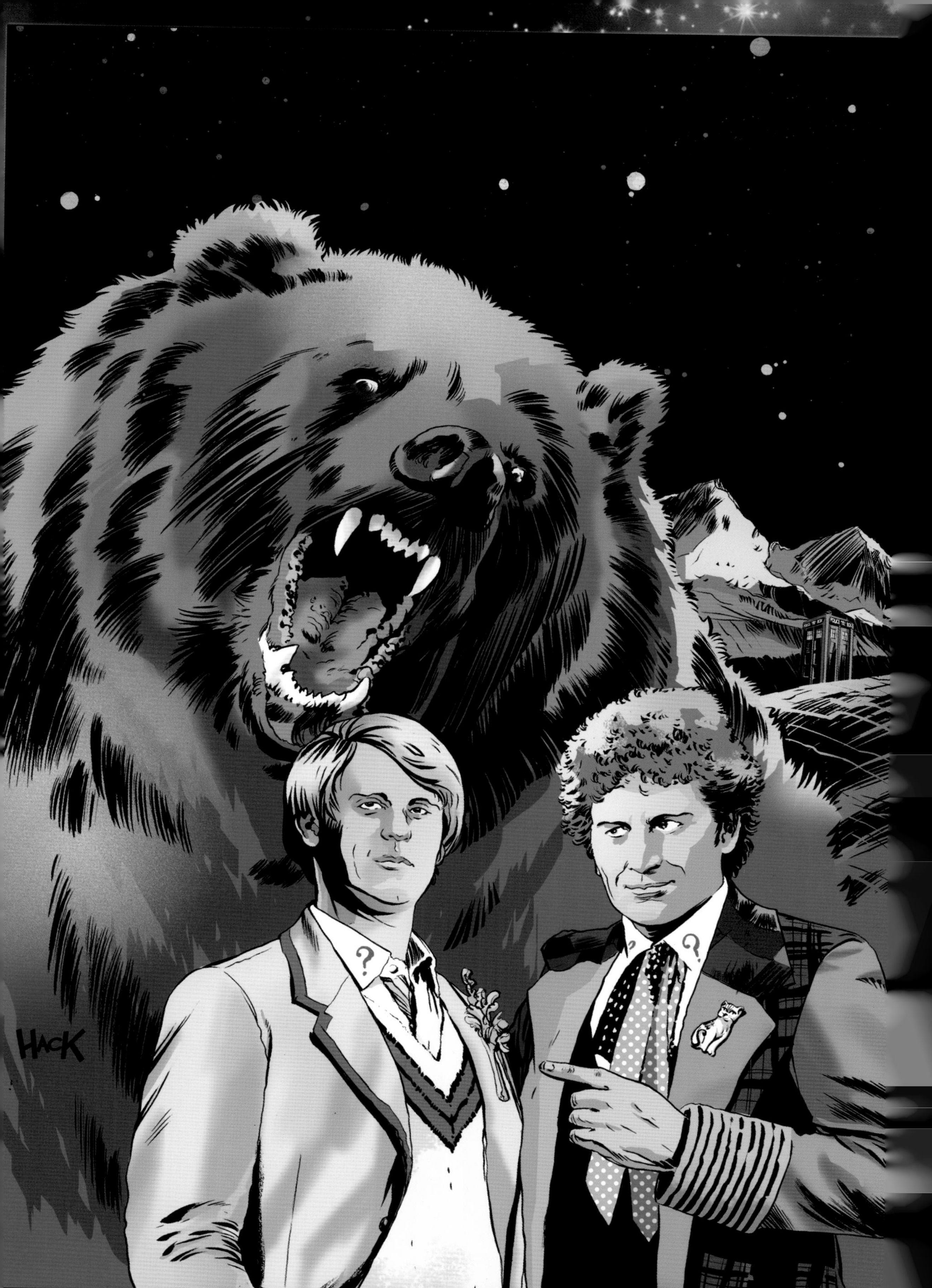
HACK

Cover Art by Robert Hack
Colors by Adrian Salmon

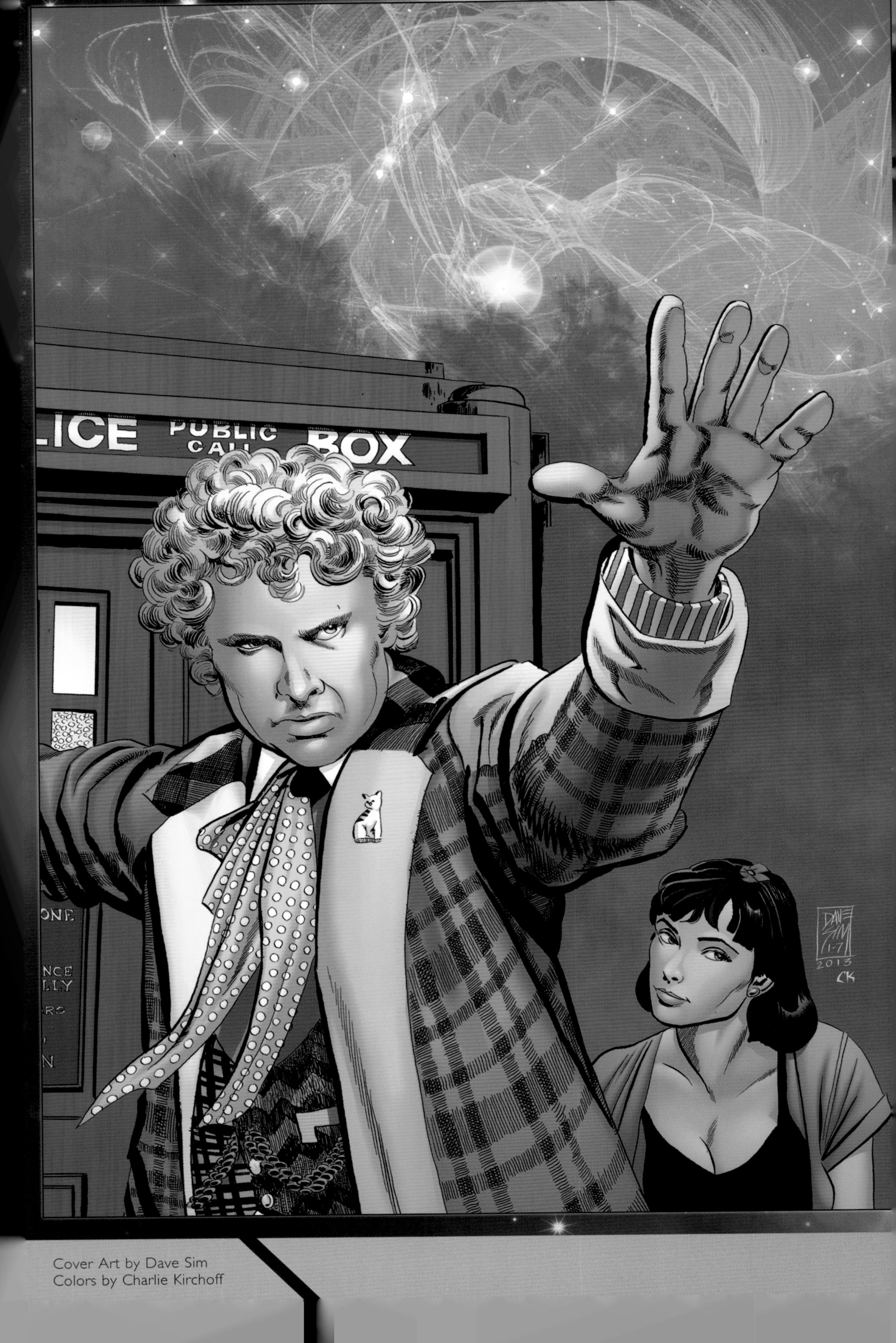
LICE
PUBLIC
CALL
BOX

Cover Art by Dave Sim
Colors by Charlie Kirchoff

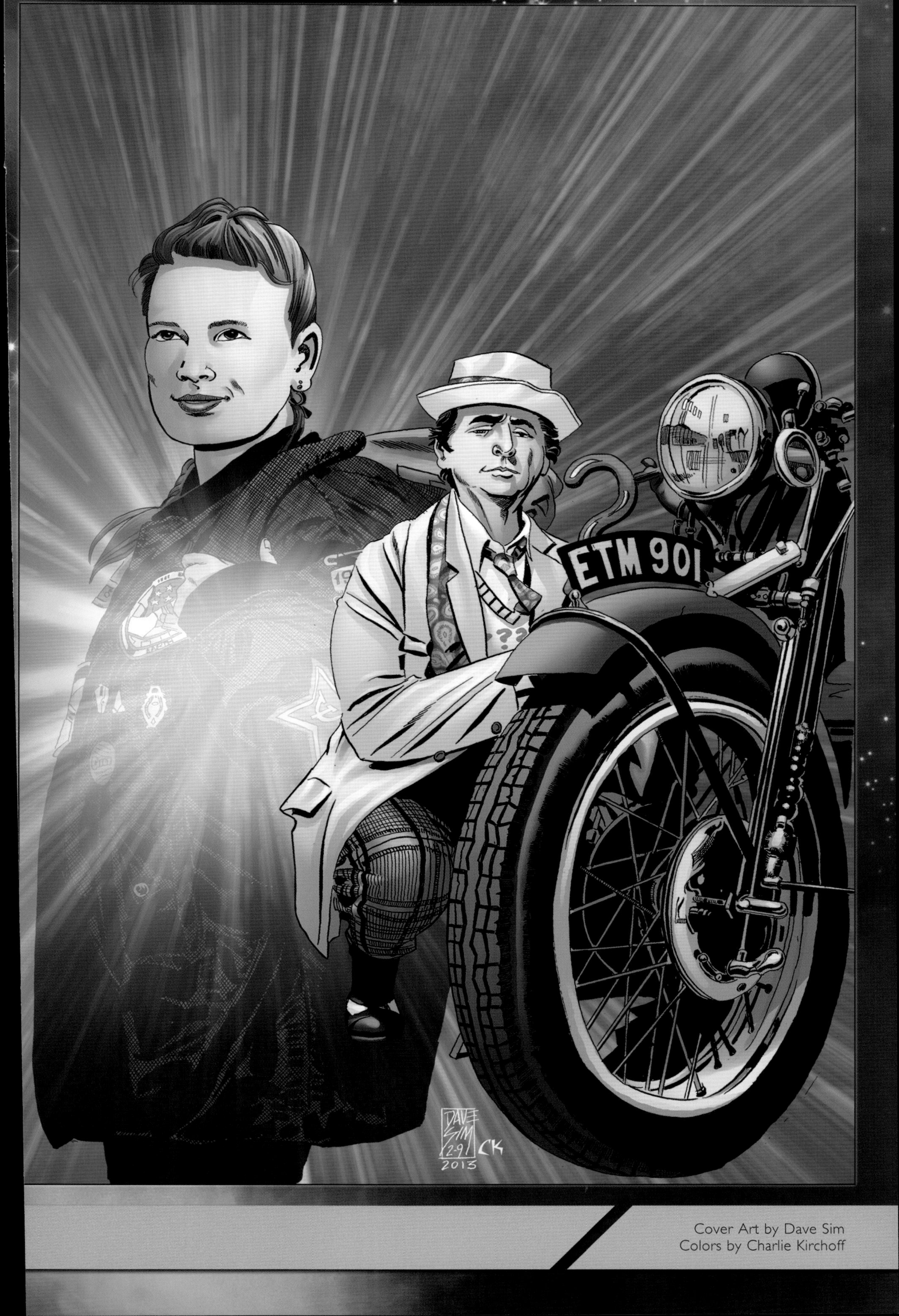
ETM 901
DAVE SIM 2-9 2013
CK

Cover Art by Dave Sim
Colors by Charlie Kirchoff

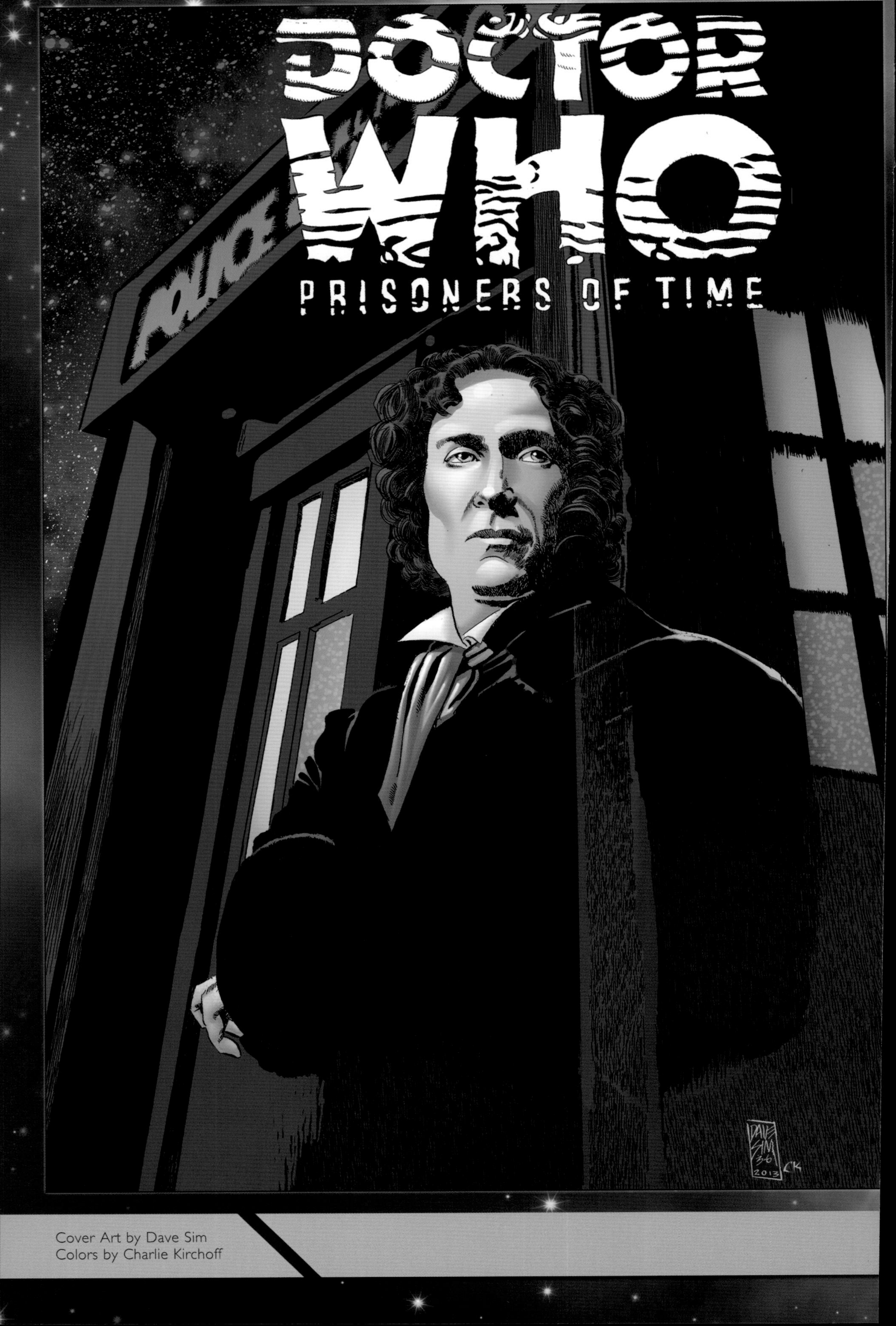
DOCTOR WHO
PRISONERS OF TIME
POLICE
DAVE SIM 3-6 2013
CK

Cover Art by Dave Sim
Colors by Charlie Kirchoff

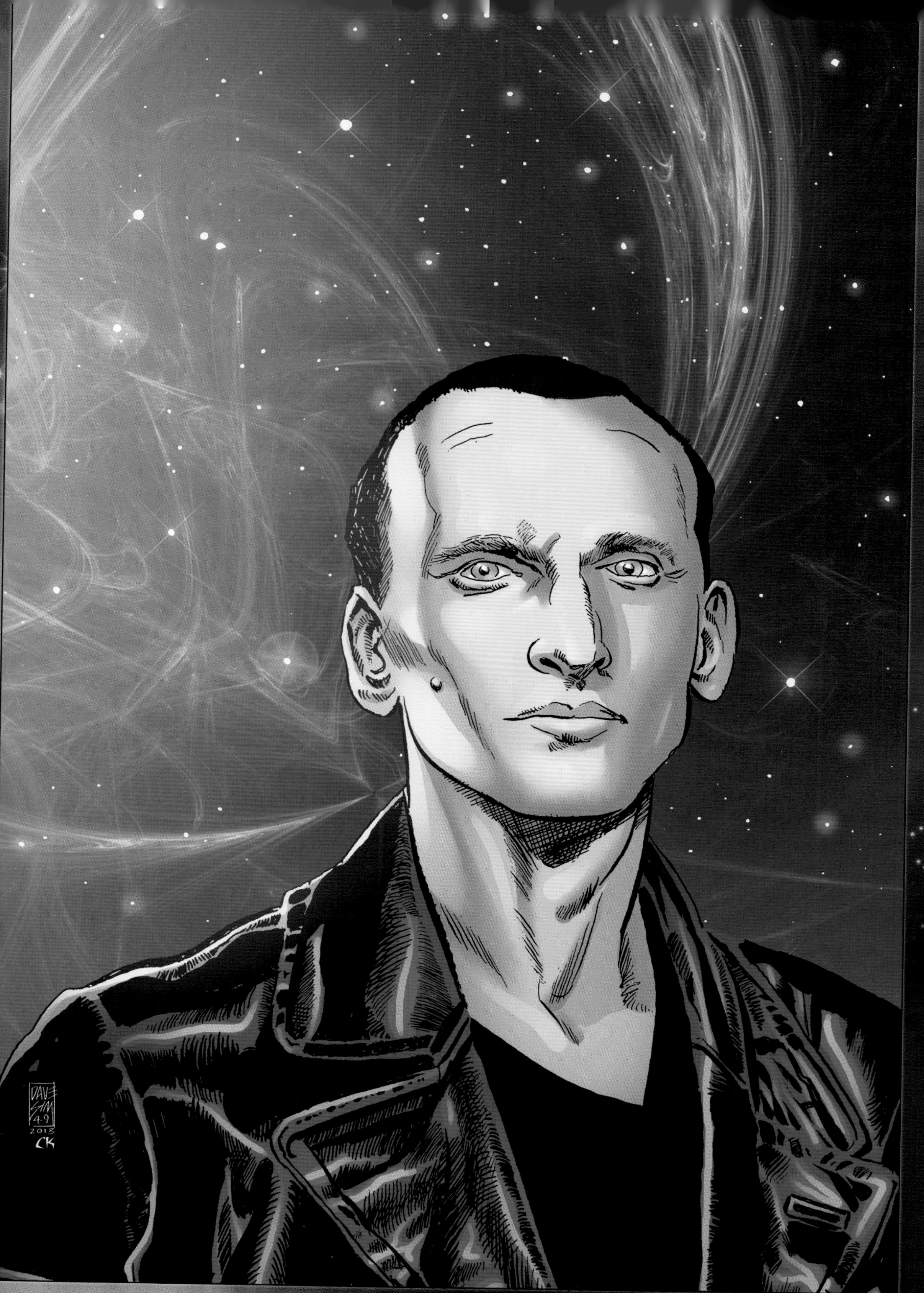
DAVE SIM 4-9 2013
CK

Cover Art by Dave Sim
Colors by Charlie Kirchoff

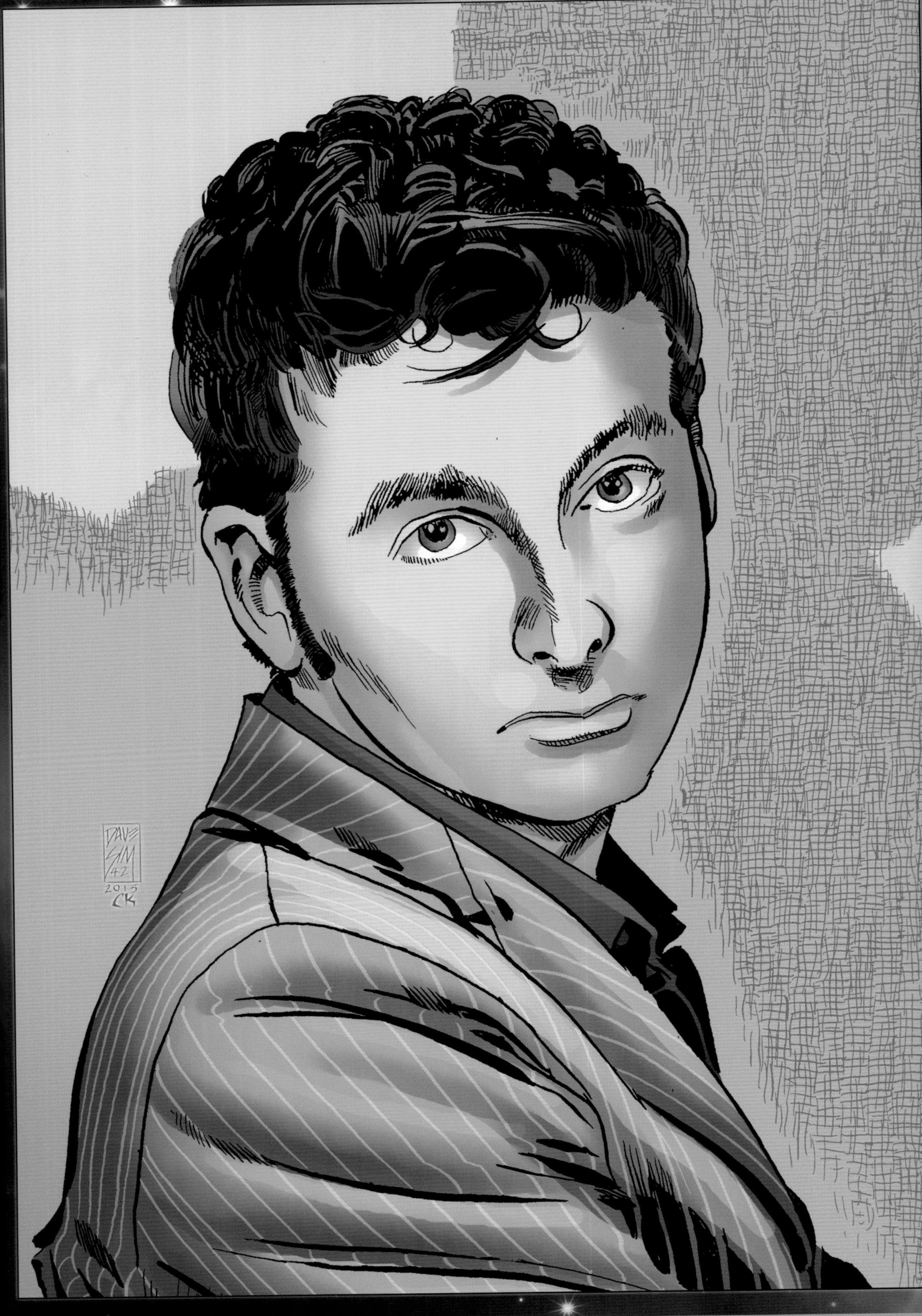
DAVE
SIM
42
2013
CK

Cover Art by Dave Sim
Colors by Charlie Kirchoff

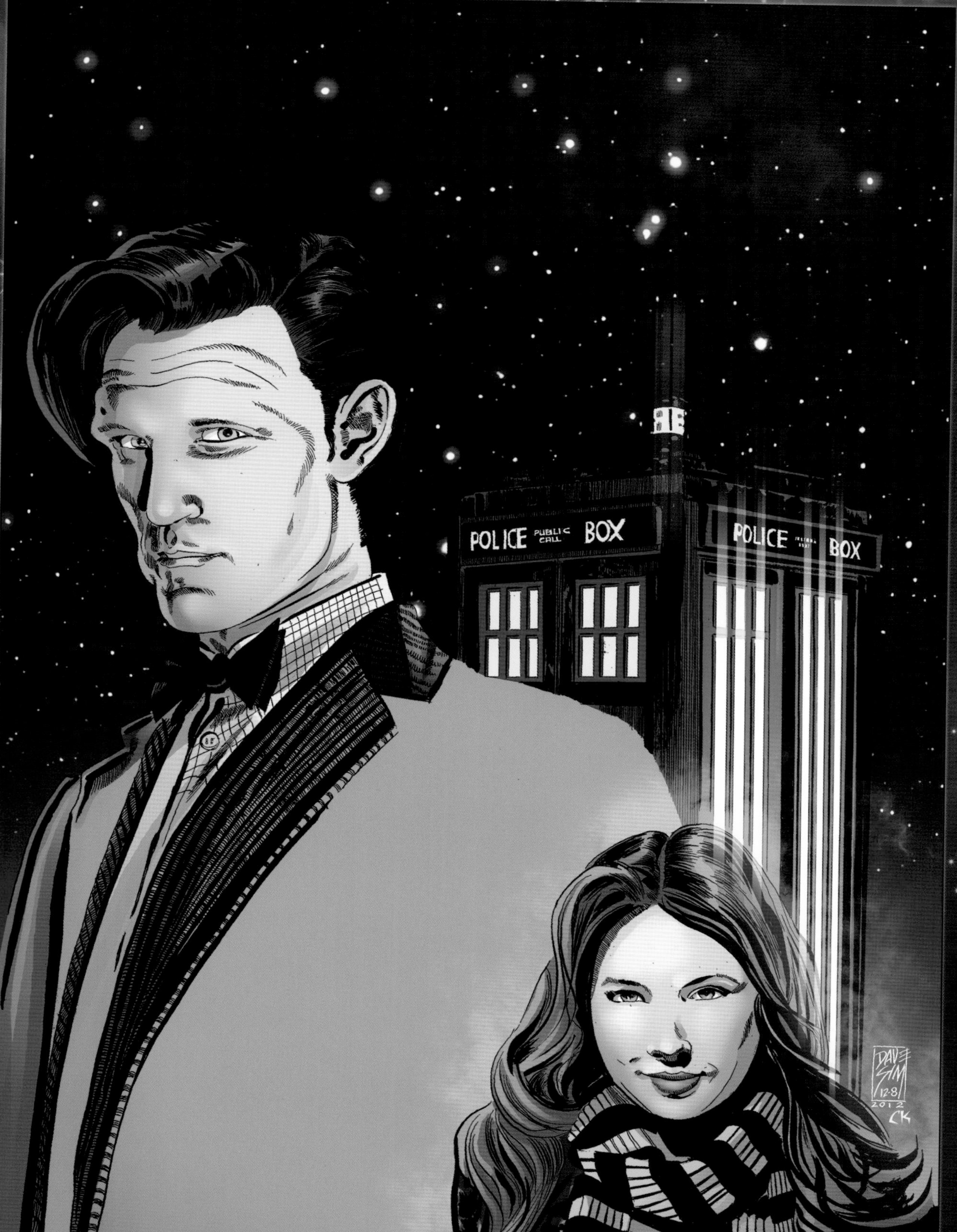
POLICE PUBLIC CALL BOX
POLICE BOX
DAVE SIM 12-8 2012 CK

Cover Art by Dave Sim
Colors by Charlie Kirchoff

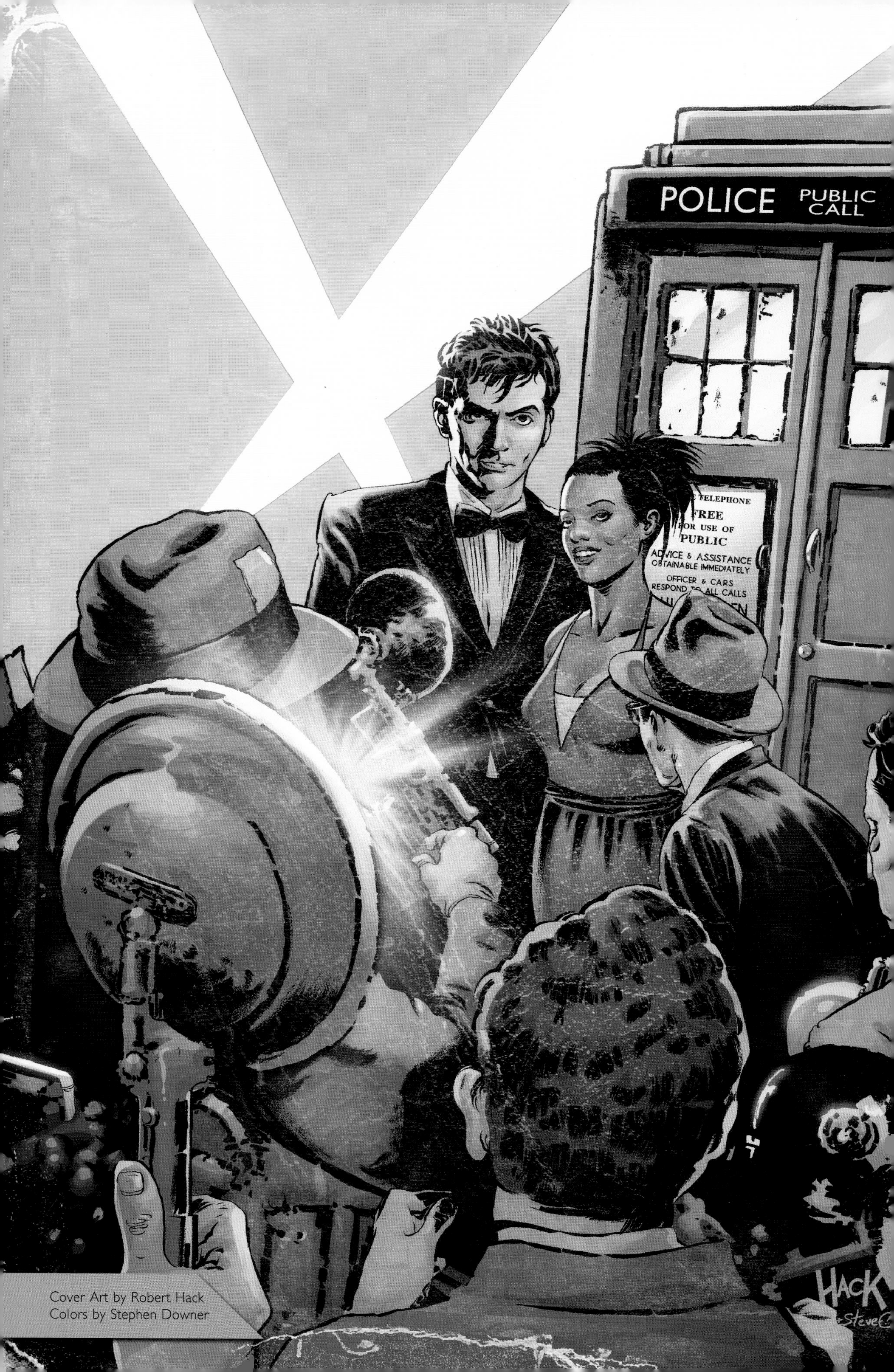
POLICE PUBLIC CALL
TELEPHONE
FREE
FOR USE OF
PUBLIC
ADVICE & ASSISTANCE
OBTAINABLE IMMEDIATELY
OFFICER & CARS
RESPOND TO ALL CALLS
HACK

Cover Art by Robert Hack
Colors by Stephen Downer

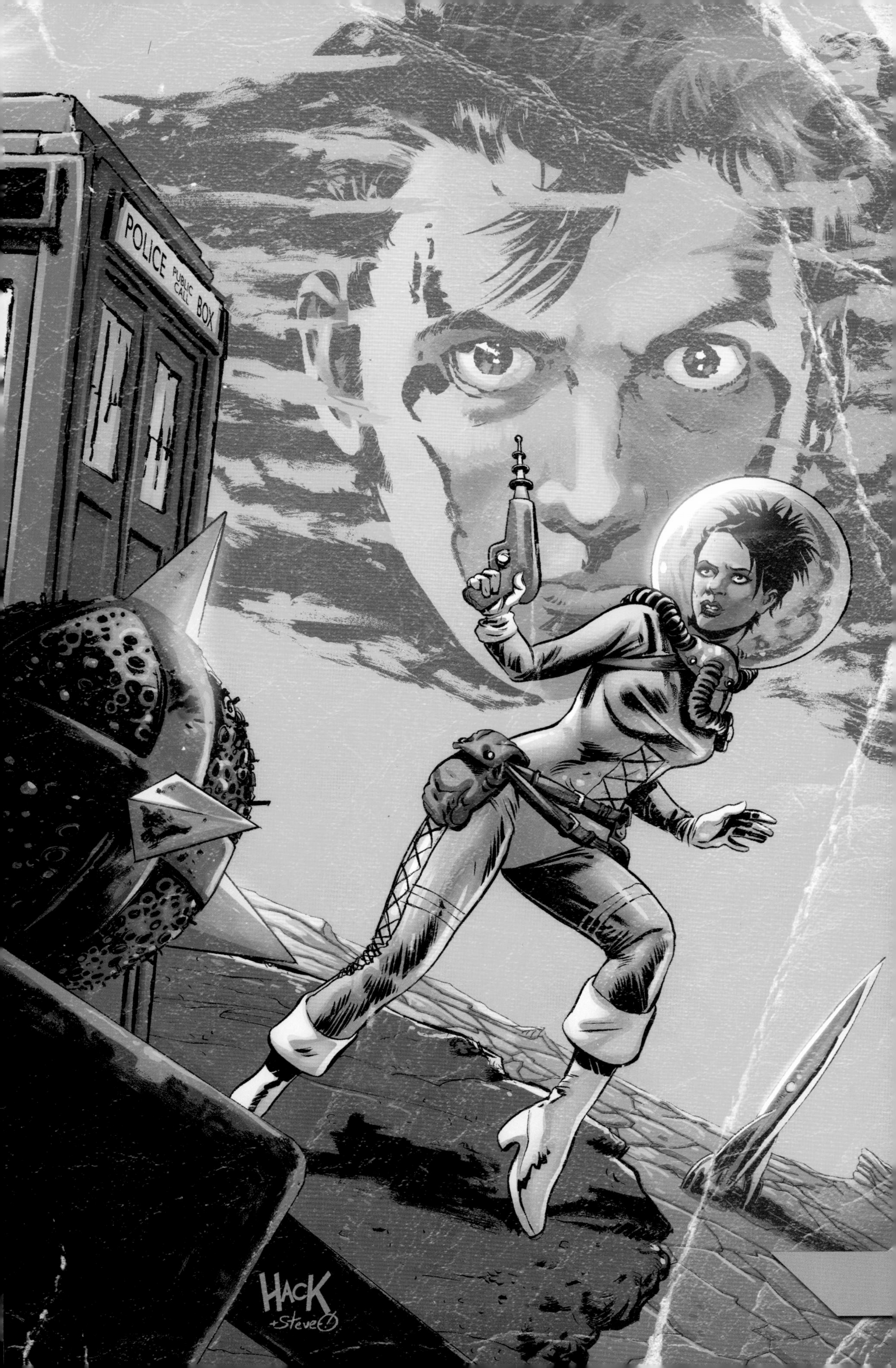
POLICE PUBLIC CALL BOX
HACK
+Steve

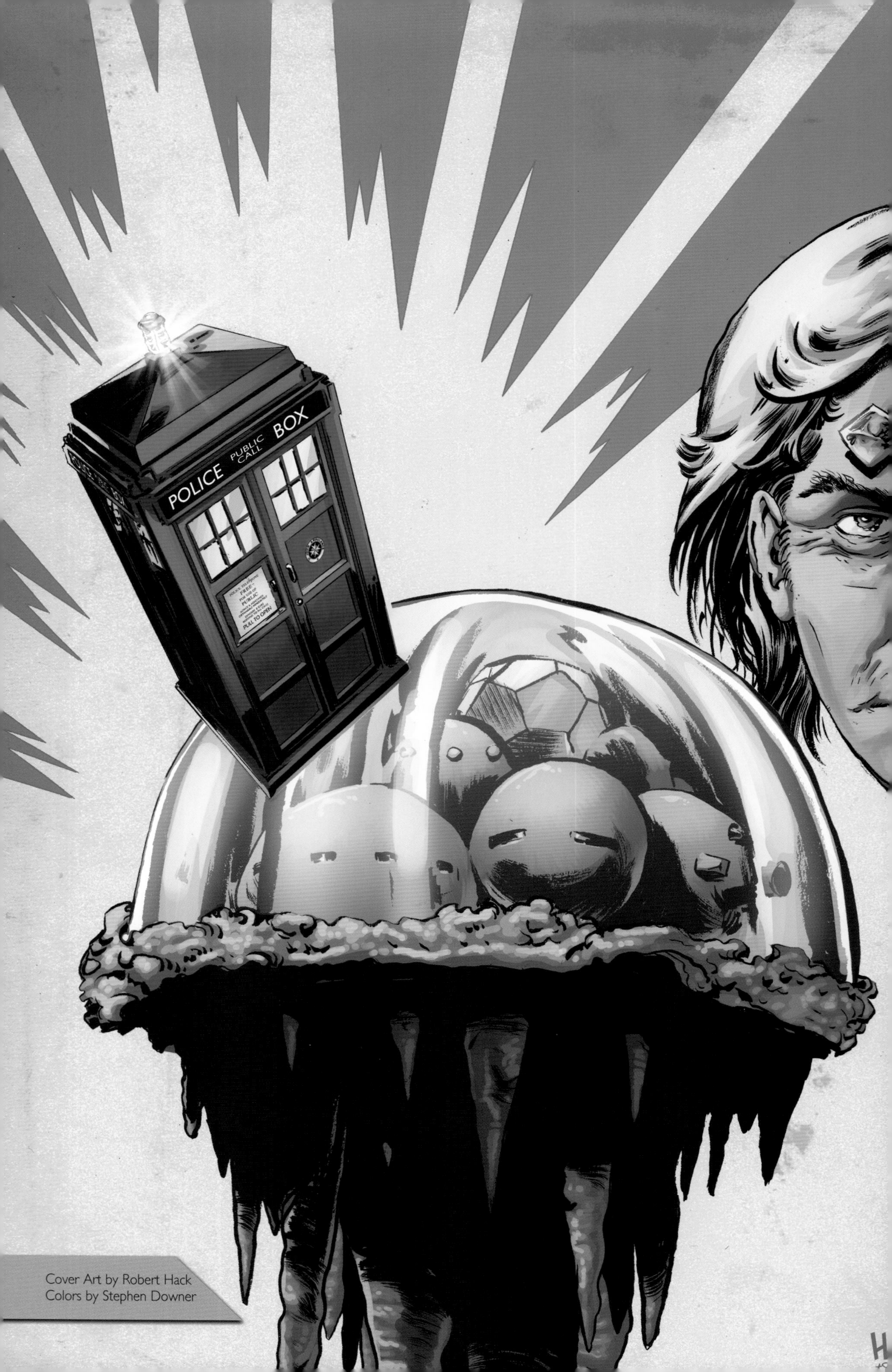
POLICE PUBLIC CALL BOX

Cover Art by Robert Hack
Colors by Stephen Downer

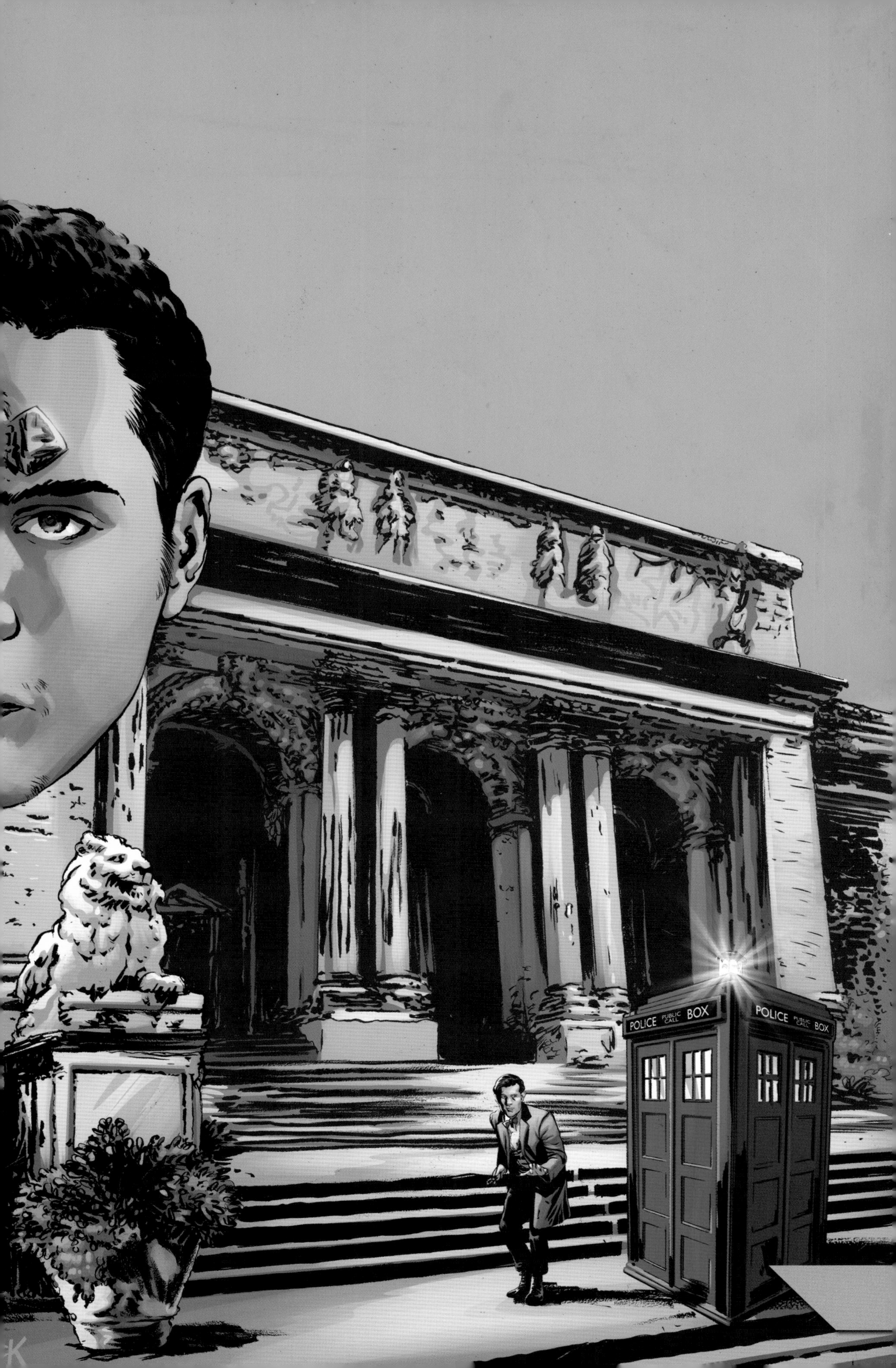
POLICE PUBLIC CALL BOX
POLICE PUBLIC CALL BOX

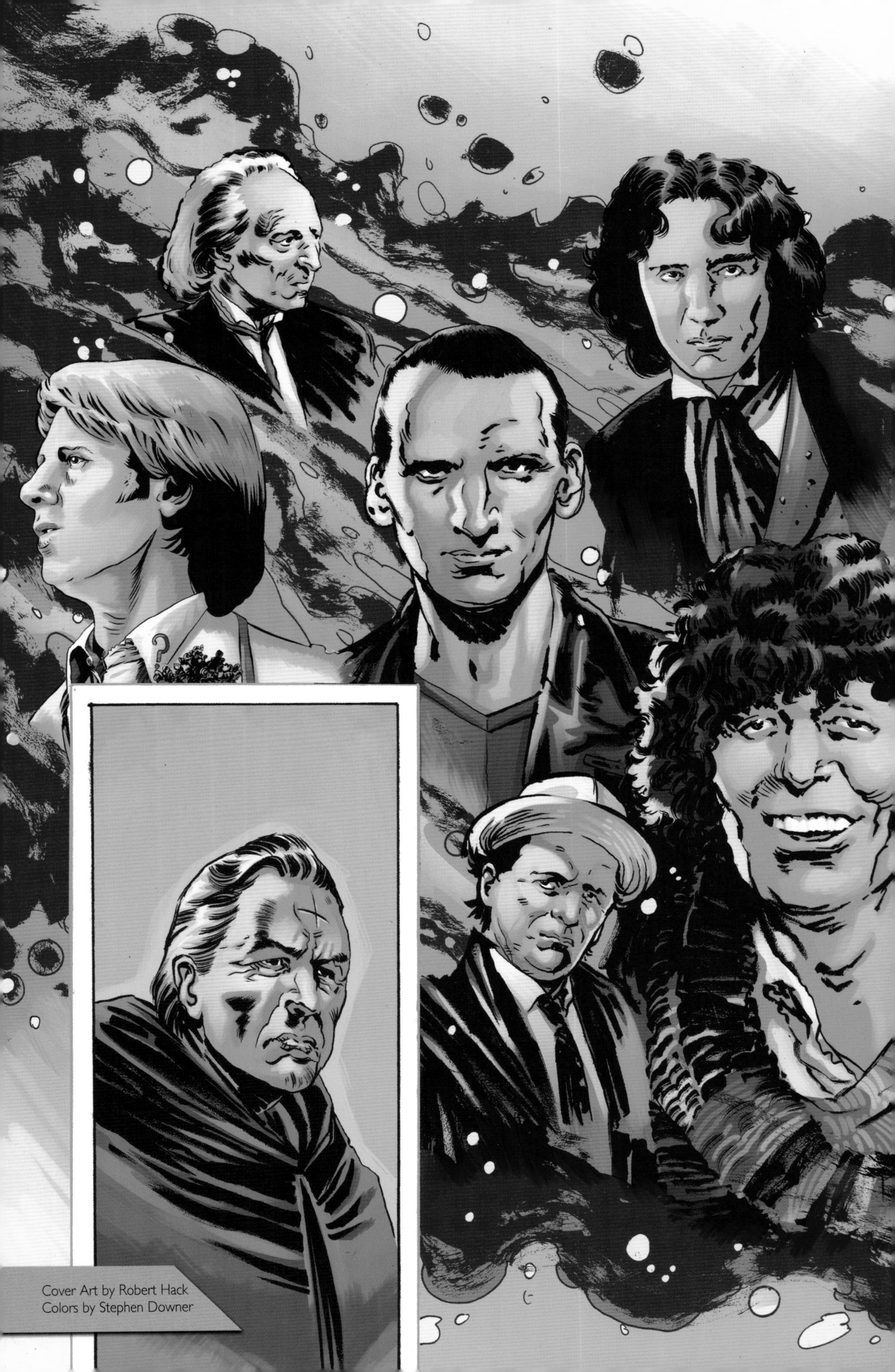

Cover Art by Robert Hack
Colors by Stephen Downer

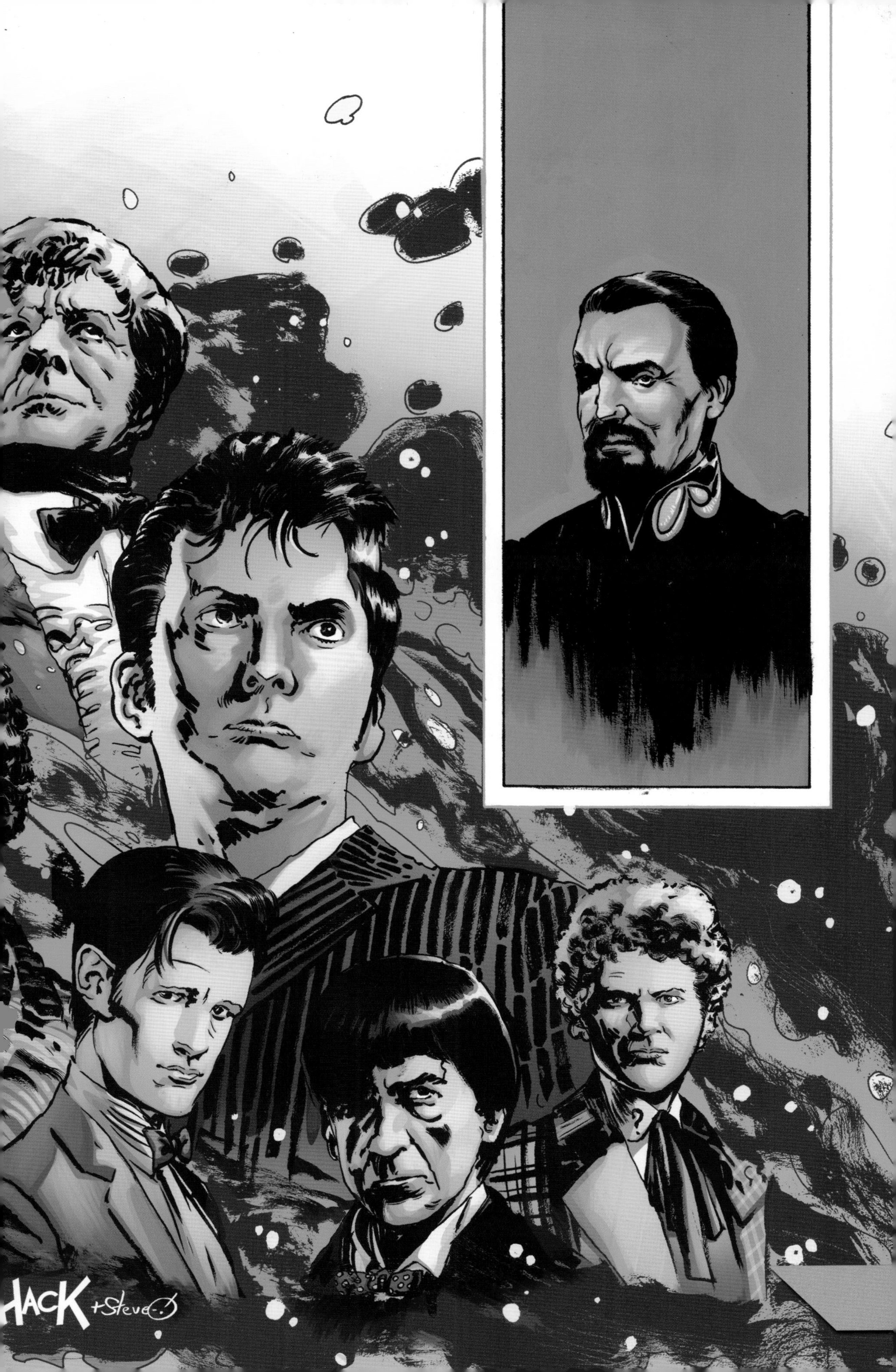
HACK +Steve

BBC

DOCTOR WHO

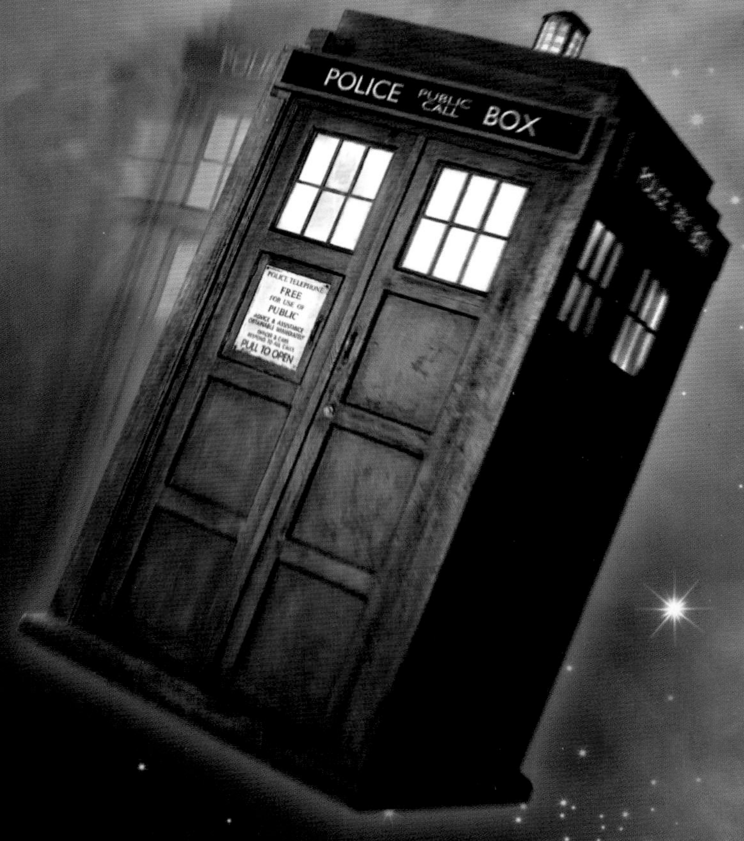
POLICE PUBLIC CALL BOX
FREE
PUBLIC
PULL TO OPEN

PRISONERS OF TIME